Lecture Notes in Computer Science 2743

Edited by G. Goos, J. Hartmanis, and J. van Leeuwen

Springer
Berlin
Heidelberg
New York
Hong Kong
London
Milan
Paris
Tokyo

Luca Cardelli (Ed.)

ECOOP 2003 – Object-Oriented Programming

17th European Conference
Darmstadt, Germany, July 21-25, 2003
Proceedings

 Springer

Series Editors

Gerhard Goos, Karlsruhe University, Germany
Juris Hartmanis, Cornell University, NY, USA
Jan van Leeuwen, Utrecht University, The Netherlands

Volume Editor

Luca Cardelli
Microsoft Research, Roger Needham Building
JJ Thomson Avenue, Cambridge CB3 0FB, United Kingdom
E-mail: luca@microsoft.com

Cataloging-in-Publication Data applied for

A catalog record for this book is available from the Library of Congress

Bibliographic information published by Die Deutsche Bibliothek
Die Deutsche Bibliothek lists this publication in the Deutsche Nationalbibliographie;
detailed bibliographic data is available in the Internet at <http://dnb.ddb.de>.

CR Subject Classification (1998): D.1-3, H.2, F.3, C.2, K.4, J.1

ISSN 0302-9743
ISBN 3-540-40531-3 Springer-Verlag Berlin Heidelberg New York

Springer-Verlag Berlin Heidelberg New York
a member of BertelsmannSpringer Science+Business Media GmbH

http://www.springer.de

© Springer-Verlag Berlin Heidelberg 2003
Printed in Germany

Typesetting: Camera-ready by author, data conversion by DA-TeX Gerd Blumenstein
Printed on acid-free paper   SPIN: 10929230   06/3142   5 4 3 2 1 0

Preface

ECOOP is the premier forum in Europe for bringing together practitioners, researchers, and students to share their ideas and experiences in a broad range of disciplines woven with the common thread of object technology. It is a well-integrated collage of events, including outstanding invited speakers, carefully refereed technical papers, real-world experiences in the form of practitioner reports, exciting panels, topic-focused workshops, late-breaking demonstrations, and an interactive posters session.

The 17th ECOOP conference marks another year of continued success for object-oriented programming, both as the subject of intensive academic study, and as a primary vehicle for industrial software development. The expanding field of applications and challenges for object technology guarantees many more years of fruitful investigation; high-quality conferences such as ECOOP reflect and support the vitality of the area.

This year, the program committee reviewed 88 submissions, of which 18 were accepted for publication after a thorough reviewing process. Each paper received at least 4 reviews, and was evaluated on relevance, novelty, significance, clarity, originality, and correctness. The topics covered include: aspects and components; patterns, architecture and collaboration; object-oriented modeling; type systems; implementation techniques; and formal techniques and methodology. Invited papers by Mary Fernández, and Carl Gunter are also included in these proceedings, as well as the abstract of an invited talk by Martín Abadi.

A major conference such as ECOOP is a significant undertaking, and I would like to thank a number of individuals and organizations that greatly facilitated my job as program committee chair. The 24 members of the program committee produced high-quality reviews with full coverage and on a precise schedule, and they (uncharacteristically) all attended the program committee meeting. The local organizer, Mira Mezini, assisted on a number of logistic issues as well as serving as a member of the program committee. The conference chair, Rachid Guerraoui, and the AITO Executive Board (Ole Lehrmann Madsen, in particular) provided guidance. Richard van de Stadt gave invaluable support in the use of his CyberChairPRO system through the reviewing and publication process. Finally, Angela Still at Microsoft Research Cambridge provided administrative and logistic assistance for the program committee meeting.

May 2003   Luca Cardelli

Organization

ECOOP 2003 was organized by the Software Technology Group, Department of Computer Science, Darmstadt University of Technology, under the auspices of AITO (Association Internationale pour les Technologies Objets), and in cooperation with ACM SIGPLAN.

Executive Committee

Conference Chair:
>   Rachid Guerraoui (École Polytechnique Fédérale de Lausanne)

Program Chair:
>   Luca Cardelli (Microsoft Research)

Organizing Chair:
>   Mira Mezini (Darmstadt University of Technology)

Organizing Committee

Tutorial Chairs:
>   Krzysztof Czarnecki (DaimlerChrysler Research)
>   Max Mühlhäuser (Darmstadt University of Technology)

Workshop Chairs:
>   Alejandro Buchmann (Darmstadt University of Technology)
>   Frank Buschmann (Siemens Corporate Technology)

Practitioner Reports Chair:
>   Michael Stal (Siemens Corporate Technology)

Doctoral Symposium Chairs:
>   Lodewijk Bergmans (University of Twente)
>   Erik Ernst (University of Aarhus)

Poster/Demonstration Chairs:
>   Thomas Kühne (Darmstadt University of Technology)
>   David Lorenz (Northeastern University)

General Conference Organization:
>   Christoph Bockisch (Darmstadt University of Technology)
>   Vasian Cepa (Darmstadt University of Technology)
>   Michael Eichberg (Darmstadt University of Technology)
>   Michael Haupt (Darmstadt University of Technology)
>   Gudrun Jörs (Darmstadt University of Technology)
>   Sven Kloppenburg (Darmstadt University of Technology)
>   Klaus Ostermann (Darmstadt University of Technology)

Program Committee

Mehmet Akşit	University of Twente, The Netherlands
Suad Alagić	University of Southern Maine, USA
Elisa Bertino	University of Milan, Italy
Andrew Black	Oregon Health & Science University, USA
Vinny Cahill	Trinity College Dublin, Ireland
Theo D'Hondt	Vrije Universiteit Brussel, Belgium
Peter Dickman	University of Glasgow, UK
Sophia Drossopoulou	Imperial College, UK
Urs Hölzle	University of California at Santa Barbara, USA
Atsushi Igarashi	Kyoto University, Japan
Mehdi Jazayeri	Technical University of Vienna, Austria
Eric Jul	DIKU, University of Copenhagen, Denmark
Doug Lea	State University of New York at Oswego, USA
Gary T. Leavens	Iowa State University, USA
Jørgen Lindskov Knudsen	Mjølner Informatics, Denmark
Boris Magnusson	Lund Institute of Technology, Sweden
Mira Mezini	Darmstadt University of Technology, Germany
Oscar Nierstrasz	University of Berne, Switzerland
Martin Odersky	École Polytechnique Fédérale de Lausanne, Switzerland
Jens Palsberg	Purdue University, USA
John Reppy	University of Chicago, USA
Guy Steele	Sun Microsystems Labs, USA
Jan Vitek	Purdue University, USA

Sponsoring Organizations

Referees

Gabriela Arévalo
Carlo Bellettini
Alexandre Bergel
Klaas van den Berg
Lodewijk Bergmans
Johan Brichau
David Briggs
Pim van den Broek
Peter A. Buhr
Brian Cabana
Jiongxiong Chen
Yoonsik Cheon
Siobhán Clarke
Thomas Cleenewerck
Cliff Click
Curtis Clifton
Markus Dahm
Wolfgang De Meuter
Jessie Dedecker
Dirk Deridder
Jim Dowling
Karel Driesen
Stéphane Ducasse
Michael Eichberg
Torbjörn Ekman
Johan Fabry
Pascal Fenkam
Robby Findler
Cédric Fournet
Markus Gaelli
Alexander Garthwaite
Tudor Girba
Maurice Glandrup
Sofie Goderis
Thomas Gschwind
Kris Gybels
Aart van Halteren
Ashif S. Harji

Michael Haupt
Roger Henriksson
David Holmes
Suresh Jagannathan
Mark Jones
Richard Jones
Clemens Kerer
Joseph Kiniry
Ivan Kurtev
Michele Lanza
Doug Lea
Jeremy Logan
Steve MacDonald
Tom Mens
Mattia Monga
István Nagy
David Naumann
Anders Nilsson
Joost Noppen
Joe Oberleitner
Klaus Ostermann
Erik Poll
Laura Ponisio
Barry Redmond
Arend Rensink
Sven G. Robertz
Nathanael Schärli
Michel Schinz
Luk Stoops
Don Syme
Wallapak Tavanapong
Tom Tourwé
Dirk Van Deun
Ellen Van Paesschen
Rebecca Wirfs-Brock
Roel Wuyts
Matthias Zenger

Table of Contents

Modeling

Algorithms, Optimization and Runtimes

Invited Talk 3

Formal Techniques and Methodology

Built-in Object Security

Martín Abadi

Computer Science Department
University of California, Santa Cruz
abadi@cs.ucsc.edu

Modern programming languages and systems provide much support for security. Through strong typing, they can substantially reduce the opportunities for low-level coding errors that could result in buffer overflows and other vulnerabilities. They also allow protection by encapsulation and the treatment of objects as unforgeable capabilities. In addition, they sometimes include rich security infrastructures, for example libraries for authentication and authorization.

Although common programming languages are not primarily concerned with security, language definitions can be the basis for security guarantees. A language specification may imply, for instance, that object references are unguessable. An implementation may resort to cryptography in order to enforce this property and others built into the language.

Conversely, for better or for worse, security machinery can have a significant effect on language semantics and implementations, even when it is regarded as an add-on. For instance, access-control techniques that depend on the contents of the execution stack give an observable role to the stack, affecting program equivalences. A language perspective can help in understanding such security mechanisms and sometimes in developing new ones.

References

[1] Martín Abadi. Protection in programming-language translations. In *Proceedings of the 25th International Colloquium on Automata, Languages and Programming*, volume 1443 of *Lecture Notes in Computer Science*, pages 868–883. Springer-Verlag, July 1998.

[2] Martín Abadi and Cédric Fournet. Access control based on execution history. In *Proceedings of the 10th Annual Network and Distributed System Security Symposium*, pages 107–121, February 2003.

[3] Martín Abadi, Cédric Fournet, and Georges Gonthier. Secure implementation of channel abstractions. *Information and Computation*, 174(1):37–83, April 2002.

[4] Leendert van Doorn, Martín Abadi, Mike Burrows, and Edward Wobber. Secure network objects. In *Proceedings of the 1996 IEEE Symposium on Security and Privacy*, pages 211–221, May 1996.

L. Cardelli (Ed.): ECOOP 2003, LNCS 2743, p. 1, 2003.

Modeling Crosscutting in Aspect-Oriented Mechanisms

Hidehiko Masuhara[1] and Gregor Kiczales[2]

[1] University of Tokyo
masuhara@acm.org
[2] University of British Columbia
gregor@cs.ubc.ca

Abstract. Modeling four aspect-oriented programming mechanisms shows the way in which each supports modular crosscutting. Comparing the models produces a clear three part characterization of what is required to support crosscutting structure: a common frame of reference that two (or more) programs can use to connect with each other and each provide their semantic contribution.

1   Introduction

A number of tools have been proposed for aspect-oriented (AO) software development. But to date there is no generally agreed upon definition of what makes a technique aspect-oriented. This paper takes a step in that direction by presenting a framework that can be used to explain how four proposed mechanisms support modular crosscutting:

- Pointcuts and advice as in AspectJ [10, 11].
- Traversal specifications as in Demeter[15], DemeterJ[16] and DJ[14, 21].
- Class composition as in Hyper/J[22, 23].
- Open classes as in AspectJ.[1]

We capture the core semantics of these mechanisms by modeling the weaving process by which they are implemented. The models define a weaving process as taking two programs and coordinating their coming together into a single combined computation. In the case of mechanisms like Hyper/J, where the semantics is defined in terms of code-processing, the model describes combining input programs to produce a single combined program.

A critical property of the models is that they describe the join points as existing in the result of the weaving process rather than being in either of the input programs. This yields a three-part description of crosscutting structure – in terms of how the two input programs *crosscut each other with respect to* the result computation or program. This three-part description is essential to model all four mechanisms, and to model an arbitrary number of crosscutting programs.

---

[1]   This functionality originated in Flavors [19, 28] where Flavor declarations did not lexically contain their methods and is found in several other languages; the term open class is due to [5, 18]. AspectJ used to call this feature introduction, and now calls it inter-type declarations.

L. Cardelli (Ed.): ECOOP 2003, LNCS 2743, pp. 2-28, 2003.

The paper is organized as follows:

Section 2 presents a simple object-oriented (OO) language that is used as a basis for discussion throughout the paper. This includes an example program in the language, and key elements of a simple interpreter for the language.

Section 3 presents the common structure of all the models.

Section 4 has four parts, each of which shows how one of the four mechanisms is modeled. The discussion in each part first outlines the core semantics to be addressed, by showing how that semantics could be embedded in the language of Section 2. This starts with an example program and an implementation of the semantics, as a modification to the implementation of Section 2.2. We then show the model and use the implementation to intuitively validate the model.

Section 5 shows that the simplifications of Section 4 do not invalidate the models of the real systems. This is done by showing that a number of features originally left out of the models in Section 4 can easily be added to the models.

Section 6 presents the model of crosscutting structure and uses it to describe the crosscutting in the examples from Section 4.

Section 7 discusses related work, Section 8 presents future work, and Section 9 is a summary.

The paper assumes prior knowledge of all four AO mechanisms and a reading familiarity with simple Scheme interpreters of OO languages. But, at least on a first pass through, the paper can be read in subsets. Readers unfamiliar with all the mechanisms can skip the corresponding sub-sections of Section 4. Readers can avoid much of the Scheme code by skipping Sections 2.2 and 4.[1-4].1; the effect of this will be to read the models, without the validation of their appropriateness.

The code in this paper is available online.[2] This includes all the model implementations, as well as the example programs written in both the full systems (AspectJ, Hyper/J, etc.) as well as our core models of those systems.

2   BASE – An Object-Oriented Language

This section describes a simple object-oriented language, called BASE, which is the basis for the rest of the paper. The description has three parts: a simple intuitive description of the language, a sample program in the language, and a simple Scheme interpreter for the language. The discussion of each of the four mechanisms in Section 4 follows this same structure, and builds on both the example program and the model interpreter.

BASE can be seen as a core subset of Java. It is a single-inheritance OO language, without interfaces, overloading or multi-methods. Programs in BASE are written in a Java-like syntax.[3]

---

[2]   See http://www.cs.ubc.ca/labs/spl/projects/asb.html.

[3]   In our actual implementation, BASE has a more Scheme-like syntax. We use a Java-like syntax in the paper to help the reader distinguish between code written in BASE and the Scheme code that implements BASE. As part of using Java syntax, we show code with a return statement, even though the actual BASE language has only expressions, no statements.

2.1   Sample Program

A simple program written in the BASE language is:

```
class Figure {
List elements = new LinkedList();
}

class FigureElement {
  Display display;
}

class Point extends FigureElement {
  int x;
  int y;

  int getX() { return x; }
  int getY() { return y; }

  void setX(int x) { this.x = x; }
  void setY(int y) { this.y = y; }
}

class Line extends FigureElement {
  Point p1;
  Point p2;

  int getP1() { return p1; }
  int getP2() { return p2; }

  void setP1(Point p1) { this.p1 = p1; }
  void setP2(Point p2) { this.p2 = p2; }
}
```

This code implements a simple figures package. A Figure is comprised of a collection of FigureElements. There are two kinds of FigureElements, Point and Line. Both points and lines have the usual structure, and getter and setter methods. See [11] for a more detailed discussion of this example.

2.2   Model Implementation

This section presents the model implementation of BASE. The implementation is an interpreter structured in a manner similar to Chapter 5 of [8]. We show the main structure of the interpreter, including key data structures and procedures. A number of minor helper procedures are not included in this presentation.

For simplicity our model implementation does not include a static type checker, we simply assume the program checks. (We can do this because the language has no overloading, or other features that cause static typing to have semantic effect on correct code.)

The interpreter is written in Scheme [9]. We use a style in which variable names represent the type of their value. (Not actual Hungarian notation.) To save space, some of these names are abbreviated. The following table shows the naming and abbreviation conventions used in the code.

abbreviation	type of value
pgm	program
cname, mname...	class, method, field and super name
decl	declaration
cdecl, mdecl...	class, method and field declaration
param	parameter
id	identifier
methods	list of methods
fields	list of fields
cdecls, mdecls...	list of class, method... declarations
...	...
env	environment
exp	expression

The main data structures of the interpreter include AST structures that represent class, method and field declarations, and expressions that represent code.

```
(define-struct class-decl  (cname s     name decls))
(define-struct method-decl (rtype mname params body))

(define-struct exp ())
(define-struct (if-exp exp) (test then else))
<and many sub-types of exp>
```

There are class and method structures that represent total effective class and method definitions. While a class declaration includes method declarations for only those methods defined lexically in the class, a class structure includes method structures for methods defined in the class as well as inherited methods.

```
(define-struct class  (cname sname fields methods))
(define-struct method (cname mname params body))
(define-struct field  (type fname))
```

There are also environment data structures that hold variable values and class definitions. The code for those is not shown here.

The entry point of the interpreter is the eval-program procedure. It first walks over the declarations to produce the class and method structures; the global variable *classes* is bound to a list of the class structures. Then eval-expression is called with an expression that calls the main entry point.[4]

```
(define eval-program
  (lambda (pgm)
    (set! *classes* (init-classes))
    (elaborate-class-decls! (program-decls pgm))
```

---

[4] In the model implementation on the website, this entry point is the main method of the class called Main. To save space, the example code in Section 2.1 doesn't include a Main class.

```
(eval-exp (parse-exp "(new Main()).main()")
          (make-empty-env)))))
```

The eval-expression procedure is a standard recursive evaluator. Within the
structure of eval-expression, we identify specific helper procedures, call-
method, get-field and set-field, for evaluating method calls and field accesses.
Separating these helper procedures, rather than inlining them in eval-expression
is done to simplify the presentation in later sections of the paper.

```
(define eval-expression
  (lambda (exp env)
    (cond
      ((literal-exp? exp) (literal-exp-datum exp))
      ((if-exp?       exp) ...)
      ...
      ((method-call-exp? exp)
       (let ((mname    (method-call-exp-mname exp))
             (obj-exp (method-call-exp-obj-exp exp))
             (rands   (method-call-exp-rands exp)))
         (call-method mname
                      (eval-exp obj-exp env)
                      (eval-rands rands env)))))
      ((get-field-exp? exp)
       (let ((obj (apply-env env 'this))
             (fname (get-field-exp-fname exp)))
         (get-field obj fname)))
      ((set-field-exp? exp)
       ...
       (set-field obj fname val)))))))

(define call-method
  (lambda (mname obj args)
    (let ((method (lookup-method mname obj)))
      (execute-method method obj args)))))

(define get-field
  (lambda (obj fname)
    <get the field value from the object>))

(define set-field
  (lambda (obj fname val)
    <set the field value in the object>))
```

The lookup-method procedure simply finds the method in the methods of the
class, if no matching method is found an error is signaled.

```
(define lookup-method (mname obj)
  (let* ((cname    (object-cname obj))
         (methods (cname->methods cname)))
    <scan methods looking for one matching mname>
    ))
```

The execute-method procedure simply evaluates the body of the method in an environment with this bound to the object, and the method parameter identifiers bound to the arguments.

```
(define execute-method (method obj args)
  (eval-expression (method-body method)
    (make-env (cons 'this (method-ids method))
              (cons obj args))))
```

Together with a modest number of helper procedures not shown here, this provides a complete implementation of the BASE language.

3   The Modeling Framework

This short section presents the modeling framework in general terms. (Readers who prefer bottom-up presentation of general concepts may want to skip directly to section 4.)

The framework models each AO mechanism as a *weaver* that combines two input programs to produce either a program or a computation. Each weaver is modeled as an 11-tuple:

$$\langle X, X_{JP}, A, A_{ID}, A_{EFF}, A_{MOD}, B, B_{ID}, B_{EFF}, B_{MOD}, META \rangle$$

A and B are the languages in which the input programs p_A and p_B are written. X is the result domain of the weaving process, which is usually a computation, but can be a third language to model systems like Hyper/J, where the semantics is defined in terms of manipulating code.

X_{JP} is the join points in X.

A_{ID} and B_{ID} are the means, in the languages A and B, of identifying elements of X_{JP} (the join points in X).

A_{EFF} and B_{EFF} are the means, in the languages A and B, of effecting semantics at identified join points.

A_{MOD} and B_{MOD} are the units of modularity in the languages A and B. All discussion of the units of modularity is deferred to Section 6.

META is an optional meta-language for parameterizing the weaving process. In cases where META is not used we simply leave it out of the model.

A *weaving process* is defined as a procedure with signature:

$$A \times B \times META \rightarrow X$$

That is, it accepts three programs, p_A, p_B and p_{META}, written in the A, B and META languages, and produces either a computation or a new program.

A critical property of this model is that it models A, B and X as distinct entities, and models weaving as combining the semantics of programs in A and B at join points in X. This differs from models that have two elements (i.e. A and B), and characterize B as merging with A at join points in A. The implications of this three-part model are discussed further in Section 6, but two points are worth discussing here.

Table 1. Summary of four models. In this table the single letters 'c', 'm' and 'f' are abbreviations for class, method and field respectively

	PA	TRAV	COMPOSITOR	OC
X	program execution	traversal execution	composed program	combined program
X_{JP}	method calls	arrival at each object	declarations in X	class declarations
A	c, m, f declarations	c, f declarations	c, m, f declarations	c declarations w/o OC declarations
A_{ID}	m signatures, etc.	c, f signatures	c, m, f signatures	method signatures
A_{EFF}	execute method body	provide reachability	provide declarations	provide declarations
B	advice declarations	traversal spec. & visitor	$(= A)$	OC method declarations
B_{ID}	pointcuts	traversal spec.	$(= A_{ID})$	effective method signatures
B_{EFF}	execute advice body	call visitor & continue	$(= A_{EFF})$	copy method declarations
META	none	none	match & merge rules	none

In general, A and B can be different. This means that A_{ID} and B_{ID} can differ, as can A_{EFF} and B_{EFF}. For example, in the model of AspectJ presented in Section 4.1, method declarations are modeled as elements of the A language, and advice are modeled as elements of B. Both method declarations and advice can affect what happens at a method call. But their means of identifying the call is different (a method signature in a method declaration vs. a pointcut in an advice), and their means of effecting semantics of the call is different (execution of a method differs from execution of after advice).

In cases where A and B are different, it is often the case that one of them can be seen as more similar in structure to X than the other. Again, in the AspectJ case, X will be the execution of the objects, which can be seen as more similar in structure to A (the classes and methods) than to B (the advice). In such cases, we will always use A as the name of the one that is more similar to X. But it will be critical to remember that A is not the same as X, it is just highly similar in structure to X. A key property of this framework is to distinguish A and X even when they are quite similar.

4   Four Mechanisms in Terms of the Model

This section presents models of four mechanisms found in current AO systems. Table 1 shows a summary of the four models. For each mechanism, we first present a simplified, or core version of its semantics, by providing an intuitive description and a short example program. These are based on the corresponding material developed for the BASE semantics in Section 2. We then present the model, which is derived from the framework by filling in the eleven parameters. Each sub-section ends with an intuitive validation of the model, which is done by showing how elements of the implementation correspond to elements of the model.

4.1   PA – Pointcuts and Advice

This section shows how the pointcut and advice mechanism in AspectJ can be modeled in terms of the modeling framework.

We first present a simplified, or core, version of the pointcut and advice mechanism semantics; we call this core semantics PA. As compared to AspectJ, PA has only method call join points, after advice declarations, and call, target, && and || pointcuts. While this leaves out significant AspectJ functionality, it suffices to capture the important elements, and later in the paper Section 5.1 shows that the missing functionality can be added without requiring changes to the model.

As an example of the PA functionality, consider the following after advice, which implements display updating functionality similar to that in [11].

```
after(FigureElement fe):
    (call(void Point.setX(int))
     || call(void Point.setY(int))
     || call(void Line.setP1(Point))
     || call(void Line.setP2(Point)))
    && target(fe) {
  fe.display.update(fe);⁵
}
```

Implementation of PA. This section presents an interpreter for PA, based on a few small changes and additions to the interpreter for BASE.

First, we define a structure used to represent dynamic join points:

```
(define-struct call-jp (mname target args))
```

This structure says that the dynamic values at a join point – remember that for now PA only has method call join points – include the name of the method being called, the object that is the target of the call, and a list of the arguments to the call.

The weave procedure is defined as:

```
(define pa:weave
  (lambda (pgm); -> computation
    (fluid-let ((pgm
                  (remove-advice-decls pgm))
                (*advice-decls*
                  (gather-advice-decls pgm)))
      (eval-program pgm)))))
```

---

⁵ In full AspectJ, this could be written as:

```
after(FigureElement fe):
    call(void FigureElement+.set*(..)) && target(fe) {
  fe.display.update(fe);
}
```

But we write the longer form because we do not implement the required type pattern and wildcarding functionality in this paper.

The weaver first separates the advice declarations from the rest of the program, leaving it with an ordinary BASE program, as well as a list of advice declarations. The weaver then proceeds to evaluate the BASE program.

The call-method procedure is modified to create method call join point structures, and check whether any advice declarations match the join point; these advice declarations are run after executing the method itself.

```
(define call-method
  (lambda (mname obj args)
    (let* ((jp (make-call-jp mname obj args))
           (method      (lookup-method jp))
           (adv-matches (lookup-advice jp)))
      (execute-advice adv-matches jp
        (lambda ()
          (execute-method method jp))))))
```

In addition to redefining call-method, we also redefine lookup- and execute-method to take a single jp structure as their argument, rather than taking mname, obj and args separately. This simple change is not shown here.

The role of lookup-advice is to take a jp structure and look in *advice-decls* to find which advice declarations have a pointcut that matches the join point. The result of lookup-advice is a list of adv-match structures. Each such structure represents the fact that a particular advice declaration matched, and includes bindings of parameters of the advice to values in the context of the join point (i.e. fe is bound to the figure element).

```
(define-struct adv-match (adv-decl ptc-match))
(define-struct ptc-match (ids vals))
```

lookup-advice works simply by looping through all the advice declarations, calling pointcut-matches to see if each advice declaration's pointcut matches the join point.

```
(define lookup-advice
  (lambda (jp)
    (remove*⁶ #f
      (map (lambda (adecl)
             (let* ((ptc (advice-decl-ptc adecl))
                    (ptc-match
                     (pointcut-matches ptc jp)))
               (if (not ptc-match)
                   #f
                   (make-adv-match adecl
                                   ptc-match))))
           *advice-decls*)))))
```

pointcut-matches is simply a case-based test to see whether a given pointcut matches the join point. If not, it returns false, otherwise it returns a ptc-match structure. Note that target is currently the only pointcut that binds parameters.

---

⁶ Remove all occurrences of an item from a list.

```
(define pointcut-matches
  (lambda (ptc jp)
    (cond ((call-pointcut? ptc)
           (and (eq? (call-pointcut-mname ptc)
                     (call-jp-mname jp))
                (make-ptc-match '() '())))
          ((target-pointcut? ptc)
           (make-ptc-match
             (list (target-pointcut-id ptc))
             (list (call-jp-target jp))))
          ((and-pointcut? ptc) ...)
          ((or-pointcut?  ptc) ...)
          )))
```

The execute-advice procedure takes a list of advice match structures, a jp structure and a thunk as arguments. The thunk implements the computation at the join point independent of any advice. As shown in the call-method procedure above, at method call join points, the thunk implements the behavior of call-method in the original BASE system. Note that execute-advice must be able to handle a list of matching advice, because join points can have more than one matching advice.

```
(define execute-advice
  (lambda (adv-matches jp thunk)
    (let ((result (thunk)))
      (for-each (lambda (adv-match)
                  (execute-one-advice adv-match
                                      jp))
                adv-matches)
      result)))
```

Model of PA. The model of PA in terms of the framework is as follows. Note that we use italics to identify parts of PA semantics that are deferred to Section 5.

X	Execution of combined programs
X_{JP}	method calls, and field gets and sets
A	Class, method *and field* declarations
A_{ID}	method *and field* signatures
A_{EFF}	execute method body, get and set field value
B	advice declarations with pointcuts
B_{ID}	Pointcuts
B_{EFF}	execute advice body *before*, after *and around* method

We use the implementation as intuitive evidence that the model is realizable and appropriate. We do this by matching the model parameters to corresponding elements in the implementation code.

A and B are clearly modeled in the implementation of pa:weave. A program p_A in the language A is the class declarations from the complete program; a program p_B in the language B is the advice declarations, with their associated pointcuts. X is the complete computation, which pa:weave produces by calling eval-program. In this case A plays a primary role over B, as the weaver proceeds by running A, calling advice from B when appropriate.

The revised implementation of `call-method` models method call join points (X_{JP}) as the points in the flow of control when a method is called. The jp structure models the kind of join point, as well as the values available in the context of the join point.[7]

In A, the complete signatures of method declarations are the means of identifying join points (A_{ID}), and execution of the method body is the means of specifying semantics at the join points (A_{EFF}). Taken together, these say, "when execution reaches a call to an object of this class with this method name, then execute this code."

In B, the means of identifying join points (B_{ID}) is pointcuts, and is modeled by `pointcut-matches`. The means of effecting semantics (B_{EFF}) is execution of the advice body after continuing with the join point, and is modeled by `execute-advice`.

4.2   TRAV – Traversals

The Demeter systems (Demeter, DemeterJ and DJ) provide a mechanism that enables programmers to implement traversals through object graphs in a succinct declarative fashion. The effect of this functionality is to allow the programmer to define, in a modular way, a traversal that would otherwise require code scattered among a number of classes. They work by defining the traversal as well as what actions to take at points along the traversal.

In this section, we work with a simple traversal semantics, called TRAV. TRAV supports declarative description of the traversal, but not whether to call the visitor at each object in the traversal; the visitor is simply called at every object in the traversal. As with PA above, while this omits important functionality, that omission does not impact the suitability of the general framework. Section 5 shows how the omitted functionality can be added.

An example of a program fragment written using TRAV is:

```
Visitor counter = new CountElementsVisitor();

traverse("from Figure to FigureElement",
         fig,
         counter);
```

This code fragment implements the behavior of visiting all the `FigureElements` reachable from a `Figure`. The first argument to `traverse` is called a traversal specification; it describes the path to follow to each object to be visited. The second argument is a root object, where the traversal starts. The third argument is a visitor, which defines behavior at each traversed object. In this case the traversal mechanism

---

[7] The semantics of values in the context of a join point and how the `this`, `target` and `args` pointcuts access those values is more complex than this in AspectJ, because proceed can change the values that `args` sees. Doing it properly makes the code more complex, but does not impact the modeling framework or the model of PA.

is taking care of iterating through the elements of the figure, and following down through line objects to reach point objects. The visitor is called on every object in the traversal, including the Figure as well as the List that holds the FigureElements. The actual visitor must decide which objects to count, i.e. not to count the List.

We preserve the critical property of Demeter that the range of traversal is based on reachability information from the class graph, in addition to information about the dynamic class of the current object. Therefore, when the traversal comes to a Line object, for example, it goes on to the Point objects referenced by the Line; but it does not go on to the Display object, because the traversal specification says it is looking for FigureElement and the class graph shows there are no ways to reach a FigureElement from a Display.

Implementation of TRAV. The weaver implementation for TRAV is the procedure **trav:weave**. We modify **eval-expression** from the BASE interpreter to call **trav:weave** to implement the new **traverse** primitive. The definition of **trav:weave** is:

```
(define trav:weave
  (lambda (trav-spec root visitor)
    (let arrive ((obj   root)  ;arrival at obj is a jp
                 (path (make-path
                          (object-cname root))))
      (call-visitor visitor obj)
      (for-each
        (lambda (fname)
          (let* ((next-obj (get-field fname obj))
                 (next-cname (object-cname next-obj))
                 (next-path
                   (extend-path path next-cname)))
            (if (match? next-path trav-spec)
                (arrive next-obj next-path))))
        (object->fnames obj)))))
```

The traversal process can be seen as a simple depth-first walk with a navigator that restricts the walk. When the walk arrives at an object, it calls the visitor with the object, and then recursively walks the objects referenced by the object. At each step along the way, it first checks with the navigator about whether or not to proceed.

The navigator checks whether to traverse to an object in two steps. It first locates possible positions of the object in the traversal specification. The traversal specifications following those positions are then tested against the class graph. The test succeeds when there exists a path on the class graph that matches a remaining specification.

We implement this in a simple way. We assume the root object is always a legal root of the traversal specification. In order to locate positions in the specification, the code manages a path that keeps track of a sequence of classes walked from the root. The match? procedure checks whether the whole path matches the traversal specification by using two sub-procedures that correspond to the two steps above.

```
(define match?
  (lambda (path trav-spec)
    (let ((residual-spec (match-path path trav-spec)))
      (match-class-graph?
        residual-spec (path-last-cname path)))))
```

The match-path procedure matches the path to the traversal specification by repeatedly matching each class in the path from the root.[8] The matching algorithm is implemented by simple conditional cases on the kind of the directive at the head of the specification. The code returns either a remaining specification for partially matched cases, an empty specification for completely matched cases, or false for unmatched cases. When a class matches more than one position in the specification, an or-specification is returned as a result.

```
(define match-path
  (lambda (path spec);->spec
    (let loop ((cnames (path->cnames path))
               (spec spec))
      (if (null? cnames) spec
          (loop (cdr cnames)
                (match-cname (car cnames) spec))))))
(define match-cname
  (lambda (cname spec);->spec or #f
    (cond ((null? spec) #f) ; unmatched
          ((to-spec? spec)
           (if (subclass? cname (to-spec-cname spec))
               (make-or-spec '()
                 (list spec (spec-next spec)))
               spec))
          ...)))
```

The match-class-graph? procedure matches the remaining specification against the class graph, and returns true or false. For a to-specification, the matching is simply subsumed by the reachability to the specified class. Note that the reachability is decided by checking the class graph. In the implementation, the procedure reachable?, not shown here, does this by using global variable *classes*.

```
(define match-class-graph?
  (lambda (spec root-cname);->boolean
    (let loop ((spec spec)
               (cname root-cname))
      (cond ((eq? spec #f) #f) ; already unmatched
            ((to-spec? spec)
             (reachable? cname (to-spec-cname spec)))
            ...))))
```

Calling the visitor involves calling the visit method with the object as its argument.

---

[8] A more sophisticated implementation would implement these steps with a state transition machine so that it could avoid complicated checks at each object.

```
(define call-visitor
  (lambda (visitor obj)
    (call-method 'visit visitor (list obj)))))
```

Model of TRAV. The TRAV model is:

X	execution of traversal through object graph (visit the objects specified by traversal spec)
X_{JP}	arrival at each object along the traversal
A	class and field declarations
A_{ID}	class names and complete field signatures[9]
A_{EFF}	provide reachability information
B	traversal specification and visitor
B_{ID}	traversal specification, overloaded visitor methods
B_{EFF}	call visitor and continue traversal (or not)

X is the actual traversal, and is implemented by `trav:weave`. Within that process, a call to `arrive` corresponds to a join point. This is analogous to the way, in the PA model, that a dynamic call to `call-method` corresponds to a join point.

p_A and p_B are clearly modeled in the implementation – p_A is the class and field declarations, which are converted into a class graph (bound to the `*classes*` global variable) by `eval-program` before executing `trav:weave`. p_B is the three arguments to `trav:weave`.

In A, the class names and field signatures are A_{ID}. The effect of A is to provide reachability information, which is modeled by the `reachable?` procedure. This combined with the traversal specification determines where the traversal goes. This combination happens in the `match?` procedure.

In B, B_{ID} is the traversal specifications, and is modeled by the `match-path` procedure. Combined with A_{EFF}, B_{EFF} determines whether to continue traversal, which is realized by the simple conditional branch on the result of the `match?` procedure.

4.3   COMPOSITOR – Class Composition

Hyper/J provides mechanisms that compose programs. This allows the programmer to implement concerns as independent (partial) programs, even when the composition of the concerns cuts across their module structure.

In this paper, we focus on the composition of classes. We omit class hierarchy composition, slicing based on concern maps and other powerful features of Hyper/J. For simplicity, we also limit ourselves to only a simple composition semantics that merges two programs based on class and member names. Using our simplified semantics, called COMPOSITOR, the display updating functionality from Section 4.1 can be implemented in two steps as follows. First we write a program with just this class:

---

[9]   Similar to a complete method signature, a complete field signature includes the class name, and is of the form: `<class> <enclosing-class>.<id>`

```
class Observable {
  Display display;
  void moved() {
    display.update(this);
  }
}
```

calling the original figures program of Section 2.1 program A, and this one program B, the two programs are composed with a call to the compositor (weaver) as follows:

```
(compositor:weave <program-a> <program-b>
  "match Point.setX with Observable.moved
   match Point.setY with Observable.moved
   match Line.setP1 with Observable.moved
   match Line.setP2 with Observable.moved")[10]
```

In the resultant composed program, the specified methods of the Point and Line classes are combined with the body of the moved method above. The effect is that they call display.update after they finish executing.

Implementation of COMPOSITOR. The weaver for COMPOSITOR is a source-to-source translator, which merges two BASE programs into one, under control of a composition description. The code for the weaver is

```
(define compositor:weave
  (lambda (pgm-a pgm-b relationships)
    (let loop ((pgm    (make-program '()))
               (seeds (compute-seeds pgm-a pgm-b)))
      (if (not (null? seeds))
          (let ((signature
                  (all-match (car seeds)
                             relationships)))
            (if signature
                (let* ((jp    (car seeds))
                       (decl (merge-decls jp
                               relationships)))
                  (loop (add-decl-to-pgm decl pgm
                                          signature)
                        (remove-subsets jp (cdr seeds))))
                (loop pgm (cdr seeds))))
          pgm))))
```

---

[10] The actual Hyper/J meta-program for this composition would look something like:

```
mergeByName;
bracket "{Point,Line}"."set*"
  after Observable.moved($OperationName);
```

But for simplicity, we do not implement pattern matching and bracketing mechanisms. Instead, we assume that two methods with the same name match regardless of the parameter types, and that when methods from programs A and B are merged, the bodies of those methods are placed in A, B order in the merged method.

It receives two programs, pgm-a and pgm-b, as well as the description of the matching and merging to use, relationships.

The first step is to compute all possible compositions of declarations in the merged program. We call these seeds, and they are produced by compute-seeds. We model this as computing the power set of the union of the declarations in pgm-a and pgm-b (of course our implementation does not actually compute the power set). The list of seeds is sorted in set-inclusion order, with subsets following supersets.

After sorting, for each seed, there are up to three steps:

1. The procedure all-match determines whether this set should actually be merged according to the composition description, and returns the signature for the composed declaration when it should. In the simplest case, a seed of two method declarations (coming from pgm-a and pgm-b) having the same signature m matches, and returns m as the signature for the composed declaration. I.e. the set:

   {<Point.setX(int)>, <Observable.moved()>}

   s merged to <Point.setX(int)> in the composed program.

2. The procedure merge-decls computes the body of the actual declaration. I.e.

   ```
   {
       this.x = x;
       display.update(this);
   }
   ```

3. The procedure add-decl-to-pgm adds the declaration to the resultant program with the computed signature.

For any seed that is merged, all subsets of that seed are removed from the remaining seeds before proceeding.

The procedure all-match first picks a signature from the declarations in the given seed, and then checks that all the declarations can contribute to the signature. In order to allow renaming, it takes a relationships parameter as an additional argument:

```
(define all-match
  (lambda (decls relationships)
    (let ((sig (pick-signature decls
                               relationships)))
      (and (every? (lambda (decl)
                     (signature-match? sig decl
                       relationships))
                   decls)
           sig))))
```

The merge-decls procedure also receives relationships as an argument. Richer merging mechanisms, such as overriding and bracketing (i.e., before/after/around-like merger), can be supported by extending the meta-language and this procedure.

Model of COMPOSITOR. The description of the COMPOSITOR model is as follows. Note that unlike the other mechanisms, A and B are in the same language, and in this case we also use the META parameter.

X	the composed program
X_{JP}	declarations in X
A, B	class, method and field declarations
A_{ID}, B_{ID}	class, method and field signatures
A_{EFF}, B_{EFF}	provide declaration
META	Rules for matching *and merging*

In the code, p_A and p_B are modeled as separate parameters to compositor:weave. p_{META} is the third parameter to this procedure. A and B are treated equally in the code, and can easily be generalized to a list of programs for composing more than two programs. X is the resultant composed program, which initially is empty, and is populated with declarations during the weaving process.

Join points are modeled as declarations in X. Each one corresponds to the merging of a subset of declarations from p_A and p_B. So seeds are in fact seeds for join points. If they match the match/merge description (p_{META}) they are merged to form an actual join point. Note that a single declaration from A or B can contribute to more than one declaration in X and vice versa.

A_{ID}, B_{ID} is the signatures of the declarations in A and B. The matching rules A_{ID}, B_{ID} work with are modeled by the META argument to the weaver.

A_{EFF}, B_{EFF} is simply to contribute the declaration from A or B to the merge. The actual merging is controlled by META.

4.4   OC – Open Classes

Open class mechanisms make it possible to locate method or field declarations for a class outside the textual body of the class declaration. Open classes are used in a variety of ways to modularize code; a common use is in visitor problems.

In this section, we work with a simple version of open classes in which method declarations are contained within class declarations, but it is possible to mark certain method declarations as defining methods on another class. We call this simple semantics OC.

Building on the running example, the following OC code defines draw methods for the different kinds of figure elements in a single DisplayMethods class – it modularizes the display aspect of the system.

```
class DisplayMethods {
  void Point.draw() { Graphics.drawOval(...); }
  void Line.draw()  { Graphics.drawLine(...); }
}
```

Implementation of OC. We implement OC as a pre-processor that operates on a program consisting of normal BASE code intermixed with open class method declarations and produces a BASE program. This pre-processor pass is defined as

```
(define oc:weave
  (lambda (pgm)
    (let ((pgm       (remove-oc-mdecls pgm))
          (oc-mdecls (gather-oc-mdecls pgm)))
      (make-pgm
        (map (lambda (cdecl)
               (let* ((cname (class-decl-cname cdecl))
                      (sname (class-decl-sname cdecl))
                      (per-class-oc-mdecls
                        (lookup-oc-mdecls cname
                                              oc-mdecls)))
                 (make-class-decl cname sname
                   (append (class-decl-decls cdecl)
                           (copy-oc-mdecls cname
                             per-class-ocmdecls)))))
             (pgm-class-decls pgm))))))
```

The first step is to remove all open class method declarations from the input program. This is done by remove-oc-mdecls and gather-oc-mdecls. The open class method declarations are then each copied into their appropriate class. The lookup-oc-mdecls procedure finds, for a given class name, which open class method declarations should be copied into it. The copy-oc-mdecls procedure then copies those declarations, changing their signature from the open class form <cname>.<mname> to the normal BASE form <mname>.

```
(define lookup-oc-mdecls
  (lambda (cname all-oc-mdecls)
    (collect-if
      (lambda (oc-mdecl)
        (eq? (oc-mdecl-cname oc-mdecl) cname))
      all-oc-mdecls)))

(define copy-oc-mdecls
  (lambda (cname per-class-oc-mdecls)
    (map (lambda (oc-mdecl)
           (make-method-decl cname
             (oc-mdecl-rtype  oc-mdecl)
             (oc-mdecl-mname  oc-mdecl)
             (oc-mdecl-params oc-mdecl)
             (oc-mdecl-body   oc-mdecl)))
         per-class-oc-mdecls)))
```

Model of OC. The description of OC in terms of the model is as follows:

X	combined program
X_{JP}	class declarations
A	class declarations without OC method declarations
A_{ID}	effective method signatures (cname from enclosing class declaration)
A_{EFF}	method declaration stays in place
B	OC method declarations
B_{ID}	effective method signatures (cname from OC method declaration)
B_{EFF}	copy method declaration to target class

X is modeled as the results of the oc:weave procedure. p_A and p_B are a BASE program stripped of open class method declarations and the sets of open class method declarations respectively. The join points are the class declarations in the result program. A_{ID} happens by inclusion – the normal methods in p_A are copied into their same enclosing classes in X. This is the same effect as saying that the complete signature of methods in A is A_{ID}. B_{ID} is also the complete signature, which is explicit in B. The matching process for B is modeled by lookup-oc-mdecls. A_{EFF}, B_{EFF} are the same, the method declaration is copied into the class it belongs in X.

5   Restoring Functionality

To have confidence in the applicability of the modeling framework, we must be sure that in our simplified semantics – PA, TRAV etc. vs. AspectJ, Demeter etc. – we did not leave out issues that cannot be captured by the framework. This section addresses that concern by showing how several key missing functionalities could be added without falling outside the scope of the models.

There are two ways to show this, the strongest is to show that the actual models of each semantics change only in their details. The second is to show that even though a new model is required, it still fits within the same framework. In all the cases below, we show the former. We show this by once again appealing to the implementation and using it to intuitively validate that the model changes are only minor. Since all these changes are highly localized in the implementation, we claim they do not change the deep model structure.

5.1   Adding Features to PA

The PA semantics is missing several key features of AspectJ, including additional kinds of join points, before and around advice, and context-sensitive pointcuts like cflow.

To add more kinds of join point, we must enrich the space of jp structures, and have more places in the interpreter perform advice lookup and execute operations. For example, join points for reading a field could be added to PA by defining a structure as follows:

```
(define-struct (get-jp jp) (fname))
```[11]

and replacing the body of get-field just as Section 4.1 does for call-method.

To add additional pointcuts (excluding cflow-like pointcuts), we simply extend pointcut-matches to identify join points matching those pointcuts. This could include pointcuts that identify only one kind of join point, such as call and get as well as pointcuts like target that identify multiple kinds of join point. In some cases implementing a new pointcut can require that additional information be added

---

[11] Assume that we first define a structure type jp, and modify call-jp to be a subtype of it.

to some or all kinds of join point. For example, adding a within pointcut would require adding information about the lexically enclosing method to call join points.

To add before or around advice, we modify execute-advice to run the pieces of advice and call the thunk in the appropriate order. Supporting proceed can be done in a manner similar to super calls. We modify execute-advice to make a lambda closure for the remaining processing at the join point and put the closure in the environment of around advice execution. We also extend eval-exp to extract the closure from the environment and execute it for proceed.

Allowing proceed to change the arguments that inner advice and the method receive is more complicated. It requires changing the thunk passed to execute-advice to take a single argument, args, which is a list of those arguments. When a proceed is evaluated, the values of its operands are passed to the closure for proceed, which eventually passes them to the thunk.

To add control flow sensitive pointcuts like cflow, we thread a call stack through the join point structures. This is done by adding a stack-prev-jp field to all jp structures. This field holds the previous join point on the call stack. This requires the code that constructs the join points to keep the last top of stack and thread it properly. We can do this with the fluid-let mechanism in Scheme:

```
(define call-method
  (lambda (mname obj args)
    (let* ((jp (make-call-jp .stack-previous-jp.
                             mname obj args))
           ...)
      (fluid-let ((.stack-previous-jp. jp))
        ...))))
```

Here .stack-previous-jp. is effectively a dynamically scoped variable. The new cflow clause of pointcut-match follow the stack-prev-jp field until it either finds a matching jp or reaches the bottom of the stack.

A frequently-proposed feature for PA like mechanisms is to add an attribute feature to method declarations [1], and allow pointcuts to identify join-points based on these attributes [26]. This feature can easily be added to PA. Doing it for method declarations and call join points requires extending the language syntax to support attributes, extending join point structures to include an attribute element, modifying call-method to include the attribute in the join point, and adding a new kind of pointcut to match based on attributes.

These changes add detail to the previous model for PA, but they do not change its structure. Field gets are, like method calls, points in the flow of execution. Similarly the new kinds of pointcuts are no more than that – new kinds of pointcuts. Before and around advice require changes only to execute-advice. Adding proceed with arguments is only a little less localized.

5.2   TRAV

Demeter, DemeterJ and DJ differ slightly in terms of whether the traversal specification itself has control over whether the visitor is called. In DJ, for example, this is controlled by whether the visitor has an overloaded method for the type of

visited object. This range of behaviors can be modeled in the implementation of
`call-visitor`. To do so we adopt a naming convention that simulates overloading;
then, before calling a visitor on an object, the traverser checks whether the visitor has
a method for the class of the object, and then calls that method if it exists:

```
(define call-visitor
  (lambda (visitor obj)
    (let ((mname (visitor-mname (object-cname obj))))
      (if (has-method? (object-cname visitor) mname)
          (call-method mname visitor (list obj))))))
```

Again, these changes are local in the model implementation, and affect only details
of the TRAV model.

5.3   Compositor

Hyper/J provides a rich meta-language that controls the composition, namely,
bracketing (inserting method bodies before, after, or around of another method body),
overriding, renaming, and wild-carding for matching. These can be supported by
extending `all-match` and `merge-decls`. Since the enriched meta-languages can
specify different merging strategies for different declarations contributing to a join
point, `all-match` has to return both a matched signature and a list of merging
directives for each matched declaration, so that `merge-decls` can know what to do.

Once again, these changes do not affect the basic structure of the COMPOSITOR
model, as evidenced by the way they are localized in the implementation.

6   Modular Crosscutting

Our models provide a basis for understanding and comparing how each of the
mechanisms enables crosscutting modularity. To do so we first need to address the
A_{MOD} and B_{MOD} model parameters. These are the units of modularity in the A and B
languages. We define these as follows:

	A_{MOD}	B_{MOD}
PA	class	advice
TRAV	class	traversal specification
COMPOSITO R	class	class
OC	class	class

These are not the only possibilities for units of modularity in each of these models.
In PA for example, we could do as AspectJ does, and B_{MOD} could be aspect
declarations. In all the models we could use higher-level units of modularity like
packages. The analysis of this section can be repeated for such alternative units of
modularity to compare how crosscutting is supported for each.

For a module m_A (from p_A) we say that the *projection* of m_A onto X is the set of
join points identified by the A_{ID} elements within m_A. The same is true for m_B. For

example, in PA, the projection of a given advice declaration is all the join points matched by the pointcut of that advice declaration.

The dots in X represent JPs, the dots in A/B represent elements that match those JPs, the dashed/dotted boxes in A/B represent modules, and the dashed/dotted boxes in X are the projections of those modules. In all these cases the modules in A and B crosscut with respect to X.

For a pair of modules m_A and m_B (from p_A and p_B) we say that *m_A crosscuts m_B with respect to X* if and only if their projections onto X intersect, and neither of the projections is a subset of the other. Fig. 1 illustrates this situation, first in general terms and then for each of the example programs as explained below.

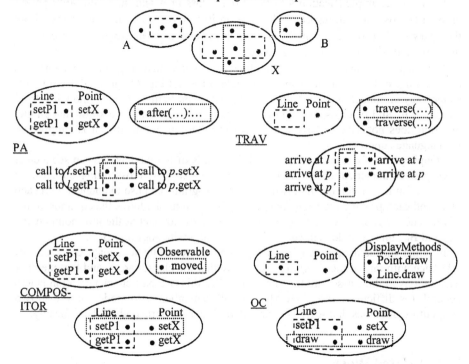

Fig. 1. Modular Crosscutting in General Terms and in the Four Example Programs

In the PA example (Section 4.1) the Point class and the display updating advice crosscut each other with respect to X. We consider the projection of the Point class onto X to include all calls to methods of the Point class.[12] The projection of the advice onto X includes calls to the setter methods of the Point and Line classes. So the projections of the Point class and the advice intersect, and neither is subset of the other.

---

[12] In AspectJ, the call join points would be considered not as being within the projection of the class, but rather as being within the projection of the calling class. Execution join points would be considered as within the projection of the class that defines the method.

In the TRAV example (Section 4.2) the Point class and the traversal description crosscut with respect to X. The projection of the Point class includes all arrivals at Point objects initiated by any traversals. The projection of the traversal description includes arrivals at Point objects as well as arrivals at objects of other classes such as Line and LinkedList.

In the COMPOSITOR example (Section 4.3) the Point class and the Observable class crosscut with respect to X. The projection of the Point class on X includes all methods of the Point class in X. The projection of the Observable in B includes all set methods of Point and Line classes in X.

In the OC example (Section 4.4) the Point class in A and the DisplayMethods class in B crosscut with respect to X. The projection of Point in A contains all but the draw method of Point in X, and the projection of DisplayMethods contains draw methods of Point and Line classes.

Note that this analysis does not allow us to say that a given mechanism is crosscutting, only that it can support modular crosscutting. Or, in model terms, we cannot say a model is crosscutting, just that a particular pair of modules from particular p_A and p_B crosscut each other. This is not surprising, we know that an OO program does not have to have a hierarchical inheritance structure; it is simply that the language supports it.

Stepping back from the examples and the details of the models, we can see a clear three part characterization of what is required to support crosscutting structure: a common frame of reference that two (or more) programs can use to connect with each other and each provide their semantic contribution. In model terms the common frame of reference is X_{JP}, the programs are p_A and p_B, they connect at the join points using A_{ID} and B_{ID}, and provide their semantic contribution with A_{EFF} and B_{EFF}.

In some mechanisms, including PA, it can be tempting to equate the frame of reference with one of the programs, i.e. to say that the classes are X and that member declarations in the classes are the join points. But this two part characterization is less general It is difficult to model COMPOSITOR semantics or to model more than two crosscutting modules that way. The three part model supports both of these cleanly.

7   Related Work

Some authors have compared two particular AO systems, for example, Lieberherr et al. have explained concepts in the Demeter systems in terms of AspectJ [14]. Our work defines a common framework in terms of which four systems are modeled.

Some authors have proposed formal models for AO mechanisms [2, 6, 13, 20, 27]. Those models are attractive in that they express deep characteristics of the systems, such as implementation issues [17] and static analysis [25], in concise ways. But they only apply to specific mechanisms, all of which are in the PA family. Again, our work differs in finding common structure for diverse AO mechanisms. We believe that our framework could also be useful in developing other kinds of models for specific mechanisms. In fact, Wand's semantics[27] is based on our earlier work on the modeling framework. Note that this is in contrast to characterizations of weaving that work only in terms of source code pre-processing.

Filman and Friedman suggest that AOP systems can be defined as enabling quantified programmatic assertions over programs written by programmers oblivious to such assertions [7]. The model they propose is a two part-model – it compares programs and assertions. Our three-part structure is essential to accounting for how the mechanisms enable modular crosscutting, a key goal identified in [12]. Our framework can also model mechanisms that involve less "obliviousness", in that it can describe mechanisms such as attribute-based pointcuts described in Section 5.1.

8   Future Work

Further development of these models is one area of future work. For example, it appears that a variant of the PA model should apply to systems like Composition Filters [3, 4], and aspect-oriented frameworks[24].

We would like to enhance the model, and the implementations, to have a single parameterized weaving process. In the models, the weaving process consists of three operations: generate a join point, use A_{ID} and/or B_{ID} to identify elements in p_A and/or p_B matching the join point, and use A_{EFF} and/or B_{EFF} to produce the proper effects from the matching elements. The following code shows these steps:

```
(lambda (pA pB)
  ...
  (let ((jp <generate a JP>))
    ...
    (apply-A (lookup-A jp ...pA...))
    ...
    (apply-B (lookup-B jp ...pB...))
    ...))
```

But differences among the models make it difficult to actually implement all four using a parameterizable procedure of this form. These differences include:

- COMPOSITOR generates candidate join points rather than actual join points.
- B_{EFF} in PA takes as input a thunk that does lookup and apply for A. This makes it possible for B_{EFF} to control execution of A.
- The lookup and apply for A is implicit in OC. COMPOSITOR has a folded lookup and apply for A and B. In TRAV, A_{ID} and B_{ID} work together on each join point.

While a single parameterized weaving process is attractive, not having it does not seem to be a cause for significant concerns. Similar modeling frameworks for OO tend to work in terms of common terms more than a single parameterized implementation. The interpreters from [8] on which our code is based are not, for example, parameterized or composable.

9   Summary

Developing a common set of concepts with which to discuss and compare AO mechanisms is a critical task. This paper takes a step in this direction by presenting a set of models that can be used to compare how different AOP mechanisms provide support for modular implementation of crosscutting concerns. The analysis yields a three-part characterization of what is required for two programs coordinate their semantic contributions in terms of a common frame of reference. Modules in the programs are said to crosscut each other with respect to the frame of reference. This simple model makes it possible to capture all four mechanisms, and expands naturally to cover more than two crosscutting modules.

Acknowledgements

The authors are grateful to Kris de Volder, Mitchell Wand, Chris Dutchyn, Gail Murphy, Harold Ossher, Karl Lieberherr, Mira Mezini, and Mario Südholt for their valuable comments and discussion on early drafts of the paper. Previous work with Wand and Dutchyn developed earlier versions of the Aspect Sandbox.

References

[1]   C# Language Specification (2nd edition), ECMA Standard-334, 2002.
[2]   Andrews, J., Process-Algebraic Foundations of Aspect-Oriented Programming. In *International Conference on Metalevel Architectures and Separation of Crosscutting Concerns*, LNCS 2192, Springer, pp.187-209, 2001.
[3]   Bergmans, L. and Aksit, M. Composing Crosscutting Concerns Using Composition Filters. *Communications of ACM*, 44(10)51-57, 2001.
[4]   Bergmans, L., Aksit, M. and Tekinerdogan, B. Aspect Composition Using Composition Filters. In *Software Architectures and Component Technology: The State of the Art in Research and Practice*, Kluwer, pp.357-382, 2001.
[5]   Clifton, C., Leavens, G., Chambers, C. and Millstein, T., MultiJava: Modular Open Classes and Symmetric Multiple Dispatch for Java. In *Conference on Object Oriented Programming Systems Languages and Applications*, pp.130-145, 2000.
[6]   Douence, R., Motelet, O. and Südholt, M. A Formal Definition of Crosscuts. In *International Conference on Metalevel Architectures and Separation of Crosscutting Concerns, LNCS 2192*, Springer, pp.170-186, 2001.
[7]   Filman, R. and Friedman, D. Aspect-Oriented Programming is Quantification and Obliviousness. In *OOPSLA 2000 Workshop on Advanced Separation of Concerns*.
[8]   Friedman, D., Wand, M. and Haynes, C.T. *Essentials of Programming Languages*. MIT Press, 2001.

[9]   Kelsey, R., Clinger, W. and Rees, J. Revised[5] Report on the Algorithmic Language Scheme. *Higher-Order and Symbolic Computation*, *11*(1)7-105, 1998.

[10]   Kiczales, G., Hilsdale, E., Hugunin, J., Kersten, M., Palm, J. and Griswold, W. Getting Started with AspectJ. *Communications of ACM*, *44*(10)59-65, 2001.

[11]   Kiczales, G., Hilsdale, E., Hugunin, J., Kersten, M., Palm, J. and Griswold, W.G. An overview of AspectJ. In *European Conference on Object-Oriented Programming, LNCS 2072*, Springer, pp.327-353, 2001.

[12]   Kiczales, G., Lamping, J., Mendhekar, A., Maeda, C., Lopes, C., Loingtier, J.-M. and Irwin, J. Aspect-Oriented Programming. In *European Conference Object-Oriented Programming, LNCS 1241*, Springer, pp.220-242, 1997.

[13]   Laemmel, R. A Semantical Approach to Method-call Interception. In *International Conference on Aspect-Oriented Software Development*, pp.41-55, 2002.

[14]   Lieberherr, K., Orleans, D. and Ovlinger, J. Aspect-Oriented Programming with Adaptive Methods. *Communications of ACM*, *44*(10)39-41, 2001.

[15]   Lieberherr, K. Adaptive Object-Oriented Software: the Demeter Method with Propagation Patterns. PWS Publishing, 1996.

[16]   Lieberherr, K. and Orleans, D. Preventive Program Maintenance in Demeter/Java (Research demonstration). In *International Conference on Software Engineering*, pp.604-605, 1997.

[17]   Masuhara, H., Kiczales, G. and Dutchyn, C., A Compilation and Optimization Model for Aspect-Oriented Programs. In *International Conference on Compiler Construction*, LNCS 2622, Springer, pp.46-60, 2003.

[18]   Millstein, T. and Chambers, C., Modular Statically Typed Multimethods. In *European Conference on Object-Oriented Programming*, LNCS 1628, Springer, pp.279-303, 1999.

[19]   Moon, D., Object-oriented programming with Flavors. In Conference on Object Oriented Programming Systems Languages and Applications, pp.1-8, 1986.

[20]   Orleans, D. Incremental Programming with Extensible Decisions. In *International Conference on Aspect-Oriented Software Development*, pp.56-64, 2002.

[21]   Orleans, D. and Lieberherr, K. DJ: Dynamic Adaptive Programming in Java. In *International Conference on Metalevel Architectures and Separation of Crosscutting Concerns*, LNCS 2192, Springer, pp.73-80, 2001.

[22]   Ossher, H. and Tarr, P. Hyper/J: Multi-dimensional separation of concerns for Java. In *International Conference on Software Engineering*, pp.729-730, 2001.

[23]   Ossher, H. and Tarr, P. The Shape of Things To Come: Using Multi-Dimensional Separation of Concerns with Hyper/J to (Re)Shape Evolving Software. *Communications of ACM*, *44*(10)43-50, 2001.

[24]   Pinto, M., Fuentes, L., Fayad, M. and Troya, J. Separation of Coordination in a Dynamic Aspect Oriented Framework. In *International Conference on Aspect-Oriented Software Development*, pp.134-140, 2002.

[25]   Sereni, D. and de Moor, O., Static Analysis of Aspects. In *International Conference on Aspect-Oriented Software Development*, pp.30-39, 2003.

[26]   Shukla, D., Fell, S. and Sells, C. Aspect-Oriented Programming Enables Better Code Encapsulation and Reuse. *MSDN Magazine, March*, 2002.

[27]   Wand, M., Kiczales, G. and Dutchyn, C. A Semantics for Advice and Dynamic Join Points in Aspect-Oriented Programming. In *Foundations of Aspect-Oriented Languages (FOAL2002)*, pp.1-8, 2002.

[28]   Weinreb, D. and Moon, D.A. Flavors: Message passing in the LISP machine, A.I. Memo 602, Massachusetts Institute of Technology A.I. Lab., 1980.

Spontaneous Container Services

Andrei Popovici, Gustavo Alonso, and Thomas Gross

Department of Computer Science, Swiss Federal Institute of Technology (ETHZ)
ETH Zentrum, CH-8092 Zürich, Switzerland
{popovici,alonso,trg}@inf.ethz.ch

Abstract. Container technology (e.g., Enterprise Java Beans) was designed for fixed network applications. This is unfortunate, because the ability of containers to adapt components transparently (e.g., with persistence and transactions) would be of great advantage in mobile computing. In this paper, we generalize the container model into a new software architecture, the *spontaneous container*. A spontaneous container allows to homogeneously extend all applications of a network, even if they spontaneously join or leave the network. In the paper we show how to build a spontaneous container by unifying different technologies into one coherent architecture: (i) dynamic aspect-oriented programming, (ii) containers, and (iii) infrastructures for mobile computing. Dynamic aspect-orientation makes a spontaneous container much more flexible than existing commercial containers. Inheriting the container programming model allows a single focus point for modifications for all applications in a network. Basing the overall architecture on dynamic service brokerage and discovery allows a seamless integration with existing infrastructures for both mobile and fixed computing. Following these ideas, we have built and evaluated a spontaneous container prototype that effectively and efficiently transforms applications within a network into a distributed system capable of transactional interaction, access control, and orthogonal persistence.

1   Introduction

Modern server architectures [14, 21] employ the *container model* to separate the business components from the system components. Through this separation, key functionality such as transactions, persistence, or security can be transparently added to the application at deployment time rather than having to implement it as part of the application.

Through separation of concerns [39], this model leads to increased re-usability and interoperability of business components. Although obviously very useful, this form of adaptation is not enough in software infrastructures for mobile computing where services appear and disappear arbitrarily and nodes cannot possibly know in advance with which other nodes they will interact. The frequent changes encountered in these new environments hamper the applicability of the container model because deployment-time adaptation would require taking applications off-line before they can be adapted to a new mobile or ad-hoc network.

L. Cardelli (Ed.): ECOOP 2003, LNCS 2743, pp. 29–53, 2003.

Instead of giving up the container model (and its benefits) for these dynamic environments, we advocate in this paper its generalization into a new software architecture for which we use the term *spontaneous container*. A spontaneous container provides a way to program and coordinate a number of entities in the same network – to have them working in a unified way in spite of their heterogeneity and their transient presence within the network boundaries.

From a software engineering point of view, the question is how to design and implement a spontaneous container. A promising way to achieve this objective is to provide explicit programming support for dynamic adaptation models [42, 20, 27] and aspect-orientation [9, 16]. By exposing the aspect-oriented run-time support in such a system, one gains the ability to unify at a small cost the programming paradigms encountered in (i) containers and in (ii) spontaneous networks for mobile computing. Thus, a spontaneous container inherits the properties of three technologies:

Spontaneous Networks Spontaneous networks are characterized by dynamic service discovery [4, 19]. As a consequence, applications do not need static binding to external resources. Instead, these resources are located at run-time as the application moves from one wireless network to another. This way, arbitrary services can discover and use each other's resources while co-located in the same computing network. By computing environment, we mean any set of two or more applications that can interact with each other (e.g., using a wireless network).

Container Programming The container model [22, 40] implies the ability to factor key functionality out of an application and make this functionality a dynamic property of the computing environment. I.e., rather than forcing the application to carry with it all the functionality necessary to interact with other applications or services, the computing environment of a spontaneous container should dynamically provide this functionality when needed.

Dynamic Adaptation New programming support infrastructures [27, 34, 8] allow changing applications at run-time. This is the kind of property needed in a spontaneous container, where applications must be adapted on-the-fly, as they join or leave a given computing environment. The nature of these adaptations (transactions, orthogonal persistence, security, logging) suggests using the concepts of aspect-oriented programming. By *explicitly exposing* an adaptation interface for dynamic, aspect-oriented adaptations, one can achieve the level of flexibility needed by these highly dynamic environments.

In this paper we present a Java-based infrastructure capable of such run-time adaptation. Using this spontaneous container, nodes can dynamically acquire extensions that make their state persistent (the state may be stored at a base station or at another node), their interactions transactional (with arbitrary levels of nesting and interacting with either base stations or on a peer-to-peer basis), and subject them to an access control policy (when accessing information in other nodes or at base stations).

We first motivate the paper by providing two example scenarios that extend existing commercial systems and that we have used as our test-bed for the ideas presented (Section 2). In Section 3 we describe how to unify existing technologies into a coherent system architecture. We show how to implement this architecture in the context of applications running on a Java Virtual Machine (JVM) in Section 4. Based on this prototype, we have implemented network policies providing container managed persistence, access control, and transactional interaction. We explain how the container works by discussing every necessary extension step by step (Section 5). We also provide an extensive experimental study of the resulting system as a first step towards identifying the problems that need to be solved to make spontaneous information systems a reality. We discuss these results in Section 6 and conclude the paper in Section 7.

2   Motivation

2.1   Location Services for Mobile Computing

Imagine a trade show or a large conference where participants are provided with computing devices such as desk-tops, lap-tops or PDAs (we will refer to these devices from now on as nodes) . Assume there is a spontaneous container that allows service publishing and discovery. Certain participants, like vendors and exhibitors use the fixed infrastructure. Other participants (e.g., visitors) use hand-held nodes. Nodes can communicate with either a base station or directly with each other. Using a spontaneous container, we want to provide the same services offered by a conventional middleware infrastructure. In particular, we would like to be able to provide the basic functionality found in a container (i.e., persistence, security and transactional interaction) but in a completely ad-hoc manner, that is, to all vendors registering at any time and to all visitors entering the fair grounds. Thus, nodes should be able to receive from the spontaneous container transparent functionality extensions and, after that, be capable of interacting transactionally among them, have their state persistently stored (in other nodes or a base station), and follow a simple access control policy. In addition to traditional service functionality (transactions, persistence, etc.), a spontaneous container may model location-specific features, such as service billing tailored to that particular fair ground.

In such a scenario, a spontaneous container provides the necessary flexibility. For example, if the access control policy of the organization evolves over time, it would be have new functionality extensions applied to all computing nodes within the organizational boundaries (in the example, a fair ground). On the other hand, if one computing node changes its location, all functionality extensions acquired within the boundaries of that location are discarded when the node leaves the area. Later on, when this node enters a new location provided with its own spontaneous container, it can be once again adapted at run-time with location-specific functionality.

As a refinement of this scenario, a spontaneous container could also be used to provide specialized policies for two distinct areas of the *same* fair ground. For example, it can be used to increase the privacy of transactions in the sale areas

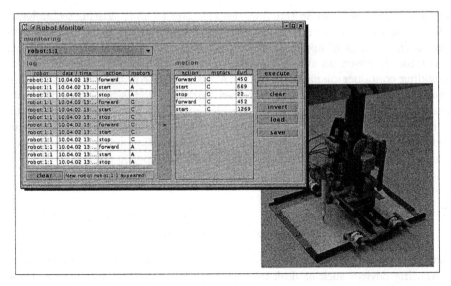

Fig. 1. A simple robot prototype (lower-right) transparently extended to show the motor actions in a graphical interface (upper-left)

of the fair ground by locally adapting nodes with the corresponding extensions, and to enforce a more permissive policy around meeting points.

2.2   Monitoring Extensions for Robotics

Consider a manufacturing plant where a large number of mobile devices, robots and possibly "smart" artifacts collaborate to manufacture goods, control quality, receive production schedules and order sub-parts needed in the production process.

As an example, Figure 1 (lower-right) shows a simple prototype of a plotter that can be used in this scenario. When the plotter is moved into a given production hall, we want its behavior extended so that all relevant commands and service calls are logged in a database. The result is a comprehensive history of the relevant activities of the plotter (service calls, motor moves, sensor reads). All commands ever issued and executed within a specific context can be later analyzed, re-executed or undone. If a failure condition is detected, then a local base-station with a global view of all actions may trigger a compensation activity involving the coordinated movements of several devices. With the appropriate software support, the context could adapt the plotter so that the movements performed by the device are replicated and monitored on a nearby screen.

A variant is a robot (e.g., a transportation appliance) that enters a production hall. Assuming a well-defined geometrical model of the production hall, the robot does not need to learn by itself how to operate in this space. Instead, the robot's functionality can be adapted by the hall so its movements match the local working conditions.

A spontaneous container addresses these problems by treating all mobile devices that enter the production hall as components "deployed" within its scope. As such, they are extended on-the fly with the monitoring functionality.

It is important to notice that neither the robots nor the other applications are aware of the functionality extensions added by the spontaneous container. The extension can be added or removed as needed. If the robot is moved to a different location, that location's spontaneous container can add a new extension that indicates where the data must be sent for persistent storage. Or, within the same location, the extension can be exchanged for a new one that indicates that the data must be sent to a program that shows the movements in a graphic display, as shown in Figure 1 (upper-left).

3 Unifying Technologies in the Spontaneous Container Architecture

Spontaneous containers inherit the container programming model, dynamic resource usage and the ability to express cross-cutting run-time changes. This section shows how to unify these technologies into one coherent system architecture. In addition, we show how the resulting architecture differs from existing solutions in each of the originating areas.

3.1 Spontaneous Container Programming

A spontaneous container allows programmers to apply a homogeneous service policy to all entities of a networking area. We assume that every networking area is characterized by a spontaneous container policy P that describes the service model to be enforced on all entities within that network. An example of such a policy is "all remote invocations must be treated as transactions". This statement does not specify how to enforce, e.g., isolation, nor does it list the services and resources (database management systems, transaction monitors) accessible in the local network that will be used in the process of enforcing transactional behavior.

To enforce P, this declarative description may be translated into functionality extensions $e_1 .. e_n$. Each e_i contains concrete functionality to be added to all services within the boundaries of the considered spontaneous container. This functionality must describe what to change (e.g., what particular service invocations) and how to change it (e.g., how to bracket service invocations). Later on, if the policy is updated with a new version P^{new}, a new set of extensions $e_1^{new}...e_n^{new}$ may be generated and applied to the services within the network, while the obsolete extensions are revoked.

The spontaneous container programming model allows a single focus point for modification in both spatial and temporal dimensions. In the spatial dimension it addresses the increasing number of mobile computing devices that must be continuously adapted to the specific conditions of an enterprise, fair ground, production hall, etc. In the temporal dimension, the ability of a spontaneous

container to deal with frequent policy changes in a uniform way addresses the
continuous evolution of modern information systems. A clear advantage of this
form of adaptability is that devices only need to carry their basic functionality.
Any additional functionality is location specific and is inserted or extracted as
need dictates. We create the spontaneous container in three steps.

3.2   Step 1: Using Dynamic AOP

In a spontaneous container one can create extensions that modify a running
program. For this purpose it is first necessary to identify *where* to change the
program. Potential points of interest may be, e.g., incoming and outgoing calls or
variable access. Once a set of such points is identified, it is necessary to establish
what additional actions are needed at those points. After this step, each time
the execution reaches one of the points of interest, the execution is intercepted,
and an additional piece of code is executed.

In a spontaneous container this information (where to change a program and
what additional code to execute) is encapsulated into a single unit of software
called *extension*. Typical examples of extensions are:

- Invoke `transactionBegin` before entering methods with names matching
  `"*transaction*"`.
- Invoke the additional code `updateDBTable` whenever a variable belonging to
  `"*EntityBean*"` classes is written.

Run-time adaptation is done by inserting extensions into applications. Extensions can also be withdrawn, leaving the program as if no insertion ever took
place. Inserting and removing extension allows treating adaptations that affect
a large number of points as a single modification operation.

The nature of extensions suggests employing aspect-orientation to program
extensions. AOP allows factoring out of an application all orthogonal *concerns*
(functionality) so that they can be treated separately [39]. Typical examples are
distribution, security and logging when this functionality cuts across the system,
i.e., it is not located in a single decomposition unit (e.g., class or package).
Once this separation has been made, AOP techniques are used to combine the
application with the orthogonal concerns when the application is compiled. This
process is called *weaving* and is based on *crosscuts*, i.e., collections of points
in the execution of a program where some additional functionality should be
invoked. In AspectJ [43], for instance, these crosscuts could be the invocations
of some method(s) of a set of classes.

Run-time changes to a program are usually performed in languages that
explicitly support run-time adaptability such as composition filters [1] or reflection [15, 13, 24]. In the context of Java, reflective architectures such as Meta-
Java [17], Guarana [25], or Iguana/J [36] can be used to support unanticipated
software adaptation. Borrowing ideas from these techniques, frameworks for dynamic AOP have recently emerged [8, 26, 28].

Every node of the network carries with it the support for program modification (extension programming, extension insertion and extension withdrawal),

which is explicitly available to all other nodes of a network. As we will show later, the support for adaptation in commercial platforms is either proprietary or not existent. By explicitly exposing this support one can express adaptations that could not have been foreseen at development or even at deployment time.

3.3   Step 2: Extending Container Models with Dynamic AOP

A good example of commercial container technology is the model included in the J2EE architectures [14]. This model, known as Enterprise Java Beans (EJB) [22] was the result of several years of evolution that lead to the separation of well understood middleware functionality from the business logic. The EJB specification describes *coding conventions* for creating business components. For example, all business logic methods must be previously defined in EJB-compliant interfaces; users must provide a number of administrative methods, prefixed by "ejb", as shown in Figure 2.a.

When developers follow this coding convention, the pure business logic can be *wrapped* in larger components that extend the business logic. The wrapping is done automatically at deployment time by the the server application called *EJB Container*. The EJB container typically generates code that deals with concerns that are orthogonal to the business logic. A simplified example of generated and deployed functionality is illustrated in Figure 2.b.

The container usage model implies that each site installs one or several containers on its site and configures this container to use the site-specific computing context (e.g., naming service, database servers). Then it acquires third-party components and deploys these components in its own container. As explained, the container automatically adapts each component with additional functionality (lines 2.b-4.b,7.b), which indirectly reflects the site's computing environment.

The main *common* trait of both commercial containers and the spontaneous container architecture is the fact that a large number of points that often cut across the business logic components are automatically enhanced with orthogonal functionality. However, there are important *differences*.

```
1.a class Account               1.b withdraw(float amount) {
2.a extends AccountEntityBean   2.b <identify remote caller>
3.a {                           3.b <authorize remote caller>
4.a     ejbActivate();          4.b <obtain a~reference to a>
5.a     withdraw(float amount); 5.b a.ejbActivate();
6.a }                           6.b a.withdraw(amount);
                                7.b <end withdraw transaction>}
```

            (a)   (b)

Fig. 2.   (a) Business logic and (b) Wrapped business logic

The first one is the limited range of adaptations addressable by commercial containers. The kind of added functionality is "de facto" determined at development time: the coding conventions must be foreseen from the start in the business logic components. In addition, commercial containers typically use a proprietary technology for adding functionality, tailored for usage with the considered coding conventions. The added functionality corresponds exactly to the middleware features foreseen in the container specification. This limitation becomes quickly unacceptable when trying to add site-specific features. In practice, this would require the ability to change the often proprietary container implementation (resulting in a lack of tailorability of container models [29]). By contrast, a spontaneous container provides explicit support for adaptations located at the run-time environment level. This more general approach allows for adaptations that could not have been foreseen at development time. Through this feature, a spontaneous container does not require applications to be developed using a specific coding standard.

The second important difference is the limited flexibility of commercial containers – they add functionality at deployment time. The reason is that containers have been built for deploying long-running server-side business components. Once deployed in a commercial container, a business application will use the *same* computing context (nearby database management servers, naming services, etc.) throughout its lifetime (or until these resources are updated). The frequent changes encountered in mobile and embedded computing do not fit in this model and are difficult to address at deployment time. The explicit support for run-time adaptation makes a spontaneous container more appropriate for these environments.

3.4   Step 3: Extending Spontaneous Networks with Dynamic AOP

Spontaneous networks [19, 4] are systems for service discovery and brokerage. They provide the flexibility needed in mobile computing: applications do not know from the start which other services they are going to use throughout their lifetime. When a computing node enters a community of services (e.g., by joining an ad-hoc network) it *discovers* the available resources (nearby services for fair exchange, stable storage, light switches, printers, message boards, etc.). It uses these services through their published interfaces until it leaves the considered network. Later on, it may join a new community of services where it discovers and uses a new set of services.

Figure 3.a illustrates the basic mechanism used to discover and use new services in Jini [4], a platform for spontaneous networking. A service (B) joins the computing environment by registering a proxy pB at a nearby lookup service (step 1). The proxy contains code and data that can be moved freely between nodes. Other nodes can query the Lookup Service (LUS) (step 2), obtain pB and use the service B through its proxy pB (step 3). For instance, the call $pB.m1()$ will result in the execution of $B.m1()$. Alternatively, nodes can ask to be notified when a service matching a certain template joins or leaves the Jini community.

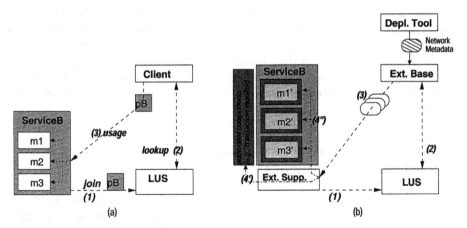

Fig. 3. (a) Typical interactions in Jini and (b) Run-time adaptation of application through a Jini interface

The main advantage of this type of spontaneous networks over container platforms is that resources are discovered and used at run-time. Because of the mobility constraint, the functionality needed for transactions, security, authentication, orthogonal data persistence is hard-coded during the development of mobile applications. This functionality must be available beforehand, even if internally it may use resources discovered at run-time. Thus, the main drawback of spontaneous networks is the lack of support for separation of concerns: they miss the properties of the container model (where business logic is reusable, while service functionality can be separately added at deployment time). This fact can cause several problems. For instance, two mobile services developed with different transaction models in mind are not inter-operable. This could not happen in a container model, where the transaction logic is uniformly added to all components by the same container. In addition, the enforcement of local policies (e.g., usage of a certain degree of encryption for all communications) is also difficult to achieve.

A spontaneous container inherits from spontaneous networks the ability to dynamically discover and use other services, but overcomes the shortcoming of hard-coded service functionality by exposing the support for dynamic aspect-oriented programming.

To achieve this goal, the spontaneous container architecture extends spontaneous networks as follows. It defines an adaptation service that allows the uploading of extension objects into a node. Each node must carry an adaptation service, which is accessible as a regular service. Figure 3.b illustrates service B running together with an adaptation service (marked in the figure with "Ext. Supp.") on the same JVM. Like any other service, the adaptation service joins the spontaneous network community (step 1) and allows other nodes to use its interface. The extension base is continuously scanning the network for new adaptation services (step 2). Once a new adaptation service is discovered, a customized set of extensions objects is sent to it (step 3). When receiving the extensions, the adaptation service instantiates in step (4') the additional sub-components received through extensions (e.g., transaction monitors, access control modules, encryption components) and then it adapts in step (4") the existing methods $m1$, $m2$, and $m3$, such that they execute additional functionality at specific joinpoints. Step (4") is performed through the explicit aspect-oriented support of the adaptation service.

4   Building Spontaneous Containers for Java Environments

To test these ideas, we have created a spontaneous container prototype for Java services. We created the prototype by filling in the architectural framework with concrete components for run-time adaptation, container programming and dynamic service discovery. For run-time changes we use PROSE [34], an aspect-oriented run-time system developed for this purpose. We add container-specific features by extending PROSE to perform container-like adaptations. Finally, we use Jini for dynamic service management and discovery so that every node can exchange, provide, and receive extensions at run-time, thereby providing the basic mechanism for spontaneous interaction.

4.1   How Extensions Work

Consider three nodes, A, B, and C that want to interact as follows. Node A initiates a distributed computation within method m_A (Figure 4.a). It first performs some local operations and then invokes method m_B on remote service B (step 1). The computation in m_B changes the state of the service B at a place denoted in the figure by ($\bullet$). m_B completes, and the results are transferred back to A (step 2) where additional operations are performed locally by A (step 3). The remaining code of m_A involves a second remote call to m_C, carried out in a similar manner (steps 4 and 5). Assume now that these nodes have acquired extensions that will enhance the computation just described with context management (CM), transaction management (TM), container managed persistence (CMP) and access control (ACM).

Figure 4.b shows the control flow once the extensions are in place. We indicate with gray shading that the control flow passes through functionality added by extensions, while the white parts correspond to functionality initially available in the methods m_A, m_B, and m_C. The time axes are not drawn to scale. As before, the computation starts in m_A. When the remote invocation to m_B is initiated, the TM extension glue traps the call (step 1). The extension glue invokes the TM functionality to create the necessary transactional context (e.g., a transaction identifier). The transactional context and A's identity are transmitted to B as implicit context (since they do not exist in the signature of m_B). The CM extension located in the communication layer, marshals the implicit context data

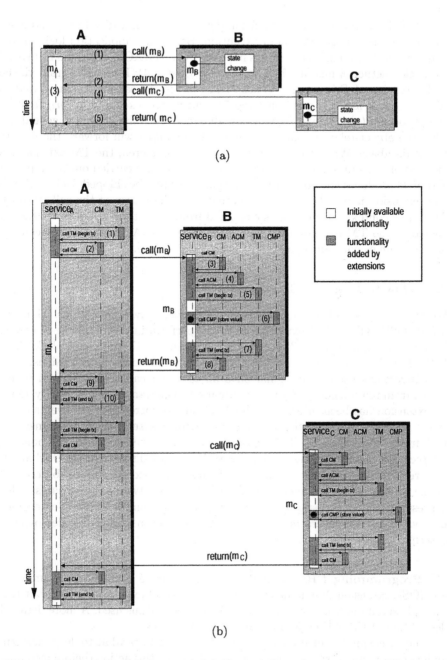

Fig. 4. (a) Initial control flow and (b) Control flow after extensions have been added

together with the parameters of the call (step 2), before the invocation takes place.

At node B, the local CM extension detaches the context data (3) and associates to it the current thread of execution. Before the application logic in m_B starts executing, a number of things happen. First, the ACM extension is invoked to check whether A has the right to access m_B (step 4). If access is granted, the TM extension of B is invoked to keep track of the transactional context and to start m_B as a local transaction (step 5). During the execution of m_B, a state change occurs ($\bullet$). The CMP extension glue intercepts the state change and notifies the object-relation mapper (step 6). The mapper will forward the update to the database. When the execution of m_B is completed, the TM extension is invoked once again (step 7) to pre-commit the changes carried out in step 6. If TM at B produces any context information that must be shipped back to A, the CM extension marshals this data together with the return of the call (step 8). At A, any context information is extracted from the return values (step 9), and passed to the TM extension for processing (step 10). After that, the execution of m_A resumes with analogous steps for the call to m_C.

4.2   How to Program Extensions

We are interested in inserting extensions in *running* Java applications. Thus, we use PROSE [34], a JVM extension that can perform interceptions at run-time. However, an application will not see any difference with a standard JVM. The PROSE JVM also provides an API for inserting and removing extensions.

PROSE extensions are regular Java objects that can be sent to and be received from remote nodes. Signatures are used to guarantee their integrity. Once an extension has been inserted in the JVM, any occurrence of the events of interest results in the execution of the corresponding extension. If an extension is withdrawn from the JVM, the extension code is discarded and the corresponding interception(s) will no longer take place. We do not discuss the PROSE architecture [34, 33] in detail, but we explain how such extensions can be created in the context of a spontaneous container. There are two basic mechanisms for expressing run-time changes: (1) by directly programming PROSE extensions in Java or (2) by generating PROSE extensions from declarative deployment descriptors.

(1) Programming PROSE Extensions. Figure 5 contains an example of a PROSE extension. We do not get into the details of extension coding, but this example should give a first impression of the mechanisms used. A more detailed description of PROSE extensions can be found in [34].

The extension is called `BeforeRemoteCall`. It defines what to do (transform an invocation into a transaction) and where to apply this action (before incoming remote calls of services of type *ServiceB*).

The method on line 3 instructs PROSE to execute its body for every method invocation (wildcard `ANYMETHOD`) of services of type `ServiceB`. The predefined

```
 1 class BeforeRemoteCall extends MethodCut() {
 2       // if we are the root, create a~transactional context
 3       public void ANYMETHOD(ServiceB thisObj, REST params) {
 4             if ( lookup(TX_CONTEXT) == null) {
 5                   txCtx = ROOT_CTX;
 6                   Transaction.bind(currentThread(),txCtx);
 7             }
 8       }
 9       { setSpecializer(ClasseS.extending(Remote.class)). AND
10                   (MethodS.BEFORE) ); }
11 }
12 }
```

Fig. 5. A Java class containing the code for a run-time extension

class REST is a wildcard that denotes arbitrary parameters list. Thus, the special signature matches invocations of the form ServiceB.*(*). This is however not enough, as we want transaction to be activated just before remote calls. This specialization is achieved on line 10 where a combination of building blocks specifies that services should extend the Remote class (thus, only methods of remote services will be intercepted by PROSE) and that the extension should be executed before the actual business logic in that method (through MethodS.BEFORE).

The body of this method represents the extension action to be executed at all code locations that match the conditions described above, that is, before incoming remote calls from other services. The extension instructs the transaction management component to create a transaction context if the current invocation is not within the scope of a transaction already (line 4). It then associates the newly created transaction with the current thread of execution. This way, all subsequent invocation to other services will be part of the newly created transaction. To activate this extension, an object of type BeforeRemoteCall must be passed to PROSE. This is done using the PROSE.addExtension method.

In PROSE it is possible to perform more accurate and complex interceptions than those used in this example. For instance, it is also possible to intercept method calls based on the type of parameters passed. The range of the interception can be widened by using wildcards, since in an ad-hoc environment the methods are not necessarily known in advance. For scenarios where more knowledge about the application is available, the interceptions can be made much more precise, by including method signatures, parameter types, etc.

An example of a very useful extension that can be written without knowing the source code is an encryption extension. Such an extension would intercept any incoming or outgoing RMI call to an application and perform the necessary encryption or decryption. Extensions can also be written knowing only the published interface of an application by using the method name, the class name, the signature, or even the parameters to specify where to intercept the execution. An example of what can be done using this information would be a logging extension that creates a log record in some remote database every time a given service is called. Finally, extensions can be written with full knowledge of the source code.

(2) Describing Policies Declaratively. To fully support the container programming model, policies applied to all entities of a network are described declaratively, usually as XML data. This has been done by extending PROSE with support for the equivalent of the *deployment descriptors* used in EJB architectures [22]. This support comes in the form of a meta-data repository (network meta-data in Figure 3.b) that specifies, in a declarative fashion, what types of services are expected to be adapted and in which way. For instance, it might say that the encryption extension is to trap all RMI calls and encrypt them; a QoS extension is to trap outgoing RMI calls and cancel them if there is not enough bandwidth available; a load balancing extension is to send requests to different servers as dictated by the current load; a billing extension is to trap calls to a specific service and generate a charge for its use.

This information, which needs to be provided by the system's programmer, is used by the *extension base* to generate extensions from these specifications. The resulting PROSE *extension object* [34] can be sent through the network to all nodes that need to be adapted.

4.3   Acquiring and Discarding Extensions

In our architecture, all nodes fall into two categories. *Extension base* nodes contain a database of extensions. They discover new nodes joining the network and send extensions to the newcomers. *Extension receivers* carry the component that receives extensions from extension bases. We assume that each extension receiver has PROSE activated on its JVM. When it obtains an extension from an extension base, it immediately inserts the extension using the PROSE API. Extension receivers also discard extensions when they leave a network or lose contact with the extension base.

By appropriately assigning extension base and extension receiver roles, one can achieve adaptations of various service communities. At one extreme, each node can contain an extension base. When it joins a new community, it distributes its extensions and receives others from the existing nodes. This peer-to-peer organization is appropriate for creating an information system infrastructure in entirely ad-hoc communities. At the other extreme, each physical location (e.g., a fair ground) may have a base station as extension base. All other nodes (e.g., the mobile nodes) are extension receivers. This organization is appropriate for adaptations that correspond to infrastructure and organizational requirements. Between the two extremes, many other configurations are possible.

When considering extension objects, we distinguish between two kinds of adaptations. These adaptations use the same PROSE mechanisms but they play different roles. The first kind is the extension *functionality*. The second kind is

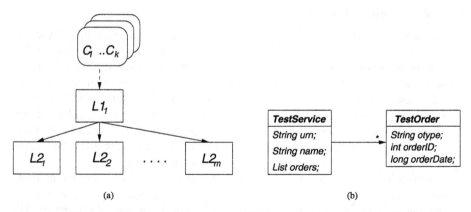

Fig. 6. (a) Three level configuration used for measurements and (b) The local data structure present at each service

needed to intercept events of the application and connect the application logic to the extension functionality. We denote this second type of adaptation extension *glue* and the points where it must be added *join-points*. Every extension we employ contains a functionality and a glue part.

We used the leasing mechanism provided by Jini [4]: the extension objects sent to each node are actually *leased*. Consequently, when a node leaves or is unplugged from the network, the leases keeping the extension alive fail to be renewed. When this occurs, the instantiated extension is discarded and the extension functionality is dynamically extracted out of the join-points.

5   Performance Results

In this section, we complete and clarify the architectural description by discussing step by step the creation of a spontaneous container with three of the extensions mentioned above (CM, CMP, and ACM); the TM extension has been described and evaluated separately [31]. We include performance measurements to give a clear idea of the costs involved and where optimizations are needed. This container has been implemented as a prototype and it is being extensively used to deploy novel applications over ad-hoc networks.

For the extensions we have used standard libraries (ACM) and developed some parts as needed (CMP and CM). We discuss only the aspects of the extensions to the extent that they are important to understand how they can be embedded within the architecture. However, there are many ways to implement this functionality and the ones we use are just an example of how to go about it.

5.1   Experimental Setup

To evaluate the performance we use a varying configuration with three layers of nodes (Figure 6.a). At level zero, nodes act as clients invoking a service implemented at level one. Clients send a request at a time but do not have idle time. As soon as a response arrives, the next request is sent. A number of k clients $(C_1..C_k)$ use concurrently a service on level one $(L1_1)$. Similarly, the service at level one does a sequence of remote invocations to the services $L2_1..L2_m$ (there are m such services) at level two. Thus, every experimental configuration is characterized by the number m. We use the notation $(1, m)$ to stress the fact that there is one service on level one and m services at level two.

On both levels, each service call performs a number of local operations that update the data structure shown in Figure 6.b. A local operation iterates over the elements in the orders list and updates the state of each TestOrder. All service invocations across levels are remote calls and all services reside in different nodes.

For the purposes of this paper, we considered all configurations $(1, 1)...(1, 5)$. For each configuration, we vary the number of clients k until the maximal throughput is reached and then measure the response time. The throughput is the average number of invocations per second (inv/sec) performed by all clients. The response time is the average time to complete a call at the client level. For the conciseness of the exposition, we present in this paper the detailed measurements of the response time (as being the most relevant for the desingn of spontaneous container). A more detailed analysis describing the throughput for all measurements and including measurements for more complex configurations (with several nodes on level one) is available [32].

The analysis is a worst case scenario in that the load across all nodes is kept artificially high. The idea is to get measurements that act as lower bounds, since in practice operations are likely to run in disjoint subsets of nodes and therefore be less demanding in terms of the resources because a typical node will not generate as much traffic nor so complex service invocations as those used in the tests.

To evaluate the feasibility of the container we perform two sets of experiments. The first set of experiments considers applications running on a fixed network, where we use Pentium III 600Mhz nodes interconnected using a 100Mbs Ethernet LAN. Since we are interested in architectures for wireless environments, the second set of experiments considers a pure wireless network, where we use Pentium III 400Mhz mobile nodes (lap-tops) interconnected using a 11Mbs wireless LAN (WLAN). The WLAN is configured in ad-hoc mode. We use Java JDK 1.2.2 on each node. We first present the fixed network measurements and then compare them with equivalent configurations in the wireless environment.

5.2   Performance with Plain Java Services

As a base line for the measurements, we run a series of tests with no extensions involved. Essentially, we are measuring the performance of Java and of making remote calls. Figure 7 gives response time for all configurations.

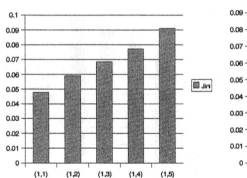

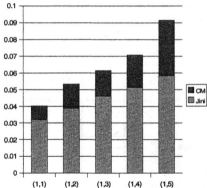

Fig. 7. Response times (s) with no extensions

Fig. 8. Response times (s) for the $(1,m)$ measurements, with CM

5.3   1st Extension: Implicit Context (CM)

In a distributed system, implicit information must be transparently attached to the parameters of the call at the caller's side and be detached at the callee. Context is transferred in the opposite direction from the callee to the caller together with the return values. Using this mechanism, non-functional information like authentication tokens or transaction identifiers can be transferred between peers.

For this purpose, the extension base distributes the CM extension, which replaces the communication layer of existing services with a new communication layer capable of transferring additional data on the same network connection. The new communication layer checks for every connection whether implicit context must be sent or received from the peer. This functionality does not use the interception mechanism of the PROSE system.

To measure the efficiency of the new communication layer, we distribute CM to all nodes. Then we run the test application when no implicit context data is transferred between peers. The observable performance decrease corresponds to the handshakes incurred by the new communication layer. Figure 8 illustrates the response time of the test system. The total height of the bars represents the response time, in seconds, of all $(1,m)$ configurations. The dark gray part represents the time spent in the new communication layer. With no implicit context data generated by the application, the response time increase is between 0.01 and 0.03 seconds.

Note that the values for Jini response times in Figure 8 (gray segments) do not build upon the values in Figure 7. The reason is that we measure the response time *when the maximal throughput of the system is reached*. E.g., the response times in Figure 7 are measured when the Jini system is loaded with 140 inv/s, while the response times in Figure 8 are obtained when the more complex Jini-CM system reaches its maximal throughput at 90 inv/s. The reason

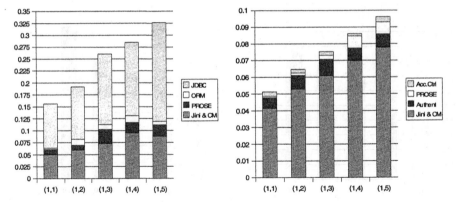

Fig. 9. Response times (s), with the CM and CMP extensions

Fig. 10. Response times (s), with the CM and ACM extensions

behind this measurement methodology is to avoid repeating information between measurement groups, while showing in each case values obtained at a system load which is relevant in practice.

5.4 2nd Extension: Implicit Context and Persistence (CMP)

In the application server area, standards that promote transparent persistence have emerged. A good example is the container managed persistence promoted by EJB [22], but more complex models (e.g., JDO [23]) have also been proposed. Their benefits have been analyzed elsewhere [7, 6].

A spontaneous container could be used similarly for securing the state of any Java-based services. Following this idea, we have developed a solution adapted to the dynamic character of a spontaneous container. It consists of an object-relational mapper (ORM) and relies on capturing object field changes at run-time using PROSE. The component is small (100KBytes) and can save, restore and update the state of entire (Java) object graphs.

The installation of the ORM is performed by the CMP extension. The CMP contains database connectivity parameters and mappings specific to the current network container. After the instantiation, the mapper searches the memory object space of the Jini node. If services, identified by their globally unique Jini IDs [4], are known to the local database, ORM attempts to restore their state. If not, it attempts to store the transitively reachable closure of objects in the local database. Like in commercial container, it is not practical to store the whole object space of an applications. We assume that the applications publish a declarative description on the persistence root-objects.

Finally, the ORM inspects once again the object space and discovers all fields that have to be synchronized with the database. For all these fields, it installs the PROSE extension glue that reports their modification. The specification of the fields to be watched is generic. As an example, consider an excerpt of a specification from the network meta-data:

```
1 <persistent_service>
2   <package_name>ch.ethz.inf.midas</package_name>
3   <class_name>MyJiniBean</class_name>
4   <primary_key>jiniServiceID</primary_key>
5   <persistent_field>foo.*</persistent_field>
6 </persistent_service>
```

This excerpt specifies on line 6 that all fields whose name matches the regular expression "foo.*" and belong to class MyJiniBean should be made persistent. It additionally specifies that the primary key of objects of type MyJiniBean is jiniServiceID.

For the specification of persistence we tried to match existing approaches in the EJB container model. PROSE allows fields to be guarded by means of regular expressions. We use this feature to provide powerful pattern-matching rules for persistence specification.

The response time of the nodes when running with implicit context and container managed persistence added to all services is depicted in Figure 9. Each bar in Figure 9 represents the total response time, in seconds, of the measurements with one L_1 service and several L_2 services. The gray section at the bottom represents the time spent together by the pure Java service and the implicit context functionality. The dark gray section above represents the time spent by PROSE to capture field modifications and submit the corresponding field modification events to the ORM. The white part represents time spent in the ORM to map field updates to database update operations. Finally, the light gray part at the top is the time spent in connections to the database (JDBC).

To measure the average time spent in each section above we incrementally configured the spontaneous container and measured the difference in response times. For the time spent in JDBC calls, e.g., we subtracted the time obtained with a persistence extension from the time we obtained when configuring the extension with a faked database connection of zero response-time.

It is easy to see that total response time increases with greater values for m: the operation is much more complex and it involves communication with the database for each service involved. Most of the response time is due to either the Jini or to the JDBC part.

5.5   3rd Extension: Security and Context (ACM)

The ACM extension is distributed to each joining node. When inserted, it either creates an ad-hoc identity (key pair) for the node or uses an existing one. The identity is generated using network-specific knowledge. For outgoing connections, the extension authenticates the node against other nodes, while for incoming ones it authenticates the peers. The transfer of authentication data is performed using the functionality provided by the implicit context extension.

The ACM extension is updated by the extension base each time a policy change occurs. It contains information on all known identities and all known services. The access control glue functionality intercepts all remote calls of services on the current node and denies or grants access according to its state. The state of an access control extension is represented by an access control list.

Figure 10 illustrates the response time of the first set of tests when nodes join a container configured to create ad-hoc identities and perform access control for each service call. Each section, from the bottom to the top, represents the time spent for Jini and the CM extension, transferring identities by ACM (dark gray), interception of remote calls by PROSE (white) and access control matrix access (top-most, light gray). As before, the overwhelming part of the time is spent in Jini and the communication layer, and just a minor part is spent in PROSE.

5.6   Throughput for Fixed and Wireless Networks

Our main objective here is to show that the spontaneous container is a feasible technology in both mobile and fixed environments and to evaluate the performance degradation due to the lower bandwidth and CPU speed. Because of hardware restrictions, we have evaluated only the (1,1) and (1,2) configurations. Figure 11 contains a comparison of the fixed network and mobile network spontaneous containers in terms of throughput. For the WLAN/mobile nodes experiments, the performance decrease is not significant, given the limitations in bandwidth and computing power. Thus, over 100 inv/s can be achieved in both configurations on a pure Jini network. Thus, when adding context management (CM), throughput reaches between 51 and 86 inv/s. With container managed persistence (CMP), the wireless spontaneous container enables between 10 and 15 inv/s.

The time spent in each component (CMP,ACM) depends on the number and kind of extensions activated in each node. This shows how the spontaneous architecture addresses the issue of energy consumption. By inserting only the extensions that are needed in a particular environment, it reduces the memory footprint and resource usage of mobile nodes.

6   Discussion and Related Work

6.1   Related Work

At the language level, solutions for adaptation problems range from Meta-Object Protocols [15, 13] to object-based inheritance models [42, 18].

AOP ideas have recently given raise to significant efforts in the area of distributed component models. The idea is to express distributed system properties like load balancing and coordination using aspects [35, 2]. Auto-adaptive systems [3] have recognized the importance of efficiently extending applications to deal with frequent context changes. Also, the limitations implied by static

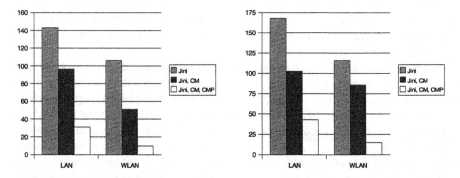

Fig. 11. (a) Comparative throughputs (inv/s) between the fixed and mobile infrastructure for the (1,1) configuration and (b) Comparative throughputs (inv/s) for the (1,2) configuration

container models are underpinned by [12]. Further on, [29] analyses the role of aspect-orientation for expressing infrastructure services and shows some of the deficiencies of the traditional container model.

There has been a significant amount of work on concrete aspects of information systems in, or in connection with, mobile computing environments (e.g., indexing, caching, update consistency, etc). Adaptability in software system architectures for mobile computing is addressed in [11]. Dynamic adaptation of objects to provide non-functional properties like persistence is addressed by incremental object composition [20], while context relations are considered in [37].

Some initial efforts have been made by extending existing middleware platforms. R-ORB [44], for instance, is a context sensitive object request broker based on reconfigurable hardware. In the context of Java, [38] provides a network-wide virtual machine that defines dynamic service components (e.g., monitoring or security). Recent efforts in reflection-based middleware [5] address the very same problem of adaptability. The goal there is to perform QoS adaptations of the CORBA service layer in response to changes in the run-time environment (e.g., network resources) [41]. This work, however, addresses only conventional middleware platforms not the type of ad-hoc networks we are exploring.

6.2 Discussion

In the general case, extensions range from service-generic to fully service-customized. For the generic ones, no specific information on services implementation is needed. For instance, one can replace the communication layer of a service with a new one that encrypts data without any particular knowledge of the adapted service. Specific adaptations may require a either a black-box view (information on particular interfaces) or glass-box view (knowledge on how a service is implemented) of the service to be adapted. For the spontaneous container to be efficient, each extension base will have many extensions ranging from generic to service-specific, while applications will provide this information if necessary. This approach, also followed by [30], accommodates incremental evolution of the software at every node (because generic extensions will still work even if the node application has changed).

One important issue is how a spontaneous container should address the security of devices entering a network (e.g., to prevent a "malicious" extension base distributing maliciuos infrastructure aspects). Cryptographically signed extensions, supported by PROSE, allow mobile nodes to define a policy policy fiels specifying trusted code bases. In general, a more flexible mechanism is needed. Such a mechanism should blend policy-based security checks and user interaction. Thus, a user should be able to specify what kinds of extensions are trusted by default (based on their signatures), and what extensions should be allowed only with an explicit user acknowledgment.

Unavoidably, mobile and ad-hoc environments face unexpected node detachments. In a spontaneous container, this is the case when a mobile node leaves the container while being actively involved in a distributed computation. Spontaneous containers rely on a RMI-like interaction between clients and servers. With RMI, abrupt node detachment may result in inconsistent distributed computations. To address node detachement, one can enance the container with a transactional extension [31]. Thus, one can avoid global inconsistencies by aborting those transactions that involve detached nodes. To address node detachment in a more general fashion, an advanced language and distribution support based on mobile computations [10] could be used.

The spontaneous container approach can be used to optimize information systems so that they can be efficiently used in an ad-hoc computing environment. In this regard, the spontaneous container is public domain software and, as our experiments have shown, can be a very powerful platform for experimenting with issues related to mobility and reconfigurability of the IT infrastructure.

Even as a first step, the results provided indicate that spontaneous adaptation of services is possible in both fixed and wireless environments. The experiments performed are really a stress test. For a distributed application, interactions are very complex (involving between 6 and 30 remote accesses) and, once persistence is involved, also very costly (every service triggers a remote transaction in the centralized database). A more realistic load, specially if it is manually generated by users, will be much less demanding and results in a considerable higher throughput. The network bandwidth plays an important role here specially given that it is quite limited in existing wireless environments. This bandwidth, however, will only grow in the future and advances in network protocols such as dynamic scatternets, multi-hop frequency access, and simply larger bandwidth will alleviate this situation.

With this in mind, the results provided are quite encouraging. We do not pretend that the container is ready to be used in a large scale network. Nevertheless, the experiments show that the mechanisms for creating a spontaneous information system do not have a significant effect in the overall performance when compared with the intrinsic cost of container managed persistence or transactions. These high costs are inherent to the nature of the extensions and have little to do with the method used to insert them into the application. Even if the insertion happens at deployment time, the experiments show that the larger part of the costs are produced at run-time and are independent of the insertion method chosen.

7 Conclusion

In this paper we have presented a system that allows computing nodes to exchange functionality and build information systems in a dynamic manner. The term we use is that of a spontaneous container. A spontaneous container dynamically adapts nodes using aspect-oriented extensions. We have presented extensions for security, transactions, and container-managed persistence. Applications of spontaneous containers range from entirely ad-hoc service communities to infrastructure-centric service adaptations. In the ad-hoc case, extensions are exchanged between nodes on a peer-to-peer basis. In the infrastructure centric case, base stations associated to, e.g., a fair ground, distribute extensions modeling the organization's policy. A spontaneous container allows organization-wide middleware properties, and service adding or removal without interrupting operations. The measurements made with the prototype, both for a fixed and a mobile network infrastructure are quite encouraging. They illustrate that the adaptation mechanism we present can be used to effectively transform a service community into a spontaneous container. The real advantage of this system is the flexibility of the architecture that allows the exploration of new forms of interaction in mobile and wireless networks.

Acknowledgements

The work presented in this paper was supported (in part) by the National Competence Center in Research on Mobile Information and Communication Systems (NCCR-MICS), a center supported by the Swiss National Science Foundation under grant number 5005-67322. We are grateful to Intel for a generous equipment grant that was used to build part of the experimental platform used in the paper. The spontaneous container prototype and its sub-components are freely available as open source modules downloadable from http://prose.ethz.ch.

References

[1] M. Aksit, K. Wakita, J. Bosch, and L. Bergmans. Abstracting Object Interactions Using Composition Filters. *Lecture Notes in Computer Science*, 791:152, 1994.

[2] M. P. Alarcon, L. Fuentes, M. Fayad, and J. M. Troya. Separation of Coordination in a Dynamic Aspect Oriented Framework. In *1st Intl. Conf. on AOSD, Enschede, The Netherlands*, April 2002.

[3] L. Andrade and J. L. Fiadeiro. An architectural approach to auto-adaptive systems. In *Proceedings of the 22nd ICDCS Workshops*, pages 439–444, Vienna, Austria, July 2002.

[4] K. Arnold, A. Wollrath, B. O'Sullivan, R. Scheifler, and J. Waldo. *The Jini Specification*. Addison-Wesley, Reading, MA, USA, 1999.

[5] D. Arregui, F. Pacull, and J. Willamowski. Rule-Based Transactional Object Migration over a Reflective Middleware. In *Middleware 2001*, volume 2218 of *LNCS*, pages 179–196, 2001.

[6] M. P. Atkinson, L. Daynes, M. J. Jordan, T. Printezis, and S. Spence. An Orthogonally Persistent Java. *SIGMOD Record*, 25(4):68–75, 1996.

[7] M. P. Atkinson and R. Morrison. Orthogonally Persistent Object Systems. *VLDB Journal*, 4(3):319–401, 1995.

[8] J. Baker and W. Hsieh. Runtime Aspect Weaving Through Metaprogramming. In *1st AOSD, Enschede, The Netherlands*, pages 86–95, April 2002.

[9] L. Bergmans and M. Aksit. Composing Crosscutting Concerns using Composition Filters. *CACM, Special Issue on Aspect-Oriented Programming*, 44(10):51 – 57, October 2001.

[10] L. Cardelli. A language with distributed scope. *Computing Systems*, 8(1):27–59, January 1995.

[11] E. de Lara, D. S. Wallach, and W. Zwaenepoel. Puppeteer: Component-based Adaptation for Mobile Computing. In *USITS-01*, Berkeley, CA, March 2001.

[12] F.Duclos, J. Estubiler, and P. Morat. Describing and Using Non Functional Aspects in Component Based Applications. In *AOSD, Enschede, The Netherlands*, April 2002.

[13] J. Itoh, Y. Yokote, and R. Lea. Using Meta-Objects to Support Optimisation in the Apertos Operating System. In *Proc. of COOTS*, Berkeley, USA, June 1995.

[14] N. Kassem. Designing Enterprise Applications with the Java 2 Plaform. Sun J2EE Blueprints, http://java.sun.com/j2ee/download.html, June 2000.

[15] G. Kiczales and J. des Rivieres. *The Art of the Metaobject Protocol*. MIT Press, Cambridge, MA, USA, 1991.

[16] G. Kiczales, J. Lamping, A. Menhdhekar, C. Maeda, C. Lopes, J. M. Loingtier, and J. Irwin. Aspect-Oriented Programming. In *ECOOP '97 ,Jyväskylä, Finland*, volume 1241, pages 220–242. Springer-Verlag, New York, NY, 1997.

[17] J. Kleinoeder and M. Golm. MetaJava — A Platform for Adaptable Operating-System Mechanisms. In *ECOOP'97 Workshop Reader*, LNCS. Springer, 1997.

[18] G. Kniesel. Type-Safe Delegation for Dynamic Component Adaptation. *LNCS*, 1543:136–137, 1998.

[19] T. J. Lehman, A. Cozzi, Y. Xiong, J. Gottschalk, V. Vasudevan, S. Landis, P. Davis, Bruce K., and P. Bowman. Hitting the distributed computing sweet spot with TSpaces. *Computer Networks (Amsterdam, Netherlands: 1999)*, 35(4):457–472, March 2001.

[20] M. Mezini. Dynamic Object Evolution without Name Collisions. In *ECOOP'97*, volume 1241 of *LNCS*, pages 190–219. Springer, 1997.

[21] Microsoft Corporation. The .NET Internet page. Accessible on-line at: http://www.microsoft.com/net/, 2001.

[22] Sun Microsystems. Enterprise Java Beans Specification, Version 2.0, August 2001.

[23] Sun Microsystems. Java Data Objects (JSR 12), May 2001.

[24] H. Ogawa, K. Shimura, S. Matsuoka, F. Maruyama, Y. Sohda, and F. Kimura. OpenJIT : An Open-Ended, Reflective JIT Compiler Framework for Java. In *Proc. of ECOOP'2000, Springer Verlag*, 2000.

[25] A. Oliva and L. E. Buzato. The design and implementation of Guaraná. In *Proc. of the 5th USENIX COOTS*, pages 203–216. The USENIX Association, 1999.

[26] D. Orleans and K. Lieberherr. DJ: Dynamic Adaptive Programming in Java. In *Reflection 2001*, Kyoto, Japan, September 2001. Springer Verlag.

[27] K. Ostermann. Dynamically Composable Collaborations with Delegation Layers. In *Proc. of ECOOP'2002)*, Malaga, Spain, 2002. Springer.

[28] R. Pawlak, L. Seinturier, L. Duchien, and G. Florin. JAC: A Flexible Solution for Aspect-Oriented Programming in Java. In *Reflection 2001*, pages 1–24, Kyoto, Japan, September 2001. Springer Verlag.

[29] R. Pichler, K. Ostermann, and M. Mezini. On Aspectualizing Component Models. *Software Practice and Experience*, 2003.

[30] S. R. Ponnekanti, B. Lee, A. Fox, P. Hanrahan, and T. Winograd. ICrafter: A Service Framework for Ubiquitous Computing Environments. *LNCS*, 2201, 2001.

[31] A. Popovici and G. Alonso. Ad-Hoc Transactions for Mobile Sevices. In *Proc. of the 3rd Intl. TES/VLDB Workshop*, Hong Kong, China, August 2002.

[32] A. Popovici, G. Alonso, and T. Gross. Design and evaluation of spontaneous container services. Technical report no. 368, CS Department, ETH Zurich, 2002.

[33] A. Popovici, G. Alonso, and T. Gross. Just in time aspects: Efficient dynamic weaving for java. In *AOSD03, Boston, USA*, March 2003.

[34] A. Popovici, T. Gross, and G. Alonso. Dynamic Weaving for Aspect Oriented Programming. In *AOSD02, Enschede, The Netherlands*, April 2002.

[35] E. Putrycz and G. Bernard. Using Aspect Oriented Programming to build a portable load balancing service. In *22nd ICDCS*, Vienna, Austria, July 2002.

[36] B. Redmond and V. Cahill. Towards a Dynamic and Efficient Reflective Architecture for Java. In *Workshop at ECOOP 2000*, Cannes, France, June 2000.

[37] Linda M. Seiter, Jens Palsberg, and Karl J. Lieberherr. Evolution of object behavior using context relations. In *Proceedings of the Fourth ACM SIGSOFT Symposium on the Foundations of Software Engineering*, ACM Software Engineering Notes, pages 46–57, New York, October 16–18 1996. ACM Press.

[38] E. G. Sirer, R. Grimm, A. J. Gregory, and B. N. Bershad. Design and Implementation of a Distributed Virtual Machine for Networked Computers. In *Symposium on Operating Systems Principles*, pages 202–216, 1999.

[39] P. Tarr, H. Ossher, W. Harrison, and S. Sutton. N Degrees of Separation: Multidimensional Separation of Concerns. In *1999 ICSE*, Los Angeles, CA, USA, 1999.

[40] The Object Management Group. The CORBA Component Model RFP. Available at http://www.omg.org/docs/orbos/97-05-22.pdf, 1997.

[41] E. Truyen, B. Joergensen, and W. Joosen. Customization of Component-Based Object Request Brokers through Dynamic Configuration. In *TOOLS Europe'2000, IEEE Press*, pages 181–194, June 2000.

[42] D. Ungar and R. B. Smith. Self: The Power of Simplicity. In *Proc. of OOPSLA*, pages 227–242, 1987.

[43] Xerox Corporation. The AspectJ Programming Guide. Online Documentation, 2002. http://www.aspectj.org/.

[44] S. S. Yau and F. Karim. Reconfigurable Context-Sensitive Middleware for ADS Applications in Mobile Ad-Hoc Network Environments. In *Proc. of the 5th ISADS*.

A Calculus of Untyped Aspect-Oriented Programs

Radha Jagadeesan, Alan Jeffrey, and James Riely

CTI, DePaul University

Abstract. Aspects have emerged as a powerful tool in the design and development of systems, allowing for the encapsulation of program transformations. The dynamic semantics of aspects is typically specified by appealing to an underlying object-oriented language via a compiler transformation known as *weaving*. This treatment is unsatisfactory for several reasons. Firstly, this semantics violates basic modularity principles of object-oriented programming. Secondly, the converse translation from object-oriented programs into an aspect language has a simple canonical flavor. Taken together, these observations suggest that aspects are worthy of study as primitive computational abstractions in their own right. In this paper, we describe an aspect calculus and its operational semantics. The calculus is rich enough to encompass many of the features of extant aspect-oriented frameworks that do not involve reflection. The independent description of the dynamic semantics of aspects enables us to specify the correctness of a weaving algorithm. We formalize weaving as a translation from the aspect calculus to a class-based object calculus, and prove its soundness.

1 Introduction

In this paper we give the dynamic semantics for an aspect-based language and prove the correctness of weaving with respect to that semantics.

Aspects: A Short Introduction. Aspects have emerged as a powerful tool in the design and development of systems [4, 14, 19, 16, 15, 2]. We begin with a short example to introduce the basic vocabulary of aspect-oriented programming and illustrate the underlying issues. Although our examples throughout the paper are couched in terms of AspectJ (http://www.aspectj.org), our study is more general in scope.

Suppose that L is a class realizing a useful library. Suppose further say that we are interested in timing information about a method foo() in L. The following AspectJ code addresses this situation. It is noteworthy and indicative of the power of the aspect framework that

- the profiling code is localized in the following aspect,
- the existing client and library source code is left untouched, and
- the responsibility for profiling all foo() calls resides with the AspectJ compiler.

```
aspect TimingMethodInvocation {
   Timer timer = new Timer();
   void around(): call (void L.foo()) {
      timer.start();  proceed();  timer.stop;
      System.out.println(timer.getTime());
   }}
```

L. Cardelli (Ed.): ECOOP 2003, LNCS 2743, pp. 54–73, 2003.
© Springer-Verlag Berlin Heidelberg 2003

This aspect is intended to trap all invocations to foo() in L. An aspect may *advise* methods, causing additional code to be executed whenever a method of interest is called. The set of interesting methods is specified using a *pointcut*, here call (void L.foo()). The advice itself is a sequence of commands. The example uses around advice. The intended execution semantics is as follows: a call to foo() invokes the code associated with the advice; in the example, the timer is started. The underlying foo() method is invoked when control reaches proceed(). Upon termination of foo(), control returns to the advice; in the example, the timer is stopped and the elapsed time displayed on the screen.

In many aspect-based languages, the intended execution semantics is realized by a compile-time process called *weaving*. Because the advice is attached to a *call pointcut* in the example, the weaving algorithm replaces each call to foo() with a call to the advice; it alters the client code, leaving the library L untouched. In this light, it is not surprising that dispatch of call pointcuts is based on the *compile-time type* of the receiver of foo().

The converse effect is achieved using an *execution pointcut*. Our example can be altered to use execution pointcuts by replacing call (void L.foo()) with execution (void L.foo()). In this case the weaving algorithm alters the library, leaving the client untouched. Dispatch of execution pointcuts is based on the *runtime type* of the receiver of foo().

In general, there may be several pieces of advice attached to a method, and therefore there must be an ordering on advice which determines the order of execution. In AspectJ, for example, the textual order of declarations is used.

Advice may also take parameters, and these parameters may be passed on to the next piece of advice via proceed. In particular, in both call and execution advice one can define a binder for target, the object receiving the message. In call advice, one can additionally bind this, the object sending the message.

Aspects interfere with OO reasoning. Much of the power in aspect-oriented programming lies in the ability to intercept method calls. This power, however, comes at the price of breaking object-oriented encapsulation and the reasoning that it allows. As a simple example, consider the following declarations:

```
class C { void foo(){..} }
class D extends C { }
```

In an object-oriented language, this definition is indistinguishable from the following:

```
class C { void foo(){..} }
class D extends C { void foo(){ super.foo(); } }
```

The following aspect, however, distinguishes them:

```
aspect SpotInheritance {
   void around(): execution (void D.foo()) {
      System.out.println("aspect in action");
   }}
```

In the first declaration, the execution advice cannot attach itself to foo in D, since D does not declare the method; it inherits it. It cannot attach itself either to C, since the advice is intended for D alone. The effect of the aspect is seen only in the second declaration where foo() is redeclared, albeit trivially.

Unfortunately, interference with object-oriented reasoning does not stop there. As a second example, consider that behavioral changes caused by aspects need not be inherited down the class hierarchy. The following aspect distinguishes objects of type C that are not also of type D:

```
aspect OnlySuperclass {
  void around(): (void execution(C.foo()))
            && !(void execution(C.foo())) {
    System.out.println("aspect in action");
  }}
```

These examples indicate that one cannot naively extend object-oriented reasoning to aspect-oriented programs.

Our aims: Reductionism and a specification for weaving. Our approach to understanding aspect-oriented programming is based on an aspect calculus. We have attempted to define the essential features of an aspect-oriented language, leaving many pragmatic programming constructs out. To begin with, we do not include the aspect container in our language, taking advice to be primitive. In addition, we study only around advice. Some other forms of advice can be derived. For example, AspectJ includes *before advice*, which executes just before a method is called; "before(){C;}" can be encoded as "around(){C; proceed();}"". We also define a simple logic to describe pointcuts, built up from the call and execution primitives described above. Aspect-oriented languages such as AspectJ have a rich collection of pointcuts, including ones that rely on reflection. While many forms of pointcuts can be encoded in our language, we do not address reflection. In this paper, we also focus strictly on dynamics, avoiding issues related to the static semantics and type checking.

Perhaps more important than providing a core calculus, the source-level semantics for aspects provides a specification for the weaving algorithm. Rather than using transformation to define the semantics, we are able to prove the *correctness* of the weaving transformation; we prove that woven programs (where all aspects have been removed) perform computation exactly as specified by the original aspect program.

In one respect, our aspect calculus is richer than statically woven languages such as AspectJ, allowing for the the dynamic addition of advice to a running program. Clearly, programs that dynamically load advice affecting existing classes cannot be woven statically. We define a notion of *weavability*, which excludes such programs, and prove the correctness of weaving with respect to weavable programs only.

The Rest of this Paper. We define a class-based language in Section 2. The class-based language is the foundation for the aspect-based language introduced in Section 3. In Section 4 we describe the weaving algorithm, which translates programs in the aspect-based languages into the class-based language. Section 5 states the correctness theorem; all proofs can be found in the full version of the paper. We conclude with a survey of related work.

2 A Class-Based Language

In this section, we describe an untyped class-based language. In contrast to untyped object calculi, our language includes a primitive notion of *class*. This approach simplifies the later discussion of aspects, whose advice is bound to classes, rather than objects.

Previous work on class-based languages has concentrated on translations from class-based languages into polymorphic λ-calculi [5] or to object-based languages such as the ς-calculus [1]. For example, this is the technique used in giving the semantics of LOOM [6], PolyTOIL [7] and Moby [11]. There is less literature on providing a direct semantics for class-based languages; notable exceptions are Featherweight Java [12] and Java$_s$ [9]. Our semantics is heavily influenced by Featherweight Java, but is for a multi-threaded language of mutable objects rather than a single-threaded language of immutable objects; in addition, we do not address issues of genericity or of translating away inner classes [13].

NOTATION. For any metavariable x, we write x for ordered sequences of x's, and $\bar{x}$ for unordered sequences of x's.

A program P has the form $(\bar{D} \vdash \bar{H})$, where $\bar{D}$ is a set of declarations and $\bar{H}$ is a set of heap allocated threads and objects. A class declaration "class $c <: d \{ ...m\,(x)\,\{C\}... \}$" must indicate the superclass d and a set of method declarations. Fields are not declared since the language is untyped. The superclass relation is terminated in the undeclared class "Object". An object declaration, "obj $o:c \{ ...f=v... \}$" must indicate the actual class of the object and the values of the fields. A thread declaration, "thrd $p\{S\}$" names a controlling object p and a stack S, which contains a sequence of commands to perform. If a thread is executing a method on behalf of object p, then p will be the controlling object. We include the controlling object only for compatibility with the aspect-based language; it is not used here.

The dynamic semantics of the class-based language is described as a transformation of programs:

$$P \rightarrow P'$$

Let us consider a few examples. As a simple example of a command, the values of fields in objects can be retrieved by dereferencing the heap.

$$\begin{array}{l} \text{obj } o:c \{ ...f=v... \} \\ \text{thrd } p\{ \text{let } x=o.f;\, \} \end{array} \quad \rightarrow \quad \begin{array}{l} \text{obj } o:c \{ ...f=v... \} \\ \text{thrd } p\{ \text{let } x=v;\, \} \end{array}$$

Symmetrically, a field in an object can be set to store a new value.

$$\begin{array}{l} \text{obj } o:c \{ ...f=u... \} \\ \text{thrd } p\{ \text{set } o.f=v;\, \} \end{array} \quad \rightarrow \quad \begin{array}{l} \text{obj } o:c \{ ...f=v... \} \\ \text{thrd } p\{\} \end{array}$$

Threads may include "inner class" declarations that are loaded dynamically:

$$\text{thrd } p\{ \text{new class } c <: d \{...\};\, \} \quad \rightarrow \quad \begin{array}{l} \text{class } c <: d \{...\} \\ \text{thrd } p\{\,\} \end{array}$$

The most important reduction rules, however, are those involving method invocation. In a dynamically dispatched message, we first look up the dynamic type of the

Table 1. Class-Based Syntax

$a, .., z$	*Name*	$C, B ::=$	*Command*
$P, Q ::= (\bar{D} \vdash \bar{H})$	*Program*	new $\bar{D};$	New Class
		new $\bar{H};$	New Heap Element
$D, E ::= \text{class } c <: d \{\bar{M}\}$	*Declaration*	return $v;$	Return
$M ::= m(x) \{C\}$	*Method*	let $x = v;$	Value
$H, G ::=$	*Heap Element*	let $x = o.m(v);$	Dynamic Message
obj $o : c \{\bar{F}\}$	Object	let $x = o.c :: m(v);$	Static Message
thrd $o\{S\}$	Thread	let $x = o.f;$	Get Field
$F ::= f = v$	*Field*	set $o.f = v;$	Set Field
$S, T ::=$	*Call Stack*		
C	Current Frame		
let $x = o\{S\}; C$	Pushed Frame		

object. Next, we move up the superclass chain till we find a class where the method is actually defined. Finally, once we have discovered the class where the method is defined, reduction proceeds via a standard substitution of parameters for the method, instantiating of this with the actual receiver of the method.

$$
\begin{array}{l}
\text{class } d <: \text{Object} \{\dots m(x) \{B\} \dots\} \\
\text{class } c <: d \{\dots\} \\
\text{obj } o : c \{\dots\} \\
\text{thrd } p\{o.m(v);\}
\end{array}
\quad \rightarrow \quad
\begin{array}{l}
\text{class } d <: \text{Object} \{\dots m(x) \{B\} \dots\} \\
\text{class } c <: d \{\dots\} \\
\text{obj } o : c \{\dots\} \\
\text{thrd } p\{B[^o/\text{this}, ^v/x]\}
\end{array}
$$

We include statically dispatched messages to encode superclass calls. In class c which extends d, "super.$m(v);$" is encoded "this.$d :: m(v);$".

2.1   Syntax

The syntax is given in Table 1. In definitions and examples, we write "_" to stand for an element of any syntactic category that is not of interest.

Lower-case letters a–z range over a set of names. "Object", "this", "target" and "proceed" are reserved names. Although all names are drawn from a single set, our use of names is disciplined to improve readability. We use c–e for class names; f for field names; m for method names; o–q for object reference names; x–z for variables; v for values (object references or variables); a–b for advice. Advice is discussed in the following section, where we will also assume a fixed total order on names, $n \prec m$. We may write a collection of names as "$a, \bar{a}$" to indicate that a is ordered before any of the names in $\bar{a}$.

Table 2. Reduction

$(L_C\text{-SUPER})$
$$\bar{D} \ni \text{class } c <: d \{\bar{M}\}$$
$$\bar{M} \not\ni m(\_) \{\_\}$$
$$\bar{D} \vdash \text{body}(d::m) = (x)C$$
$$\bar{D} \vdash \text{body}(c::m) = (x)C$$

$(L_C\text{-THIS})$
$$\bar{D} \ni \text{class } c <: \_ \{\bar{M}, m(x) \{C\}\}$$
$$\bar{D} \vdash \text{body}(c::m) = (x)C$$

$(R_C\text{-LET})$
$$(\bar{D} \vdash \bar{H}, \text{thrd } q\{S\})$$
$$\to (\bar{D}' \vdash \bar{H}', \text{thrd } q\{S'\})$$
$$(\bar{D} \vdash \bar{H}, \text{thrd } p\{\text{let } x=q\{S\}; C\})$$
$$\to (\bar{D}' \vdash \bar{H}', \text{thrd } p\{\text{let } x=q\{S'\}; C\})$$

$(R_C\text{-VALUE})$
$$(\bar{D} \vdash \bar{H}, \text{thrd } p\{\text{let } x=v; C\})$$
$$\to (\bar{D} \vdash \bar{H}, \text{thrd } p\{C[^v\!/x]\})$$

$(R_C\text{-RETURN})$
$$(\bar{D} \vdash \bar{H}, \text{thrd } p\{\text{let } x=q\{\text{return } v; B\}; C\})$$
$$\to (\bar{D} \vdash \bar{H}, \text{thrd } p\{\text{let } x=v; C\})$$

$(R_C\text{-GARBAGE})$
$$(\bar{D} \vdash \bar{H}, \text{thrd } p\{\text{return } v; C\})$$
$$\to (\bar{D} \vdash H)$$

$(R_C\text{-DYN-MSG})$
$$\bar{H} \ni \text{obj } o:c \{\_\}$$
$$\bar{D} \vdash \text{body}(c::m) = (x)B$$
$$(\bar{D} \vdash \bar{H}, \text{thrd } p\{\text{let } x=o.m(v); C\})$$
$$\to (\bar{D} \vdash \bar{H}, \text{thrd } p\{\text{let } x=o\{B[^o\!/\text{this}, ^v\!/x]\}; C\})$$

$(R_C\text{-DEC})$
domains of $\bar{D}$ and $\bar{E}$ are disjoint
$$(\bar{D} \vdash \bar{H}, \text{thrd } p\{\text{new } \bar{E}; C\})$$
$$\to (\bar{D}, \bar{E} \vdash \bar{H}, \text{thrd } p\{C\})$$

$(R_C\text{-STC-MSG})$
$$\bar{D} \vdash \text{body}(c::m) = (x)B$$
$$(\bar{D} \vdash \bar{H}, \text{thrd } p\{\text{let } x=o.c::m(v); C\})$$
$$\to (\bar{D} \vdash \bar{H}, \text{thrd } p\{\text{let } x=o\{B[^o\!/\text{this}, ^v\!/x]\}; C\})$$

$(R_C\text{-HEAP})$
domains of $\bar{H}$ and $\bar{G}$ are disjoint
$$(\bar{D} \vdash \bar{H}, \text{thrd } p\{\text{new } \bar{G}; C\})$$
$$\to (\bar{D} \vdash \bar{H}, \bar{G}, \text{thrd } p\{C\})$$

$(R_C\text{-GET})$
$$\bar{H} \ni \text{obj } o:c \{\bar{F}, f=v\}$$
$$(\bar{D} \vdash \bar{H}, \text{thrd } p\{\text{let } x=o.f; C\})$$
$$\to (\bar{D} \vdash \bar{H}, \text{thrd } p\{\text{let } x=v; C\})$$

$(R_C\text{-SET})$
$$(\bar{D} \vdash \bar{H}, \text{obj } o:c \{\bar{F}, f=u\}, \text{thrd } p\{\text{set } o.f=v; C\})$$
$$\to (\bar{D} \vdash \bar{H}, \text{obj } o:c \{\bar{F}, f=v\}, \text{thrd } p\{C\})$$

We define the notion of *bound name* for method declarations and command sequences. The method declaration "$m(x) \{C\}$" binds x and this, the scope is C. The class declaration "new class $c <: d \{\bar{M}\}; C$" binds c, with scope $\bar{M}$ and C. The object declaration "new obj $o:c \{\bar{F}\}; C$" binds o, with scope $\bar{F}$ and C. Each let-command sequence "let $x=\ldots; C$", binds x, with scope C. Command sequences associate to the right, so "$C_1 \, C_2 \, C_3$" should be read "$C_1(C_2 \, C_3)$"; the scope of variables bound in C_1 includes C_2 and C_3. Note that there are no binders for method or field names; the usual semantics requires a static typing system, which we purposefully avoid here. We identify programs up to renaming of bound names and define substitution $C[^v\!/x]$ as usual.

2.2 Dynamic Semantics

Computation proceeds by executing the command sequences contained in threads. Commands may include declaration of classes "new $\bar{D}$;" or heap elements "new $\bar{H}$;". The value stored in an object field can be retrieved "let $x = o.f$;" and set "set $o.f = v$;". Method calls may be dispatched using the dynamic type of the object "let $x = o.m(v)$;" or a statically chosen type "let $x = o.c :: m(v)$;".

A pushed frame "let $x = p\{S\}; C$" successfully terminates in a return command which removes the remainder of S, leaving C to execute; "let $x = p\{$ return $v; B\}; C$" reduces to "let $x = v; C$", which is then further reduced via substitution to "$C[^v/_x]$". A top level return "thrd $p\{$ return $v; C\}$" causes the thread to be garbage collected.

The reduction rules $P \rightarrow P'$ are given in Table 2. The rules (R_C-LET), (R_C-RETURN) and (R_C-GARBAGE) deal with pushed frames. The rule (R_C-VALUE) allows returned values to be substituted through for the variables to which they are bound. The rules (R_C-DEC) and (R_C-HEAP) allow threads to create new classes, objects and threads. These rules require alpha-renaming to make the domains disjoint, allowing generation of new class, object and thread names. The rules (R_C-GET) and (R_C-SET) allow for the manipulation of fields.

The rules (R_C-DYN-MSG) and (R_C-STC-MSG) perform beta reduction on method calls; in the dynamic case, the method is determined by the actual class of the object o; in the static case, the method is determined by the annotated method call $c :: m$. These rules use an auxiliary relation for method lookup "$\bar{D} \vdash \text{body}(c :: m) = (x) C$", also defined in Table 2. The rule (L_C-THIS) allows for a method body to be retrieved from the class which declares it, whereas (L_C-SUPER) specifies that if a method is not declared in a class, then the superclass should be checked. Note that *body* defines a partial function.

3 An Aspect-Based Language

The move from a class-based language to an aspect-based language involves three new pieces of syntax: aspect declarations, advised method calls and proceed calls.

An aspect declaration, "adv $a(x) : \phi \{C\}$" has three essential components. The name a allows references to the aspect from elsewhere in the program. The command sequence C species *what* to execute and the pointcut ϕ specifies *when*. A pointcut specifies the set of methods that are affected by this aspect; formally pointcuts are presented as elements of the boolean algebra whose atoms are execution pointcuts, $\text{exec}(c :: m)$, and call pointcuts, $\text{call}(c :: m)$.

An advised method call "let $x = o.m[\bar{a}; \bar{b}](v)$;" specifies a set $\bar{a}$ of call advice and a set $\bar{b}$ of execution advice. For simplicity, we assume that there is a fixed total ordering on the names of advice ($n \prec m$) which determines the execution order; we do not allow declarations of advice precedence. The advice sets $\bar{a}$ and $\bar{b}$ determine the semantics of advised method calls; the method name m is an annotation required only to define the weaving function for call advice in the Section 4.

The final new command is "let $x = \text{proceed}(v)$;" which is intended to appear in the body of advice. This command plays a crucial role in the operational semantics as sketched below.

Due to the presence of call advice, we must know the static (declared) type of an object reference, in addition to its dynamic (actual) type. Thus, in the aspect language, each dynamically dispatched method call "let $x = o : c.m(v)$;" must be annotated with a static type c. We follow AspectJ in ignoring call advice for super calls, here modeled by statically dispatched messages. We could easily adapt our semantics to execute call advice on static messages as well.

In the aspect language, classes have the form "class $c <: d$ { ... $m[\bar{a}; \bar{b}]$ ... }". There are no commands directly associated with classes, rather, they are indirectly associated using the advice sets $\bar{a}$ and $\bar{b}$. Method bodies in class declarations would be redundant, as demonstrated below.

Let us first consider a few examples. Given a method call in the aspect-oriented calculus, we first lookup the call and execution advice associated with the method to build an advised method call. Call advice lookup is based on the declared type, whereas execution advice lookup is based on the actual type.

$$
\begin{array}{ll}
\text{adv } a\,(...) : \text{call}\,(c::m)\;\{\,...\,\} & \text{adv } a\,(...) : \text{call}\,(c::m)\;\{\,...\,\} \\
\text{adv } b\,(...) : \text{exec}\,(d::m)\;\{\,...\,\} & \text{adv } b\,(...) : \text{exec}\,(d::m)\;\{\,...\,\} \\
\text{obj } o : d\;\{\,...\,\} & \to \quad \text{obj } o : d\;\{\,...\,\} \\
\text{thrd } p\{\,o : c.m(v)\,;\,\} & \text{thrd } p\{\,o.m[a;\,b]\,(v)\,;\,\}
\end{array}
$$

Now, consider an advised message where the call advice list is nonempty:

$$
\begin{array}{ll}
\text{adv } a\,(x) : ...\;\{B\} & \text{adv } a\,(x) : ...\;\{B\} \\
\text{thrd } p\{\,o.m[a;\,b]\,(v)\,;\,\} & \to \quad \text{thrd } p\{\,B[{}^{p}/\text{this},\,{}^{o}/\text{target},\,{}^{o.m[0;\,b]}/\text{proceed},\,{}^{v}/x]\,\}
\end{array}
$$

Reduction proceeds as follows: First, we choose the aspect to execute, in this case a. Next, the aspect declaration is looked up to extract the advice body, in this case B. Finally, some substitutions are performed. In addition to the formal parameters, this is bound to the sender of the message p, and target is bound to the recipient o. Most significantly, proceed is bound to a new advised method call, referencing the remaining aspects, in this case $o.m[0; b]$. Using the substitution on proceed, the semantics walks through the advice given in the call advice set, then the advice given in the execution advice set, using global order on aspect names to determine precedence within each of the two sets. If proceed does not occur in an advice body, then subsequent advice is ignored. On the other hand, if a name occurs in both the call and execution advice sets, the advice body may be executed twice. An advised method call with no advice is treated as an error; it cannot reduce.

The encoding of the class-based language into the aspect calculus provides insight into the operational semantics of the aspect calculus. The translation must account for the fact that methods in the aspect calculus do not have any method bodies. Write "cbl_c_m" to identify a fresh name generated from class name c and method name m. Given a method definition "class $d <: c$ { ... $m(x)$ { C } ... }" create the advice:

$$
\text{adv cbl\_}d\text{\_}m\,(x) : \text{exec}\,(d::m)\;\{\,C[^{\text{proceed}}/\text{super}]\,\}
$$

For this encoding to work, it must be the case that if d is a subclass of c, then the name cbl_d_m precedes cbl_c_m in the advice ordering. Thus, the first aspect pulled out of the

Table 3. Aspect-Based Syntax

$D,E ::= ...$	*Declaration*	$C,B ::= ...$	*Command*
adv $a\,(x):\phi\,\{\,C\,\}$	Advice	let $x = o : c.m(v)\,;$	Dynamic Message
$M ::= m\,[\bar{a}\,;\,\bar{b}]$	*Method*	let $x = o.m\,[\bar{a}\,;\,\bar{b}]\,(v)\,;$	Advised Message
		let $x = \text{proceed}\,(v)\,;$	Proceed
$L ::= c :: m$	*Label*		
		Replace the dynamic message syntax from Table 1	
$\phi,\psi ::=$	*Pointcut*		
false	False		
$\neg\phi$	Negation		
$\phi \vee \psi$	Disjunction		
call (L)	Call		
exec (L)	Execution		

aspect list is the closest definition of m in the class hierarchy. Finally, note that method bodies in a class-based language do not contain proceed; thus proceed can be used to encode calls to super. If no such calls exist, then subsequent advice is not executed.

3.1 Syntax

In Table 3 we extend the grammar for declarations and commands, replace the grammar for method declarations, and define a new grammar for pointcuts. The method declaration "$m\,[\bar{a}\,;\,\bar{b}]$" no longer includes a command sequence, but rather two sets of advice; the idea is that $\bar{a}$ is executed by the *caller* (call advice), $\bar{b}$ is executed by the *callee* (execution advice). The advice declaration "new adv $a\,(x):\phi\,\{\,B\,\};C$" binds a, with scope B and C, and also binds x, this and target, with scope B.

Pointcuts are used to indicate the set of methods to which advice should be attached. A point cut ϕ allows one to specify a calling point "call$(c::m)$", an execution point "exec$(c::m)$", or a combination thereof. The full set of boolean connectives can prove useful, given that point cuts apply not only to the specified class, but to all subclasses as well; negation can be used to change this.

An advised method call "let $x = o.m\,[\bar{a}\,;\,\bar{b}]\,(v)\,;$" indicates the collections of call advice $\bar{a}$ and execution advice $\bar{b}$ yet to be performed; the method name m is ignored. Source programs need not contain advised method calls; rather advised method calls are included because they arise during the dynamics of programs. An advised call with no advice "let $x = o.m\,[\emptyset\,;\,\emptyset]\,(v)\,;$" is unable to reduce. The proceed command "let $x = \text{proceed}\,(v)\,;$" causes control to advance to the next named advice, where the global order on names ($n \prec m$) is used to determine which advice is next.

3.2 Dynamic Semantics

The semantics of pointcuts is defined in Table 4. We write "$\bar{D} \vdash c :: m \in \text{execadv}(\phi)$" when pointcut ϕ applies to the execution of method m in class c, and similarly for call

Table 4. Semantics of Pointcuts

$$(\text{S-EXTENDS})$$
$$\bar{D} \ni \text{class } c <: d \{\_\}$$
$$\overline{\bar{D} \vdash c <: d}$$

$$(\text{S-REFLEX})$$
$$\overline{\bar{D} \vdash c <: c}$$

$$(\text{S-TRANS})$$
$$\bar{D} \vdash c <: d$$
$$\bar{D} \vdash d <: e$$
$$\overline{\bar{D} \vdash c <: e}$$

$$(\text{PC-EXEC})$$
$$\bar{D} \vdash c <: d$$
$$\overline{\bar{D} \vdash c :: m \in \text{execadv}(\text{exec}(d :: m))}$$

$$(\text{PC-CALL})$$
$$\bar{D} \vdash c <: d$$
$$\overline{\bar{D} \vdash c :: m \in \text{calladv}(\text{call}(d :: m))}$$

$$(\text{PC-ENOT})$$
$$\bar{D} \vdash L \notin \text{execadv}(\phi)$$
$$\overline{\bar{D} \vdash L \in \text{execadv}(\neg\phi)}$$

$$(\text{PC-EORL})$$
$$\bar{D} \vdash L \in \text{execadv}(\phi)$$
$$\overline{\bar{D} \vdash L \in \text{execadv}(\phi \vee \psi)}$$

$$(\text{PC-EORR})$$
$$\bar{D} \vdash L \in \text{execadv}(\psi)$$
$$\overline{\bar{D} \vdash L \in \text{execadv}(\phi \vee \psi)}$$

$$(\text{PC-CNOT})$$
$$\bar{D} \vdash L \notin \text{calladv}(\phi)$$
$$\overline{\bar{D} \vdash L \in \text{calladv}(\neg\phi)}$$

$$(\text{PC-CORL})$$
$$\bar{D} \vdash L \in \text{calladv}(\phi)$$
$$\overline{\bar{D} \vdash L \in \text{calladv}(\phi \vee \psi)}$$

$$(\text{PC-CORR})$$
$$\bar{D} \vdash L \in \text{calladv}(\psi)$$
$$\overline{\bar{D} \vdash L \in \text{calladv}(\phi \vee \psi)}$$

pointcuts. The definition relies on a notion of subtyping "$\bar{D} \vdash c <: d$", given in the same table. Note that these definitions ignore the advice sets declared by methods.

The semantics of aspect programs is defined in Table 5. Rather than use the semantics of pointcuts directly, the rules for method invocation $(\text{R}_A\text{-DYN-MSG})$ and $(\text{R}_A\text{-STC-MSG})$, rely on the advice sets declared by methods. We do this to emulate realistic advice lookup, which should be be based on the class hierarchy alone. The more naive approach would require that each method dispatch lock all advice in the heap; our semantics is intended to be efficiently implementable. Write "$\bar{D} \vdash \text{advice}(c :: m) = [\bar{a} \; ; \; \bar{b}]$" if $\bar{a}$ *(resp. $\bar{b}$)* is the call advice *(resp. execution advice)* declared for m in c. The definition is also given in Table 5. The rule $(\text{L}_A\text{-TOP})$ is required to ensure that $(\text{R}_A\text{-DYN-MSG})$ always succeeds in looking up execution advice, even if the method m is not defined. This is required for consistency with the woven program, where call advice is executed even if the object o does not exist. Note that $(\text{R}_A\text{-DYN-MSG})$ looks up the call and execution advice at different types. The rule $(\text{R}_A\text{-ADV-MSG1})$ describes the reduction of execution advice. The rule $(\text{R}_A\text{-ADV-MSG2})$ describes the reduction of call advice.

Clearly, the advice that appears in a method declaration must be consistent with that which is attached to a pointcut. We formalize this intuition as *coherence* and define a function *close* which creates coherent declaration sets. To maintain coherence, the rule for inner declarations $(\text{R}_A\text{-DEC})$ uses *close* to saturate the declaration set with new classes and advice.

Table 5. Aspect-Based Reduction

Include all rules from Table 2, except $(R_C\text{-DEC})$, $(R_C\text{-DYN-MSG})$ and $(R_C\text{-STC-MSG})$.

$(L_A\text{-TOP})$
$$\bar{D} \vdash \text{advice}(\text{Object} :: m) = [0 \; ; \; 0]$$

$(L_A\text{-THIS})$
$$\frac{\bar{D} \ni \text{class } c <: \_ \{ \bar{M}, m[\bar{a} \; ; \; \bar{b}] \}}{\bar{D} \vdash \text{advice}(c :: m) = [\bar{a} \; ; \; \bar{b}]}$$

$(L_A\text{-SUPER})$
$$\frac{\bar{D} \vdash \text{advice}(d :: m) = [\bar{a} \; ; \; \bar{b}] \quad \bar{M} \not\ni m(\_) \{\_\} \quad \bar{D} \ni \text{class } c <: d \{ \bar{M} \}}{\bar{D} \vdash \text{advice}(c :: m) = [\bar{a} \; ; \; \bar{b}]}$$

$(R_A\text{-DEC})$
$$\frac{\text{domains of } \bar{D} \text{ and } \bar{E} \text{ are disjoint}}{(\bar{D} \vdash \bar{H}, \text{thrd } p\{ \text{new } \bar{E}; C \}) \; \rightarrow \; (\text{close}(\bar{D}, \bar{E}) \vdash \bar{H}, \text{thrd } p\{ C \})}$$

$(R_A\text{-DYN-MSG})$
$$\frac{\bar{H} \ni \text{obj } o{:}d \{\_\} \quad \bar{D} \vdash \text{advice}(c :: m) = [\bar{a} \; ; \; \_] \quad \bar{D} \vdash \text{advice}(d :: m) = [\_ \; ; \; \bar{b}]}{(\bar{D} \vdash \bar{H}, \text{thrd } p\{ \text{let } x{=}o{:}c.m(v) ; C \}) \; \rightarrow \; (\bar{D} \vdash \bar{H}, \text{thrd } p\{ \text{let } x{=}o.m[\bar{a} \; ; \; \bar{b}] (v) ; C \})}$$

$(R_A\text{-STC-MSG})$
$$\frac{\bar{D} \vdash \text{advice}(c :: m) = [\_ \; ; \; \bar{b}]}{(\bar{D} \vdash \bar{H}, \text{thrd } p\{ \text{let } x{=}o.c{::}m(v) ; C \}) \; \rightarrow \; (\bar{D} \vdash \bar{H}, \text{thrd } p\{ \text{let } x{=}o.m[0 \; ; \; \bar{b}] (v) ; C \})}$$

$(R_A\text{-ADV-MSG1})$
$$\frac{\bar{D} \ni \text{adv } b(x) : \_ \{ B \}}{(\bar{D} \vdash \bar{H}, \text{thrd } p\{ \text{let } x{=}o.m[0 \; ; \; b, \bar{b}] (v) ; C \}) \; \rightarrow \; (\bar{D} \vdash \bar{H}, \text{thrd } p\{ \text{let } x{=}o\{ B[^o/\text{this}, ^{o.m[0 \; ; \; \bar{b}]}/\text{proceed}, ^v/x] \} ; C \})} \quad b \prec \bar{b}$$

$(R_A\text{-ADV-MSG2})$
$$\frac{\bar{D} \ni \text{adv } a(x) : \_ \{ B \}}{(\bar{D} \vdash \bar{H}, \text{thrd } p\{ \text{let } x{=}o.m[a, \bar{a} \; ; \; \bar{b}] (v) ; C \}) \; \rightarrow \; (\bar{D} \vdash \bar{H}, \text{thrd } p\{ \text{let } x{=}p\{ B[^p/\text{this}, ^o/\text{target}, ^{o.m[\bar{a} \; ; \; \bar{b}]}/\text{proceed}, ^v/x] \} ; C \})} \quad a \prec \bar{a}$$

Definition 1 (Coherence). *A collection of declarations $\bar{D}$ is* coherent *(resp.* semi-coherent*) whenever, for any*

$$\text{if } \bar{D} \ni \text{adv } b(\_) : \phi \{\_\}$$
$$\text{and } \bar{D} \ni \text{class } c <: \_ \{ \dots m[\bar{a} \; ; \; \bar{a}'] \dots \}$$
$$\text{then } b \in \bar{a} \text{ iff (resp. implies) } \bar{D} \vdash c :: m \in \text{calladv}(\phi)$$
$$\text{and } b \in \bar{a}' \text{ iff (resp. implies) } \bar{D} \vdash c :: m \in \text{execadv}(\phi)$$

Definition 2 (Close). *We define the function* $\text{close}(\bar{D})$, *which saturates class declarations with advice:*

(C-FIX)

$\bar{D}$ *is coherent*

$\text{close}(\bar{D}) = \bar{D}$

(C-CALL)

$\bar{D} \ni \text{adv } a\,(\_) : \phi\,\{\_\}$

$\bar{D} \vdash c :: m \in \text{calladv}(\phi)$

$\bar{D} = \bar{E}, \text{class } c <: d\,\{\bar{M}, m[\bar{a}\,;\,\bar{b}]\,\}$

$\text{close}(\bar{D}) = \text{close}(\bar{E}, \text{class } c <: d\,\{\bar{M}, m[\bar{a}\,;\,\bar{b}, b]\,\})$

(C-EXEC)

$\bar{D} \ni \text{adv } b\,(\_) : \phi\,\{\_\}$

$\bar{D} \vdash c :: m \in \text{execadv}(\phi)$

$\bar{D} = \bar{E}, \text{class } c <: d\,\{\bar{M}, m[\bar{a}\,;\,\bar{b}]\,\}$

$\text{close}(\bar{D}) = \text{close}(\bar{E}, \text{class } c <: d\,\{\bar{M}, m[\bar{a}, a\,;\,\bar{b}]\,\})$

Lemma 1 (Close). *If $\bar{D}$ is semi-coherent, then* $\text{close}(\bar{D})$ *is coherent.*

Lemma 2 (Coherence Preservation). *Coherence is preserved by reduction.*

Note that any program where each class declaration is taken from the class-based language is semi-coherent by construction.

4 Weaving

The weaving algorithm translates aspect-based programs into programs in the class-based language. The algorithm is not novel, being closely modeled on that used by AspectJ. Rather our contribution is that we have developed a specification of the correctness of *any* weaving algorithm.

Our goal is to show that the weaving algorithm preserves transitions made by the source aspect program. We achieve this up to a trivial renaming on methods ($\simeq$) defined below. Corectness is formalized by demanding that the following diagram can be completed.

$$
\begin{array}{ccc}
P \overset{weave}{\Longrightarrow} Q & & P \overset{weave}{\Longrightarrow} Q \\
\Big\downarrow & \text{as} & \Big\downarrow \qquad \Big\downarrow \\
P' & & P' \overset{weave}{\Longrightarrow} \simeq Q'
\end{array}
$$

We also expect that a woven program not have spurious new reductions. This is formalized by demanding that the following diagram can be completed.

$$
\begin{array}{ccc}
P \overset{weave}{\Longrightarrow} Q & & P \overset{weave}{\Longrightarrow} Q \\
\Big\downarrow & \text{as} & \Big\downarrow \qquad \Big\downarrow \\
Q' & & P' \overset{weave}{\Longrightarrow} \simeq Q'
\end{array}
$$

4.1 Weaving as Macro Expansion

In order to motivate the ideas, we first describe a macro-expansion approach to weaving, limiting our attention to execution pointcuts. Recall that weaving is intended as a compile-time process. Thus, the weaving process works through the entire program text. The effect of the weaving process will be to change method calls to incorporate all of the aspects advising the method.

Read $\bar{D} \vdash \text{weave}(\cdot)$ as the weaving of program fragment $(\cdot)$ in the context of declarations $\bar{D}$. The heart of the macro expansion approach to weaving is the following rule. The body of a method is determined by selecting the body of the first advice named in the advice list. The rule is applied again, after substituting the remaining advice through for proceed. Note that in the case that the advice list $\bar{b}$ is empty, then any calls to proceed will be blocked in the consequent.

$$\frac{\bar{D} \ni \text{adv } b\,(x) :\_ \{C\} \qquad \bar{D} \vdash \text{weave}(C[^{\text{this}.m\,[\emptyset\,;\,\bar{b}]}/_{\text{proceed}}]) = C'}{\bar{D} \vdash \text{weave}(m\,[\emptyset\,;\,b,\bar{b}]) = m\,(x)\,\{C'\}} \quad \bar{b} \neq \emptyset$$

This treatment directly captures the idea from the dynamic semantics that a call to proceed is a call to the succeeding aspect in the aspect list.

This implementation of weaving is not useful in practice because it is not guaranteed to terminate. Since weaving is intended to occur at compile time, non-termination is a bad thing.

4.2 Weaving by Introducing New Methods

We now describe a practical weaving algorithm which mimics macro expansion using run-time method invocation. Our algorithm closely follows that of AspectJ. Intuitively, given a method m affected by advice $\bar{a}$, we create an auxiliary method for each suffix of the list $\bar{a}$. Call advised methods are placed in the class of the caller, whereas execution advised methods are placed in the class of the callee.

We begin with an example in the aspect language, showing the reduction of a dynamically dispatched message. Consider the following declarations:

```
obj p : Main {}
class Main{ m [∅ ; ma] }
adv ma () : exec (Main :: m) { let x = o : c.m () ; return () ; }

obj o : c {}
class c{ m [ca ; cb] }
adv ca () : call (c :: m) { let y = proceed () ; return () ; }
adv cb () : exec (c :: m) { return () ; }
```

In the presence of these declarations, we can observe the following reductions:

$$thrd\ p\{\ let\ x=o:c.m()\ ;\ \}$$

$(R_A\text{-DYN-MSG})$	$\rightarrow$	thrd p$\{$ let x=o.m$[$ca ; cb$]$ () ; $\}$
$(R_A\text{-ADV-MSG2})$	$\rightarrow$	thrd p$\{$ let x=p$\{$ let y=o.m$[0$; cb$]$ () ;return () ; $\}$; $\}$
$(R_A\text{-ADV-MSG1})$	$\rightarrow$	thrd p$\{$ let x=p$\{$ let y=o$\{$return () ; $\}$;return () ; $\}$; $\}$
$(R_A\text{-RETURN})$	$\rightarrow$	thrd p$\{$ let x=p$\{$ let y= () ;return () ; $\}$; $\}$
$(R_A\text{-VAL})$	$\rightarrow$	thrd p$\{$ let x=p$\{$ return () ; $\}$; $\}$
$(R_A\text{-RETURN})$	$\rightarrow$	thrd p$\{$ let x= () ; $\}$
$(R_A\text{-VAL})$	$\rightarrow$	thrd p$\{\}$

Weaving the declarations produces:

```
obj p: Main {}
class Main{ m () { skip; let x=this.call_ca_m(o) ;return () ; }
            exec_ma () { skip; let x=this.call_ca_m(o) ;return () ; }
            call_ca_m (z) { let y=z.m() ;return () ; }}
obj o:c {}
class c{ m () { return () ; }
         exec_cb () { return () ; }}
```

Here "skip; C" is defined as "let $x=x;C$", where x does not appear free in C. The resulting class-based reductions are as follows:

$$thrd\ p\{\ skip; let\ x=p.call\_ca\_m(o)\ ;\ \}$$

$(R_C\text{-VAL})$	$\rightarrow$	thrd p$\{$ let x=p.call_ca_m(o) ; $\}$
$(R_C\text{-DYN-MSG})$	$\rightarrow$	thrd p$\{$ let x=p$\{$ let y=o.m() ;return () ; $\}$; $\}$
$(R_C\text{-DYN-MSG})$	$\rightarrow$	thrd p$\{$ let x=p$\{$ let y=o$\{$return () ; $\}$;return () ; $\}$; $\}$
$(R_C\text{-RETURN})$	$\rightarrow$	thrd p$\{$ let x=p$\{$ let y= () ;return () ; $\}$; $\}$
$(R_C\text{-VAL})$	$\rightarrow$	thrd p$\{$ let x=p$\{$ return () ; $\}$; $\}$
$(R_C\text{-RETURN})$	$\rightarrow$	thrd p$\{$ let x= () ; $\}$
$(R_C\text{-VAL})$	$\rightarrow$	thrd p$\{\}$

It is worth noting several things in this example. First, the method exec_ma is introduced into Main, corresponding to the execution advice on m in Main. In addition, call_ca_m is introduced into Main and exec_cb is introduced into c, corresponding to call and execution advice on m in c. Second, note that in call_ca_m, the call to proceed has been replaced with a dynamically dispatched call on m, sent to the extra parameter z. Since woven call advice is not defined in the target object's class, the target object must be passed using this additional parameter. Finally, note the gratuitous use of "skip;"; the extra reduction is required to match the advice lookup step (R_A-DYN-MSG) in the aspect language.

The definition of weaving is split over two tables. Table 6 gives the rules for handling execution advice; Table 7 gives the rules for handling call advice. The definition proceeds by structural induction on program fragments. For clarity, we use different names when weaving different syntactic categories: *weave* for programs, *wdec* for declarations, *wheap* for heaps, *wmth* for methods, and *wstack* for stacks. Each of these is a total function on the respective domains.

Table 6. Execution Advice Weaving

$$(\text{W-PROG})$$
$$\frac{\text{close}(\bar{D}) \vdash \text{wdec}(\text{close}(\bar{D})) = \bar{D}' \qquad \text{close}(\bar{D}) \vdash \text{wheap}(\bar{H}) = \bar{H}'}{\text{weave}(\bar{D} \vdash \bar{H}) = (\bar{D}' \vdash \bar{H}')}$$

$$(\text{W-ADVICE})$$
$$\frac{}{\bar{D} \vdash \text{wdec}(\text{adv}\_(\_):\_\{\_\}) = \emptyset}$$

$$(\text{W-OBJECT})$$
$$\frac{}{\bar{D} \vdash \text{wheap}(\text{obj}\, o:c\, \{\bar{F}\}) = \text{obj}\, o:c\, \{\bar{F}\}}$$

$$(\text{W-CLASS})$$
$$\frac{\bar{D} \vdash \text{wmth}(\bar{M}) = \bar{M}'}{\bar{D} \vdash \text{wdec}(\text{class}\, c <: d\, \{\bar{M}\}) = \text{class}\, c <: d\, \{\bar{M}'\}}$$

$$(\text{W-THREAD})$$
$$\frac{\bar{D} \vdash \text{wstack}(p\{S\}) = (M\, ;\, S')}{\bar{D} \vdash \text{wheap}(\text{thrd}\, p\{S\}) = \text{thrd}\, p\{S'\}}$$

$$(\text{W-METHOD})$$
$$\frac{\bar{D} \vdash \text{genExecMth}(\bar{b}) = \bar{M} \qquad \bar{M} \ni \text{exec}\_\bar{b}\,(x)\,\{C\}}{\bar{D} \vdash \text{wmth}(m\,[\bar{a}\, ;\, \bar{b}]) = \bar{M}, m\,(x)\,\{C\}}$$

$$(\text{GEN-EXEC})$$
$$\frac{\bar{D} \ni \text{adv}\, b\,(x):\_\{C\} \qquad \bar{D} \vdash \text{wstack}(\text{this}\{C^{[\text{this}.m\,[\emptyset\, ;\, \bar{b}']}/_{\text{proceed}}]\}) = (\bar{M}'\, ;\, C') \qquad \bar{D} \vdash \text{genExecMth}(\bar{b}') = \bar{M}}{\bar{D} \vdash \text{genExecMth}(\bar{b}) = \bar{M}, \bar{M}', \text{exec}\_\bar{b}\,(x)\,\{C'\}} \qquad \begin{array}{l}\bar{b} = b, \bar{b}' \\ b \prec \bar{b}\end{array}$$

$$(\text{W-LET})$$
$$\frac{\bar{D} \vdash \text{wstack}(q\{S\}) = (\bar{M}\, ;\, S') \qquad \bar{D} \vdash \text{wstack}(p\{C\}) = (\bar{M}'\, ;\, C')}{\bar{D} \vdash \text{wstack}(p\{\text{let}\, x = q\{S\}; C\}) = (\bar{M}, \bar{M}'\, ;\, \text{let}\, x = q\{S'\}; C')}$$

$$(\text{W-DYN-MSG1})$$
$$\frac{\bar{D} \vdash \text{advice}(c::m) = [\emptyset\, ;\, \_] \qquad \bar{D} \vdash \text{wstack}(p\{C\}) = (\bar{M}\, ;\, C')}{\bar{D} \vdash \text{wstack}(p\{\text{let}\, x = o.c.m(v)\, ; C\}) = (\bar{M}\, ;\, \text{skip}; \text{let}\, x = o.m(v)\, ; C')}$$

$$(\text{W-DEC})$$
$$\frac{\text{close}(\bar{D}, \bar{E}) \vdash \text{wdec}(\text{close}(\bar{E})) = \bar{E}' \qquad \text{close}(\bar{D}, \bar{E}) \vdash \text{wstack}(p\{C\}) = (M\, ;\, C')}{\bar{D} \vdash \text{wstack}(p\{\text{new}\, \bar{E}; C\}) = (M\, ;\, \text{new}\, \bar{E}'; C')}$$

$$(\text{W-STC-MSG})$$
$$\frac{\bar{D} \vdash \text{wstack}(p\{C\}) = (\bar{M}\, ;\, C')}{\bar{D} \vdash \text{wstack}(p\{\text{let}\, x = o.c::m(v)\, ; C\}) = (\bar{M}\, ;\, \text{skip}; \text{let}\, x = o.c::m(v)\, ; C')}$$

$$(\text{W-HEAP})$$
$$\frac{\bar{D} \vdash \text{wheap}(\bar{H}) = \bar{H}' \qquad \bar{D} \vdash \text{wstack}(p\{C\}) = (\bar{M}\, ;\, C')}{\bar{D} \vdash \text{wstack}(p\{\text{new}\, \bar{H}; C\}) = (M\, ;\, \text{new}\, \bar{H}'; C')}$$

$$(\text{W-ADV-MSG1})$$
$$\frac{\bar{D} \vdash \text{wstack}(p\{C\}) = (\bar{M}\, ;\, C')}{\bar{D} \vdash \text{wstack}(p\{\text{let}\, x = o.m[\emptyset\, ;\, \bar{b}]\,(v)\, ; C\}) = (\bar{M}\, ;\, \text{let}\, x = o.\text{exec}\_\bar{b}(v)\, ; C')}$$

$$(\text{W-OTHER})$$
no other command rules applies
$$\frac{\bar{D} \vdash \text{wstack}(p\{C\}) = (\bar{M}\, ;\, C')}{\bar{D} \vdash \text{wstack}(p\{B\, C\}) = (\bar{M}\, ;\, B\, C')}$$

$$(\text{W-NONE})$$
$$\frac{}{\bar{D} \vdash \text{wstack}(p\{\}) = (\emptyset\, ;\, \emptyset)}$$

Table 7. Call Advice Weaving

(W-DYN-MSG2)

$$\frac{\begin{array}{l} \bar{D} \vdash \text{advice}(c::m) = [\bar{a}\,;\,\_] \\ \bar{D} \vdash \text{genCallMth}(m;\,\bar{a}) = \bar{M} \\ \bar{D} \vdash \text{wstack}(p\{\,C\,\}) = (\bar{M}'\,;\,C') \end{array}}{\begin{array}{l} \bar{D} \vdash \text{wstack}(p\{\,\text{let } x=o:c.m(v)\,;C\,\}) \\ \quad = (\bar{M}, \bar{M}'\,;\,\text{skip}\,;\text{let } x=p.\text{call\_}\bar{a}\_m(o,v)\,;C') \end{array}}\quad \bar{a} \neq \emptyset$$

(W-ADV-MSG2)

$$\frac{\begin{array}{l} \bar{D} \vdash \text{genCallMth}(m;\,\bar{a}) = \bar{M} \\ \bar{D} \vdash \text{wstack}(p\{\,C\,\}) = (\bar{M}'\,;\,C') \end{array}}{\begin{array}{l} \bar{D} \vdash \text{wstack}(p\{\,\text{let } x=o.m\,[\bar{a}\,;\,\_]\,(v)\,;C\,\}) \\ \quad = (\bar{M}, \bar{M}'\,;\,\text{let } x=p.\text{call\_}\bar{a}\_m(o,v)\,;C') \end{array}}\quad \bar{a} \neq \emptyset$$

(GEN-CALL1)

$$\frac{\begin{array}{l} \bar{D} \ni \text{adv } a\,(x):\_\{\,C\,\} \\ \bar{D} \vdash \text{wstack}(\text{this}\{\,C[^p/_\text{target}, {}^{y.m}/_\text{proceed}]\,\}) = (\bar{M}'\,;\,C') \end{array}}{\bar{D} \vdash \text{genCallMth}(m;\,a) = \bar{M}', \text{call\_}a\_m\,(y,x)\,\{\,C'\,\}}$$

(GEN-CALL2)

$$\frac{\begin{array}{l} \bar{D} \ni \text{adv } a\,(x):\_\{\,C\,\} \\ \bar{D} \vdash \text{wstack}(\text{this}\{\,C[^p/_\text{target}, {}^{\text{this}.m\,[\bar{a}\,;\,\emptyset]}/_\text{proceed}]\,\}) = (\bar{M}'\,;\,C') \end{array}}{\bar{D} \vdash \text{genCallMth}(m;\,\bar{a}) = \bar{M}', \text{call\_}\bar{a}\_m\,(y,x)\,\{\,C'\,\}}\quad \begin{array}{l} \bar{a} = a, \bar{a}' \\ a \prec \bar{a}' \\ \bar{a}' \neq \emptyset \end{array}$$

The resulting of weaving is a class-based program without any advice declaration; thus (W-ADVICE) returns the empty set. Instead, (W-CLASS) specifies that in a class declaration, the method bodies must be woven. This in turn causes (W-METHOD) to be applied to each method in the class. The result of weaving a method m is a method suite with a new method generated for each suffix of the aspect list affecting m. The names of the new methods are based on the declared advice; roughly speaking, the method exec_$\bar{b}$ handles the advice list $\bar{b}$.

The rule (GEN-EXEC) specifies that the body of the newly created method is given by the advice associated with the first aspect in the list, with the proceed bound to the method corresponding to the rest of the list. (GEN-EXEC) generates the methods one at a time, substituting for proceed, in each, the progressively smaller advice set. Informally, this definition can be viewed as performing the macro-expanded code described in previous subsection inside of the newly created method body. Thus, in effect, the actual expansion is postponed to runtime.

The commands in a method are woven as stacks with controlling object this; the controlling object is used only when weaving call advice. Weaving the commands in (GEN-EXEC) may produce call advised methods $\bar{M}'$. In the end, all of the collected methods are added back into the class using (W-METHOD) and (W-CLASS).

The rules for commands themselves are mostly straightforward. Note however, that (W-DYN-MSG1) and (W-STC-MSG) introduce an extra reduction, corresponding to advice lookup. Also note that (W-ADV-MSG1) substitutes $\mathrm{exec}\_\bar{b}$ for $m[\emptyset \ ; \ \bar{b}]$.

The extension to call pointcuts is given in Table 7. Recall that the call aspects associated with a message are determined by the static type of the object. Apart from this difference, the weaving process for call advised methods (W-DYN-MSG2) follows the structure enunciated for execution advice. One difference stands out, however; rather than sending a message to the target o, call advised methods remain with the sender p, passing o as an additional parameter.

This extra parameter is substituted for target when weaving the advice body in (W-GEN-CALL1) and (W-GEN-CALL2), giving the call advice access to the target object. Note in (W-GEN-CALL2) that $\mathrm{this}.m[\bar{a} \ ; \ \emptyset]$ is substituted through for proceed, which is later converted to $\mathrm{this}.\mathrm{call}\_\bar{a}\_m$ by (W-ADV-MSG2).

Note that if a subclass inherits a method it also inherits the associated call advice.

5   The Correctness of Weaving

Weaving is not correct for all programs. In particular weaving does not support the dynamic loading of advice that affects existing classes, although it is admissible to load classes that are affected by existing advice. Because we allow for the weaving of running threads — not something typically allowed in aspect languages—we also must make a few other sanity requirements. In particular, we require that the controlling object of all threads must be defined, and that all advised messages $m[\_ \ ; \ \_]$ in a thread with controlling object p should arise because some method defined in the class of p is declared to send a message to m. In addition, we require that programs contain no dangling references; along with the other requirements, this ensures that all of the required methods have been generated. We formalize these intuitions in the following notion of *weavability*.

Definition 3 (Weavability). *We define* $\bar{D}; \bar{H}; \bar{n} \vdash \mathrm{weavable}(\cdot)$ *on stacks in Table 8. Extend the definition to programs and advice declarations as follows:*

$$\frac{\bar{D}; \bar{H}; \mathrm{bn}(\bar{H}) \vdash \mathrm{weavable}(\bar{D}) \quad \bar{D}; \bar{H}; \mathrm{bn}(\bar{H}) \vdash \mathrm{weavable}(\bar{H})}{\mathrm{weavable}(\bar{D} \vdash \bar{H})} \qquad \frac{\bar{D}; \bar{H}; \bar{n}, x, \mathrm{this}, \mathrm{target} \vdash \mathrm{weavable}(\mathrm{this}\{C\})}{\bar{D}; \bar{H}; \bar{n} \vdash \mathrm{weavable}(\mathrm{adv}\ a\ (x) : \_\{C\})}$$

Extend the definition to all other program constructs homorphically using conjunction.

Lemma 3. *Weavability is preserved by reduction.*

Even given weavability, our definition of weaving is not quite exact with respect to the reduction semantics. As seen in the example in the last section, in the aspect language a dynamic message is converted to an advised message in one reduction. The names generated by weaving these are different in the case that there is no call advice. The discrepancy cannot be handled during weaving, since the list of execution advice cannot be determined statically. We therefore must work up to a relation that equates m with $\mathrm{exec}\_\bar{b}$ in the appropriate circumstances.

Table 8. Weavability of Stacks

To simplify the definition we write "wheap$_{\bar{D}}(\bar{H})$" for "$\bar{D} \vdash \text{wheap}(H)$", and "wdec$_{\bar{D}}(E)$" for "$\bar{D} \vdash \text{wdec}(E)$". Also, "write bn($\bar{H}$)" for the set of object names bound by heap $\bar{H}$.

(WC-DEC)
$$\frac{\begin{array}{c}\text{wheap}_{\bar{D}}(\bar{H}) = \text{wheap}_{\text{close}(\bar{D}, \bar{D}')}(\bar{H}) \\ \text{close}(\text{wdec}_{\bar{D}}(\bar{D}), \bar{D}') = \text{wdec}_{\text{close}(\bar{D}, \bar{D}')}(\text{close}(\bar{D}, \bar{D}')) \\ \text{close}(\bar{D}, \bar{D}'); \bar{H}; \bar{n} \vdash \text{weavable}(p\{\,C\,\})\end{array}}{\bar{D}; \bar{H}; \bar{n} \vdash \text{weavable}(p\{\,\text{new } D'; C\,\})}$$

(WC-HEAP)
$$\frac{\bar{D}; \bar{H}, \bar{H}'; \bar{n}, \text{bn}(\bar{H}') \vdash \text{weavable}(p\{\,C\,\})}{\bar{D}; \bar{H}; \bar{n} \vdash \text{weavable}(p\{\,\text{new } \bar{H}'; C\,\})}$$

(WC-ADV-MSG)
$$\frac{\begin{array}{c}\bar{H} \ni \text{obj } o:c\,\{\,\_\,\} \\ \bar{H} \ni \text{obj } p:d\,\{\,\_\,\} \\ \text{wdec}_{\text{close}(\bar{D})}(\text{close}(\bar{D})) \vdash \text{body}(c::\text{exec}\_\bar{b}) \text{ defined} \\ \text{wdec}_{\text{close}(\bar{D})}(\text{close}(\bar{D})) \vdash \text{body}(d::\text{call}\_\bar{a}\_m) \text{ defined} \\ \bar{D}; \bar{H}; \bar{n}, x \vdash \text{weavable}(p\{\,C\,\})\end{array}}{\bar{D}; \bar{H}; \bar{n} \vdash \text{weavable}(p\{\,\text{let } x=o.m[\bar{a}\,; \bar{b}]\,(v)\,; C\,\})}$$

(WC-LET)
$$\frac{\begin{array}{c}\bar{D}; \bar{H}; \bar{n} \vdash \text{weavable}(o\{\,S\,\}) \\ \bar{D}; \bar{H}; \bar{n}, x \vdash \text{weavable}(p\{\,C\,\})\end{array}}{\bar{D}; \bar{H}; \bar{n} \vdash \text{weavable}(p\{\,\text{let } x=o\{\,S\,\}; C\,\})}$$

(WC-DYN-MSG)
$$\frac{\begin{array}{c}o \in \bar{n} \\ \bar{D}; \bar{H}; \bar{n}, x \vdash \text{weavable}(p\{\,C\,\})\end{array}}{\bar{D}; \bar{H}; \bar{n} \vdash \text{weavable}(p\{\,\text{let } x=o:c.m(v)\,; C\,\})}$$

(WC-OTHER1)
$$\frac{\begin{array}{c}\text{no other let rule applies} \\ \bar{D}; \bar{H}; \bar{n}, x \vdash \text{weavable}(p\{\,C\,\})\end{array}}{\bar{D}; \bar{H}; \bar{n} \vdash \text{weavable}(p\{\,\text{let } x=...; C\,\})}$$

(WC-STC-MSG)
$$\frac{\begin{array}{c}o \in \bar{n} \\ \bar{D}; \bar{H}; \bar{n}, x \vdash \text{weavable}(p\{\,C\,\})\end{array}}{\bar{D}; \bar{H}; \bar{n} \vdash \text{weavable}(p\{\,\text{let } x=o.c::m(v)\,; C\,\})}$$

(WC-OTHER2)
$$\frac{\begin{array}{c}\text{no other command rule applies} \\ \bar{D}; \bar{H}; \bar{n}, x \vdash \text{weavable}(p\{\,C\,\})\end{array}}{\bar{D}; \bar{H}; \bar{n} \vdash \text{weavable}(p\{\,B\,C\,\})}$$

Definition 4 (Name Equivalence). *Let $\simeq$ be the equivalence on class-based commands generated by:*

$$\frac{\begin{array}{c}\bar{H} \ni \text{obj } o:d\,\{\,\_\,\} \\ \bar{D} \vdash \text{advice}(d::m) = [\_\,; \bar{b}]\end{array}}{\bar{D}; \bar{H} \vdash \text{let } x=o.m(v)\,; \simeq \text{let } x=o.\text{exec}\_\bar{b}(v)\,;}$$

$$\frac{\bar{D} \vdash \text{advice}(c::m) = [\_\,; \bar{b}]}{\bar{D}; \bar{H} \vdash \text{let } x=o.c::m(v)\,; \simeq \text{let } x=o.\text{exec}\_\bar{b}(v)\,;}$$

$$\frac{C \text{ is not a method call}}{\bar{D}; \bar{H} \vdash C \simeq C}$$

Extend the definition to all other program constructs homorphically using conjunction. Let $P = (\bar{D} \vdash \bar{H})$ and $P' = (\bar{D}' \vdash \bar{H}')$. We write "$P \simeq P'$" when $\bar{D}; \bar{H} \vdash P \simeq P'$ and $\bar{D}'; \bar{H}' \vdash P \simeq P'$.

Theorem 1. *Suppose that an aspect-based program P is coherent and weavable, and that $P \twoheadrightarrow P'$. Then there exists some Q', such that $\text{weave}(P) \twoheadrightarrow Q'$ and $Q' \simeq \text{weave}(P')$. Suppose that an aspect-based program P is coherent and weavable, and that $\text{weave}(P) \twoheadrightarrow Q'$. Then there exists some P', such that $P \twoheadrightarrow P'$ and $P' \simeq \text{weave}(Q')$.*

6   Related Work

We refer the reader to the October 2001 issue of CACM for a comprehensive survey and references to the range of approaches and applications of AOP. Here, we restrict ourselves to the several recent efforts to formalize and provide simple conceptual models of some features of aspect-oriented languages.

There are several efforts focused largely on weaving and the understanding of pointcuts. For example, The Aspect SandBox [10] provides a testbed to experiment with weaving strategies. Wand, Kiczales, and Dutchyn [21], give a denotational semantics for a mini-language that embodies the key features of dynamic join points, pointcut designators, and advice. R. Douence and O. Motelet and M. Südholt [8] describe a domain-specific language for the definition of crosscuts and sketch a prototype implementation in Java which has been systematically derived from the language definition. H. Masuhara, Kiczales and Dutchyn [17] present a semantics-based compilation framework for an aspect-oriented programming language. Using partial evaluation, the framework studies which aspects can be woven in at compile time and which dispatches must be executed at run-time.

In contrast to this line of research, our aim has been to develop an independent *specification* of weaving. We have taken the point of view that the operational semantics of the aspect language validates a given implementation of weaving. In this sense, our approach is complementary to this body of work. One might daresay that a suitable mixture of these ideas could result in a model of a real-life aspect-oriented programming language.

The research closest to the spirit of our paper is the concurrent and independent work of Walker, Zdancewic and Ligatti [20]. This paper studies a powerful core calculus of aspects, not including subtyping, where both advice and join-points are first class entities that can be created and manipulated at runtime. On the one hand, their paper proves a type soundness theorem for a calculus with features that are not available in our core calculus. On the other hand, their study focuses on the case of execution pointcuts by assuming that the source code of the advised method is available for transformation.

From a more foundational viewpoint, Meuter [18] describe a view of aspects as monads. In this view, the weaver then becomes a lifter to transform programs through different monads. Andrews [3] views aspects in a process-algebraic context. Both these papers can be viewed as attempts to translate aspects into other frameworks. In contrast, our work follows the line of research into object calculi and their adaptations to particular programming languages such as Java. In this spirit, we study aspects as a primitive computational entity in their own right.

References

[1] Martin Abadi and Luca Cardelli. *A theory of objects*. Springer-Verlag, 1996.
[2] M. Aksit, K. Wakita, J. Bosch, L. Bergmans, and A. Yonezawa. Abstracting object-interactions using composition-filters. In *In object-based distributed processing, LNCS*, 1993.
[3] J. Andrews. Process-algebraic foundations of aspectoriented programming. In *In Reflection, LNCS 2192*, 2001.

[4] L. Bergmans. *"Composing Concurrent Objects - Applying Composition Filters for the Development and Reuse of Concurrent Object-Oriented Programs"*. Ph.d. thesis, University of Twente, 1994. http://wwwhome.cs.utwente.nl/ bergmans/phd.htm.

[5] Kim B. Bruce, Luca Cardelli, and Benjamin C. Pierce. Comparing object encodings. *Information and Computation*, 155, 1999. an extended abstract appeared in Proceedings of TACS '97, LNCS 1281, Springer-Verlag, pp. 415-438.

[6] Kim B. Bruce, Adrian Fiech, and Leaf Petersen. Subtyping is not a good "match" for object-oriented languages. In *European Conference on Object-Oriented Programming (ECOOP)*, 1997.

[7] Kim B. Bruce, Adrian Fiech, Angela Schuett, and Robert van Gent. A type-safe polymorphic object-oriented language. In *European Conference on Object-Oriented Programming (ECOOP)*, 1995.

[8] R. Douence, O. Motelet, and M. Südholt. A formal definition of crosscuts. In *Proceedings of the 3rd International Conference on Reflection and Crosscutting Concerns*, LNCS. Springer Verlag, September 2001. long version is http://www.emn.fr/info/recherche/publications/RR01/01-3-INFO.ps.gz.

[9] Sophia Drossopoulou, Susan Eisenbach, and Sarfraz Khurshid. Is the java type system sound? *Theory and Practice of Object Systems*, 5(11):3–24, 1999.

[10] Christopher Dutchyn, Gregor Kiczales, and Hidehiko Masuhara. http://www.cs.ubc.ca/labs/spl/projects/asb.html.

[11] Kathleen Fisher, John Reppy, and Jon G. Riecke. A calculus for compiling and linking classes. In *European Conference on Object-Oriented Programming (ECOOP)*, 2000.

[12] Atsushi Igarashi, Benjamin Pierce, and Philip Wadler. Featherweight Java: A minimal core calculus for Java and GJ. In *Proceedings of OOPSLA*, October 1999. Full version in ACM Transactions on Programming Languages and Systems (TOPLAS), 23(3), May 2001.

[13] Atsushi Igarashi and Benjamin C. Pierce. On inner classes. In *European Conference on Object-Oriented Programming (ECOOP)*, 2000. Also in informal proceedings of the Seventh International Workshop on Foundations of Object-Oriented Languages (FOOL). To appear in *Information and Computation*.

[14] Gregor Kiczales, Erik Hilsdale, Jim Hugunin, Mik Kersten, Jeffrey Palm, and William G. Griswold. An overview of AspectJ. *Lecture Notes in Computer Science*, 2072:327–355, 2001.

[15] Gregor Kiczales, John Lamping, Anurag Mendhekar, Chris Maeda, Cristina Videira Lopes, Jean-Marc Loingtier, and John Irwin. Aspect-oriented programming. In *European Conference on Object-Oriented Programming (ECOOP)*, 1997.

[16] K. J. Lieberherr. *Adaptive Object-Oriented Software: The Demeter Method with Propagation Patterns*. PWS Publishing Company, 1996.

[17] Hidehiko Masuhara, Gregor Kiczales, and Chris Dutchyn. Compilation semantics of aspect-oriented programs.

[18] W. De Meuter. Monads as a theoretical foundation for aop. In *International Workshop on Aspect-Oriented Programming at ECOOP*, 1997.

[19] H. Ossher and P. Tarr. Multi-dimensional separation of concerns and the hyperspace approach. In *Proceedings of the Symposium on Software Architectures and Component Technology: The State of the Art in Software Development*, 2001.

[20] David Walker, Steve Zdancewic, and Jay Ligatti. A theory of aspects. Submitted for publication.

[21] Mitchell Wand, Gregor Kiczales, and Christopher Dutchyn. A semantics for advice and dynamic join points in aspect-oriented programming. appeared in Informal Workshop Record of FOOL 9, pages 67-88; also presented at FOAL (Workshop on Foundations of Aspect-Oriented Languages), a satellite event of AOSD 2002, 2002.

Language Support for Connector Abstractions

Jonathan Aldrich, Vibha Sazawal, Craig Chambers, and David Notkin

Department of Computer Science and Engineering
University of Washington, Box 352350, Seattle, Washington, USA 98195-2350
Phone: +1 206 616-1846
{jonal,vibha,chambers,notkin}@cs.washington.edu

Abstract. Software connectors are increasingly recognized as an important consideration in the design and implementation of object-oriented software systems. Connectors can be used to communicate across a distributed system, coordinate the activities of several objects, or adapt one object's interface to the interface of another. Mainstream object-oriented languages, however, do not provide explicit support for connectors. As a result, connection code is intermingled with application code, making it difficult to understand, evolve, and reuse connection mechanisms.

In this paper, we add language support for user-defined connectors to the ArchJava language. Our design enables a wide range of connector abstractions, including caches, events, streams, and remote method calls. Developers can describe both the run-time semantics of connectors and the typechecking semantics. The connector abstraction supported by ArchJava cleanly separates reusable connection code from application logic, making the semantics of connections more explicit and allowing engineers to easily change the connection mechanisms used in a program. We evaluate the expressiveness and the engineering benefits of our design in a case study applying ArchJava to the PlantCare ubiquitous computing application.

1   Introduction

The high-level design of a software system is often expressed as a software architecture, consisting of a set of components and the connections through which the components interact [GS93,PW92]. Object-oriented languages provide a natural *object* abstraction for components, and encourage developers to compose systems out of interacting objects. However, mainstream object-oriented languages do not provide explicit support for connections. Instead, connections are implicit in the object references in the heap, or are expressed indirectly using design patterns such as Proxy and Adaptor [GHJ+94].

Despite this lack of language support, connections are increasingly recognized as a crucial element of software systems. The software architecture literature has proposed a *connector* abstraction for connections, complementing the class abstraction for

L. Cardelli (Ed.): ECOOP 2003, LNCS 2743, pp. 74–102, 2003.

components. In this context, a connector is a reusable design element that supports a particular style of component interactions. In a comprehensive taxonomy of connectors, Mehta et al. describe the wide variety of connectors used in software, including method calls, events, shared variables, adaptors, streams, semaphores, and many others [MMP00]. Connectors are particularly important in the context of distributed systems, where connector attributes such as bandwidth, synchronicity, security, reliability, and the wire protocol used may be crucial to the functionality and performance of the application.

Implementation Approaches. Because of the lack of language abstractions for connectors, developers are forced to make engineering compromises when implementing them. One approach integrates connector code into the interacting components. Unfortunately, this tightly couples the component and connector, making each of them harder to evolve or reuse. Alternatively, connectors can be written as reusable libraries. However, these libraries must often be written to a generic interface (perhaps based on type Object), giving up many of the advantages of static typechecking. Furthermore, even if a connector library is reusable, dependencies on the connector often pervade a component's implementation, making it difficult to understand the component in isolation or reuse it with other connectors. Our discussion of the PlantCare application in sections 4.2-4.4 illustrates many of these issues.

Tool Support. Communication infrastructures such as RMI [Jav97], CORBA [OMG95], and COM [Mic95] address these challenges by using tools to automatically generate proxies for communication with remote objects. These proxies encapsulate the connector code in a distributed system, allowing application components to make remote method calls using the same syntax as local calls. Many CASE tools and code generation tools provide similar benefits. However, these infrastructures and tools fix a particular semantics for distributed communication— semantics based on synchronous method calls using particular encodings and wire protocols. While such tools may be ideal for applications that can leverage the built-in semantics, they are inappropriate for applications that need different connector semantics. For example, the PlantCare application discussed in our case study uses a custom message-passing library designed to support the very lightweight and adaptive communication style that is required in the ubiquitous computing domain. Although tools play an important role in implementing connectors, we believe that no single connection infrastructure will be sufficient for the diverse needs of all applications in the foreseeable future.

Our Approach. In this paper, we propose explicit language support for user-defined connectors. It is difficult to integrate user-defined connectors directly in a conventional object-oriented language such as Java, because connections between objects are not explicit in the source code, but are expressed implicitly through the run time structure of references. Instead, we present our design in the context of ArchJava, an extension to Java that allows developers to specify the software architecture of a system within the implementation [ACN02a]. Because ArchJava already supports explicit connections between component objects, it can be easily extended to enable user-defined connectors that override the built-in connection semantics.

Our design allows developers to implement connectors using arbitrary Java code, supporting a very wide range of connector types. We evaluate the expressiveness of our design by implementing a representative subset of the connectors from Mehta et al.'s catalogue [MMP00]. A novel feature of our approach is that connectors define not just the run-time semantics of the connector, but also the typechecking strategy that should be used. Thus, connectors can be used to link components with interfaces that would not match using the normal Java semantics. As long as connector developers implement typechecking correctly for the domain of their connectors, our system provides a static guarantee of type safety to connector clients.

Our approach provides a clean separation of concerns. Each connector is modularly defined in its own class. Components interact with connectors in a clean way using Java's existing method call syntax. In our approach, the connector used to bind two components together is specified in a higher-level component, so that the communicating components are not aware of and do not depend on the specific connector being used. Due to this design, it is easy to change the connectors in a system. In contrast, changing connectors may be more difficult in languages without explicit support for connector abstractions.

Organization. The rest of this paper is organized as follows. In the next section, we review the ArchJava language design through a simple peer-to-peer system example. Section 3 extends ArchJava with explicit support for connector abstractions, describing by example how they can be defined and used. We evaluate the expressiveness and the engineering benefits of our system in section 4, both by implementing a wide range of connectors and by applying ArchJava to part of the PlantCare ubiquitous computing application. We discuss related work in section 5 before concluding in section 6.

2   The ArchJava Language

ArchJava is an extension to Java that allows programmers to express the architectural structure of an application within the source code [ACN02a]. ArchJava's type system verifies *communication integrity*, the property that implementation code communicates only along connections declared in the architecture [MQR95,LV95,ACN02b]. This paper extends ArchJava by supporting much more flexible kinds of interactions along connections.

We illustrate the ArchJava language through PoemSwap, a simple peer-to-peer program for sharing poetry online. To allow programmers to describe architectural structure, ArchJava adds new language constructs to support *components*, *connections*, and *ports*. The next subsection describes ArchJava's features for representing components and ports, while subsection 2.2 shows how developers can specify an architecture using components and connections. These sections review an earlier presentation of ArchJava [ACN02a].

2.1   Components and Ports

A *component* in ArchJava is a special kind of object that communicates with other components in a structured way. Components are instances of *component classes*, such as the PoemPeer component class in Figure 1. The PoemPeer component represents the network interface of the PoemSwap application.

Components in ArchJava communicate with each other through connected ports. A *port* represents a logical communication channel between a component and one or more components that it is connected to. For example, PoemPeer has a search port that provides search services to the PoemSwap user interface, and it has a poems port that it uses to access the local database of poems.

```
public component class PoemPeer {
  public port search {
    provides PoemDesc[] search(PoemDesc partialDesc) throws
IOException;
    provides void downloadPoem(PoemDesc desc) throws IOException;
  }

  public port poems {
    requires PoemDesc[] getPoemDescs();
    requires Poem getPoem(PoemDesc desc);
    requires void addPoem(Poem poem);
  }

  public port interface client {
    requires client(InetAddress address) throws IOException;
    requires PoemDesc[] search(PoemDesc partialDesc, int hops, Nonce
n);
    requires Poem download(PoemDesc desc);
  }

  public port interface server {
    provides PoemDesc[] search(PoemDesc partialDesc, int hops, Nonce
n);
    provides Poem download(PoemDesc desc);
  }

  void downloadPoem(PoemDesc desc) throws IOException {
    client peer = new client(desc.getAddress());
    Poem newPoem = peer.download(desc);
    if (newPoem != null) {
      poems.addPoem(newPoem);
    }
  }
  // other method definitions...
}
```

Fig. 1. The PoemPeer class represents the network interface of the PoemSwap application. PoemPeer communicates with other components through its ports. It provides a network search service to the rest of the application through the search port, and it accesses the poem database through the poems port. Finally, it communicates with other PoemSwap applications over a wide-area network using complimentary client and server ports

Ports declare two sets of methods, specified using the **requires** and **provides** keywords. A *provided* method is implemented by the component and is available to be called by other components connected to this port. For example, the search port provides searching and downloading methods that can be invoked from the user interface. Provided methods must be given definitions in the surrounding component class, as shown by the implementation of downloadPoem in Figure 1.

Conversely, each *required* method is provided by some other component connected to this port. In Figure 1, the poems port requires methods that get descriptions of all the poems in the database, retrieve a specific poem by its description, and add a poem to the database. A port may have both required and provided methods, but as shown in the example, it is common for a port to have only one or the other.

A component can invoke a required method declared in one of its ports by sending a message to the port. For example, in Figure 1, after downloading a new poem from a peer, the downloadPoem method adds the new poem to the poem database with the call poems.addPoem(newPoem). As this example shows, ports such as poems are concrete objects, and required methods can be invoked on ports using Java's standard method call syntax.

If a component communicates with multiple different components using the same interface, it can declare a *port interface* and then create a port of that interface type for each component it needs to communicate with. A port interface defines the type of a port, just as a class defines the type of an object. In fact, concrete port declarations such as **public port** search { ... } are a convenient shorthand for declaring a port interface together with a single instance of that interface type. In the example, PoemPeer must communicate with many other PoemSwap peers through its client port interface, and it may serve requests from many peers through its server port interface. The two interfaces are symmetric, as each peer may act as both a client and a server.

The client port interface contains a *required connection constructor*, named client after the surrounding port interface, which the PoemPeer can invoke in order to create a connection to a peer at the given InetAddress. The downloadPoem method instantiates a port of type client with the same **new** syntax used to create objects in Java. The method can then call the required method download on the newly created port instance.

The goal of ports is to specify both the services implemented by a component and the services a component needs to do its job. Required interfaces make dependencies explicit, reducing coupling between components and promoting understanding of components in isolation. For example, the PoemPeer component is implemented without any knowledge of what connection protocol will be used to connect it to its peers. PoemPeer expects a connector that has synchronous method call semantics, but any connector that conforms to this constraint can be used.

2.2   Software Architecture in ArchJava

In ArchJava, a hierarchical software architecture is expressed with a *composite component*, which is made up of a number of subcomponents connected together. A *subcomponent* is a component instance nested within another component. For example, Figure 2 shows how PoemSwap, the main component of the PoemSwap application, is composed of three subcomponents: a user interface, a poem database, and a PoemPeer instance. The subcomponents are declared as fields within PoemSwap.

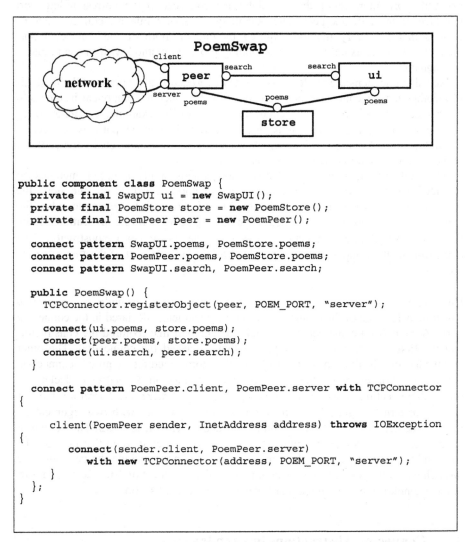

```
public component class PoemSwap {
  private final SwapUI ui = new SwapUI();
  private final PoemStore store = new PoemStore();
  private final PoemPeer peer = new PoemPeer();

  connect pattern SwapUI.poems, PoemStore.poems;
  connect pattern PoemPeer.poems, PoemStore.poems;
  connect pattern SwapUI.search, PoemPeer.search;

  public PoemSwap() {
    TCPConnector.registerObject(peer, POEM_PORT, "server");

    connect(ui.poems, store.poems);
    connect(peer.poems, store.poems);
    connect(ui.search, peer.search);
  }

  connect pattern PoemPeer.client, PoemPeer.server with TCPConnector
  {

    client(PoemPeer sender, InetAddress address) throws IOException
  {

      connect(sender.client, PoemPeer.server)
        with new TCPConnector(address, POEM_PORT, "server");
    }
  };
}
```

Fig. 2. A graphical and textual description of the PoemSwap architecture. The PoemSwap component class contains three subcomponents—a user interface, a poem store, and the network peer. Connect patterns show statically how these components may be connected, and the connect expressions in the constructor link the components together following these patterns. A final connect pattern shows how peers on different machines communicate via a TCPConnector. The client connection constructor creates a connection when the PoemPeer requests one

In ArchJava, architects declare the set of permissible connections in the architecture using *connect patterns*. A connect pattern specifies two or more port interfaces that may be connected together at run time. For example, the first three connect patterns in Figure 2 specify that both the user interface and the network interface connect to the `poems` port interface of the `PoemStore`, and that the `search` port interface of the user interface connects to the corresponding port interface of the network peer. The default typechecking rule for connect patterns ensures that for every method required by one or more of the connected port interfaces, there is exactly one corresponding provided method with the same name and signature.

Actual connections are made using *connect expressions* that appear in the methods of a component. A connect expression specifies the concrete component instances to be connected in addition to the connected ports. In the example, the `PoemSwap` constructor makes three connections, one for each of the connect patterns declared in the architecture. A static check ensures that the types of the connected ports conform to the types declared in one of the connect patterns.

The built-in semantics of ArchJava connections binds required methods to provided methods, so that when a required method is called on one port, the corresponding provided method of the other port is invoked. For example, when the `PoemPeer` in Figure 1 invokes `addPoem` on its `poems` port, the invocation will be forwarded across the connection created in the `PoemSwap` constructor. The `addPoem` method implementation provided by the `poems` port of the `PoemStore` (not shown) will be invoked.

Connection Constructors. Each connect pattern must provide a *connection constructor* for each of the required connection constructors declared in the connected ports. A connection constructor is named after the port that required the constructor, and the first argument is the component that requested the connection. The other arguments match the ones declared in the corresponding required connection constructor. For example, the `client` port interface in `PoemPeer` declares a required connection constructor that accepts an `InetAddress`. Therefore, the last connect pattern in Figure 2 declares a connection constructor with two arguments— the `PoemPeer` that requested the connection and an `InetAddress`. The body of a connection constructor must contain exactly one connect expression that matches the surrounding connect pattern. The connect expression must include the port interface through which the `sender` component requested the connection (`sender.client` in the example). We explain the **with** keyword in the next section.

3   Connector Abstractions in ArchJava

In this section, we describe the new language features and libraries that support connector abstractions in ArchJava. We extend the syntax of connect patterns and connect expressions to describe which connector abstractions should be used to typecheck and implement the connections. Subsection 3.1 demonstrates these language features by examples, showing how a user-defined TCP/IP connector can be used to connect different PoemSwap peers across a wide-area network. New connectors can be written using the archjava.reflect library, described in Subsection 3.2, which reifies connections and required method invocations. Subsection 3.3 shows how the TCP/IP connector can be implemented using this library. Finally, subsection 3.4 discusses the use of connector abstractions, identifying when connector abstractions are beneficial and when a more conventional connector implementation may be appropriate.

3.1   Using Connector Abstractions

Connector Typechecking. Instead of using ArchJava's default typechecking rules, connect patterns can specify that a user-defined connector class should be used for typechecking instead. For example, the connect pattern at the end of Figure 2 specifies a user-defined connector class to be used for typechecking using the syntax **with** <*connector class*>. Every connector class has a static typecheck method that defines the typechecking semantics of that connector (see Figure 3 below). In the example, when the PoemSwap component class is compiled, the compiler loads the TCPConnector class and invokes the typecheck method to check the validity of the connect pattern (see Figure 5 and the discussion in subsection 3.3). This typechecking replaces the default ArchJava typechecking semantics, allowing the connector abstraction to define arbitrary typechecking rules.

In the case of TCPConnector, the typecheck method first invokes the standard ArchJava typechecker, and then additionally checks that all arguments and results of all methods in the connection are subtypes of the Serializable interface. Because the TCPConnector uses Java's serialization mechanism to send method arguments and results across a network, a run-time error will result if the method arguments and results are not serializable. By defining its own typechecking semantics to extend those of ArchJava, the TCPConnector can detect this error at compile time[1].

Instantiating Connectors. Connectors are instantiated whenever a connect expression that specifies a user-defined connector object is executed at run time. A connect expression uses the syntax **with** <*expression*> to specify the connector instance that should be used for the connection it is creating. For example, the connection constructor in Figure 2 executes a connect expression when it is called, and the connect expression creates a user-defined TCPConnector object, passing the address, TCP/IP port, and the name of the remote peer to the constructor of the connector. The expression in the **with** clause must be have a type that is a subclass of the connector type declared in the corresponding connect pattern, to ensure that the connector implementation used at run time matches the connector that was used to typecheck the connection statically.

---

[1] This check would have been handy when testing the PoemSwap application. Before customized typechecking was implemented, we got run time errors because we forgot to make class Poem serializable.

```
public class Connector {
  public static Error[] typecheck(Connection c);
  public Object invoke(Call c) throws Throwable;

  public Connector();
  protected Connector(Object components[], String portNames[]);

  public final Connection getConnection();
}

public final class Connection {
  public Port[] getPorts()
  public Connector getConnector()
}

public final class Port {
  public String getName();
  public Method[] getRequiredMethods();
  public Method[] getProvidedMethods();
  public Object getEnclosingObject();
}

public final class Method {
  public String getName();
  public Type[] getParameterTypes();
  public Object invoke(Object args[]) throws Throwable;
}

public final class Type {
  public String getName();
  public boolean isAssignableFrom(Type other);
  public static Type forName(String qualifiedName);
}

public final class Call {
  public Method getMethod();
  public Object[] getArguments();
}
```

Fig. 3. The `archjava.reflect` library includes classes reifying connectors, connections, ports, methods, types, and calls. User-defined connector classes extend the `Connector` class, overriding the `invoke` method to define customized dynamic semantics and providing a `typecheck` method that implements typechecking

In the case of `PoemSwap`, the component to be connected to the `PoemPeer` is a peer on a remote machine, and so we cannot use a direct reference to it in the connect expression. ArchJava allows developers to specify connections to remote components (to which they cannot have a direct reference) by specifying the type of the connected component rather than an actual concrete instance. This type allows the compiler to check the connect expression against the surrounding connect pattern. The `TCPConnector` is responsible for identifying and communicating with the remote component, and it does this using the `InetAddress` passed to the constructor.

3.2   The archjava.reflect Library

Connector abstractions are defined using the archjava.reflect library, whose most important classes and methods are shown in Figure 3. This library defines a Connector class that user-defined connector classes extend, as well as classes that reify connections, ports, and methods.

Class Connector provides a hook for defining customized connectors. Connector abstractions can define custom typechecking semantics by defining a static typecheck method, which is called at compile time to typecheck a connect pattern, returning a possibly empty array of errors. For example, the default implementation of typecheck returns an error for each required method that has no matching provided method, or has more than one matching provided method. If a connector defines no typecheck method, the compiler looks in that connector's superclass for a typecheck method, and so on until the compiler gets to the default typecheck method in class Connector.

Run-time connection behavior can be defined by overriding the invoke method, which accepts a Call object reifying an invocation on a required method. The default implementation finds the corresponding provided method and invokes it, passing the resulting return value or exception back to the caller.

Connector provides a default public constructor that is used by all direct clients and most subclasses. A second constructor creates a connection programmatically (i.e., without a connect expression) from the specified arrays of components and corresponding port names. This constructor is provided since some connectors (including TCPConnector) must be able to create a connector object that represents the "local end" of a connection that was originally made on a remote machine. Since this constructor allows connections to be created dynamically without being typechecked statically, it is accessible only to Connector subclasses, not to clients.

Classes Connection, Port, Method, and Type reify the connection that is associated with the connector, along with its ports and method signatures. Figure 3 shows only a fraction of the interface of these classes. User-defined connectors do not extend these classes, but instead may use them as a library for getting information about the current connection. This information, accessible through the getConnection method of Connector, can be used statically when typechecking or dynamically when dispatching a required method invocation. For example, the connector can invoke provided methods at run time by calling invoke on the relevant Method object.

3.3   Implementing Connector Abstractions

Figure 4 shows how the run-time semantics of TCPConnector can be defined in Java code. The example shows primarily the interface of the connector and how it uses the archjava.reflect library. We omit the code in two helper classes: TCPDaemon, which listens for incoming network connections on a TCP/IP port, and TCPEndpoint, which serializes and deserializes data going through a connection endpoint.

```
public class TCPConnector extends Connector {
  // data members
  protected TCPEndpoint endpoint;

  // public interface
  public TCPConnector(InetAddress host, int prt, String objName)
                                                           throws
IOException {
     endpoint = new TCPEndpoint(this, host, prt, objName);
  }

  public Object invoke(Call call) throws Throwable {
    Method meth = call.getMethod();
    return endpoint.sendMethod(meth.getName(),
meth.getParameterTypes(),
                             call.getArguments());
  }

  public static void registerObject(Object o, int prt, String
objName)
                                                           throws
IOException {
    TCPDaemon.createDaemon(prt).register(objName, o);
  }

  // interface used by TCPDaemon
  TCPConnector(TCPEndpoint endpoint, Object receiver, String
portName) {
     super(new Object[] { receiver }, new String[] { portName });
     this.endpoint = endpoint;
     endpoint.setConnector(this);
  }

  Object invokeLocalMethod(String name, Type parameterTypes[],
                           Object arguments[]) throws Throwable {
    // find method with parameters that match parameterTypes
    Method meth = findMethod(name, parameterTypes);
    return meth.invoke(arguments);
  }

  // typechecking semantics defined in Figure 5
}
```

Fig. 4. The TCPConnector class extends the archjava.reflect.Connector class to define the dynamic semantics of a connector based on a TCP/IP network connection. The invoke method passes the method name, parameter types, and arguments to a daemon that uses Java's serialization facilities to send them over a TCP/IP network connection. The daemon at the other end of the connection, created when the other peer called registerObject, calls invokeLocalMethod on a TCPConnector object, which identifies the right method to call and invokes it

When the downloadPoem method in Figure 1 creates a new instance of the client port interface, the corresponding connection constructor links the client port instance to a remote server by creating a TCPConnector object, passing the

Internet address of the remote machine together with a port and string identifying the server. The TCPConnector constructor shown in Figure 4 creates a TCPEndpoint object that opens a network connection to the remote host.

When a required method is called on the client port instance, the runtime system reifies the call and redirects it to the invoke method on the TCPConnector. TCPConnector's invoke method determines which required method was called, and then passes the name of the method, its parameter types, and the actual call arguments to the TCPEndpoint. The TCPEndpoint sends this data over the TCP/IP network connection.

At the other side of the network, the PoemSwap application uses registerObject to register a PoemPeer component under the name "server" (see Figure 2). The registerObject method starts a TCPDaemon listening at the assigned TCP/IP port. When the daemon receives an incoming connection, it creates a TCPEndpoint object representing that TCP/IP connection and creates a TCPConnector object to represent the connector locally. The daemon uses the non-public TCPConnector constructor, passing the local TCPEndpoint object as well as the object to be connected and the name of its connected port to the constructor. Since the originating connection was created on the other machine, there is no information about this connection in the runtime system, and so it is necessary to specify the components and ports to be connected when calling the protected constructor of the Connector superclass.

When the TCPEndpoint receives an incoming method, it calls invokeLocalMethod on the TCPConnector associated with the receiver object. invokeLocalMethod uses the findMethod helper function (not shown) to identify the matching provided method, and then invokes the method through a reflective call. The result, or any exception that is thrown, will be packaged back up by the TCPEndpoint, sent back over the network, returned to the implementation of invoke in the source TCPConnector, and returned to the caller.

User-Defined Typechecking. For each connect pattern in the system, the compiler loads the appropriate connector class and calls its typecheck method at compile time. The compiler passes typecheck a Connection object that reifies the port interfaces in the connect pattern, so that the typechecker can examine the methods and types in the connected port interfaces.

The typecheck method returns a possibly empty array of Error objects describing any semantic errors in the connect pattern. The Error class encapsulates a String describing the problem as well as a syntax element (a Connection, Port, or Method) that describes where the error occurred, allowing the compiler to determine an accurate line number for the reported error.

Figure 5 shows the definition of the typecheck method of TCPConnector. The code begins by running the standard typecheck method defined in class Connector, which ensures that for each required method there is exactly one provided method with an identical name and signature. It returns any errors found by this method. If standard typechecking succeeds, the TCPConnector visits every required and provided method in the connection, making sure that all method arguments and results are `Serializable`, so that the `TCPEndpoint` will be able to serialize them successfully at run time.

```
public class TCPConnector extends Connector {
  public static Error[] typecheck(Connection c) {
    // First invoke the default Java typechecker
    Error [] errors = Connector.typecheck(c);
    if (errors.length > 0)
      return errors;

    // ensure all arguments and results are Serializable
    Type serializable = Type.forName("java.lang.Serializable");
    for (int pI = 0; pI < c.getPorts().length; ++pI) {
      for (int mI = 0; mI < c.getPorts()[pI].getMethods().length;
++mI) {
        Method method = c.getPorts()[pI].getMethods()[mI];
        Type returnType = method.getReturnType();
        if (!serializable.isAssignableFrom(returnType))
          return new Error[] { new Error("type not serializable", c)
};
        // similar check for method arguments
      }
    }
  }

  // dynamic semantics defined in Figure 4
}
```

Fig. 5. The `typecheck` method in the `TCPConnector` class ensures that method arguments and results are serializable

3.4   Connector Implementation

Connectors can be implemented in a wide variety of ways, each with its own benefits and drawbacks. For example, in addition to our connector abstractions, connectors could be built into the language, expressed idiomatically through a design pattern, or described using ArchJava's component construct.

The key benefit of using connector abstractions is that the same connector can be reused to support the same interaction semantics across many different interfaces, while still providing a strong, static guarantee of type safety to clients. For example, the `TCPConnector` can connect any two ports with matching signatures, as long as the arguments to methods in those ports are `Serializable`. Other solutions that guarantee type safety require separate stub and skeleton code to be written for each interface, causing considerable code duplication and hindering reuse and evolution. Alternatively, a standard library for sending objects across a TCP/IP connection could be used, but this solution does not guarantee that the messages sent and received across the connection have compatible types, so run time errors are possible.

The main drawback of using connector abstractions is that they are defined using a reflective mechanism. Although connectors can define typechecking rules for their clients, there is no way to statically check that a connector's implementation performs the communication in a type-safe way. Also, there is some run-time overhead associated with reifying a method call so that a connector can process it dynamically. Thus, in situations where a connector is not reused across different interfaces, it may be better to use objects or components to implement the connector.

4   Evaluation

We have implemented language support for connector abstractions in the ArchJava compiler, which is available for download at the ArchJava web site [Arc02]. Thus, all examples in this paper, including PoemSwap and PlantCare, are simplified versions of working code.

We evaluate our design in two ways. In the next subsection, we evaluate the expressiveness of our connector abstraction mechanism by describing how a wide range of connectors can be implemented. In the following subsection, we evaluate the engineering benefits of connector abstractions with a small case study on the PlantCare ubiquitous computing application. Subsection 4.3 discusses the case study and reports feedback from the developers of PlantCare. Finally, subsection 4.4 compares our connector abstraction approach to an alternative approach using design patterns in the PlantCare system.

4.1   Expressiveness

In order to evaluate the expressiveness of our connector abstraction mechanisms, we use Mehta et al.'s taxonomy of connectors as a benchmark for our design [MMP00]. The taxonomy describes eight major types of connectors: procedure call, event, data access, linkage, stream, arbitrator, adaptor, and distributor connectors. We discuss each connector type in turn, describing which species of that connector can benefit from using connector abstractions. All of the connector abstraction examples described here are available for download as part of the ArchJava distribution [Arc02].

Procedure Call. Procedure call connectors enable the transfer of control and data through various forms of invocation. Although most programming languages provide explicit support for procedure calls, there are a number of semantic issues that justify user-defined procedure call connectors. For example, parameters could be passed by reference, by value, by (deep) copy, etc.; calls could be synchronous or asynchronous; calls could use one-to-many broadcast semantics, many-to-one collecting semantics, or conceivably even a many-to-many semantics.

ArchJava's connector abstractions are well suited to implementing procedure call connectors because the interface for defining connectors reifies method calls on ports. As an example, we have implemented an AsynchronousConnector that accepts incoming required method calls, returns to the sender immediately, and then invokes the corresponding provided method asynchronously in another thread.

We have also implemented a SummingBroadcastConnector that accepts an incoming method call, broadcasts it to all connected components, and sums the results of all the invocations before returning the sum to the original caller. This second connector relies on ArchJava's multi-way connections, which can connect more than two ports. Both connectors implement appropriate typechecking; for example, the `AsynchronousConnector` ensures that all methods in connected ports return `void`, while the `SummingBroadcastConnector` ensures that all of the methods return an integer. The `TCPConnector` shown in Figure 4 above is a procedure call connector that connects components running on different virtual machines.

Event. Event connectors support the transfer of data and control using an implicit mechanism, where the producer and consumer of an event are not aware of each other's identity. Semantic issues with event connectors include the cardinality of producers and consumers, event priority, synchronicity, and the event notification mechanism.

Events are often implemented as inner-class callback objects in languages such as Java, but this technique can make programs very difficult to reason about and evolve, as it is hard to see which components might be communicating through an event channel. In contrast, using a custom ArchJava event connector may aid in program understanding, because the connection between components is explicit in the software architecture of the system. Connector abstractions provide additional benefit by allowing components to communicate using different event semantics. For example, we have implemented an `EventDispatchConnector` that enqueues event notifications and dispatches them asynchronously to consumers.

The PlantCare application, described below in subsection 4.2, uses a user-defined connector to support asynchronous event-based communication across a loosely coupled ad-hoc network.

Data Access. Data access connectors are used to access a data store, such as a SQL database, the file system, or a repository such as the Windows registry. Issues in data access components include initialization and cleanup of connections to data sources, and the conversion and presentation of data. Conventional library-based techniques are appropriate for implementing many kinds of data access connectors. However, connector abstractions can be used to provide a convenient view of the data source, or adding semantic value to a data source in a reusable way. For example, one could imagine a connector that provides an object-oriented view of a relational database, translating each row of each table into an object and providing a collection-like access to clients. As a more concrete example, Figure 6 shows a `CachingConnector` that caches the results of method calls to a data store and returns the same result if the method is called again with identical arguments.

Linkage. Linkage connectors bind a name in one module to the implementation provided by another module. Examples of linkage connectors include imported names and references to names defined in other source files. ArchJava's connector abstractions are intended to connect object instances at run time, not link names at compile time. Therefore, Linkage connectors are outside of the scope of ArchJava's connector abstraction design.

```
public class CachingConnector extends Connector {
  protected Map cache = new Hashtable();

  public Object invoke(Call call) throws Throwable {
    List arguments = Arrays.asList(call.getArguments());
    Object result = cache.get(arguments);
    if (result != null)
      return result;

    result = super.invoke(call);

    if (result != null)
      cache.put(arguments, result);
    return result;
  }
}
```

Fig. 6. A CachingConnector that caches method invocations to avoid recomputation

Stream. Stream connectors support the exchange of a sequence of data between loosely coupled producer and consumer components. Semantic issues with streams include buffering, bounding, synchronicity, data types, data conversion, and the cardinality of the producers and consumers. Many of these issues can be encapsulated within a reusable connector abstraction. For example, we have developed a BufferedStreamConnector that implements a stream with a bounded buffer size, supporting one producer but an arbitrary number of consumers. The BufferedStreamConnector is reusable for streams of many different data types, but checks that the types of data produced and consumed match. A plain Java implementation would either sacrifice reusability or use Object as the data type, giving up the checking benefits of a typed stream. Here connector abstractions provide an advantage similar to generics proposals for Java such as GJ [BOS+98].

Arbitrator. Arbitrator connectors provide services that coordinate and facilitate interactions among components. Examples of arbitrators include semaphores, locks, transactions, fault handling connectors with failover, and load balancing connectors. Semaphores and locks typically have the same interface no matter which components they connect, and so they are probably best implemented using ordinary objects or as ArchJava components. However, more sophisticated arbitrators can benefit from ArchJava's connector abstraction mechanism. For example, we have built a LoadBalancingConnector that accepts incoming method calls from a client and distributes them to a bank of server components based on the current server loads. The LoadBalancingConnector is reusable across any client interface, while still providing typechecking between clients and services.

We have also implemented a BarrierSynchronizationConnector. Components invoke a different method on the barrier after each stage of work, and the barrier ensures that all its clients have called a given barrier method before it allows any of the method calls to return.

Adaptor. Adaptor components retrofit components with different interfaces so that they can interact. Adaptors may convert data formats, adapt to different invocation mechanisms, transform protocols, or even make presentation changes like internationalization conversions. Well-known design patterns such as Adaptor, Wrapper, and Façade are often used to implement adaptors [GHJ+94]. However, connector abstractions can be useful for performing similar adaptations to different interfaces. For example, the `RainConnector` in section 4.2 below adapts data types using structural subtyping, so that two components can communicate with different datatypes as long as the data sent in a message has a superset of the information expected by the receiver.

Distributor. Distributor connectors identify paths between components and route communication along those paths. Distributors are not first-class connectors, but provide routing services to other connectors. Both the `EventDispatchConnector` described above and the `RainConnector` described below include distributor functionality.

Summary. As the discussion above makes clear, ArchJava's connector abstractions are very flexible, supporting a wide range of different connector types. Some kinds of connectors are most clearly expressed using conventional mechanisms such as objects and components. However, connector abstractions provide a unique level of reusability across port interfaces while still providing clients with a strong static guarantee of type safety.

4.2   PlantCare Case Study

In order to evaluate the engineering benefits of user-defined connector abstractions, we performed a small case study with the PlantCare ubiquitous computing application [LBK+02]. PlantCare is a project at Intel Research Seattle that uses a collection of sensors and a robot to care for houseplants autonomously in a home or office environment. This application illustrates many of the challenges of ubiquitous computing systems: it must be able to configure itself and react robustly to failures and changes in its environment.

The Gardening Service. Figure 7 shows the architecture of the gardening service, one of several services in the PlantCare system. The gardening service consists of a central gardener component that uses three external services as well as a client for a well-known discovery service. The gardener periodically executes a cycle of code that cares for plants as follows. First, the gardener requests from the `PlantStore` a list of all the plants in the system and the sensor readings from each plant. For each plant, it queries the `Encyclopedia` to determine how that plant should be cared for. After comparing the recommended and actual plant humidity levels, it adds or removes watering tasks from the `TaskServer` so that each plant remains in good health.

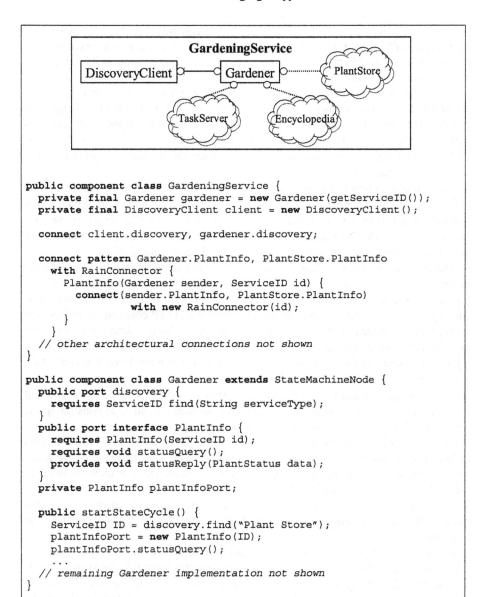

```
public component class GardeningService {
  private final Gardener gardener = new Gardener(getServiceID());
  private final DiscoveryClient client = new DiscoveryClient();

  connect client.discovery, gardener.discovery;

  connect pattern Gardener.PlantInfo, PlantStore.PlantInfo
    with RainConnector {
      PlantInfo(Gardener sender, ServiceID id) {
        connect(sender.PlantInfo, PlantStore.PlantInfo)
               with new RainConnector(id);
      }
    }
  // other architectural connections not shown
}

public component class Gardener extends StateMachineNode {
  public port discovery {
    requires ServiceID find(String serviceType);
  }
  public port interface PlantInfo {
    requires PlantInfo(ServiceID id);
    requires void statusQuery();
    provides void statusReply(PlantStatus data);
  }
  private PlantInfo plantInfoPort;

  public startStateCycle() {
    ServiceID ID = discovery.find("Plant Store");
    plantInfoPort = new PlantInfo(ID);
    plantInfoPort.statusQuery();
    ...
  // remaining Gardener implementation not shown
}
```

Fig. 7. The architecture of the PlantCare gardening service

We have chosen to include the interfaces of relevant external services as part of the gardening service architecture, because then we can use the connectors in the architecture to reason about the protocols used to communicate with these services. A more conventional architectural depiction would represent these protocols as connectors in an enclosing architecture. However, in ubiquitous computing systems, there is no way to statically specify the entire enclosing architecture, because the services available in a system may change frequently as devices move and connections fail. Instead, the gardening service architecture includes a partial view of the surrounding architecture, including the external components with which the gardener communicates.

Below the visual architectural diagram in Figure 7 is the ArchJava code describing the architecture (the complete gardener service code is about 500 lines long). The concrete Gardener and DiscoveryClient component instances are declared with final fields. The connect declaration linking the discovery ports of the client and the gardener is syntactic sugar for a connect pattern and a corresponding connect expression.

The connect pattern links the PlantInfo port interfaces of the gardener and the plant store. When the gardener requests a new connection, the provided connection constructor specifies that it should be connected with a RainConnector, using a ServiceID to identify the location of the remote PlantStore component. The other connect patterns, although omitted from this diagram, are similar.

The RainConnector class implements the Rain communication protocol used in the PlantCare system. When methods are invoked through connections of type RainConnector, the user-defined connector code will package the method name and arguments as an XML message, send them over a HTTP connection, and call the appropriate provided method on the other side. Since Rain messages are asynchronous and do not return a response, RainConnector also defines a custom typechecker that verifies that methods in the connected ports have a **void** return type. Although RainConnector is similar to TCPConnector in that both connect components that may be located on different hosts, it provides very different semantics (asynchronous messages vs. synchronous method calls), demonstrating the versatility of ArchJava's connector abstractions.

The RainConnector implementation is similar to the TCPConnector defined earlier. The connector uses the name of the method called as the name of the XML message to be sent. The method arguments are serialized and sent over the network using the same Rain library that is currently used by the PlantCare application. Because Rain messages are asynchronous, the RainConnector returns immediately after sending a message, without waiting for an acknowledgement or response.

The Gardener class has a concrete port for discovery, but port interfaces for communicating with other components. This is a natural choice, because discovery is a fundamental service that must be in place in order for the Gardener to dynamically discover other available services. The discovery interface allows the Gardener to look up a service by its type. It returns a ServiceID data structure that can then be used in a connection constructor to connect to other components.

The code in startStateCycle shows the beginning of the cycle of code that the Gardener executes when caring for plants. The code uses the discovery service to find the ServiceID of an available PlantStore service. It then allocates a new PlantInfo port instance and stores it in a variable. The final line of code shown sends an asynchronous message through the newly allocated port, querying the status of the plants in the system. The PlantStore will reply with another asynchronous message, which will be translated by the `RainConnector` into a call to the `statusReply` method, which carries out the next stage in the cycle. If an internal timer (not shown) expires before the `statusReply` message is received, the gardener assumes that the `PlantStore` component (or an intervening network link) has failed, and restarts the state cycle, using the discovery service once again to connect to a functioning `PlantStore`.

Java Version:

```java
Protected void handleMessageIn(Message m) {
    if ... { ... // cases for plant status messages above...
    } else if (msg instanceof PlantInfoReply) {
        // case for plant info message
        PlantInfoReply p = (PlantInfoReply) msg;
        careMap.put(p.name,p);
        state = AWAITING_TASKS;
        sendTasksRequest();
        return;
    } else if (msg instanceof TaskListReply) {
        // case for task reply message below...
}

protected void sendTasksRequest() {
    try {
        TaskListQuery q = new TaskListQuery();
        q.list = "Water Plants";
        sendMessage(taskServer,q,newClosure());
    } catch (Exception ex) {
        // an error occurred, restart the cycle
        ex.printStackTrace();
        resetState();
    }
}
```

ArchJava Version:

```java
void infoReply(PlantInfoReply data) {
    careMap.put(data.name, data);
    state = AWAITING_TASKS;
    try {
        taskPort.taskQuery("Water Plants");
    } catch (Exception ex) {
        // an error occurred, restart the cycle
        ex.printStackTrace();
        resetState();
    }
}
```

Fig. 8. A comparison of the old and new versions of the Gardener code that responds to the PlantInfoReply message

4.3   Discussion

In this section, we analyze the results of our case study according to three criteria: program understanding, program correctness, and software evolution. Finally, we report feedback from the developers of the PlantCare application.

Program Understanding. The ArchJava version of the gardening service code has a number of characteristics that make it easier to understand the service's implementation. In the Java version, the information about which messages are sent and received is spread throughout the source code. Figure 7 shows how the ArchJava architecture documents the sent and received messages explicitly as required and provided methods in the ports of Gardener, making it easier to understand the interactions between the gardener and other services.

Figure 7 also shows how the ArchJava source code documents the architecture of the service, showing which other services the gardener depends on. This information is obscured in the original gardener source code; it would have to be deduced from the types of messages exchanged. Another benefit is that the connector specification explicitly documents that the Rain communication protocol is used between components. This would be especially valuable if the gardener used different protocols to communicate with different external services, as may often be the case in heterogeneous ubiquitous computing systems.

Figure 8 compares the Java and ArchJava versions of the code that responds to a PlantInfoReply message from the encyclopedia. Here, ArchJava's abstraction mechanisms for inter-component communication make the application logic of the gardener clearer. In the original Java code, a single handleMessageIn method responds to all incoming messages. The PlantInfoReply message is one case in a long list of messages; the code stores the plant care information in an internal data structure and then calls a separate sendTasksRequest function to send out the next batch of messages. In the ArchJava version, this response code is more cleanly encapsulated in a single method, which responds to the original message and then sends the next set of messages through the task port. The process of sending a message is also simpler and cleaner in ArchJava. The programmer simply calls a method in the taskPort, rather than constructing a custom message and sending it using the Rain library.

Correctness. The ArchJava language performs a number of checks that help to ensure the correctness of the GardeningService implementation. For example, the RainConnector typechecker verifies interface compatibility between the ports of Gardener and the connected ports of the external services at compile time. In the original Java code, this problem would show up as a run time error when a component does not recognize a message that was sent to it.

ArchJava also verifies communication integrity [MQR95,LV95,ACN02b], a property which guarantees that the Gardener only communicates with the services declared in the GardeningService architecture (We assume that the gardener does not directly use Java's networking library, a property that could also be checked in a straightforward way). This property guarantees that the architecture can be relied on as an accurate representation of the communication in the system, increasing the program understanding benefits of architecture.

Software Evolution. Because of ArchJava's explicit abstractions for ports and connectors, some evolutionary steps are easier to perform. For example, if a service needs to interact with a device that cannot generate XML messages, we can replace `RainConnector` with a new connector type that can communicate with the more restricted device. Also, we can reuse an existing service in a new environment by simply inserting adaptor components or connectors that retrofit the old service to the message protocol expected by the new environment. In both cases, ArchJava's explicit descriptions of component interfaces and connections make architectural evolution easier.

An important criterion to consider in the evolvability of a system is the degree to which the system's modularization hides information within a single module. One benefit of the ArchJava version of the gardening service is that the gardener's functionality is encapsulated in `Gardener` while the communication protocol used is encapsulated in `GardeningService`. The ports of `Gardener` serve as the interfaces used to hide this information. Thus, in the ArchJava code, the gardening functionality can be changed independently of the communication protocol, facilitating evolution of this service.

Developer Feedback. Perhaps the most important evaluation criterion is feedback from the developers of PlantCare. We found that the developers were able to understand the ArchJava notation fairly quickly. They said that the `GardeningService` architecture captured their informal architectural view of the system well. Finally, they agreed that ArchJava was able to provide the benefits describe in the analysis above. We are currently working with them to put ArchJava to production use in a future ubiquitous computing system.

4.4   Design Pattern Alternatives to Connector Abstractions

In this section, we compare the connector abstraction technique we used in the PlantCare application to an alternative solution using conventional object-oriented design techniques. Many design patterns are intended to provide benefits like separation of concerns and ease of change, similar to the benefits provided by connectors [GHJ+94]. In order to be concrete, our comparison focuses on the PlantCare application.

For example, Figure 9 shows the PlantCare code for responding to the `PlantInfoReply` message, rewritten using the Proxy design pattern. In this example, the application-defined response code is contained in an `infoReply` method that is similar to the `infoReply` message in the ArchJava example. Instead of invoking the `taskQuery` method on the `taskPort`, as in ArchJava, it invokes the method on a proxy that sends the message on to the task server. Like the ArchJava version, this solution cleanly separates communication code from application logic.

The main difference between the design pattern code and the ArchJava code is that in the design pattern solution, custom code must be written to dispatch each message to the handler function (`infoReply` in this example) and to send each message using the Rain library (`taskQuery` in this example). By comparison, in ArchJava the dispatch code and the message sending code are written once in the connector, and can then be reused for each connection in the system.

Analysis. The primary disadvantages of our approach, relative to design patterns, are twofold. First, our approach involves a new language construct. Although it is a very tiny addition to the ArchJava language, it does increase the complexity of the language, and this comes on top of the (more substantial) ArchJava additions to Java. Second, our approach uses reflection, thereby losing some understandability and efficiency relative to custom-written object-oriented code.

Design Patterns Version:

```
protected void handleMessageIn(Message m) {
  if ... { ... // cases for plant status messages above...
  } else if (msg instanceof PlantInfoReply) {
    // case for plant info message
    infoReply(msg);
  } else if (msg instanceof TaskListReply) {
    // case for task reply message below...
}

void infoReply(PlantInfoReply data) {
  careMap.put(data.name, data);
  state = AWAITING_TASKS;
  try {
    taskProxy.taskQuery("Water Plants");
  } catch (Exception ex) {
    // an error occurred, restart the cycle
    ex.printStackTrace();
    resetState();
  }
}

protected class TaskProxy {
  public void taskQuery(String task) {
    TaskListQuery q = new TaskListQuery();
    q.list = task;
    sendMessage(taskServer,q,newClosure());
  }
  // methods for other TaskServer messages...
}
```

Fig. 9. The response code for the PlantInfoReply message, written using design patterns to separate communication code from application logic

On the other hand, our approach offers key advantages over conventional object-oriented solutions. Perhaps the most significant advantage is that connector abstractions can define typechecking rules that verify different properties than the default Java rules. Thus, connectors can statically verify that certain classes of connector-specific errors will not occur at run time.

In many cases, connector abstractions allow programmers to reuse connector code that would be duplicated in a conventional solution using adaptors or proxies. Since code does not have to be duplicated or customized for each communication interface, the resulting system is easier to evolve when connector abstractions are used. For example, changing the connector used takes only one line of code in ArchJava, but in the design pattern solution, a new Proxy class must be written that adapts the communication interface to the new connection protocol. Our design also expresses the intent of a connector directly through the abstraction, rather than indirectly through a design pattern. Finally, ArchJava explicitly documents the software architecture of the system, providing benefits for reasoning about and evolving code.

Our design shares many benefits with the design-pattern solution described above. Connector code is isolated from application code, and the interfaces used to communicate between objects are documented and checked. However, in the design-pattern case, these benefits only accrue if the developer anticipates the need to evolve the connectors in a system, and chooses to use the appropriate design pattern in the system. An important advantage of language support for connector abstractions is that it encourages developers to think and program in terms of connectors, gaining all of the benefits described above. In contrast, developers may balk at implementing design patterns that may result in duplicated code if they seem unnecessary at the time, discovering only later that the system would have been easier to understand or evolve had design patterns been used.

5   Related Work

Software Architecture. Most architecture description languages (ADLs) support the specification or implementation of software connectors [MT00]. For example, Wright specifies the temporal relationship of events on a connector and provides tools for checking properties such as freedom from deadlock [AG97]. SADL formalizes connectors in terms of theories and describes how abstract connectors in a design can be iteratively refined into concrete connectors in an implementation [MQR95]. Rapide specifies connectors within a reactive system using event traces [LV95].

Several ADLs provide tools that can generate executable code from an architectural description. UniCon's tools use an architectural specification to generate connector code that links components together [SDK+95]. C2 provides runtime libraries in C++ and Java that implement C2 connectors [MOR+96]. Darwin provides infrastructure support for implementing distributed systems specified in the Darwin ADL [MK96]. These code generation tools, however, support a limited number of built-in connector types, and developers cannot easily define connectors with custom semantics.

User-Defined Connectors. The work most similar to our own is a specification of how user-defined connector types can be added as plugins to the UniCon compiler [SDZ96]. UniCon connector plugins are fairly heavyweight, as connector developers must understand the details of several phases of the compiler. However, this design allows new connectors to be tightly integrated into the compiler system, permitting new kinds of architectural analysis to be defined over these connectors. In contrast, ArchJava's connector abstractions are lightweight, and a wide range of connectors can be implemented with knowledge of a small library interface.

Dashofy et al. describe how off-the-shelf middleware can be used to implement C2 connectors [DMT99]. Their work differs from ours in that the semantics of the connectors is fixed by the C2 architectural style, while our connector abstractions are intended to support a wide range of architectural styles.

Mezini and Ostermann describe language support for adaptor connections that allow components with different data models to work together [MO02]. Their language makes wrapper code less tedious to write, and provides support for the difficult problem of maintaining consistent wrapper identity. ArchJava's connector abstractions provide weaker support for adaptors, but facilitate a range of connector types beyond adaptors.

Object-Oriented Languages. A number of proposals have added connection support to object-oriented languages such as Java. For example, ComponentJ [SC00] and ACOEL [Sre02] as well as the original design of ArchJava [ACN02a] all provide primitives for linking components together with connections. However, these languages all fix the semantics of connections to the same synchronous method call semantics used by Java.

Aspect-Oriented Programming. Aspect-oriented programming (AOP) languages allow programmers to more effectively separate code that implements different application concerns. For example, Soares et al. showed how the AspectJ language can be used to implement distribution and persistence in a health complaint system [SLB02]. Aspect-oriented programming developed out of meta-object protocols, which allow programmers to define how an object should react to events like method calls [KRB91]. Relative to languages such as AspectJ and the more powerful meta-object protocol technique, ArchJava's connector abstractions provide a more limited kind of separation of concerns, restricted to the semantics of connectors. However, because connectors are bound in the surrounding architecture of a component, they support more local reasoning about connector aspect code.

Composition filters is the aspect-oriented approach most similar to ArchJava's connector abstractions. In this technique, developers interpose filter objects that can inspect incoming method calls and perform operations like translation, adaptation, and forwarding on the messages [BA01]. ArchJava's connector abstractions are similar to composition filters, but instead of processing all messages called on a single object, they process messages exchanged between two component objects in an architecture.

Distributed System Infrastructures. A number of libraries and tools have been defined to support distributed programming. Commercial examples include RPC [BCL+87] as well as COM [Mic95], CORBA [OMG95], and RMI [Jav97]. These systems offer a convenient method-call interface for remote communication, much like the interface provided by ArchJava's connector abstractions. Furthermore, these systems check statically that communication through their connections is well typed. Infrastructures support some flexibility—for example, RMI allows the developer to specify the wire protocol to be used, and CORBA provides an event service that can be used in place of remote method calls. However, each of these commercially available systems defines a particular semantics (usually synchronous method call) for the connections it supports, rather than providing a general interface that programmers can implement in various ways to support their application-specific needs.

Recently, researchers have been developing extensible middleware such as the OpenORB [BCA+01] and the Universally Interoperable Core [Ubi02]. These systems allow developers to customize middleware aspects such as the network transport protocol, object marshalling, and method invocation semantics. DADO provides features of aspect-oriented programming in the context of a reflective middleware system, supporting connector functionality like caching and performance monitoring [WJD03]. Compared to ArchJava's connector abstractions, these middleware systems provide a great deal of built-in services, but are not tightly integrated into programming languages and do not provide customized connection typechecking.

CASE Tools. Several computer-aided software engineering tools, including Consystant and Rational Rose RealTime, generate code to connect components together. This connection code can range from stubs and skeletons for an infrastructure like CORBA or RMI to wires that connect different processors in an embedded system. Like many of the technologies discussed above, these tools typically support a fixed set of connectors.

6 Conclusion

This paper described a technique for adding explicit support for connector abstractions to the ArchJava programming language. In our system, connector abstractions can be defined using a very flexible reflective library-based mechanism. We have evaluated the expressiveness of our technique by implementing representative connectors from a wide range of connector types, and we have evaluated the engineering tradeoffs in a small case study on the PlantCare ubiquitous computing application. The benefits of connector abstractions include separating communication code from application logic, documenting and checking connector interfaces, and reusing connector abstractions more effectively compared with alternative techniques.

In future work, we intend to implement more connectors and evaluate their expressiveness on a wider variety of systems. We also hope to develop a library-based framework for composing connectors together so that complex connectors can be easily created from simple building blocks. Another important area of future work is more effective support for adaptor-style connections, extending recently developed adaptation techniques such as on-demand remodularization [MO02]. Finally, we would like to provide specification and checking of connector properties that go beyond simple typechecking. We believe that enhanced language and system support for connectors is crucial to the effective development and evolution of many classes of software systems.

Acknowledgements

We would like to thank Sorin Lerner, Anthony LaMarca, Stefan Sigurdsson, Matt Lease, and the anonymous reviewers for their helpful comments. We especially thank Intel Research Seattle for access to the PlantCare application. This work was supported in part by NSF grants CCR-9970986, CCR-0073379, and CCR-0204047, and gifts from Sun Microsystems and IBM.

References

[ACN02a]   Jonathan Aldrich, Craig Chambers, and David Notkin. ArchJava: Connecting Software Architecture to Implementation. Proc. International Conference on Software Engineering, Orlando, Florida, May 2002.

[ACN02b]   Jonathan Aldrich, Craig Chambers, and David Notkin. Architectural Reasoning in ArchJava. Proc. European Conference on Object-Oriented Programming, Málaga, Spain, June 2002.

[AG97]   Robert Allen and David Garlan. A Formal Basis for Architectural Connection. ACM Transactions on Software Engineering and Methodology 6(3):213-249, July 1997.

[Arc02]   ArchJava web site. http://www.archjava.org/

[BA01]   Lodewijk Bergmans and Mehmet Aksit, Composing Crosscutting Concerns Using Composition Filters, Communications of the ACM 44(10):51-57, October 2001.

[BCA+01]   Gordon S. Blair, Geoff Coulson, Anders Andersen, Lynne Blair, Michael Clarke, Fabio Costa, Hector Duran-Limon, Tom Fitzpatrick, Lee Johnston, Rui Moreira, Nikos Parlavantzas, and Katia Saikoski. The Design and Implementation of Open ORB 2. IEEE Distributed Systems Online Journal 2(6): 2001.

[BCL+87]   Brian Bershad, Dennis Ching, Edward Lazowska, Jan Sanislo, and Michael Schwartz. A Remote Procedure Call Facility for Interconnecting Heterogeneous Computer Systems. IEEE Trans. Software Engineering 13(8):880-894, August 1987.

[BOS+98]   Gilad Bracha, Martin Odersky, David Stoutamire, and Philip Wadler. Making the Future Safe for the Past: Adding Genericity to the Java Programming Language. Proc. Object Oriented Programming Systems, Languages, and Applications, Vancouver, British Columbia, October 1998.

[DMT99]   Eric M. Dashofy, Nenad Medvidovic, and Richard N. Taylor. Using Off-the-Shelf Middleware to Implement Connectors in Distributed Software Architectures. Proc. International Conference on Software Engineering, Los Angeles, California, May 1999.

[GHJ+94]   Erich Gamma, Richard Helm, Ralph Johnson and John Vlissides. Design Patterns: Elements of Reusable Object-Oriented Software. Addison-Wesley, 1994.

[GS93]   David Garlan and Mary Shaw. An Introduction to Software
            Architecture. In Advances in Software Engineering and Knowledge
            Engineering, I (Ambriola V, Tortora G, Eds.) World Scientific
            Publishing Company, 1993.
[Jav97]   Javasoft Java RMI Team. Java Remote Method Invocation
            Specification, Sun Microsystems, 1997.
[JLH88]   Eric Jul, Hank Levy, Norman Hutchinson, and Andrew Black. Fine-
            Grained Mobility in the Emerald System. ACM Trans. Computer
            Systems 6(1):109-133, February 1988.
[KRB91]   Gregor Kiczales, James des Rivières, and Daniel G. Bobrow. The Art of
            the Meta-Object Protocol. MIT Press, Cambridge, MA, 1991.
[LBK+02]   A. LaMarca, W. Brunette, D. Koizumi, M. Lease, S. B. Sigurdsson,
            K. Sikorski, D. Fox, and G. Borriello. PlantCare: An Investigation in
            Practical Ubiquitous Systems. Proc. International Conference on
            Ubiquitous Computing, Göteborg, Sweden, September 2002.
[LV95]   David C. Luckham and James Vera. An Event Based Architecture
            Definition Language. IEEE Trans. Software Engineering 21(9),
            September 1995.
[Mic95]   Microsoft Corporation. The Component Object Model Specification,
            Version 0.9. October 1995.
[MK96]   Jeff Magee and Jeff Kramer. Dynamic Structure in Software
            Architectures. Proc. Foundations of Software Engineering, San
            Francisco, California, October 1996.
[MMP00]   Nikunj R. Mehta, Nenad Medvidovic, and Sandeep Phadke. Towards a
            Taxonomy of Software Connectors. Proc. International Conference on
            Software Engineering, Limerick, Ireland, June 2000.
[MO02]   Mira Mezini and Klaus Ostermann. Integrating Independent
            Components with On-Demand Remodularization. Proc. Object-Oriented
            Programming Systems, Languages, and Applications, Seattle,
            Washington, November 2002.
[MOR+96]   Nenad Medvidovic, Peyman Oreizy, Jason E. Robbins, and
            Richard N. Taylor. Using Object-Oriented Typing to Support
            Architectural Design in the C2 Style. Proc. Foundations of Software
            Engineering, San Francisco, California, October 1996.
[MQR95]   Mark Moriconi, Xiaolei Qian, and Robert A. Riemenschneider. Correct
            Architecture Refinement. IEEE Trans. Software Engineering, 21(4):356-
            372, April 1995.
[MT00]   Nenad Medvidovic and Richard N. Taylor. A Classification and
            Comparison Framework for Software Architecture Description
            Languages. IEEE Trans. Software Engineering, 26(1):70-93, January
            2000.
[OMG95]   Object Management Group. The Common Object Request Broker:
            Architecture and Specification (CORBA), revision 2.0. 1995.
[PW92]   Dewayne E. Perry and Alexander L. Wolf. Foundations for the Study of
            Software Architecture. ACM SIGSOFT Software Engineering Notes,
            17:40-52, October 1992.

[SC00]   João C. Seco and Luís Caires. A Basic Model of Typed Components. Proc. European Conference on Object-Oriented Programming, Cannes, France, June 2000.

[SDK+95]   Mary Shaw, Rob DeLine, Daniel V. Klein, Theodore L. Ross, David M. Young, and Gregory Zelesnik. Abstractions for Software Architecture and Tools to Support Them. IEEE Trans. Software Engineering, 21(4):314-335, April 1995.

[SDZ96]   Mary Shaw, Rob DeLine, and Gregory Zelesnik. Abstractions and Implementations for Architectural Connections. Proc. International Conference on Configurable Distributed Systems, Annapolis, Maryland, May 1996.

[SLB02]   Sergio Soares, Eduardo Laureano, and Paulo Borba. Implementing Distribution and Persistence Aspects with AspectJ. Proc. Object-Oriented Programming Systems, Languages, and Applications, Seattle, Washington, November 2002.

[Sre02]   Vugranam C. Sreedhar. Mixin' Up Components. Proc. International Conference on Software Engineering, Orlando, Florida, May 2002.

[Ubi02]   UbiCore LLC. Universally Interoperable Core. Description at http://www.ubi-core.com/Documentation/Universally_Interoperable_ Core/universally_interoperable_core.html.

[WJD03]   Eric Wohlstadter, Stoney Jackson and Premkumar Devanbu. DADO: Enhancing Middleware to Support Cross-Cutting Features in Distributed, Heterogeneous Systems. Proc. International Conference on Software Engineering, Portland, Oregon, May 2003.

Walkabout Revisited: The Runabout

Christian Grothoff

S^3 lab, Department of Computer Sciences, Purdue University
grothoff@cs.purdue.edu
http://www.ovmj.org/runabout/

Abstract. We present a variation of the visitor pattern which allows programmers to write visitor-like code in a concise way. The Runabout is a library extension that adds a limited form of multi-dispatch to Java. While the Runabout is not as expressive as a general multiple dispatching facility, the Runabout can be significantly faster than existing implementations of multiple dispatch for Java, such as MultiJava. Unlike MultiJava, the Runabout does not require changes to the syntax and the compiler.

In this paper we illustrate how to use the Runabout, detail its implementation and provide benchmarks comparing its performance with other approaches.

1 Introduction

A fundamental problem in programming language design is to make software extensible while avoiding changes to existing code and retaining static type safety [19]. For example, we may want to add functionality that operates on a number of existing objects, or we may want to introduce a new object to existing code. For such purposes, a strength of object-oriented programming is that it is easy to introduce a new class. Adding functionality to existing classes is more difficult, particularly because this typically requires access to the source code. It also may be undesireable to add the functionality to all subclasses.

> **Extensibility Problem:** Devise a mechanism for adding functionality and classes to existing code while avoiding recompilation and retaining efficiency and static type safety.

One traditional solution to this problem is to use the visitor pattern [14]. The visitor pattern allows adding functionality in the form of **visit** methods that are invoked from an **accept** method which is defined in each visitee object. The **accept** is only specific with respect to the type of an abstract visitor. Visitors do not completely solve the extensibility problem. If the set of visitee classes changes, the type of the abstract visitor changes. Using visitors, it becomes more difficult to change the set of visitees since all visitors must be adjusted to provide a **visit** method matching the visitee types. Another solution to the extensibility problem is to use multi-methods which allow both new functionality and new

L. Cardelli (Ed.): ECOOP 2003, LNCS 2743, pp. 103–125, 2003.

classes to be added in a flexible and concise manner. The Runabout is a step towards achieving many of the benefits of multi-methods without requireing a new language.

In this paper we address the extensibility problem for Java, giving a solution that does support changing sets of visitee types, and provides both acceptable performance (only 2-10 times slower than visitors) and the minimum amount of programming effort. Our solution is based on an approach that was proposed by Palsberg and Jay [26] called Walkabout. Their approach takes advantage of Java's reflection mechanism to implement double-dispatch.

The Runabout presented in this paper is an extension of the Java libraries that adds two-argument dispatch to Java. The Runabout is itself implemented in Java (without any native methods). The code for the Runabout is about 1,000 lines of code, which is available on our webpage. Like the Walkabout [26], the Runabout uses reflection to *find* visit methods. But instead of invoking the visit methods with reflection, the Runabout uses dynamic code generation to create verifying bytecode that will invoke the appropriate visit method. The dynamically generated bytecode is type-safe and can be analyzed and optimized by the compiler.

Generating bytecode for multi-dispatching is also what the MultiJava compiler [7] does. MultiJava compiles Java with multi-methods to ordinary Java bytecode. Unlike MultiJava, the Runabout generates the invocation code when the application is executed, not at compile time. Thus the Runabout does not require changes to the compiler or the virtual machine. Contrary to previous beliefs [26], the approach using reflection to determine visit targets does not automatically imply an extraordinary run-time overhead. In fact, for 100 million visit invocations on 2,000 visitee classes, the Runabout is slower by less than a factor of two compared to visitors (217s vs. 137s).

The remainder of the paper is structured as follows. First, an example for programming with runabouts is given and the semantics of the Runabout are described in detail. In section 3 the implementation of the Runabout is presented. Performance evaluations are detailed in section 4. Section 5 discusses some related work.

2   Using the Runabout

Writing runabouts is similar to writing visitors or using multi methods. In order to demonstrate how to write code with Runabouts, an example that implements the same functionality using dedicated methods, visitors, MultiJava and the Runabout is first presented. Next, the semantics of the `visitAppropriate` method of the Runabout are described. Then the specific benefits and drawbacks of each of the implementations in terms of expressiveness and restrictions imposed on the programmer are discussed.

```
interface A˜{
   int dedicated ();
}
class A0 implements A˜{
   int dedicated () { return 0; }
}
class A1 implements A˜{
   int dedicated () { return 1; }
}
class A2 implements A˜{
   int dedicated () { return 2; }
}
long run(A[] a) {
   long sum = 0;
   for (int j=0;j<a.length;j++)
     sum += a[j].dedicated ();
   return sum;
}
```

Fig. 1. The visitee classes with a dedicated method (`dedicated`)

2.1 A Simple Example

For our example, we are going to use a set of visitee classes A_i that implement
the common interface A. Given an array a of instances of type A, the goal is to
compute $\sum_{a \in A} I(a)$ where $I(a) = i$ if a is of type A_i.

Dedicated Methods Dedicated methods can be used to solve the problem
efficiently. The problem with dedicated methods is, that for every operation
that is to be performed on the visitee classes, a method must be added to each
of the visitee classes. This spreads the code used by a particular operation over
many classes and makes it often hard to maintain. Fig. 1 shows the solution
using a dedicated method.

Cascading Conditionals Another possibility would be to use a sequence of
`instanceof` tests, which is certainly impractical for larger numbers of visitee
types and requires modification each time a visitee is added (Fig. 2).

Visitors Fig. 3 details the code for expressing a solution with visitors. The
example uses overloading for the `visit` methods. Overloading is not needed for
visitors and it is used here to emphasize the similarities with MultiJava and the
Runabout. For simplification, we assume here that only one visitor is being used
and that thus there is no need for a visitor interface for the `accept` methods
to dispatch upon. In practice, the code would consist of multiple visitors for
multiple computations that would be performed over the visitee objects.

```
interface A~{}
class A0 implements A~{}
class A1 implements A~{}
class A2 implements A~{}
long run(A[] a) {
  long sum = 0;
  for (int j=0;j<a.length;j++) {
    A~ aj = a[j];
    if (aj instanceof A2)
      sumInstanceof += 2;
    else if (aj instanceof A1)
      sumInstanceof += 1;
    else if (aj instanceof A0)
      sumInstanceof += 0;
    else
      throw new Error("Illegal_call");
  }
  return sum;
}
```

Fig. 2. No changes to the visitees are required with cascading conditionals

Multi-methods An implementation using MultiJava (Fig. 4) does not require the accept methods. Instead, the compiler can see that multi-dispatch is declared (@) and generates code to invoke the appropriate visit method.

Runabouts The Runabout code (Fig. 5) is somewhere between visitors and MultiJava. The visit methods do not require any additional syntax; all that is required is that the class extends Runabout and that `visitAppropriate` (a method provided by the parent class) is invoked instead of `visit`. As in Multi-Java, no `accept` method is required in the visitees.

2.2   Semantics

In order to create a Runabout, the client code must create a public subclass of `Runabout`. The `Runabout` class provides the method `visitAppropriate` which can be used for two-argument dispatch. The two-arguments of the two-argument dispatch are the receiver of `visitAppropriate` and the first and only argument of `visitAppropriate`. The callee of the dispatch is determined by the `lookup` method.

visitAppropriate The callee in the dispatch performed by `visitAppropriate` is either `visitDefault` or exactly one of the `visit` methods defined in or inherited by the class of the receiver. The concrete selection of the `visit` method is performed by the `lookup` function, which, given a `Class`, returns `Code` to invoke one of the visit methods. lookup(T) may only select non-static visit methods that have a return type of void and take only a single argument of public type S where S must be a supertype of T. lookup may return null in which case visitDefault is invoked. If not overridden, visitDefault throws a run-time exception to indicate that no visit method was found. lookup may also throw run-time exceptions (for example, to indicate ambiguities in the method resolution).

Note that visitAppropriate does *not* require that all visit methods have a common base-class other than Object. Thus the Runabout does not require the interface A that most of the other implementations use to declare the dedicated method, to declare the accept method, or as a help for the type system in the form of the A@.

The fact that the Runabout does not require accept methods or a common interface in the visitees is often beneficial when dealing with code where adding an accept method is not possible, like for String. A simple example for this is given in Fig. 6.

```
interface A˜{
   void accept(Visitor v);
}
class A0 implements A˜{
   void accept(Visitor v) { v.visit(this);   }
}
class A1 implements A˜{
   void accept(Visitor v) { v.visit(this);   }
}
class A2 implements A˜{
   void accept(Visitor v) { v.visit(this);   }
}
class Visitor {
   long sum = 0;
   public void visit(A0 a) { sum += 0; }
   public void visit(A1 a) { sum += 1; }
   public void visit(A2 a) { sum += 2; }
}
long run(A[] a) {
   Visitor v = new Visitor();
   for (int j=0;j<a.length;j++)
      a[j].accept(v);
   return v.sum;
}
```

Fig. 3. Visitors require accept methods in the visitees

```
interface A~{}
class A0 implements A~{}
class A1 implements A~{}
class A2 implements A~{}
class MultiJavaSum {
  long sum = 0;
  public void visit(A a)     { throw new Error(); }
  public void visit(A@A0 a) { sum += 0; }
  public void visit(A@A1 a) { sum += 1; }
  public void visit(A@A2 a) { sum += 2; }
}
long run(A[] a) {
  MultiJavaSum v = new MultiJavaSum();
  for (int j=0;j<a.length;j++)
    v.visit(a[j]);
  return v.sum;
}
```

Fig. 4. MultiJava indicates multi-dispatch using minimal changes to the syntax

```
public class A0 {}
public class A1 {}
public class A2 {}
public class RunaboutSum extends Runabout {
  long sum = 0;
  public void visit(A0 a) { sum += 0; }
  public void visit(A1 a) { sum += 1; }
  public void visit(A2 a) { sum += 2; }
}
long run(Object[] a) {
  RunaboutSum v = new RunaboutSum();
  for (int j=0;j<a.length;j++)
    v.visitAppropriate(a[j]);
  return v.sum;
}
```

Fig. 5. Runabouts extend the Runabout class to inherit `visitAppropriate`

lookup Which `visit` method is invoked by `visitAppropriate` is specified by the *lookup strategy* that is implemented by `lookup`. Defining a lookup strategy is similar to defining how a compiler (like `javac`) resolves method invocations for overloaded methods [15, section 15.11.2]. The main difference is that instead of the static type, the dynamic type of the argument object is used. As with overloading, multiple methods may be applicable. In the case of `javac`, the method with the closest matching signature is chosen, and a compile-error is generated in the case of ambiguities.

```
public static void main(String[] arg) {
  MyRunabout mr = new MyRunabout();
  mr.visitAppropriate("Hello");
  mr.visitAppropriate(new Integer(1));
  assertTrue(mr.cnt == 3);
}
public class MyRunabout extends Runabout {
  int cnt = 0;
  public void visit(String s)  { cnt += 2; }
  public void visit(Integer i) { cnt += i.intValue(); }
}
```

Fig. 6. Using the Runabout on any kind of visitee

Client code can define a specific lookup strategy by overriding the lookup function[1]. As an input, the lookup function is passed the dynamic type of the object on which the dispatch takes place. The dynamic type is a node in the inheritance hierarchy (a directional acyclic graph), which can then be traversed by the function to find a matching type for which a visit method exists. A simple example for an implementation of lookup that does not consider interfaces is given in Fig. 7. The helper method getCodeForClass(c) tests if a visit method for the type c exists and if so returns the Code instance for that visit method.

```
protected Code lookup(Class c) {
  while (c != null) {
    Code co = getCodeForClass(c);
    if (co != null)
      return co;
    c = c.getSuperclass();
  }
  return null;
}
```

Fig. 7. Example of a lookup method

---

[1] Functions are methods that do not access any state except for the arguments and that have no side-effects. We restrict the lookup strategy to a function since this restriction allows a static checker to verify that the lookup strategy always succeeds when run in a closed-world setting. This is not a significant restriction since a lookup strategy that depends on the state of the application is likely to have an unexpected behavior for the programmer and thus such a design should in fact be made impossible for other reasons.

The Runabout has the following default lookup strategy. If visit methods for both classes and interfaces are applicable to the given dynamic type, the visit method for the *class* closest to the dynamic type is chosen. If no visit method for a superclass of the dynamic type exists and if there is only one visit method matching any of the interfaces implemented by the dynamic type, then that visit method is selected. If visit methods for multiple interfaces implemented by the dynamic type (but none for its parent classes) exist, a run-time exception indicating the ambiguity is thrown. If no applicable visit method exists at all, null is returned, causing the invocation of visitDefault.

2.3 Discussion

The Runabout as described so far is more expressive than typical visitors and has fewer requirements for the visitees. Primarily, the Runabout does not require accept methods in the visitees. On the other hand, additional restrictions imposed by the Runabout are that all the visitee classes and all subclasses of Runabout must be public (the Runabout must internally cast to these types) and that all visit methods must be public. These restrictions are minor since if the visitees are legacy code, the classes are probably already public; adding accept methods (or even dedicated methods) would typically be much harder. Making the subclass of Runabout or its visit methods public is even less likely to be a problem. A slightly more limiting constraint is that the Runabout requires visit methods to return void and take just one argument. A more sophisticated implementation should be able to relax this requirement.

MultiJava does not impose restrictions on the access modifiers, the specialized compiler takes care of these problems. Extending the language has the advantage that MultiJava is more expressive than any other solution. For example, it is possible to dispatch on more than one argument. MultiJava also does not have the requirement that the methods that are multi-dispatched are named visit, which also allows MultiJava to support many multiply-dispatched method families in the same class.

While the Runabout could be extended to allow names other than visit, we feel that in practice this limitation will hardly ever be a problem and that in fact several multi-dispatch method families in the same class without any syntax to mark these methods would instead likely confuse programmers. MultiJava's approach of extending the Java syntax solves this problem but prevents users from deploying other language extensions like GJ [2] or AspectJ [18] in the same code. The current implementation of MultiJava uses linear sequences of instanceof tests, making the tool impractical for large numbers of visitee classes. We expect that a better implementation of MultiJava will take care of this major performance issue.

A drawback of visitors is that they often require writing excessive amounts of trivial code. All visit methods must be declared in a base-class (or interface) which is used by the accept method. The accept methods themselves can be tedious if the code has many visitees. Also, the visitor pattern is less expressive than the Runabout since it requires the programmer to occasionally add additional code to perform the intended dispatch. For example, suppose some of the visitee types form a hierarchy where A, B and C represent similar visitees and thus extend the common parent P. In this case, the visit methods for P, A, B and C are sometimes identical. In the case of the Runabout, only one visit method for P needs to be implemented, the `lookup` for A, B and C will automatically result in the invocation of `visit(P)`. For visitors, either the code is replicated or the default visitor pattern [17] where `visit(A a)` calls `this.visit((P)a);` must be used, forcing the user to write additional methods that merely indirect the control flow.

3   Implementation

In this section, we describe our implementation of Runabout. In particular, we describe how the constructor builds the *dynamic code map* and how the `visitAppropriate` method uses that map to invoke the appropriate `visit` method. We then discuss extensions to the core functionality, such as handling of primitive visitees and addition of `visit` methods that are not declared in the subclass of Runabout.

3.1   The Dynamic Code Map

Central to the implementation of the Runabout is the dynamic code map. This hash table maps the dynamic type of the argument to an implementation of Code (see Fig. 8), an abstract class. Instances of `Code` are stateless and can be seen as the Java equivalent of C function pointers. The virtual method table of the code objects refers to a piece of code that is to be invoked for arguments of the corresponding dynamic type.

The constructor of Runabout scans the Runabout class (using reflection) and creates a specialized object of type `Code` for every visit method that is found. The class for each instance of `Code` (Fig. 8) is generated on-the-fly and dynamically loaded into the VM using Java's class-loading mechanism. The generated code is illustrated best with an example. If the concrete instance of Runabout is of type `RunaboutExample` and the visit method takes `String` as the argument, the dynamically generated code will correspond to the Java code in Fig. 9. The X is replaced with a unique number to avoid name-clashes. An instance of `GenCodeX` is instantiated and installed in the dynamic code map.

```
public static abstract class Code {
   public abstract void visit(Runabout r, Object o);
}
```

Fig. 8. The Code class is an inner class of the Runabout that defines the interface for the dynamically generated and loaded code tunks

```
class GenCodeX
  extends Runabout.Code {
  public void visit(Runabout r, Object o) {
    ((RunaboutExample) r).visit((String)o);
  }
}
```

Fig. 9. Source equivalent of the code that is dynamically generated code when reflection finds the method `RunaboutExample.visit(String)`. An instance of this type is returned by `map.get(String.class)` in `visitAppropriate`

3.2 Lookup

The implementation of `Runabout.visitAppropriate` is now simple (Fig. 10). `visitAppropriate` does a `get` on the dynamic code `map`, to find an object of type `Code`. If no matching code is found, the `lookup` procedure is invoked to find a matching piece of code and the dynamic code map is updated. Finally, the code found in the code map is invoked. Note that lookup returns a code object `nocode` with an implementation of `visit` that just returns if no matching visit method was found in the lookup. Note that lookup runs at most once for every dynamic type passed to `visitAppropriate` per Runabout class. Lookup also never needs to perform dynamic loading; the initial population of the dynamic code table in the constructor has created all the `Code` instances that are needed.

3.3 Caching Generated Code

Like [3], the Runabout uses caching to improve the performance. The dynamic code map as described above caches the results of the lookup. While this is effective to improve the time of running `visitAppropriate`, creating a Runabout

```
public final void visitAppropriate(Object o) {
  Class cl = o.getClass();
  Code co = map.get(cl);
  if (co == null) {
    co = lookup(cl);
    if (co == null)
      co = visitDefaultCode;
    map.put(c, co);
  }
  co.visit(this, o);
}
```

Fig. 10. visitAppropriate finds the dynamically generated code for an object in the hash table `map`

instance is also a performance concern. Creating a Runabout involves the use of reflection to find the declared `visit` methods and dynamic code generation, class loading and reflective instantiation of `Code` objects. The performance of Runabout creation can be improved by sharing the dynamic code map between instances of the same Runabout types. For this, the implementation uses a second second `Cache` that is basically a thread-local hash table that maps subclasses of Runabout to instances of the dynamic code map. The `Cache` is thread-local to eliminate the need for synchronization on the maps. Every new instance of a Runabout is checked against the cache, limiting the use of reflection and dynamic code generation to once per Runabout class. Since the code maps are shared, this also further limits the use of the lookup function to only once for each combination of thread, runabout class and dynamic type that is used in the dispatch. The Runabout uses the same class loader for all instances that share the same `Cache`.

3.4   Extensions

In order to support primitive visitees, our Runabout implementation provides a second `visitAppropriate` method, which takes an additional argument of type `java.lang.Class`. This second argument is used to distinguish between primitive types and their wrapper classes. The Runabout provides empty `visit` methods for the 8 primitive types that can be overridden by subclasses.

A typical use of this facility would be the iteration over an object graph using reflection. Fig. 11 shows the code of a simple iterator that counts the number of primitive `int`s that are reachable from any argument passed to `visitAppropriate`. Note that the example code does not handle cycles in the object graph.

Another simple extension is adding methods to the code map that are not `visit` methods in the subclass of the Runabout. The Runabout interface provides the method `addExternalVisit(Class cl, Code co)` to allow adding an *external* visit method to the Runabout. If the Runabout encounters an object of the specified class, it calls the visit method defined in `Code`. Note that the `visit` method declared in `Runabout.Code` is declared to take `Object` as the type of the visitee argument, and while the Runabout guarantees that the object passed will be a subtype of `cl`, it cannot verify that casts in `Code` are safe. Note that the cost of the dispatch in the Runabout is not changed at all by this extension.

Adding external visit methods to an instance of Runabout should not modify the behavior of other instances. Thus the shared dynamic code that was obtained from the `Cache` is copied when the first *private* extension is added.

4   Experimental Results

In this section we present experimental results. We first present micro-benchmarking results which demonstrate that the Runabout is comparable in performance with the other designs. We then describe our experience with refactoring the Kacheck/J to use the Runabout instead of visitors.

```
public class CountInt extends Runabout {
  int count = 0;
  public void visit(int i) {
    count++;
  }
  public void visit(Object o) {
    Field[] fields = o.getClass().getDeclaredFields();
    for (int i=0;i<fields.length;i++)
      if (! Modifier.isStatic(fields[i].getModifiers()))
        visitAppropriate(fields[i].get(o),
                         fields[i].getType());
  }
}
void run() {
  CountInt ci = new CountInt();
  ci.visitAppropriate("Example");
  System.out.println(ci.count + "_int_fields_reachable");
}
```

Fig. 11. Using the Runabout with primitives: counting the number of reachable fields of type int in an object graph without cycles

4.1 Synthetic Micro-Benchmarks

In order to evaluate the performance of the Runabout, we have run variations of the example presented in section 2.1. The four major designs were run on IBM JDK 1.4.0 and Sun JDK 1.4.1 on a PIII-1000 running Linux 2.4.18. The time measured corresponds to a total of 10 million invocations. The reported numbers are the average over 10 runs in single user mode. All methods are invoked with equal frequency.

Two parameters have a significant impact on the benchmark. First of all, the number of visit methods (and visitee classes) is important to see if the design scales to complex visitee structures. The graphs contain the results for one to 20 visitee types, appendix A shows the results for up to 200 visitee types. For 2,000 types MultiJava is currently unable to compile the test-case.

The second important parameter is the hierarchy of the visitee types. The graphs show the numbers for a totally flat hierarchy (every visitee extends Object) and for a hierarchy of maximum depth (visitee class n extends $n-1$). Note that in the case of the deep hierarchy, the number of visit methods is equal to the depth of the hierarchy. The choice of hierarchy impacts the runtime of subtype tests, performed frequently by the MultiJava and the Runabout implementation.

As the benchmarks in Fig. 12 and 14 show, the differences between the approaches in execution speed are small. The Runabout has the highest cost for just one visit method; MultiJava degrades with higher numbers of visitee types. If the hierarchy is deep (Fig. 13 and 15), the instanceof tests in MultiJava be-

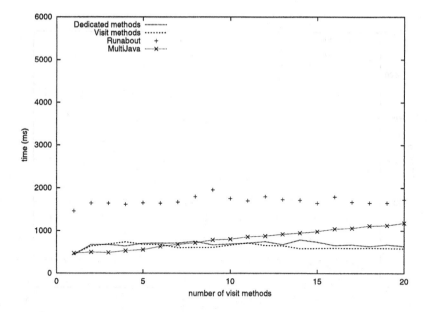

Fig. 12. Sun JDK 1.4.1, flat hierarchy

come more expensive. The performance of dedicated methods, visitors and the Runabout is not changed significantly.

In practice, the differences between all five approaches (with the potential exception of MultiJava for large hierarchies) are minor. In particular, the fact that the double dispatch of the visitor turns out to be faster than the dedicated method can not be explained and is presumabably just an artefact of the optimzing compiler. Overall, the numbers from the micro benchmark are too close to rule out any of the variants: the runtime of any application using any of the variants of the visitor pattern is typically not determined by the tiny cost of the dispatch but rather by the actions performed in the visit methods. Also, hierarchies in real applications are typcially not very deep, thus Fig. 12 is more realistic than Fig. 13.

The measurements above just reflect the time required for the invocation. But the Runabout is also a bit more costly to create compared to instances of ordinary visitors. Fig. 16 shows the cost of creating 100,000,000 instances of Runabout (with caching enabled) compared with the creation of 100,000,000 instances of an equivalent visitor. As the numbers show, creating a Runabout can be only about a factor of two slower than creating a visitor. But this is only half-true. The Runabout implementation caches reflective information, in particular instances of the dynamically generated and loaded classes, in a thread-local cache. The creation of the first instance of a given Runabout type in a new thread is more expensive. Fig. 17 shows the cost of creating 100,000 Runabouts without the cache. The numbers show that caching the reflective information per-thread

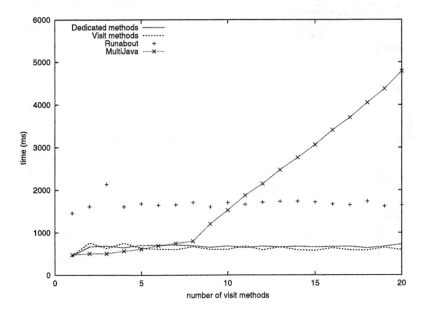

Fig. 13. Sun JDK 1.4.1, deep hierarchy

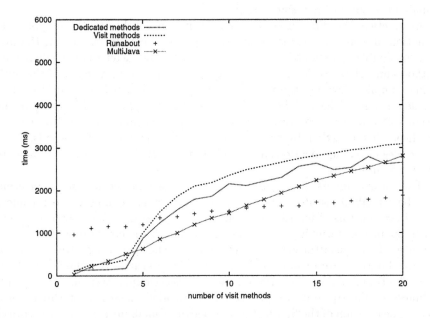

Fig. 14. IBM JDK 1.4.1, flat hierarchy

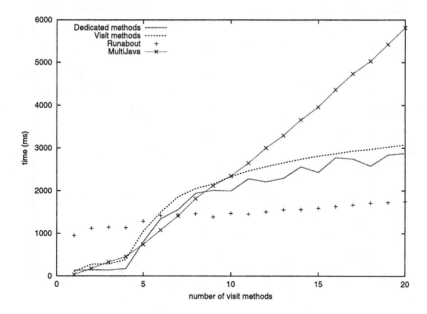

Fig. 15. IBM JDK 1.4.1, deep hierarchy

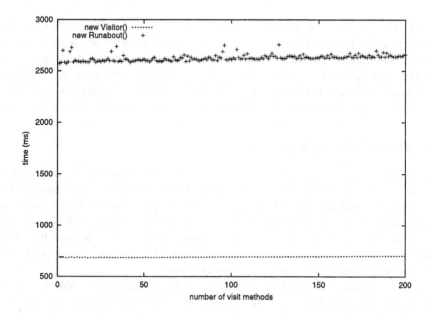

Fig. 16. This graph compares the time to create 10,000,000 instances of the same Runabout with the time to create 10,000,000 visitors on Sun JDK 1.4.1. The creation of a Runabout with the cache is about a factor of 3.8 slower

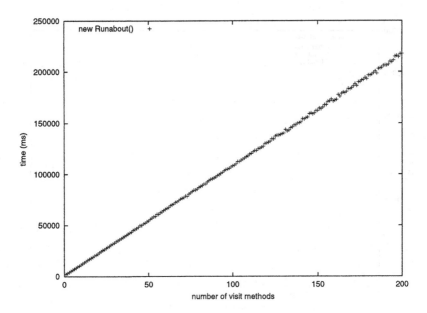

Fig. 17. This graph shows the time it takes to create 1,000 Runabouts *without* the cache on Sun JDK 1.4.1

reduces the overhead of creating a Runabout by a factor of up to 810,000 for 200 visit methods. Note that while it would be possible to cache the information globally and not just per thread, this would introduce synchronization operations in visitAppropriate, which would probably be worse in most applications. Profiling Runabout creation shows that dynamic class loading and reflective instantiation are each responsible for over 30% of the time of Runabout creation.

4.2 Refactoring Kacheck/J

Kacheck/J is a bytecode analysis tool to infer confined types [16]. Kacheck/J is written using the Ovm bytecode framework [25]. Ovm [24] is a customizable Java Virtual Machine. The Ovm framework contains a bytecode analysis and manipulation framework which was previously based on visitors. In particular, the framework provides an abstract interpretation engine that uses flyweight instruction objects as visitees to support abstract execution. Kacheck/J uses this abstract execution framework to analyze code.

In the previous version of the framework, every instruction object had an accept method. In addition to that, every instruction had an execute method which would perform the state manipulation on the abstract interpreter for this instruction during abstract interpretation. In its main loop, the abstract interpreter would call the execute method to simulate the instruction interleaved with accepting on a visitor which would do the analysis. Some additional code in the main loop took care of control flow handling and merging of abstract states. The **execute** method can be seen as a dedicated method for abstract execution.

We have refactored the analysis framework to use Runabouts instead of the dedicated **execute** method and the **accept** method. An immediate benefit of this change was that adding new instruction types for analysis on VM specific bytecodes (for example, quick opcodes), no longer requires adding visit methods to parts of the framework that are not concerned with these types of instructions. Factoring out the **execute** method into a Runabout makes it easier to change its behavior. In order to ease the selective manipulation of the abstract execution, each abstract interpretation step was split into two Runabouts: one that manipulates the local variables and the stack of the abstract machine and one that is responsible for control flow, exception handling and merging of states.

In addition to saving hundreds of **accept** methods and hundreds of **visit** methods in the matching abstract visitor, the introduction of the Runabout also allowed other code reductions. Many analyses were grouping **visit** methods for closely related instructions, such as *invokevirtual, invokeinterface, invokespecial* and *invokestatic*. This was achieved with the default visitor pattern [17]. Since the hierarchy of instructions is fairly complex, multiple default visitors (where one visit method was just dispatching to another visit method) existed in the old framework. Maintaining these default visitors, especially with changes in the hierarchy of the instructions, has always been a problem. With the Runabout, most of what we were trying to achieve with the default visitors was covered by the lookup algorithm, making all of these classes obsolete.

The new framework also has some additional features that impact Kacheck/J's performance (for example, an extensible set of abstract values for application-specific abstract execution domains). Additionally, Kacheck/J's implementation is slightly more powerful; for example it records and reports much more detailed information about the constraint system. These and other changes make the code not entirely comparable. The original Kacheck/J tool takes about 57 seconds to analyze the entire Sun JDK 1.4.0 from the Purdue Benchmark Suite (JDK5) running on top of Sun JDK 1.4.1 on a PIII-800.

The performance of the redesigned Kacheck/J is about 77s to analyze the entire Sun JDK 1.4.0.[2] During the analysis, the innermost loop performs slightly more than 10 million invocations of **visitAppropriate**.

To evaluate the impact of the **visitAppropriate** calls on the overall performance of the application, additional calls to **visitAppropriate** were put into the inner loop. The additional calls invoke cheap but not entirely trivial **visit** methods that computes the sum of the opcodes of the instructions visited. The original inner loop contains three Runabout invocations, using additional invocations to these opcode-counting Runabouts the number of calls in the inner loop was increased to up to a total of 9 calls. Overall, the inner loop is run about 3.3

---

[2] On a dual-processor system, the difference between the original tool (44s real time, 60s CPU time) and the new implementation (62s real time, 95s CPU time) is slightly different.

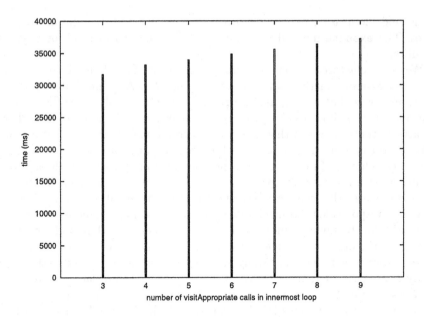

Fig. 18. Timings for the abstract execution phase of Kacheck/J with 0 to 6 additional Runabout invocations in the innermost loop

million times, resulting in 10 to 30 million runabout invocations for the profiling. For 30 million calls, the total runtime increases to about 95s. Fig. 18 shows the runtime of the abstract execution and the solving of the constraint system for three to nine Runabout invocations in the inner loop. The cost of parsing is nearly constant at 90s.

The cost of the introduction of the Runabout call in the innermost loop of Kacheck/J is thus about 12% of the time spent for abstract execution without constraint solving. While 12% might sound rather large, most steps in the abstract execution in practice consist of extremely cheap operations where even the traditional double-dispatch would take a fair share of the runtime. For example, for a POP, our implementation calls a visitor to do stack manipulation (which reduces the height of the stack by one) and a visitor to record Kacheck/J specific constraints (which only does something for 11 out of 200 Java opcodes), and finally calls a third visitor which most of the time just increments the program counter. That the three calls are taking a large share (and with the Runabout even 12%) of the runtime is thus more an effect of the way the code is written.

For the overall application with parsing and constraint solving, the cost of the Runabout drops down to less than 3%. Considering that double dispatch and even dedicated methods also incur some cost, the actual cost of using the Runabout instead of traditional visitors is more around 2%.

5   Related Work

The walkabout pattern as described in [26] allows the traversal of an arbitrary object graph without double dispatch. Instead of double dispatch, reflection is used to find the matching visit method. The authors noted that their implementation was impractically slow. Bravenboer [3] improved the performance of the walkabout by caching reflective results, but their performance is still poor; they report being about 100 times slower than visitors. The implementation given in [26] also requires that the type of the argument to the visit method matches exactly the type of the object that is being visited.

Space and time efficient implementations of virtual method dispatch have been the subject of a large body of research [6, 9, 20, 27]. In a statically typed single inheritance setting, the most common approach is to use virtual function tables. More advanced languages, such as Java, require more complicated designs [1] to handle features like multiple-inheritance and dynamic class loading. [29] provides a good overview of recent research. The Runabout is not concerned with these low-level compilation techniques and instead uses a large hashtable which puts it close to dynamic perfect hashing [8], a design that is not suitable for general dispatch techniques since it comes with a large space penalty. For the Runabout, space is not really a concern since there are typically very few Runabout classes in any given application. Furthermore, the type-safe high-level implementation of the dispatch in the Runabout cannot use some of the low-level techniques that compilers would use for dispatching.

A technique to provide multi-dispatch in the JVM is described in [10]. The authors have extended the virtual machine to use multi-dispatch for classes that were marked for multi-dispatch. While their approach is compatible with existing java compilers and libraries, it requires modifications to the VM. The authors also implemented MDLint, a tool to statically analyze code and warn programmers about ambiguities in the multi-dispatch.

While the Runabout and other multi-dispatch related research has focused on the dispatch element in visitors, other researchers [3, 23] have made suggestions on how to specify the visit strategy, that is the order in which objects are visited. In the same way that the Runabout allows for a concise and dynamic specification of how to find the target of the dispatch, the Demeter Java project has focused on designing specifications for the visit order, allowing programmers to specify the order in which objects in a graph should be visited [23]. A guiding visitor [3] can be used to specify the order of the traversal, allowing programmers to make the actual code independent from the specification of the traversal order. Note that both research areas (dispatch strategy and visit strategy) are orthogonal and thus most solutions can be easily composed.

Various techniques to extend traditional programming languages in order to allow programmers to write more extensible, reusable code have been proposed in the past [11, 12, 13, 18, 21, 22, 28]. These implementations are often incompatible with each other and require specialized compilers. While these techniques are more general than the Runabout, the Runabout is a more lightweight solution for Java. Other examples for lightweight extentions of the Java language that also use dynamic code generation and reflection are the dynamic generation of helper classes for structural conformance, automatic delegation or mixins [4].

6   Conclusion

The Runabout is a viable alternative solution to the extensibility problem. Unlike other designs, the Runabout does not require extensions to the Java language. The Runabout can perform about as fast as other solutions, including MultiJava, visitors or dedicated methods. While the current implementation of the Runabout only supports double-dispatch, future work may extend this approach to support full multi-dispatch.

Acknowledgements

My thanks go to the anonymous reviewers for helpful suggestions, Jan Vitek and Jens Palsberg for editing and to Tom VanDrunen, Suresh Jagannathan and James Noble for discussions.

References

[1] Bowen Alpern, Anthony Cocchi, Stephen J. Fink, David Grove, and Derek Lieber. Efficient Implementation of Java Interfaces: Invokeinterface Considered Harmless. In *OOPSLA 2001 Conference on Object-Oriented Programming, Systems, Languages, and Applications, Tampa, Florida*, pages 108–124, 2001.

[2] Gilad Bracha, Martin Odersky, David Stoutamire, and Philip Wadler. Making the future safe for the past: Adding genericity to the Java programming language. In *OOPSLA Proceedings*. ACM Press, Vancouver, BC, October 1998.

[3] M. Bravenboer and E. Visser. Guiding visitors: Separating navigation from computation. Technical report, Institute of Information and Computing Sciences, Utrecht University, 2001.

[4] T. M. Breuel. Implementing dynamic language features in java using dynamic code generation. In *Proceedings 39th International Conference and Exhibition on Technology of Object-Oriented Languages and Systems. TOOLS 39*, pages 143–52, 2001.

[5] Craig Chambers. Object-oriented multi-methods in Cecil. In Ole Lehrmann Madsen, editor, *Proceedings of the 6th European Conference on Object-Oriented Programming (ECOOP)*, volume 615, pages 33–56, Berlin, Heidelberg, New York, Tokyo, 1992. Springer-Verlag.

[6] Craig Chambers and Weimin Chen. Efficient multiple and predicate dispatching. In *Proceedings of the 1999 ACM Conference on Object-Oriented Programming Languages, Systems, and Applications (OOPSLA '99)*, volume 34(10) of *ACM SIGPLAN Notices*, pages 238–255, Denver, CO, November 1999. ACM.

[7] Curtis Clifton, Gary T. Leavens, Craig Chambers, and Todd Millstein. MultiJava: Modular open classes and symmetric multiple dispatch for Java. In *OOPSLA 2000 Conference on Object-Oriented Programming, Systems, Languages, and Applications, Minneapolis, Minnesota*, volume 35(10), pages 130–145, 2000.

[8] Martin Dietzfelbinger, Anna R. Karlin, Kurt Mehlhorn, Friedhelm Meyer auf der Heide, Hans Rohnert, and Robert Endre Tarjan. Dynamic perfect hashing: Upper and lower bounds. In *IEEE Symposium on Foundations of Computer Science*, pages 524–531, 1988.

[9] Karel Driesen, Urs Hölzle, and Jan Vitek. Message dispatch on pipelined processors. *Lecture Notes in Computer Science*, 952:253–283, 1995.

[10] C. Dutchyn. Multi-dispatch in the Java Virtual Machine: Design and implementation. Master's thesis, Department of Computing Science, University of Alberta, Edmonton, Alberta, Canada, 2001.

[11] Matthew Flatt. Programming Languages for Reusable Software Components. Technical Report TR99-345, 20, 1999.

[12] Matthew Flatt and Matthias Felleisen. Units: Cool modules for HOT languages. In *Proceedings of the ACM SIGPLAN '98 Conference on Programming Language Design and Implementation*, pages 236–248, 1998.

[13] Matthew Flatt, Shriram Krishnamurthi, and Matthias Felleisen. Classes and Mixins. In *Conference Record of POPL 98: The 25TH ACM SIGPLAN-SIGACT Symposium on Principles of Programming Languages, San Diego, California*, pages 171–183, New York, NY, 1998.

[14] Erich Gamma, Richard Helm, Ralph Johnson, and John Vlissides. *Design Patterns: Elements of Reusable Object-Oriented Software*. Addison Wesley, Massachusetts, 1994.

[15] James Gosling, Bill Joy, and Guy Steele. *The Java Language Specification*. Addison Wesley, 1996.

[16] Christian Grothoff, Jens Palsberg, and Jan Vitek. Encapsulating Objects with Confined Types. In *OOPSLA 2001 Conference on Object-Oriented Programming, Systems, Languages, and Applications, Tampa, Florida*, pages 241–253, 2001.

[17] Martin E. Nordberg III. Variations of the Visitor Pattern. 1996.

[18] Gregor Kiczales, Erik Hilsdale, Jim Hugunin, Mik Kersten, Jeffrey Palm, and William G. Griswold. An Overview of AspectJ. *Lecture Notes in Computer Science*, 2072:327–355, 2001.

[19] Shriram Krishnamurthi, Matthias Felleisen, and Daniel P. Friedman. Synthesizing Object-Oriented and Functional Design to Promote Re-use. *Lecture Notes in Computer Science*, 1445:91–113, 1998.

[20] M. Naik and R. Kumar. Efficient message dispatch in object-oriented systems. volume 35(3) of *ACM SIGPLAN Notices*, pages 49–58. ACM, March 2000.

[21] Nathaniel Nystrom, Michael R. Clarkson, and Andrew C. Myers. Polyglot: An Extensible Compiler Framework for Java. In *Compiler Construction 2003, LNCS 2622, Warsaw, Poland*, pages 138–152, 2003.

[22] M. Odersky and P. Wadler. Pizza into Java: Translating Theory into Practice. In *Proceedings of the 24th ACM Symposium on Principles of Programming Languages (POPL'97), Paris, France*, pages 146–159. ACM Press, New York (NY), USA, 1997.

[23] Johan Ovlinger and Mitchell Wand. A Language for Specifying Traversals of Object Structures. Technical report, College of Computer Science, Northeastern University, Boston, MA, November 1998.

[24] OVM Consortium. http://www.ovmj.org/. 2002.

[25] Krzysztof Palacz, Jason Baker, Chapman Flack, Christian Grothoff, Hiroshi Yamauchi, and Jan Vitek. Engineering a Customizable Intermediate Representation. In *ACM SIGPLAN 2003 Workshop on Interpreters, Virtual Machines and Emulators (IVME 2003)*. ACM SIGPLAN, 2003.

[26] Jens Palsberg and C. Barry Jay. The Essence of the Visitor Pattern. In *Proc. 22nd IEEE Int. Computer Software and Applications Conf., COMPSAC*, pages 9–15, 1998.

[27] B. Stroustrup. Multiple Inheritance for C++. In *Proceedings of the Spring 1987 European Unix Users Group Conference*, Helsinki, 1987.

[28] Matthias Zenger and Martin Odersky. Implementing Extensible Compilers. In *Workshop on Multiparadigm Programming with Object-Oriented Languages*, Budapest, Hungary, June 2001.

[29] Yoav Zibin and Joseph (Yossi) Gil. Fast Algorithm for Creating Space Efficient Dispatching Tables with Application to Multi-Dispatching. In *OOPSLA 2002 Conference on Object-Oriented Programming, Systems, Languages, and Applications, Seattle, Washington*, pages 142–160, 2002.

A   Micro-Benchmarks: One to 200 Visit Methods

In this appendix the results for the micro-benchmarks that were shown for one to twenty visit methods in figures 12, 13, 14 and 15 are repeated, just this time for one to 200 visit methods. Note that a different y-scale is used for the flat and the deep hierarchy.

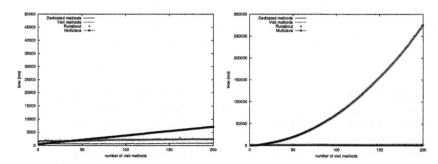

Fig. 19. Sun JDK 1.4.1 with flat (left) and deep (right) hierarchy

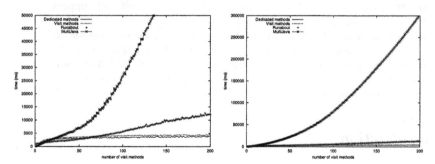

Fig. 20. IBM JDK 1.4.1 with flat (left) and deep (right) hierarchy

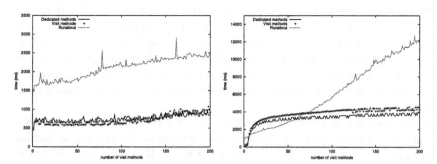

Fig. 21. SUN (left) and IBM (right), flat hierarchy without MultiJava

MX: Mobile Object Exchange
for Collaborative Applications*

Liuba Shrira and Hong Tian

Department of Computer Science
Brandeis University
Waltham, Massachusetts 02454, USA
liuba@brandeis.edu hongtian@cs.brandeis.edu

Abstract. MX is a new mobile caching system for collaborative applications accessing data residing in large storage repositories. MX supports *mobile exchange* − a direct user-to-user object transfer. Mobile exchange (MX) makes mobile computing more effective because it enables certain kinds of collaborative work that would be impossible otherwise. MX allows disconnected peers to learn of recent unknown updates, and to apply these updates to locally-cached data. MX validates the exchange, merging the more recent and modified data. MX combines efficient support for coarse-grained data transfer with efficient fine-grained validation, in a way that avoid the problem of false sharing. Performance evaluation of the MX prototype indicates that for transactional applications, the extra cost required to support mobile exchange is moderate. Moreover, the extra cost is offset by the cost of accessing remote repositories over high-latency networks.

1 Introduction

As mobile computing becomes more pervasive, users expect levels of data consistency and integrity that are not supported by current systems.

Disconnected access to consistent shared files is by now a well-understood problem [29]. Mobile users manipulate locally-cached copies of files and periodically validate their changes against the "master copy" of the file stored at the server. Validation encompasses two problems: first, detecting conflicts, which usually is done with timestamps on files, and second, reconciliation of conflicts which is usually done in an application specific way (sometimes by just asking the user).

Disconnected access becomes a harder problem if the shared persistent data is not files but instead consists of many small component objects, e.g. molecular structures or construction designs manipulated by CAD applications. Since the component objects can be small, much smaller than files, its is not feasible to associate a timestamp with each small modified object. Putting timestamp on

---

* This research is supported in part by the National Science Foundation (CCR-9901699).

L. Cardelli (Ed.): ECOOP 2003, LNCS 2743, pp. 126–150, 2003.

coarser grain objects, such as physical memory pages, creates the problem of *false sharing* when accesses to unrelated objects appear to conflict because they occur on the same physical page. Fine-grained validation techniques that avoid the problem of false sharing in disconnected systems are subject of ongoing research [9, 10, 25, 43].

The contribution of this paper is to extend the validation and reconciliation techniques to systems that support *mobile exchange*, the ability of a user to acquire missing and more recent versions of shared data directly from another user while disconnected from the master copy. Mobile exchange makes mobile computing more useful because it allows to accomplish collaborative work that would be impossible otherwise.

Consider a design team from a large engineering firm visiting a client company. The team is preparing a presentation using the design documents for an initial proposal. The design documents are cached on laptops, while the master copies are stored at the firm's home repositories. Part-way through the visit, the team needs to revise the proposal, incorporating design elements from a laptop of another team member. The team needs to change the design and merge the changes in a safe and coherent way. The modifications need eventually to be propagated to the home repository. The problem is the team does not have connectivity to the repository servers.

Direct data exchange would allow the team to prepare a revised proposal using the laptop copies of the data while disconnected. Fine-grained validation and reconciliation would avoid false conflicts upon reconnection, and multi-object atomicity would ensure that all the modifications are installed atomically, avoiding the potential danger of creating an inconsistent set of data objects in the presence of conflicts and independent reconciliation actions [24]. No mobile storage system today provides all these features. Peer-to-peer replication systems that support direct data exchange either use "update anywhere" replication that allows replicas to diverge [24], or require (for validation) a complete replica of the storage system to be available at each peer, ruling out large systems [27, 32, 42]. Master-copy systems, such as databases [24, 25], or file systems [38], that do not require full-replication, provide no support for direct data exchange between users.

MX is a new mobile caching system for collaborative applications accessing large-scale object storage systems. It allows mobile users to exchange complex data in an efficient way, supports fine-grained validation and coarse-grained reconciliation, and insures that a consistent copy of the persistent objects exists at all times at designated storage system servers (called *base nodes*). MX presents two main technical challenges. One challenge is to balance direct object exchange with transactional consistency in disconnected operation. Another is to support fine-grained updates without introducing false sharing penalties.

False sharing is universally recognized to be a problem in multiprocessor and distributed shared memory systems [19, 7, 20]. But is false sharing a problem for mobile systems? We think that false sharing will become more of a problem for mobile systems for several reasons. One reason is that with mobile computing entering mainstream, users expect their desktop applications to follow them wherever they go. Adapting existing applications to mobile environment is attractive to avoid the cost of re-writing applications from scratch. When modern object-oriented languages, e.g. Java, are used to program persistent object applications, however, it is hard to ensure that non-conflicting accesses do not end up on the same physical page. Moreover, hardware trends indicate that page sizes are likely to grow while object sizes are unlikely to change much. Furthermore, in a disconnected system, the likelihood of conflicting read/write accesses increases as users disconnect for long time periods.

MX has a simple architecture that combines a disconnected client/server system and cooperative caching [13, 18, 22, 45]. Persistent objects are stored in highly-available and reliable repository servers in data centers interconnected by high-bandwidth networks. Less reliable machines, e.g. laptops or PDAs, run disconnected client applications on cached copies of the persistent objects. Like other disconnected storage systems, MX uses optimistic concurrency control [4, 35]. A disconnected client commits tentative transactions on cached data. Upon reconnection, the tentative transactions are validated and, in the case of a conflict, aborted or reconciled. Disconnected mobile clients form ad-hoc groups that support mobile exchange of data. In a mobile exchange, a client (the helper) provides missing or more current physical pages to a collaborating client (the requester). Since the requester may have read stale objects, the requester validates his tentative transactions against the newer data and merges new and modified pages. The requester manages the bookkeeping needed to commit upon reconnection the modifications based on exchanged data. MX validation protocols are efficient. The mobile exchange uses a fast coarse-grained validation, falling back to the more expansive fine-grained validation when coarse-grained validation fails. In contrast, the reconnection protocol takes advantage of the invalidations available at the base servers, providing low-cost, fine-grained validation.

To evaluate our techniques, we have implemented an MX prototype and carried out a cost benefit analysis of the mobile exchange performance for a range of shared workloads and a range of ad-hoc network configurations. Preliminary results indicate that the extra cost required to support mobile exchange in a transactional storage system is moderate. Moreover, this extra cost is offset by the cost of accessing remote repository servers over high-latency networks. Nonetheless, some of the mobile exchange benefits can not be quantified. When nearby collaborators can communicate over an ad-hoc network, and have no connectivity to the repository servers, MX enables to accomplish work that would be impossible in other systems.

2   Related Work

Work on cooperative caching systems considers client-to-client access to shared read-only data [13, 18, 22] or shared mutable data [3, 8, 45]. These systems provide direct exchange of data in connected operation.

Recent work in peer-to-peer storage systems, for example [12, 44], considers server side architectures. These systems provide scalable and reliable access to content-addressable shared data and provide limited support for mutable data.

Update-anywhere replication systems support peer-to-peer exchange of shared mutable objects. Many of the approaches utilize the epidemic model [6, 14, 15, 31, 36, 41]. Some of the systems [41] use an optimistic reconciliation-based approach that works in non-transactional single-object domains such as file systems. These approaches only provide weak eventual consistency semantics. Bayou and Lazy Replication [15, 36] take a more pessimistic approach that ensures that all committed updates are serialized in the same order at all replicas using a primary-copy scheme, but they require (for validation) a complete replica of the storage system to be available at each peer, limiting the applicability to small-scale systems. As pointed out by analysis in Gray [24], the traditional update-anywhere approaches suffer from replica divergence as reconciliation fails at individual replicas due to read/write conflicts. Some of the more recent update anywhere replication schemes [6, 27, 32] avoid the replica divergence problem using epidemic quorum techniques that provide strong multi-object consistency and serializability. However, like other epidemic approaches, they require full replication.

Many traditional mobile storages systems in the literature and popular commercial products are based on the client server master copy approach. For example, mobile access to a distributed file system is provided in Coda [33] and Little Work [28] systems, isolation-only transactions for files are considered in [38], The Rover [30] system provides mobile access to general objects, mobile access to persistent objects is described in [9, 10, 25]. A comprehensive survey of existing systems can be found in [29]. These systems provide a consistent master version at the servers but provide no support for client-to-client data exchange.

Oceanstore [34] is a global storage system that deals with access to shared mobile data in wide-area network environment. The architecture is based on nomadic cache pools, similar to MX cache groups, and primary servers. Like MX, Oceanstore uses optimistic concurrency control at the servers to provide strict consistency for persistent data, and a transactional cache consistency protocol [21] in cache pools. Oceanstore does not consider complex data and fine-grained validation.

3   MX

The MX wide-area mobile storage system consists of connected (immobile) base nodes, and mobile collaborating nodes. The base nodes, located in secure data centers connected by high-bandwidth networks, provide reliable and highly-available disk storage for the master versions of persistent objects. A persistent object is owned by a single base node. Since objects may be small (order of 100 bytes for programming language objects [37]), objects on disk are clustered into physical pages. The mobile nodes run client applications accessing the cached copies of the persistent objects. Earlier studies in object storage systems(e.g. [16])

show that for small objects, page-based client caching and page-based transfer from server provide a significant performance advantage compared to single object transfer. Mobile MX client nodes therefore fetch pages from the base nodes and cache pages locally.

The client population is dynamic but not changing fast since access to the shared persistent storage system requires an authenticated account. Mobile client nodes dynamically form collaborating groups, interacting at a close range. We expect a typical group size not to exceed 5-10 clients, smaller groups being the common case. The mobile nodes have the networking capability that allows them to communicate among themselves, and are not limited by the cache capacity.

A typical MX storage system is large: it serves a distributed organization with many branches and mobile employees, such as a large medical research company, or an engineering design firm. Given current technology trends, we expect the system assumptions to be the norm in such organizations.

Before disconnecting from the base nodes, a mobile node pre-loads the cache with up-to-date copies of the master versions of the persistent objects of interest. Techniques similar to hoarding [33] and prefetch queries [25] can be used to assist pre-loading but since the storage system is large, it is not feasible for the mobile nodes to cache the entire storage system.

While disconnected, a mobile node runs tentative transactions accessing the local copies of the cached objects. A tentative transaction records intention to commit, and allows a client to start up a next transaction. Tentative commits lead to "dependent commits" [25, 38, 39]: transaction $T2$ *depends* on $T1$ if it uses objects modified by $T1$ because if $T1$ ultimately aborts so must $T2$. A tentative commit that is not a "dependent commit", defines an "independent action" [23]: a transaction $T2$ that does not use objects modified by $T1$ can commit even if $T1$ ultimately aborts.

At any time the mobile node has access to two cached data versions: a local version and a best-known master version. A tentative transaction updates the local version of the cached data, and generates a standard log record containing modified and new object values to be committed, read and write object sets used for validation, along with undo records that allow to reset the objects to the pre-transaction state. A tentative transaction never modifies the best-known master version.

3.1   Mobile Exchange

A disconnected mobile node can join another mobile peer (or peers) to form a mobile collaborating group. The group *join* protocol identifies the most recent master versions of data available in a group, and notifies the peers with out-of-date versions. A peer (the requester) receiving a notification about an out-of-date versions, reads in the pages from the peer with the most recent master version (the helper) and executes a *catch-up* protocol.

If requesters' transaction has read an outdated master version, it needs to abort. The *catch-up* protocol validates the requesters' tentative transactions against the more recent versions of the data and, if needed, uses the requesters' tentative commit log to undo or reconcile transaction modifications, and install the newer master versions. The requester can then redo the aborted transactions, committing new tentative transactions.

While running within a mobile group, a peer may discover it needs access to an object it does not have. If another peer in the group has a version of this object, the *acquire* protocol provides the missing object directly from that peer. As with catch-up, the acquire protocol provides the best-known master version.

Currently MX only supports the exchange of committed versions. The exchange of uncommitted versions makes the system significantly more complicated. Specifically, it introduces non-local "dependent commits" that reduce the availability of the master versions in mobile environments. Under certain specialized circumstances, exchange of uncommitted changes may be useful, but under most other circumstances the benefits remain unproven. For now, we believe it is more important to support conflict detection and roll-back because these services complement the kind of manual coordination (synchronization) one would expect in collaborative groups.

A mobile node reconnects to the base nodes to commit the tentative transactions. The base nodes validate the transactions using an optimistic concurrency control protocol that checks if a transaction has read the most recent version of the master copies [4]. A tentative transaction that passes validation creates new durable versions of the modified master copies. A transaction that fails validation is aborted at the mobile node that has generated it, and is undone or reconciled. After all the tentative transactions that pass validation commit, the mobile node synchronizes its cache with the base nodes by fetching up-to-date master versions. The tentative transactions that were aborted and undone, can be redone at this point, while the node is connected, or alternatively, redone as tentative transactions after the node disconnects.

3.2 Validation

Keeping track of individual object versions could introduce high system overheads when objects are small. Fetching single objects from a peer during mobile exchange, could increase the cost of communication. Similarly, checking for the most recent master versions of all cached objects in a mobile group, could increase the cost of the mobile exchange. MX addresses this granularity problem by keeping track of page versions. Nevertheless, since the applications modify individual objects rather then entire pages, it is important to avoid the penalty of false sharing. To deal with this problem, MX adds fine-grained validation procedures at mobile exchange and at reconnection.

The mobile exchange protocol identifies page-level conflicts using page versions and then checks objects read from an outdated page by performing a bitwise comparison with the objects in the new page. The approach resembles the adaptive granularity validation schemes [40, 47].

The reconnection protocol takes advantage of the object invalidations available at the servers. The invalidation-based protocol is adapted from [4] and works as follows. Base node directories keep track of which pages are cached at which nodes. When a transaction modifying an object on a page commits, object invalidations are generated for the mobile peers caching that page. When a peer reconnects to validate tentative transactions, the base nodes use the pending object invalidations to check the read sets of the tentative transactions. The invalidations generated for a mobile node are retained at the base node until the mobile node reconnects and completes validation. This assumes mobile nodes reconnect before the resources for retaining invalidations are depleted.

Certain invalidations must be transitive. When a mobile helper node provides a requester with a page the requester does not have, the base node must retain object invalidations for the requester as well. When the helper provides such a page to the requester, it registers this fact, and informs the base node upon reconnection. If the requester node has not yet reconnected, the base node retains the object invalidations until it does.

When peers exchange master versions, persistent objects could get corrupted by a careless peer that scribbles over the cached MX objects. To avoid corrupted objects, master versions can contain embedded checksums created and signed by the base nodes when the new versions of pages are committed. Requesters can verify the checksums for pages they obtain from the helpers in catch-up and acquire requests. Incremental techniques described in [46] can be used to update the checksums inexpensively at commit time, without requiring access to the entire modified page.

Note that because only committed page versions are exchanged, peer group management, i.e. peer node joins and leaves do not interfere with the base transactional system correctness. Appendix A summarizes MX protocol correctness invariants. The invariants guarantee that MX combined with the base invalidation-based protocol [4] provides transaction serializability.

3.3   Undo, Redo and Reconcile

Like other optimistic systems, MX applications need to deal with transactions that abort due to conflicts. The general approach works as follows. When MX detects a serializability conflict, it identifies to the application the actions that violate serializability. Sometimes the application's actions can be undone and redone, and sometimes not. When undo and redo is possible, MX rolls back the object state, invalidates the stale objects, and returns control to the application to redo the transaction. Otherwise, if the action cannot be undone, the application asks the user to compensate in an application-appropriate way.

Applications receive a two levels of support from MX. The MX system itself provides conflict detection in terms of read and write sets, and it provides the ability to restore an earlier pre-transaction state. In addition, MX stores application-specific information provided by the application that identifies the application-level actions associated with each tentative transaction, e.g. the application may identify to MX the portion of the application log recording application operations. The application, however, is responsible for logging the application-level actions associated with the tentative transaction, and for re-executing them if the transaction needs to be redone. The application can also specify to MX when automatic undo and redo is not possible, and interaction with the user is needed. During validation, MX examines each tentative commit record for conflicts. If a tentatively committed transaction has read stale data, MX informs the application, which allows the application to retrieve the application-level actions based on the stale data. Application can choose an appropriate redo action, or a compensating action in place of an undo followed by a redo. For example, the application may consult the user. The comprehensive treatment of application-specific techniques for collaborative redo and reconciliation is outside the scope of this paper. In the rest of the paper we restrict the discussion to applications where undo and redo are appropriate.

Validation and reconciliation can occur under two distinct circumstances: at mobile exchange between disconnected peers, and at reconnection between a mobile host and the base node server. As explained above, disconnected validation produces tentative (non-durable) transactions, which are ultimately validated at reconnection. At reconnection, by contrast, validation produces durable transactions. Similarly, mobile exchange time reconciliation actions are tentative, while reconnection time reconciliation actions are durable.

3.4 Workloads

MX supports peer group access to shared objects. The benefits of MX depend on the patterns of object sharing in the workload. We consider the workloads where we expect MX to be beneficial and workloads where MX offers no benefit. In a disconnected transactional system, obtaining missing shared objects from peers may not be beneficial if peer accesses are conflicting since the tentative transactions accessing the shared object will fail validation and will abort. However, in closely collaborating groups it is more likely that read-write sharing can be manually coordinated by the peers themselves, so that conflicts can be avoided. Nevertheless, for application workloads that exhibit high rates of conflicting accesses, we do not expect MX to be beneficial.

Catch-up allows a peer to obtain more recent objects available at another peer. Catch-up may be expensive if a modifying transaction T at the requester peer has read the outdated page version. In this case validation requires to perform bitwise comparison of objects read from outdated pages, and catch-up potentially requires undo and redo of the modifying tentative transactions. If peer coordination can establish that the requester needs the more recent objects, the undo is not wasted and avoids future aborts.

On the other hand, if peer coordination can establish that the requester transaction T that has read objects from an outdated page has seen up-to-date values (since these objects have not been modified in the more recent page version), the requester can refuse the fine-grained validation and avoid the cost of bitwise comparison. In this case, the fine-grained validation at reconnection time would allow the tentative transaction T to pass validation if T indeed did not read stale objects, and would abort T if it did.

4   Implementation

This section provides some of the MX protocol implementation details. We describe the basic support for disconnected operation, the mobile exchange, and connected and disconnected validation.

MX uses the Thor client/server object-oriented database [37] extended to support disconnected operation as the base storage system. Thor is a good choice because it provides transactional (ACID) storage for objects, supports optimistic concurrency control, supports pages and provides high performance in distributed environments [37].

4.1   Base Storage System

This section outlines the relevant components of the Thor architecture. Thor servers provide persistent storage for objects, clients cache copies of these objects. Applications run at the clients and interact with the system by making calls on methods of cached objects. All method calls occur within atomic transactions. Clients communicate with servers to fetch pages or to commit a transaction.

The servers have a disk for storing persistent objects, a stable transaction log, and volatile memory. The disk is organized as a set of pages which are the units of disk access. The stable log holds commit information and object modifications for committed transactions. The server memory contains cache directory that keeps track of which pages are cached by which clients.

Transactions are serialized using optimistic concurrency control [4]. The client keeps track of objects that are read and modified by its transaction; it sends this information, along with new copies of modified objects, to the servers when it tries to commit the transaction. The servers determine whether the commit is possible, using a two-phase commit protocol if the transaction used objects at multiple servers. If the transaction commits, the new copies of modified objects are appended to the stable log and eventually propagated to the disk.

Since objects are not locked before being used, a transaction commit can cause caches to contain obsolete objects. Servers will abort a transaction that used obsolete objects. However, to reduce the probability of aborts, servers notify connected clients when their objects become obsolete by sending them *invalidation* messages; a server uses its directory and the information about the committing transaction to determine what invalidation messages to send. Invalidation messages are small because they simply identify obsolete objects. Furthermore, they are sent in the background, batched and piggybacked on other messages.

When a client receives an invalidation message, it removes obsolete objects from its cache and aborts the current transaction if it used them. The client continues to retain pages containing invalidated objects; these pages are now *incomplete* with "holes" in place of the invalidated objects. Performing invalidation on an object basis means that false sharing does not cause unnecessary aborts; keeping incomplete pages in the client cache means that false sharing does not lead to unnecessary cache misses. Invalidation messages prevent some aborts, and accelerate those that must happen — thus wasting less work and offloading detection of aborts from servers to clients.

Clients acknowledge all invalidations. The transaction validation protocol treats an acknowledgement as an indication that stale data has been removed from the cache and therefore will not be read by a transaction. Like invalidations, acknowledgements are sent in the background, batched and piggybacked on other messages.

When a transaction aborts, its client restores the cached copies of modified objects to the state they had before the transaction started; this is possible because a client makes a copy of an object the first time it is modified by a transaction.

4.2 Disconnected Operation

To support disconnected operation, we extended Thor to deal with disconnected cache management and tentative commit. The design uses the object management techniques similar to [11] adapted for MX. When a mobile node disconnects it preloads the cache with the most recent copies of the pages potentially needed by the user. Since the storage system can be very large, disconnected cache misses can not be eliminated entirely. Such a miss results in transaction abort and exception propagated to the user.

While disconnected, client applications run tentative transactions that modify the cached copies of pages. When an application issues a commit, the system adds a commit record to the tentative transaction log maintained at the mobile node. The record identifies all the objects read, modified, and created by this transaction, and contains the modified and newly created object values. The commit record also includes the application-level information for dealing with transaction aborts as discussed in section 3.3.

To abort a transaction, the client has to undo the modification made by this transaction, and by all the dependent tentative transactions that read objects modified by this transaction. The client uses the tentative commit log as follows. The value of an object that has been modified by an aborted transaction is restored to the value committed by the most recent preceding tentative transaction in the log. If no such transaction was committed, the value is restored to the value in the most recent master version.

Upon reconnection to the base, MX client sends the tentative commit log records one by one to commit at the server. The client maintains a list of objects undone by aborted transactions so far (undone list). It checks this list against the read and write sets in each subsequent tentative transaction commit record before sending the record for validation to a base node. If an object *read* by the transaction is in the undo list, the transaction is aborted and its modifications are undone; if an object *modified* by the aborted transaction is already in undone list, this value has already been undone and therefore no further undo is needed since the cache contains the correct value.

After the entire tentative transaction log is validated, the client acknowledges all the invalidations sent by the base, re-fetches the invalidated pages. At this point the client interacts with the application in order to redo the aborted transactions using the application level redo information provided by the application.

4.3 Versions

A disconnected mobile peer node can provide pages to other peer nodes. Page version numbers allow the peers to determine which node has the the most recent version of a page. When a version of a page is modified for the first time by a tentative transaction, a clean (unmodified) version stays in an auxiliary cache. Only the clean version of a page are provided to another peer.

The page version numbers are updated by the base node each time a transaction commits modifications to the page. Page version numbers are included with the read sets in the commit records clients send to the base nodes for validation to identify the page version numbers from which the transaction read the objects.

When a mobile node disconnects, the cache directories at the base node keep track of the versions of pages cached in the mobile node at time of disconnection. In addition, object invalidations have the page version number created at the commit time associated with them. If a transaction has read an object from version l and there is pending invalidation for this object associated with page version k, $k > l$, the transaction has read a stale object.

4.4 Catch-Up

If a peer discovers that a more recent version of a page it caches is available at a nearby peer, the client requests the page and performs catch-up. If the client has not read the outdated page, the catch-up requires no additional work except reading in the page.

Note however, that since the page versions can increase in the client cache during disconnected operation without the base node knowing this, the client needs to have enough information to determine at reconnection time what were the page version numbers from which a tentative transaction has read. The mapping *TransactionToPage* provides this information. To maintain the mapping, the client first records the initial snapshot of the version numbers corresponding to the cached pages at disconnection time, and then records in the corresponding position in the tentative transaction log the version numbers corresponding to pages acquired from the peers. At reconnect time, the validation procedure uses *TransactionToPage* mapping to reconstruct the correct version numbers for objects read by the transaction and sends them to the base node with the commit record.

At catch-up time, MX validates the tentative transactions that have read or modified outdated pages and the dependent transactions. If a tentative modifying transaction has read an outdated page, it may have read stale objects and modifications may need to abort. On the other hand, if the modified objects read from outdated page were not stale, the newly arrived page needs to be updated to reflect the tentative modifications.

The mapping *PageToTransaction* determines the earliest tentative transaction in the tentative log that has read or modified a given page. To perform fine-grained catch-up validation, the client scans the log from the earliest transaction that read an outdated page. Client performs a bitwise comparison of an object that was read from the page (using the master version of the outdated page in case the object has been modified by later transactions) comparing it to the object in the new page version. If the object have changed, transaction gets aborted together with the dependent transactions. If the bits have not changed, the newer version of the page and the modifications are merged.

In the case when the bitwise comparison provides a false negative, i.e. no change is detected in the bits because the object has been modified and later reset to the same value, the connected validation procedure using invalidations will detect the conflict since the mapping *TransactionToPage* reconstructs at commit time the actual version number of the page from which the transaction read.

After undoing the aborted tentative transactions, the system interacts with the application to redo the aborted transactions using the information provided by the application as explained in Section 3.3. The new portion of the log, generated for the redone transactions, includes the appropriate new page version numbers records.

Compared to the invalidation-based reconnection-time validation at the base server, the disconnected validation introduces the cost of bitwise object comparison and page merging. The cost depends on the workload, specifically, the number of the different objects read and modified on outdated pages, and the sizes of the objects.

4.5   Acquire

A cache miss at one peer in a group can be served by acquiring the page from another peer cache. Since the base node cache directory is unaware of the acquired page, to support fine-grained validation for the transactions that access such an acquired page, the client maintains information on sending and acquiring missing pages and reports this information to the base nodes at the reconnect time. This information is used to efficiently generate invalidations for the acquired missing pages and to garbage collect the invalidations when they are no longer needed.

4.6   Object Creation and Deletion

Object creation and deletion can present a problem for disconnected protocols [36]. We briefly consider how creation and deletion interacts with the mobile exchange. MX follows the proposal in [11] for disconnected object creation and deletion. New objects created by a disconnected MX client only become persistent when committed at the base servers. Since in MX uncommitted data is never provided in a mobile exchange, object creation poses no additional issues for MX.

Objects are never explicitly deleted in MX because, as in Thor, MX uses the persistence by reachability model and relies on a transactional garbage collector to reclaim the free storage. An object, unreachable in the persistent object graph, may become tentatively persistent if a disconnected client commits a tentative transaction that creates a reference to it. Therefore, the garbage collector considers all objects cached in disconnected clients to be the roots of garbage collection. To support mobile exchange, the garbage collector needs to track where objects are cached. It uses the page tracking technique similar to the one used by the validation protocol to generate invalidations. The disconnected garbage collector has not been implemented yet.

4.7   Hooking Up with a Peer

To hook-up with a collaborating peer, a node starts up a connector module that runs a simple discovery procedure that lets the client to join an existing group, or start a new group. The discovery procedure makes use of the INS intentional naming system [2]. The details of the discovery protocol, and of the group management protocol dealing with client joins and leaves, are omitted for lack of space.

The connector module, available in each peer, coordinates the page transfers for catch-up and acquire. At the hook-up time a peer sends its page table with the version numbers to the connector who compares the version numbers and sends out to each peer the list of pages available for catch-up. A peer with an outdated version reads in the more recent versions by fetching them via the connector module. Hook-up cost increases with the group size, but for the small groups typical in MX, we do not expect the cost to be significant.

To support page acquire, the connector maintains a directory of pages available in the peer group. While a peer runs connected to a group a cache miss experienced by a peer reaches the connector, and if the missing page is available in the directory, the request is forwarded to the helping peer. This scheme is very similar to one used in the BuddyCache [8] system.

5   Performance Evaluation

We have implemented an MX prototype and conducted a performance study to evaluate the costs and benefits of mobile exchange, the novel feature in MX. Our experiments highlight a collaborative situation when a mobile team operates far away from base servers because this is the typical environment MX is designed for. Nevertheless, an MX client sometimes needs to run in a non-collaborative situation. To support mobile exchange, MX introduces extra mechanism at the mobile peer nodes and the base nodes. We evaluate the cost of the extra mechanism a client needs to pay in MX for being mobile exchange enabled.

In a collaborative situation mobile exchange can provide a benefit that can not be measured: the ability to obtain data and continue work while disconnected. However, mobile exchange can also provide a performance benefit that can be measured: fetching missing or more recent data from a nearby peer, instead of reconnecting to the remote repository. The benefit is similar to cooperative caching but, because of the validation, the overheads are different. We evaluate this benefit.

The evaluation compares the performance of MX to the performance of a mobile transactional object storage system without the mobile exchange (Mobile). To evaluate the overheads, we analyze the costs of MX protocol components and consider the effect of varying sharing in the workload. To evaluate the benefits, we compare the time it takes to complete a task using MX and Mobile in different peer network confgurations.

The results indicate that in a transactional object storage system the extra cost required to support mobile exchange and fine-grain validation is moderate. Furthermore, the extra cost is offset by the cost of accessing the base repository when network latency is high.

5.1   Experimental Setup

The experiments use two system configurations: the *MX* system runs our implementation of MX protocols in Thor system, extended to support disconnected operation as described in Section 4.2, the *Mobile* system runs Thor extended to support disconnected operation but without the support for mobile exchange.

Unfortunately, there is no standard benchmark available for collaborative systems at this time. We are considering to develop such a benchmark in our future work. Our workloads are based on the multi-user OO7 benchmark [17]; this benchmark is intended to capture the characteristics of complex data in many different CAD/CAM/CASE applications, but does not model any specific application. We use OO7 because it allows to control the sharing of complex data and because it is a standard benchmark for measuring object storage system performance. Appendix B contains a detailed decription of our implementation of the multi-user OO7 benchmark with the traversals T1 (read-only), T2a (read-write sparse modifications), and T2b (dense modifications).

Our experiments compare the performance costs of MX and Mobile when running tentative transactions, and validation, fetch and commit operations. These costs are determined by either the actions of a single peer or the interactions between two peers, the requester and the helper in MX, and a peer and a base node in Mobile. The costs are independent of the size of the collaborative group for the small group sizes expected in MX. We use therefore a system configurations containing a base node and two peers in our experiments.

The server (base node), and the two clients ran each on a 600MHz Intel Pentium III processor based PC, 128MB of memory, and Linux Red Hat 6.2. Unless otherwise specified, the clients were connected by a 100Mb/s Ethernet; the long distance connection to the base node used an estimated network latency of 70 msec (70 milliseconds) and 1 Mb/s connection approximating a cable modem. The OO7 database was stored on the server disk; in all the experiments the fetched data was cached in the server cache. The experiments ran in Utah experimental testbed emulab.net [1] on a dedicated, unloaded and isolated system.

5.2   Clean Versions

Compared to the Mobile system, MX requires extra space and CPU for the clean versions of modified pages, and extra space in the tentative transaction log to store the peer exchange records identifying page versions for the *TransactionToPage* mapping. The clean versions are by far the main space expense. The CPU cost of creating a clean copy of a page including the cost of page copy, and unswizzle references, averages 0.32 msec in our workloads.

5.3   Acquire

To evaluate the costs and benefits of acquiring missing objects using MX in wide-area environment, consider the scenario described in Section 1 where a team of design engineers (here called Mary and John), travels to present a design proposal to another company (called FarAway), and needs to revise the joint design. In MX, after coordinating the revision details, John acquires Mary's proposal data directly from Mary, and produces a draft modifying the documents to produce an internally consistent proposal. After the sales presentation, the proposal gets revised some more, until John returns home, reconnects to the repository and commits the revised version. In *Mobile*, the team actions are identical, except to acquire the proposal data, John fetches it remotely from the home repository. We compare the time to accomplish the task in MX and Mobile.

To model the above scenario in MX, Mary runs a cold T1 traversal (read-only) pre-loading her laptop before disconnecting. John disconnects without the objects. At the *FarAway* company site, it takes Mary and John time *HookUp* of 2 msec to hook up (i.e. send page tables to the connector and receive (empty) stale page lists), and it takes John time *MXCold* of 2.58 sec to run a cold T1 $(50, 0, 50, 0)$ traversal fetching from Mary missing objects contained in 1255 pages. To commit 100 tentative transactions running a hot T2a $(0, 50, 0, 50)$ traversal (sparse modifications), John needs time *HotTentative* of 35.01sec. T2a $(0, 50, 0, 50)$ single traversal takes 0.234 sec, single tentative commit 0.0989 sec. For comparison, T2b $(0, 50, 0, 50)$ traversal (dense modifications) takes 0.243 sec, tentative commit time 0.147 sec (not shown). Tentative commit is expensive in our (unoptimized) implementation of the disconnected system because it includes copying read and write sets, and object update and undo information into the log. We are working on optimizing these costs. To commit the modifications at home repository on a fast local network John executes the invalidation generation step that takes time *InvalGen* of 1.31 msec, and validates and commits in time *Commit* of 2.29 sec.

In the *Mobile* system, John reads in over the long distance network the project data in time *MobileCold* of 296.911 sec, runs 100 tentative T2a $(0, 50, 0, 50)$ transactions in time *HotTentative* of 33.29 sec, and validates and commits in time *Commit* of 2.29 sec. Running tentative transactions including modifications is more expensive in MX than in Mobile because of the cost of creating a clean version of a modified page. The reason it takes John such a long time to get Mary's objects in Mobile is that his application is acquiring the objects by faulting the missing pages synchronously. If the missing pages are known in advance, John can prefetch Mary's objects asynchronously in a pipeline constrained only by the bandwidth of the link to the base repository. Section 5.4 discusses pipelined fetching. Nevertheless, in general applications, dynamic prefetch is known to be a hard problem.

Table 1 summarizes the results. The results indicate that the overhead of acquiring missing objects including extra validation costs, slower tentative transactions and the cost of hookup, is offset by the cost of acquiring the missing objects from the home repository when the latency of access to the repository is high. Of course, in situations when the access to remote repository is impossible, this may be the only available choice.

5.4   Catch-Up

To evaluate the performance of catch-up, we consider a variation of the scenario where Mary and John are making collaborative changes at the *FarAway* company site. Mary loads shared proposal objects into her laptop, disconnects, and travels to the *FarAway* company. John stays behind, commits last minute modifications to the proposal in response to some late breaking news, and disconnects to travel to *FarAway*. At *FarAway*, when John informs Mary about his changes, he finds out Mary has already made some tentative modifications to the proposal. Mary suggests she gets John's modifications and they coordinate the next set of changes to prevent future conflicts.

In *MX*, Mary hooks up with John, performs catch-up with undo and redo since her changes were based on stale objects. In *Mobile*, to get *John's* modifications, *Mary* needs to reconnect to the base, abort the tentative transactions that accessed objects modified by John, refetch the modified pages, and redo her tentative modifications.

To model this scenario, in the *MX* experiment *Mary* runs cold T1 $(50, 0, 50, 0)$ traversal (read only) to pre-load cache before disconnecting. Then *John* runs connected T2a $(0, 0, 0, 100)$ transactions modifying the shared module and commits. At the *FarAway* site *Mary* commits 50 tentative transactions T2a $(40, 40, 10, 10)$ while running disconnected in time $HotTentative1$ of 15.64 sec. It takes Mary and John 11.49 msec to hook up and it takes Mary the time of $FetchMx$ of 0.76 sec to read in from *John* the 532 modified pages. It takes Mary time $ValidateMX$ of 4.61 sec to catch up. 24% of Mary's transactions get aborted in this workload. To redo her changes, Mary commits 12 tentative transactions T2a $(40, 40, 10, 10)$ while running disconnected in time $HotTentative2$ of 3.75 sec.

In *Mobile*, to obtain John's modifications, Mary needs to reconnect to the remote home repository. She receives invalidations, validates and aborts the tentative transactions that accessed stale pages modified by John(24% aborts) in time $ValidateMobile$ of 4.00 sec (local validation time). Mary fetches the 532 modified pages in time $FetchMobile$ of, 115.146 sec and re-executes and com-

Table 1. Costs of Acquire

Time (sec)	MX	MOBILE
MobileCold	0	296.911
HookUp	0.002	0
MXCold	2.58	0
HotTentative	35.01	33.29
InvalGen	0.00131	0
Commit	2.29	2.29

Table 2. Costs of catch-up

Time (sec)	MX	MOBILE
HotTentative1	15.64	15.64
ValidateMobile	0	4.00
HookUp	0.012	0
ValidateMX	4.61	0
FetchMX	0.76	0
FetchMobile	0	115.146(33.39 piped)
HotTentative2	3.75	3.75
Total	24.77	138.8(57.04 piped)

mits 12 tentative transactions T2a $(40, 40, 10, 10)$ while running disconnected in time $HotTentative2$ of 3.75 sec.

Here, unlike in the scenario in Section 5.3, Mary could easily pipeline fetches of the invalidated pages, since the list of invalidated pages is known after the validation and abort. We do not measure pipelined fetches because our system currently supports only a limited form of prefetch in the form of clustered pages that takes advantage of object clustering for both fetching from a peer ($FetchMX$) and from base ($FetchMobile$). The pipelined fetch costs for Mobile, computed assuming a 1 Mb/s cable modem are included for comparison. Table 2 summarizes the results.

Validation Costs. Table 3 breaks down the MX catch-up costs ($ValidateMX$ in table 2). These are read set check ($WithBitwiseCompare$), including checks against the set of undone objects $(2, 283, 816$ objects checked) and bitwise comparison for objects read from the stale pages (0.257 sec for $276, 385$ objects checked); undo of aborted transactions using the log ($Undo$); tracking committed modifications on new pages (CollectUpdates), and merging the modifications with the new pages ($Merge$). To avoid repeated swizzling, unmodified objects (that did not change size) are currently merged from the new page into the old swizzled page. Read set check dominates the catch-up cost; the check against the undone objects beeing the main cost in this workload.

Table 4 breaks down the validation with base costs ($ValidateMobile$ in Table 2) that include read set check $WithInvalidations$ against the invalidations of the cached shared pages, and against the set of undone objects; and undo of the aborted transactions using the log ($Undo$). The $Undo$ costs in Mobile and MX are different, because MX uses a somewhat different undo protocol that takes advantage of merging. As in MX, the read set check dominates the validation cost.

Sharing. When transactions access many objects, failed validation (with undo and merge) may take less time than successful validation since detection of a conflict terminates the remaining check, while successful validation completes the

Table 3. Validation with a Peer

Validation Action	Time(sec)
WithBitwiseCompare	4.41
CollectUpates	0.014
Merge	0.13
Undo	0.0044
Other	0.052
Total	4.61

Table 4. Validation with Base

Validation Action	Time(sec)
WithInvalidations	3.98
Undo	0.0061
Other	0.014
Total	4.00

entire read set check. Figure 1 shows this trend as conflict rate increases for workloads with sparse (T2a) and dense (T2b) modifications for validation with base (*Mobile*) and peer (*MX*). Validation costs are higher for T2b because of larger undo sets and increased undo cost. Validation cost increases initially, because for low abort rates the size of the undo set dominates the cost of the validation. As abort rate increases, the benefit of avoided checks due to aborts dominates the total validation cost.

In above experiments the difference between the validation cost with a peer and with a base is small. In general, the difference between validation with peer and with base may depend on the page clustering and the amount of false sharing in the workload, parameters that are not directly controlled in the standart 007 benchmark.

To evaluate the effect of false sharing, we created a modifed 007 database and two new traversals derived from T2b. In the modified datatabase, the atomic parts and conections in a composite part are numbered and connected in a way that allows the new traversal $T2b_{odd}$ ($T2b_{even}$) to only read and modify the odd (even) atomic parts. In the scenario with John and Mary in Table 2, when John commits modifications to the database using $T2b_{odd}$ traversal, and disconnected Mary concurrently runs tentative $T2b_{even}$ traversals, the transactions do not conflict but the workload contains false sharing since the odd and even parts share the same pages. Figure 2 compares the time it takes Mary to validate with John in MX, and with base in Mobile, after Mary commits 50 tentative $T2b_{even}$ transactions. The experiment measures validation costs for different amount of false sharing by controlling in the validation procedure for a fixed size transaction read set, the percentage of objects Mary reads and writes on pages modified by John. Note, that validation costs here differ from ones in Table 2 because a tentative T2a transaction reads more and modifies less objects then the tentative $T2b_{even}$ ($T2b_{odd}$) transactions ($T2b_{odd}$ reads $1,406,203$ objects and modifies $61,470$ objects on 1199 pages). The cost of validation increases for both Mobile and MX as more objects are read and modified on pages containing false sharing since more objects need invalidation-based checks in Mobile and bitwise comparison checks in MX. The cost of the check against the undo set and the coarse-grain check against modified pages performed for the entire read-set is the same in Mobile and MX and is fixed in this experiment since the read-set size is fixed. The invalidation check cost is higher then bitwise comparison

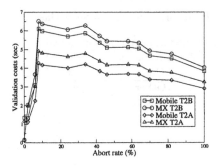

Fig. 1. Workloads with aborts   **Fig. 2.** Workloads with false sharing

and update merge cost when many objects are checked and invalidation sets
are large since merge costs do not increase as more objects are modified in our
implementation. Overall, the experiment indicates that for OO7 workloads with
and without false sharing, the cost of validation with the peer is comparable to
the invalidation-based validation with the base.

5.5 Performance Benefit

The performance benefit of fetching from peer instead of base depends on peer
connectivity. The experiments so far assumed co-located peers connected by 100
Mb/s Ethernet. Below we consider this benefit in other network configurations.
The benefit is defined as the time difference between fetching from the base (in
Mobile), and from the peer (*MX*) using acquire or catch-up, relative to the
fetch from the base. The MX time when using catch-up (*Catch − up*) includes
hook-up, fetch from peer, and validation; the MX time using acquire (*Acquire*)
include no validation. The scenario corresponds to Table 2 with 532 modified
pages fetched and validation costs *ValidateMX*.

Figure 3 shows the benefit for co-located peers connected by a wireless 801.11
ad-hoc network with a 5 millisecond latency and a range of bandwidth corresponding to varying distance between peers. Both the measured benefit using
non-piped fetches, and the computed benefit assuming piped fetches for MX and
Mobile are shown. The results indicate that with non-piped fetches e.g. when
prefetch information is unavailable for acquire, fetch from the peer has a high
60%-90% performance benefit. With piped fetches, the catch-up validation costs
limit the benefit when the peer network bandwidth is below 2 Mb/sec. Above 2
Mb/sec fetching from peer provides a substantial 40% − 80% benefit.

To show the limits of the benefit, the next experiment considers MX in a configuration it was not originally intended for, where instead of beeing co-located,
mobile peers roam within a metropolitan area using a 1 Mb/sec wireless 801.11
network connection to base stations interconnected via a metropolitan Internet.
The results in Figure 4 show that with typical metropolitan Internet laten-
cies, fetch from the peer provides no performance benefit even for acquire (no

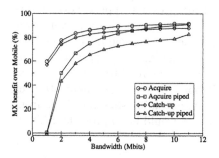

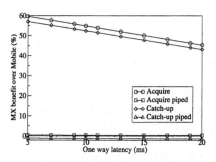

Fig. 3. MX benefit: wireless ad-hoc network

Fig. 4. MX benefit: wireless via Internet

validation) unless non-piped fetches are used because prefetch information is unavailable.

In summary, the performance benefit results indicate that unless peer network has good connectivity, fetch and validation with a peer is rather costly. Validation with a home may be preferable because it is less expensive and because it insures transactions indeed commit. However, fetch and validation with a peer is attractive on a remote location provided peer coordination insures the validation is not wasted due to conflicting accesses.

6 Conclusion

Direct exchange of shared objects is useful for mobile collaborators. Mobile storage systems address the issue of how to do this for simple data but efficient direct exchange of complex data remains an open problem. This issue will become even more important as mobile computing becomes pervasive, and mobile use of collaborative applications manipulating complex data becomes common.

The paper describes MX, a new mobile caching system for collaborative applications, that provides the first systematic approach to solving this problem. MX clients can obtain missing or more recent objects from nearby collaborators. MX validates the exchange, manages the bookkeeping to allow modification based on exchanged data to commit upon reconnection, and insures that a consistent master copy of the persistent objects exists at all times at designated repository servers. MX supports well the exchange of complex data because it provides efficient (page-based) data transfer and fine-grained object validation that avoids the problem of false sharing. Moreover, the validation protocols do not restrict repository size because MX is a caching system and does not require full replication. The paper describes MX caching and validation protocols and specifies the invariants that insure correctness of the mobile exchange.

The paper also describes a prototype implementation based on the Thor object storage system. Preliminary performance results using the OO7 benchmark indicate that the extra validation cost required to support mobile exchange is moderate. For nearby collaborators communicating over a typical ad-hoc network this extra cost is offset by the cost of accessing repository servers over high-latency networks, making the exchange attractive on remote locations. The MX scheme does have some costs. The cost of catch-up with the more recent shared objects is proportional to the number of objects read from the outdated pages. Nevertheless, when members of a collaborating team communicate over ad-hoc network and have no global connectivity, obtaining shared objects from a collaborator may allow to accomplish work that would be impossible in other systems.

Our paper makes the following contributions:

- It describes a new technique, mobile exchange, that allows mobile collaborating clients to acquire from each other complex data residing in large-scale repositories.
- It presents fine-grained transaction validation protocols for the exchanged objects.
- It describes a prototype implementation that supports mobile exchange in a transactional object storage system.
- It presents a performance study of the costs and benefits of mobile exchange for a range of shared data workloads and a range of client network configurations.

Acknowledgements

We thank Jay Lepreau and the staff of Utah experimental testbed emulab.net [1], especially Leigh Stoller, for their help with the testbed, Sidney Chang and Dorothy Curtis for the help with implementing object referencing in disconnected operation, and Jim Gray and Maurice Herlihy for helpful comments.

References

[1] 'emulab.net', the Utah Network Emulation Facility. supported by NSF grant ANI-00-82493.
[2] W. Adjie-Winoto, E.Schwartz, H.Balakrishnan, and J. Lilley. The design and implementation of an intentional naming system. In *ACM SOSP*, 1999.
[3] A. Adya, M. Castro, B. Liskov, U. Maheshwari, and L. Shrira. Fragment Reconstruction: Providing Global Cache Coherence in a Transactional Storage System. In *Proceedings of the International Conference on Distributed Computing Systems*, May 1997.
[4] A. Adya, R. Gruber, B. Liskov, and U. Maheshwari. Efficient Optimistic Concurrency Control Using Loosely Synchronized Clocks. In *Proceedings of the ACM SIGMOD International Conference on Management of Data*, May 1995.
[5] A. Adya and B. Liskov. Lazy Consistency Using Loosely Synchronized Clocks. In *Proceedings of the ACM Symposium on Principles of Distributed Computing*, August 1997.

[6] D. Agrawal, A. E. Abbadi, and R. Steinke. Epidemic Algorithms in Replicated Databases. In *Proceedings of the 16th ACM Symposium on Principles of Database Systems*, May 1997.

[7] C. Amza, A.L. Cox, S. Dwarkadas, P. Keleher, H. Lu, R. Rajamony, W. Yu, and W. Zwaenepoel. TreadMarks: Shared Memory Computing on Networks of Workstations. In *IEEE Computer, Vol. 29, No. 2*, February 1996.

[8] M. Bjornsson and L. Shrira. BuddyCache: High-Performance Object Storage for Collaborative Strong-Consistency Applications. In *OOPSLA Conference*, November 2002.

[9] M. Butrico, H. Chang, A. Cocchi, N. Cohen, D. Shea, and S. Smith. Gold Rush: mobile transaction middleware with Java-object replication. In *Proceedings of the Third USENIX Conference on Object-Oriented Technologies and Systems (COOTS)*, June 1997.

[10] S. Chang and D. Curtis. An Approach to Disconnected Operation in an Object-Oriented Database. In *Proceedings of Third International Conference on Mobile Data Management, Singapore*, January 2002.

[11] Sidney Chang. Adapting Object-oriented Database for Disconnected Operation, M.Eng. Thesis. Technical report, Massachussetts Institute of Technology, May 2001.

[12] Frank Dabek, M. Frans Kaashoek, David Karger, Robert Morris, and Ion Stoica. Wide-area cooperative storage with CFS. In *ACM SOSP*, October 2001.

[13] M. D. Dahlin, R. Y. Wang, T. E. Anderson, and D. A. Patterson. Cooperative caching: Using Remote Client Memory to Improve File System Performance. *Proceedings of the USENIX Conference on Operating Systems Design and Implementation*, November 1994.

[14] A. Demers, D. Gren, C. Hauser, W. Irsh, J. Larson, S. Shenker, H. Sturgis, D. Swinehart, and D. Terry. Epidemic Algorithms for Replicated Database Maintenance. In *Proceedings of the 6th ACM Symposium on Principles of Distributed Computing (PODC)*, August 1987.

[15] A. J. Demers, K. Petersen, M. J. Spreitzer, D. B. Terry, M. M. Theimer, and B. B. Welch. The Bayou Architecture: Support for Data Sharing among Mobile Users. *Proceedings of the Workshop on Mobile Computing Systems and Applications*, December 1994.

[16] D. DeWitt, P. Futtersack, D. Majer, and F. Velez. A Study of Three Alternative Workstation-Server Architectures for Object Oriented Database Systems. In *The Sixteenth International Conference on VLDB*, August 1990.

[17] M. Carey et al. A Status Report on the OO7 OODBMS Benchmarking Effort. *Proceedings of OOPSLA Conference*, October 1994.

[18] M. Feeley, W. Morgan, F. Pighin, A. Karlin, and H. Levy. Implementing Global Memory Management in a Workstation Cluster. *Proceedings of the 15th ACM Symposium on Operating Systems Principles*, December 1995.

[19] M. J. Feeley, J. S. Chase, V. R. Narasayya, and H. M. Levy. Integrating coherency and recoverablity in distributed systems. In *Proceedings of the First Usenix Symposium on Operating sustems Design and Implementation*, May 1994.

[20] P. Ferreira and M. Shapiro et al. PerDiS: design, implementation, and use of a PERsistent DIstributed Store. In *Recent Advances in Distributed Systems, LNCS 1752, Springer-Verlag*, October 1999.

[21] M. Franklin, M. Carey, and M. Livny. Transactional client-server cache consistency: Alternatives and performance. *ACM Transactions on Database Systems*, September 1997.

[22] Michael Franklin, Michael Carey, and Miron Livny. Global Memory Management for Client-Server DBMS Architectures. In *Proceedings of the 19th Intl. Conference on Very Large Data Bases (VLDB)*, August 1992.

[23] D. Gifford and J. Donahue. Coordinating Independent Atomic Actions. In *Proceedings of IEEE COMPCON Digest of Papers*, February 1985.

[24] J. Gray, P. Helland, P. O'Neil, and D. Shasha. The Dangers of Replication and a Solution. In *Proceedings of ACM SIGMOD Conference*, June 1996.

[25] R. Gruber, F. Kaashoek, B. Liskov, and L. Shrira. Disconnected Operation in the Thor Object-Oriented Database System. In *Proceedings of the IEEE Workshop on Mobile Computing Systems and Applications*, December 1994.

[26] M. Herlihy and M. McKendry. Timestamp-Based Orphan Elimination. *IEEE Transactions on Software Engineering*, July 1989.

[27] J. Holliday, R. Steinke, D. Agrawal, and A. E. Abbadi. Epidemic Quorums for Managing Replicated Data. In *Proceedings of the 19th IEEE International Conference on Performance, Computing, and Communication*, February 2000.

[28] L. B. Huston and P. Honeyman. Disconnected Operation for AFS. In *Proceedings of the USENIX Symposium on Mobile and Location Independent Computing*, August 1995.

[29] J. Jing, A. Helal, and A. Elmagarmid. Client-Server Computing in Mobile Environments. *ACM Computing Surveys*, 31(2), Jun 1999.

[30] A. Joseph, A. Lespinasse, J. Tauber, D. Gifford, and F. Kaashoek. Rover: A toolkit for mobile information access. In *Proceedings of the 15th ACM Symposium on Operating Systems Principles*, December 1995.

[31] L. Kawell, S. Beckhardt, T. Halvorsen, R. Ozzie, and I. Greif. Replicated document management in a group communication system. In *Proceedings of the ACM CSCW Conference*, September 1988.

[32] P. J. Keleher. Decentralized Replicated-Object Protocols. In *Proceedings of the 18th ACM Symposium on Principles of Distributed Computing*, May 1999.

[33] J. Kistler and M. Satyanarayanan. Disconnected operation in the Coda file system. *ACM TOCS*, February 1992.

[34] J. Kubiatowicz, D. Bindel, Y. Chen, S. Czerwinski, P. Eaton, D. Geels, R. Gummadi, S. Rhea, H. Weatherspoon, W. Weimer, C. Wells, and B. Zhao. OceanStore: An Architecture for Global-Scale Persistent Storage. In *Proceedings of the Ninth International Conference on Architectural Support for Programming Languages and Operating Systems*, November 2000.

[35] H. Kung and J. Robinson. On optimistic methods for concurrency control. In *ACM TODS 6(2)*, June 1981.

[36] R. Ladin, B. Liskov, L. Shrira, and S. Ghemawat. Providing High Availability Using Lazy Replication. In *ACM TOCS 22(3)*, November 1992.

[37] B. Liskov, M. Castro, L. Shrira, and A. Adya. Providing Persistent Objects in Distributed Systems. In *Proceedings of the 13th European Conference on Object-Oriented Programming (ECOOP '99)*, June 1999.

[38] Qi Lu and M. Satyanarayanan. Improving Data Consistency in Mobile Computing Using Isolation-Only Transactions. In *Fifth IEEE HotOS Topics Workshop*, May 1995.

[39] W. Montgomery. Robust concurrency control for distributed information system. Technical report, MIT Laboratory for Computer Science,Cambridge, December 1978.

[40] L. Mummert and M. Satyanarayanan. Large Granularity Cache Coherence For Intermittent Connectivity. In *Usenix Summer Technical Conference*, June 1998.

[41] T. W. Pager, Jr. R. G. Guy, J. S. Heidemann, D. H. Ratner, P. L. Reiher, G. H. Kuenning A. Goel, and G. J. Popek. Perspectives on optimistically replicated peer-to-peer filing. *Software - Practice and Experience*, February 1998.

[42] K. Petersen, M. J. Spreitzer, M. M. Theimer D. B. Terry, and A. J. Demers. Flexible update propagation for weakly consistent replication. In *Proceedings of the 16th ACM Symposium on Operationg Systems Principles*, October 1997.

[43] S. Phatak and B. Badrinath. Conflict Resolution and Reconciliation in Disconnected Databases. In *MDDS*, September 1999.

[44] A. Rowstron and P. Druschel. Storage management and caching in PAST, a large-scale, persistent peer-to-peer storage utility. In *ACM SOSP*, October 2001.

[45] P. Sarkar and J. Hartman. Efficient Cooperative Caching Using Hints. In *Proceedings of the Usenix Symposium on Operation Systems Design and Implementation*, October 1996.

[46] Liuba Shrira and Ben Yoder. Trust but Check: Mutable Objects in Untrusted Cooperative Caches. In *POS8*, Sept 1998.

[47] M. Zaharioudakis, M. J. Carey, and M. J. Franklin. Adaptive, Fine-Grained Sharing in a Client-Server OODBMS: A Callback-Based Approach. *ACM Transactions on Database Systems*, 22(4):570–627, December 1997.

7 Appendix A: MX Invariants

Below we summarize MX protocol by stating its invariants. The MX protocol maintains the following simple invariants I1 and I2 that insure protocol correctness. In the following, $Max(C,i)$ ($Min(C,i)$) denote the highest (lowest) master versions of the page C possibly cached at node i since disconnection, $Master(C)$ is the master version of C at the base node, and $Invalid(C,i)$ is the set of invalidations of C retained at the base node since node i disconnection. We say a tentative transaction $T2$ *depends* on a tentative transaction $T1$ if $T2$ reads objects modified by transaction $T1$.

Invariant I1. If a mobile node i has provided a page C to a mobile node j, then either node j has disconnected without the page C, or $Max(C,i) > Max(C,j)$ at the time of the exchange.

Invariant I2. Let i be a mobile node reconnecting to a base node with a page C, where $Min(C,i) = k$, and i has either disconnected with C, or has disconnected without it and has acquired C from a mobile node j. If at reconnection time at the base node $Master(C) = m$, $k < m$, then $Invalid(C,i)$ contains all the invalidations for C that correspond to versions $k + 1$ through m of C.

Invariants $I1$ and $I2$ insure that if a tentative transaction T at the mobile node i has read an object x from a master version l of a page C while disconnected, and i reconnects with $Min(C,i) <= l <= Max(C,i)$ and T passes validation, then value x read by T is not stale. Moreover, if at validation time none of the objects read by T are stale and T does not depend on a tentative transaction S that has aborted, T will pass validation.

MX protocol insures that the master versions at the base nodes reflect a state generated by a globally serializable sequence of update transactions. Tentative transactions that fail validation and need to abort, however, may observe an inconsistent state if they access objects on multiple pages. This is undesirable for applications that rely on the invariants maintained by the transactions. This problem, related to the orphan detection problem in distributed systems using locking [26], and lazy consistency problem in optimistic systems [5] has efficient solutions in connected environments using timestamps and safe reconnection intervals that are not applicable for the disconnected environment.

One possible solution is to require mobile hosts to hoard page sets that are "invariant-complete" i.e. contain all objects in a multi-object invariant. At disconnect time, the hoarding procedure runs as a read-only transaction to make sure the hoarded set reflects a transactionally consistent "invariant-complete" state. Since mobile exchange always involves "invariant-complete" set of pages, tentative transactions will always observe a transactionally consistent state.

8   Appendix B: The OO7 Benchmark

The OO7 database contains a tree of assembly objects with leaves pointing to three *composite* parts chosen randomly from among 500 such objects. Each composite part contains a graph of *atomic* parts, accessible from a single root atomic part, and linked by *connection* objects; each atomic part has 3 outgoing connections. We use a *small* database that has 20 atomic parts per composite part. The multi-user database allocates for each client a "private" module consisting of one tree of assembly objects, and adds an extra "shared" module that scales proportionally to the number of clients. To run experiments with a 2 client team we generate OO7 database with modules for 2 clients. The objects in the database are clustered in 8K pages, which are also the unit of transfer in the fetch requests. We expect a typical MX configuration to not be cache limited and therefore focus on workloads where the objects in the client working set fit in the cache.

The OO7 workload consists of two types of transactions, *read-only* and *read-write*. Read-only transactions use the T1 traversal that performs a depth-first traversal of entire composite part graph. Read-Write transactions use the T2b traversal that is identical to T1 except it modifies all the atomic parts, or the T2a traversal that modifies only the root part. A T1 traversal accesses 52389 objects if it traverses a private module, and 55924 objects if traverses the shared module. T2a modifies 1064 objects (on 532 pages) and T2b modifies 21280 objects (on 613 pages) when traversing the shared module. A transaction includes one traversal.

A OO7 client workload is specified by a $4-tuple$ that defines the mix of the read-only and read-write transactions accessing the private and the shared modules of the database. E.g. a $(40, 40, 10, 10)$ $4-tuple$ defines a workload with 40% read-only, 40% read-write transactions in the private module and 10% read-only, 10% read-write transactions in the shared part. Note that read-write transactions do no modify all the objects it accesses e.g. T2b modified 49% of the objects it accesses. The level of contention (conflict) in the workload is controlled by the read-write accesses to shared module.

Regular Object Types[*]

Vladimir Gapeyev and Benjamin C. Pierce

University of Pennsylvania
{vgapeyev,bcpierce}@cis.upenn.edu

Abstract. Regular types have been proposed as a foundation for statically typed processing of XML and other forms of tree-structured data. To date, however, regular types have only been explored in special-purpose languages (e.g., XDUCE, CDUCE, and XQUERY) with type systems designed around regular types "from the ground up." The goal of the XTATIC language is to bring regular types to a broad audience by offering them as a lightweight extension of a popular object-oriented language, C#.

We develop here the formal core of the XTATIC design—a combination of the tree-structured data model of XDUCE and the classes-and-objects data model of a conventional object-oriented language. Our tool for this investigation is a tiny language called FX with features drawn from Featherweight Java (FJ) and from the core of XDUCE. Points of interest include (1) a smooth interleaving of the two data models, in which XDUCE's tree structures are grafted into of FJ's class hierarchy while objects and object types play the role of XDUCE's label values and label types; (2) an intuitive "semantic" definition of the subtype relation, inherited from XDUCE and extended to objects; and (3) a natural encoding of XML documents and their schemas using a simple form of singleton classes.

1 Introduction

The popularity of XML can be attributed, in part, to the existence of a number of formalisms for specifying the structure of XML documents. By supporting dynamic consistency checking, ensuring that information being exchanged (e.g., between modules in an application or nodes in a distributed system) has the expected structure, these schema languages can significantly increase the robustness of complex XML-based information systems.

However, the exploitation of schema languages by current XML technologies falls far short of what is possible. In particular, schemas play little part in the static analysis of programs that operate on XML structures: they are not used for checking code for inconsistencies at compile time, or for optimization—in short, they are not used as types in the usual programming-language sense of the term. Taking advantage of this missed opportunity, and thereby improving

---

[*] An early version of this paper was presented at the 2003 workshop on Foundations of Object-Oriented Languages.

L. Cardelli (Ed.): ECOOP 2003, LNCS 2743, pp. 151–175, 2003.

both the robustness and the efficiency of XML-based information systems, is the long-range goal of the XTATIC project at the University of Pennsylvania.

The key technology for this project is *regular types* (sometimes called *regular expression types*). Regular types are based on well-known constructions from automata theory—they are a mild generalization of nondeterministic tree automata. Their basic constructors (union, concatenation, repetition, etc.) are similar to those found in existing XML schema formalisms such as DTDs [36] and XML-Schema [39]. In a programming language based on regular types, however, XML trees are built-in values and static analysis of the shapes of trees that may appear at run time (as values of variables, parameters to methods, results of complex expressions, etc.) becomes part of the ordinary behavior of the type-checker.

Past work on regular types led to a language prototype called XDUCE [17, 19, 16, 18, 13]. XDUCE is a statically typed language for writing recursive tree transformers—roughly, a statically typed fragment of the popular XSLT language [40]. Beyond regular types, its main innovation is a powerful form of *regular pattern matching*—a statically typed "tree grep" primitive that arises naturally from types [16]. The XDUCE implementation demonstrates efficient algorithms for subtyping and typechecking [19].

XDUCE has had a significant impact on parts of the XML world; in particular, its influence can be seen in the type system of the XML Query Algebra [11], the core of the W3C draft standard query language for XML [37, 38], as well as newer schema languages such as TREX [8] and Relax NG [9]. However, significant work remains before the benefits of regular types can be made available to the vast majority of XML programmers. In particular, we must understand how to integrate the simple tree-data model of XDUCE with the conventional data models and type systems of mainstream programming languages, in particular with object-oriented features.

We have begun a new phase of the XDUCE project—a redesign and re-implementation along more ambitious lines, dubbed XTATIC, whose main focus is on inter-operability both at source level and at run time with an established, object-oriented host language. We have chosen compatibility with $C^\#$ as our immediate target; a similar exercise could easily be carried out for a related language such as Java. The goal is to make XTATIC as lightweight an extension of $C^\#$ as possible, smoothly merging the tree values and types of XDUCE with the familiar object model of $C^\#$ and re-using existing $C^\#$ features wherever possible in the design, rather than introducing new, XML-specific mechanisms.

This paper develops the formal core of the XTATIC design—a combination of the tree-structured data model of XDUCE with the classes-and-objects model of $C^\#$. Our tool for this investigation is a tiny language called FX, which combines Featherweight Java [20] with the core features of XDUCE. The main points of interest in FX may be summarized as follows.

- The two original data models are tightly interwoven in FX. On one hand, the subtype hierarchy of tree types is grafted into the class hierarchy, allowing tree values to be passed to generic library facilities (e.g., collection classes),

```
<Person>                                    [ <Person>[
  <Name>Queen Elisabeth</Name>                 <Name>['Queen Elisabeth'],
  <Email>queen@buckingham.uk</Email>           <Email>['queen@buckingham.uk']
</Person>                                     ],
<Person>                                      <Person>[
  <Name>Tony Blair</Name>                        <Name>['Tony Blair'],
  <Phone>+44 55 6666</Phone>                     <Phone>['+44 55 6666']
</Person>                                      ]
                                            ]
```

Fig. 1. An XML fragment and the corresponding XTATIC value

stored in fields of objects, etc. Conversely, the roles of labels and label types in XDUCE are played by objects and classes in FX.

- Subtyping in FX is a natural extension of both the object-oriented subclass relation and the richer subtype relation of regular types. XDUCE's simple "semantic" definition of subtyping (sans inference rules) is extended to objects and classes.
- FX enriches XDUCE's regular pattern matching construct with a natural form of type-based pattern-matching on objects.

The paper is organized as follows. Section 2 gives a brief illustrative example of XTATIC code. In Section 3, we review some details of XDUCE and FJ's data models. Section 4—the heart of the paper—combines these to produce the data model of FX. The remainder of the the FX language is informally described in Section 5; standard soundness properties are sketched in Section 6. In Section 7, we show how the FX data model encodes XML types and values. Section 8 discusses related work, and Section 9 sketches our plans for the future development of XTATIC.

2   Example

XTATIC provides a general mechanism for representing and manipulating tree-structured data. In Section 7, we will explain in detail how this mechanism can be used to encode XML. Here, we briefly illustrate the key features of the language through a simple example, treating the encoded features as though they were primitive.

Figure 1 shows a sample XML fragment and its representation as an XTATIC expression. XML opening tags (e.g. <Name>) look the same in XTATIC. For brevity in this paper, however, closing tags are not used—instead, we separate trees by commas and use brackets [...] to explicitly delimit tree sequences. Textual fragments are delimited by backquotes. (The full language implemented by our Xtatic prototype uses concrete syntax closer to actual XML.)

A possible type for this expression can be written

```
[ <Person>[
    <Name>[pcdata],
    (<Email>[pcdata] | <Phone>[pcdata]) ]*
]
```

The type constructor "|" is type alternation (union), and "*" is repetition. The type pcdata is used for XML textual data ("parsed character data" in XML jargon).

Sequence values can be examined using type-based pattern matching. For example, assuming the variables list and phonebook each contain a sequence of the type given above and spamlist holds pcdata text, the code fragment

```
match (list) {
  case [ <Person>[ <Name>[pcdata], <Email>[pcdata e] ],
         any rest ]:
    spamlist = [ spamlist, ',', e ];
    //...
  case [ <Person>[ <Name>[pcdata], <Phone>[pcdata] ] p,
         any rest]]:
    phonebook = [[ phonebook, p ]];
    //...
  case []:
    //...
}
```

inspects the first tree in the sequence list and, if the corresponding person has an email, extracts the address into a pcdata variable e and uses it to extend the text in spamlist. Otherwise, the person must have a phone, and the second match clause binds the whole entry to the variable p and adds it to the end of the phonebook sequence. The last clause handles the case when list is an empty sequence. The type any that trails both first patterns matches an arbitrary sequence of trees (which gets assigned to the variable rest). Tree values, types, and patterns always appear inside of brackets [...], explicitly signaling the shift from the world of host language ($C^\#$) values and types to the world of trees.

3   Technical Background

The *data model* of a language is the collection of *values* that programs in the language manipulate, their *types*, and fundamental relations such as *value typing* and *subtyping*. The data model is the bedrock on which the full language definition (the syntax, typing rules, and evaluation rules for expressions) rests. Because the primary topic of this paper is the combination of trees and objects (and their types), the data model of FX is where we will concentrate our attention. As background for this development, we begin in this section by sketching the data models found in XDuce and in FJ.

3.1   The XDuce Data Model

The data model of XDuce is parameterized on a language of *labels*. The details of these labels can vary (and do vary, across the several published XDuce papers and implementations), but all variations offer the following common structure:

- a set L of *label values*, ranged over by 1,
- a set of *label types*, ranged over by L,
- a denotation function $[\![\cdot]\!]$ giving the set $[\![L]\!] \subseteq L$ of label values that are members of each label type L.

The subtyping relation on label types, written $L_1 \sqsubseteq : L_2$, is generated by $[\![\cdot]\!]$—that is $L_1 \sqsubseteq : L_2$ iff $[\![L_1]\!] \subseteq [\![L_2]\!]$.

One simple choice of label language is to select an arbitrary set of identifiers as the set L of label values; for each value $1 \in L$, we consider 1 to be a label type as well (i.e., 1 is the *singleton type* whose denotation contains just 1); we also introduce the wildcard label type ˜, denoting the whole set L. A yet simpler choice would be to omit ˜, but having a maximal label type turns out to be quite useful in pattern matching, where it functions as a "don't care" pattern. If desired, the language of label types can also be enhanced by adding a notion of "sub label" and/or operators such as union, intersection and difference.

Having selected the language of labels, the XDuce data model can be defined in a uniform way. First, a *tree value* t consists of a label value and a sequence of children tree values:

$$t ::= \langle\!\langle 1 \rangle\!\rangle [t_1, \dots, t_n] \quad \text{where } n \geq 0$$

Now, a *sequence value* is a sequence $t_1, \dots, t_n$ of zero or more tree values placed next to each other. (We use the shorthand notation $\bar{t}$ throughout the paper for sequences, and [] to denote the empty sequence. We write $\bar{s}, \bar{t}$ for the concatenation of the sequences $\bar{s}$ and $\bar{t}$.)

XDuce types—*regular types*—are traditional regular expressions over a non-traditional "alphabet" consisting of the tree types $\langle\!\langle L \rangle\!\rangle [X]$:

T ::=	
$\langle\!\langle L \rangle\!\rangle [X]$	tree
[]	empty sequence
T,T	concatenation
T|T	union
T*	repetition

The tree types refer to type names X from a globally defined collection of type definitions; we write *def*(X) for the definition T corresponding to the name X. Note that type names X are restricted to occur only in the contents of a tree type, and the only possible tree type content is a type name. This restriction guarantees that the above grammar generates only regular types. (The full Xtatic language uses a more permissive type grammar, where general types, not just variables, may appear as the contents of tree types—with additional well-formedness checks to ensure that we remain within the world of regular type expressions.[1])

Next, the denotation function $[\![\cdot]\!]$ mapping types T to sets of sequence values $\bar{t}$ is defined as the least solution of the following equations:

$$
\begin{aligned}
[\![\langle\!\langle L \rangle\!\rangle [X]]\!] &= \{\, \langle\!\langle 1 \rangle\!\rangle [\bar{t}] \mid 1 \in [\![L]\!] \text{ and } \bar{t} \in [\![T]\!] \text{ where } \mathit{def}(X) = T \,\} \\
[\![[\,]]\!] &= \{\,[\,]\,\} \\
[\![T_1 , T_2]\!] &= \{\, \bar{t}_1 , \bar{t}_2 \mid \bar{t}_1 \in [\![T_1]\!], \bar{t}_2 \in [\![T_2]\!] \,\} \\
[\![T_1 \mid T_2]\!] &= [\![T_1]\!] \cup [\![T_2]\!] \\
[\![T*]\!] &= \{\, \bar{t}_1 \ldots \bar{t}_n \mid n \geq 0 \wedge \forall k \in 1 \ldots n. \ \bar{t}_k \in [\![T]\!] \,\}
\end{aligned}
$$

The subtyping relation for regular types is defined in the simplest imaginable way:

$$ T_1 <: T_2 \text{ iff } [\![T_1]\!] \subseteq [\![T_2]\!]. $$

The fact that subtyping can be defined in this "semantic" fashion is actually quite important in XDuce. The alternative—writing down a collection of inference rules characterizing the same relation inductively—would be much heavier and harder to understand than the subtype relations of most languages, since the regular type constructors satisfy many algebraic laws arising from the associativity of comma and the associativity, commutativity, and distributivity (over sequencing and $\langle\!\langle L \rangle\!\rangle [\ldots]$) of the (*non*-disjoint!) union. An inference-rule presentation of the subtyping relation can certainly be given—indeed, it must be, since it is the basis for the algorithm for subtype checking [19]—but it is not pretty.

3.2   The FJ Data Model

Featherweight Java [20] (or FJ) is a tiny calculus designed to capture the essential typing mechanisms of class-based object-oriented languages such as Java and $C^{\#}$. It was first used by Igarashi, Pierce, and Wadler [20] to formalize the GJ [5] type system, and has since formed the basis of numerous formal studies of Java and related languages [21, 31, 2, 3, 41, 1, 29, 23, etc.]. FJ embodies the core mechanisms of object creation, field access, method invocation, and inheritance (and—in the most common presentation, though not here—casting) in exactly the same form as they are found in Java, while omitting everything else... from reflection and concurrency to interfaces, overloading, static members, and even assignment.

An FJ program consists of a collection of class declarations plus a single expression to be evaluated. The types in an FJ program are just class names C. FJ values are objects, which (since FJ is a declarative language, the only things that distinguish one object from another are its class and the arguments passed to its constructor) are simply identified with new expressions.

$$ o ::= \text{new } C(o_1, \ldots, o_n) \qquad (n \geq 0) $$

---

[1] See [19] for a formal presentation of the more permissive grammar and corresponding well-formedness conditions. The presentation used here is that of [14].

The constructor arguments $o_1, \ldots, o_n$ (usually written just $\overline{o}$) are required to correspond exactly to the fields of the class C. For example, if C has fields a and b and its immediate subclass D declares fields e and f, then an instance of D will have the form new $D(o_1, o_2, o_3, o_4)$, where o_1 is the value for the a field of the new object, o_2 is the value of the b field, o_3 of the e field, and o_4 of the f field.

The global set of class definitions in an FJ program is formalized as a *program context*—a collection of sets, relations, and functions summarizing different aspects of the class definitions: the set of all defined classes (which always includes the special class Object); the immediate-subclass relation, which must be tree-structured with Object at the root; the list of field names and types in each class; the method names and signatures in each class; and the method bodies for each class. This program context is used to define the typing and evaluation relations. For purposes of discussing the FJ data model, we can restrict attention to the part of the static context comprising just the set of class names, the immediate-subclass relation and class field declarations.

The subtype relation in FJ, written $C_1 \sqsubseteq: C_2$, is the reflexive and transitive closure of the immediate-subclass relation. As in XDUCE, this definition of subtyping is pleasingly simple; however, it has a completely different—more syntactic—character. In order to combine the two data models, we need a more "semantic" presentation of this one (as we remarked above, a syntactic presentation of XDUCE subtyping is not an attractive alternative). This can be achieved as follows.

We say that a value new $C(\overline{o})$ is a *valid* object of the class C if its field values $\overline{o}$ conform to the field types declared for C in the program context. The *denotation* of a class C is then the set of all valid objects of this class and all its subclasses:

$$[\![C]\!] = \{ \text{new } D(\overline{o}) \mid D \sqsubseteq: C, \mathit{fields}(D) = \overline{F} \ \overline{f}, o_i \in [\![F_i]\!] \}.$$

The clause $\mathit{fields}(D) = \overline{F} \ \overline{f}$ here is read "where the sequence $\overline{f}$ is the names of the fields defined in class D and $\overline{F}$ is the types of these fields. (Formally, this equation should be considered as the definition of a monotone function on pairs (o, C) whose least fixed point is the relation $o \in [\![C]\!]$. For FJ, which omits assignment, the least fixed point is sufficient; in a more general setting where objects can form cyclic structures in the heap, we would need the greatest fixed point of the same function—cf. [34].)

It is obvious from the definition that the "semantic" subtyping relation derived from it coincides exactly with the syntactic subclass relation:

$$C_1 \sqsubseteq: C_2 \text{ iff } [\![C_1]\!] \subseteq [\![C_2]\!].$$

This formulation of subtyping fits smoothly with the semantic subtyping from XDuce, as we shall see in the following section.

4   The FX Data Model

The interweaving of XDUCE's and FJ's data models in FX is founded on two observations.

Values		Types	
		Full FX language	
a ::=	FX value	A ::=	FX type
new C(ā)	object	C	class name
[t̄]	delimited sequence	[X]	regular type name
		[T]	regular type
	Regular expression sublanguage		
t ::=		T ::=	regular type
《a》[t̄]	tree value	《A》[X]	tree type
		[]	empty sequence
		T,T	concatenation
		T|T	union
		T*	repetition

Fig. 2. FX values and types

1. We can treat sequences of trees as objects simply by "grafting" the whole collection of regular types into the class hierarchy, inventing a special *class* Seq whose sub*types* are all the regular types. This grafting is justified by our intended compilation model—reminiscent of GJ's homogeneous translation [5, 20]—in which all regular types in an FX program are "erased" to the single class type Seq and all tree values are translated into objects of class Seq.

2. The data model of objects and classes qualifies as a "label language" in the sense discussed in Section 3.1, so we can use arbitrary objects as the labels in XDUCE trees and classes as label types. (Indeed, tree labels in FX can even be other trees! We doubt that this generality will be very useful for programming, but allowing it does not hurt anything, whereas explicitly disallowing it would require additional work in the definitions.)

Formally, the data model is defined in three steps. First, we give the syntax of values and types. Next, we give the notion of a static context, which summarizes the definitions appearing in a program. Finally, fixing a static context, we define the membership relation for values in types.

Figure 2 defines the syntax. An FX value a can have one of two forms: it is either an object new C(ā) or a sequence [t̄] delimited by brackets. Observe that, inside an object new C(ā), the values of fields may be arbitrary FX values ā; in particular, they can be sequences. The organization of FX types A is similar, combining class types C and regular types [T]. Regular values t̄ and regular types T are essentially those of XDUCE, where any FX value can be used as a label in a tree value and any class type C can be used as a label in a tree type.

As in the presentation of XDUCE in Section 3.1, the grammar of types restricts the contents of a tree type 《A》[X] to be a type name. In examples, however—and in the full Xtatic language—we allow tree types of the form

⟪A⟫[T], assuming that T is permissible, i.e. the tree type and the corresponding table of type definitions can be translated into an equivalent form that does belong to the official grammar. We also write ⟪A⟫[] instead ⟪A⟫[[]].

A *program context* is a tuple

$$Ctx = \langle\, \textit{Typenames, def, Classes, } \sqsubseteq:, \textit{fields, mtype, mbody}\,\rangle,$$

where

- *Typenames* is a set of names for regular types, ranged over by X;
- *def* is a function that maps each name X from *Typenames* to a regular type T (its *definition*) so that if a type name X′ appears in *def*(X), then X′ ∈ *Typenames*;
- *Classes* is a set of class names, ranged over by C and containing special names Object and Seq;
- $\sqsubseteq$: is a binary relation on *Classes*, generated as the reflexive and transitive closure of an "immediate predecessor" relation *Parent* : *Classes*\{Object} → *Classes*, with
  - for each C ∈ *dom*(*Parent*) there is $n \geq 1$ such that $Parent^n(C) = $ Object;
  - *Parent*(Seq) = Object;
  - for every C ∈ *Classes*, *Parent*(C) ≠ Seq;
- *fields* : C ↦ $\overline{F}$ $\overline{f}$ is a function defined on *Classes* with *fields*(C) being the list F_1 $f_1,\ldots,F_n$ f_n of types and names of C's fields such that
  - *fields*(Object) and *fields*(Seq) are empty;
  - if C $\sqsubseteq$: D, then the list *fields*(D) is a prefix of the list *fields*(C);
- *mtype* : C ↦ m ↦ ($\overline{A}$→A) is a function defined on *Classes* with *mtype*(C) being a partial mapping from method names m to method signatures ($\overline{A}$→A) such that if C $\sqsubseteq$: D, then *dom*(*mtype*(D)) ⊆ *dom*(*mtype*(C));
- *mbody* : C ↦ m ↦ (D, $\overline{x}$, e) is a function defined on *Classes* with *mbody*(C) being a partial mapping that associates a type name m with the triple (D, $\overline{x}$, e) of the class D (a superclass of C) where the method definition is located, method parameters $\overline{x}$, and method body e, such that *dom*(*mbody*(C)) = *dom*(*mtype*(C)) for all C ∈ *Classes*. (The method body is an expression. The syntax of expressions is introduced later—we don't need them for defining the data model.)

In the following we assume that a fixed program context *Ctx* is given and that functions and relations *Typenames, def, Classes*, $\sqsubseteq$:, *fields, mtype, mbody* refer to the components of this context. (We assume, moreover, that *Ctx* is well-formed, in the sense defined in the Appendix.)

The syntax of values a given in Figure 2 allows ill-formed object values new C($\overline{a}$) where actual field values $\overline{a}$ do not conform to the field types declared for class C in the program context. To correct this, we introduce the type membership relation a ∈ A as the least fixed point of the rules in Figure 3. A value a is *valid* if there is a type A such that a ∈ A. *Type denotations*, as sets of values inhabiting a type, are induced by the membership relation as

$$[\![A]\!] = \{\, a \mid a \in A \,\}.$$

$$\frac{\begin{array}{cc} D \sqsubseteq : C & D \neq \mathsf{Seq} \\ \textit{fields}(D) = \overline{F}\ \overline{f} & \overline{a} \in \overline{F} \end{array}}{\mathsf{new}\ D(\overline{a}) \in C}\ \text{M-ObjCls} \qquad \frac{[\overline{t}] \in [T] \qquad \mathsf{Seq} \sqsubseteq : C}{[\overline{t}] \in C}\ \text{M-SeqCls}$$

$$\frac{\textit{def}(X) = T \qquad a \in [T]}{a \in [X]}\ \text{M-RegDef} \qquad \frac{a \in A \qquad [\overline{t}] \in [T]}{[\langle\!\langle a \rangle\!\rangle [\overline{t}]] \in [\langle\!\langle A \rangle\!\rangle [T]]}\ \text{M-Tree}$$

$$\frac{[\overline{t}_1] \in [T_1] \qquad [\overline{t}_2] \in [T_2]}{[\overline{t}_1, \overline{t}_2] \in [T_1, T_2]}\ \text{M-Seq} \qquad \frac{[\overline{t}] \in [P_1]}{[\overline{t}] \in [P_1 \mid P_2]}\ \text{M-Alt1}$$

$$\frac{[\overline{t}] \in [P_2]}{[\overline{t}] \in [P_1 \mid P_2]}\ \text{M-Alt2} \qquad \frac{m \geq 0 \qquad \forall k \in 1\ldots m.\ [\overline{t}_k] \in [T]}{[\overline{t}_1, \ldots, \overline{t}_m] \in [T*]}\ \text{M-Rep}$$

Fig. 3. FX type membership relation

Note the special role of the class Seq, whose denotation does not contain objects (in fact, new Seq($\overline{a}$) is not in the denotation of any type), but instead contains all valid sequence values.

Subtyping on FX types is then defined semantically:

$$A_1 <: A_2 \qquad \Longleftrightarrow \qquad [\![A_1]\!] \subseteq [\![A_2]\!].$$

This is the official subtyping relation of FX that is to be used in typechecking everywhere where FJ used the subclassing relation.

As we remarked above, the FX data model allows tree values and types of the form $\langle\!\langle [\overline{s}] \rangle\!\rangle [\overline{t}]$ and $\langle\!\langle [S] \rangle\!\rangle [T]$ correspondingly, with sequences appearing as tree labels. This is a consequence of the special role of the Seq type: since the type $\langle\!\langle \mathsf{Seq} \rangle\!\rangle [T]$ should clearly be permitted, and since sequences are the members of Seq, the above types have to be permitted as well.

5   The FX Language

The FX data model described in the previous section establishes a skeleton, on which a full-blown programming language can be constructed—providing ways of interrogating and destructing values, as well as abstraction mechanisms and all the other usual apparatus. Naturally, FX's value-destruction mechanisms are contributed by the corresponding sublanguages: FJ provides field projection on objects and XDuce brings in regular pattern matching on sequences and trees. The abstraction mechanisms of FX—classes, methods, and inheritance—are taken entirely from FJ.

Figure 4 gives the syntax of FX expressions and their constituent patterns. The behavior of most of these constructs is standard; therefore we discuss the

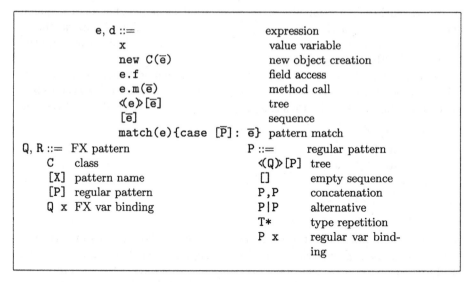

e, d ::=		expression
	x	value variable
	new C(ē)	new object creation
	e.f	field access
	e.m(ē)	method call
	⟪e⟫[ē]	tree
	[ē]	sequence
	match(e){case [P̄] : ē}	pattern match
Q, R ::=	FX pattern	P ::=	regular pattern
C	class	⟪Q⟫[P]	tree
[X]	pattern name	[]	empty sequence
[P]	regular pattern	P,P	concatenation
Q x	FX var binding	P|P	alternative
		T*	type repetition
		P x	regular var binding

Fig. 4. FX language syntax

language semantics mostly informally, commenting in more detail on the issues that are novel in FX. (Full definitions are provided in the appendix.)

The only significant difference between the FX contexts introduced in the previous section and the information provided by an FJ program is that the types of fields and the types appearing in method signatures are arbitrary FX types, i.e. they can be regular types as well as classes. Consequently, the subtyping relation used for checking the method overriding constraints (as part of the process of checking that a class is well-formed) is the semantic subtyping relation <:. Similarly, FX variables x (which can only originate in FX as method argument names or as binders in patterns) can hold any FX values, either objects or sequences. As in FJ, there is a variable this that can be used in expressions to refer to the current object. The typing and evaluation rules treat this variable specially.

The FX data model permits only tree values to be members of sequences. That is, something like [[t̄], (new C(ā)), [s̄]] is not a well-formed value. The syntax of *expressions*, however, does allow nested sequences. The reason is that we want an expression like

```
[db.getPapers("POPL"), db.getPapers("ICFP")]
```

to be legal—provided the method getPapers() returns values of a sequence type—and to mean the concatenation of the sequences returned by the two calls. Therefore, a nested sequence [[ē], [d̄]] is a valid FX expression, which evaluates to the same value as [ē, d̄]. Generally, FX typing rules ensure that an expression [e_1, e_2] is legal only when e_1 and e_2 both have valid regular types.

On the other hand, an object is never legal as a member of a sequence and, symmetrically, a tree expression $\langle\!\langle e \rangle\!\rangle[\bar{d}]$ is never allowed outside the sequence parentheses [...]. Since both are permitted syntactically, this condition is checked by the typing rules.

Deconstruction of sequence values is done by matching them against patterns using the match construct, which syntactically resembles the $C^\#$ switch statement but behaves like XDUCE's match. That is, the behavior of an expression

```
match (d) {
    case [P₁]: e₁;
    case [P₂]: e₂;
...
    case [Pₙ]: eₙ;
}
```

is to evaluate d and match the result against each of the patterns in turn until the first one, say $[P_i]$, matching the value is encountered. The successful match produces an environment that maps variables declared in $[P_i]$ to the appropriate portions of the value computed from d. The result of the whole expression is the result of evaluating e_i, assuming variable mappings from the environment. So, the case bodies do not have the "fall through" behavior by definition—in contrast to $C^\#$ switch that requires explicit control transfer from a branch (via return, break, exit, etc.). The value of match's input d must be a sequence, and all case patterns must be sequence patterns.

The syntax of FX sequence patterns [P] is essentially that of XDUCE: a pattern is just a type annotated with variable binders.[2] This intuition is extended in FX to class types. A *class pattern* has the form C x, where C is a class name and x is a variable to be bound. Correspondingly, the pattern-matching relation $a \in Q \Rightarrow \Sigma$, which defines when a value a matches a pattern Q to produce a value environment Σ, is based on the pattern-matching relation $[\bar{t}] \in [P] \Rightarrow \Sigma$ of XDUCE. Additional rules are needed only to handle class patterns:

$$\frac{D \sqsubseteq: C}{\texttt{new } D(\bar{a}) \triangleright C \Rightarrow \bullet} \text{ P-OBJCLS} \qquad \frac{\texttt{Seq} \sqsubseteq: C}{[\bar{t}] \triangleright C \Rightarrow \bullet} \text{ P-SEQCLS}$$

$$\frac{a \triangleright R \Rightarrow \Sigma}{a \triangleright R \ x \Rightarrow x : a, \Sigma} \text{ P-BINDFX}$$

Observe that, in contrast to the type membership relation (Figure 3) the rule P-OBJCLS of pattern matching does not examine object fields for conformance with the declared field types—only the class tag of the object is checked. Similarly, in the rule P-SEQCLS the validity of sequences is not checked. This will

---

[2] As in XDUCE, we demand that each pattern P satisfy the same regularity constraint as for types, and that it be *linear*. Intuitively, linearity means that no variable is bound in P twice, except in alternation patterns, where branches must bind exactly the same variables (see [16], appendix A.2, for the formal definition).

turn out to be safe, as only valid objects and sequences exist at run-time. Moreover, this agrees with a natural implementation of run-time class determination in a statically typed OO language.

Since classes can be types of labels in tree types, it is natural to use a class pattern in the label position in a tree pattern. This allows one to extract a label from a tree as an object for later use in the program. It is worthwhile noticing that this is a benefit of our goal to use, whenever possible, C$^\#$ features for the needs of regular types. To compare, in XDUCE a label is an integral part of a tree and cannot be extracted from it as a first-class value.

The typing of match expressions relies on a judgement for extracting the types of variables bound in patterns. We write $\triangleright Q \Rightarrow \Gamma$ to mean that the bound variables in Q have the types specified in the context Γ. Intuitively, this is just a matter of reading off the annotations on pattern variables. However, in the case of alternation patterns, we generalize slightly, using the *join* of the types from the alternatives, defined as their smallest expressible common upper bound.

The typing rule for match expressions guarantees exhaustiveness by checking that the input type is a subtype of the union of the types of all the patterns. It also provides a restricted form of pattern redundancy checking by comparing, for each prefix of the pattern list, the union of the prefix's patterns and the input type.

In XDUCE, the pattern typing judgment has the more general form $T \triangleright P \Rightarrow \Gamma$, mapping an input type T (the type of values being matched against) and a pattern P into a typing environment Γ recording the types of the variables in P. Instead of just recording the declared types of pattern variables, this judgment intersects each declaration with the portion of the input type that may possible "flow to" this point in the pattern. This analysis can be used to *infer* types for pattern variables (declarations can be left out, if desired) that is *precise*, in the sense that, for each type $\Gamma(x)$, each value from its denotation can possibly be bound to x at run time as a result of matching some value from T's denotation against P, and $[\![\Gamma(x)]\!]$ does not contain values that cannot be thus obtained. The precision is achieved thanks to the availability of unrestricted union, intersection, and difference operations on XDUCE types—which, unfortunately, cannot be defined in Xtatic (because the subclass hierarchy $\sqsubseteq:$ is not necessarily closed under union, intersection, and difference).[3]

6   Properties

We can now state for FX the standard results of static type safety ("preservation" and "progress"). The proofs, which are straightforward inductive arguments, are

---

[3] We are currently exploring (with Alan Schmitt) some ideas on how to eliminate this limitation. It appears possible to extend the type system of FJ with the boolean operations of intersection, union, and difference on *class* types, with the restriction that these extended types are used only in variable and method declarations and in patterns, not in new expressions. This would re-open the possibility of precise type inference for XTATIC pattern variables.

omitted. All the results are stated assuming there is a well-formed static context corresponding to an FX program.

Value environments Σ and typing environments Γ are mappings from variables x to values a, and, correspondingly, to types A. An environment with the empty domain is written •.

A value environment Σ *conforms* to a typing environment Γ, written $\Sigma \in \Gamma$, if $dom(\Sigma) = dom(\Gamma)$ and $\Sigma(x) \in \Gamma(x)$, for all x.

The typing and operational semantics of FX is formalized using the following relations:

- $\Gamma \vdash e \in A$, "in the typing environment Γ, expression e gets type A",
- $\Sigma \vdash e \Downarrow a$, "in the value environment Σ, expression e evaluates to value a".

To state the progress property, we need one more relation, written $\Sigma \vdash e \Downarrow\hspace{-0.6em}/$ and pronounced "evaluation of e gets stuck in finite number of steps." (this relation is specific to big-step semantics, the analogous property for small-step semantics says that e gets reduced to a non-value, an expression to which none of the evaluation rules is applicable.)

The proofs below depend on the following property of pattern matching, which is interesting in itself. Recall that the rules P-OBJCLS and P-SEQCLS of our pattern matching relation $a \rhd Q \Rightarrow \Sigma$ do not check for the validity of objects and sequences. The property says that, despite of this, if pattern matching is done against a valid value a, any binding in the resulting environment is also valid.

6.1 Proposition [Pattern Matching Preserves Validity]: Let $a \in A$ and Q be a pattern. If $a \rhd Q \Rightarrow \Sigma$ and $\rhd Q \Rightarrow \Gamma$, then $A <: tyof(Q)$ and $\Sigma \in \Gamma$. (We write $tyof(Q)$ for the type obtained from the pattern Q by erasing value binding annotations.)

6.2 Theorem [Preservation]: For $\Sigma \in \Gamma$, if $\Gamma \vdash e \in A$ and $\Sigma \vdash e \Downarrow a$, then $a \in A$.

6.3 Theorem [Soundness]: If • $\vdash e \in A$, then not • $\vdash e \Downarrow\hspace{-0.6em}/$.

7   XML in FX

So far, none of the mechanisms we have described have been especially tied to XML—we have simply established a generic foundation for representing and manipulating ordered, labeled tree structures in an object-oriented setting. Our final job is to show how this foundation supports a natural encoding of most of XML itself (missing, notably, attributes), based on a simple form of singleton types and a modicum of syntactic sugar.

We begin by explaining how the textual "leaf data" of XML documents, known as PCDATA (parsed character data), can be treated. Our first step is to extend, conceptually, the C$^\#$ data model by introducing singleton classes for individual characters. We assume that the program context *Ctx* provides a class Char, corresponding to the standard $C^\#$ character class, plus, for each character c, a class $Char_c$ extending Char. These classes have no fields and have nullary constructors—thus, each class $Char_c$ contains only a single object, new $Char_c$(), which we can identify with the character c itself. Now, a $C^\#$ character literal, say $'a'$, is considered as syntactic sugar for either the object new $Char_a$(), when used in an expression, or the class $Char_a$, when used in a type.

We can now define a regular type pcdata for representing XML character data:

$$\mathit{def}(\text{pcdata}) \quad = \quad (\text{ «Char»[] })*$$

That is, an XML text value is represented by a sequence of trees, where each tree has no children and has a character object as its label. The type pcdata contains arbitrary text strings, so we can write patterns like «Object»[pcdata], which matches a tree whose body contains only character data.

Why not adopt the more obvious choice of using $C^\#$'s String class to hold XML character data? One reason is that the pcdata representation opens the way to interesting uses of pattern matching for string regular expression processing. Since each $Char_a$ is a subtype of Char, we can write types that restrict text to a particular form. For example, all character sequences starting with $'a'$ and ending with $'b'$ belong to the regular type

$$\text{«}'a'\text{»[], pcdata, «}'b'\text{»[].}$$

This type, like any XTATIC type, can be annotated with variable binders to obtain a pattern. The general pattern-matching facility, then, offers functionality somewhat similar to that of Perl's regular expression string patterns, but with static typing support. (This idea also appears in the CDuce design [4]; it is explored in more depth in [33].)

Another reason for using pcdata instead of String is that, in XML, two character sequences following each other are indistinguishable from a single larger character sequence. The pcdata type satisfies this requirement,

$$[\![\text{pcdata, pcdata}]\!] = [\![\text{«Char»[]*, «Char»[]*}]\!] = [\![\text{«Char»[]*}]\!] = [\![\text{pcdata}]\!]$$

but a String-based representation does not, since $[\![\text{«String»[],«String»[]}]\!] \neq [\![\text{«String»[]}]\!]$.

The encoding of XML documents in XTATIC now follows naturally—all we need is an encoding for XML tags, and this can be obtained by following exactly the same intuitions that we used for characters. We assume that the program context *Ctx* contains a special class Tag and, for each XML tag <g>, a singleton class $Tag_{<g>}$ (with the object new $Tag_{<g>}$() as its only inhabitant) as an immediate subclass of Tag. Then, for an XML fragment

```
<basket> <apple/> <banana/> </basket>
```

the corresponding XTATIC value is

<new Tag_{basket}()>[<new Tag_{apple}()>[], <new Tag_{banana}()>[]]

and the corresponding type is

<Tag_{basket}>[<Tag_{apple}>[], <Tag_{banana}>[]]

Of course, an implementation needs special syntax that makes these values and types readable. The concrete syntax in our current prototype implementation looks very close to standard XML.

Together, the encodings of character data and tags allow a good-size fragment of XML to be represented very directly in FX. (There are still important parts missing, though. Most urgently, we still lack a good treatment of attributes which, until very recently [15], was also lacking in XDUCE.)

The only basic data type provided by the XML standard is character sequences. Some schema formalisms, however, introduce *datatypes*—a set of conventions by which a schema can specify that a particular textual fragment in an XML document is supposed to represent a non-textual value, e.g. a float or a date. Some of these datatype descriptions can be captured using subtypes of pcdata built from regular expression operators to mimic the string regular expressions that describe particular datatype formats. Alternatively, the FX framework could accommodate a Schema-datatype-aware encoding of XML, when a text representing a Schema datatype value gets translated directly into a value of an appropriate $C^\#$ type (placed as a label of a childless tree), bypassing the pcdata representation.

8   Related Work

There is a substantial literature (and many formalisms and tools) addressing dynamic validation of XML documents against expected schemas, either by stand-alone processors or during document construction (as has been proposed for DOM Level 3 [10]). While XTATIC shares some formal background with these techniques, its central goal—to support *static* checking of XML-manipulating code—falls completely outside their purview.

Among static approaches, there are two overlapping kinds of work that are directly relevant to ours: (1) work on providing XML processing capabilities in pre-existing programming languages with static guarantees of correctness, and (2) work on combining object-orientation with XML-like data models.

A popular direction for work of the first kind is to provide a translation that generates type definitions (and value constructors) in the original language corresponding to XML types of interest. Examples include JAXB [32], Relaxer [28], HaXML [35], and XMλ [24, 30]. One disadvantage of these translations is that they tend to introduce "spurious structure," destroying some useful flexibility in the subtype relation. This point is discussed in detail in [18] and [13].

There are varying degrees of possible integration of a "foreign" data model into the object-oriented data model. One is creating a combined data model that includes the features of both on an equal basis, but without mixing them. A successful example is the ODMG data model [6], an accepted standard for object-oriented databases, which offers a class-based object-oriented type system analogous to that of programming languages like $C^{\#}$, together with a few other built-in type constructors: records, sets, bags, lists and arrays (all of them typed).

A greater degree of integration can be achieved by taking the object-oriented data model as primary and the other data model as subsidiary, in the sense that its values can also be viewed as objects. This approach has the advantage of better integration with legacy software written entirely under the original object-oriented model. Examples of this approach can be found in both the programming language and database communities.

The Pizza [26] project extended Java with parametric polymorphism, higher-order functions, and tagged union types with pattern matching. (The polymorphism component became the basis for the GJ [5] proposal for adding generic types to Java.) All these features are implemented by a "homogeneous translation" into pure Java; we plan to use a similar translation scheme to implement XTATIC. Current work on the programming language Scala [25] is aimed at incorporating many of the same ideas as Pizza in a language aimed at programming Web services, including XML processing.

Even before XML became popular, the database community was actively investigating the management of "semistructured" data; the Object Exchange Model (OEM) [27] is a popular formalism in this area. An OEM data value is a directed graph (often just a tree) with edges labeled by tags, internal nodes containing unique identifiers, and leaf nodes containing atomic values (integers, strings, etc.).

The combination of ordinary algebraic types with objects in the ODMG data model proves to be rather inflexible for working with semistructural data, as it involved encodings within the structural ODMG model, which are usually complex and difficult to manage and evolve. The Ozone project [22] approached this problem by integrating the OEM data model into the ODMG data model. Their solution is similar to ours at the level of values: first, the OEM model is generalized to allow arbitrary ODMG values, including objects and structural values as leaves; second, a special ODMG class, OEM, is designated to hold all OEM values. The OEM values are ultimately implemented as objects of OEM subclasses. The OEM data model, however, is not statically typed. The motivation for Ozone was to allow convenient manipulation of semistructured data in an object-oriented database while avoiding the overly strict ODMG typing restrictions. Our contribution can be viewed as proceeding from the observation that an Ozone-like integration of objects and semistructured data can be carried out in a fully typed way, once an appropriate alternative to algebraic types (i.e., regular types) is identified.

Two ongoing language design efforts that are very close to XTATIC in intentions and approach are CDUCE and JWIG. JWIG [7] is an extension of Java intended for programming interactive sessions between Web servers and clients. Although quite different in style from XTATIC (it uses data flow analysis to check well-formedness of XML expressions constructed by filling in "templates", rather than a conventional type system and tree expression language), the basic expressive power of Jwig's analysis is close to that of XDUCE's type system; see [7] for a detailed discussion of this point.

CDUCE [4], like to XTATIC, aims to introduce XDUCE features into an object-oriented type system. The latter, in case of CDUCE, is λ-&—a variant of λ-calculus with overloading, commonly used as a formalism for multiple-dispatch OO languages. Like XTATIC, CDUCE adapts the semantic interpretation of subtyping to a larger type system [12]. The major difference is the need to give a semantic interpretation of arrow types, which does not arise in XTATIC (we avoid it because of the "nominal" character of the underlying type system). A further dimension of complexity in CDUCE is its support for arbitrary boolean type constructors, including intersection and difference in addition to union.

9   Future Work

We are currently experimenting with a prototype interpreter for XTATIC. Though it still lacks many of the features of $C^\#$, the language implemented by the interpreter goes quite a bit beyond the simple FX core described here—in particular, it includes imperative features, interfaces, and overloading; we have used it to experiment with a number of small demos. Our immediate goals include handling a larger fragment of $C^\#$, building more ambitious demos, and replacing the simple interpreter by a back end targeting the .NET Common Language Runtime.

Another important near-term goal is to extend the type system to encompass a larger part of XML—most urgently, attributes. Hosoya and Murata [15] have recently proposed a typing mechanism and corresponding algorithms based on the attribute-element constraints of Relax NG; we hope to be able to adapt this proposal to XTATIC. We also plan to implement translators from standard XML schema languages (in particular, a subset of the XML-Schema standard) into XTATIC.

Our longer-term goals concentrate in two major areas: improving the efficiency of the underlying algorithms and run-time representations, and refining and extending the design of the core language. On the efficiency side, the main development currently in the works is high-performance compilation of pattern matching. We also need to come up with better run-time representations for certain special cases, while keeping compliance with the basic data model. One case in point is the PCDATA type. The typing and pattern-matching properties of the PCDATA definition given in Section 7 are attractive, but the naive representation that we sketched is clearly too heavy to perform well; something more clever will be needed. At the level of the core language design, there are also numerous questions to be considered. Can objects and trees be further unified? E.g., could pattern matching be used to extract object fields? Could attributes and fields be unified? Can we offer other kinds of pattern matching primitives, e.g. support for XPath? And, last but not least, can the XTATIC design be extended to cope with parametric polymorphism ("generics" in C# parlance)?

Acknowledgements

Michael Levin and Alan Schmitt have been closely involved in the XTATIC design and contributed many ideas to this formalization of the core. We are also grateful to Haruo Hosoya, originator of XDUCE, and to Eijiro Sumii for numerous conversations, to Matthias Zenger, Vincent Cremet, and Martin Odersky for helping work out some of the basic insights in the XML encoding, to Todd Proebsting, Eric Meijer, and Wolfram Schulte for insights into the world of XML processing in C# and its implications on language design, to Peter Buneman for the name XTATIC, and to Arnaud Sahuguet for making us aware of Ozone and for general encouragement and enthusiasm.

Our work on XDUCE and XTATIC has been supported by the National Science Foundation under Career grant CCR-9701826 and ITR CCR-0219945 and by a gift from Microsoft.

References

[1] J. Aldrich, V. Kostadinov, and C. Chambers. Alias annotations for program understanding. In *ACM Symposium on Object Oriented Programming: Systems, Languages, and Applications (OOPSLA)*, Nov. 2002.

[2] D. Ancona, G. Lagorio, and E. Zucca. A core calculus for Java exceptions. In *ACM Symposium on Object Oriented Programming: Systems, Languages, and Applications (OOPSLA)*, pages 16–30, 2001.

[3] D. Ancona and E. Zucca. True modules for Java-like languages: Design and foundations, Aug. 2000. Technical Report DISI-TR-00-12, Dipartimento di Informatica e Scienze dellInformazione, Università di Genova.

[4] V. Benzaken, G. Castagna, and A. Frisch. CDuce: a white paper. ftp:// ftp.ens.fr/pub/di/users/castagna/cduce-wp.ps.gz, 2002. Workshop on Programming Language Technologies for XML (PLAN-X).

[5] G. Bracha, M. Odersky, D. Stoutamire, and P. Wadler. Making the future safe for the past: Adding genericity to the Java programming language. In C. Chambers, editor, *ACM Symposium on Object Oriented Programming: Systems, Languages, and Applications (OOPSLA)*, ACM SIGPLAN Notices volume 33 number 10, pages 183–200, Vancouver, BC, Oct. 1998.

[6] R. Catell, editor. *The Object Database Standard: ODMG-93*. Morgan Kaufmann, 1994.

[7] A. S. Christensen, A. Moller, and M. I. Schwartzbach. Extending Java for high-level web service construction. http://www.brics.dk/~mis/jwig.ps, 2002.

[8] J. Clark. TREX: Tree Regular Expressions for XML. www.thaiopensource.com/ trex/, 2001.

[9] J. Clark and M. Murata. RELAX NG. http://www.relaxng.org, 2001.

[10] Document Object Model (DOM) Level 3 validation specification, W3C working draft. http://www.w3.org/TR/DOM-Level-3-Val, 2002.

[11] M. F. Fernández, J. Siméon, and P. Wadler. A semi-monad for semi-structured data. In J. V. den Bussche and V. Vianu, editors, *Proceedings of 8th International Conference on Database Theory (ICDT 2001)*, volume 1973 of *Lecture Notes in Computer Science*, pages 263–300. Springer, 2001.

[12] A. Frisch, G. Castagna, and V. Benzaken. Semantic subtyping. In *IEEE Symposium on Logic in Computer Science (LICS)*, 2002.

[13] H. Hosoya. *Regular Expression Types for XML*. PhD thesis, The University of Tokyo, Japan, 2000.

[14] H. Hosoya. Regular expression pattern matching - a simpler design. Technical Report 1397, RIMS, Kyoto University, 2003.

[15] H. Hosoya and M. Murata. Validation and boolean operations for attribute-element constraints. In *Workshop on Programming Language Technologies for XML (PLAN-X)*, 2002.

[16] H. Hosoya and B. Pierce. Regular expression pattern matching. In *ACM Symposium on Principles of Programming Languages (POPL)*, London, England, 2001. Full version to appear in *Journal of Functional Programming*.

[17] H. Hosoya and B. C. Pierce. XDuce: A typed XML processing language (preliminary report). In D. Suciu and G. Vossen, editors, *International Workshop on the Web and Databases (WebDB)*, May 2000. Reprinted in *The Web and Databases, Selected Papers*, Springer LNCS volume 1997, 2001.

[18] H. Hosoya and B. C. Pierce. XDuce: A statically typed XML processing language. *ACM Transactions on Internet Technology*, 2003. To appear.

[19] H. Hosoya, J. Vouillon, and B. C. Pierce. Regular expression types for XML. In *Proceedings of the International Conference on Functional Programming (ICFP)*, 2000.

[20] A. Igarashi, B. Pierce, and P. Wadler. Featherweight Java: A minimal core calculus for Java and GJ. In *ACM Symposium on Object Oriented Programming: Systems, Languages, and Applications (OOPSLA)*, Oct. 1999. Full version in ACM Transactions on Programming Languages and Systems (TOPLAS), 23(3), May 2001.

[21] A. Igarashi and B. C. Pierce. On inner classes. *Information and Computation*, 177(1):56–89, Aug. 2002. A special issue with papers from the 7th Workshop on Foundations of Object-Oriented Languages (FOOL), informal proceedings. An earlier version appeared in *Proceedings of the 14th European Conference on Object-Oriented Programming (ECOOP)*, Springer LNCS 1850, pages 129–153.

[22] T. Lahiri, S. Abiteboul, and J. Widom. Ozone: integrating structured and semistructured data. In *International Workshop on Database Programming Languages*, volume 1949 of *Lecture Notes in Computer Science*, pages 297–32. Springer, 1999.

[23] C. League, Z. Shao, and V. Trifonov. Type-preserving compilation of Featherweight Java. *ACM Transactions on Programming Languages and Systems*, 24(2):112–152, 2002.

[24] E. Meijer and M. Shields. XMλ: A functional programming language for constructing and manipulating XML documents. Submitted for publication, 1999.

[25] M. Odersky. Report on the programming language Scala. http://lamp.epfl.ch/~odersky/scala/reference.ps, 2002.

[26] M. Odersky and P. Wadler. Pizza into Java: Translating theory into practice. In *ACM Symposium on Principles of Programming Languages (POPL)*, Paris, France, 1997.

[27] Y. Papaconstantinou, H. Garcia-Molina, and J. Widom. Object exchange across heterogeneous information sources. In *International Conference on Data Engineering*, Mar. 1995.

[28] Relaxer.   `http://www.asahi-net.or.jp/~dp8t-asm/java/tools/Relaxer/index.html`.

[29] U. P. Schultz. Partial evaluation for class-based object-oriented languages. In *Programs as Data Objects (PADO), Aarhus, Denmark*, volume 2053 of *Lecture Notes in Computer Science*, pages 173–197, 2001.

[30] M. Shields and E. Meijer. Type-indexed rows. In *ACM Symposium on Principles of Programming Languages (POPL), London, England*, 2001.

[31] T. Studer. Constructive foundations for Featherweight Java. In R. Kahle, P. Schroeder-Heister, and R. Stärk, editors, *Proof Theory in Computer Science*. Springer-Verlag, 2001. Lecture Notes in Computer Science, volume 2183.

[32] Sun Microsystems. The Java architecture for XML binding (JAXB). `http://java.sun.com/xml/jaxb`, 2001.

[33] N. Tabuchi, E. Sumii, and A. Yonezawa. Regular expression types for strings in a text processing language. In G. Barthe and P. Thiemann, editors, *Proceedings of Workshop on Types in Programming (TIP'02)*, volume 75 of *Electronic Notes in Theoretical Computer Science*, pages 1–19. Elsevier Science, July 2002.

[34] M. Tofte. Type inference for polymorphic references. *Information and Computation*, 89(1), Nov. 1990.

[35] M. Wallace and C. Runciman. Haskell and XML: Generic combinators or type-based translation? In *Proceedings of the Fourth ACM SIGPLAN International Conference on Functional Programming (ICFP'99)*, volume 34-9 of *ACM SIGPLAN Notices*, pages 148–159, N.Y., 1999. ACM Press.

[36] Extensible Markup Language (XML™), Feb. 1998. XML 1.0, W3C Recommendation, `http://www.w3.org/XML/`.

[37] XQuery 1.0: An XML Query Language, W3C Working Draft. `http://www.w3.org/TR/xquery/`, Nov. 2002.

[38] XQuery 1.0 and XPath 2.0 Formal Semantics, W3C Working Draft. `http://www.w3c.org/TR/query-semantics/`, Nov. 2002.

[39] XML Schema Part 0: Primer, W3C Working Draft. `http://www.w3.org/TR/xmlschema-0/`, 2000.

[40] XSL Transformations (XSLT), 1999. `http://www.w3.org/TR/xslt`.

[41] M. Zenger. Type-safe prototype-based component evolution. In *European Conference on Object-Oriented Programming (ECOOP), Malaga, Spain*, June 2002.

A   Appendix: Additional Definitions

This appendix presents in full some parts of the FX language definition that were just sketched in the body of the paper.

The *typing* judgment $\Gamma \vdash e \in A$, "in the type environment Γ, expression e gets type A", and its prerequisite *pattern typing* judgment, $\triangleright R \Rightarrow \Gamma$ are defined in Figure 5. We write *tyof*(R) for the type obtained from the pattern R by erasing value binding annotations.

A program context $Ctx = \langle Typenames, def, Classes, \sqsubseteq:, fields, mtype, mbody \rangle$, is *valid* provided the following holds

- if $D \sqsubseteq: C$, then for any $m \in dom(C)$, if $mtype(D)(m) = (\overline{A} \to A)$ and $mtype(C)(m) = (\overline{B} \to B)$, then $\overline{A} <: \overline{B}$, $\overline{B} <: \overline{A}$ and $A <: B$.
- for any C and m, if $mtype(C)(m) = \overline{A} \to A$ and $mbody(C)(m) = (D, \overline{x}, e)$, then this $: D, \overline{x} : \overline{A} \vdash e \in B$ for some $B <: A$.

A valid context corresponds to a program that has passed all the typing checks and for which we can guarantee absence of type errors at run time (Section 6).

Figure 6 defines the big-step *evaluation* judgment $\Sigma \vdash e \Downarrow a$, "in the value environment Σ, expression e evaluates to value a", and its prerequisite *pattern matching* judgment $a \triangleright Q \Rightarrow \Sigma$, read "an FX value expression a matches a pattern Q, yielding an environment Σ".

Figure 7 introduces the judgment $\Sigma \vdash e \not\Downarrow$, "evaluation of e gets stuck in finite number of steps". This judgment is specific to big-step semantics and is necessary to state the soundness theorem. The analogous property for small-step semantics says that e gets reduced to a non-value, an expression to which none of the evaluation rules is applicable.

Expression typing: $\Gamma \vdash e \in A$

$$\frac{\Gamma(x) = A}{\Gamma \vdash x \in A} \quad \text{T-Var}$$

$$\frac{C \neq \text{Seq} \quad \textit{fields}(C) = \overline{F}\ \overline{f} \quad \Gamma \vdash \overline{e} \in \overline{A} \quad \overline{A} <: \overline{F}}{\Gamma \vdash \text{new } C(\overline{e}) \in C} \quad \text{T-New}$$

$$\frac{\Gamma \vdash e \in C \quad \textit{fields}(C) = \overline{F}\ \overline{f}}{\Gamma \vdash e.f_k \in F_k} \quad \text{T-Field}$$

$$\frac{\Gamma \vdash e \in C \quad \textit{mtype}(C)(m) = \overline{F} \rightarrow B \quad \Gamma \vdash \overline{d} \in \overline{A} \quad \overline{A} <: \overline{F}}{\Gamma \vdash e.m(\overline{d}) \in B} \quad \text{T-Invk} \qquad \Gamma \vdash [] \in [[]] \quad \text{T-Eps}$$

$$\frac{n \geq 2 \quad \Gamma \vdash [e_k] \in [T_k]}{\Gamma \vdash [\overline{e}] \in [T_1,\ \ldots,\ T_n]} \quad \text{T-Seq} \qquad \frac{\Gamma \vdash d \in A \quad \Gamma \vdash [\overline{e}] \in T}{\Gamma \vdash [\langle\!\langle d \rangle\!\rangle[\overline{e}]] \in [\langle\!\langle A \rangle\!\rangle[T]]} \quad \text{T-Tree}$$

$$\frac{\Gamma \vdash [e] \in [T]}{\Gamma \vdash [[e]] \in [T]} \quad \text{T-Collapse}$$

$$\frac{\begin{array}{c} \Gamma \vdash d \in [T] \quad [T] <: [P_1 | \ldots | P_n] \\ \forall k \in 1 \ldots n-1.\ [T] \not<: [P_1 | \ldots | P_k] \\ \forall k \in 1 \ldots n.\ \rhd [P_k] \Rightarrow \Gamma_k \quad \Gamma, \Gamma_k \vdash e_k \in A_k \end{array}}{\Gamma \vdash \text{match}(d)\{\text{case } [\overline{P}] : \overline{e}\} \in A_1 \sqcup A_2 \sqcup \ldots \sqcup A_n} \quad \text{T-Match}$$

Pattern typing: $\rhd [X] \Rightarrow \Gamma$

$$\rhd C \Rightarrow \bullet \quad \text{PI-Class} \qquad \frac{\textit{def}(X) = T \quad \rhd [T] \Rightarrow \Gamma}{\rhd [X] \Rightarrow \Gamma} \quad \text{PI-REtype}$$

$$\frac{\rhd Q \Rightarrow \Gamma \quad \textit{tyof}(R) = A}{\rhd R\ x \Rightarrow x : A, \Gamma} \quad \text{PI-BindFX} \qquad \frac{\rhd Q \Rightarrow \Gamma_1 \quad \rhd [P] \Rightarrow \Gamma_2}{\rhd [\langle\!\langle Q \rangle\!\rangle[P]] \Rightarrow \Gamma_1, \Gamma_2} \quad \text{PI-Tree}$$

$$\rhd [[]] \Rightarrow \bullet \quad \text{PI-Eps} \qquad \frac{\rhd [P_1] \Rightarrow \Gamma_1 \quad \rhd [P_2] \Rightarrow \Gamma_2}{\rhd [P_1, P_2] \Rightarrow \Gamma_1, \Gamma_2} \quad \text{PI-Cat}$$

$$\frac{\rhd [P_1] \Rightarrow \Gamma_1 \quad \rhd [P_2] \Rightarrow \Gamma_2}{\rhd [P_1 | P_2] \Rightarrow \Gamma_1 \sqcup \Gamma_2} \quad \text{PI-Alt} \qquad \rhd [T*] \Rightarrow \bullet \quad \text{PI-Rep}$$

$$\frac{\rhd [P] \Rightarrow \Gamma \quad \textit{tyof}([P]) = [T]}{\rhd [P\ x] \Rightarrow x : [T], \Gamma} \quad \text{PI-BindRE}$$

Type join and type environment join

$$
\begin{array}{ll}
C \sqcup D & = \sup_{\sqsubseteq:}\{C, D\} \\
C \sqcup [T] & = \sup_{\sqsubseteq:}\{C, \text{Seq}\} \\
[T] \sqcup C & = \sup_{\sqsubseteq:}\{\text{Seq}, C\} \\
[T_1] \sqcup [T_2] & = [T_1 | T_2] \\
\Gamma_1 \sqcup \Gamma_2 & = \lambda x.\Gamma_1(x) \sqcup \Gamma_2(x)
\end{array}
$$

Fig. 5. FX typing

Expression evaluation: $\Sigma \vdash \mathtt{e} \Downarrow \mathtt{a}$

$$\frac{\Sigma(\mathtt{x}) = \mathtt{a}}{\Sigma \vdash \mathtt{x} \Downarrow \mathtt{a}} \ \text{E-Var} \qquad\qquad \frac{\Sigma \vdash \overline{\mathtt{e}} \Downarrow \overline{\mathtt{a}}}{\Sigma \vdash \mathtt{new\ C(\overline{e})} \Downarrow \mathtt{new\ C(\overline{a})}} \ \text{E-New}$$

$$\frac{\Sigma \vdash \mathtt{e} \Downarrow \mathtt{new\ C(\overline{a})} \qquad \mathit{fields}(\mathtt{C}) = \overline{\mathtt{F}}\ \overline{\mathtt{f}}}{\Sigma \vdash \mathtt{e.f}_k \Downarrow \mathtt{a}_k} \ \text{E-Field}$$

$$\frac{\begin{array}{c}\Sigma \vdash \mathtt{e}_0 \Downarrow \mathtt{new\ C(\overline{a})} \qquad \mathit{mbody}(\mathtt{C},\mathtt{m}) = (\mathtt{D},\overline{\mathtt{x}},\mathtt{e}) \\ \Sigma \vdash \overline{\mathtt{d}} \Downarrow \overline{\mathtt{b}} \qquad \overline{\mathtt{x}} : \overline{\mathtt{b}}, \mathtt{this} : \mathtt{new\ C(\overline{a})} \vdash \mathtt{e} \Downarrow \mathtt{a}\end{array}}{\Sigma \vdash \mathtt{e}_0.\mathtt{m}(\overline{\mathtt{d}}) \Downarrow \mathtt{a}} \ \text{E-Invk} \qquad \Sigma \vdash [] \Downarrow [] \ \text{E-Eps}$$

$$\frac{n \geq 2 \qquad \Sigma \vdash [\mathtt{e}_k] \Downarrow [\overline{\mathtt{t}}_k]}{\Sigma \vdash [\overline{\mathtt{e}}] \Downarrow [\overline{\mathtt{t}}_1, \ldots, \overline{\mathtt{t}}_n]} \ \text{E-Seq} \qquad \frac{\Sigma \vdash \mathtt{d} \Downarrow \mathtt{a} \qquad \Sigma \vdash [\overline{\mathtt{e}}] \Downarrow [\overline{\mathtt{t}}]}{\Sigma \vdash [\langle\!\langle \mathtt{d}\rangle\!\rangle[\overline{\mathtt{e}}]] \Downarrow [\langle\!\langle \mathtt{a}\rangle\!\rangle[\overline{\mathtt{t}}]]} \ \text{E-Tree}$$

$$\frac{\Sigma \vdash [\overline{\mathtt{e}}] \Downarrow [\overline{\mathtt{t}}]}{\Sigma \vdash [[\overline{\mathtt{e}}]] \Downarrow [\overline{\mathtt{t}}]} \ \text{E-Collapse}$$

$$\frac{\Sigma \vdash \mathtt{d} \Downarrow [\overline{\mathtt{t}}] \qquad [\overline{\mathtt{t}}] \notin [\mathtt{P}_1] \quad \ldots \quad [\overline{\mathtt{t}}] \notin [\mathtt{P}_{k-1}] \qquad [\overline{\mathtt{t}}] \in [\mathtt{P}_k] \Rightarrow \Sigma' \qquad \Sigma, \Sigma' \vdash \mathtt{e}_k \Downarrow \mathtt{a}}{\Sigma \vdash \{\mathtt{match(d)}\{\mathtt{case}\ [\overline{\mathtt{P}}] : \overline{\mathtt{e}}\} \Downarrow \mathtt{a}} \ \text{E-Match}$$

Pattern matching: $\mathtt{a} \triangleright \mathtt{Q} \Rightarrow \Sigma$

$$\frac{\mathtt{D} \sqsubseteq : \mathtt{C}}{\mathtt{new\ D(\overline{a})} \triangleright \mathtt{C} \Rightarrow \bullet} \ \text{P-ObjCls} \qquad\qquad \frac{\mathtt{Seq} \sqsubseteq : \mathtt{C}}{[\overline{\mathtt{t}}] \triangleright \mathtt{C} \Rightarrow \bullet} \ \text{P-SeqCls}$$

$$\frac{\mathit{def}(\mathtt{X}) = \mathtt{T} \qquad [\overline{\mathtt{t}}] \triangleright [\mathtt{T}] \Rightarrow \Sigma}{[\overline{\mathtt{t}}] \triangleright [\mathtt{X}] \Rightarrow \Sigma} \ \text{P-RegDef} \qquad\qquad \frac{\mathtt{a} \triangleright \mathtt{Q} \Rightarrow \Sigma}{\mathtt{a} \triangleright \mathtt{Q}\ \mathtt{x} \Rightarrow \mathtt{x} : \mathtt{a}, \Sigma} \ \text{P-BindFX}$$

$$\frac{\mathtt{a} \triangleright \mathtt{Q} \Rightarrow \Sigma_1 \qquad [\overline{\mathtt{t}}] \triangleright [\mathtt{P}] \Rightarrow \Sigma_2}{[\langle\!\langle \mathtt{a}\rangle\!\rangle[\overline{\mathtt{t}}]] \triangleright [\langle\!\langle \mathtt{Q}\rangle\!\rangle[\mathtt{P}]] \Rightarrow \Sigma_1, \Sigma_2} \ \text{P-Tree} \qquad\qquad [] \triangleright [[]] \Rightarrow \bullet \ \text{P-Eps}$$

$$\frac{\begin{array}{c}[\overline{\mathtt{t}}_1] \triangleright [\mathtt{P}_1] \Rightarrow \Sigma_1 \\ [\overline{\mathtt{t}}_2] \triangleright [\mathtt{P}_2] \Rightarrow \Sigma_2\end{array}}{[\overline{\mathtt{t}}_1,\ \overline{\mathtt{t}}_2] \triangleright [\mathtt{P}_1,\ \mathtt{P}_2] \Rightarrow \Sigma_1, \Sigma_2} \ \text{P-Cat} \qquad\qquad \frac{[\overline{\mathtt{t}}] \triangleright [\mathtt{P}_1] \Rightarrow \Sigma}{[\overline{\mathtt{t}}] \triangleright [\mathtt{P}_1 | \mathtt{P}_2] \Rightarrow \Sigma} \ \text{P-Alt1}$$

$$\frac{\begin{array}{c}[\overline{\mathtt{t}}] \triangleright [\mathtt{P}_1] \not\Rightarrow \\ [\overline{\mathtt{t}}] \triangleright [\mathtt{P}_2] \Rightarrow \Sigma\end{array}}{[\overline{\mathtt{t}}] \triangleright [\mathtt{P}_1 | \mathtt{P}_2] \Rightarrow \Sigma} \ \text{P-Alt2} \qquad\qquad \frac{n \geq 0 \qquad \forall k \in 1 \ldots n.\ [\overline{\mathtt{t}}_k] \triangleright [\mathtt{T}] \Rightarrow \bullet}{[\overline{\mathtt{t}}_1, \ldots, \overline{\mathtt{t}}_n] \triangleright [\mathtt{T}*] \Rightarrow \bullet} \ \text{P-Rep}$$

$$\frac{[\overline{\mathtt{t}}] \triangleright [\mathtt{P}] \Rightarrow \Sigma}{[\overline{\mathtt{t}}] \triangleright [\mathtt{P}\ \mathtt{x}] \Rightarrow \mathtt{x} : [\overline{\mathtt{t}}], \Sigma} \ \text{P-BindRE}$$

Fig. 6. FX evaluation

- $\Sigma \vdash$ new C($\overline{\text{e}}$) $\Downarrow\!\!\!\!/$ if $\Sigma \vdash$ e$_i$ $\Downarrow\!\!\!\!/$ for either one of e$_i$ from $\overline{\text{e}}$;
- $\Sigma \vdash$ d.f $\Downarrow\!\!\!\!/$ if either
    1. $\Sigma \vdash$ d $\Downarrow\!\!\!\!/$ or
    2. $\Sigma \vdash$ d $\Downarrow$ [$\overline{\text{t}}$], or
    3. $\Sigma \vdash$ d $\Downarrow$ new C($\overline{\text{b}}$), but f is not among *fields*(C);
- $\Sigma \vdash$ d.m($\overline{\text{e}}$) $\Downarrow\!\!\!\!/$ if either
    1. $\Sigma \vdash$ d $\Downarrow\!\!\!\!/$ or
    2. $\Sigma \vdash$ d $\Downarrow$ [$\overline{\text{t}}$], or
    3. $\Sigma \vdash$ d $\Downarrow$ new C($\overline{\text{b}}$) but *mbody*(C)(m) is not defined, or
    4. $\Sigma \vdash$ d $\Downarrow$ new C($\overline{\text{b}}$), *mbody*(C)(m) is defined, but $\Sigma \vdash$ e$_i$ $\Downarrow\!\!\!\!/$ for either one of e$_i$ from $\overline{\text{e}}$;
    5. $\Sigma \vdash$ d $\Downarrow$ new C($\overline{\text{b}}$), *mbody*(C)(m) = (D,$\overline{\text{x}}$,e), $\Sigma \vdash \overline{\text{e}} \Downarrow \overline{\text{a}}$, but this : new C($\overline{\text{b}}$),$\overline{\text{x}}$: $\overline{\text{a}} \vdash$ e $\Downarrow\!\!\!\!/$
- $\Sigma \vdash$ [$\langle\!\langle$d$\rangle\!\rangle$[$\overline{\text{e}}$]] $\Downarrow\!\!\!\!/$ if either
    1. $\Sigma \vdash$ d $\Downarrow\!\!\!\!/$, or
    2. $\Sigma \vdash$ d $\Downarrow$ a, but $\Sigma \vdash$ [$\overline{\text{e}}$] $\Downarrow\!\!\!\!/$;
- $\Sigma \vdash$ [$\overline{\text{e}}$] $\Downarrow\!\!\!\!/$ if $|\overline{\text{e}}| \geq 2$ and $\Sigma \vdash$ e$_i$ $\Downarrow\!\!\!\!/$ for either one of e$_i$ from $\overline{\text{e}}$;
- $\Sigma \vdash$ [[$\overline{\text{e}}$]] $\Downarrow\!\!\!\!/$ if $\Sigma \vdash$ [$\overline{\text{e}}$] $\Downarrow\!\!\!\!/$
- $\Sigma \vdash$ match(d){case [$\overline{\text{P}}$] : $\overline{\text{e}}$} $\Downarrow\!\!\!\!/$ if either
    1. $\Sigma \vdash$ d $\Downarrow\!\!\!\!/$, or
    2. $\Sigma \vdash$ d $\Downarrow$ new C($\overline{\text{b}}$), or
    3. $\Sigma \vdash$ d $\Downarrow$ [$\overline{\text{t}}$], but [$\overline{\text{t}}$] $\in$ [P$_i$] $\not\Rightarrow$ for all i, or
    4. $\Sigma \vdash$ d $\Downarrow$ [$\overline{\text{t}}$], and, for some i, [$\overline{\text{t}}$] $\in$ [P$_1$] $\not\Rightarrow$, [$\overline{\text{t}}$] $\in$ [P$_{i-1}$] $\not\Rightarrow$, [$\overline{\text{t}}$] $\in$ [P$_i$] $\Rightarrow \Sigma'$, but $\Sigma,\Sigma' \vdash$ e$_i$ $\Downarrow\!\!\!\!/$.

Fig. 7. FX stuck evaluation relation $\Sigma \vdash$ e $\Downarrow\!\!\!\!/$

External Uniqueness Is Unique Enough

Dave Clarke[1] and Tobias Wrigstad[2]

[1] Institute of Information and Computing Sciences
Utrecht University, Utrecht, The Netherlands.
dave@cs.uu.nl
[2] Deptartment of Computer and Systems Sciences
Stockholm University/KTH, Stockholm, Sweden.
tobias@dsv.su.se

Abstract. *External uniqueness* is a surprising new way to add unique references to an OOPL. The idea is that an externally unique reference is the only reference into an aggregate from outside the aggregate. Internal references which do not escape the boundary of the aggregate are innocuous and therefore permitted. Based on ownership types, our proposal not only overcomes an abstraction problem from which existing uniqueness proposals suffer, it also enables many examples which are inherently not unique, such as a unique reference to a set of links in a doubly-linked list, without losing the benefits of uniqueness.

1 Introduction

Two essentially different approaches to managing aliasing in object-oriented programming exist. On one hand sits unique or alias-free references. These are based on a very simple idea: any variable or field annotated with the keyword unique contains the only reference to the object it holds, otherwise it contains null [29, 35, 11, 13, 9, 1]. Apart from helping reason about programs, unique references safely enable, for example, idioms essential in concurrent programming such as the transfer of ownership pattern [32], and help enforce software protocols [19]. In all cases, the same notion of uniqueness applies.

Unfortunately, all extant uniqueness proposals suffer from an *abstraction problem* which we identify in this paper: *as software evolves, programs which use uniqueness are forced to change their interfaces when purely internal implementation changes are made.* The interface changes propagate through a program.

The second approach to managing aliasing employs alias encapsulation, as exemplified by ownership types [17]. Simply put, these impose a form of object-level privacy by preventing objects (rather than just fields) from being accessed outside of their enclosing encapsulation boundaries [17, 36, 15, 9, 7, 16, 1, 5]. Ownership types have been employed for reasoning about programs [16, 36], for alias management [17, 37], in program understanding [1], to eliminate data-races [9] and deadlocks [7] from concurrent programs, and to enable safe lazy updates in object-oriented databases [8].

L. Cardelli (Ed.): ECOOP 2003, LNCS 2743, pp. 176–200, 2003.

Existing attempts to unify uniqueness and ownership typing [9, 1] unfortunately offer little additional benefit from their combination, while perpetuating the abstraction problem.

We believe that the key to the abstraction problem is that most systems cannot distinguish between external references and innocuous, internal references which do not escape encapsulation boundaries. There are essentially two kinds of ownership types, based on the degree of protection provided. The stronger form, namely those with deep ownership [17, 16], provide the machinery necessary to make this distinction. These form the basis for our proposal.

In this paper, we introduce a different kind of uniqueness called *external uniqueness*. External uniqueness loosens the conventional uniqueness constraint, requiring that there be only one reference to an aggregate from outside of the aggregate, without limiting the number of references to the aggregate from its inside. Interestingly, it turns out that the externally unique reference is the only active reference to an object, so it is effectively unique.

Our proposal not only overcomes the abstraction problem, it also enables a number of interesting examples which result from the synergy between uniqueness and deep ownership: we enable, for example, the transfer of entire aggregates between objects, or even the combination of the encapsulated representation of data structures such as doubly-linked lists, even in the presence of aliasing within such aggregates, without leaving any unwanted aliases which would break encapsulation. Above all, we do so for a class-based object-oriented programming language with subtyping.

Outline Our paper is organised as follows. In Section 2 we describe the abstraction problem with uniqueness, and point to a way around it. As ownership types are the key to a solution, we review them in Section 3. We then describe external uniqueness in Section 4, before illustrating its power through example in Section 5. Section 6 covers the essence of our formalisation. We discuss our proposal in Section 7 and related work in Section 8, before concluding in Section 9.

2   Challenging Uniqueness

Existing approaches to uniqueness in object-oriented programming are broken. We now outline how the two different approaches both suffer from the same abstraction problem, before indicating a way out of the mess.

2.1   An Abstraction Problem

To add unique references to an OOPL, one must consider how a class treats its instances internally via this (or self). Approaches in the literature reflect the treatment of this in a class' interface in one of two ways:

Via Class Annotation classes are divided into two kinds, those which may assign this internally, and those which do not. Only instances of the latter may be referenced uniquely [35].

Via Method Annotation methods are annotated to indicate that they may consume `this` [29, 11]. Calling such a method requires (at least conceptually) that its target be destructively read.

Proposals combining ownership types and uniqueness follow suit: Boyapati and Rinard [9] adopt the first approach, whereas Aldrich, Kostadinov and Chambers [1] adopt the latter. In both cases, a problem surfaces when the implementation of a class changes the way it uses `this`. For concreteness, assume that we have the following class with a single method:

```
class BlackBox {            and a variable (or field):
    void xyzzy() { .. }         unique BlackBox bb;
}
```

When we change the implementation of the `BlackBox` class so that the `xyzzy` method assigns `this` internally, we are *forced*, under existing proposals, to change `BlackBox`'s interface.

Using class annotations we would have to modify `BlackBox` to indicate that its instances cannot be referred to uniquely: `class neverunique BlackBox`. As a result, variable declarations such as the one above would no longer be valid, and would have their uniqueness stripped. It may also be the case that all destructive reads of `BlackBox` objects throughout the entire program would have to be changed to ordinary reads, perhaps with destructive read implemented manually.

When using method annotations, we would have to modify the `xyzzy` method to indicate that it consumes `this`, such as `void xyzzy() consumes { .. }`. The call `bb.xyzzy()` may create an internal reference to its target, requiring that the target `bb` be consumed to preserve uniqueness. The consequence here is even more drastic, as the semantics of method call changes: calls to this method suddenly consume their target, whereas in the original program they did not.

In both cases, a purely internal change to the implementation of `BlackBox` forces changes to its interface, which propagate through the program — either statically or dynamically. Not only does this introduce the opportunity for errors, since the behaviour of a program changes, it means that objects cannot be treated like black boxes. Thus extant uniqueness proposals break *abstraction*.

2.2   Distinguishing Internal and External References

The abstraction problem occurs, we believe, because the distinction cannot readily be made between internal and external references. For example, traditional object-oriented programming languages cannot distinguish the references between the links of a linked list, which are internal to the data structure, from references that go *into* a data structure from *outside* of it, such as the reference from the handle object to the first link.

A purely internal reference to an object which has only one external reference cannot be used by objects other than the holder of the external reference. This means that no changes to the object can be made via the internal reference violating the "uniqueness" of the external reference, since the internal reference is only accessible once already inside the object. Thus, purely internal references are innocuous. Their existence should not affect how an aggregate is viewed externally; they ought to be preserved to maintain the internal consistency of an aggregate. Otherwise, knowledge of internal reference behaviour exposes an object's implementation details and thus violates abstraction, as we have shown.

Fortunately, the desired distinction can be made in a programming language with ownership types, as originally proposed by Clarke, Potter and Noble [17]. This form of ownership types provide strong protection against external aliasing of an object's internals, enabling a strong notion of aggregate object. Technically, each object has an owner through which all external access paths into the object must pass, meaning that owners are dominators in the object graph (take a peek at Figure 1). The resulting anti-aliasing guarantees are compatible with the containment implicit in object-oriented programming.

Based on the machinery of ownership types, we propose a new take on uniqueness called *external uniqueness*. External uniqueness restricts the external references to an object to be at most one, while permitting arbitrary internal aliasing. Consequently, external uniqueness refines the object graph property underlying ownership types from dominating nodes to dominating edges (see again Figure 1). Using external uniqueness, we treat this non-uniquely and allow it to be arbitrarily assigned internally. Methods cannot steal this, and hence need not be annotated, keeping the syntactic overhead down and avoiding clutter in interfaces. Furthermore, under very mild conditions, we need not annotate classes,[1] since instances from every class can be referred to uniquely. Thus external uniqueness can solve the abstraction problem.

Since ownership types are crucial to our proposal, we shall now review what they do and how they do it.

3   How Ownership Types Work

Ownership types package together into a class-based type system a number of conditions which together act locally to restrict the global structure of object graphs. The underlying idea is very simple.

Objects have owners and can be the owners of other objects. Ownership forms a tree, where an object is *inside* the object which owns it. Also, an object is inside itself. An additional owner called world forms the root of the tree, hence all objects are inside world. Finally, there is a condition which governs whether one object can refer to another (ι, ι' are object ids, $\Rightarrow$ is logical implication):

$$\iota \text{ refers to } \iota' \Rightarrow \iota \text{ inside } \mathsf{owner}(\iota')$$

This says that object ι can only access an object ι' whose owner is outside of itself, or alternatively, an object cannot be accessed from outside of its owner. The owner can be seen as the permission required to access an object, and

---

[1] Assigning this to a static variable prohibits unique references to the objects of its class. This behaviour is rare, so we will not even consider it here.

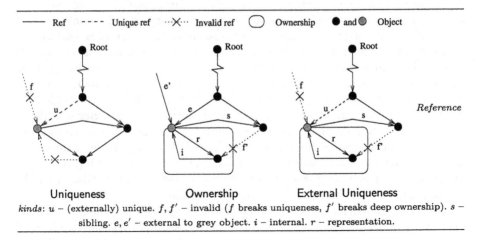

kinds: u – (externally) unique. f, f' – invalid (f breaks uniqueness, f' breaks deep ownership). s – sibling. e, e' – external to grey object. i – internal. r – representation.

Fig. 1. Comparing uniqueness, deep ownership and external uniqueness

an object's position in the inside relation determines whether the object has enough permission. A nice little theorem [38, 15] states that if we have all of these conditions, then an object's owner will be on all paths from the root of the graph to that object, which is to say that an object's owner is its *dominator*. We call this property *owners-as-dominators*, and type systems which enjoy it are said to offer *deep ownership*.

Deep ownership is illustrated in the centre picture in Figure 1. If one considers the objects an object owns to be nested inside it, as depicted by the rounded box, then deep ownership can be stated as: *no reference can pass through an object's boundary from outside to the inside.*

The tricky part is realising these ideas in a class-based OOPL. Firstly, owners become a syntactic category and are indicated in an object's type. Types take the form $p_0 : c\langle p_{i \in 1..n}\rangle$, where c is a class name, p_0 is the owner of objects of that type, and each $p_{i \in 1..n}$ is a binding for the parameters of the class. Constraints on owners are recorded in the type system using both inside ($\prec^*$) and its converse outside ($\succ^*$). These constraints are specified in class headers (and elsewhere) and must be satisfied when forming types. In code examples, we write `inside` for $\prec^*$ and `outside` for $\succ^*$.

Outside of a class there is only one owner, the global `world`. Within the body of a class, `this` is used to denote objects owned by the current instance. These objects are directly inside the current instance — objects inside these objects are also inside, but inaccessible. A class implicitly takes a parameter for the owner of its instances, denoted `owner` within the class body — objects with this owner are called *siblings*. In addition, the class may have parameters, such as a and b in the following:

```
class c<a, b outside a> {
    // valid owners: this, owner, world, a, b
    // relationship: this inside owner inside a~inside b inside world
}
```

Table 1. Syntax of Joline

$c \in$ **ClassName**, $f \in$ **FieldName**, $m \in$ **MethodName**, $x, y \in$ **TermVar**,
$\alpha \in$ **OwnerVar**.

$P \in$ **Program**	::=	$class_{i \in 1..n}\ s\ e$
$class \in$ **Class**	::=	class $c\langle \alpha_i\ R_i\ p_{i \in 1..m}\rangle$ extends $c'\langle p'_{i' \in 1..n}\rangle$ { $fd_{j \in 1..r}\ meth_{k \in 1..s}$ }
		where R is either inside or outside ($\prec^*$ or $\succ^*$).
$fd \in$ **Field**	::=	$t\ f = e;$
$meth \in$ **Method**	::=	$\langle \alpha_i\ R_i\ p_{i \in 1..m}\rangle\ t\ m(t_i\ x_{i \in 1..n})$ { s return e }
$lval \in$ **Lvalue**	::=	$x\ \mid\ e.f$
$e \in$ **Expr**	::=	this $\mid$ $lval$ $\mid$ $lval$-- $\mid$ new t $\mid$ null $\mid$ $e.m\langle p_{j \in 1..m}\rangle(e_{i \in 1..n})$
$s \in$ **Stat**	::=	skip; $\mid$ $t\ x = e;$ $\mid$ $e;$ $\mid$ $lval = e;$ $\mid$ $s\ s$ $\mid$ if (e) { s_1 } else { s_2 }
		$\mid$ (α) { s } $\mid$ { s } $\mid$ borrow $lval$ as $\langle \alpha \rangle$ x { s }
$p, q \in$ **Owner**	::=	this $\mid$ α $\mid$ world $\mid$ owner $\mid$ unique
		$\mid$ unique$_p$ (*in elaborated language only*)
$t \in$ **Type**	::=	$p\!:\!c\langle p_{i \in 1..n}\rangle$

External objects have **owner**, **world** or some parameter as owner. In addition to these owners, additional owner variables may be introduced via owner polymorphic methods, scoped regions, or borrowing. Whether these are internal or otherwise is determined from their relationship (if any) with **this**.

That takes care of owners, now for the nesting between them. Firstly, every owner is inside **world**. Within a class body we have **this** $\prec^*$ **owner**, and **owner** $\prec^* \alpha$ for each of the class' parameters α. Since the ordering of owners is required when forming types, we also can specify the ordering, such as the constraint **b** $\succ^*$ **a** above, in the class header. (The default constraint is **outside owner**.)

The final constraint required is that the owner part of a type be preserved through subtyping, as this acts as the permission governing access to the object.

More detailed descriptions of ownership types are available in the literature [15, 16]. From now on, when we refer to ownership types, we assume a deep model of ownership, and we use "unique" to indicate external uniqueness, adding the appropriate qualifiers either where required or for emphasis.

4   A Tour of External Uniqueness

We now present our proposal for external uniqueness. It is a minor extension to ownership types with major consequences. For concreteness, we work in the context of a core programming language called Joline, much of which ought to be familiar (see Table 1). We first describe external uniqueness, then the operations required to support it, and address a few technicalities required to maintain soundness of the system, before diving into examples in the next section.

4.1   External Uniqueness in a Nutshell

A reference to an object is *externally unique* if it is the only reference from outside an object to it. Aliasing from inside the object is still permitted, because such references form a part of the aggregate objects' implementation. External uniqueness takes uniqueness, but only applies it externally, using the distinction between the inside and outside of an object offered by ownership types. Figure 1 illustrates the distinction between uniqueness, deep ownership, and external uniqueness. The graph-theoretic property that external uniqueness enjoys is a refinement of the owners-as-dominators property. An externally unique reference corresponds to a *dominating edge* to its target, which is an edge that must occur on all paths from the root of an object graph to the target. This can be seen in the third picture in Figure 1: the dotted edge u denotes an externally unique reference. Notice that internal references to the grey object are still permitted. The dominating edge property implies that if the dominating edge u is removed, then all internal objects (within the rounded box) become inaccessible from the rest of the system. Contrast this with ownership typing in the centre picture, where the removal of the grey dominator object would result in its internal objects becoming inaccessible.

The formal property of external uniqueness is:

$$\iota \text{ refers uniquely to } \iota' \wedge \iota_o \text{ refers to } \iota' \Rightarrow \iota_o \text{ inside } \mathsf{owner}(\iota')$$

This property states that all non-unique references to an object referred to via a unique reference are from objects internal to the object. Combined with the fact that there can be only one unique reference and the original owners-as-dominators property, we get that unique references are dominating edges.

Externally unique references are denoted using types such as $\mathsf{unique} : c\langle p_{i \in 1..n}\rangle$. The unique annotation can only appear in the owner position, and thus no $p_{i \in 1..n}$ may be "unique." (For technical reasons, we have types like $\mathsf{unique}_p : c\langle p_{i \in 1..n}\rangle$ — see Section 4.3.) As ownership types maintain the dominators property, to obtain external uniqueness we need only add machinery to ensure the uniqueness of references of type $\mathsf{unique} : c\langle p_{i \in 1..n}\rangle$ whenever viewed externally.

4.2   Operations on External Uniques

Unique values, fields and variables are affected in two ways: *movement* and *borrowing*. Movement is simpler, so we discuss it first.

Movement Movement allows an externally unique reference to be moved from one field or variable into another, possibly losing its uniqueness along the way. Movement is the only operation which can be directly performed on a unique field or variable. To preserve uniqueness the original value must no longer be accessible through its source after the movement. Either the source must be nullified, the approach we take, or a technique such as alias burying, which

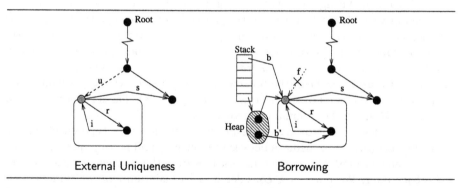

Fig. 2. Mediating between external uniqueness and borrowing—*b* is the original borrowed reference. *b, b'* are only valid during the borrowing. (Stack grows downwards)

statically ensures that all aliases to an object are dead when a unique variable or field is read [11], must be applied.

Moving is really a compound operation which combines a means for obtaining a unique value with a means for consuming it. A unique value, as opposed to a unique field or variable, can be obtained through object creation, the destructive read of a unique field or variable (*lval--*), or as the result of a method call. To simplify the formal account of the language, destructive reads are made explicit. Thus a programmer writes x = y-- or return x--, for example, instead of x = y or return x, respectively. Ultimately, a unique value is consumed by assigning it to a field or variable, or by passing it as an argument to a method.

The presence of internal references causes no problems when moving, because the dominating edge property guarantees that these are all (effectively) moved also. When consuming a unique value, however, we must ensure that deep ownership be maintained. The appropriate constraints on movement are incorporated into the subtype relation.

Borrowing Performing an operation other than the moving of a unique reference, such as accessing a field or calling a method, requires that it first be borrowed. The borrowing construct creates a non-unique reference, *x*, to the borrowed entity, *lval*, for a limited lexical scope, *s*:

borrow *lval* as $\langle \alpha \rangle$ *x* { *s* }

For example, we could call the add method of the object in variable unique:B bus as follows: borrow bus as <bo> b { b.add(...); }.

To make this a little more concrete, consider the phases of borrowing depicted in Figure 2. The left-hand picture indicates the state of play before the borrowing occurs. Initially, all access paths from the root to the grey object and its inside contain the unique reference *u*, which is inactive, and thus the objects are also inactive. During the borrowing, right-hand picture, the original reference is placed in variable x which can be treated non-uniquely. The type of x is not unique, having owner α, which must always be a "fresh owner", for the duration of the borrowing, and we can access its fields and methods, pass it to methods, or even store it in subsequent stack frames or on locally created heaps. Since α is only available in the scope of the borrowing, no references with types containing α are active at then end of the borrowing. Only internal aliases remain, and the situation returns to the original inactive state.

To some degree, borrowing exists primarily to facilitate type checking, by providing a construct to mediate between uniqueness and non-uniqueness. Ownership typing ensures that no reference escapes from the borrowing construct via some back door. We must now consider how to maintain external uniqueness, since one could simply walk in the front door and move the reference contained in $lval$ (indicated as u in Figure 2). There are essentially three approaches:

Do Nothing rather than invalidate the original $lval$, we could simply weaken the definition of uniqueness, permitting both the reference in the $lval$ and the borrowed references, and even allowing movement of the $lval$ underfoot. We dismiss this case for now.

Destructive we could nullify the $lval$ during borrowing, and then:
  - simply restore the original contents of $lval$ when the borrowing ceases;
  - restore the final contents of the borrowing variable x at the end of the borrowing. Restoring the initial value is consistent with conventional uniqueness, whereas enabling a different reference into the same aggregate to be reinstated is consistent with external uniqueness; or
  - rather than simply nullify $lval$, we could record the state of its contents. The three possible states are: *available*, *null*, and *borrowed*, indicating that $lval$ contains something, nothing, or is disabled due to some borrowing. In the presence of multiple threads, more states could be added to indicate whether a different thread is borrowing the reference.

Alias Burying the last possibility is to employ alias burying, as mentioned above. This would ensure that when $lval$ is read that all aliases are unusable [11]. Alias burying eliminates the need for destructive reads, but unfortunately comes at cost. As it is based on program analysis, its strength is sensitive to the underlying analysis. To achieve modular checking, classes must be further annotated to indicate which unique fields are read [12]. This may well reintroduce the abstraction problem. Furthermore, we do not know whether alias burying works in a multi-threaded setting.

In the last two cases, there is no active reference to the target object extracted from $lval$. Thus, the combination of a borrowing mechanism and ownership types ensures that an externally unique reference is the only active reference to its target. We proceed with the second variation of the destructive approach, preventing a reference such as f in Figure 2. This keeps our formal system simple, while retaining a strong definition of uniqueness.

A drawback of destructive reads is that it precludes simultaneous non-conflicting operations on unique references, *e.g.*, allowing read-only methods on unique references even during a borrowing (not necessarily a good thing).

4.3 Movement Bounds

Moving an object to a new location could result in residual aliasing of the internals of its original location, thus violating the invariants of deep ownership and external uniqueness. To avoid this problem, all occurrences of **unique** have an associated *movement bound* and appear in the formal system as **unique**$_p$. The movement bounds bound the outwards movement of unique references — a unique reference may only be moved to variables inside its movement bound. Choosing p requires a trade-off: an outer p enables more movement, but limits what the object can access (*i.e.*, what ownership parameters can appear in its type); whereas an inner p would enable less movement, but permits more access. A unique reference with movement bound **world** can be moved anywhere in the system. (See our workshop version of this paper for an example elaboration function which provides movement bounds automatically [18].)

4.4 Do Constructors Return Externally Unique References?

Clearly, the act of creation results in a unique object, so we must consider what could go wrong in a method call, which is effectively what a constructor call is. Here external uniqueness would be violated if the method assigns **this** to a preexisting external object. This object would have to have **owner** as its owner and be accessible from an object passed to the method. But, if the **owner** was merely acting as the movement bound, then there would be no problem, because such an argument to the constructor would be unique and could be consumed by the constructor into the new object. Thus the fix is simple: *the parameters of a constructor cannot have* **owner** *in their type, except as a movement bound.* This is a minor restriction.

For simplicity, we omit constructors from our language description.

5 External Uniqueness at Work and Play

We now illustrate external uniqueness with a number of examples, highlighting aspects which would be impossible under existing uniqueness proposals.

External Uniqueness In Figure 3 a server manages a number of clients. The clients are part of the representation of whatever object owns the server. Each client stores a back pointer to its server, *e.g.*, to access other clients via the **clients** array or to compare the server's object id with the source of some event. In ordinary models of uniqueness, this reference would either make it impossible have a unique reference to the server, or it would consume the server the first time it was passed to a client. With external uniqueness, this reference is permitted — the internal use of **this** in the server class does not effect its interface or how the server may be used or referenced externally.

```
class Server {
    this:Client<owner>[10] clients; // internal array of clients
    void accept(int num) {
        clients[num].setServer(this);
    }
}
class Client<serverowner outside owner> {
    serverowner:Server server; // server is external
    void setServer(serverowner:Server server) {
        this.server = server;
    }
}
```

Fig. 3. External uniqueness

The Initialisation Problem ([20]) To keep objects such as the following lexer flexible, we must be able to initialise its internal stream with an externally created object, without leaving any external aliasing to the stream object. Proposed solutions suffer from the weaknesses of shallow ownership [1, 9] (see Section 8).

```
class Lexer {
    this:InputStream stream;        // internal
    Lexer(unique:InputStream s) { stream = s--; }
}
void lexerClient() {
    unique:InputStream stream = new FileInputStream(file);
    unique:Lexer l = new Lexer(stream--);
}
```

Simulating Borrowing Previous approaches to uniqueness use *lent* parameters to avoid the capture of unique references passed to methods. We can simulate this using borrowing and a call to an owner polymorphic method. Apart from making them applicable to objects with different owners, owner polymorphic methods cannot capture any argument whose owner is a parameter:

```
class Printer {
    static <o inside world> void print(o:Printable p) { .. }
}
unique:B b;      // B implements Printable
borrow b as <a> b' { Printer.print<a>(b'); }
```

Another benefit of this scheme is that the borrowed object may be stored temporarily on the heap during the borrowing. This is discussed shortly.

Transfer of Ownership Transfer of ownership is an important design pattern in concurrent object-oriented programming [32]. In the following token ring, the token object is passed from one thread to the next by calling the **give**

```
class TokenRing {
    owner:TokenRing next;   // sibling
    unique:Token token;
    void give() { next.receive(token--); }
    void receive(unique:Token tkn)
        { token = tkn--; }
}
```

Fig. 4. A Token Ring.   Transfer token B from A to its sibling C

method. For example, Figure 4 illustrates the move of **Token** B from **TokenRing** element A to C. This idiom relies on the movement bound of B being the owner of the surrounding object A, that is D, to ensure that B has no references to the objects inside A. That is, the token ring elements must be siblings.

External uniqueness allows the token object to be a fully-fledged aggregate which may be the resource shared between the elements in the token ring. Of course, there is no reason why this couldn't be a movement from one machine to another.

Merging Representations External uniqueness enables the protected, self-referential internals of two data structures to be merged, without copying, into a new data structure, which offers the same degree of protection, *without* any residual aliasing from the original data structures. For example, Figure 5 shows the merging of one doubly-linked list into another. The phases of operation are: (1) borrow the local interior, **head**, using temporary owner **ho**; (2) move the other interior, **other.head**, so that it has owner **ho**; perform the merge (an append in this case); and then reinstate with the resulting value of **bh**, which may have been set in line (*). Note that **other.head** is consumed in this operation.

David Holmes posed this example as a challenge when he saw the original ownership types proposal [17]. No existing combination of uniqueness and ownership types can handle it, but we finally do so in an elegant manner.

Moving Parts In the previous example, there is a single unique reference into the internal links of the doubly-linked list from the **List** object. It is simple to modify this example to account for multiple references into a data structure. For concreteness, we consider a doubly-linked list with a tail pointer. The key is to introduce a proxy object to hold both references into the list, and have a unique reference to this object.

```
class HeadAndTail<data> {          class List<data> {
    owner:Link<data> head, tail;        unique:HeadAndTail<data> handle;
}                                  }
```

Local Objects and Orthogonality Joline also has a construct which enables the creation of temporary heap objects which may refer to existing objects, including borrowed unique references. The statement (α) { s } creates a new owner

```
class Link<data> {
  data:Object data;
  owner:Link<data> next, prev;
}
class List<data> {
  unique:Link<data> head;
  void append(owner:List<data> other) {
    borrow head as <ho> bh {                    (1)
      ho:Link<data> ohead = other.head--;       (2)
      if (bh == null) { bh = ohead; }           (*)
      else if (ohead != null) {
        ho:Link<data> h = bh;
        while (h.next != null) { h = h.next; }
        h.next = ohead; h.next.prev = h;
      }
    }
  }
}
```

Fig. 5. Merging two doubly-linked lists. ho is the temporary owner of the list head while borrowed. head

which is implicitly nested inside some existing collection of owners, giving access to existing objects. Through the invariants of ownership types, the lifetime of objects of types containing α is limited to the scope of s. Objects created within the block can be used normally, even passed to owner polymorphic methods, but are discarded at the end of the block.

For example, the print method in an earlier example could have the body which follows. Here the LayoutManager object, which has owner a, can access the external Printable object, but cannot persist when the scope exits.

```
static void print<o inside world>(o:Printable p) {
  (a) {                        // temporary owner
    a:LayoutManager<o> lm = new a:LayoutManager<o>(p);
    lm.addBorder();
    lm.print("/dev/printer");
  }
}
```

This feature is impossible without deep ownership, unless one uses an effects system. Scoped regions resemble an abstract, statically safe, type-level version of ScopedMemories from Real-time Java [6], which requires no dynamic checks.

6   A Touch of Formality

In this section, we present the static semantics for Joline, focusing on the most important rules. The remainder are relatively standard and straightforward and can be found in Appendix A. Type checking is defined for programs which have movement bounds in place (see further [18]). As a notational shortcut, we present rules with multiple conclusions, denoting one copy of the rule for each conclusion. The type environment E records the nesting relation on owner parameters, and the types of free term variables:

$$E ::= \emptyset \mid E, x :: t \mid E, \alpha \prec^* \bigsqcup \{p_{i \in 1..n}\} \mid E, \alpha \succ^* p$$

$(\alpha \prec^* \bigsqcup \{p_{i \in 1..n}\}$ means α is inside all $p \in \{p_{i \in 1..n}\})$. The test $\mathsf{unique}(t)$ is true if and only if the type t is unique, that is, that its owner is unique_p. $\mathcal{F}_c$ and $\mathcal{M}_c$ are maps for each class c from the field names or method names in that class (or superclass) to their declared types, modulo the substitution of superclass parameters. The function $\mathsf{owners}()$ when applied to an environment gives all the owner parameters defined in that environment, including the global world, and when applied to a type gives all the owner arguments in the type. Substitutions of owners for owner parameters are denoted σ. The act of substituting is denoted $\sigma(\cdots)$. The notation σ^p represents the substitution $\sigma \cup \{\mathsf{owner} \mapsto p\}$. A type may be written either as $p : c\langle p_{i \in 1..n}\rangle$ or $p : c\langle\sigma\rangle$, where $\sigma = \{\alpha_i \mapsto p_{i \in 1..n}\}$ for appropriate $\alpha_{i \in 1..n}$, i.e., the names of the owner parameters declared in the class.

––––––––– *Types* –––––––––

$$\text{(TYPE)}$$
$$\frac{\mathsf{class}\ c\langle\alpha_i\ \mathsf{R}_i\ p_{i \in 1..n}\rangle \cdots \in P \qquad \sigma = \{\mathsf{owner} \mapsto q, \alpha_i \mapsto q_{i \in 1..n}\} \quad E \vdash \sigma(\alpha_i\ \mathsf{R}_i\ p_i)_{i \in 1..n}}{\begin{array}{c} E \vdash q : c\langle q_{i \in 1..n}\rangle \\ E \vdash \mathsf{unique}_q : c\langle q_{i \in 1..n}\rangle \end{array}}$$

A type is well-formed whenever the substituted owner arguments satisfy the ordering on parameters prescribed in the class. The type can be either unique or not. In the case of unique types, the movement bound must satisfy the same constraint which it would satisfy as the actual owner.

––––––––– *Subtyping* –––––––––

$$\text{(SUB-LOSE-UNIQUE)}$$
$$\frac{E \vdash p : c\langle\sigma\rangle}{E \vdash \mathsf{unique}_p : c\langle\sigma\rangle \leq p : c\langle\sigma\rangle}$$

$$\text{(SUB-CLASS)}$$
$$\frac{E \vdash p : c\langle\sigma^p\rangle \quad \mathsf{class}\ c\langle\ldots\rangle\ \mathsf{extends}\ c'\langle p'_{i \in 1..n}\rangle \cdots \in P}{\begin{array}{c} E \vdash p : c\langle\sigma\rangle \leq p : c'\langle\sigma^p(p'_{i \in 1..n})\rangle \\ E \vdash \mathsf{unique}_p : c\langle\sigma\rangle \leq \mathsf{unique}_p : c'\langle\sigma^p(p'_{i \in 1..n})\rangle \end{array}}$$

$$\text{(SUB-MOVE)}$$
$$\frac{E \vdash p' \prec^* p \quad E \vdash p : c\langle p_{i \in 1..n}\rangle}{E \vdash \mathsf{unique}_p : c\langle p_{i \in 1..n}\rangle \leq \mathsf{unique}_{p'} : c\langle p_{i \in 1..n}\rangle}$$

Subtyping is derived from subclassing, modulo the binding of superclass parameters. As this corresponds to the composition of two order-preserving functions, it is order-preserving, required to preserve deep ownership [15]. In particular, subtyping preserves the owner. Letting the owner vary, as in Cyclone [27], would be unsound in our system [16]. Finally, subtyping may preserve uniqueness or forget it, in which case the movement bound becomes the regular owner of the object. The movement bound may also move inwards, to get a stronger movement restriction.

─────────── *Statements* ───────────

$$(\text{STAT-UPDATE})$$
$$\frac{E \vdash lval :: t \ \textbf{ref} \quad E \vdash e :: t}{E \vdash lval = e; \ ; E}$$

$$(\text{STAT-SCOPED-REGION})$$
$$\frac{E, \alpha \prec^* \bigsqcup P \vdash s \ ; E' \quad P \subseteq \textsf{owners}(E)}{E \vdash (\alpha) \ \{ \ s \ \} \ ; E}$$

$$(\text{STAT-BORROW})$$
$$\frac{E \vdash lval :: \textbf{unique}_p : c\langle p_{i \in 1..n} \rangle \ \textbf{ref} \quad E, \alpha \prec^* p, x :: \alpha : c\langle p_{i \in 1..n} \rangle \vdash s \ ; E'}{E \vdash \textbf{borrow} \ lval \ \textbf{as} \ \langle \alpha \rangle \ x \ \{ \ s \ \} \ ; E}$$

The rule (STAT-UPDATE) simply enforces that updates can be performed to l-values only if the types match, modulo subtyping. The rule (STAT-SCOPED-REGION) introduces a new owner variable for the duration of the given block. The bounds P, though unspecified in code, determine which objects may be accessed by objects created in this scope. From the rule (STAT-BORROW) any uniquely typed l-value may be borrowed. This is achieved by introducing a new owner variable which is restricted in scope to act as the owner of the temporary non-unique reference to the borrowed value. To ensure that this reference, or other references into the borrowed value do not escape this scope, we require that this owner is inside the unique type's movement bound. The remainder of the type *must* correspond exactly to the type of the l-value, so that it is reinstated with a correctly typed value when the borrowing ends.

─────────── *l-values* ───────────

$$(\text{LVAL-VAR})$$
$$\frac{x :: t \in E \quad x \neq \textbf{this}}{E \vdash x :: t \ \textbf{ref}}$$

$$(\text{LVAL-FIELD})$$
$$\frac{E \vdash e :: p : c\langle \sigma \rangle \quad \mathcal{F}_c(f) = t}{E \vdash e.f :: \sigma^p(t) \ \textbf{ref}}$$
$$\textbf{this} \in \textsf{owners}(t) \Rightarrow e \equiv \textbf{this}$$

These rules give the types of l-values, which are variables (other than **this**) and fields. Their type is given exactly as declared, modulo substitution of parameters. l-values may be updated or destructively read. The condition **this** $\in$ owners$(t) \Rightarrow e \equiv$ **this**, which was called the *static visibility* in the original ownership types system [17], ensures that types contain **this** in them can only be accessed internally to the object. It amounts to saying that fields (and methods) which return or require the object in internals are private. This is not essential; we could have used *dynamic aliasing* [16], but the type system would have been a little too complex to present our ideas. Subsumption *does not* apply to l-value types to ensure the validity of reinstatement at the end of borrowing.

Expressions ―――――――――――――――――――――――――――――――――――

$$\frac{(\text{EXPR-LVAL})}{E \vdash lval :: t} \quad \frac{(\text{EXPR-DREAD})}{E \vdash lval :: t \; \textbf{ref}}{E \vdash lval\text{--} :: t}$$

(EXPR-LVAL)
$$\frac{E \vdash lval :: t \; \textbf{ref} \quad \neg\text{unique}(t)}{E \vdash lval :: t}$$

(EXPR-DREAD)
$$\frac{E \vdash lval :: t \; \textbf{ref}}{E \vdash lval\text{--} :: t}$$

(EXPR-CALL)
$$E \vdash e :: p\!:\!c\langle\sigma\rangle \quad \mathcal{M}_c(m) = \forall(\alpha_i \, \mathsf{R}_i \, p_{i\in 1..n})t_{j\in 1..m} \to t_0$$
$$\textbf{this} \in \text{owners}(\forall(\alpha_i \, \mathsf{R}_i \, p_{i\in 1..n})t_{j\in 1..m} \to t_0) \Rightarrow e \equiv \textbf{this}$$
$$\frac{\sigma' = \{\alpha_i \mapsto q_{i\in 1..n}\} \quad E \vdash \sigma'(\sigma^p(\alpha_i \, \mathsf{R}_i \, p_{i\in 1..n})) \quad E \vdash e_j :: \sigma'(\sigma^p(t_j)) \quad \text{for all } j \in 1..m}{E \vdash e.m\langle q_{i\in 1..n}\rangle(e_{j\in 1..m}) :: \sigma'(\sigma^p(t_0))}$$

Not all l-values can be directly treated as values. The rules (EXPR-LVAL) and (EXPR-DREAD) correspond to extracting the value within the l-value. If the type is non-unique, then the (contents of) l-value can automatically be used as a value. If the type is unique, then a destructive read must be used to convert its contents into an expression. Destructive reads can apply to non-unique l-values.

The rule for method call is a behemoth. Firstly, it applies only to non-unique types (as does the rule for field access). The second line is the static visibility test which restricts expressions containing $\textbf{this}$ in their type (as declared in the class) to being used only internally, that is, on $\textbf{this}$. The owner arguments of the target type and the owner arguments supplied to the method form two substitutions to transform the method's argument and return types into types terms of the owners in scope. The value supplied to each argument of the method must have the type expected by the method. The method may return a uniquely typed value.

Note that there are no rules for accessing the fields and methods of unique references. To do so a borrowing must first be issued.

As usual, subsumption *does* apply to expression typing.

7 Discussion

We believe that our model of uniqueness is more appropriate and more stable than existing approaches in that it overcomes their limitations.

The Abstraction Problem Ownership types distinguish internal and external references. With them, we can permit arbitrary internal aliasing within a uniquely referenced aggregate, without the loss of effective uniqueness. From a software engineering perspective, our proposal is better suited to software evolution than traditional uniqueness, since it does not require interfaces to change when the internal implementation does, as illustrated by the Client-Server example in Figure 3. In addition, we need not clutter interfaces with annotations on methods or constructors indicating calls that destructively consume their targets, as in other proposals, because methods cannot be called on a unique reference and their targets cannot be consumed. The price is the loss of uniqueness on $\textbf{this}$, precluding moves initiated within an object. The gains are much greater.

Orthogonality Borrowing was introduced in existing uniqueness proposals so that unique references can be operated upon without consuming their targets. Existing uniqueness proposals impose the restriction that a borrowed reference cannot be stored in the field of an object, making borrowed references a kind of second class citizen. These proposals lack mechanisms in their type systems to treat borrowed references as usual non-unique references and maintain the invariant that after the borrowing has ceased, the reference is again unique.

Rather than introducing borrowed references as another kind of reference, our borrowing is a construct which mediates between unique and non-unique perspectives. Any non-unique reference, including those introduced in a borrowing and those internal to an object, can be passed to owner polymorphic methods, or stored on the heap in objects created within scoped regions. Ownership types guarantees that any aliases created are temporary or appropriately contained. The result is a cleaner language which employs orthogonal constructs in a flexible manner.

A Unique is a Unique is a Unique A potential problem when dealing with unique references in the presence of borrowing is that reading a field or variable containing a uniquely typed reference while aliases exist violates the uniqueness expectation of those accessing the field. As we mentioned in Section 4, there are a number of ways for dealing with this. Recapping, we could weaken the definition of unique and not nullify a variable when borrowing, or we could nullify when borrowing thus introducing null pointers and potential race conditions, or we could employ alias burying and accept a sophisticated program analysis which does not work in a multi-threaded setting. In the last two solutions, external uniqueness becomes effectively unique. That is, while not strictly unique, the dominating edge property means that there is only ever one active reference to an externally unique object, since internal references only become active during a borrowing when the original reference is unavailable. Thus there is either a single active unique reference to an object, or many references with limited scope, but never both.

Reentrancy and Internal Threads An interesting consequence of our proposal regarding the reentrancy of objects is that, once a reference has been borrowed, an object can only be reentered from references inside the original object. It is not possible to call a method from an external object which then results in a call to the original object. We expect that this *localised reentrancy* will be handy when reasoning about objects.

An important conclusion for concurrency is that an object referred to uniquely can only be entered by one thread. However, if threads are created within an object while it is being borrowed, then their mere existence threatens the possibility of retaining a strong notion of uniqueness. We feel that this should be avoided — a better approach is to pass the unique references between threads.

Uniqueness, Non-null and Finality The stronger form of uniqueness interacts badly if we wish to have final fields containing unique values or non-null unique types [22]. The problems encountered are similar, though independent. When a final field contains a unique reference, a destructive borrowing violates the finality of the field and similarly, the non-nullity of a non-null type. We suspect that alias burying again will come to the rescue in the sequential setting, but beyond that we cannot yet have non-null or final unique references. Yet another approach is to weaken external uniqueness for final fields.

Uniqueness and Shallow Ownership Dominating edges are possible only when dominators can be enforced. But this is impossible in systems lacking deep ownership, such as AliasJava [1] and some in the first author's thesis [15], and hence they cannot support external uniqueness. Adding ordinary uniqueness in such cases is easy, since the invariants underlying deep ownership need not be considered. (This originally caused us to baulk when contemplating uniqueness.)

Weakness and Limitations Apart from the difficulty maintaining the uniqueness invariant in a sensible and cheap manner, external uniqueness also inherits the weaknesses of deep ownership. In brief, one must program with the single entry point to aggregate objects requirement. Consequently a choice must be made between the amount encapsulation desired and the flexibility gained. The difficulties arise when trying to implement patterns such as iterators or command objects which require multiple, sometimes temporary, access paths into the internals of an object, or observers which require multiple permanent references [23]. Shallow ownership overcomes these weaknesses [1], though some attempts have been made to overcome some them while maintaining deep ownership [16].

8   Related Work

Table 2 presents a comparison between different proposals in the literature with regard to the kinds of uniqueness, alias encapsulation, and borrowing they provide. For reasons of space, we restrict our discussion mainly to object-oriented programming languages. For a few pointers into less closely related literature, see *e.g.*, [11, 13], or for a recent discussion on aliasing in general, see [16].

We consider three kinds of uniqueness:

Free values can be unique (*e.g.*, from object construction).
Conventional Uniqueness fields and variables may contain unique references to an object. Such a reference is the only one stored in the heap, and possibly the stack, modulo any borrowing.
External Uniqueness fields and variables may contain externally unique reference *into* an aggregate. Internal references to unique object are permitted.

Both forms of uniqueness subsume free. Freedom without uniqueness means that the freeness is lost as soon as the value is stored in a field or variable. Commonly used synonyms for uniqueness include linear and unshareable.

We consider three kinds of ownership/encapsulation:

Table 2. Comparison. Legend: − not applicable; *a-e* see text

	Uniqueness	Encapsulation	Borrowing
This paper	External	Deep	Orthogonal
PRFJ [9] [a]	Conventional	Deep	Parameter
Flexible Alias Protection [37]	Free	Deep	−
Vault [19, 21] [b]	∼Conventional	Shallow	Orthogonal
AliasJava [1]	Conventional	Shallow	Parameter
Pivot Uniqueness [33] [c]	<Conventional	Shallow	Parameter
Capabilities for sharing [13] [d]	∼Conventional	∼Shallow	∼Parameter
Islands [29] [e]	Conventional	Full	∼Parameter
Balloons [2]	Conventional	Full	Parameter
OOFX/Alias Burying [11, 26]	Conventional	None	Parameter
Eiffel* [35]	Conventional	None	Parameter
Virginity [34]	Free	None	Parameter

Shallow direct access to certain objects is limited.

Deep the only access (transitively) to the internal state of an object is through a single-entry point. References to external state is possible.

Full same as deep ownership, except that no references to objects outside the encapsulating object from within the encapsulating boundary are permitted.

While shallow ownership prevents direct access to the encapsulated objects, proxy objects may be created (internally or externally) which access the encapsulated objects and may escape the encapsulation boundary. Deep ownership goes further by lifting the nesting of objects into the type system and ensuring that no references to deeply nested objects pass through their enclosing boundary. This is also called flexible alias encapsulation [37]. Full alias encapsulation [37] is like deep ownership except that references to external objects are not permitted from within the encapsulation boundaries. In graph theoretic terms, deep ownership imposes that owners are dominators which break path connectivity when removed, whereas full alias encapsulation imposes that "owners" are cut points which break graph connectivity when removed. Other forms of encapsulation, such as the package level restrictions in Confined Types [28], are too coarse-grained to enable external uniqueness.

Kim, Bertino and Garza [30] define semantics for references capable of expressing a shallow form of ownership and traditional uniqueness for *composite references*. This system is however not statically checked nor does it provide deep ownership or external uniqueness, though the machinery seems to be in place to implement the latter via dynamic checks. A more detailed comparision with this and other models from the OODB community would be instructive.

We consider two kinds of borrowing of unique references:

Borrowed Parameters method parameters, this, and/or local variables may borrow a unique reference. Borrowed references may not be assigned to fields.

Orthogonal Borrowing references are either unique or non-unique. Scope restrictions apply to a borrowed unique reference to ensure that the uniqueness invariant can be regained.

In Eiffel* [35], AliasJava [1], Balloons [2], Pivot Uniqueness [33] and Capabilities for sharing [13], borrowing weakens uniqueness since the unique reference is still visible and usable despite the existence of the temporary borrowed aliases. This is avoided in PRFJ [9], Vault [19] and our proposal by using nullification or scope restrictions, and in Alias Burying [11] by invalidating all borrowings if a unique field or variable is read while borrowed. Checking the constraints underlying alias burying modularly leads to an interdependence between uniqueness and read effects [12]. Guava [3] also uses lent parameters to avoid capturing of objects.

Some remarks regarding Table 2 follow. (a) PRFJ [9] permits object graphs which violates deep ownership, but it uses an effects system to prevent access through the offending references. The result is *effectively deep ownership*. In addition, to increase flexibility, PRFJ allows unique to be used even as a non-owner parameter. For example, to allow a list class where the data in the links is unshared, see Figure 5, unique is used in the data owner position. This requires that the list class be written with this in mind. Unfortunately, no formalisation exists, and so we have remained conservative and permit unique to appear only as the owner. (b) DeLine and Fähndrich [21] give a practical linear type system for a non object-oriented, imperative language. Our borrowing resembles their adopt operation, where a linear reference temporarily becomes non-linear. They also have a focus operation which enables non-linear references to linear entities to be treated linearly, avoiding destructive read. The inflexible nature of classes makes this difficult to achieve in our setting. (c) Pivot uniqueness [33] only enables unique fields to be assigned with newly created objects or null. (d) Capabilities for sharing [13] offers primitive and dynamic constructs that combine to give various kinds uniqueness, read-only references *etc.*, though no one specific policy is enforced. Furthermore, no static type system exists. Finally, (e) Islands [29] only allows borrowing through read-only references.

Uniqueness and Linearity Girard's linear logic [25] created the opportunity for stronger control of resources in programming languages. However, a number of researchers have realised that programming with uniqueness or linearity in its strictest form is painful [41, 4]. Wadler's let! construct, quasi-linear types [31], and Vault's adoption and focus [21], for example, introduce means for alleviating this pain. Our notion of external aliasing and to a lesser extent our borrowing construct were designed for a similar goal in an object-oriented setting.

Region-Based Memory Management Our scoped region construct is similar to lexically scoped letregion construct used in region-based memory management [39, 40]. There are a number of differences. Firstly, our construct is under programmer control, as in Cyclone [27], whereas the regions calculus is the basis for a compiler's intermediate language. Secondly, the principal aim of region-based memory management differs from ours, which is to limit the aliasing between objects. The final difference is the technical machinery used to achieve safety: our approach is structural, maintaining a specific nesting relationship between objects to ensure that no references into a deleted region remain (see also [15]), whereas the regions calculus uses effects to determine that references into a deleted region are never dereferenced. Both Cyclone [27] and Gay and Aiken's RC [24] manage a nesting relationship which captures when one object *outlives* another. While some attempts to explicitly add region-based memory management to Java exist [42, 14], they require interfaces to be extended with effects annotations to ensure modular checking, whereas our structural approach uses ownership and owner annotations. Recently , however, Boyapati *et.al.,* did add regions and ownership to Java to address the problems of Real-time Java [10]. Although the structural approach lacks the delicacy of the regions calculus, we believe that it is closer to the spirit of object-oriented programming.

9   Conclusions and Future Work

In this paper we introduced a new take on uniqueness called external uniqueness. This was a natural extension of ownership types; while not free, it is, in a sense, already paid for once you have ownership types.[2] On the surface our proposal seems to violate the very essence of uniqueness, permitting arbitrary internal references to an object which is referred to by an externally unique pointer, but, as we have demonstrated, the external references is the only active reference to the object, and is thus effectively unique. Furthermore, our definition solves an abstraction problem from which existing approaches to uniqueness suffer.

This work forms part of a general program to localise references, behaviour, control, *etc.* to simplify reasoning about programs. We wish to further our work in this direction. In addition, we are adding external uniqueness to our Joe compiler [16] so that we can then explore more programming patterns and apply our ideas to concurrency, mobility, memory management and so forth.

References

[1] Jonathan Aldrich, Valentin Kostadinov, and Craig Chambers. Alias annotations for program understanding. In *OOPSLA Proceedings*, November 2002.

[2] Paulo Sérgio Almeida. Balloon Types: Controlling sharing of state in data types. In *ECOOP Proceedings*, June 1997.

[3] David F. Bacon, Robert E. Strom, and Ashis Tarafdar. Guava: a dialect of Java without data races. In *OOPSLA Proceedings*, pages 382–400, 2000.

[4] Henry G. Baker. 'Use-once' variables and linear objects – storage management, reflection and multi-threading. *ACM SIGPLAN Notices*, 30(1), January 1995.

[5] Anindya Banerjee and David A. Naumann. Representation independence, confinement, and access control. In *Proceedings of the 29th ACM Symposium on Principles of Programming Languages (POPL'02)*, Portland, Oregon, January 2002.

---

[2] Quoting Simon Peyton Jones.

[6] Greg Bollella, James Gosling, Benjamin Brosgol, Peter Dibble, Steve Furr, and Mark Turnbull. *The Real-Time Specification for Java*. Addison-Wesley, 2000.

[7] Chandrasekhar Boyapati, Robert Lee, and Martin Rinard. Ownership types for safe programming: Preventing data races and deadlocks. In *OOPSLA Proceedings*, November 2002.

[8] Chandrasekhar Boyapati, Barbara Liskov, and Liuba Shrira. Ownership types and safe lazy upgrades in object-oriented databases. Technical Report MIT-LCS-TR-858, Laboratory for Computer Science, MIT, July 2002.

[9] Chandrasekhar Boyapati and Martin Rinard. A parameterized type system for race-free Java programs. In *OOPSLA Proceedings*, 2001.

[10] Chandrasekhar Boyapati, Alexandru Salcianu, William Beebee, and Martin Rinard. Ownership types for safe region-based memory management in real-time java. In *ACM SIGPLAN 2003 Conference on Programming Language Design and Implementation (PLDI)*, June 2003.

[11] John Boyland. Alias burying: Unique variables without destructive reads. *Software – Practice and Experience*, 31(6):533–553, May 2001.

[12] John Boyland. The interdependence of effects and uniqueness. In *3rd Workshop on Formal Techniques for Java Programs*, June 2001.

[13] John Boyland, James Noble, and William Retert. Capabilities for Sharing: A Generalization of Uniqueness and Read-Only. In *ECOOP Proceedings*, June 2001.

[14] M. V. Christiansen and P. Velschrow. Region-based memory management in Java. Master's thesis, Department of Computer Science (DIKU), University of Copenhagen, May 1998.

[15] David Clarke. *Object Ownership and Containment*. PhD thesis, School of Computer Science and Engineering, University of New South Wales, Sydney, Australia, 2001.

[16] David Clarke and Sophia Drossopolou. Ownership, encapsulation and the disjointness of type and effect. In *OOPSLA Proceedings*, November 2002.

[17] David Clarke, John Potter, and James Noble. Ownership types for flexible alias protection. In *OOPSLA Proceedings*, 1998.

[18] David Clarke and Tobias Wrigstad. External uniqueness. In *10th Workshop on Foundations of Object-Oriented Languages (FOOL)*, New Orleans, LA, January 2003.

[19] Robert DeLine and Manuel Fähndrich. Enforcing high-level protocols in low-level software. In *Proceedings of the ACM Conference on Programming Language Design and Implementation*, pages 59–69, June 2001.

[20] David L. Detlefs, K. Rustan M. Leino, and Greg Nelson. Wrestling with rep exposure. Technical Report SRC-RR-98-156, Compaq Systems Research Center, July 1998.

[21] Manuel Fähndrich and Robert DeLine. Adoption and focus: Practical linear types for imperative programming. In *Proceedings of the ACM Conference on Programming Language Design and Implementation*, June 2002.

[22] Manuel Fähndrich and K. Rustan M. Leino. Non-null types in an object-oriented language. In Erik Poll, editor, *Formal Techniques for Java-like Programs*, Málaga, Spain, June 2002. Appears in Technical report NIII-R0204, Computing Science Department, University of Nijmegen, 2002.

[23] Erich Gamma, Richard Helm, Ralph E. Johnson, and John Vlissides. *Design Patterns*. Addison-Wesley, 1994.

[24] David Gay and Alex Aiken. Language support for regions. In *ACM SIGPLAN 2001 Conference on Programming Language Design and Implementation (PLDI)*, Snowbird, Utah, June 2001.

[25] J.-Y. Girard. Linear logic. *Theoretical Computer Science*, 50:1–102, 1987.

[26] Aaron Greenhouse and John Boyland. An object-oriented effects system. In *ECOOP'99*, 1999.

[27] Dan Grossman, Greg Morrisett, Trevor Jim, Michael Hicks, Yanling Wang, and James Cheney. Region-based memory management in Cyclone. In *Proceedings of the ACM Conference on Programming Language Design and Implementation*, June 2002.

[28] Christian Grothoff, Jens Palsberg, and Jan Vitek. Encapsulating objects with confined types. In *OOPSLA Proceedings*, 2001.

[29] John Hogg. Islands: Aliasing protection in object-oriented languages. In *OOPSLA Proceedings*, November 1991.

[30] Won Kim, Elisa Bertino, and Jorge F Garza. Composite objects revisited. In *Proceedings of the 1989 ACM SIGMOD International Conference on Management of Data*, pages 337–347, Portland, Oregon, 1989.

[31] Naoki Kobayashi. Quasi-linear types. In *26th ACM Symposium on Principles of Programming Languages*, January 1999.

[32] Doug Lea. *Concurrent-Programming in Java: Design Principles and Patterns*. Java Series. Addison-Wesley, 1998.

[33] K. Rustan M. Leino, Arnd Poetzsch-Heffter, and Yunhong Zhou. Using data groups to specify and check side effects. In *Proceedings of the ACM Conference on Programming Language Design and Implementation*, June 2002.

[34] K. Rustan M. Leino and Raymie Stata. Virginity: A contribution to the specification of object-oriented software. *Information Processing Letters*, 70(2):99–105, April 1999.

[35] Naftaly Minsky. Towards alias-free pointers. In *ECOOP Proceedings*, July 1996.

[36] P. Müller and A. Poetzsch-Heffter. Universes: A type system for controlling representation exposure. In A. Poetzsch-Heffter and J. Meyer, editors, *Programming Languages and Fundamentals of Programming*. Fernuniversität Hagen, 1999.

[37] James Noble, Jan Vitek, and John Potter. Flexible alias protection. In Eric Jul, editor, *ECOOP'98— Object-Oriented Programming*, volume 1445 of *Lecture Notes In Computer Science*, pages 158–185, Berlin, Heidelberg, New York, July 1988. Springer-Verlag.

[38] John Potter, James Noble, and David Clarke. The ins and outs of objects. In *Australian Software Engineering Conference*, Adelaide, Australia, November 1998. IEEE Press.

[39] J.-P Talpin and P. Jouvelot. Polymorphic type, region, and effect inference. *Journal of Functional Programming*, 2(3):245–271, July 1992.

[40] Mads Tofte and Jean-Pierre Talpin. Region-Based Memory Management. *Information and Computation*, 132(2):109–176, 1997.

[41] Phil Wadler. Linear types can change the world! In M. Broy and C. B. Jones, editors, *IFIP TC 2 Working Conference on Programming Concepts and Methods*, pages 561–581, Sea of Gallilee, Israel, April 1990. North-Holland.

[42] Bennett Norton Yates. A type-and-effect system for encapsulating memory in Java. Master's thesis, Department of Computer and Information Science and the Graduate School of the University of Oregon, August 1999.

A Type Rules

The complete collection of type rules are given here.

$E \vdash \diamond$ Good environment

$$(\text{ENV-}\emptyset) \qquad (\text{ENV-}x) \qquad\qquad (\text{ENV-}\alpha \succ^*) \qquad\qquad (\text{ENV-}\alpha \prec^*)$$

$$\frac{}{\emptyset \vdash \diamond} \qquad \frac{E \vdash t \quad x \notin \text{dom}(E)}{E, x :: t \vdash \diamond} \qquad \frac{E \vdash p \quad \alpha \notin \text{dom}(E)}{E, \alpha \succ^* p \vdash \diamond} \qquad \frac{E \vdash p_{i \in 1..n} \quad \alpha \notin \text{dom}(E)}{E, \alpha \prec^* \bigsqcup \{p_{i \in 1..n}\} \vdash \diamond}$$

$E \vdash p$ Good owner

$$(\text{OWNER-VAR}) \qquad (\text{OWNER-THIS}) \qquad (\text{OWNER-WORLD})$$

$$\frac{\alpha \, \mathsf{R}_- \in E}{E \vdash \alpha} \qquad \frac{\text{this} :: t \in E}{E \vdash \text{this}} \qquad \frac{E \vdash \diamond}{E \vdash \text{world}}$$

$E \vdash p \prec^* q$ Owner p is inside q

$$(\text{IN-ENV1}) \qquad\qquad (\text{IN-ENV2}) \qquad (\text{IN-WORLD})$$

$$\frac{\alpha \prec^* \bigsqcup P \in E \quad p \in P}{E \vdash \alpha \prec^* p} \qquad \frac{\alpha \succ^* p \in E}{E \vdash p \prec^* \alpha} \qquad \frac{E \vdash p}{E \vdash p \prec^* \text{world}}$$

$$(\text{IN-THIS}) \qquad (\text{IN-REFL}) \qquad (\text{IN-TRANS})$$

$$\frac{\text{this} :: t \in E}{E \vdash \text{this} \prec^* \text{owner}} \qquad \frac{E \vdash p}{E \vdash p \prec^* p} \qquad \frac{E \vdash p \prec^* q \quad E \vdash q \prec^* q'}{E \vdash p \prec^* q'}$$

$\vdash P, \vdash class$ Good Program and Class

$$(\text{PROGRAM}) \qquad\qquad\qquad\qquad (\text{CLASS-OBJECT})$$

$$\frac{\vdash class \text{ for all } class \in P \quad \vdash s \,; E \quad E \vdash e :: t}{\vdash class_{i \in 1..n} \ s \ e :: t} \qquad \frac{}{\vdash \text{class Object \{ \}}}$$

$$(\text{CLASS})$$

$$E_0 = \text{owner} \prec^* \text{world}, \alpha_i \, \mathsf{R}_i \, p_{i \in 1..m} \quad E_0 \vdash \text{owner} \prec^* \alpha_{i \in 1..m}$$

$$E_0 \vdash \text{owner} : c'\langle \sigma \rangle \quad \text{owner} \notin \text{rng}(\sigma) \quad E = E_0, \text{this} :: \text{owner} : c\langle \alpha_{i \in 1..m} \rangle$$

$$\{f_{i \in 1..n}\} \cap \text{dom}(\mathcal{F}_{c'}) = \emptyset \quad E \vdash e_i :: t_{i \in 1..r} \quad E \vdash meth_{j \in 1..s}$$

$$\mathcal{M}_c(m) \equiv \sigma(\mathcal{M}_{c'}(m)) \quad \forall m \in \text{names}(meth_{j \in 1..s}) \cap \text{dom}(\mathcal{M}_{c'})$$

$$\frac{}{\vdash \text{class } c\langle \alpha_i \, \mathsf{R}_i \, p_{i \in 1..m} \rangle \text{ extends } c'\langle \sigma \rangle \ \{t_i \ f_i = e_{i \in 1..r} \ meth_{j \in 1..s}\}}$$

$E \vdash meth$ Good Method

$$(\text{METHOD})$$

$$\frac{E'' = E, \alpha_i \, \mathsf{R}_i \, p_{i \in 1..n}, x_j :: t_{j \in 1..m} \quad E'' \vdash s; E' \quad E' \vdash e :: t_0}{E \vdash \langle \alpha_i \, \mathsf{R}_i \, p_{i \in 1..n} \rangle \ t_0 \ m(t_i \ x_{i \in 1..m})\{ \ s \ \text{return } e \ \}}$$

$E \vdash t$ Good Type

$$(\text{TYPE})$$

$$\text{class } c\langle \alpha_i \, \mathsf{R}_i \, p_{i \in 1..n} \rangle \cdots \in P$$

$$\frac{\sigma = \{\text{owner} \mapsto q, \alpha_i \mapsto q_{i \in 1..n}\} \quad E \vdash \sigma(\alpha_i \, \mathsf{R}_i \, p_i)_{i \in 1..n}}{E \vdash q : c\langle q_{i \in 1..n} \rangle}$$

$$E \vdash \text{unique}_q : c\langle q_{i \in 1..n} \rangle$$

$E \vdash t \leq t'$ $\hfill$ t is a subtype of t'

$$\text{(SUB-LOSE-UNIQUE)} \quad \frac{E \vdash p\!:\!c\langle\sigma\rangle}{E \vdash \mathbf{unique}_p\!:\!c\langle\sigma\rangle \leq p\!:\!c\langle\sigma\rangle}$$

$$\text{(SUB-CLASS)}$$
$$\frac{E \vdash p\!:\!c\langle\sigma^p\rangle \quad \mathbf{class}\ c\langle\ldots\rangle\ \mathbf{extends}\ c'\langle p'_{i\in 1..n}\rangle \cdots \in P}{\begin{array}{c} E \vdash p\!:\!c\langle\sigma\rangle \leq p\!:\!c'\langle\sigma^p(p'_{i\in 1..n})\rangle \\ E \vdash \mathbf{unique}_p\!:\!c\langle\sigma\rangle \leq \mathbf{unique}_p\!:\!c'\langle\sigma^p(p'_{i\in 1..n})\rangle \end{array}}$$

$$\text{(SUB-REFL)} \quad \frac{E \vdash t}{E \vdash t \leq t} \qquad \text{(SUB-TRANS)} \quad \frac{E \vdash t \leq t' \quad E \vdash t' \leq t''}{E \vdash t \leq t''}$$

$$\text{(SUB-MOVE)} \quad \frac{E \vdash p' \prec^* p \quad E \vdash p\!:\!c\langle p_{i\in 1..n}\rangle}{E \vdash \mathbf{unique}_p\!:\!c\langle p_{i\in 1..n}\rangle \leq \mathbf{unique}_{p'}\!:\!c\langle p_{i\in 1..n}\rangle}$$

$E \vdash s \ ; E'$ $\hfill$ Good statement. Resulting environment E'

$$\text{(STAT-SKIP)} \quad \frac{E \vdash \Diamond}{E \vdash \mathbf{skip}; \ ; E}$$

$$\text{(STAT-LOCAL)} \quad \frac{x \notin \mathrm{dom}(E) \quad E \vdash e :: t}{E \vdash t\ x = e; \ ; E, x :: t}$$

$$\text{(STAT-EXPR)} \quad \frac{E \vdash e :: t}{E \vdash e; \ ; E}$$

$$\text{(STAT-UPDATE)} \quad \frac{E \vdash lval :: t\ \mathbf{ref} \quad E \vdash e :: t}{E \vdash lval = e; \ ; E}$$

$$\text{(STAT-SEQUENCE)} \quad \frac{E \vdash s_1 \ ; E'' \quad E'' \vdash s_2 \ ; E'}{E \vdash s_1\ s_2 \ ; E'}$$

$$\text{(STAT-SCOPED-REGION)} \quad \frac{E, \alpha \prec^* \bigsqcup P \vdash s \ ; E' \quad P \subseteq \mathrm{owners}(E)}{E \vdash (\alpha)\ \{\ s\ \} \ ; E}$$

$$\text{(STAT-BLOCK)} \quad \frac{E \vdash s \ ; E'}{E \vdash \{s\} \ ; E}$$

$$\text{(STAT-IF-THEN-ELSE)} \quad \frac{E \vdash e :: \mathbf{bool} \quad E \vdash s_1 \ ; E' \quad E \vdash s_2 \ ; E''}{E \vdash \mathbf{if}\ (e)\ \{\ s_1\ \}\ \mathbf{else}\ \{\ s_2\ \} \ ; E}$$

$$\text{(STAT-BORROW)} \quad \frac{E \vdash lval :: \mathbf{unique}_p\!:\!c\langle p_{i\in 1..n}\rangle\ \mathbf{ref} \quad E, \alpha \prec^* p, x :: \alpha\!:\!c\langle p_{i\in 1..n}\rangle \vdash s \ ; E'}{E \vdash \mathbf{borrow}\ lval\ \mathbf{as}\ \langle\alpha\rangle\ x\ \{\ s\ \} \ ; E}$$

$E \vdash lval :: t\ \mathbf{ref}$ $\hfill$ l-value of type t

$$\text{(LVAL-VAR)} \quad \frac{x :: t \in E \quad x \neq \mathbf{this}}{E \vdash x :: t\ \mathbf{ref}}$$

$$\text{(LVAL-FIELD)} \quad \frac{E \vdash e :: p\!:\!c\langle\sigma\rangle \quad \mathcal{F}_c(f) = t \quad \mathbf{this} \in \mathrm{owners}(t) \Rightarrow e \equiv \mathbf{this}}{E \vdash e.f :: \sigma^p(t)\ \mathbf{ref}}$$

$E \vdash e :: t$ $\hfill$ Expression e has type t

$$\text{(EXPR-LVAL)} \quad \frac{E \vdash lval :: t\ \mathbf{ref} \quad \neg \mathrm{unique}(t)}{E \vdash lval :: t}$$

$$\text{(EXPR-DREAD)} \quad \frac{E \vdash lval :: t\ \mathbf{ref}}{E \vdash lval\text{--} :: t}$$

$$\text{(EXPR-THIS)} \quad \frac{\mathbf{this} :: t \in E}{E \vdash \mathbf{this} :: t}$$

$$\text{(EXPR-NEW)} \quad \frac{E \vdash t}{E \vdash \mathbf{new}\ t :: t}$$

$$\text{(EXPR-NULL)} \quad \frac{E \vdash t}{E \vdash \mathbf{null} :: t}$$

$$\text{(EXPR-SUBSUMPTION)} \quad \frac{E \vdash e :: t \quad E \vdash t \leq t'}{E \vdash e :: t'}$$

$$\text{(EXPR-CALL)}$$
$$\frac{\begin{array}{c} E \vdash e :: p\!:\!c\langle\sigma\rangle \quad \mathcal{M}_c(m) = \forall(\alpha_i\ \mathsf{R}_i\ p_{i\in 1..n})t_{j\in 1..m} \to t_0 \\ \mathbf{this} \in \mathrm{owners}(\forall(\alpha_i\ \mathsf{R}_i\ p_{i\in 1..n})t_{j\in 1..m} \to t_0) \Rightarrow e \equiv \mathbf{this} \\ \sigma' = \{\alpha_i \mapsto q_{i\in 1..n}\} \quad E \vdash \sigma'(\sigma^p(\alpha_i\ \mathsf{R}_i\ p_{i\in 1..n})) \quad E \vdash e_j :: \sigma'(\sigma^p(t_j)) \quad \text{for all}\ j \in 1..m \end{array}}{E \vdash e.m\langle q_{i\in 1..n}\rangle(e_{j\in 1..m}) :: \sigma'(\sigma^p(t_0))}$$

A Nominal Theory of Objects
with Dependent Types

Martin Odersky, Vincent Cremet, Christine Röckl, and Matthias Zenger

École Polytechnique Fédérale de Lausanne
INR Ecublens, 1015 Lausanne, Switzerland
martin.odersky@epfl.ch

Abstract. We design and study *νObj*, a calculus and dependent type system for objects and classes which can have types as members. Type members can be aliases, abstract types, or new types. The type system can model the essential concepts of JAVA's inner classes as well as virtual types and family polymorphism found in BETA or GBETA. It can also model most concepts of SML-style module systems, including sharing constraints and higher-order functors, but excluding applicative functors. The type system can thus be used as a basis for unifying concepts that so far existed in parallel in advanced object systems and in module systems. The paper presents results on confluence of the calculus, soundness of the type system, and undecidability of type checking.

1   Introduction

The development in object and module systems has been largely complementary. Module systems in the style of SML or CAML excel in abstraction; they allow very precise control over visibility of names and types, including the ability to partially abstract over types. Object-oriented languages excel in composition; they offer several composition mechanisms lacking in module systems, including inheritance and unlimited recursion between objects and classes. On the other hand, object-oriented languages usually express abstraction only in a coarse grained way, e.g. through modifiers *private* or *protected* which limit accessibility of a name to some predetermined part of a system. There is usually no analogue to the signatures with abstract types in module systems, which can hide information about a binding outside the unit defining it.

Recently, we see a convergence of the two worlds. Module systems have acquired a form of inheritance through mixin modules [18, 2, 3, 9, 7], first-class modules [37] can play a role similar to objects, and recursive modules are also being investigated [16]. On the object side, nested classes with virtual or abstract types [31, 39, 12] can model the essential properties of signatures with abstract types in ML-like module systems [29]. In principle, this is not a new development. Class nesting has been introduced already in SIMULA 67 [17], whereas virtual or abstract types are present in BETA [30], as well as more recently in GBETA [19], RUNE [42] and SCALA [33]. An essential ingredient of these systems are objects with type members. There is currently much work that explores the

L. Cardelli (Ed.): ECOOP 2003, LNCS 2743, pp. 201–224, 2003.
© Springer-Verlag Berlin Heidelberg 2003

uses of this concept in object-oriented programming [38, 40, 20, 36]. But its type theoretic foundations are just beginning to be investigated.

As is the case for modules, dependent types are a promising candidate for a foundation of objects with type members. Dependent products can be used to represent functors in SML module systems as well as classes in object systems with virtual types [26]. But where the details in ML module systems build on a long tradition, the corresponding foundations of object systems with abstract and virtual types have so far been less well developed. One possible approach would be to extend the formalizations of ML module systems to object systems, but their technical complexity makes this a difficult task. An alternative would be to apply the intuitions of dependent types to a smaller calculus of objects and classes, with the aim of arriving on a combined foundation for objects and classes as well as modules. This is what we want to achieve in this paper. Our main contribution is a formal study of a type theory for objects based on dependent types. The theory developed here can be used as a type-theoretic foundation for languages such as BETA, GBETA or SCALA, as well as for many concepts that have so far been presented only in an informal way.

A characteristic of our calculus and type system is that it is *nominal*. Nominality comes into play in two respects. First, objects are given unique names in the reduction system. It is always the name of an object which is passed, instead of a copy of the object itself. A name passing strategy for objects is necessary because our regime of dependent types is based on object identity: If L is a type label then $x.L$ and $y.L$ are the same type only if x and y can be shown to refer to the same object. If objects were copied, type equalities would not be maintained during reduction.

Second, we introduce a nominal binding for types: $L \prec T$ defines L as a name of a new type which unfolds to type T. Two such definitions always define two different types, even if they unfold to the same type. This corresponds closely to the notion of interfaces in a language like JAVA. An interface defines a new type whose structure is completely known. It is possible to define values of an interface type by giving implementations for all members of the interface. In our type system we represent the members of an interface by a record type T. The relationship between the interface name I and its unfolding T is then neither an equality $I = T$ (because then I would not represent a new type), nor is I an abstract type $I <: T$ (because then one could not create new values of I from implementations of type T). Hence, the need of the third type binding $I \prec T$.

A perhaps more standard alternative to our nominal new-type bindings would be *branding*. That is, one would define type equality and subtyping structurally and introduce a binder to create new type names. Branding then means creating a new type by combining a structurally defined type and a freshly created type name. An advantage of the branding approach is that it is orthogonal to traditional structural type systems for objects or modules. A disadvantage is that it corresponds less well to the definitions and implementations of existing object-oriented languages (with the exception of MODULA-3 [13]).

A more technical reason for abandoning the structural types with brands approach has to do with recursion: In a system with dependent types, type recursion can involve terms, which means that recursive types are not necessarily regular trees. For instance if p is a qualified identifier of an object with a term member l and a type member L, then the type $p.L$ might depend on the type $p.l.L$. The resulting tree would then not be regular. There is little hope that practical semi-algorithms for checking equality and subtyping of non-regular trees can be found. To sidestep these problems we follow the strategy of many existing programming languages: we restrict ourselves to non-recursive type aliases, and introduce a new kind of type definition that makes the defined type a subtype of its right-hand side. Note that similar problems for type-checking are caused by parameterized algebraic types where recursive use of a type constructor can also lead to non-regular trees. The common approach to deal with such types is again to make them nominal.

In summary, we design and study in this paper νObj, a core calculus and type system for objects and classes with type members. Type members can be aliases, abstract types, or new types. Classes are first-class and can be composed using mixin-composition. Our type system supports via encodings:

- Most concepts of SML-style module systems, including sharing constraints and higher-order functors, but excluding applicative functors.
- System $F_{<:}$ [14], with the full subtyping rule.
- Virtual types and family polymorphism [20].

Because all these constructs are mapped to the same small language core, it becomes possible to express unified concepts. In particular, our theory promotes the following identifications.

$$
\begin{array}{ll}
Object & = Module \\
Object\ type & = Signature \\
Class & = Method\ =\ Functor
\end{array}
$$

The same identifications are made in BETA and GBETA, where classes and methods are subsumed under the notion of "patterns". Our own language SCALA follows the same approach, except that it maintains a distinction between methods and classes on the syntactical level. Generally, many of our intuitions are inspired by BETA and by the work of Erik Ernst [19] and Mads Torgerson, which build on it. A contribution of our work is the definition and study of these ideas in a formal calculus and type system. The main technical results of the paper are

- Confluence of the reduction relation.
- Undecidability of type checking by reduction to the problem in $F_{<:}$.
- Type soundness – a well-typed program that does not diverge reduces to an answer of the same type.

Other Related Work This paper extends a previous workshop contribution [35]. Nominal type systems have also been formalized in the Java context, examples are [21, 27, 32]. A difference between these approaches and ours is that they rely on a global class graph that describes membership and inheritance. Another difference is that these systems are almost completely nominal, in the sense that most types can be described by a name (exceptions are only array types and generic types in FGJ [27]). By contrast, classes can be local in νObj and nominal types are just one construction in an otherwise structural type system.

There are two other attempts at formalizations of virtual or abstract types in object-oriented programming that we are aware of. The first, by Torgersen [41], sketches a nominal type system for virtual types. It argues informally that if certain restrictions are imposed on the usage of virtual types (which in fact makes them equivalent to abstract types in our terminology), type soundness can be ensured. Igarashi and Pierce [25] proposed a foundation of virtual types using a type system that adds dependent types to an $F_{<:}$ core. However, no formal study of the type system's properties was attempted, and in fact their initial formalization lacked the subject reduction property (that formalization was dropped in the journal version of their paper [26]).

The rest of this paper is structured as follows. Section 2 presents context-free syntax, operational semantics, and type assignment rules of our object calculus, νObj. Section 3 illustrates in a series of examples how the calculus expresses common object-oriented idioms. Section 4 presents the type structure of νObj types, including derivation rules for well-formedness, equality and subtyping. Section 5 presents an encoding of $F_{<:}$ in νObj. Section 6 presents the meta-theory of νObj with results on confluence, soundness and undecidability. Section 7 concludes.

2   The νObj Calculus

We now present a core language for objects and classes. Compared to the standard theory of objects [1], there are three major differences. First, we have classes besides objects as a primitive concept. Classes are even "first-class" in the sense they can result from evaluation of a term and they may be associated with a label. Second, the calculus has a notion of object identity in that every object is referenced by a name and it is that name instead of the object record which is passed around. Third, we can express object types with type components, and some of these components can be nominal.

2.1   Context-Free Syntax

Figure 1 presents the νObj calculus in terms of its abstract syntax, and its structural equivalence and reduction relations. There are three alphabets. Proper term names x, y, z are subject to α-renaming, whereas term labels l, m, n and type labels L, M, N are fixed.

A *term* denotes an object or a class. It can be of the following five forms.

– A *simple name* x, which denotes an object.

Syntax

x, y, z	Name		
l, m, n	Term label	L, M, N	Type label
$s, t, u ::=$	Term	$S, T, U ::=$	Type
x	Variable	$p.\mathbf{type}$	Singleton
$t.l$	Selection	$T \bullet L$	Type selection
$\nu x \leftarrow t \,;\, u$	New object	$\{x\mid \overline{D}\}$	Record type (=:: R)
$[x\!:\!S\mid \overline{d}]$	Class template	$[x\!:\!S\mid \overline{D}]$	Class type
$t \,\&_S\, u$	Composition	$T \,\&\, U$	Compound type
$d \quad ::=$	Definition	$D \quad ::=$	Declaration
$l = t$	Term definition	$l : T$	Term declaration
$L \preceq T$	Type definition	$L \preceq: T$	Type declaration
$p \quad ::=$	Path	$\preceq: \quad ::=$	Type binder
$x \mid p.l$		$=$	Type alias
$v \quad ::=$	Value	$\prec$	New type
$x \mid [x\!:\!S\mid \overline{d}]$		$<:$	Abstract type
		$\preceq \quad ::=$	Concrete type binder
		$= \mid \prec$	

Structural Equivalence α-renaming of bound variables x, plus

(extrude) $\qquad\qquad e\langle \nu x \leftarrow t \,;\, u\rangle \equiv \nu x \leftarrow t \,;\, e\langle u\rangle$
$$\textbf{if } x \notin \mathit{fn}(e),\ \mathit{bn}(e) \cap \mathit{fn}(x, t) = \emptyset$$

Reduction

(select) $\quad \nu x \leftarrow [x\!:\!S\mid \overline{d}, l = v] \,;\, e\langle x.l\rangle \;\rightarrow\; \nu x \leftarrow [x\!:\!S\mid \overline{d}, l = v] \,;\, e\langle v\rangle$
$$\textbf{if } \mathit{bn}(e) \cap \mathit{fn}(x, v) = \emptyset$$

(mix) $\qquad\quad [x\!:\!S_1\mid \overline{d}_1] \,\&_S\, [x\!:\!S_2\mid \overline{d}_2] \;\rightarrow\; [x\!:\!S\mid \overline{d}_1 \uplus \overline{d}_2]$

where evaluation context

$e ::= \langle\rangle \mid e.l \mid e \,\&_S\, t \mid t \,\&_S\, e \mid \nu x \leftarrow t \,;\, e \mid \nu x \leftarrow e \,;\, t \mid \nu x \leftarrow [x\!:\!S\mid \overline{d}, l = e] \,;\, t$

Fig. 1. The νObj Calculus

- A *selection* $t.l$, which can denote either an object or a class.
- An *object creation* $\nu x \leftarrow t \,;\, u$, which defines a fresh instance x of class t. The scope of this object is the term u.
- A *class template* $[x : S\mid \overline{d}]$ where $\overline{d}$ is a sequence of *definitions* which associate term labels with values and type labels with types. This acts as a template to construct objects with the members defined by the definitions. The name x of type S stands for "self", i.e. the object being constructed from the template. Its scope is the definition sequence $\overline{d}$. A term or type can refer via $x.l$ to some other member of that object. No textual sequence constraint applies

to such references; in particular it is possible that a binding refers to itself or to bindings defined later in the same record. This distinguishes our type system from earlier type systems for records [15] or modules [23].

- A *mixin composition* t $\&_S$ u, which forms a combined class from the two classes to which t and u evaluate. Here, S is the type of "self" in the combined class.

A *value* is a simple name or a class template. A *path* p is a name x followed by a possibly empty sequence of selections, e.g. $x.l_1$. ... $.l_n$.

The syntax of *types* in our system closely follows the syntax of terms. A type can be of the following five forms.

- A *singleton type* $p.$**type**. This type represents the set of values which has as only element the object referenced by the path p. Singleton types are the only way a type can depend on a term in νObj.
- A *type selection* $T \bullet L$, which represents the type component labelled L of type T.
- A *record type* $\{x | \overline{D}\}$ where $\overline{D}$ is a sequence of *declarations* which can be value bindings or type bindings. A *value binding* $l : T$ associates a term label l with its type T. *Type bindings* come in three different forms: First, the binding $L = T$ defines L to be an *alias* for T. Second, the binding $L \prec T$ defines L to be a *new type* which *expands* to type T. That is, L is a subtype of T which has exactly the members defined by T; furthermore, one can create objects of type L from a class which defines all members of T. Third, the binding $L <: T$ defines L to be an *abstract type* which is known to be a subtype of its bound T. We let the meta-variable $\preceq$ range over $=$ and $\prec$, and let $\preceq:$ range over $=$, $\prec$, and $<:$. The name x stands for "self"; its type is assumed to be the record type itself. We let the letter R range over record types.
- A *compound type* T & U. This type contains all members of types T and U. The subtyping relation for compound types is the same as the one for intersection types [4], but the formation rules are more restrictive. Where T and U have a member with the same label, the compound type contains the member defined in U. That member definition must be more specific (see Section 4) than the corresponding member definition in T.
- A *class type* $[x : S | \overline{D}]$, which contains as values classes that instantiate to objects of type $\{x | \overline{D}\}$, or some subtype of it. x is again the name for "self". It now comes with an explicit type S which may be different from $\{x | \overline{D}\}$. Definitions in S which are missing from $\overline{D}$ play the role of abstract members. Such members can be referred to from other definitions in the class, but they are not defined in the class itself. Instead, these members must be defined in other classes which are composed with the class itself in a mixin composition. Definitions which are present in $\overline{D}$ but missing in S play in some sense the role of non-virtual members – they are not referred to via "self" from inside the class, so overriding them does not change existing behavior. Definitions present in both S and $\overline{D}$ play the role of virtual members.

Discussion Most notably missing from the core language are functions, including polymorphic ones, and parameterized types. In fact, type variables are missing completely — the only α-renameable identifiers denote ν-bound terms. However, these omitted constructs can still be expressed in νObj using context-free encodings. This will be shown later in the paper. Section 3 explains how named monomorphic functions are encoded. Section 5 generalizes the encoding to system $F_{<:}$.

The type syntax defines a singleton type $p.\textbf{type}$ and a selection $T \bullet L$ which operates on types T. More conventional would have been a type selection $p.L$ which operates on terms p instead of types. The latter selection operation can be expressed in our syntax as $p.\textbf{type} \bullet L$. Besides having some technical advantages, this decomposition can express two concepts which the conventional type selection $p.L$ cannot. First, the self-type of a class can be expressed as a singleton type *this.type*. This can accurately model covariant self-types. For contravariant self-types one would need a matching operation [11, 10] instead of – or in addition to – the subtyping relation that we introduce. Second, an inner class of the kind it exists in JAVA [22, 24] can be referenced by a type selection $Outer \bullet Inner$ where $Outer$ and $Inner$ are types. Such a selection risks being non-sensical in the presence of abstract type members in the outer class $Outer$. Consequently, our typing rules prevent formation of the type $T \bullet L$ if L's definition depends on some abstract member of T. Note that this is not a problem for JAVA, which does not have abstract type declarations.

Syntactic Sugar

1. The type $p.L$ is a shorthand for $p.\textbf{type} \bullet L$.
2. The class type $[x|\ \overline{D}]$ is a shorthand for $[x\colon\{x|\ \overline{D}\}|\ \overline{D}]$.
3. The class template $[x|\ \overline{d}]$ is a shorthand for $[x\colon\{x|\ \overline{D}\}|\ \overline{d}]$ where $\overline{D}$ is the most specific set of declarations matching definitions $\overline{d}$.
4. The types $\{\overline{D}\}$, $[\overline{D}]$ and the term $[\overline{d}]$ are shorthands for $\{x|\ \overline{D}\}$, $[x|\ \overline{D}]$ and $[x|\ \overline{d}]$ where x does not appear in $\overline{D}$ or $\overline{d}$.
5. new t is a shorthand for $\nu x \leftarrow t\ ;\ x$.
6. $t_1\ \&\ t_2$ is a shorthand for $t_1\ \&_{S_1\ \&\ (S_2\ \&\ \{x|\ D_1 \uplus D_2\})}\ t_2$ if t_i has least type $[x : S_i|\ \overline{D}_i]$ for $i \in 1..2$.

The last shorthand implements an overriding behavior for mixin composition where a concrete definition always overrides an abstract definition of the same label. Furthermore, between two abstract definitions or between two concrete definitions of the same label it is always the second which overrides the first. This scheme, which corresponds closely with the rules in Zenger's component calculus [44], is often more useful than the straight "second overrides first" rule of systems where mixins are seen as functions over classes [8, 21, 5].

2.2   Operational Semantics

Figure 1 specifies a structural equivalence and a small-step reduction relation for our calculus. Both relations are based on the notion of an *evaluation context*, which determines where in a term reduction may take place. The grammar for evaluation contexts given in Figure 1 does not yet yield a deterministic reduction relation, but still leaves a choice of a strict or lazy evaluation strategy, or some hybrid in-between. Particular evaluation strategies are obtained by tightening the grammar for evaluation contexts.

Notation We write $\bar{a}$ for a sequence of entities $a_1, \ldots, a_n$. We implicitly identify all permutations of such a sequence, and take the empty sequence ϵ as a unit for (,). The *domain* $dom(\bar{d})$, $dom(\bar{D})$ of a sequence of definitions $\bar{d}$ or declarations $\bar{D}$ is the set of labels it defines. The restriction $\bar{d}|_{\mathcal{L}}$, $\bar{D}|_{\mathcal{L}}$ of definitions $\bar{d}$ or declarations $\bar{D}$ to a set of labels $\mathcal{L}$ consists of all those bindings in $\bar{d}$ or $\bar{D}$ that define labels in $\mathcal{L}$. The $\uplus$ operator on definitions or declarations denotes concatenation with overwriting of common labels. That is, $\bar{a} \uplus \bar{b} = \bar{a}|_{dom(\bar{a}) \backslash dom(\bar{b})}, \bar{b}$.

A name occurrence x is *bound* in a type T, a term t, a definition d, a declaration D, or an evaluation context e if there is an enclosing object creation $\nu x \leftarrow u \; ; \; t$, a class template $[x : S| \bar{d}]$, a class type $[x : S| \bar{D}]$, or a record type $\{x| \bar{D}\}$ which has the occurrence in the scope of the name x. The free names $fn(X)$ of one of the syntactic classes X enumerated above is the set of names which have unbound occurrences in X. The bound names $bn(e)$ of an evaluation context e are all names x bound by a subterm of e such that the scope of x contains the hole $\langle \rangle$ of the context.

Structural Equivalence As usual we identify terms related by α-renaming. We also postulate a scope extrusion rule (extrude), which allows us to lift a ν-binding out of an evaluation context, provided that this does not cause capture of free variable names. Formally, α-renaming equivalence $\equiv_\alpha$ is the smallest congruence on types and terms satisfying the four laws

$$\nu x \leftarrow t \; ; \; u \equiv_\alpha \nu y \leftarrow t \; ; \; [y/x]u \quad \text{if } y \notin fn(u)$$
$$[x{:}S| \bar{d}] \equiv_\alpha [y{:}S| [y/x]\bar{d}] \quad \text{if } y \notin fn(\bar{d})$$
$$[x{:}S| \bar{D}] \equiv_\alpha [y{:}S| [y/x]\bar{D}] \quad \text{if } y \notin fn(\bar{D})$$
$$\{x| \bar{D}\} \equiv_\alpha \{y| [y/x]\bar{D}\} \quad \text{if } y \notin fn(\bar{D})$$

Structural equivalence $\equiv$ is the smallest congruence containing $\equiv_\alpha$ and satisfying the (extrude) law in Figure 1.

Reduction The reduction relation $\rightarrow$ is the smallest relation that contains the two rules given in Figure 1 and that is closed under structural equivalence and formation of evaluation contexts. That is, if $t \equiv t' \rightarrow u' \equiv u$, then also $e\langle t\rangle \rightarrow e\langle u\rangle$. The first reduction rule, (*select*), connects a definition of an object with a selection on that object. The rule requires that the external object reference and the internal "self" have the same name x (this can always be arranged by α-renaming). The second rule, (mix), constructs a class from two operand classes by mixin composition, combining the definitions of both classes with the $\uplus$ operator. Multi-step reduction $\twoheadrightarrow$ is the smallest transitive relation that includes $\equiv$ and $\rightarrow$.

$$(\text{VAR}) \quad \frac{x{:}T \in \Gamma}{\Gamma \vdash x : T} \qquad\qquad \frac{\Gamma \vdash t : T, \ \ T \ni (l : U)}{\Gamma \vdash t.l : U} \quad (\text{SEL})$$

$$(\text{VARPATH}) \quad \frac{\Gamma \vdash x : R}{\Gamma \vdash x : x.\textbf{type}} \qquad \frac{\Gamma \vdash t : p.\textbf{type}, \ \ t.l : R}{\Gamma \vdash t.l : p.l.\textbf{type}} \quad (\text{SELPATH})$$

$$(\text{SUB}) \quad \frac{\Gamma \vdash t : T, \ \ T \leq U}{\Gamma \vdash t : U} \qquad \frac{\begin{array}{c}\Gamma \vdash t : [x{:}S|\ \overline{D}], \ \ S \prec \{x|\ \overline{D}\} \\ \Gamma, x{:}S \vdash u : U \qquad x \notin fn(U)\end{array}}{\Gamma \vdash (\nu x \leftarrow t \ ; u) : U} \quad (\text{NEW})$$

$$(\text{CLASS}) \quad \frac{\begin{array}{c}\Gamma \vdash S \ \text{wf} \qquad \Gamma, x{:}S \vdash \overline{D} \ \text{wf}, \ \ t_i : T_i \\ t_i \ \text{contractive in} \ x \qquad (i \in 1..n)\end{array}}{\Gamma \vdash [x{:}S|\ \overline{D}, l_i = t_i{}^{i \in 1..n}] : [x{:}S|\ \overline{D}, l_i{:}T_i{}^{i \in 1..n}]}$$

$$(\&) \quad \frac{\Gamma \vdash t_i : [x{:}S_i|\ \overline{D}_i] \qquad \Gamma \vdash S \ \text{wf}, \ \ S \leq S_i \qquad (i = 1, 2)}{\Gamma \vdash t_1 \ \&_S \ t_2 : [x{:}S \ | \ \overline{D}_1 \uplus \overline{D}_2]}$$

Fig. 2. Type assignment

2.3 Type Assignment

Figure 2 presents the rules for assigning types to terms. These are expressed as
deduction rules for type judgments $\Gamma \vdash t : T$. Here, Γ is a type environment,
i.e. a set of bindings $x : T$, where all bound names x are assumed to be pairwise
different.

There are the usual tautology and subsumption rules. Rule (SEL) assigns to
a selection $t.l$ the type U provided t's type has a member $l : U$. Rules (VARPATH)
and (SELPATH) assign singleton types $p.\textbf{type}$ to terms which denote unique objects.

Rule (NEW) types a ν-expression $\nu x \leftarrow t \ ; \ u$. The term t needs to have
a class type $[x{:}S \ | \ \overline{D}]$ such that the self type S expands to a record type which
contains exactly the declarations $\overline{D}$. This means that all declarations present in S
must be defined in D, with the same type. In particular, classes with abstract
members cannot be instantiated. The body u is then typed under an augmented
environment which contains the binding $x : S$. The type of u is not allowed to
refer to x.

Rule (CLASS) types class templates. All term definitions $l_i = t_i$ in the template
are typed under a new environment which includes a binding $x : S$ for the self-
name of the class. However, it is required that all terms t_i are contractive in self.
This means that they do not access self during the instantiation of an object of
the class. Contractiveness is defined formally as follows.

Definition. The term t is *contractive* in the name x if one of the following holds.

- $x \notin fn(t)$, or
- t is a class template $[y : S | \overline{d}]$, or
- t is a mixin composition $t_1 \&_S t_2$ and t_1, t_2 are contractive in x, or
- t is an object creation $\nu y \leftarrow t_1 ; t_2$, $x \notin fn(t_1)$ and t_2 is contractive in x.

The contractiveness requirement prevents accesses to fields of an object before these fields are defined. In conventional object-oriented languages this would correspond to the requirement that self can be accessed only from methods, not from initializers of object fields. More liberal schemes are possible [6], but require additional technical overhead in the type assignment rules. One can also envisage to allow accesses to self without restrictions, preinitializing fields to some default value, or raising a run-time exception on access before definition.

The last rule, (&) types compositions of class terms. The self type S of the composition is required to be a subtype of the self types of both components. The definitions of the composed class are then obtained by concatenating the definitions of the components.

These deduction rules are based on several other forms of judgments on types, specifically the well-formedness judgment $\Gamma \vdash T \ wf$, the membership judgment $\Gamma \vdash T \ni D$, the expansion judgment $\Gamma \vdash T \prec T'$, and the subtyping judgment $\Gamma \vdash T \leq T'$. Deduction rules for these judgments are motivated in Section 4 and given in full in an accompanying technical report [34].

As usual, we assume that terms can be alpha-renamed in type assignments in order to prevent failed type derivations due to duplicate variables in environments. That is, if $\Gamma \vdash t : T$ and $t \equiv_\alpha t'$ then also $\Gamma \vdash t' : T$.

The type assignment judgment is extended to a judgment relating definitions and declarations as follows.

Definition. A declaration D *matches* a definition d in an environment Γ written $\Gamma \vdash d : D$, if one of the following holds:

$\Gamma \vdash (l = t) : (l : T)$ if $\Gamma \vdash t : T$.
$\Gamma \vdash (L \preceq T) : D$ if $\Gamma \vdash (L \preceq T) \leq D$ (see Section 4.5 for a definition of $\leq$ on declarations).

3   Examples

Before presenting the remaining details of the theory, we demonstrate its usage by means of some examples. Since the νObj calculus is quite different from standard object-oriented notations, we first present each example in the more conventional object-oriented language SCALA [33]. SCALA's object model is a generalization of the object model of JAVA. The extensions most important for the purposes of this paper are abstract types, type aliases, and mixin composition of classes. A subset of SCALA maps easily into νObj, and we will restrict the example code to that subset. Other constructs, such as higher-order functions, generics, or pattern matching can be defined by translation into the subset, and, ultimately, into the object calculus.

3.1   Modules, Classes, and Objects

We start with a class for representing points in a one dimensional space. Class *Point* is defined as a member of the singleton object *pt*. In SCALA, such top-level singleton objects play the role of modules. In addition to the coordinate *x*, class *Point* defines a method *eq* for comparing a point with another point.

```
object pt {
    abstract class Point {
        def x: Int;
        def eq(p: Point): Boolean = (x == p.x);
    }
}
```

In the subset of SCALA used here, classes do not have explicit constructor parameters. Instead, parameters are represented as abstract class members. For creating an object, one has to subclass *Point* and provide concrete implementations for the abstract members. In the following code we do this twice by using a mixin composition of class *Point* with an anonymous class that defines the missing coordinate *x*.

```
val a = new pt.Point with { def x = 0; };
val b = new pt.Point with { def x = 1; };
a.eq(b)
```

We now devise a translation of the previous SCALA code into our calculus. In addition to the syntax defined in Figure 1, we also make use of λ-abstractions and applications. Later in this section we will explain how to encode these constructs in νObj.

$$\nu\, pt \leftarrow [pt \mid$$
$$Point \prec \{x: Int, eq: pt.Point \rightarrow Boolean\},$$
$$point = [this: pt.Point \mid eq = \lambda\, (p: pt.Point)\, p.x == this.x\,]$$
$$];$$
$$\nu\, a \leftarrow pt.point\, \&_{pt.Point}\, [x = 0];$$
$$\nu\, b \leftarrow pt.point\, \&_{pt.Point}\, [x = 1];$$
$$a.eq(b)$$

A class is represented by two entities: an object type that is used to type instances of the class and a class value, which is used to construct objects. We use the name of the class as the name of the type and the same name, but starting with a lower-case letter, as the name of the class value. While the type includes the signatures of all class members, the class value only provides implementations for the non-abstract members. In general, abstract members are present in the self-type S of a class $[x : S \mid \overline{d}]$, but are missing from the class definitions $\overline{d}$. Non-abstract members are present in both S and $\overline{d}$.

3.2   Functions

For encoding λ-abstractions and applications we use a technique similar to the one for passing parameters during class instantiations. A λ-abstraction $\lambda(x : T)\, t$ is represented as a class with an abstract member *arg* for the function argument and a concrete member *fun* which refers to the expression for computing the function's result:

$[x: \{arg: T\} \mid fun = [res = t']]$

where t' corresponds to term t in which all occurrences of x get replaced by $x.arg$. As explained in Section 2, we cannot access arg directly on the right-hand-side of fun. Therefore fun packs the body of the function into another class. The instantiation of this class will then trigger the execution of the function body. For instance, function λ $(p: pt.Point)$ $p.x == this.x$ could be encoded as a class $[p: \{arg: pt.Point\} \mid fun = [res = p.arg.x == this.x]]$ of type $[p: \{arg: pt.Point\} \mid fun: [res: Boolean]]$ that contains an abstract member arg and a concrete member fun.

In νObj, an application $g(e)$ gets decomposed into three subsequent steps:

$\nu\, g_{app} \leftarrow g \; \& \; [arg = e];$

$\nu\, g_{eval} \leftarrow g_{app}.fun;$

$g_{eval}.res$

First we instantiate function g with a concrete argument yielding a thunk g_{app}. Then we evaluate this thunk by creating an instance g_{eval} of it. Finally we extract the result by querying field res of g_{eval}. For instance, the call to function eq from the previous code could be encoded as $\nu\, g_{app} \leftarrow a.eq \; \& \; [arg = b]; \nu\, g_{eval} \leftarrow g_{app}.fun; g_{eval}.res$.

3.3 Abstract Types

Suppose we would now like to extend the *Point* class for defining a new class *ColorPoint* that includes color information. Since extended classes define subtypes in SCALA, we cannot override method *eq* contravariantly such that the parameter of *eq* now has type *ColorPoint*. But exactly this would allow us to compare *ColorPoints* only with *ColorPoints*. Instead, we have to refactor our code and abstract over the parameter type explicitly in anticipation of future extensions. The following code fragment defines an abstract type *This* in class *Point* with bound *Point* which gets covariantly refined in subclasses like *ColorPoint*.

```
object pt {
    abstract class Point {
        type This <: Point;
        def x: Int;
        def eq(p: This): Boolean = (x == p.x);
    }
}
object cpt {
    abstract class ColorPoint extends pt.Point {
        type This <: ColorPoint;
        def col: String;
        override def eq(p: This): Boolean = (x == p.x) && (col == p.col);
    }
}
```

We now make use of the two classes and define a *Point* and two *ColorPoint* instances.

val c = **new** pt.Point **with**
            {**type** This = pt.Point; **def** x=0;};
val d = **new** cpt.ColorPoint **with**
            {**type** This = cpt.ColorPoint; **def** x=1; **def** col="blue";};
val e = **new** cpt.ColorPoint **with**
            {**type** This = cpt.ColorPoint; **def** x=2; **def** col="green";};

The type system has to ensure that we are able to compare only compatible objects; i.e. we have to be able to execute d.eq(e) and e.eq(d) as well as c.eq(d) and c.eq(e), whereas terms like d.eq(c) are ill-typed and therefore rejected by the typechecker.

An encoding of the previous two classes in our object calculus is given by the following term.

ν pt ← [pt |
    Point ≺ {this | This <: pt.Point, x: Int, eq: this.This → Boolean},
    point = [this: pt.Point | eq = λ (p: this.This) p.x == this.x]
];
ν cpt ← [cpt |
    ColorPoint ≺ pt.Point & {This <: cpt.ColorPoint, col: String},
    colorPoint = [this: cpt.ColorPoint |
        eq = λ (p: this.This) p.x == this.x && p.col == this.col]
];
ν c ← pt.point & [This = pt.Point, x = 0];
ν d ← cpt.colorPoint & [This = cpt.ColorPoint, x = 1, col = "blue"];
c.eq(d)

This example does not only explain how to use abstract types, it also shows that our calculus is expressive enough to model virtual types in a type-safe way.

3.4   Generic Types

We now present a more evolved example that shows how to use νObj to encode generic classes. The following code defines a "module" lst which contains an implementation for generic lists consisting of three classes List, Nil, and Cons.

```
object lst {
    abstract class List {
        type T <: scala.Object;
        def isEmpty: Boolean;
        def head: T;
        def tail: List with {type T = List.this.T;};
    }
    abstract class Nil extends List {
        def isEmpty = true;
        def head: T = error;
        def tail: List with {type T = Nil.this.T;} = error;
    }
    abstract class Cons extends List {
        def isEmpty = false;
    }
}
```

Since classes are neither parameterized by values nor types, we model the element type of a list with an abstract type T in class *List*. Similarly, class parameters like the head and the tail of a cons-cell are represented by abstract functions. Note that the type of the *tail* value of a list object is a mixin composition of *List* with a record type which consists of the type binding {**type** T = *List*.**this**.T}. This forces the element type of a list and its tail to be the same. [1] In general, mixin composition with type bindings subsumes in expressive power the sharing constraints of SML module systems [28].

Class *Nil* provides all the abstract functions of its superclass *List*. For the implementation of *head* and *tail* we make use of a predefined value *error* that produces errors at run-time when accessed. *error* is of any type. Even though our formal treatment does not include such a bottom type, adding one would be straightforward.

Class *Cons* only defines function *isEmpty*. The other abstract functions constitute constructor parameters and have to be provided at instantiation time.

Here is an example how the list abstraction is applied. The following code fragment constructs two lists of integers [ ] and [*1*] and returns the *head* of the second list. Again, we use a mixin class composition to emulate parameter passing.

```
val x0 = new lst.Nil with {type T = Int;};
val x1 = new lst.Cons with {type T = Int; def head = 1; def tail = x0;};
x1.head
```

Here is the translation of the previous SCALA code into our object calculus.

```
ν lst ← [lst |
    List ≺ {this |
        T <: {}, isEmpty: Boolean, head: this.T, tail: lst.List & {T = this.T}},
    Nil ≺ lst.List,
    Cons ≺ lst.List,
    nil = [this: lst.Nil | isEmpty = true, head = error, tail = error],
    cons = [this: lst.Cons | isEmpty = false]
];
ν x0 ← lst.nil & [T = Int];
ν x1 ← lst.cons & [T = Int, head = 1, tail = x0];
x1.head
```

We now augment class *List* of the previous example with a function *len* that computes the length of the list. In SCALA, this can be done without changing the source code of *List*, by using a class as a mixin:

```
object llst {
    abstract class ListWithLen extends lst.List {
        def tail: ListWithLen with { type T = ListWithLen.this.T; };
        def len(): Int = if (this.isEmpty) 0 else 1 + this.tail.len();
    }
}
```

---

[1] Like in JAVA, *Outer*.**this** denotes the identity of an enclosing *Outer* object in the scope of an inner class of *Outer*.

Class *ListWithLen* extends class *List*. It adds a new *len* member and narrows the type of the existing *tail* member to *ListWithLen*. To build lists with *len* members, we add this class as a mixin. Here is an example usage:

```
val y0 = new lst.Nil with {
    type T = Int;
    def tail: ListWithLen with {type T = Int;} = error;
} with llst.ListWithLen;
val y1 = new lst.Cons with {
    type T = Int;
    def head = 1;
    def tail = y0;
} with llst.ListWithLen;
y1.len()
```

The translation of this program into νObj is given in the following code fragment. Please note that this time, we encode function *len* directly as a class, similar to the description given before. This time we can use a slightly simpler encoding since our function is not parameterized.

```
ν llst ← [llst |
    ListWithLen ≺ lst.List & {this |
        tail: llst.ListWithLen & {T = this.T},
        len: [res: Int ]
    },
    listWithLen = [this: llst.ListWithLen |
        len = [res = if (this.isEmpty) 0 else 1 + (ν t ← this.tail.len; t.res)]]
];
ν y0 ← lst.nil & [T = Int] & llst.listWithLen;
ν y1 ← lst.cons & [T = Int, head = 1, tail = y0] & llst.listWithLen;
ν l ← y1.len;
l.res
```

Note that type *ListWithLen* is represented as a composition of type *List* and a record type containing added and overridden members. This turns type *ListWithLen* into a subtype of type *List*.

4   Type Structure

The type structure of νObj is defined by deduction rules for the following kinds of judgments:

$\Gamma \vdash T$ wf	Type T is well-formed.
$\Gamma \vdash D$ wf	Declaration D is well-formed.
$\Gamma \vdash T \ni D$	Type T contains declaration D.
$\Gamma \vdash T = U$	Types T and U are equal.
$\Gamma \vdash T \prec U$	Type T expands to type U.
$\Gamma \vdash T <: U$	Type T is upper-bounded by type U.
$\Gamma \vdash T \leq U$	Type T is a subtype of type U.
$\Gamma \vdash \overline{D}_1 \leq \overline{D}_2$	Declarations D_1 are more specific than declarations D_2.

Compared to standard type systems there are three non-standard forms of judgments: First, the membership judgment $\Gamma \vdash T \ni D$ factors out the essence of path-dependent types. Second, the expansion judgment $\Gamma \vdash T \prec U$ captures the essential relation between a new type and its unfolding. Third, the upper-binding judgment $\Gamma \vdash T <: U$ provides exact type information about which record type is a supertype of a given type. This information is needed for the correct treatment of type bindings in records. The essential typing rules for all these judgments are discussed in the following.

Notation We sometimes write judgments with several predicates on the right of the turnstile as an abbreviation for multiple judgments. E.g. " $\Gamma \vdash T\ wf,\ T'\ wf$ " is an abbreviation for the two judgments " $\Gamma \vdash T\ wf$ " and " $\Gamma \vdash T'\ wf$ ".

4.1   Membership

The membership judgment $\Gamma \vdash T \ni D$ states that type T has a member definition D. The judgment is derived by the following two rules, which capture the principles of path-dependent types.

$$(\text{Single-}\ni) \quad \frac{\Gamma \vdash p.\textbf{type} <: \{x|\ \overline{D'}, D\}}{\Gamma \vdash p.\textbf{type} \ni [p/x]D}$$

$$(\text{Other-}\ni) \quad \frac{\Gamma, x : T \vdash x.\textbf{type} \ni D \qquad x \notin \mathit{fn}(\Gamma, D)}{\Gamma \vdash T \ni D}$$

Rule (Single-$\ni$) defines membership for singleton types. In this case, the self-reference x in the definition is replaced by the path p. Rule (Other-$\ni$) defines membership for arbitrary types in terms of (Single-$\ni$). To determine a member D of a type T which is not a singleton, invent a fresh variable x of type T and determine the corresponding member of type $x.\textbf{type}$. The resulting member is not allowed to depend on x. Note that, if T is a singleton type, rule (Other-$\ni$) either fails or yields the same judgments as rule (Single-$\ni$).

Example Consider the type $T \prec \{x : T \mid L <: \{\ \}, l_1 : x.L, l_2 : Int\}$. Further consider a path p and some other term t which is not a path, both of type T. Then p contains the definitions $L <: \{\ \}$, $l_1 : p.L$, and $l_2 : Int$. On the other hand, t contains only the definitions $L <: \{\ \}$ and $l_2 : Int$ since rule (Other-$\ni$) does not derive a binding for l_1. Indeed, substituting t for the self reference x in the binding for l_1 would yield the type $t.L$ which would not be well-formed.

4.2   Equality

The type equality judgment $\Gamma \vdash T = T'$ states that the two types T and T' are the same or aliases of each other. Type equality is the smallest congruence which is closed under the following two derivation rules.

$$(\text{ALIAS-=}) \quad \frac{\Gamma \vdash T \ni (L = U), \quad T \; wf}{\Gamma \vdash T{\bullet}L = U} \qquad \frac{\Gamma \vdash p : q.\mathbf{type}}{\Gamma \vdash p.\mathbf{type} = q.\mathbf{type}} \quad (\text{SINGLE-=})$$

Rule (ALIAS-=) is standard; it states that type $T{\bullet}L$ is equal to U, provided T has an alias member definition $L = U$. Rule (SINGLE-=) expresses the following property: if a path p has a singleton type $q.\mathbf{type}$, we know that p and q are aliases, hence the singleton types $p.\mathbf{type}$ and $q.\mathbf{type}$ should be equal. Without the rule, one would only have that $p.\mathbf{type}$ is a subtype of $q.\mathbf{type}$.

4.3   Expansion

The type expansion judgment $\Gamma \vdash T \prec T'$ states that type T expands (or: unfolds) into type T'. Expansion is the smallest transitive relation which contains type equality and is closed under the following three derivation rules.

$$(\text{TSEL-}\prec) \quad \frac{\Gamma \vdash T \ni (L \prec U)}{\Gamma \vdash T{\bullet}L \prec U} \qquad \frac{\Gamma \vdash T \prec T', \quad U \prec U'}{\Gamma \vdash T \,\&\, U \prec T' \,\&\, U'} \quad (\&\text{-}\prec)$$

$$(\text{MIXIN-}\prec) \quad \frac{\Gamma, x : \{x|\ \overline{D}_1 \uplus \overline{D}_2\} \vdash \overline{D}_2 \leq \overline{D}_1|_{\mathrm{dom}(\overline{D}_2)}}{\Gamma \vdash \{x|\ \overline{D}_1\} \,\&\, \{x|\ \overline{D}_2\} \prec \{x|\ \overline{D}_1 \uplus \overline{D}_2\}}$$

Rule (TSEL-$\prec$) expresses expansion of type selections in the usual way. Rule (MIXIN-$\prec$) states that the combination of two record types R_1 and R_2 expands to a record type containing the concatenation of the definitions in R_1 and R_2. If some label is defined in both R_1 and R_2, the definition in R_2 overrides the definition in R_1. In this case we must have that the definition in R_2 is more specific than the definition in R_1.

4.4   Upper Bounds

The upper bound judgment $\Gamma \vdash T <: T'$ states that T' is an expansion of T or a (tight) upper bound of it. The primary use of this relation is in determining for a type T the least record type which is a supertype of T. This information is needed for deriving the membership judgment by rule (SINGLE-$\in$).

Upper-binding is the smallest transitive relation which contains expansion and which is closed under the following three derivation rules.

$$(\text{TSEL-}<:) \quad \frac{\Gamma \vdash T \ni (L <: U)}{\Gamma \vdash T{\bullet}L <: U} \qquad \frac{x : T \in \Gamma}{\Gamma \vdash x.\mathbf{type} <: T} \quad (\text{VAR-}<:)$$

$$(\text{SEL-}<:) \quad \frac{\Gamma \vdash p.\mathbf{type} \ni (l : U)}{\Gamma \vdash p.l.\mathbf{type} <: U}$$

The first rule (TSEL-$<:$) defines upper bounds of abstract types in the usual way. The other two rules take as the upper bound of a singleton type $p.\mathbf{type}$ the type which p has in the current environment. Note that we could not have replaced these two rules by a simpler rule which states that $\Gamma \vdash p.\mathbf{type} <: T$, provided $\Gamma \vdash p : T$. The reason is that the subsumption for type assignments would allow one to forget information about a path's type. Hence, one could not guarantee with the simpler rule that upper bounds are tight.

4.5 Subtyping

The subtyping judgment $\Gamma \vdash T \leq T'$ states that T is a subtype of T'. Subtyping is the smallest transitive relation that contains upper-binding (<:) and that is closed under the following four rules.

$$(\&\text{-}\leq) \quad \frac{\Gamma \vdash T_1 \,\&\, T_2 \leq T_1}{\Gamma \vdash T_1 \,\&\, T_2 \leq T_2} \qquad\qquad \frac{\Gamma \vdash T \leq T_1, \; T \leq T_2}{\Gamma \vdash T \leq T_1 \,\&\, T_2} \quad (\leq\text{-}\&)$$

$$(\text{Rec-}\leq) \quad \frac{\Gamma, x : \{x|\; \overline{D}, \overline{D'}\} \vdash \overline{D} \leq \overline{D''}}{\Gamma \vdash \{x|\; \overline{D}, \overline{D'}\} \leq \{x|\; \overline{D''}\}}$$

$$(\text{Class-}\leq) \quad \frac{\Gamma \vdash R \text{ wf}, \; S \,\&\, R \leq S', \; S' \leq S \quad \Gamma, x : S' \vdash \overline{D} \leq \overline{D'}}{\Gamma \vdash [x : S|\; \overline{D}] \leq [x : S'|\; \overline{D'}]}$$

Rules (&-$\leq$) and ($\leq$-&) state that & behaves like type intersection in subtyping: That is, the type $T_1 \,\&\, T_2$ is a subtype of both T_1 and T_2 and to show that a type U is a subtype of $T_1 \,\&\, T_2$ one needs to show that U is a subtype of both T_1 and T_2.

The remaining two rules (Rec-$\leq$) and (Class-$\leq$) determine subtyping for record and class types. For record types, subtyping is covariant in the declarations $\overline{D}$, and declarations in the subtype may be dropped in the supertype. For class types, subtyping is contravariant in the self-type S and covariant in the declarations $\overline{D}$. However, both premises are restricted for type checking reasons.

First, unlike for record types, a class type always declares the same labels as its supertypes, so declared labels may not be forgotten. This ensures that the type of labels in a composition is fully determined. For instance, in $[l = 1]$ $\&_{\{\}} \; [l = \text{``}abc\text{''}]$ the label l is always known to be bound to a string, not an integer. If labels could be forgotten, the second operand of the composition could be widened via subsumption to the empty class, which would assign l the integer in an alternative typing derivation of the composite class term.

Second, contravariance of self types is limited so that the smaller self type S' must result from the larger self type S composed with some record type. On the other hand, it is not allowed to take as S' some nominal subtype of S. This restriction is necessary to ensure that there is always a least type that can be assigned to instances created from a class in a ν-expression.

The ($\leq$) relation is also defined between declarations. $D \leq D'$ means that declaration D is *more specific* than declaration D'. This predicate is expressed by the following two derivation rules.

$$(\text{Bind-}\leq) \quad \frac{\Gamma \vdash T \leq T'}{\Gamma \vdash (l : T) \leq (l : T')} \qquad\qquad \frac{\Gamma \vdash T \leq T'}{\Gamma \vdash (L \preceq: T) \leq (L <: T')} \quad (\text{Tbind-}\leq)$$

Subtyping on value declarations is defined as usual. For type labels one has that an arbitrary type declaration $L \preceq: T$ is more specific than an abstract type declaration $L <: T$, provided $T \leq T'$. Hence, abstract types can be overridden with other abstract or concrete types as long as the overriding type conforms to the abstract type's bound. Aliases and new types, on the other hand, cannot be overridden.

4.6 Well-Formedness

The well-formedness judgment is of the form $\Gamma \vdash T$ wf. Roughly, a type is well-formed if it refers only to names and labels which are defined and if it does not contain any illegal cyclic dependencies. These requirements are formalized in the four rules given below. The remaining rules propagate these requirements over all forms of types; they are given in full in the accompanying technical report [34].

$$(\text{SINGLE-WF})\frac{\Gamma \vdash p : R}{\Gamma \vdash p.\textbf{type} \ wf} \qquad \frac{\Gamma \vdash T \ wf, \ T \ni (L = U), \ U \ wf}{\Gamma \vdash T{\bullet}L \ wf} (\text{TSEL-WF}_1)$$

$$(\text{TSEL-WF}_2) \ \frac{\Gamma \vdash T \ wf, \ T \ni (L \prec U), \ U \prec R}{\Gamma \vdash T{\bullet}L \ wf}$$

$$(\text{TSEL-WF}_3) \ \frac{\Gamma \vdash T \ni (L <: U), \ U <: R}{\Gamma \vdash T{\bullet}L \ wf}$$

Rule (SINGLE-WF) states that $p.\textbf{type}$ is well-formed if p is a path referring to some object. The next three rules cover well-formedness of a type selection $T{\bullet}L$. They distinguish between the form of definition of L in T.

If L is defined to be an alias of some type U, $T{\bullet}L$ is well-formed only if U is well-formed. This requirement excludes recursive types, where a type label is defined to be an alias of some type containing itself. Such a recursive type would not have a finite proof tree for well-formedness. On the other hand, if L is defined to be a new type which expands to some type U, one requires only that U in turn expands to some record type. This requirement excludes cyclic definitions such as $\{x|\ L \prec x.L \ \& \ R\}$. But recursive references to the label from inside a record or class are allowed; e.g. $\{x|\ L \prec \{next : x.L\}\}$. Finally, if L is defined to be an abstract type bounded by U, one requires that U in turn is bounded by a record type. This requirement excludes situations where a type is bounded directly or indirectly by itself, such as in $\{x|\ L_1 <: x.L_2, L_2 <: x.L_1\}$. But it admits F-bounded polymorphism, where the abstract type appears inside its bound, as in $\{x|\ L <: \{next : x.L\}\}$.

5 Relationship with $F_{<:}$

System $F_{<:}$ can be encoded in νObj by the translation $\langle\!\langle \cdot \rangle\!\rangle$, which is defined on types, terms, and environments. The translation of $F_{<:}$ types into νObj types is defined as follows.

$$\langle\!\langle \forall X <: S.T \rangle\!\rangle = \{ val : [\, X : \{ Arg <: \langle\!\langle S \rangle\!\rangle \}|\ fun : [res : \langle\!\langle T \rangle\!\rangle] \,] \}$$
$$\langle\!\langle T \to U \rangle\!\rangle = \{ val : [\, x : \{ arg : \langle\!\langle T \rangle\!\rangle \}|\ fun : [res : \langle\!\langle U \rangle\!\rangle] \,] \} \qquad (x\ fresh)$$
$$\langle\!\langle X \rangle\!\rangle = X.Arg$$
$$\langle\!\langle \top \rangle\!\rangle = \{\,\}$$

The translation of $F_{<:}$ terms into νObj terms is defined as follows.

$$\langle\!\langle \lambda x : T.t \rangle\!\rangle = new [\, val = [\, x : \{ arg : \langle\!\langle T \rangle\!\rangle \}|\ fun = [res = \langle\!\langle t \rangle\!\rangle] \,] \,]$$
$$\langle\!\langle t\ u \rangle\!\rangle = \nu x \leftarrow \langle\!\langle t \rangle\!\rangle.val\ \&\ [arg = \langle\!\langle u \rangle\!\rangle]\ ;\ \nu y \leftarrow x.fun\ ;\ y.res$$
$$\langle\!\langle \Lambda X <: S.t \rangle\!\rangle = new [\, val = [\, X : \{ Arg <: \langle\!\langle S \rangle\!\rangle \}|\ fun = [res = \langle\!\langle t \rangle\!\rangle] \,] \,]$$
$$\langle\!\langle t[T] \rangle\!\rangle = \nu x \leftarrow \langle\!\langle t \rangle\!\rangle.val\ \&\ [Arg = \langle\!\langle T \rangle\!\rangle]\ ;\ \nu y \leftarrow x.fun\ ;\ y.res$$
$$\langle\!\langle x \rangle\!\rangle = x.arg$$

Finally, here is the translation of $F_{<:}$ environments into νObj environments.

$$\langle\!\langle x : T \rangle\!\rangle = x : \{ arg : \langle\!\langle T \rangle\!\rangle \}$$
$$\langle\!\langle X <: T \rangle\!\rangle = X : \{ Arg <: \langle\!\langle T \rangle\!\rangle \}$$
$$\langle\!\langle \epsilon \rangle\!\rangle = \epsilon$$
$$\langle\!\langle \Gamma, \Sigma \rangle\!\rangle = \langle\!\langle \Gamma \rangle\!\rangle, \langle\!\langle \Sigma \rangle\!\rangle$$

In the translation, we use letters x and X for names, words consisting of lower-case letters for value labels, and words consisting of upper-case letters for type labels. Specifically, arg labels a value parameter, Arg labels a type parameter, res labels a function result, and val labels a class value.

Given this translation, here is how $F_{<:}$'s polymorphic identity function $\Lambda X <: \top.\lambda x : X.x$ is expressed in our calculus.

new [val = [X: {Arg <: {}}|
    fun = [res = new [val = [x: {arg: X.Arg} | fun = [res = x.arg]]]]]]

To give some sense to our encoding we can easily show the following properties.

Lemma 1 *For any environment Γ, types T and U, term t in $F_{<:}$:*

1. $\Gamma \vdash_{F_{<:}} T <: U$ *implies* $\langle\!\langle \Gamma \rangle\!\rangle \vdash \langle\!\langle T \rangle\!\rangle \leq \langle\!\langle U \rangle\!\rangle$.
2. $\Gamma \vdash_{F_{<:}} t : T$ *implies* $\langle\!\langle \Gamma \rangle\!\rangle \vdash \langle\!\langle t \rangle\!\rangle : \langle\!\langle T \rangle\!\rangle$.

Lemma 2 $\vdash_{F_{<:}} t : T$ *and* $t \to u$ *implies* $\langle\!\langle t \rangle\!\rangle \to^+ e_G\langle\!\langle\!\langle u \rangle\!\rangle\!\rangle$, *where e_G is a "garbage context" of the form $\nu x_1 \leftarrow u_1\ ;\ \ldots\ ;\ \nu x_n \leftarrow u_n\ ;\ \langle\rangle$ such that no name x_i is free in $\langle\!\langle u \rangle\!\rangle$.*

The introduction of the garbage context e_G in the previous lemma is necessary because translation of λ-abstraction and λ-application involves the creation of objects, which are persistent, contrary to the λs that disappear during the lambda reduction rule.

Lemma 3 $\langle\!\langle t \rangle\!\rangle \to$ *implies* $t \to$.

The reduction relation $\to$ that we use for $F_{<:}$ in 3 is the call-by-value small-step semantics, i.e. we never reduce under the λs and an argument has to be reduced to a value before being passed to a function. Together with the previous lemma, this lemma has as corollary that if a well-typed term reduces to an irreducible term then its translation reduces to the translation of this term, which is also irreducible.

6   Meta-theory

In this chapter, we establish three results for νObj. First, that the reduction relation is confluent. Second, that the typing rules are sound with respect to the operational semantics. Third, that the subtyping relation (and with it type checking) is undecidable. For reasons of space we refer to an accompanying technical report [34] for proofs.

6.1   Confluence

Theorem 6.1 The $\twoheadrightarrow$ relation is confluent: If $t \twoheadrightarrow t_1$ and $t \twoheadrightarrow t_2$ then there exists a term t' such that $t_1 \twoheadrightarrow t'$ and $t_2 \twoheadrightarrow t'$.

6.2   Type Soundness

We establish soundness of the νObj type system using the syntactic technique of Wright and Felleisen [43]. We first show a subject reduction result which states that typings are preserved under reduction. We then characterize a notion of evaluation result called an *answer* and show that every well-typed, non-diverging term reduces to an answer that has the same type as the original term.

Theorem 6.2 [Subject Reduction] Let Γ be an environment. Let t, t' be terms such that $bn(t, t') \cap dom(\Gamma) = \emptyset$ and let T be a type. If $\Gamma \vdash t : T$ and $t \rightarrow t'$, then $\Gamma \vdash t' : T$.

To establish type soundness from subject reduction, we still need to show that well-typed non-diverging terms reduce to answers. These notions are defined as follows.

Definition. A term t *diverges*, written $t \Uparrow$ if there exists an infinite reduction sequence $t \rightarrow t_1 \rightarrow \ldots \rightarrow t_n \rightarrow \ldots$ starting in t.

Definition. An *answer* is a value, possibly nested in ν-binders from classes all of whose definitions are fully evaluated. Thus, the syntax of answers a is:

$$a ::= v \mid \nu x \leftarrow [x : S \mid \overline{f}] \, ; a$$
$$f ::= l = v \mid L \preceq T \ .$$

Theorem 6.3 [Type Soundness] If $\epsilon \vdash t : T$ then either $t \Uparrow$ or $t \twoheadrightarrow a$, for some answer a such that $\epsilon \vdash a : T$.

6.3   Undecidability of Type Checking

Theorem 6.4 There exists no algorithm that can decide if a judgment $\Gamma \vdash t : T$ is derivable or not.

7 Conclusion

This paper develops a calculus for reasoning about classes and objects with type members. We define a confluent notion of reduction, as well as a sound type system based on dependent types.

There are at least three areas where future work seems worthwhile. First, there is the problem of undecidablility of νObj. We need to develop decidable subsystems, or describe type reconstruction algorithms that are incomplete but can be shown to work reasonably well in practice. Second, we would like to explore extensions of the calculus, such as with imperative side effects or with richer notions of information hiding. Third, we would like to study in more detail the relationships between νObj and existing object-oriented languages and language proposals. We hope that the work presented here can be used as a foundation for these research directions.

Acknowledgments

We thank Luca Cardelli, Erik Ernst, Benjamin Pierce, Mads Torgersen, Philip Wadler, and Christoph Zenger for discussions on the subject of this paper. We thank Philippe Altherr and Stéphane Micheloud for comments on previous versions of it.

References

[1] Martin Abadi and Luca Cardelli. *A Theory of Objects*. Monographs in Computer Science. Springer Verlag, 1996.

[2] Davide Ancona and Elena Zucca. A primitive calculus for module systems. In *Principles and Practice of Declarative Programming*, LNCS 1702, 1999.

[3] Davide Ancona and Elena Zucca. A calculus of module systems. *Journal of Functional Programming*, 2002.

[4] H.P. Barendregt, M. Coppo, and M. Dezani-Ciancaglini. A filter lambda model and the completeness of type assignment. *Journal of Symbolic Logic*, 48(4):931–940, 1983.

[5] Viviana Bono, Amit Patel, and Vitaly Shmatikov. A core calculus of classes and mixins. In *Proceedings of the 13th European Conference on Object-Oriented Programming*, pages 43–66, Lisbon, Portugal, 1999.

[6] Gérard Boudol. The recursive record semantics of objects revisited. Technical Report 4199, INRIA, jun 2001. to appear in Journal of Functional Programming.

[7] Gilad Bracha. *The Programming Language Jigsaw: Mixins, Modularity and Multiple Inheritance*. PhD thesis, University of Utah, 1992.

[8] Gilad Bracha and D. Griswold. Extending Smalltalk with mixins. In *OOPSLA '96 Workshop on Extending the Smalltalk Language*, April 1996.

[9] Gilad Bracha and Gary Lindstrom. Modularity meets inheritance. In *Proceedings of the IEEE Computer Society International Conference on Computer Languages*, pages 282–290, Washington, DC, 1992. IEEE Computer Society.

[10] Kim B. Bruce. *Foundations of Object-Oriented Programming Languages: Types and Semantics.* MIT Press, Cambridge, Massachusetts, February 2002. ISBN 0-201-17888-5.

[11] Kim B. Bruce, Adrian Fiech, and Leaf Petersen. Subtyping is not a good "Match" for object-oriented languages. In *Proceedings of the European Conference on Object-Oriented Programming*, pages 104–127, 1997.

[12] Kim B. Bruce, Martin Odersky, and Philip Wadler. A statical safe alternative to virtual types. In *Proceedings of the 5th International Workshop on Foundations of Object-Oriented Languages*, San Diego, USA, 1998.

[13] Luca Cardelli, James Donahue, Lucille Glassman, Mick Jordan, Bill Kalsow, and Greg Nelson. Modula-3 language definition. *ACM SIGPLAN Notices*, 27(8):15–42, August 1992.

[14] Luca Cardelli, Simone Martini, John C. Mitchell, and Andre Scedrov. An extension of system F with subtyping. *Information and Computation*, 109(1-2):4–56, 1994 1994.

[15] Luca Cardelli and John Mitchell. Operations on records. *Mathematical Structures in Computer Science*, 1:3–38, 1991.

[16] Karl Crary, Robert Harper, and Sidd Puri. What is a recursive module? In *SIGPLAN Conference on Programming Language Design and Implementation*, pages 50–63, 1999.

[17] Ole-Johan Dahl, Bjørn Myhrhaug, and Kristen Nygaard. Simula: Common base language. Technical report, Norwegian Computing Center, October 1970.

[18] Dominic Duggan and Constantinos Sourelis. Mixin modules. In *Proceedings of the ACM SIGPLAN International Conference on Functional Programming*, pages 262–273, Philadelphia, Pennsylvania, June 1996.

[19] Erik Ernst. *gBeta: A language with virtual attributes, block structure and propagating, dynamic inheritance.* PhD thesis, Department of Computer Science, University of Aarhus, Denmark, 1999.

[20] Erik Ernst. Family polymorphism. In *Proceedings of the European Conference on Object-Oriented Programming*, pages 303–326, Budapest, Hungary, 2001.

[21] Matthew Flatt, Shriram Krishnamurthi, and Matthias Felleisen. Classes and mixins. In *Proceedings of the 25th ACM Symposium on Principles of Programming Languages*, pages 171–183, San Diego, California, 1998.

[22] James Gosling, Bill Joy, Guy Steele, and Gilad Bracha. *The Java Language Specification.* Java Series, Sun Microsystems, second edition, 2000. ISBN 0-201-31008-2.

[23] Robert Harper and Mark Lillibridge. A type-theoretic approach to higher-order modules with sharing. In *Proceedings of the 21st ACM Symposium on Principles of Programming Languages*, January 1994.

[24] Atsushi Igarashi. On inner classes. In *Proceedings of the European Conference on Object-Oriented Programming*, Cannes, France, June 2000.

[25] Atsushi Igarashi and Benjamin C. Pierce. Foundations for virtual types. *Proc. ECOOP'99, Lecture Notes in Computer Science*, 1628, 1999.

[26] Atsushi Igarashi and Benjamin C. Pierce. Foundations for virtual types. *Information and Computation*, 175(1):34–49, 2002.

[27] Atsushi Igarishi, Benjamin Pierce, and Philip Wadler. Featherweight Java: A minimal core calculus for Java and GJ. In *Proc. OOPSLA*, November 1999.

[28] Xavier Leroy. A syntactic theory of type generativity and sharing. In *ACM Symposium on Principles of Programming Languages (POPL)*, Portland, Oregon, 1994.

[29] David MacQueen. Modules for Standard ML. In *Conference Record of the 1984 ACM Symposium on Lisp and Functional Programming*, pages 198–207, New York, August 1984.

[30] O. Lehrmann Madsen, B. Møller-Pedersen, and K. Nygaard. *Object-Oriented Programming in the BETA Programming Language*. Addison-Wesley, June 1993. ISBN 0-201-62430-3.

[31] Ole Lehrmann Madsen and Birger Møller-Pedersen. Virtual Classes: A powerful mechanism for object-oriented programming. In *Proceedings OOPSLA'89*, pages 397–406, October 1989.

[32] Tobias Nipkow and David von Oheimb. Java-light is type-safe — definitely. In L. Cardelli, editor, *Conference Record of the 25th Symposium on Principles of Programming Languages (POPL'98)*, pages 161–170, San Diego, California, 1998. ACM Press.

[33] Martin Odersky. Report on the programming language Scala, 2002. École Polytechnique Fédérale de Lausanne, Switzerland. http://lamp.epfl.ch/~odersky/scala.

[34] Martin Odersky, Vincent Cremet, Christine Röckl, and Matthias Zenger. A nominal theory of objects with dependent types. Technical report IC/2002/70, EPFL, Switzerland, September 2002. http://lamp.epfl.ch/papers/technto.pdf.

[35] Martin Odersky, Vincent Cremet, Christine Röckl, and Matthias Zenger. A nominal theory of objects with dependent types. In *Proc. FOOL 10*, January 2003. http://www.cis.upenn.edu/~bcpierce/FOOL/FOOL10.html.

[36] Klaus Ostermann. Dynamically composable collaborations with delegation layers. In *Proceedings of the 16th European Conference on Object-Oriented Programming*, Málaga, Spain, 2002.

[37] Claudio Russo. First-class structures for Standard ML. In *Proceedings of the 9th European Symposium on Programming*, pages 336–350, Berlin, Germany, 2000.

[38] Yannis Smaragdakis and Don Batory. Implementing layered designs with mixin layers. *Lecture Notes in Computer Science*, 1445, 1998.

[39] Kresten Krab Thorup. Genericity in Java with virtual types. In *Proceedings of the European Conference on Object-Oriented Programming*, LNCS 1241, pages 444–471, June 1997.

[40] Kresten Krab Thorup and Mads Torgersen. Unifying genericity: Combining the benefits of virtual types and parameterized classes. *Lecture Notes in Computer Science*, 1628, 1999.

[41] Mads Torgersen. Virtual types are statically safe. In *5th Workshop on Foundations of Object-Oriented Languages*, San Diego, CA, USA, January 1998.

[42] Mads Torgersen. Inheritance is specialization. In *The Inheritance Workshop, with ECOOP 2002*, June 2002. http://www.cs.auc.dk/~eernst/inhws/.

[43] Andrew K. Wright and Matthias Felleisen. A syntactic approach to type soundness. *Information and Computation*, 115, 1994.

[44] Matthias Zenger. Type-safe prototype-based component evolution. In *Proceedings of the European Conference on Object-Oriented Programming*, Málaga, Spain, June 2002.

Open APIs for Embedded Security

Carl A. Gunter

Department of Computer and Information Science
University of Pennsylvania
3330 Walnut Street
Philadelphia PA 19104-6389
gunter@cis.upenn.edu
http://www.cis.upenn.edu/gunter

Abstract. Embedded computer control is increasingly common in appliances, vehicles, communication devices, medical instruments, and many other systems. Some embedded computer systems enable users to obtain their own programs from parties other than the maker of the device. For instance, PDAs and some cell phones offer an open application programming interface that enables users to better customize devices to their needs and support an industry of independent software vendors. This kind of flexibility will be more difficult for other kinds of embedded devices where safety and security are a greater risk. This paper discusses some of the challenges and architectural options for open APIs for embedded systems. These issues are illustrated through an approach to implementing secure programmable payment cards.

1   Introduction

Embedded computer systems are computers that are installed in devices such as appliances, vehicles, cell phones, medical devices, and so on. They typically differ from computers in servers and desktop systems like PCs because of limits on size, power consumption, form factor, and location (*eg.* mobility), resulting in limits on computational power, memory, and communication connectivity. Embedded systems are increasingly common; they control important devices in military, government, industrial, and, increasingly, consumer contexts. Because of the many constraints on such devices and the fact that they are used in contexts with safety and security concerns, embedded systems typically do not enjoy many of the desirable features of servers and desktop systems. For instance, a computer embedded in a car or vacuum cleaner probably is not accessible from the Internet, and its software probably cannot be easily updated to new versions. On the other hand, computers in PDAs are somewhat like desktop systems except they trade off power, connectivity, and features like a large monitor to enhance mobility. In particular, current PDAs have in common with desktop computer systems the ability to run programs developed by parties other than the maker of the PDA. Such programs can be installed by the user of the device after she has purchased it. Most embedded computers, such as those in appliances

L. Cardelli (Ed.): ECOOP 2003, LNCS 2743, pp. 225–247, 2003.

and vehicles, do not offer this level of user control and flexibility. Some systems are at a boundary in this respect. For instance, there are now cell phones that allow users to download and run programs from third parties. Common software engineering practice leads software developers to create software in layers and such layered systems often provide an *Application Programming Interface (API)* to aid software evolution. The APIs may also enable the device vendor to work more easily with subcontractors to obtain application software for their platform. The key difference that is the interest of this paper is what it takes to allow the API to be *open* so that application developers not under the direct control of the platform vendor can provide programs to customize the platform.

There are a collection of barriers that prevent the deployment of open APIs. Many of these barriers are commercial: platform vendors often consider it more profitable to write their own applications, or may be concerned about losing control of their platform if its API is open. There are also many technical challenges. This paper focuses on ways in which control can be balanced between the embedded computer, its host device, and remote host devices. The discussion is divided into seven sections. Section 2 considers various options for delivering code to an embedded device with an open API. Section 3 focuses on the trade-offs in using remote control and illustrates this with smart cards implementing the SET payment protocol. Section 4 introduces the concept of a programmable payment card. Section 5 surveys technologies that could aid the implementation of such cards. Section 6 introduces the refinement architecture and the filter implementation as a means of realizing programmable payment cards. Section 7 concludes.

2   Delivery Architectures

One of the challenges for open APIs is how to *deliver* code to the device. Because of the diverse nature of the contexts in which embedded systems are used, there is a similar diversity of challenges and options for delivery. Some of the basic options are shown in Figure 1. The primary components of the system are the *embedded computer* itself and its *user*. The embedded computer is contained within a *host device*, which could be a car, a vacuum cleaner, a cell phone, or many similar devices. The embedded computer may be permanently encased in the host device, as in most appliances, or it may be removable, as in smart cards for financial transactions or cell phones. The host may include a capable computer itself, or it may derive its intelligence from the embedded device. If the embedded computer has an open API and the user is able to program it, then it must have some way to access new programs. There are at least four common options. The user may be able to customize the device in rudimentary manner though some input interface provided by the host. For serious programming, the device could accept some kind of *removable media* that carries programming or get its programming across a *network link*. In the networked case, the code could be derived from *remote data* and moved to the device or the program could reside elsewhere and operate by *remote control*.

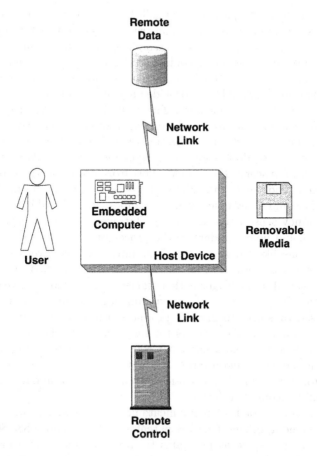

Fig. 1. Communication Options

Typical desktop computers are characterized in part by their easy access to most or all of these options. By contrast, embedded computers often offer a far more limited range of possibilities. We illustrate the options by considering the problem of *programmable cooking devices*, specifically multi-modal ovens. A multi-modal oven is one that offers several different cooking options. For instance, the GE Advantium provides three actuators (a microwave function and two sets of halogen lamps) and two sensors (for heat and humidity). Such ovens offer the ability to perform actions that cannot be performed by current single-mode ovens; for instance, they can cook food quickly like a microwave and brown it like a traditional oven. Other functions like jet impingement can provide faster heat transfer and crust development with more retention of moisture. However, hardware vendors are constrained by the existing means of programming ovens. A typical microwave is programmed by the user keying in a recipe (simple program) taken from a cookbook or off a frozen food package. Such recipes must be very simple given the patience and skill level of the user. A recipe that uses multiple sensors and actuators in a non-trivial way is difficult to describe with this constraint. This is done to some extent. The Advantium can be programmed with three numbers representing cook times for its actuators, and these recipes appear on some kinds of frozen foods. Let us consider some of the alternatives.

A simple approach would be to provide programs in storage on the host device using something like flash memory. The host device would provide a library of recipes from which the user could select. High end microwaves provide this functionality now, at least for a collection of typical recipes. A more ambitious goal would be to provide a library of recipes for frozen foods available off the shelf of the local grocery. This would allow frozen food vendors to use recipes that cook their food better than recipes keyed in by the user from the packages. First of all, it would allow much complex recipes, possibly taking real advantage of all those fancy sensors and actuators. But even at a more elementary level, the program could help standardize the processing. For instance, recipes often have instructions like 'cook for 3 to 5 minutes' because ovens vary from 600 watts to 1000 watts, indicate that the food should be turned in ovens that do not turntables, and so on. To make this process easier, vendors have explored the idea of putting bar code readers on experimental microwave ovens. Linear bar codes are used by stores to identify products based on the Universal Product Code (UPC) standard. The readers for such codes are cheap, so a user could scan a frozen food package using a bar code reader on the oven, and the oven could run the indexed program from its database of recipes. The real drawback to this approach is the fact that changes occur and a static database of recipes will eventually become out-of-date.

Some means is needed to communicate new recipes to the embedded control in the oven. One approach (see US patents 5,812,393 and 5,883,801) is to let the linear barcodes serve as programs themselves. One cannot provide a real programming language with programs that are expressed as 10 digits, but the standardization problem can be partially addressed in this way. For instance, ovens with different power capabilities can translate the supplied parameters themselves so the user does not need to calculate what the cook time should be for their specific oven. A technique explored by the OpEm Project at Penn is the use of two-dimensional barcodes [7, 9]. These can be printed inexpensively on paper and contain far more data than linear barcodes. A recipe can be represented as a small program of about 1 to 2 kilobytes, placed on a package, and read by the oven using a charged coupled device. This provides programs through inexpensive 'removable media'. The OpEm work explored the use of a subset of Java to control a 'microwave oven object'. It is possible to create interesting recipe bytecodes with one or two kilobytes of space; Java bytecodes are redundant enough to benefit from compression, even for programs of only one kilobyte. There are a variety of benefits in doing this. Aside from addressing the problem with diverse oven capabilities, there are things that a program can do that are too complicated to assign to users, such as adjusting cooking times based on user-instigated pauses.

A commercial disadvantage to 2D barcode programs is the fact that food vendors do not provide such recipes currently, so a 'chicken and egg' problem exists: without barcode recipes on packages there is no benefit to manufacturing or owning an oven that reads barcodes, and, when few ovens read barcodes, there is limited incentive to supply barcode recipes on packages. This problem did not exist with the database solution since one could develop a recipe suite that covered the products from most frozen food vendors and put this on the programmable oven at the outset. If the problem of keeping this database up-to-date can be addressed, then this could provide a practical approach. Microwave vendors have considered adding serial ports to ovens. This would enable the device to download recipes in a manner similar to TiVo (www.tivo.com), which gets schedules for television programs by short periodic telephone calls. This essentially corresponds to the remote data approach in Figure 1. A more sophisticated variation would be to put the oven on the Internet. Ovens that attach to computers and can therefore download programs over the Internet were explored in the Rutgers-Samsung IMWO project, and Sharp introduced such an oven in March of 2002 (http://www.sharp-world.com/corporate/news/020130.html). It seems plausible that ovens and other kitchen appliances will offer WiFi links in the future.

3   Remote Control

The previous section used programmable microwaves to illustrate each of the delivery approaches in Figure 1 except remote control. In a sense remote control is the anti-thesis of embedded control, since it shifts intelligence from the embedded computer and its host to a remote host. The effects of this shift can be particularly appreciated in the contrast between *magnetic stripe* tokens versus *smart cards*. Both of these are familiar contents of wallets, used for purposes like payment cards and loyalty programs. Magnetic stripe cards contain data and their processing is based solely on control from a local or remote host; smart cards contain a processor and are able to supply a limited amount of embedded control when inserted in a suitable host port.

An example helps illustrate the distinction. In my wallet I carry a Starbucks card, used to purchase drinks from participating branches of this coffee shop vendor. This is a magnetic stripe card that indexes my account with Starbucks. I periodically put money into the account by giving the card and some cash to a clerk. The card works at branches other than the one that took the cash and acts as a kind of electronic wallet. When I want to make a purchase with the card, the index is used to determine my balance, from which the charges are deducted. By contrast, I once had a smart card embedded into a Penn ID card. This smart card served as an electronic wallet, able to hold a digital representation of money for use with Penn services, including, for instance, the vending machines in my building. The main difference between the magnetic stripe card and the smart card is where the processing is carried out. The magnetic stripe card has no embedded control; it provides only data, possibly encrypted to protect sensitive data like a Personal ID Number (PIN). The smart card, by contrast, is able to do some on-board processing and is able to protect cleartext data on the card by physical means and interface limits as well as encryption. The smart card is especially well-suited to offline operation since it cannot easily be duplicated,[1] so this is a good fit for vending machines, which may not have the option of checking an account balance over a network link.

Network connectivity is a crucial factor in whether remote control is feasible. When it exists, it can contribute significantly to security and simplicity. Network connectivity may partially explain the wider use of smart cards in Europe compared to the United States. Balances for payment cards in the U.S. were initially checked by a telephone call, whereas European transactions commonly relied on the embedded control in a smart card. Let us now consider models for payment card transactions in more detail as a way to study tradeoffs between embedded and remote control. For more on the tradeoffs between magnetic stripes and smart cards see [22].

Payment cards are a major means for carrying out consumer purchases, competing with other means such as cash and checks. They come in several flavors: credit cards provide a loan capability, demand cards allow for payments to be delayed for a month or so, and debit cards deduct costs immediately from a cardhold's bank account. They typically provide for three to five participants, illustrated in Figure 2. A typical scenario is a *cardholder* visiting the premises of a *merchant* such as a department store. The user has obtained his card from an *issuer*. Issuers are often banks such as Citibank or MBNA. The card is inserted into a host (terminal) provided by the merchant, which contacts an entity known as the *acquirer*. The acquirer may be a computer operated by the bank of the merchant. The acquirer contacts a *payment system* with information like the amount of payment requested. Common payment systems include MasterCard and Visa. The payment system may contact the issuer of the card holder to determine whether the cardholder has enough money to make the payment. An approval propagates back through the acquirer to the merchant, who obtains an authorizing signature or PIN from the customer and provides him a receipt. There are a number of variations on this scenario. For instance, the issuer may be a store, like Sears, rather than a bank, and the payment system may be different. For example, when American Express is used as the payment system, the merchant contacts the payment system directly rather than contacting an acquirer bank. For our purposes, the main point is the fact that the transaction is distributed, online, realtime, and the card does not provide embedded control to the host of the merchant. For more information about payment cards see [6].

The basic scenario described in Figure 2 has changed in important ways with changes in buying habits. For instance, cardholder users may not be physically present at the site of the merchant. At first this occurred primarily because of telephone purchases, but more recently consumers have used the Internet to make

---

[1] Magnetic stripes are also more vulnerable to offline attack: if data is encrypted with a PIN on a magnetic stripe, it would be easy to check all possible PINs to determine the encrypted value.

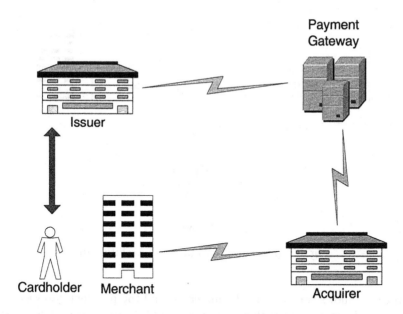

Fig. 2. Common Payment Card Architecture

remote purchases. This has a significant impact not only on the convenience of the transaction for the consumer but also on the risks for the merchant and payment system. In particular, fraud in Internet payment card purchases is a major cost. In response to this, a collection of organizations developed a standard for Secure Electronic Commerce (SET) to provide improved protections. Figure 3 illustrates the approach. A *user* runs SET from a *host* computer, which may be her personal computer at home. SET can run from the host computer alone, but it may also be used with embedded control provided by a smart card for running (portions of) the SET protocol. The user host and embedded system exchange a series of messages over the Internet with the *merchant*. The merchant, in turn, exchanges SET protocol messages with a *payment gateway* to ensure payment for the transaction.

SET is described in a hefty series of documents [16, 17, 18, 19]. We focus on the protocol in which a user C makes a purchase from a merchant M, who is paid by a payment gateway P. Before the protocol begins, the user C and the merchant M negotiate a description OrderDesc of the item to be purchased and an amount PurchAmt to be paid for it. The aim of the protocol is to assure the merchant that he will be paid for the order without revealing what it is to the payment gateway. At the same time, the user and merchant need to convince the payment gateway that it is a legitimate purchase through the use of secret information, namely CardSecret and PANData. The PANData includes information such as the user's Primary Account Number (PAN) that should not be revealed to the merchant. The cryptographic technique is called a *dual*

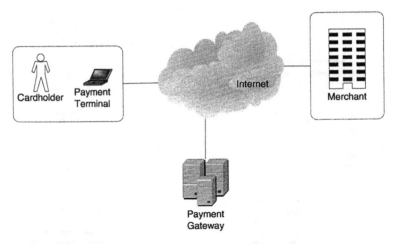

Fig. 3. Internet Payment Card Architecture

signature. It allows two parties (the merchant and the payment gateway in this case) to participate in (what they can prove to be) the same transaction without revealing all information to both parties. We describe a simplified version of the purchase request protocol based on the formal treatment in [3], which, in turn, was derived from [18]. SET uses PCKS envelops and X.509 certificates. To keep things simple, we omit information in messages about certificates and use a simplified notation. We write $[X]_S$ for message X together with a signature by subject S, and $\{X\}_S$ for message X encrypted for subject S, and $H(X)$ for the hash of message X.

The messages in the SET purchase request are given in Figure 4. In PInitReq, the user sends a challenge Chall_C to the merchant, together with a local identifier LID_M. In PInitRes, the merchant responds to this with a unique transaction identifier XID, a challenge Chall_M of his own, as well as the local identifier and challenge from the user, all signed with his private key. The third message in the protocol, PReq, is its essence. The user sends the merchant the dual signature. It consists of two parts. A first part, OIDualSign, contains information for the merchant. In particular, it includes the order instruction data, OIData, which connects the request to the agreed purchase item and payment amount. A second part, PIDualSign, contains information for the payment gateway. In particular, it connects the request to the payment instruction data PIData, which includes the PANData and a hash of the card secret. Both of these parts are sent to the merchant, who is able to check a signature in PIDualSign to connect the purchase and order information, but is unable to learn the purchase information because it is encrypted under the public key of the payment gateway. The merchant forwards PIDualSign to the payment gateway, who then confirms the transaction.

The SET protocol is characterized by a number of secrets and authentication operations. While the protocol could be implemented on a host PC and these secrets could be stored there, it is beneficial to keep some of the sensitive

PInitReq	$C \to M$:	LID_M, Chall_C
PInitRes	$M \to C$:	$[\text{LID}_M, \text{XID}, \text{Chall}_C, \text{Chall}_M]_M$
PReq	$C \to M$:	OIDualSign, PIDualSign
AuthReq	$M \to P$:	$\{[\text{LID}_M, \text{XID}, H(\text{OIData}), \text{HOD}, \text{PIDualSign}]_M\}_P$
AuthRes	$P \to M$:	$\{[\text{LID}_M, \text{XID}, \text{PurchAmt}, \text{authCode}]_P\}_M$
PRes	$M \to C$:	$[\text{LID}_M, \text{XID}, \text{Chall}_C, H(\text{PurchAmt})]_M$

where

HOD	$= H(\text{OrderDesc}, \text{PurchAmt})$
OIData	$= \text{XID}, \text{Chall}_C, \text{HOD}, \text{Chall}_M$

PIHead	$= \text{LID}_M, \text{XID}, \text{HOD}, \text{PurchAmt}, M, H(\text{XID}, \text{CardSecret})$
PIData	$= \text{PIHead}, \text{PANData}$

OIDualSign $= \text{OIData}, H(\text{PIData})$

PIDualSign $= [H(\text{PIData}), H(\text{OIData})]_C, \{\text{PIHead}, \text{PANData}, H(\text{OIData})\}_P$

Fig. 4. SET Purchase Request Protocol

information on a tamper-resistant smart card. There have been a variety of attempts to support SET with embedded control provided by smart cards. The *Chip Electronic Commerce (CEC)* specification aimed to provide SET for Europay Mastercard Visa (EMV) smart cards. The *Chip SET (C-SET)* pilot from CyberCard provided a translater that enabled SET to work with a smart card. The vWALLET smart card was a SET card developed as part of the e-COMM pilot initiated by Gemplus, VISA International, France Telecom, BNP, Societe Generale and Credit Lyonnais. Recent work has produced a SET implementation for the Java Card [14, 12, 13]. This work, and a number of related technologies for the Java Card, will be discussed further below.

4 Programmable Payment Cards

I now introduce an architecture and application that provides a range of interesting challenges for open embedded control. The application is a *Programmable Payment Card (PPC)*. It is common for an issuer, such as a bank, to provide payment cards to an enterprise so the enterprise can enable its employees to make purchases with the cards. This improves efficiency by empowering employees. It does have the limitation that employees must be trusted to some extent to use the cards properly in accordance with policies under which they were given the card. A simple policy would be to restrict the value of the purchases that can be made with a given card within a given time frame such as a month. Another possibility is to issue a card that is specific to a particular vendor, so an employee with a card can purchase only from the authorized vendor. Families also act like enterprises in this respect, offering cards to older children to be used in emergencies or for other purposes. Some policy can be enforced. For instance, a parent could open a bank account and obtain a debit card against this account to prevent a child from spending more than the balance of the account. In general, however, the policies that govern cards in enterprises and families are too complex to be enforced by the issuing bank and the payment gateway. Moreover, issuers and payment gateways may not be eager to know or enforce policies of *secondary issuers* such as enterprises and parents since this adds transaction complexity and may create liabilities. Another factor is privacy: secondary issuers may not want to communicate policies to banks, stores, payment gateways, and other external entities.

Is it possible to design a payment card that could accept policies from secondary issuers after the card was originally issued? For instance, an enterprise could 'create' a card that could be given a specific budget each month, or a family could 'create' a card that could only be used to purchase hotel accommodations. To some extent issuers do try to distinguish their cards by offering special ways to customize them. For instance, there are cards targeted at small businesses that help the owner control risks for employees charged with card-based procurement. If, however, the owner of a small business wanted a policy that was not wanted by thousands of other similar businesses, then it is unlikely that an issuer would be willing to create such a custom card. Looking at Figures 1 and 2, one possibility is to provide for some form of customizable remote control. For instance, we could augment Figure 2 so that the payment gateway not only consulted the '*primary* issuer' (typically a bank) but also the secondary issuer. Suppose, for instance, that Penn wanted to issue cards to employees that could only be used to make purchases from a specified collection of merchants. When an employee attempted a purchase, the payment gateway would contact a server at Penn with information about the purchase. Penn's server would need to approve the request before the payment gateway would authorize the purchase. This approach, based on remote control, has a number of the desired benefits, including significant customizability. It complicates the approval process, however, and the merchant and payment gateway may consider it too cumbersome to include additional online checks involving a diverse range of parties.

Another idea is to use embedded control for policy. In this approach, policy is installed on the card itself by the secondary issuer. This has the significant limit that it only works for payment cards that are smart cards using a protocol like SET, with a sufficient amount of memory and protection to enforce the policy. The rest of this paper will argue that this is at least *technically* feasible at the current time in a limited way, and trends will make it somewhat more feasible in the future. It provides a non-trivial case study in the analysis of embedded control architectures and assurance technologies.

5   Open Smart Cards

The value of an open API for smart cards was recognized in the 1990's and, in particular, the Java Card is a widely accepted instantiation of this today. This section sketches background for some of the relevant technologies that could contribute to the development of PPCs. These technologies include: smart cards, the Java Card, the GlobalPlatform, byte code verification on the Java Card, and payment protocols on the Java Card.

Smart Cards

Smart cards, also known as integrated circuit cards, where invented in the late 1960's and are now commonly used for personal identification, payment, communication, and physical access applications. There are many smart card vendors and the ISO 7816 series of standards provides an industry-wide baseline. There are a number of kinds of smart cards. Our focus is on microprocessor contact cards. These include a microprocessor that enables the card to do certain kinds of calculations and a set of contacts that allow the card to get power and communicate through a Card Acceptance Device (CAD). They are commonly distributed in a credit-card-sized plastic substrate and provide a degree of tamper-resistance against physical efforts to learn the contents of the card memory or subvert its computational functions. Aside from the ISO 7816 standards there are standards for smart card Subscriber Identity Modules (SIMs) in telephones that support the Global System for Mobile Communications (GSM), as defined by the European Telecommunications Standards Institute (ETSI). These include GSM 11.11 and GSM 11.14, which define interfaces and toolkits respectively, and GSM 03.19, which defines a SIM API for the Java Card platform. Also, EMV provides standards for cards to suit the needs of the financial industry (www.emvco.com).

Smart cards typically provide three kinds of memory: Read Only Memory (ROM), Electrical Erasable Programmable Read-Only Memory (EEPROM), and RAM (Random Access Memory). ROM is used to store fixed programming and parameters. It holds data even without power, but cannot be written after the card is fabricated. ROM holds the OS of the card and permanent applications. A typical card might have 64 kilobytes of ROM. EEPROM can also be preserved when the card has no power and, unlike ROM, it can be modified during the service life of the card. It can be used to hold data and applications that are added after the card is made. However, it is slow to write to EEPROM and it supports only a limited number of such writes, so EEPROM is not appropriate for often-changing variables. A typical card might have 16 kilobytes of EEPROM. RAM provides the necessary workspace for computation. It is quick to modify RAM, and it does not wear out with many modifications. However, RAM is expensive on a smart card, and memory in RAM is lost when the card is not powered. A typical card may have only 1 kilobyte of RAM.

Java Cards

An API for using Java to program smart cards was introduced in 1996 by Slumberger. This effort was expanded to include other companies in an industry consortium called the Java Card Forum. This has evolved to a collection of specifications supported by Sun (java.sun.com/products/javacard) covering the Java Card API, the Java Card Runtime Environment (JCRE), and the Java Card Virtual Machine (JCVM). The current specification is 2.2 and it offers a good platform for open embedded programming. In particular, it supports a restricted subset of Java that can be compiled to JCVM byte code and a runtime system that enables this code to run in a restricted *context*. The rules for communicating between contexts enables multi-application programming with a limited degree of sharing.

The Java Card supports many of the familiar Java programming constructs such as packages, classes, interfaces, exceptions, inheritance, and dynamic object creation. It has a limited collection of data structures including booleans, bytes, short integers and one-dimensional arrays, but not long integers, double, float, characters, strings, or multi-dimensional arrays. There is no dynamic class loading, object serialization, or threads and no garbage collection. The Java Card does not support the Java Security Manager, but instead provides *applet firewalls*, which, as mentioned above, protect distinct groups of applets through contexts.

Other approaches to open multi-application smart cards include MultOS (www.multos.com) and Smart Card for Windows.

GlobalPlatform

Java Card programs are created by first making Java bytecode and then processing this to create a Converted APplet (CAP), which is then loaded and installed on the card. An especially important aspect of this process is the fact that type checking is carried out in these steps rather than on the card. This raises a challenge if the development environment is not trusted by the card. In a multi-application open card this is not an unusual state of affairs since applications from different vendors may not trust each other. One approach to deal with this problem is to rely on the issuer to certify that programs are well-formed and secure.

Visa developed an architecture in the 1990s to instantiate this approach. The architecture was first called the Open Platform and is now subsumed in an industry consortium called the GlobalPlatform (www.globalplatform.org). The architecture is intended to be independent of the underlying smart card runtime system, but assumes that the system supports features like the ability to protect confidentiality and integrity between applications installed post-issuance by parties that do not wish to trust each other. It also aims to keep the issuer in substantial control of the card while not requiring the issuer to know all details of the providers. Some examples help motivate the aims. Suppose a merchant would like to provide a loyalty application that gives the user credit for shopping with that merchant. If a patron is visiting the merchant, it would be convenient to use the terminal of the merchant to download the new application to the patron's card without the need to contact the card issuer. Referring to Figure 1, this enables software to be provided from the local host without the need to contact some kind of remote storage, or at least to contact remote storage under

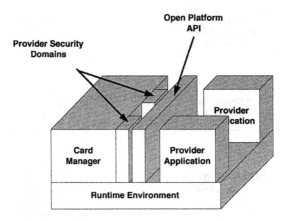

Fig. 5. GlobalPlatform Architecture

the control of the party that owns the local host. Another class of examples that motivate the GlobalPlaform are applications that hold sensitive information. Examples include a car rental company that keeps information about a driver or a medical application that keeps health care and insurance records.

This GlobalPlatform architecture is illustrated in Figure 5. A *Runtime Environment* underlies the system, and card functions are controlled by a *Card Manager*. The Card Manager uses a collection of *Provider Security Domains* to determine the rights of parties to add *Provider Applications* to the card using the *Open Platform API*. Each security domain includes keys needed to authenticate the provider through a CAD before authorizing the installation of the provider's application. This authentication is carried out by the card manager through the functions in the API.

The problem of how to ensure that programs satisfy the necessary properties before they are installed and how to place control in the hands of the issuer is illustrated in the steps involved in how the provider loads and installs an application. This process is illustrated in Figure 6. In Step 1, the issuer produces a card with a collection of security domains and, in Step 2, the card is activated. In Step 3 the provider creates an application and, in Step 4, obtains the rights to a security domain. In Step 5, the provider obtains the necessary cryptographic keys to prove her rights. The application provider submits her program to a certifier in Step 6, who reviews it for security and other concerns. The submitted program does not need to contain private information of the party that will receive the card. Moreover, the certifier could be the issuer or an independent certification authority. In Step 7, the certifier then supplies necessary authentication data such as a signature on the program that can be checked by the card manager. In Step 8, the provider uses a CAD to download the approved application onto the card, which is installed in Step 9 once all of the security checks have succeeded.

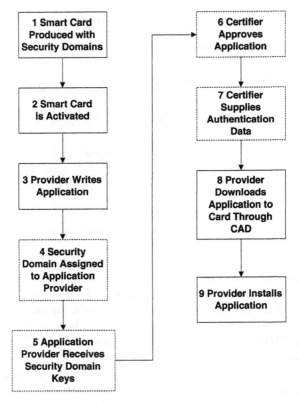

Fig. 6. Steps in the GlobalPlatform Provider Loading

5.1 Byte Code Verification on Java Cards

The use of certification by digital signature to ensure security features of provider applications has a number of drawbacks. In particular, it takes back some of the primary benefit of post-issuance installation of applications by making it contingent on Steps 4-7 indicated with dotted lines in Figure 6. Eliminating these steps by developing some form of practical on-card verification has been an interesting research objective for the last 5 years. One possibility is to use a *defensive* virtual machine on the card that checks types at runtime. This is expensive, however. If the types are checked statically off-card, then there is no way for the card to ensure security without repeating the checks, so on-card static verification is the only alternative. Static verification of Java programs in the JVM implementation is too expensive to perform on-card, so some alternative is needed. One approach is to augment the usual verification so that it provides 'hints' to aid re-verification on the card. This approach [20, 8] can be realized by providing type maps with additional type information for stack and register contents as a supplement to the usual Java byte code. Although generating the type maps may be expensive, it is easier to verify the code with them, so this

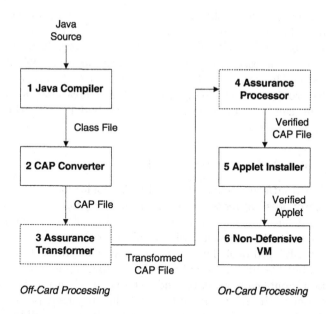

Fig. 7. Steps in On-Card Byte Code Verification for Smart Cards

can be exploited by the on-card verification. A practical way to structure this is shown in Figure 7. The basic idea is to insert an 'assurance layer' at the end of the off-card code generation and before the on-card installation. The figure depicts the following steps. In Step 1 a Java compiler creates a class file, which is input in Step 2 to a CAP converter to create a standard CAP file. In Step 3 this CAP file is converted to include assurance information such as a type map that can be processed in Step 4 to confirm on-card that the code is well-typed. This step uses the type map information to deal with the limitations of on-card verification. The verified CAP file is now used in Step 5 to create a verified applet that can be run in a non-defensive virtual machine. A similar strategy was developed for the Sun virtual machine for mobile devices [23], where a 'preverifier' is used to create the type maps.

Another strategy for on-card verification based on the steps in Figure 7 is described in [11]. The idea in this case is to transform the CAP file into a form where byte code verification can be carried out on-card. The basic observation is that two assumptions about the Java program to be processed and one assumption about the Java runtime environment suffice to eliminate the space overhead imposed by type maps. The runtime environment is assumed to initialize nonparameter registers on method entry to a safe value such as a null reference. Assuming that this is satisfied, the output of a standard Java compiler can be transformed to satisfy the two assumptions on programs: the operand stack is empty at all branch and branch target instructions, and, for each method evaluation, each register has only one type. If one accepts that the restriction on the runtime is acceptable for JCRE, then the main questions concern: (1) the overhead imposed by the transformations to achieve the other two assumptions, and (2) the cost of the on-card verifier in time and memory. Tests show [11] that the transformation increases code sizes only slightly (less than 3%) if at all. The space required by the verifier code can be estimated at 10 kilobytes, and it is estimated that verification can be carried out on a Java Card at one kilobyte per second. This can be compared to an EEPROM budget of 32-64 kilobytes for all provider applications.

Payment Protocols for the Java Card

With the GlobalPlatform architecture and technologies for on-card verification there is a range of possibilities for ensuring the desired properties of post-issuance provider code. A question remains about the specifics of these guarantees when the card must share its processing with local and remote hosts, as it does, for example, in the SET protocol. There are many payment protocols other than the SET protocol, but the SET protocol is an interesting representative. Moreover, its specification is publically available and has become a benchmark for academic case studies. Hence the focus on SET here: other payment protocols may be more interesting commercially, but the technologies required will be comparable to those needed for SET.

Let us look now as the SET protocol with respect to the potential responsibilities of the embedded computer, that is, the smart card. The host device provides network connectivity and power and can carry out parts of the computation that are not considered sensitive. The terminal is likely to be chosen by the user or the merchant, although it may sometimes be chosen by the issuer. Let us assume for the current discussion that the host consists of a PC and terminal chosen by the user and is trusted by the user, but that risk mitigation is desirable. For example, a corrupted PC should be unable to complete transactions if the card is not present in the reader and should not be able to confer the ability to make purchases to other machines. If the SET protocol is implemented entirely on the PC, then these guarantees cannot generally be made. If the PC has access to the keys that authorize transactions, then it can carry out transactions whenever it is attached to the network, and, if the physical security of the PC is lost, then the keys can be exported to other machines so they can make transactions. Given these risks, which of the steps in Figure 4 should be carried out on the smart card?

To see the challenge, consider the checking of certificates used to encrypt messages. In the PReq message the user (comprising both the host and embedded computer for now), includes information for the payment gateway such as the PANData, encrypted with the public key for the payment gateway. Suppose that the smart card is responsible for the signing and encrypting operations but checking of the certificate for the payment gateway is carried out by the host PC. The host PC could substitute a fake certificate so that the card put the PANData in a message encrypted under a key selected by the host, which could now obtain and store or distribute the PANData. It appears necessary to assign certificate checking to the card. However, checking certificates typically involves checking a chain of certificates starting from a root certificate and also checking revocation status by inspecting referenced Certificate Revocation Lists (CRLs). Full certificate checking is a complicated operation that requires significant memory and (if CRLs must be obtained remotely) network connectivity. Even assuming that the smart card could muster the space and computational capacity to do this, there is an more intrinsic problem: the lack of a clock with which to check expiration times.

Indeed it is general challenge regarding the use of a smart cards to ask which parts of the protocols can run on the terminal under various models of the trust level for the terminal. Work in [15] describes a general approach to this division based on a form of multi-level security. Sensitive values such as the private key for the card and the PAN are given high security level, while other data such as the OIData and XID are given low security level. The method partitions the code implementing the protocol into components that are assigned high and low values based on their treatment of sensitive values. High valued components must run on the card, whereas low valued components can be implemented on the terminal. There are also techniques to deal with the verification of certificates by the smart card. Lacking garbage collection, a Java Card is not able to do ordinary certificate checking, but it can engage the host in a sequence of messages that restrict the amount of memory the card needs to allocate at each step. Another idea is to entrust certificate checking to a remote control service, although this complicates the networking in transactions and raises questions about how the card knows what certificate is being checked given its inability to store and parse the certificate itself. It is possible to check the certificate locally in pieces while using a remote service to confirm the time [15].

6   Refinement Architecture

We have now described a variety of technologies that could contribute to developing the concept of 'programmable payment cards' as sketched in Section 4. Smart cards provide the ability to embed some level of protected control in a host. Java Cards provide the ability to add post-issuance programs that might serve as approval policies. Such programs can be checked by the card using a digital signature, if the card supports the GlobalPlatform API, or verified on-card, if the card supports the assurance architecture in Figure 7. Sensitive steps of the protocol can be protected by the card while letting the host deal with less sensitive steps to help address card limitations. However, we still lack an overall model for reasoning about the security objective of a programmable payment card. The architecture in [15] provides a significant part of what is needed by modeling secrecy requirements. Secrecy is pivotal to controlling authorization, which is the main objective of the programmable payment card. However, it is not equivalent. For instance, a protocol that does not provide replay protection might allow an adversary to duplicate a transaction even if he is unable to decrypt the transaction messages.

The *refinement architecture* is based on the simple idea that the post-issuance programs on the card should always limit, and never expand, the sensitive transactions that a card is able to carry out. In a basic form, this is similar to a network firewall. Filtering firewalls examine packets and reject packets that match certain undesirable patterns. So, applying this concept to payment cards, we could impose a 'firewall' filter on the card that prevents undesirable messages from leaving the card. Communication units on smart cards are called Application Protocol Data Units (APDUs); they are classified into APDU commands and responses. However, it may make more sense to view communication units at a higher level. For instance, with a SET-based payment card, our primary attention may be on filtering PReq (purchase request) messages, or, more precisely, preventing the host from sending PReq messages that do not satisfy the policy of secondary provider but will be accepted as valid by the merchant and payment gateway. For example, suppose that merchants provide an OrderDesc (order description) that includes a service class such as whether the service is for accommodation or entertainment. Then the card filter could insist, for instance, that a PReq message will be created only with an OrderDesc for accommodation. This would refine the possible card events to include only acceptable accommodation purchases while eliminating unacceptable entertainment purchases. This approach makes at least two key assumptions that should be noted. First, message elements like OrderDesc must contain information on which policy can be based. If there is no service classification then it would be impossible for the card to make the necessary distinction. Second, the filter provider must trust that the merchant and payment gateway respect the payment protocol and the merchant provides an honest OrderDesc. In particular, the user should not be able to collaborate with the merchant to formulate an order description that circumvents the filter. For instance, the merchant must insist on classifying entertainment as such even if it might cause a lost sale because of the policy filter on the card.

Is it possible to implement the refinement architecture using the filtering concept? Let us attempt a sketch of how this can be done assuming that all of the technologies in the previous section are at our disposal. We also need to assume some key trust relations. First, the user trusts the host he uses. Since this is likely to be his PC, this is a credible assumption. Second, the issuer and secondary provider trust the merchants and payment gateways as far as this is required for the SET protocol. Trust in the merchants includes trusting that OrderDesc provides an accurate description of the item being purchased. It does *not* include trusting the merchant to use the same PurchAmt with the payment gateway that it used with the user since this is already ensured by the SET protocol. Third, the card needs to protect its integrity against physical attack by the user, and against logical attacks from the host, merchant, and other parties to whom the card could be connected by a network link. A variety of additional assumptions would needed to prove the security claims formally, but these give a good start. The idea is to formulate the refinement as a conjunction of filters that are registered by secondary providers and invoked by the program that creates the PReq message. These filters are applied to the pair (OrderDesc,

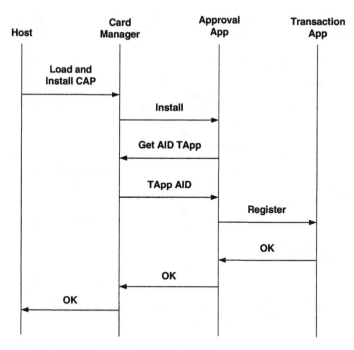

Fig. 8. Messages in Filter Refinement Installation

PurchAmt) together with auxiliary data such as the identity of the merchant and the time of purchase. Let us call this the *filter* refinement implementation.

The steps in the filter refinement implementation can be divided into installation steps by which a provider adds a filter, and transaction steps in which a user creates a purchase message. Messages for installation are described in Figure 8. The host of the provider loads and installs a CAP for an approval applet (filter) with the aid of the card manager. The approval applet has its own installation method, which is invoked by the card manager to initialize the approval applet. As part of this set-up, the approval applet obtains the Application IDentifier (AID) object of the transaction applet by providing a well-known reference value to the card manager. It uses this to access the Shared Interface Object (SIO) of the transaction applet. It invokes a registration method in this SIO to provide a reference that can be used by the transaction applet to later get the SIO of the approval applet. If this registration is successful then this is indicated to the approval applet, the card manager, and, finally, the host.

The steps in the transaction process are shown in Figure 9. When the host attempts to send a payment message, it needs to have the card create the signatures. To do this, the host passes purchase information D to the transaction applet on the card. This information includes OrderDesc, PurchAmt and other information. The transaction applet has a list of approval applets that it devel-

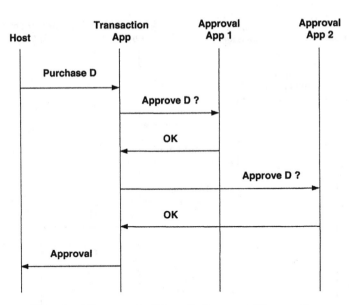

Fig. 9. Messages in Filter Refinement Transactions

oped as these applets registered themselves. It now and invokes each of these and provides them with D to get approvals. In the figure there are two approval applets that have been installed by providers. They act as filters on the information D. Only if both of them approve of D will the transaction applet create the signatures that the host needs to complete the purchase transaction. In particular, without the ability to create PReq, the user and host are unable to convince the merchant and the payment gateway to approve the purchase of the items in OrderDesc.

Now, what is needed to ensure the integrity of the filters? For instance, could a user install his own filter and use this filter to force approval of unauthorized purchases? The protocols in Figures 8 and 9 do not allow a filter to do more than *refine* the set of allowed events unless either (1) they have been given access to keys and other data necessary to complete transactions themselves or (2) they can corrupt the card memory to obtain these keys or otherwise trick the card into creating needed parts of PReq messages. The first of these is handled by choosing the programming interface for the card and transaction managers so that resources available to approval applets are limited to the purchase information they need. The second problem can be handled in either of two ways. In the GlobalPlatform approach, the approval applets can be inspected in advance by a certifying authority (Step 6 in Figure 6). The card will not load an approval applet without the necessary signatures. The certifier can perform checks such as showing that the CAP file is well-formed. In the method of Figure 7, the certifier is unnecessary and providers are able to place 'assurance transformed' CAP files on the card without needing a signature. The card then verifies such applets (Step 5 in Figure 7) and they are subsequently invoked by the transaction applet to obtain approvals.

There are some immediate questions that arise about the filter implementation. What happens if someone installs a bad filter that prevents the card from performing *any* transactions. Or, what if two filters interact to have this effect? We can assume that someone in physical possession of the card has the ability to destroy it, so the main threat arises if providers are are somehow able to gain unwelcome remote access to the card. Thus we must assume that whoever is in possession of the card uses a host that is capable of checking the credentials of a provider before allowing the provider to make an installation. Note that this is different from insisting that the *card* must be able to do this (as it does in the GlobalPlatform architecture). This can be viewed as an aspect of the requirement that the cardholder trusts his terminal.

Another question concerns how can a provider know what filters are already present to avoid redundancy? This raises also the question of what APDUs might be implemented by providers. It was argued above that we can prevent new APDUs from threatening the transactions that the card is able to make since the applet firewalls provided by the Java runtime will protect sensitive information. In the filter model as described above, the only SIO provided by the transaction applet is the one for registration, so there is a limited ability to usurp functions of the transaction applet. For convenience, filters could provide an APDU that allows them to be queried for some kind of description of what they filter. However, an applet with a rich set of APDUs (or SIOs) might risk its own security if the interface enabled tampering by some unexpected means.

The filter implementation has the advantage that it can be used without certifying or authenticating the filter code if on-card verification is possible. If it is possible or necessary to certify provider policies offline, then there are ways to go beyond the filter implementation and exploit technologies for proving refinement relations between policies. There is a considerable body of work on refinement, including automated systems linked to programming languages [5, 10, 24]. One example of a line of work on refinement [1, 2] breaks the process down into steps such as assume/guarantee reasoning, witness selection, and algorithmic state-space analysis to check transition invariants. Methods like execution monitoring [21] will be challenged by the size and time limitations of cards, but an executable monitoring language such as NERL [4] could be useful to define effective high-level monitoring.

7   Conclusion

A key challenge in the design of embedded control systems lies in deciding which functions should be performed in the embedded device and which should be performed remotely or locally in a more capable host. This tradeoff becomes more complex when the embedded control offers an open API. Open smart cards provide an early insight into specific challenges in this area since they have advanced to widespread recognition of the value of open APIs for embedded systems. Programmable payment cards offer a case study for architectural and assurance issues. Existing platforms and technologies, combined with the refinement architecture and filter implementation suggest that such cards are feasible even for comparatively complex transaction protocols. Platform support based on authenticated code could also enable the use of more advanced refinement techniques.

Acknowledgements

The work described here is based primarily on work in the OpEm project at Penn, so special thanks belong to the people participating in OpEm: Rajeev Alur, Watee Arsjamat, Alwyn Goodloe, Michael McDougall, and Jason Simas. OpEm is supported by ARO DAAD-19-01-1-0473, NSF CCR02-08990, and NSF EIA00-88028. I would like to thank David Tennenhouse for starting me thinking about programmable embedded devices, and Helen Gill for suggesting the idea of focusing on smart cards. I would also like to thank Fabio Massacci for helping me understand the SET protocol. Mykhailo Lyubich's work on SET for Java cards contributed in many ways to the OpEm project's understanding of the opportunities for an open API on payment cards.

References

[1] Rajeev Alur, Radu Grosu, and Bow-Yaw Wang. Automated refinement checking for asynchronous processes. In *3rd International Conference on Formal Methods in Computer-Aided Design*, 2000.

[2] Rajeev Alur and Bow-Yaw Wang. Verifying network protocol implementations by symbolic refinement checking. In *13th International Conference on Computer-Aided Verification*, 2001.

[3] Glampaolo Bella, Fabio Massacci, and Lawrence C. Paulson. The verification of an industrial payment protocol. In Vijay Atluri, editor, *Proceedings of the 9th ACM Conference on Computer and Communications Security*, Washington, DC, November 2002. ACM Press.

[4] Karthikeyan Bhargavan and Carl A. Gunter. Requirements for a network event recognition language. *Electronic Notes in Theoretical Computer Science*, 70(4), December 2002.

[5] David L. Detlefs, K. Rustan M. Leino, Greg Nelson, and James B. Sax. Extended static checking. Research Report 159, Compaq Systems Research Center, 1998.

[6] David Evans and Richard I. Schmalensee. *Paying with Plastic*. MIT Press, 1999.

[7] Alwyn Goodloe, Michael McDougall, Rajeev Alur, and Carl A. Gunter. Predictable programs in barcodes. In Ahmed Jerraya and Wayne Wolf, editors, *Proceedings of CASES 2003 International Conference on Compilers, Architecture, and Synthesis for Embedded Systems*, pages 298–303, Grenoble, France, October 2002. ACM Press.

[8] Gilles Grimaud, Jean-Louis Lanet, and Jean-Jacques Vandewalle. FACADE: A typed intermediate language dedicated to smart cards. In O. Nierstrasz and M. Lemoine, editors, *Software Engineering – ESEC/FSE'99*, number 1687, pages 476–493. Springer-Verlag, Berlin Germany, 1999.

[9] Carl A. Gunter. Micro mobile programs. In Ricardo Baeza-Yates, Ugo Montanari, and Nicola Santoro, editors, *Foundations of Information Technology in the Era of Network and Mobile Computing*, pages 356–369, Montreal, Canada, August 2002. IFIP 17th World Computer Congress — TC1 Stream / International Conference on Theoretical Computer Science (TCS 2002), Kluwer.

[10] Greg Nelson K. Rustan M. Leino and James B. Saxe. ESC/java user's manual. Technical Note 2000-002, Compaq Systems Research Center, October 2000.

[11] Xavier Leroy. Bytecode verification for Java smart card. *Software Practice & Experience*, 32:319–340, 2002.

[12] M. Lyubich. Eine SET Kundembörse mit der Java Card Unterstützung. In *GI Informatiktage 2000*. Konradin-Verlag, November 2000.

[13] M. Lyubich. Die architekturen von SET mit der Java Card. In A. Bode and W. Karl, editors, *ITG Fachbericht, APC 2001 Arbeitsplatzcomputer*, 2001.

[14] M. Lyubich and C. Cap. Eine implementierung von SET für Java. In *Tagesband Netzinfrustruckhur und Anwendugen für Informationsgesellschaft*, pages 208–214. Dr. Wilke Verlag, 1998.

[15] Mykhailo Lyubich. *Architectural Concepts for Java Card Running a Payment Protocol and Their Application in a SET Wallet*. PhD thesis, University of Rostock, 2003.

[16] Mastercard and Visa. *SET Secure Electronic Transaction Specification: Business Description*, May 1997.

[17] Mastercard and Visa. *SET Secure Electronic Transaction Specification: External Interface Guide*, May 1997.

[18] Mastercard and Visa. *SET Secure Electronic Transaction Specification: Formal Protocol Definition*, May 1997.

[19] Mastercard and Visa. *SET Secure Electronic Transaction Specification: Programmer's Guide*, May 1997.

[20] E. Rose and K. H. Rose. Lightweight bytecode verification. In *Workshop "Formal Underpinnings of the Java Paradigm", OOPSLA'98*, 1998.

[21] Fred B. Schneider. Enforceable security policies. *ACM Transactions on Information and System Security*, 3:30–50, 2000.

[22] Bruce Schneier. *Secrets and Lies*. John Wiley & Sons, 2000.

[23] Sun Microsystems. *Java 2 Platform Icro Edition (J2ME) Technology for Creating Mobile Devices*, May 2000. White paper, http://java.sun.com/products/cldc/wp/KVMwp.pdf.

[24] Joachim van den Berg and Bart Jacobs. The LOOP compiler for Java and JML. In T. Margaria and W. Yi, editors, *Tools and Algorithms for the Construction and Analysis of Software (TACAS)*, volume 2031 of *Springer LNCS*, pages 299–312, 2001.

Traits: Composable Units of Behaviour*

Nathanael Schärli[1], Stéphane Ducasse[1],
Oscar Nierstrasz[1], and Andrew P. Black[2]

[1] Software Composition Group
University of Bern, Switzerland
{schaerli,ducasse,oscar}@iam.unibe.ch
[2] OGI School of Science & Engineering
Oregon Health and Science University
black@cse.ogi.edu

Abstract. Despite the undisputed prominence of inheritance as the fundamental reuse mechanism in object-oriented programming languages, the main variants — single inheritance, multiple inheritance, and mixin inheritance — all suffer from conceptual and practical problems. In the first part of this paper, we identify and illustrate these problems. We then present *traits*, a simple compositional model for structuring object-oriented programs. A trait is essentially a group of pure methods that serves as a building block for classes and is a primitive unit of code reuse. In this model, classes are *composed* from a set of traits by specifying *glue code* that connects the traits together and accesses the necessary state. We demonstrate how traits overcome the problems arising from the different variants of inheritance, we discuss how traits can be implemented effectively, and we summarize our experience applying traits to refactor an existing class hierarchy.

Keywords: Inheritance, mixins, multiple inheritance, traits, reuse, Smalltalk

1 Introduction

Although single inheritance is widely accepted as the *sine qua non* of object-orientation, programmers have long realized that single inheritance is not expressive enough to factor out common features (*i.e.*, instance variables and methods) shared by classes in a complex hierarchy. As a consequence, language designers have proposed various forms of multiple inheritance [7, 23, 29, 35, 41], as well as other mechanisms such as mixins [3, 10, 18, 27, 32], that allow classes to be composed incrementally from sets of features.

Despite the passage of nearly twenty years, neither multiple inheritance nor mixins have achieved wide acceptance [44]. Summarizing Alan Snyder's contribution to the inheritance panel discussion at OOPSLA '87, Steve Cook wrote:

---

* This research was partially supported by the National Science Foundation under award CCR-0098323.

L. Cardelli (Ed.): ECOOP 2003, LNCS 2743, pp. 248–274, 2003.
© Springer-Verlag Berlin Heidelberg 2003

"Multiple inheritance is good, but there is no good way to do it." [11]

The trend seems to be away from multiple inheritance; the designers of recent languages such as Java and C# decided that the complexities introduced by multiple inheritance far outweighed its utility. It is widely accepted that multiple inheritance creates some serious implementation problems [14, 43]; we believe that it also introduces serious *conceptual* problems. Our study of these problems has led us to the present design for traits.

Although multiple inheritance makes it possible to reuse any desired set of classes, a class is frequently not the most appropriate element to reuse. This is because classes play two competing roles. A class has a primary role as a *generator of instances*: it must therefore be complete. But as a *unit of reuse*, a class should be small. These properties often conflict. Furthermore, the role of classes as instance generators requires that each class have a unique place in the class hierarchy, whereas units of reuse should be applicable at arbitrary places.

Moon's Flavors [32] were an early attempt to address this problem: Flavors are small, not necessarily complete, and they can be "mixed in" at arbitrary places in the class hierarchy. More sophisticated notions of mixins were subsequently developed by Bracha and Cook [10], Mens and van Limberghen [27], Flatt, Krishnamurthi and Felleisen [18], and Ancona, Lagorio and Zucca [3]. These approaches all permit the programmer to create components that are designed for reuse, rather than for instantiation. However, as we shall show, they can have a negative influence on understandability.

Mixins use the ordinary single inheritance operator to extend various base classes with the same set of features. However, although this inheritance operator is well-suited for deriving new classes from existing ones, it is not appropriate for composing reusable building blocks. Specifically, inheritance requires that mixins be composed linearly; this severely restricts one's ability to specify the "glue code" that is necessary to adapt the mixins so that they fit together.

In our proposal, lightweight entities called *traits* serve as the primitive units of code reuse. The design of traits started with the observation that the conflict between reuse and understandability is more apparent than real. In general, we believe that understanding a program is easier if it is possible to view the program in multiple forms. Even though a class may have been *constructed* by composing small traits in a complex hierarchy, there is no need to require that it be *viewed* in the same way. It should be possible to view the class *either* as a flat collection of methods *or* as a composite entity built from traits. The flattened view promotes understanding; the composite view promotes reuse. There is no conflict so long as both of these views can coexist, which requires that composition be used only as a structuring tool and have *no effect on the meaning of the class*.

Traits satisfy this requirement. They provide structure, modularity and reusability *within* classes, but they can be ignored when one considers the relationships between one classeand another. Traits provide an excellent balance between reusability and understandability, while enabling better conceptual modeling. Moreover, because traits are concerned solely with the reuse of behaviour and not with the reuse of state, they avoid the implementation difficulties that characterize multiple inheritance and mixins.

Traits have the following properties.

- A trait *provides* a set of methods that implement behaviour.
- A trait *requires* a set of methods that serve as parameters for the provided behaviour.
- Traits do not specify any state variables, and the methods provided by traits never access state variables directly.
- Classes and traits can be composed from other traits, but the composition order is irrelevant. Conflicting methods must be *explicitly* resolved.
- Trait composition does not affect the semantics of a class: the meaning of the class is the same as it would be if all of the methods obtained from the trait(s) were defined directly in the class.
- Similarly, trait composition does not affect the semantics of a trait: a composite trait is equivalent to a *flattened* trait containing the same methods.

A class can be constructed by inheriting from a superclass, and adding a set of traits, the necessary state variables and the required methods. These methods represent *glue* that specifies how the traits are connected together and how conflicts are resolved. This approach allows a class to be decomposed into sets of coherent features —*i.e.*, traits— and factors out the glue code that connects the features together. Because the semantics of a method is independent of whether it is defined in a trait or in a class that uses the trait, it is always possible to *flatten* a composite trait structure at any level.

The contributions of this paper are the identification of the problems associated with multiple inheritance and mixins, and the introduction of traits as a composition model that solves these problems. We proceed as follows: in section 2 we describe the problems of multiple inheritance and mixins, and in section 3 we introduce traits and illustrate their use on some small examples. In section 4 we discuss the most important design decisions and evaluate traits against the problems we identified in section 2. In section 5 we present our implementation of traits. In section 6 we summarize the results of a realistic application of traits: a refactoring of the Smalltalk-80 collection hierarchy. We discuss related work in section 7. We conclude the paper and indicate future work in section 8.

2   Reusability Problems with Inheritance

Inheritance is commonly regarded as one of the fundamental features of object-oriented programming, but at the same time, inheritance is also a mechanism with many competing meanings and interpretations [44]. Over the years, researchers have developed various inheritance models including single inheritance, multiple inheritance, and mixin inheritance. In this section, we give a brief overview of these models and point out their conceptual and practical short-comings with respect to reusability. In particular we describe specific problems of mixin composition that have not been identified previously in the literature.

Note that this section is focused on reusability issues. Other problems with inheritance such as implementation difficulties [14, 43] and conflicts between inheritance and subtyping [2, 25, 26] are outside the scope of this paper.

Single Inheritance is the simplest inheritance model; it allows a class to inherit from at most one superclass. Although this model is well-accepted, it is not expressive enough to allow the programmer to factor out all the common features shared by classes in a complex hierarchy. Hence single inheritance sometimes forces *code duplication*. Note that extending single inheritance with interfaces as promoted by Java addresses the issues of subtyping and conceptual modeling, but does nothing to avoid the need to duplicate code.

Multiple Inheritance enables a class to inherit features from more than one parent class, thus providing the benefits of better code reuse and more flexible modeling. However, multiple inheritance uses the notion of a class in two competing roles: the generator of instances and the unit of code reuse. This gives rise to the following difficulties.

Conflicting Features. With multiple inheritance, ambiguity can arise when conflicting features are inherited along different paths [17]. A particularly troublesome situation is the "diamond problem" [10, 38] (also known as "fork-join inheritance" [33]), which occurs when a class inherits from the *same* base class via multiple paths. Since classes are instance generators, they must all provide some minimal common features (*e.g.*, the methods =, hash, and asString), which are typically inherited from a common root class such as Object. Thus, when several of these classes are reused, the common features conflict.

There are two kinds of conflicting feature: *methods* and *state variables*. Whereas method conflicts can be resolved relatively easily (*e.g.*, by overriding), conflicting state is more problematic. Even if the declarations are consistent, it is not clear whether conflicting state should be inherited once or multiply [34].

Accessing Overridden Features. Since identically named features can be inherited from different base classes, a single keyword (*e.g.*, **super**) is not enough to access inherited methods unambiguously. For example, C++ [42] forces one to explicitly name the superclass to access an overridden method; recent versions of Eiffel [29] suggest the same technique[1]. This tangles class references with the source code, making the code fragile with respect to changes in the architecture of the class hierarchy. Explicit class references are avoided in languages such as CLOS [40] that impose a linear order on the superclasses. However, such a linearization often leads to unexpected behaviour [15, 16] and violates encapsulation, because it may change the parent-child relationships among classes in the inheritance hierarchy [38, 39].

---

[1] The ability to access an overridden method using the keyword **precursor** followed by an optional superclass name was added to Eiffel in 1997 [29]. In earlier versions of Eiffel, access to original methods required repeated inheritance of the same class [28].

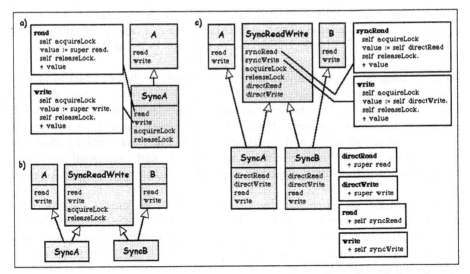

Fig. 1. In (a), the synchronization code is implemented in the subclass SyncA. In (b) we show an attempt to reuse the synchronization code in both SyncA and SyncB. However, this does not work because the methods in SyncReadWrite cannot refer to the read and write methods defined in A and B. In (c), we show how the synchronization code can be reused, but this still requires the duplication of four methods in SyncA and SyncB

Factoring out Generic Wrappers. Multiple inheritance enables a class to reuse features from multiple base classes, but it does not allow one to write a reusable entity that "wraps" methods implemented in as-yet unknown classes[2].

This limitation is illustrated in figure 1. Assume that class A contains methods read and write that provide unsynchronized access to some data. If it becomes necessary to synchronize access, we can create a class SyncA that inherits from A and wraps the methods read and write. That is, SyncA defines read and write methods that call the inherited methods under control of a lock (see figure 1a).

Now suppose that class A is part of a framework that also contains another class B with read and write methods, and that we want to use the same technique to create a synchronized version of B. Naturally, we would like to factor out the synchronization code so that it can be reused in both SyncA and SyncB.

With multiple inheritance, the natural way to share code among different classes is to inherit from a common superclass. This means that we should move the synchronization code into a class SyncReadWrite that will become the superclass of both SyncA and SyncB (see figure 1b). Unfortunately this

---

[2] In C++ and Eiffel, parameterized structures such as templates [42] and generic classes [28] compensate for this limitation.

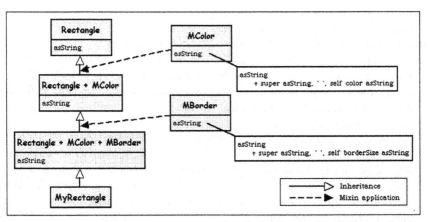

Fig. 2. The code that interconnects the mixins is specified in the mixin MBorder. The composite entity MyRectangle cannot access the implementations of asString in the mixin MColor and the class Rectangle. The classes with + in their names are intermediaries generated by applying mixins

cannot work, because super-sends are statically resolved. The super-sends in the read and write methods of SyncReadWrite cannot possibly refer in one case to methods inherited from A and in the other case to methods inherited from B.

It is possible to parameterize the methods in SyncReadWrite by using self sends of abstract methods rather than explicit super sends. These abstract methods will be implemented by the subclass (see figure 1c). However, this still requires duplication of methods in each subclass. Furthermore, avoiding name clashes between the synchronized and unsynchronized versions of the read and write methods makes this approach rather clumsy, and one has to make sure that the unsynchronized methods are *not* publicly available in SyncA and SyncB.

Mixin Inheritance. A mixin is a subclass specification that may be applied to various parent classes in order to extend them with the same set of features. Mixins allow the programmer to achieve better code reuse than single inheritance while maintaining the simplicity of the inheritance operation. However, although inheritance works well for extending a class with a single orthogonal mixin, it does not work so well for composing a class from many mixins. The problem is that usually the mixins do not *quite* fit together, *i.e.*, their features may conflict, and that inheritance is not expressive enough to resolve such conflicts. This problem manifests itself under various guises.

Total Ordering. Mixin composition is linear: all the mixins used by a class must be inherited one at a time. Mixins appearing later in the order override *all* the identically named features of earlier mixins. When we wish to resolve conflicts by selecting features from different mixins, we may find that a suitable total order does not exist.

Dispersal of Glue Code. With mixins, the composite entity is not in full control of the way that the mixins are composed: the conflict resolution code must be hardwired in the intermediate classes that are created when the mixins are used, one at a time. Obtaining the desired combination of features may require modifying the mixins, introducing new mixins, or, sometimes, using the same mixin twice.

Dispersal is illustrated in figure 2, where a class MyRectangle uses two mixins MColor and MBorder that both provide a method asString. The implementations of asString in the mixins first call the inherited implementation and then extend the resulting string with information about their own state. When we compose the two mixins to make the class MyRectangle, we can choose which of them should come first, but we cannot specify how the different implementations of asString are glued together. This is because the mixins must be added one at a time: in Rectangle + MColor + MBorder we can access the behaviour of MBorder and the *mixed* behaviour of Rectangle + MColor, but *not* the original behaviour of MColor and Rectangle. Thus, if we want to adapt the way the implementations of asString are composed (*e.g.*, changing the separation character between the two strings), we need to modify the involved mixins.

Fragile Hierarchies. Because of linearity and the limited means for resolving conflicts, the use of multiple mixins results in inheritance chains that are fragile with respect to change. Adding a new method to one of the mixins may silently override an identically named method of a mixin that appears earlier in the chain. Furthermore, it may be impossible to reestablish the original behaviour of the composite without adding or changing several mixins in the chain. This problem is especially critical if one modifies a mixin that is used in many places across the class hierarchy.

As an illustration, suppose that in the previous example (see figure 2) the mixin MBorder does not initially define a method asString. This means that the implementation of asString in MyRectangle is the one specified by MColor. Now suppose that the method asString is subsequently added to the mixin MBorder. Because of the total order, this new method overrides the implementation provided by MColor. Worse, the original behaviour of the composite class MyRectangle cannot be reestablished without changing several more mixins.

3   Traits

We propose a compositional model as a solution to the problems illustrated in the previous section. Our model is based on lightweight entities called *traits*, which serve as the basic building blocks for classes and the primitive units of code reuse. Thus, traits satisfy the needs for structure, modularization and reusability *within* a class.

Traits, and all the examples given in this paper, are implemented in the Squeak dialect of Smalltalk-80 [22], but we believe that the same concept could

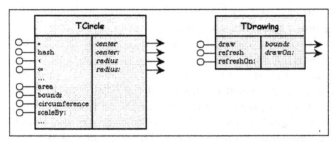

Fig. 3. The traits TDrawing and TCircle with provided methods in the left column and required methods in the right column

also be applied to other single inheritance languages (see section 8). In the remainder of this section, we present traits in detail using a running example. We show how classes are composed from traits, how traits are composed from other traits, and how naming conflicts are resolved. Space constraints prevent us from giving a formal specification of traits and the composition operations; this is available in a companion paper [37].

3.1 Running Example and Notational Conventions

Suppose that we want to represent graphical objects such as circles or squares that can be drawn on a canvas. We will use traits to structure the classes and factor out the reusable behaviour. We focus on the representation of circles, but the same techniques can be applied to the other classes.

In the examples, trait names start with the letter T, and class names do not. Because the traits are implemented in Squeak, we present the code in Smalltalk. The notation ClassName>>methodName indicates that the method methodName is defined in the class ClassName.

3.2 Specifying Traits

A trait contains a set of methods that implement the behaviour that it *provides*. In general, a trait may *require* a set of methods that serve as parameters for the provided behaviour. Traits cannot specify any state, and never access state directly. Trait methods can access state indirectly, using required methods that are ultimately satisfied by accessors (getter and setter methods).

The purpose of traits is to decompose classes into reusable building blocks by providing first-class representations for the different aspects of the behaviour of a class. Note that we use the term "aspect" to denote an independent, but not necessarily cross-cutting, concern. Traits differ from classes in that they do not define any kind of state, and that they can be composed using mechanisms other than inheritance.

Example. In our example, each graphical object can be decomposed into two aspects — its geometry, and the way that it is drawn on a canvas. In case of a circle, we represent the geometry with the trait TCircle and the drawing behaviour with the trait TDrawing.

Figure 3 shows these traits in an extension to UML. For each trait, the left column lists the provided methods and the right column lists the required methods. The trait TDrawing provides the methods draw, refreshOn:, and refresh, and it is parameterized by the required methods bounds and drawOn:. The code implementing this trait is shown below. The existence of the requirements is captured by methods (shown in italics) with body self requirement.

```
Trait named: #TDrawing uses: {}

draw                                    bounds
    ↑ self drawOn: World canvas            self requirement

refresh                                 drawOn: aCanvas
    ↑ self refreshOn: World canvas         self requirement

refreshOn: aCanvas
    aCanvas form
        deferUpdatesIn: self bounds
        while: [self drawOn: aCanvas]
```

The trait TCircle represents the geometry of a circle; it contains methods such as area, bounds, circumference, scaleBy:, =, <, and <=. TCircle requires methods center, center:, radius, and radius:, which parameterize its behaviour.

3.3   Composing Classes from Traits

Traits are a completely backward-compatible with single inheritance. In particular, trait composition complements, rather than subsumes, single inheritance. Whereas inheritance is used to derive one class from another, traits are used to achieve structure and reusability *within* a class definition. We summarize this relationship with the equation

$$Class = Superclass + State + Traits + Glue$$

This means that a class is derived from a superclass by adding the necessary state variables, using a set of traits, and implementing the *glue methods* that connect the traits together and serve as accessors for the state variables. In order for a class to be *complete*, all the requirements of the traits must be satisfied, *i.e.*, methods with the appropriate names must be provided. These methods can be implemented in the class itself, in a direct or indirect superclass, or by another trait that is used by the class.

Trait composition enjoys the *flattening property*. This property says that the semantics of a class defined using traits is exactly the same as that of a class constructed directly from all of the non-overridden methods of the traits. So, if class A is defined using trait T, and T defines methods a and b, then the

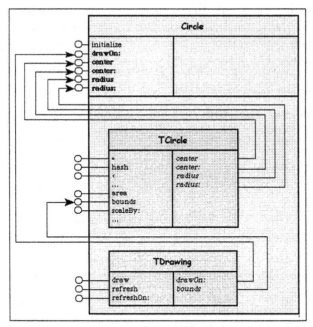

Fig. 4. The class Circle is composed from the traits TCircle and TDrawing. The requirement for TDrawing>>bounds is fulfilled by the trait TCircle. All the other requirements are fulfilled by accessor methods specified by the class

semantics of A is the same as it would be if a and b were defined directly in the class A. Naturally, if the glue code of A defines a method b directly, then this b would override the method b obtained from T. Specifically, the flattening property implies that the keyword **super** has no special semantics for traits; it simply causes the method lookup to be started in the superclass of the class that *uses* the trait.

Another property of trait composition is that the composition order is irrelevant, and hence conflicting trait methods must be explicitly disambiguated (cf. section 3.5). Conflicts between methods defined in classes and methods defined by incorporated traits are resolved using the following two precedence rules.

– *Class methods take precedence over trait methods.*
– *Trait methods take precedence over superclass methods.* This follows from the flattening property, which states that trait methods behave as if they were defined in the class itself.

Example. As illustrated in figure 4 and by the class definition hereafter, we create the class Circle by composing the traits TCircle and TDrawing. The trait TDrawing requires the methods bounds and drawOn:. The trait TCircle provides a method bounds, which already fulfills one of the requirements. Therefore, the class Circle has to provide only the methods center, center:, radius, and radius: for the trait TCircle and the method drawOn: for the trait TDrawing.

The methods center, center:, radius, and radius: are simply accessors to two instance variables. The method drawOn: draws a circle on the canvas that is passed as the argument. In addition, the class also implements a method for initializing the two instance variables.

```
Object subclass: #Circle
    instanceVariableNames: ' center radius'
    uses: { TCirle . TDrawing }

    initialize
        center := 0@0.
        radius := 50

    center                          center: aPoint
        ↑ center                        center := aPoint

    radius                          radius: aNumber
        ↑ radius                        radius := aNumber

    drawOn: aCanvas
        aCanvas fillOval: self bounds
            color: Color black
```

3.4 Composite Traits

In the same way that classes are composed from traits, traits can be composed from other traits. Unlike classes, most traits are not complete, which means that they do not define all the methods that are required by their subtraits. Unsatisfied requirements of subtraits simply become required methods of the composite trait. Again, the composition order is not important, and methods defined in the composite trait take precedence over the methods of its subtraits.

Even in case of multiple levels of composition, the flattening property remains valid. The semantics of a method does not depend on whether it is defined in a trait or in an entity that directly or indirectly uses that trait (cf. section 4.1).

Example. The trait TCircle contains two different aspects: comparison operators and geometric functions. In order to separate these aspects and improve code reuse, we redefine this trait as the composition of the traits TMagnitude and TGeometry as shown in figure 5(a). In addition, the trait TMagnitude is specified as a composite trait; it uses the trait TEquality, which requires the methods hash and =, and provides the method ~=. The trait TMagnitude itself requires <, and provides methods such as max:, <=, between:and:, and >=. Note that TMagnitude does not provide any of the methods required by its subtrait TEquality; this means that the requirements of TEquality are propagated as requirements of TMagnitude. Finally, as shown below, theTrait TCircle is composed from the traits TMagnitude and TGeometry. TCircle defines the methods =, hash, and < required by the trait TMagnitude. Below we show only the definition of TCircle. The first line of this definition contains the *composition clause*, which specifies that TCircle uses the subtraits TMagnitude and TGeomery.

Trait named: #TCircle uses: { TMagnitude . TGeometry }

   = other
      ↑ self radius = other radius and: [self center = other center]

   hash
      ↑ self radius hash and: [self center hash]

   < other
      ↑ self radius < other radius

3.5   Conflict Resolution

A conflict arises if and only if we combine two traits providing identically named methods that do not originate from the same trait. In particular, this means that if the *same* method (*i.e.*, from the same trait) is obtained more than once via different paths, there is no conflict. This rule is semantically sound because traits cannot specify state (cf. section 4.1).

Based on the trait composition rules presented in section 3.3, method conflicts must be explicitly resolved by defining a method in the class or in the composite trait. Trait composition enforces this by overriding the conflicting methods with a special marker method that indicates a method conflict. This guarantees that the conflict is resolved on the level of the composite, and not by another subtrait that happens to provide an appropriately named method. This behaviour makes trait composition associative as well as commutative.

To grant access to conflicting methods (and thereby avoid duplicating them), traits support an *alias* operation. Aliases are used to make a trait method available under another name; this is particularly useful if the original name is excluded by a conflict. Aliases are discussed further in section 4.1.

Trait composition also supports *exclusion*, which allows one to avoid a conflict before it occurs. The composition clause allows a programmer to exclude methods from a trait when it is composed. This suppresses these methods and allows the composite entity to acquire the otherwise conflicting implementation provided by another trait.

Example. Colored circles must contain color behaviour. To make this behaviour reusable, we define it in the trait TColor shown in figure 5(b). This trait provides the usual color methods such as red, green, saturation, *etc.* Because colors can also be tested for equality, TColor uses the trait TEquality, and implements the required methods = and hash as shown below.

Trait named: #TColor uses: { TEquality }

hash	= other
↑ self rgb hash	↑ self rgb = other rgb

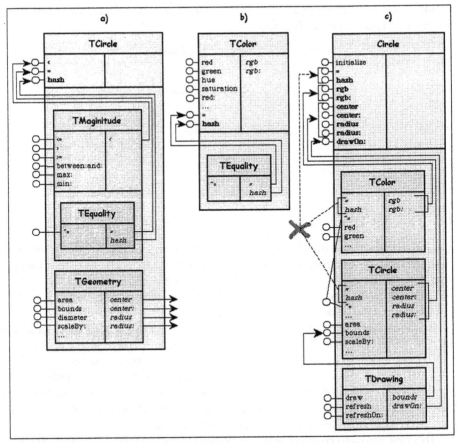

Fig. 5. Figure (a) shows how a trait TCircle is composed from a trait TGeometry and a composite trait TMagnitude, which contains the subtrait TEquality. Note that the provided services of the subtraits are propagated to the composite trait (*e.g.*, max:, ∼=, and area), and similarly, the unsatisfied requirements of the subtraits (*e.g.*, center and radius:) are turned into required methods of the composite trait. In (b), we again use the trait TEquality to specify the comparison behaviour of the trait TColor. Figure (c) shows how a class Circle is specified by composing the traits TCircle, TColor, and TDrawing

When the trait TColor is incorporated into the class Circle, a conflict arises because the traits TColor and TCircle provide different implementations for the methods = and hash, as shown in figure 5(c). Note that the method ∼= does not give rise to a conflict because in both TCircle and TColor the implementation originates from the same trait, namely TEquality.

Figure 5(c) shows that the conflicting methods are excluded and thereby turned into requirements that have to be implemented in the class TCircle to make it complete. In the code shown below, we define the method = so that two colored circles are equal if and only if they have the same geometrical properties and the same color. To avoid code duplication, we specify aliases circleEqual:, circleHash, colorEqual:, and colorHash for the conflicting methods and use them to define the semantics of the composite.

```
Object subclass: #Circle
    instanceVariableNames: 'center radius rgb'
    uses:    {    TCircle @ {#circleHash -> #hash. #circleEqual: -> #=} .
                  TDrawing .
                  TColor @ {#colorHash -> #hash. #colorEqual: -> #=} }
```

```
hash                                    = anObject
    ↑ self circleHash                       ↑ (self circleEqual: anObject)
        bitXor: self colorHash                  and: [self colorEqual: anObject]
```

Alternatively, we might decide that equality of colored objects is independent of their color and takes into account only their geometrical properties. In this case, we could remove the conflicting methods = and hash from TColor. This avoids the conflicts and has the effect that the class Circle simply uses the comparison behaviour provided by the trait TCircle. The corresponding composition clause is as follows.

```
Object subclass: #Circle
    instanceVariableNames: 'center radius rgb'
    uses: { TCircle . TDrawing − {#=. #hash} . TColor }
```

4   Discussion and Evaluation

In this section, we discuss some design decision that significantly influenced the properties of traits. We focus on reusability and understandability of programs that are written using traits. Finally, we present an evaluation of traits against the reusability problems discussed in section 2.

4.1   Design Decisions

Traits were designed with other reusability models in mind: we tried to combine their advantages, while avoiding their disadvantages. Here, we discuss the most important design decisions.

Untangling Reusability and Classes. Although they are inspired by mixins, traits are a new concept. They are a finer-grained unit of reuse than a class and are not tied to a specific place in the inheritance hierarchy. We believe that these two properties are essential for improving code reuse and conceptual modeling. Fine-grained reuse is important because the gulf that lies between entire classes and individual methods is too wide. Traits allow classes to be built by composing reusable behaviours rather than by implementing a large and unstructured set of methods. Hierarchy independence is important because it maximizes reusability. Because classes have a primary role as instance generators they must be complete, and are thus typically embedded in a hierarchy. This very property makes classes inapproprate for the secondary role that they are made to play in conventional languages: reusable method repositories [5].

Single Inheritance and the Flattening Property. Rather than replacing single inheritance, we decided to extend it with trait composition. These two operations are similar but complementary and work together nicely.

Single inheritance lets one reuse all the features (*i.e.*, methods and state variables) that are available in a class. If a class can inherit only from a single superclass, inheriting state does not cause complications, and a simple keyword (*e.g.*, **super**) is enough to access overridden methods. This mechanism for accessing inherited features is convenient, but it also gives semantics to the place of a method in the inheritance hierarchy.

Trait composition operates at a finer granularity than inheritance; it is used to modularize the behaviour defined *within* a class. As such, trait composition is designed to compose only behaviour and not state. In addition, trait composition enjoys the flattening property, which means that it does not assign any semantics to the place where a method is defined.

The flattening property combines with single inheritance to demonstrate that traits are a logical evolution of the single inheritance paradigm. A system based on traits naturally allows one to write and execute traditional single inheritance code. Moreover, with appropriate tool support, it also allows one to *view and edit* classes that are built from thousands of deeply composed traits in *exactly* the same way as one would if they were implemented without using traits at all.

Aliasing. Many multiple inheritance implementations provide access to overridden features by requiring the programmer to explicitly name the defining superclass in the source code. C++ uses the scope operator ::, whereas Eiffel uses the keyword **precursor**. With traits, we chose method aliasing in preference to placing named trait references in method bodies; this avoids the following problems.

- Named trait references contradict the *flattening property*, because they prevent the creation of a semantically consistent flattened view without adapting these references in the method bodies.
- Named trait references require the trait structure to be hardcoded in all the methods that use them. This means that changing the trait structure, or simply moving methods from one trait to another, potentially invalidates many methods.
- Named trait references would require an extension of the syntax of the underlying single inheritance language.

Method aliasing avoids all of these problems. It works with the flattening property because the flattening process can simply introduce a new name for the aliased method body.

Although there are some similarities between aliasing and method renaming as provided by Eiffel, there are also essential differences. Whereas aliasing just establishes an alternative name without affecting the original one, with renaming the original method name becomes undefined. As a consequence, method renaming must change all the references to the old name in other methods so that they refer to the new one. In contrast, aliasing has no effect on any references in other methods: requiring that they are changed would violate the flattening property.

Unintentional Naming Conflicts With traits, as with any other name-based approach to composing software features, unintentional naming conflicts may arise. For example, consider a Java class that should implement two interfaces, where each of these interfaces specifies a method with *precisely the same name* (and signature), but with different semantics.

At present, traits offer no real solution to this problem — when two traits are composed, it may be that each requires a semantically different method that happens to have the same name. Aliases alleviate the problem only to a small extent. In our view, a complete solution requires both good refactoring tools and explicit namespaces [1, 4].

Conflict Strategies and the Diamond Problem Although traits are based on single inheritance, a form of diamond problem may arise when features from the same trait are obtained multiple times via different paths. For example, consider a trait X that uses two traits Y1 and Y2, which in turn both use the trait Z.

Since traits contain no state, the most nefarious diamond problem does not arise. Nevertheless, in our example, a method foo provided by Z will be obtained by X twice. The key language design question is: *should this be considered a conflict?*

As explained in section 3.5, we decided that there should be no conflict if the *same* method is obtained more than once via different paths. This "same-operation exception", as it is called by Snyder [38], has the advantage of having a simple, intuitive semantics, but it can lead to surprises if the underlying traits are changed. Suppose that trait Y2 is re-implemented so that it no longer uses Z but still supports the same behavior (*e.g.*, the method Z>>foo is copied to the trait Y2). This causes a conflict because trait X now obtains two *different* methods foo. Thus, what may have appeared to be a strictly *internal* change to trait Y2 is visible to one of its clients.

Although it may seem that this situation will lead to fragile hierarchies, we argue that it does not. When Y2 re-implements foo, it is changing what it provides to its clients in a way that is less severe, but just as significant, as when it adds or removes methods. Any of these changes may introduce naming conflicts. However, the resulting conflict is a purely *local* matter, that is, it can be corrected by the *direct clients* of Y2 alone. X can easily resolve the resulting conflict by suppressing one foo or the other.

Let us examine two alternatives to our current rule. One alternative is for X to "automatically" obtain either one foo or the other, as happens with linearly-ordered mixins. The problem with this is that the change to Y2 would give the programmer no feedback, even though the semantics of X might have changed.

The alternative suggested by Snyder is to abandon the "same-operation exception", and announce a conflict even if the *same* method is obtained multiple times [38]. In our example, this means that there would already be a conflict in the original scenario, and that the programmer must *arbitrarily* decide which of the two foo methods should be available in X. We argue that this is more dangerous, because a later change to the foo provided by either Y1 or Y2 will not be signalled as having a possible consequence on X. With the current approach, the conflict is signalled at precisely the point in time when it arises, which is when the programmer is able to make an informed resolution.

4.2   Evaluation against the Identified Problems

In section 2 we identified a set of conceptual and practical reusability problems that are associated with various forms of inheritance. The design of traits was significantly influenced by the attempt to solve these problems. In the following, we present a point by point evaluation of the results.

Conflicting Features. Traits avoid state conflicts entirely by forbidding traits from expressing state. Method conflicts may be resolved within traits by explicitly selecting one of the conflicting methods, but more commonly conflicts are resolved in classes by overriding conflicts. In general, fewer conflicts arise than with multiple inheritance, because traits tend to remain lean, focussing on a small set of collaborating features.

Accessing Overridden/Conflicting Features. Because traits are an extension of single inheritance, *classes* can still access overridden features by means of **super** calls. However, sometimes a *trait* needs to access a conflicting feature, *e.g.*, in order to resolve the conflict. These features are accessed by aliases, rather than by explicitly naming the trait that provides the desired feature. This leads to more robust trait hierarchies, since aliases remain *outside* the implementations of methods. Contrast this approach with multiple inheritance languages in which one must explicitly name the class that provides a method in order to resolve an ambiguity. The aliasing approach both avoids tangled class references in the source code, and eliminates code that is hard to understand and fragile with respect to change.

Factoring out Generic Wrappers. Generic wrappers, such as the synchronization wrappers discussed in section 2, can be expressed easily with traits. In fact, solution (b) in figure 1 would work if SyncReadWrite were a trait, since **super** in a trait is just a placeholder for the superclass of the class that will actually use that trait. If SyncA is defiend to be a subclass of A and SyncB a subclass of B, and both use trait SyncReadWrite, then the **super** send in the trait's read and write methods will be statically bound to A or B *when the trait is used to define the class*. Other kinds of generic wrappers can be defined in much the same way.

Total Ordering. Trait composition is symmetric, so ordering is irrelevant. However, trait composition can be productively combined with inheritance to obtain a large variety of different partially ordered compositions. The basic idea is that if we want a class C to use two traits T1 and T2 in that order, we first introduce a superclass C' that uses T1, and then we define C to inherits from C' and use T2. This has the consequence that the methods in T2 override the methods in T1. This strategy has proved itself in practice when we refactored the Smalltalk collection hierarchy (see section 6 and figure 6).

Dispersal of Glue Code. When traits are combined, the glue code is always located in the combining entity, reflecting the idea that the combining entity is in complete control of plugging together the components that implement its aspects. This property nicely separates the glue code from the code that implements the different aspects, and it makes a class easy to understand, even if it is composed from many different components.

Fragile Hierarchies. Any hierarchical approach to composing software is bound to be fragile with respect to certain kinds of change: if a feature that is used by many clients changes, the change will clearly impact all the clients. The important question is: how severely will the change impact the features of direct and indirect clients? Do we need to change implementations, or only glue code? Will there be a ripple effect throughout the entire hierarchy due to apparently innocuous changes?

Adding or deleting methods provided by a trait may well impact clients by introducing new conflicts or requirements, but ripple effects are generally avoided. A direct client can generally resolve a conflict without reimplementing any features. Furthermore, if the direct client can preserve the interface it provides, no ripple effect will occur.

5   Implementation

Traits as described in this paper are implemented in Squeak [22], an open-source dialect of Smalltalk-80. Our implementation consists of two parts: an extension of the Smalltalk-80 language and an extension of the programming tools.

5.1   Language Extension

To add traits to Squeak, we extended the implementation of a class to include an additional instance variable to contain the information in the composition clause. This variable defines the traits used by the class, including any exclusions and aliases. In addition, we introduced a representation for traits, which are essentially stripped down classes that can define neither state nor a superclass. When a class C uses a trait T, the method dictionary of C is extended with an entry for all the methods in T that are not overridden by C. For an alias, we add to the method dictionary a second entry that associates the new name with the aliased method. Since compiled methods in traits do not usually depend on the location where they are used, the bytecode for the method can be shared between the trait that defines the method and all the classes and traits that use it. However, methods using the keyword **super** store an explicit reference to the superclass in their literal table. So we need to copy those methods and change the entry for the superclass appropriately. This copy could be avoided by modifying the virtual machine to compute **super** when needed.

In Smalltalk, classes are first-class objects; every class is instance of a metaclass that defines the shape and the behaviour of its singleton instance [19]. In our implementation, we support this concept by introducing the notion of a *metatrait*; a metatrait can be associated with every trait. When a trait is used in a class, the associated metatrait (if there is one) is automatically used in the metaclass. Note that a trait without a metatrait can be applied to both classes and metaclasses. To preserve metaclass compatibility [8, 20], metatraits are automatically generated for traits that send messages to the metalevel using the pseudo-message class.

Because traits are simple and completely backwards compatible with single inheritance, implementing traits in a reflective single inheritance language like Squeak is unproblematic. The fact that traits cannot specify state is a major simplification. We avoid most of the performance and space problems that occur with multiple inheritance, because these problems are related to compiling methods without knowing the indices of the instance variables in the object [14].

Our implementation requires no duplication of source code, and byte code is duplicated only if it includes sends to **super**. A program with traits shows essentially the same performance as a corresponding single inheritance program where all the methods provided by traits are implemented directly in the classes using the traits. This is especially remarkable because our implementation did not make any changes to the Squeak virtual machine. There may be a small performance penalty resulting from the use of accessor methods, but such methods are in any case widely used because they improve maintainability. JIT compilers routinely inline accessors, so we feel that requiring their use is entirely justifiable.

5.2 Programming Tools

Besides an extension of the language, our implementation also includes an extension of the programming tools, *i.e.*, the Smalltalk browser. In the following, we give a brief overview of this extended browser; a more detailed description can be found in a companion paper [36].

For each class (and each trait), the browser shows the various traits from which it is composed. The flattening property allows the browser to flatten this hierarchical structure at any level. In addition, the browser shows the programmer the *provided* and *required* methods, the *overridden* methods, and the *glue* methods, which specify how the class meets the requirements of its component traits. These features help the programmer to work with different views of the code. On the one hand, the programmer can work with the code in a flattened view, where a class consists of an unstructured set of methods and it does not matter whether the class is built from traits and whether a method is defined in a trait or in the class itself. On the other hand, the programmer can work in a composition view, where he sees how the responsibilities of the class are decomposed into several traits and how these traits are glued together in order to achieve the required behaviour. This view is especially valuable because it allows a user to understand a class by knowing the involved traits and understanding the glue methods.

As in standard Smalltalk, the browser supports incremental compilation. Whenever a trait method is added, changed or excluded, all the users of that trait are instantaneously updated. The modifications are also analyzed to infer the set of required methods. If a modification causes a new conflict or an unspecified requirement anywhere in the system, the affected classes and traits are automatically added to a "to do" list.

Our implementation features several tools that support the programmer in composing traits and generating the necessary glue code. Required methods that correspond to instance variable accessors are generated on request. Conflict elimination is also semi-automated. The programmer is presented with a list of alternative implementations; choosing one of these automatically generates the composition clause that excludes the others, and thus eliminates the conflict.

6   An Application of Traits

As a realistic evaluation of their usability, we used traits to refactor the Smalltalk-80 collection hierarchy as it is implemented in Squeak 3.2. In this section, we summarize the results of this work; interested readers are referred to a companion paper that contains more details [6].

The core classes of the Smalltalk-80 collection hierarchy have been improved over more than 20 years and are often considered a paradigmatic example of object-oriented programming. Each kind of collection can be characterized by properties such as being explicitly ordered (*e.g.*, Array), implicitly ordered (*e.g.*, SortedCollection), unordered (*e.g.*, Set), extensible (*e.g.*, Bag), immutable (*e.g.*, String), keyed (*e.g.*, Dictionary), or element-wise comparable (*e.g.*, using identity or a higher-level comparison operator).

However, single inheritance is not expressive enough to model such a diverse set of related classes that share many different properties in various combinations. Consequently, the implementors of the hierarchy were forced to duplicate code or to move methods higher in the hierarchy and then disable them in the subclasses to which they do not apply [12].

We solved these problems by creating traits for the different collection properties and combining them to build the required collection classes. In order to achieve maximum flexibility, we separated the properties specifying the implementation of a collection from the properties specifying the interface. This allowed us to freely combine different interfaces (*e.g.*, "sorted-extensible interface" and "sorted-extensible-immutable interface") with any of the suitable implementations (*e.g.*, "linked-list implementation" and "array-based implementation"). We use inheritance to partially order the traits; optimized methods in the more

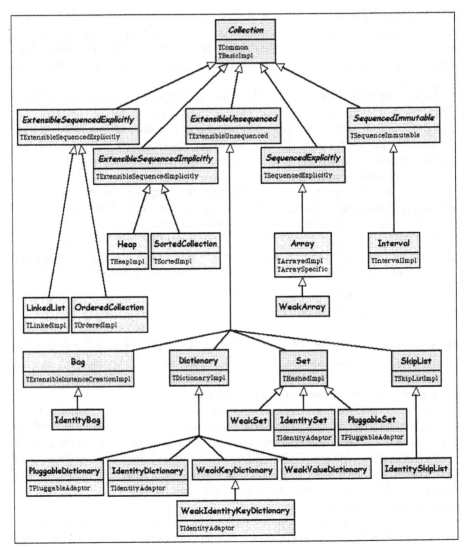

Fig. 6. The refactored collection hierarchy. Classes with italicized names are abstract; below the class name we show the traits that are used by the class directly

specific implementation traits take precedence over generic methods provided by the more general interface traits.

In addition to the traits that were necessary to achieve a sound hierarchy and avoid code duplication, we used additional subtraits to structure the code more finely. These subtraits allow us to reuse parts of the code outside of the collection hierarchy. As an example, we introduced traits representing the behaviour

"emptiness" (which requires size and provides isEmpty, notEmpty, ifEmpty:, *etc.*)
and "enumeration" (which requires do: and provides collect:, select:, detect:, *etc.*).

Although some of the collection classes are now built as the composition of as
many as 22 traits, the flattening property combined with the our programming
tools means that this does not impair understandability. If the trait structure is
not useful for a particualr task, it is always possible to work with the hierarchy
as if it were implemented with ordinary single-inheritance.

Figure 6 shows the refactored hierarchy for 21 of the more common collection
classes. Besides the class name, the figure also shows the traits that each class
uses. However, it does not show that each of these traits has many subtraits.
The abstract class Collection is at the top; it provides a small amount of general
behaviour for all collections. Then we have a layer of abstract classes that provide different combinations of traits that represent interface properties. At the
bottom, we have concrete classes that use traits to provide implementations.

In total, these classes use 48 different traits and implement 567 methods.
This is just over 10% fewer methods than in the original implementation. In
addition, the code for the trait implementation is 12% smaller than the original.
This is especially remarkable because another 9% of the methods in the original
implementation are implemented "too high" in the hierarchy, specifically to enable code sharing. With inheritance, the penalty for implementing a method too
high is the repeated need to cancel inherited behaviour in subclasses where that
behaviour does not make sense. In the trait implementation, there is no need to
resort to this tactic.

7   Related Work

In the section 2 we have shown how multiple inheritance and mixins attempt
to promote code reuse, and the problems that these approaches encounter. In
this section we compare traits to some other approaches to structuring complex
artifacts.

There are several other models that use entities called "traits" to share and
reuse implementation. One of them is the prototype-based language Self [45]. In
Self, there is no notion of class; each object conceptually defines its own format,
methods, and inheritance relations. Objects are derived from other objects by
cloning and modification. In addition, Self also has the notion of *traits objects*
that serve as repositories for sharing behaviour and state among multiple objects.
One or more traits objects can be dynamically selected as the parent(s) of any
object. Selector lookups unresolved in the child are passed to the parents; it is
an error for a selector to be found in more than one parent.

The programming language Mesa, used for implementing the software for
the Xerox Star workstation, also provided entities called *traits* as an approach to
multiple inheritance [13]. This approach has more in common with other multiple
inheritance approaches than with the trait model presented in this paper. Some
of the main differences from our model are that the Star traits have a different

semantics regarding inheritance, have different conflict resolution capabilities, carry state, and allow multiple implementations for a single method.

The Larch family of specification languages [21] is also based on a construct called a trait; the relationship turns out to be more than name deep. Larch traits are fragments of specifications that can be freely reused at fine granularity. For example, it is possible to define a Larch trait such as IsEmpty that adds a single operation to an existing container data-type. There are, of course, significant differences, since our traits are not intended to be used to prove properties of programs, and adding a trait to a class does not formally constrain the behavior of existing methods.

The Jigsaw modularity framework, developed by Bracha in his doctoral dissertation [9], defines module composition operators merge, override, copy·as and restrict that are strikingly similar to the sum, override, alias and exclusion operators on traits. For example, Bracha's merge, like our sum, is commutative. Although there are differences in the details of the definitions (for example, in how conflicts are handled), the more significant differences are in motivation and setting. Jigsaw is intended as a complete framework for module manipulation in the large, and makes assumptions appropriate to that setting: namespaces, declared types and requirements, full renaming, and semantically meaningful nesting. Traits are intended to supplement existing languages by promoting reuse in the small, and consequently do not define namespaces, do not declare types, infer their requirements, do not allow renaming, and do not give a meaning to nesting. The Jigsaw operation set also aims for completeness, whereas in the design of traits we explicitly gave up completeness for simplicity. Nevertheless, the similarity of the core operation sets is encouraging, given that they were defined independently.

Caesar's collaboration interfaces are similar to traits in that they include the declaration of *expected* methods, *i.e.*, those that classes must provide when bound to an interface [31]. Thus, Caesar's interface concept can simulate traits by binding an interface to a class and then combining it with a specific implementation. However, Caesar has no special compositional construct for dealing with conflicts. Instead, Caesar is designed to use one of the conflict resolution strategies known from multiple inheritance languages such as C++, leading to problems similar to those described in section 2. Moreover, Caesar is based on explicit wrappers, which can be costly at runtime, while the semantics of traits is compatible with single inheritance and does not create a run-time penalty.

Mezini proposed an approach to behavior composition in a class-based environment that is based on the encapsulated object model of class-based inheritance, but introduces an explicit combination layer between objects and classes [30]. The behavior definition of an evolving object is dispersed between a class that provides the standard behavior of the object and a set of mixin-like software modules, called adjustments. One of the main differences from traits is that Mezini's approach is more dynamic and complex. In fact, a combiner-metaobject is associated with each evolving object, responsible for the compositional aspects of the object's behavior. This means that the combiner-metaobject uses the adjustments to define the environment in which to evaluate the messages sent to the object.

Delegation (also known as "object-based inheritance") is another form of composition that side-steps many of the problems related to class-based inheritance [24]. In contrast to traits, delegation is designed to support *dynamic* component adaptation.

8   Conclusions and Future Work

This paper has introduced traits, a simple compositional model for building and structuring object-oriented programs. Traits are composed using a set of operators — symmetric combination, exclusion, and aliasing — that are carefully designed so that they allow a fair amount of composition flexibility without being subject to the problems and limitations that we have identified for mixins and multiple inheritance.

Thanks to the favorable composition properties, traits are an ideal extension for single inheritance languages. Traits are completely backwards compatible with Smalltalk and do not require modifying or extending the method syntax of the underlying language. Furthermore, the flattening property guarantees optimal understandability of the resulting code, because it is always possible to both view and edit the code as if it were written using single inheritance.

Having the right programming tools has proven to be crucial for giving the programmer the maximum benefit from traits. In our Squeak-based implementation, we changed the browser so that it allows the programmer to switch seamlessly between the different views and emphasizes the glue methods that define how the traits are connected.

We successfully used traits for refactoring the collection hierarchy, which is a strong indication for the usability of traits for realistic and non-trivial problems. It also showed that traits are suitable for modularizing classes that are already built, and that they raise the level of abstraction when building new classes. As we worked with the refactored hierarchy, we were impressed with the power of the flattening property, which made understanding classes that are built from composite traits quite a simple matter.

As future work we would like to (1) evaluate the impact of the introduction of namespaces and encapsulation on the flattening property, (2) consider the effects of allowing traits to specify state variables, (3) extend trait composition so that it can replace inheritance, (4) evaluate the possibility of using traits to modify the behaviour of individual instances at run-time, (5) develop a type systems for traits and identify the relationships between traits and interfaces, and (6) further explore the application of traits to the refactoring of complex class hierarchies.

We also plan to consider how best to add traits to Java, where both the type system and the syntax make the simple approach that works so well for Smalltalk more problematic. For example, the type of a method in a trait may depend on the class in which it is eventually used; Java's current type system cannot express this. There are also some annoying syntactic problems, such as the name of a constructor being the same as the name of the class: what should be the name of a constructor in a trait? However, we believe that these problems can be overcome without making major changes to the spirit of Java.

Acknowledgements

We would like to thank Gilad Bracha, William Cook, Erik Ernst, Robert Hirschfeld, Andreas Raab, and Roel Wuyts for their willingness to interact with us while we were developing traits and for their comments on this paper. We also thank the ECOOP referees for their valuable suggestions, which have helped to improve the presentation in many ways.

References

[1] Franz Achermann and Oscar Nierstrasz. Explicit Namespaces. In Jürg Gutknecht and Wolfgang Weck, editors, *Modular Programming Languages*, volume 1897 of *LNCS*, pages 77–89, Zürich, Switzerland, September 2000. Springer-Verlag.

[2] Pierre America. Designing an object-oriented programming language with behavioural subtyping. In *Proceedings REX/FOOLS Workshop*, Noordwijkerhout, June 1990.

[3] Davide Ancona, Giovanni Lagorio, and Elena Zucca. Jam - a smooth extension of java with mixins. In *Proceedings ECOOP 2000*, volume 1850 of *Lecture Notes in Computer Science*, pages 145–178, 2000.

[4] Alexandre Bergel, Stéphane Ducasse, and Roel Wuyts. Classboxes: A minimal module model supporting local rebinding. In *Proceedings of the Joint Modular Languages Conference 2003*. Springer-Verlag, 2003. To appear.

[5] Andrew Black, Norman Hutchinson, Eric Jul, and Henry Levy. Object structure in the Emerald system. In *Proceedings OOPSLA '86, ACM SIGPLAN Notices*, volume 21, pages 78–86, November 1986.

[6] Andrew Black, Nathanael Schärli, and Stéphane Ducasse. Applying traits to the Smalltalk collection hierarchy. Technical Report IAM-02-007, Institut für Informatik, Universität Bern, Switzerland, November 2002. Also available as Technical Report CSE-02-014, OGI School of Science & Engineering, Beaverton, Oregon, USA.

[7] Alan H. Borning and Daniel H.H. Ingalls. Multiple inheritance in Smalltalk-80. In *Proceedings at the National Conference on AI*, Pittsburgh, PA, 1982.

[8] Noury M. N. Bouraqadi-Saadani, Thomas Ledoux, and Fred Rivard. Safe metaclass programming. In *Proceedings OOPSLA '98*, pages 84–96, 1998.

[9] Gilad Bracha. *The Programming Language Jigsaw: Mixins, Modularity and Multiple Inheritance*. Ph.D. thesis, Dept. of Computer Science, University of Utah, March 1992.

[10] Gilad Bracha and William Cook. Mixin-based inheritance. In *Proceedings OOPSLA/ECOOP '90, ACM SIGPLAN Notices*, volume 25, pages 303–311, October 1990.

[11] Steve Cook. OOPSLA '87 Panel P2: Varieties of inheritance. In *OOPSLA '87 Addendum To The Proceedings*, pages 35–40. ACM Press, October 1987.

[12] William R. Cook. Interfaces and specifications for the Smalltalk-80 collection classes. In *Proceedings OOPSLA '92, ACM SIGPLAN Notices*, volume 27, pages 1–15, October 1992.

[13] Gael Curry, Larry Baer, Daniel Lipkie, and Bruce Lee. TRAITS: an approach to multiple inheritance subclassing. In *Proceedings ACM SIGOA, Newsletter*, volume 3, Philadelphia, June 1982.

[14] R. Dixon, T. McKee, M. Vaughan, and P. Schweizer. A fast method dispatcher for compiled languages with multiple inheritance. In *Proceedings OOPSLA '89, ACM SIGPLAN Notices*, volume 24, pages 211–214, October 1989.

[15] R. Ducournau, M. Habib, M. Huchard, and M.L. Mugnier. Monotonic conflict resolution mechanisms for inheritance. In *Proceedings OOPSLA '92, ACM SIG-PLAN Notices*, volume 27, pages 16–24, October 1992.

[16] R. Ducournau and Michel Habib. On some algorithms for multiple inheritance in object-oriented programming. In J. Bézivin, J-M. Hullot, P. Cointe, and H. Lieberman, editors, *Proceedings ECOOP '87*, volume 276 of *LNCS*, pages 243–252, Paris, France, June 15-17 1987. Springer-Verlag.

[17] Dominic Duggan and Ching-Ching Techaubol. Modular mixin-based inheritance for application frameworks. In *Proceedings OOPSLA 2001*, pages 223–240, October 2001.

[18] Matthew Flatt, Shriram Krishnamurthi, and Matthias Felleisen. Classes and mixins. In *Proceedings of the 25th ACM SIGPLAN-SIGACT Symposium on Principles of Programming Languages*, pages 171–183. ACM Press, 1998.

[19] Adele Goldberg and David Robson. *Smalltalk 80: the Language and its Implementation*. Addison Wesley, Reading, Mass., May 1983.

[20] Nicolas Graube. Metaclass compatibility. In *Proceedings OOPSLA '89, ACM SIGPLAN Notices*, volume 24, pages 305–316, October 1989.

[21] John V. Guttag, James J. Horning, and Jeannette M. Wing. The larch family of specification languages. *IEEE Transactions on Software Engineering*, 2(5):24–36, September 1985.

[22] Dan Ingalls, Ted Kaehler, John Maloney, Scott Wallace, and Alan Kay. Back to the future: The story of Squeak, A practical Smalltalk written in itself. In *Proceedings OOPSLA '97*, pages 318–326, November 1997.

[23] Sonia E. Keene. *Object-Oriented Programming in Common-Lisp*. Addison Wesley, 1989.

[24] Günter Kniesel. Type-safe delegation for run-time component adaptation. In R. Guerraoui, editor, *Proceedings ECOOP '99*, volume 1628 of *LNCS*, pages 351–366, Lisbon, Portugal, June 1999. Springer-Verlag.

[25] Wilf LaLonde and John Pugh. Subclassing ≠ Subtyping ≠ Is-a. *Journal of Object-Oriented Programming*, 3(5):57–62, January 1991.

[26] Ole Lehrmann Madsen, Boris Magnusson, and Birger Moller-Pedersen. Strong typing of object-oriented languages revisited. In *Proceedings OOPSLA/ECOOP '90, ACM SIGPLAN Notices*, volume 25, pages 140–150, October 1990.

[27] Tom Mens and Marc van Limberghen. Encapsulation and composition as orthogonal operators on mixins: A solution to multiple inheritance problems. *Object Oriented Systems*, 3(1):1–30, 1996.

[28] Bertrand Meyer. *Eiffel: The Language*. Prentice-Hall, 1992.

[29] Bertrand Meyer. *Object-Oriented Software Construction*. Prentice-Hall, second edition, 1997.

[30] Mira Mezini. Dynamic object evolution without name collisions. In *Proceedings ECOOP '97*. Springer-Verlag, June 1997.

[31] Mira Mezini and Klaus Ostermann. Integrating independent components with on-demand remodularization. In *Proceedings OOPSLA 2002*, pages 52–67, November 2002.

[32] David A. Moon. Object-oriented programming with flavors. In *Proceedings OOP-SLA '86, ACM SIGPLAN Notices*, volume 21, pages 1–8, November 1986.

[33] Markku Sakkinen. Disciplined inheritance. In S. Cook, editor, *Proceedings ECOOP '89*, pages 39–56, Nottingham, July 10-14 1989. Cambridge University Press.

[34] Markku Sakkinen. The darker side of C++ revisited. *Structured Programming*, 13(4):155–177, 1992.

[35] Craig Schaffert, Topher Cooper, Bruce Bullis, Mike Killian, and Carrie Wilpolt. An Introduction to Trellis/Owl. In *Proceedings OOPSLA '86, ACM SIGPLAN Notices*, volume 21, pages 9–16, November 1986.

[36] Nathanael Schärli and Andrew Black. A browser for incremental programming. Technical Report CSE-03-008, OGI School of Science & Engineering, Beaverton, Oregon, USA, April 2003.

[37] Nathanael Schärli, Oscar Nierstrasz, Stéphane Ducasse, Roel Wuyts, and Andrew Black. Traits: The formal model. Technical Report IAM-02-006, Institut für Informatik, Universität Bern, Switzerland, November 2002. Also available as Technical Report CSE-02-013, OGI School of Science & Engineering, Beaverton, Oregon, USA.

[38] Alan Snyder. Encapsulation and inheritance in object-oriented programming languages. In *Proceedings OOPSLA '86, ACM SIGPLAN Notices*, volume 21, pages 38–45, November 1986.

[39] Alan Snyder. Inheritance and the development of encapsulated software systems. In *Research Directions in Object-Oriented Programming*, pages 165–188. MIT Press, 1987.

[40] Guy L. Steele. *Common Lisp The Language*. Digital Press, second edition, 1990. book.

[41] Bjarne Stroustrup. *The C++ Programming Language*. Addison Wesley, Reading, Mass., 1986.

[42] Bjarne Stroustrup. *The Design and Evolution of C++*. Addison Wesley, 1994.

[43] Peter F. Sweeney and Joseph (Yossi) Gil. Space and time-efficient memory layout for multiple inheritance. In *Proceedings OOPSLA '99*, pages 256–275. ACM Press, 1999.

[44] Antero Taivalsaari. On the notion of inheritance. *ACM Computing Surveys*, 28(3):438–479, September 1996.

[45] David Ungar and Randall B. Smith. Self: The power of simplicity. In *Proceedings OOPSLA '87, ACM SIGPLAN Notices*, volume 22, pages 227–242, December 1987.

A Type System and Analysis
for the Automatic Extraction and Enforcement
of Design Information*

Patrick Lam and Martin Rinard

Laboratory for Computer Science, Massachusetts Institute of Technology
Cambridge, MA 02139, USA
{plam,rinard}@lcs.mit.edu

Abstract. We present a new type system and associated type checker, analysis, and model extraction algorithms for automatically extracting models that capture aspects of a program's design. Our type system enables the developer to place a *token* on each object; this token serves as the object's representative during the analysis and model extraction. The polymorphism in our type system enables the use of general-purpose classes whose instances may serve different purposes in the computation; programmers may also hide the details of internal data structures by placing the same token on all of the objects in these data structures.
Our combined type system and analysis provide the model extraction algorithms with sound heap aliasing information. Our algorithms can therefore extract both structural models that characterize object referencing relationships and behavioral models that capture indirect interactions mediated by objects in the heap. Previous approaches, in contrast, limited by an absence of aliasing information, have focused on control-flow interactions that take place at procedure call boundaries. We have implemented our type checker, analysis, and model extraction algorithms and used them to automatically extract design models. Our experience indicates that it is straightforward to produce the token annotations and that the extracted models provide useful insight into the structure and behavior of the program.

1 Introduction

Design abstractions such as object models [12] and module dependency diagrams are a central feature of many software development processes. In this capacity they provide a way to quickly and easily explore design alternatives and give the members of the design team a common and effective language for communicating important aspects of the design.

* This research was supported in part by a fellowship from Canada's Natural Sciences and Engineering Research Council, DARPA/AFRL Contract F33615-00-C-1692, NSF Grant CCR-0086154, NSF Grant CCR-0073513, NSF Grant CCR-0209075, an Eclipse Innovation Grant, and the Singapore-MIT Alliance.

In principle, the design abstractions should remain a primary source of information about the program for its entire lifetime. But the standard practice is for programmers to manually implement the design once it has been finalized, raising the possibility of the implementation diverging from the design. This divergence becomes ever more likely over the lifetime of the program, limiting the credibility of the original design and therefore its utility as a source of information about the program. In most cases, the design is eventually discarded and the code becomes the primary source of information about the program.

This paper presents a new type system and an associated analysis that together support the automatic extraction of design-level information from the source code. The goal is to establish a guaranteed connection between the program and its design, restore the credibility of the design as a reliable source of information about the program, and enable developers to use design abstractions effectively throughout the entire lifetime of the program.

We focus on abstractions that involve the structure of the heap and the information flow (or lack of such flow) between different subsystems. One particularly novel aspect of our technique is that it accurately captures even indirect interactions mediated by objects in the heap. Existing approaches, in contrast, focus only on the direct interactions that take place at procedure or method calls.

The key idea behind our approach is to allow the developer to use the type system to place a *token* (chosen from a finite set of tokens fixed at program analysis time) on each object in the program; this token serves as the object's representative during the analysis that extracts the design information from the program. This approach addresses several common problems that complicate the effective automatic extraction of design information:

- **Multiple Design Elements, Single Code Element:** Well-structured programs factor common behavior and structure into a single, general-purpose code element (for example, a container class or object factory). Different instantiations of such an element often have distinct conceptual purposes in the computation and should therefore correspond to different elements in the design. But standard analysis approaches treat each code element as a unit, conflating the attributes of its different instantiations and failing to capture important design-level distinctions.
  The polymorphism in our type system eliminates this problem. It allows the developer to place different tokens on different instantiations of the same class so that the analysis separates objects with different conceptual purposes even if the objects happen to be instances of the same general-purpose class.
- **Single Design Element, Multiple Code Elements:** Because the design captures aspects of the computation at a higher level of abstraction than the code, multiple code elements are often required to implement a single design element. For example, a primary object may maintain complex internal data structures that the design abstracts as conceptually part of the object. Any approach that fails to abstract these internal data structures will deliver an overly detailed model that obscures key aspects of the design.

Our type system addresses this problem by allowing the developer to place the same token on both the primary object and all of the objects that implement its internal data structures. The analysis then treats the entire collection of objects as a unit and appropriately coalesces the combined information from all of the objects into a single design element.

Consider, for example, a set object with an internal linked list of references to items in the set. Our system allows the developer to place the same token on both the set object and all of the linked list objects, with a separate token on the items that the list nodes reference. In the extracted models, the set and all of its internal linked list nodes comprise a single abstraction. Because the items in the set have a different token, they correspond to a separate abstraction.

- **Aliasing:** To accurately extract structural information (for example, referencing relationships between objects) and behavioral information (for example, how information flows between subsystems), the analysis needs to have information about the aliasing relationships in the heap. An expensive whole-program pointer analysis is the standard way to obtain this information. Pointer analyses typically use the creation site of each object to represent the object during the analysis, in which case the analysis results conflate all objects allocated at the same site and fail to appropriately coalesce internal objects.

  In our type system, the type of each object completely characterizes the referencing relationships (at the granularity of tokens) in the part of the heap reachable from that object. Instead of processing all of the load and store statements to construct a model of the heap, our analysis can simply propagate token information across procedure boundaries to substitute out the token variables in the polymorphic types. The resulting ground types provide the required aliasing information.

We present the extracted design information to the developer via a set of models. Each model is designed to capture a specific kind of design information; together, the models provide a comprehensive summary of the relationships between the structural and behavioral aspects of the design. In particular, our models help the developer visualize referencing relationships between objects in the heap and understand the full range of interaction relationships between subsystems.

1.1   Object Models

An object model identifies the kinds of objects in the heap and characterizes the relationships between these different kinds of objects [12]. We model the objects and relationships at the granularity of tokens. Specifically, there is a node in the model for each token. There is a labelled edge between two tokens if the heap may contain two objects represented by the tokens and one object may contain a reference to the other. The label identifies the field containing the reference.

Building the model at the granularity of the tokens separates conceptually distinct instances of the same class and enables the model to appropriately capture the different structural relationships associated with these different instances. The standard approach, in contrast, operates at the granularity of classes and fails to capture these distinctions [18].

1.2 Subsystem Access Models

These models characterize how subsystems access objects. Each of these models is a bipartite graph. There is a node for each token and a node for each subsystem, with an edge from a subsystem to a token if the subsystem may access an object represented by the token.

1.3 Interaction Models

Interaction models characterize interactions between subsystems at the granularity of tokens. We support two kinds of models:

- **Call/Return Interaction Model:** This model characterizes the direct interactions that take place at method calls and returns. The nodes in the call/return model are subsystems. There is a solid directed edge from subsystem s_1 to s_2 if a method in s_1 invokes a method in s_2. The edge is labelled with the tokens that represent the objects passed as parameters in any s_1 method calling s_2. There is a dashed directed edge from s_2 to s_1 if some method in the s_2 subsystem returns a result to a method in s_1. The edge is labelled with all tokens representing objects returned from s_2 to s_1.
- **Heap Interaction Model:** This model characterizes the indirect interactions that take place at reads and writes to and from objects in the heap. The nodes in this model are tokens. There is a solid directed edge between two tokens if a subsystem writes a reference to an object represented by the first token into an object represented by the second token. The label on the edge identifies the subsystem that performed the write. There is a dashed directed edge between two tokens if a subsystem reads a field in an object represented by the first token and obtains a reference to an object represented by the second token. The label on the edge is the subsystem that performed the read.

  This model smoothly generalizes to support higher-level actions (such as insertions and removals) on abstract data types (such as hashtables and lists).

Together, these models enable the developer to trace all of the dependences between and flow of information through the subsystems in the program. They also support useful projection operations — to focus on a particular aspect of the interactions, the developer selects the relevant subsystems or tokens, then hides those parts of the model that do not involve these subsystems or tokens. The resulting projected models clearly expose the properties of interest.

Our enhanced subsystem models succinctly capture all of the information in standard subsystem interaction models (which focus on aspects of the control flow; in particular, on how methods in one subsystem invoke methods in other subystems). But the availability of a sound, relevant model of the heap also enables the analysis to characterize not only the control flow but also the information flow that occurs at method calls. Perhaps more significantly, it can also characterize how subsystems access data and capture indirect subsystem interactions mediated by objects in the heap.

1.4 Contributions

This paper makes the following contributions:

- **Polymorphic Token Type System:** It presents a polymorphic type system that allows developers to place a token on each object. This type system is structured as an extension to Java, and includes a type checking algorithm that determines if the type declarations are correct.
- **Analysis and Model Extraction Algorithms:** It presents an analysis algorithm and model extraction algorithms that, together, use the type system to extract models that capture aspects of the design of the program. This extraction-based approach ensures that the models correctly reflect the design of the program. In contrast with many previous approaches, the presence of sound heap aliasing information enables the extraction of both structural models that characterize object referencing relationships and behavioral models that capture indirect interactions mediated by objects in the heap.
- **Experience:** We have implemented our type system, analysis, and model extraction algorithms. We have used these algorithms to produce design models. Our experience indicates that it is straightforward to produce the token annotations and that the extracted models provide useful insight into the structure and behavior of the program.

2 Example

We next present an example that illustrates how our analysis produces interaction models. Figure 1 presents a program in which a driver coordinates the activities of a producer and a consumer. The producer and consumer interact via a stack of objects; the driver creates the stack, then repeatedly invokes the producer (which pushes some Int items on to the stack) and the consumer (which pops the Int items off of the stack). There are two kinds of interactions: *call/return interactions* in which the stack flows between the driver, the producer, and the consumer, and *heap interactions* in which the produced items flow from the producer through the stack to the consumer. We next discuss how our analysis produces models that present information about this program.

2.1 Subsystems

Our analysis describes the behavior of the system at the granularity of *subsystems*. Each subsystem corresponds to a set of method invocations that serve

```
token     P, C, D, PCS, PCI;
subsys    EP, EC, ED;

class Int<i> {                          class Consumer<c,s,i> enter EC {
    int v;                                  Int<i> r;
    Int(int v) { this.v = v; }              public void consume
}                                                   (Stack<s,i> s) {
class Node<s,i> {                               r = s.pop();
  Node<s,i> next;                           }
  Int<i> data;                          }
}                                       class Driver<d> enter ED {
class Stack<s,i> {                          public void enter() {
  private Node <s,i> first;                   Stack<PCS,PCI> s =
  public void push (Int<i> k) {                 new Stack<PCS,PCI>();
    Node <s,i> n =                            Producer<P,PCS,PCI> p =
      new Node<s,i>();                          new Producer<PT,PCS,PCI>();
    n.data = k;                               Consumer<C,PCS,PCI> c =
    n.next = first;                             new Consumer<C,PCS,PCI>();
    first = n;                                while (true) {
  }                                             p.produce(s);
  public Int<i> pop() {                         c.consume(s);
    Int<i> r = first.data;                    }
    first = first.next;                     }
    return r;                           }
  }                                     class ProducerConsumer {
}                                           public static void main
class Producer<p,s,i> enter EP {                    (String[] argv) {
  int n = 0;                                  new Driver<D>().enter();
  public void produce                       }
        (Stack<s,i> s) {                }
    s.push(new Int<i>(n++));
  }
}
```

Fig. 1. Example Producer/Consumer Program

the same conceptual purpose in the computation. Our example contains four subsystems: the MAIN subsytem that executes the main method, the EP (Event Producer) subsystem that produces the data, the EC (Event Consumer) subsystem that consumes the data, and the ED (Event Driver) subsystem that invokes the EP and EC subsystems.[1]

The program identifies some of the classes as subsystem entry points. In our example, the program uses the enter EP clause to identify all of the methods in the Producer class as entry points to the EP subsystem, and similarly for the EC and ED subsystems. In particular, any call to a static or instance method on

---

[1] In practice, we would expect the subsystems to be much larger. We adopt this fine subsystem granularity in our example for expository purposes.

a class which is a subsystem entry point triggers a subsystem change; we define an entry method to be any method on an entry class.

Once the program enters a subsystem, it remains within that subsystem until it invokes a method in a class that is an entry point for a different subsystem. So in our example, execution starts within the MAIN subsystem, then moves into the ED subsystem when the main method invokes the enter method. The ED subsystem then invokes the EP and EC subsystems to produce and consume the data.

Note that because the push and pop methods are not subsystem entry points, invocations of these methods are part of the same subsystem that invoked them. This approach enables the construction of general-purpose classes that may be used for different purposes in different subsystems.

2.2   Polymorphic Token Types

Each class has a set of token parameters. The first parameter identifies the token placed on the class; the other parameters are used to declare the types of the reference fields of instances of the class. In our example, the Stack <s, i> class has two parameters: the token variable s identifies the token placed on stack instances and the token variable i identifies the token placed on items in the stack. The class can use these token variables to declare the types of its reference fields and the types of the parameters of its methods.

The program specifies values for the token parameters at object creation sites. In our example, the enter method uses the statement

```
Stack<PCS,PCI> s = new stack<PCS,PCI>();
```

to create a new instance s of the Stack class with tokens PCS (producer/consumer stack) and PCI (producer/consumer item). This object creation site uses concrete token values (PCS and PCI). It is possible, however, for the program to use token variables to specify the tokens at object creation sites. Consider, for example, the object creation site new Int<i>(n++); inside the produce method. This site uses the token variable i to identify the token placed in the newly created Int object.

As our example illustrates, token variables support a form of polymorphism in which different instantiations of the same class can have different tokens. This mechanism supports general classes whose instances serve different conceptual purposes in the computation.

2.3   Analysis

The goal of our analysis is to compute, at the granularity of tokens, the referencing relationships within the program. This information allows the analysis to characterize structural relationships in the heap. It also serves as a foundation for computing behavioral information about how subsystems access and share information.

Our analysis processes the object creation and method call statements to propagate token variable binding information from callers to callees. In effect, the analysis substitutes out all of the token variables from all of the types, replacing the variables with the concrete tokens on objects that actually appear when the program runs.

In our example, the analysis propagates token bindings from the enter method to the produce and consume methods as follows. At the call to the produce method, the analysis uses the declared types of p and s to generate the binding $[p \mapsto P, s \mapsto PCS, i \mapsto PCI]$ for the token variables in the produce method. It then propagates these bindings to generate the binding $[s \mapsto PCS, i \mapsto PCI]$ for the token variables in the push method. In a similar way, the analysis can substitute out the token variables in the consume and pop methods to obtain a complete set of bindings for all of the token variables in the program.

The token propagation algorithm also propagates the current subsystem identifier between invoked methods. The combined analysis result contains both the token variable bindings and a binding that indicates the subsystems that may execute each method. So, in our example, the analysis computes that the push method may execute as part of the EP subsystem, and that the pop method may execute as part of the EC subsystem.

At this point, the analysis can use the bindings to compute, for each local variable, the set of tokens that represent the objects to which the variable may refer. As described below in Sections 3.4, 3.5, and 3.6, this information enables the analysis to produce models that characterize the objects that each subsystem may access and the ways that information may flow between subsystems.

As described below in Section 3.3, the bindings at object creation sites, when combined with the type declarations for object fields, enable the analysis to produce an object model that characterizes the referencing relationships between objects at the granularity of tokens.

Finally, the question may arise how to combine binding information when different invocations of a single method may have different token variable bindings. Our framework supports both context sensitive approaches (which provide a separate result for each different combination of the values of the token variables and subsystems in each method) and context-insensitive approaches (which combine the different contexts to generate a single mapping of token variables to possible values valid for all executions). An intermediate approach combines contexts from the same subsystem but keeps contexts from different subsystems apart. Our implementation uses a context sensitive approach, which keeps distinct sets of token variable bindings for each distinct invocation of a method.

2.4   Object Models

In our system, the concrete type of each object, in combination with the types of the objects that it (transitively) references, characterizes the structure of the heap reachable from the object. Once our analysis has computed the bindings for the token variables at each object allocation site, it can use the type declarations for the fields of the object to build an object model that characterizes the referencing relationships in the part of the heap reachable from that object. This object model is a labelled, directed graph. The nodes in the graph correspond to tokens; there is an edge between two tokens if one of the objects represented by the first token may contain a reference to an object represented by the second token. The label on the edge is the name of the field that may contain the reference.

By combining the object models from each of the object creation sites, the analysis can produce a single object model that characterizes, at the granularity of tokens, all of the referencing relationships in the entire heap. In some cases it is also desirable to summarize local variable referencing relationships in the object model. Our tool can therefore process the local variable declarations to insert an unlabelled edge between two tokens if a method of an object represented by the first token has a local variable that may refer to an object represented by the second token. Figure 2 presents the object model from our example; this object model contains the unlabelled edges from local variables. [2]

2.5   Subsystem Access Models

Our analysis processes the statements in each method in the context of the token variable binding information to extract a subsystem access model. This model characterizes how subsystems access objects at the granularity of tokens. Each subsystem access model is a bipartite graph. The nodes in the graph correspond to subsystems and tokens; there is an edge connecting a subsystem and a token if the subsystem may access objects represented by the token.

Figure 3 presents the subsystem access model from our example program. The square nodes represent subsystems; the ellipse nodes represent tokens. The edge between EP and PCS, for example, indicates that EP may access the stack used to pass values between the producer and consumer.

Note that this model is not designed to reflect object creation relationships. For example, the ED (example driver) subsystem creates the Stack object (represented by the token PCS), the Producer object (represented by the token P), and the Consumer object (represented by the token C). The subsystem interaction model is not intended to present these relationships—our analysis does have enough information to present this object creation information, but we believe it would be best presented in a separate model that deals only with object creation relationships. Note also that this model is not designed to present relationships

---

[2] We have implemented our type system, analysis, and model extraction algorithms. To ease the construction of the parser, it accepts a language whose surface syntactic details differ a bit from those in our example. For example, our implemented system encloses token parameters in *< and *> instead of < and >. We use the dot graph presentation system [13] to automatically produce graphical representations of our extracted models. All of the pictures in this paper were automatically produced using our implemented system.

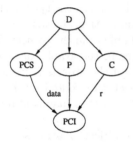

Fig. 2. Object Model

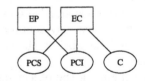

Fig. 3. Subsystem Access Model

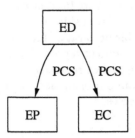

Fig. 4. Call/Return Interaction
Model

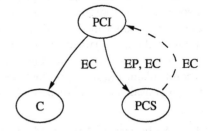

Fig. 5. Heap Interaction Model

involving primitive fields—the EP subsystem accesses the primitive field n in the
Producer object, but the model does not contain this information. Once again,
the analysis has the information required to present such relationships, but we
believe it would be better presented elsewhere.

2.6   Call/Return Interaction Models

Call/return interaction models characterize the control and data flow transfers
that take place when a method in one subsystem invokes a method in a different
subsystem. The model itself is a labelled, directed graph. The nodes correspond
to subsystems; there is a solid edge between two subsystems if a method in the
first subsystem may invoke a method in the second subsystem. There is a dashed
edge if the second method may return an object to the first subsystem. The labels
on the edges are the tokens that represent the objects passed as parameters or
returned as values.

We use the analysis results to extract the call/return interaction model as
follows. At each method call site, we retrieve the bindings that the analysis has
computed for each of the token variables in the types of the parameters. These
bindings identify the tokens that represent the objects passed as parameters
from the caller to the callee. We also extract the subsystems for the caller and
the callee.

If the callee is an entry method, the analysis generates a solid edge between
the two subsystems and labels the edge with the set of tokens that represent the

parameters. If the invoked method returns an object, it also generates a return edge, using the analysis results at the return statement(s) in the callee to extract the tokens on the label of the return edge. Figure 4 presents the call/return interaction model in our example.

Note that the call/return model treats a callback as just another method call in the program code. Like all other method calls, we draw the call and return edges in the call/return model for callbacks.

2.7   Heap Interaction Models

Heap interaction models capture the indirect interactions that take place via objects in the heap. The nodes in this model correspond to tokens. There is a solid edge between two tokens if a subsytem may write a reference to an object represented by the first token into an object represented by the second token; there is a dashed edge (in the opposite direction) if a subsystem may read that reference. The label on each edge is the subsystem that performed the write or the read.

We use the analysis results to compute the heap interaction model as follows. At each statement that reads or writes a reference from one object to another object, we retrieve the subsystems that may execute the statement, and, for each subsystem, the tokens that represent the two objects. There is an edge between each possible pair of tokens that represent the source and target objects. The label on each such edge is the corresponding retrieved subsystem.

Figure 5 presents the heap interaction model for our example. The solid lines indicate that the EP subsystem may write a PCI object into a PCS object and that the EC subsystem may write a PCI object into a C object. The dashed line indicates that the EC subsystem may read the PCI object back out of the PCS object.

Note that we have placed the PCS token on both the Stack object and the Node objects that implement the Stack's internal state, in effect collapsing all of the objects into a single abstraction in the heap interaction model (and other models as well). This is an example of how tokens allow the developer to hide irrelevant detail in the generated models.

2.8   Discussion

As this example illustrates, extracting and using pointer analysis information is relatively straightforward given the polymorphic token declarations. This information allows us to create a broad range of models that characterize the heap structure of the program, its information access behavior, and both the direct and the indirect information flow between its subsystems.

We note that our analysis has more information about the program than it presents in the extracted models. We have chosen our specific set of models based on our expectations of what developers would find most useful. We envision, however, a much richer interactive program exploration system that would allow developers to customize the models to include more or less detail depending on their current needs. To cite just one example, the developer could choose to display the name and method of each local variable that generated a given unlabelled edge in the object model. Such a system would give developers appropriate access to all of the information that the analysis extracts.

3   Analysis and Model Extraction

We next present the analysis and model extraction algorithms. The purpose of the analysis is to determine all of the possible token variable bindings for each method. The model extraction algorithms use the bindings to produce the models.

3.1   Preliminaries and Notation

The program defines a set of tokens $t \in T$, token variables $p, v \in V \cup T$, a set of methods $m \in M$, a set of subsystem identifiers $s \in S$, a set of classes $k \in K$, a set of call sites $c \in C$, and a set of object creation sites $o \in O$. Each class k has a set of object reference fields $f \in \text{fields}(k)$. Each call site c may invoke a set of methods $m \in \text{callees}(c)$; we compute the call graph information using a variant of class hierarchy analysis. Each call site c is contained in a method $\text{method}(c)$ and each object creation site o is contained in a method $\text{method}(o)$. If a method m is an entry method, then $\text{entry}(m)$ is its subsystem identifier s, otherwise $\text{entry}(m) = \text{same}$, where same is a special identifier indicating that each invocation of m is part of the same subsystem as its caller. The type of an object created at an object creation site o is $k \langle v_1, \ldots, v_l \rangle = \text{type}(o)$, where k is the class of the new object and $v_1, \ldots, v_l$ are the actual token parameters of the new object. Each local variable $lv \in LV$ has a type $k \langle v_1, \ldots, v_l \rangle = \text{type}(lv)$. Each class k has a set of formal token parameters $\langle p_1, \ldots, p_l \rangle = \text{parms}(k)$ and a set of object references $f\ k\langle v_1, \ldots, v_l \rangle$, where $k\langle v_1, \ldots, v_l \rangle$ is the type of the object which field f references.

The analysis produces bindings $b \in B = T \cup V \rightarrow T$; we require that $b(t) = t$ for all $t \in T$. The identity function on tokens is $\text{Id} = \lambda t.t$.

3.2   Analysis

The analysis propagates binding information from caller to callee to compute a set of calling contexts for each method. More specifically, for each method m, it produces a set of tuples $\langle s, b \rangle \in \text{contexts}(m)$. This set of tuples satisfies the following context soundness condition:[3]

---

[3] Note that constructors are treated just like any other method in this analysis.

If:

- c is a call site with $l + 1$ actual parameters[4] whose types are
  $$k_0 \langle v_1^0, \ldots, v_{n_0}^0 \rangle, \ldots, k_l \langle v_1^l, \ldots, v_{n_l}^l \rangle,$$
- c is inside a method $m_c = \mathsf{method}(c)$,
- $\langle s, b \rangle \in \mathsf{contexts}(m_c)$, $m \in \mathsf{callees}(c)$, and
- m has $l + 1$ formal parameters whose types are
  $$k_0 \langle p_1^0, \ldots, p_{n_0}^0 \rangle, \ldots, k_l \langle p_1^l, \ldots, p_{n_l}^l \rangle,$$

then $\langle s', [p_i^j \mapsto b(v_i^j).0 \leq j \leq l, 1 \leq i \leq n_j] \cup \mathsf{Id} \rangle \in \mathsf{contexts}(m)$, where $s' = s$ if $\mathsf{entry}(m) = \mathsf{same}$, otherwise $s' = \mathsf{entry}(m)$.

The analysis produces an analysis result that satisfies this condition by propagating token bindings in a top-down fashion from callers to callees starting with the main method. It initializes the analysis by setting $\mathsf{contexts}(\mathtt{main}) = \{\langle \mathtt{MAIN}, \mathsf{Id} \rangle\}$. It uses a fixed-point computation within strongly connected components of the call graph to ensure that the final result satisfies the context soundness condition. Note that this algorithm produces a completely context-sensitive solution in that it records each context separately in the analysis result. It is also possible to adjust the algorithm to merge contexts and produce a less context-sensitive result.

3.3 Object Model Extraction

Figure 6 presents the object model extraction algorithm. This algorithm produces a set of nodes $N \subseteq T$ and a set of labelled edges E of the form $\langle t_1, f, t_2 \rangle$; each such edge indicates that the field f in an object represented by token t_1 may contain a reference to an object represented by token t_2. The algorithm processes all of the object creation sites o in the program; for each site, it uses the token variable bindings produced by the analysis to determine the potential token instantiations for objects created at that site. It then uses the bindings to trace out the part of the heap reachable from objects created at that site. The visit algorithm uses a set V of visited class/binding pairs to ensure that it terminates in the presence of recursive data structures.

Note that this algorithm produces only the labelled edges for the heap references. Our implemented algorithm also processes the local variable declarations to add the unlabelled edges that summarize potential referencing relationships associated with the local variables in each class.

3.4 Subsystem Access Model Extraction

Figure 7 presents the subsystem access model extraction algorithm. It produces a set of nodes $N \subseteq S \cup T$ and a set of edges E of the form $\langle s, t \rangle$; each such edge indicates that the subsystem s may access an object represented by token t. The

---

[4] By convention, the receiver is parameter 0.

```
set N = ∅, E = ∅, V = ∅                    visit(k, b)
for all object creation sites o ∈ O           if ⟨k, b⟩ ∉ V then
    let m = method(o)                             let ⟨v₁, . . . , vₗ⟩ = parms(k)
    let k⟨v₁, . . . , vₗ⟩ = type(o)               set N = N ∪ {b(v₁)}
    let ⟨p₁, . . . , pₗ⟩ = parms(k)               set V = V ∪ {⟨k, b⟩}
    for all ⟨s, b⟩ ∈ contexts(m)                  for all f k′⟨v′₁, . . . v′ⱼ⟩ ∈ refs(k)
        visit(k, [pᵢ ↦ b(vᵢ).1 ≤ i ≤ l] ∪ Id)        set E = E ∪ {⟨b(v₁), f, b(v′₁)⟩}
                                                      let ⟨p₁, . . . , pⱼ⟩ = parms(k′)
                                                      visit(k′, [pᵢ ↦ b(v′ᵢ).1 ≤ i ≤ j] ∪ Id)
```

Fig. 6. Object Model Extraction Algorithm

algorithm processes all of the accesses in the program, retrieving the binding information produced by the analysis to determine 1) the subsystems that can execute the access and 2) the tokens that represent the accessed objects. Note that, as described earlier in Section 2, this model is not designed to capture accesses to primitive fields.

3.5   Call/Return Interaction Model Extraction

Figure 8 presents the call/return model extraction algorithm. It produces a set of nodes $N \subseteq S$ and a set of edges E of the form $\langle s_1, t, s_2 \rangle$. The algorithm processes all of the call sites in the program, retrieving the binding information produced by the analysis to determine 1) if the call site may invoke an entry method of a different subsystem, and 2) if so, the tokens that represent the objects passed as parameters between the subsystems. Note that there is an edge for each such token. To eliminate visual clutter, our model display algorithm coalesces all edges between the same two subsystems, producing a single edge with a list of the tokens passed as parameters between the subsystems.

The algorithm in Figure 8 does not generate the return edges. Our implemented algorithm generates these edges by similarly processing the return statements of entry methods.

```
set N = ∅, E = ∅
for each method m
    for each access lv.f in m
        let k ⟨v₁, . . . , vₗ⟩ = type(lv)
        for each ⟨s, b⟩ ∈ contexts(m)
            set N = N ∪ {s, b(v₁)}
            set E = E ∪ {⟨s, b(v₁)⟩}
```

Fig. 7. Subsystem Access Model Extraction Algorithm

```
set N = ∅, E = ∅
for each call site c
  for each ⟨s, b⟩ ∈ contexts(method(c))
    for each m ∈ callees(c)
      let s' = entry(m)
      if s' ≠ same and s' ≠ s then
        set N = N ∪ {s, s'}
        let k₀ ⟨v₁⁰,...,vₙ₀⁰⟩,..., kₗ ⟨v₁ˡ,...,vₙₗˡ⟩ be the types
          of the actual parameters at the call site c
        set E = E ∪ {⟨s, b(v₁ⁱ), s'⟩.1 ≤ i ≤ l}
```

Fig. 8. Call/Return Model Extraction Algorithm

3.6 Heap Interaction Model Extraction

The heap interaction model extraction algorithm produces a set of nodes $N \subseteq T$ and two sets of edges. The write edges $W \subseteq T \times S \times T$ summarize the write interactions; an edge $\langle t_1, s, t_2 \rangle \in W$ indicates that the subsytem s may write a reference to an object represented by token t_1 into an object represented by token t_2. The read edges $R \subseteq T \times S \times T$ summarize the read interactions; an edge $\langle t_1, s, t_2 \rangle \in R$ indicates that the subsytem s may read a reference to an object represented by token t_2 from an object represented by token t_1.

Figure 9 presents the algorithm that extracts the write interactions W. The algorithm processes all of the write accesses in the program, retrieving the binding information produced by the analysis to determine 1) the subsystems that may perform the write and 2) the tokens that represent the accessed objects. The algorithm that extracts the read interactions is similar. The set of nodes N is initialized to $\emptyset$ before the read and write interaction algorithms execute.

```
set W = ∅
for each method m
  for each write access lv₁.f = lv₂ in m
    let k¹ ⟨v₁¹,...,vₗ₁¹⟩ = type(lv₁)
    let k₂ ⟨v₁²,...,vₗ₂²⟩ = type(lv₂)
    for each ⟨s, b⟩ ∈ contexts(m)
      if (b(v₁¹) ≠ b(v₁²)) then
        set N = N ∪ {b(v₁¹), b(v₁²)}
        set W = W ∪ {⟨b(v₁¹), s, b(v₁¹)⟩}
```

Fig. 9. Heap Interaction Model Extraction Algorithm

4   Type System

We next present a formal treatment of the type system. The type system is used to check token consistency constraints. Its primary purpose is to verify that the token declarations match at assignment and method invocation statements. These checks help ensure that our models are sound; in particular, they ensure that the type declarations in object fields correctly reflect the structure of the heap. We realize our type system as a set of typing rules for a simplified core language, whose grammar is in Figure 10. To simplify the presentation, we omit subsystems from the formal treatment.

Figure 12 presents the static type rules that define the type checker; their meaning is explained in Figure 11. Formally, a program consists of a sequence of class definitions, containing method, field and token definitions, as well as token definitions (see Rule [PROG] in Figure 12). The goal is to derive the type judgement $\vdash P$, indicating that the program satisfies the static type constraints.

The type system checks each method in turn by using the type declarations of its class in conjunction with the method parameter definitions to construct an initial typing environment for the method (see Rule [METH]). The type

$$
\begin{aligned}
P &::= \textit{token}^* \; \textit{defn}^* \\
\textit{defn} &::= \textbf{class} \; \textit{cn}\langle t^* \rangle \; \{\textit{field}^* \textit{meth}^*\} \\
\textit{field} &::= \tau \; \textit{fd} \\
\tau &::= \textit{cn}\langle t^+ \rangle \mid \texttt{Object}\langle t \rangle \\
\textit{meth} &::= \textit{pn}\langle t^* \rangle (\textit{arg}^*) \; \{\textit{local}^* \; s^*\} \\
\textit{token} &::= \textit{tn} \\
t &::= \textsf{formal} \mid \textit{tn} \\
\textit{arg} &::= \tau \; x \\
\textit{local} &::= \tau \; y \\
s &::= x = e \mid x.\textit{fd} = y \mid x = \textbf{new} \; c\langle t^+ \rangle \mid \\
&\quad\; e.\textit{pn}\langle t^* \rangle (e^*) \mid \\
&\quad\; l : \; \mid \textbf{goto} \; l \mid \textbf{if} \; \textit{cond} \; \textbf{then} \; l \; \textbf{else} \; l \\
e &::= y \mid y.\textit{fd} \\
\textit{cond} &::= e\texttt{==}e \mid e\texttt{!=}e
\end{aligned}
$$

formal $\in$ formal token names
$cn \in$ class names
$fd \in$ field names
$mn \in$ method names
$tn \in$ token names
$x, y \in$ variable names
$l \in$ statement labels

Fig. 10. Grammar for core language

Judgement	Meaning
$\vdash P$	program P is well-typed
$P \vdash$ *token*	*token* is a well-formed token
$P \vdash$ *defn*	*defn* is a well-formed class definition
$P;E \vdash$ *meth*	*meth* is a well-formed method
$P;E \vdash$ *field*	*field* is a well-formed field
$P \vdash$ *field* $\in cn\langle f_{1..n}\rangle$	class cn with formal parameters $f_{1..n}$ declares field *field*
$P;E \vdash$ *wf*	E is a well-formed typing environment
$P;E \vdash_{\text{token}} t$	t is a token defined in the program or the environment
$P;E \vdash \tau$	τ is a well-formed type
$P;E \vdash e{:}\tau$	expression e has type τ
$P;E \vdash$ *cond*	condition *cond* is well-typed
$P;E \vdash s$	statement s is well-typed

Fig. 11. Meaning of Judgements in Type System

system then checks each statement of the method in turn (Rules [STMT NEW] through [STMT INVOKE]). For each statement, it attempts to derive a typing judgement of the form $P; E \vdash s$, which indicates that the statement type-checks in the context of the program P and the typing environment E. The typing environment E binds variables to types and provides the list of formal token variables. The Rule [STMT INVOKE] ensures that a method call may only occur when the necessary conditions hold.

5   Experience

We have implemented a prototype version of our system by extending the Kopi Java compiler.[5] We tested our approach on Tagger, a text formatting system written by Daniel Jackson. Tagger consists of 1721 lines of Java code and 14 classes (not counting the standard Java libraries). It accepts a text file augmented with formatting commands as input and produces as output another text file in the Quark document definition language.

We first augmented Tagger with subsystem and token annotations. This augmentation increased the number of lines of code to 1755. We added token and/or subsystem annotations to a total of 201 lines of code. There was no perceptible compile-time overhead associated with analyzing the annotated code and producing models. Our system does not incur any run-time overhead because we exclusively use static techniques.

5.1   Subsystems of Tagger

We first discuss the subsystems we added to Tagger. Our augmented version has the following subsystems, with one subsystem entry point class per subsystem:

---

[5] Available at http://www.dms.at/kopi/.

$\boxed{\vdash P}$

[PROG]

$$\frac{\begin{array}{c} ClassesOnce(P) \quad FieldsOnce(P) \\ MethodsOnce(P) \quad TokensOnce(P) \quad JumpsLocal(P) \\ P = token_{1..m}\, defn_{1..n} \quad P \vdash token_i \quad P \vdash defn_i \end{array}}{\vdash P}$$

$\boxed{P \vdash defn}$

[CLASS]

$$\frac{g_i = \mathsf{token}f_i \quad E = g_{1..n} \\ P;E \vdash field_i \quad P;E \vdash meth_i}{P \vdash \mathsf{class}\ cn\langle f_{1..n}\rangle\ \{field_{1..j}\ \ meth_{1..m}\}}$$

$\boxed{P;E \vdash meth}$

[METH]

$$\frac{\begin{array}{c} P \vdash \mathsf{class}\ c\langle f_{1..n}\rangle\ \{\cdots meth_{mn}\cdots\} \\ arg_i = cn_i\langle f_{i_1..i_{m_i}}\rangle vn_i \quad local_j = cn_j\langle f_{j_1..j_{m_j}}\rangle ln_j \\ E = E_0, arg_{1..n}, local_{n+1..n+l} \quad \forall i \in [1..t].\ P;E \vdash s_i \\ \forall n,k.\ (\exists m.\ f_{n_k} = f_m \vee P \vdash_{\mathsf{token}} f_{n_k}) \quad P;E_0 \vdash wf \end{array}}{P;E \vdash mn\langle f_{1..r}\rangle(arg_{1..n})\ \{local_{n+1..n+l}\ s_{1..t}\}}$$

$\boxed{P;E \vdash wf}$

[ENV ∅]

$$\frac{}{P;\emptyset \vdash wf}$$

[ENV TOKEN FORMAL]

$$\frac{P;E \vdash wf \quad tn \notin Dom(E)}{P;E, \mathsf{token}\ tn \vdash wf}$$

$\boxed{P;E \vdash field}$ $\boxed{P;E \vdash field \in c}$ $\boxed{P \vdash token}$

[ENV X]

$$\frac{P;E \vdash \tau \quad x \notin Dom(E)}{P;E, \tau\ x \vdash wf}$$

[FIELD INIT]

$$\frac{P;E \vdash \tau}{P;E \vdash \tau\ fd}$$

[FIELD DECLARED]

$$\frac{P;E \vdash \mathsf{class}\ c\langle f_{1..n}\rangle\ \{\cdots fd\cdots\} \\ P;E \vdash \tau\ fd}{P;E \vdash fd \in c\langle f_{1..n}\rangle}$$

[TOKEN]

$$\frac{}{P \vdash \mathsf{token}\ tn}$$

$\boxed{P;E \vdash_{\mathsf{token}} t}$ $\boxed{P;E \vdash \tau}$

[TOKEN GB'L REF]

$$\frac{P = \cdots \mathsf{token}\ t \cdots}{P;E \vdash_{\mathsf{token}} t}$$

[TOKEN FORMAL]

$$\frac{E = E_1, \mathsf{token}\ t, E_2 \\ P;E \vdash wf}{P;E \vdash_{\mathsf{token}} t}$$

[TYPE OBJECT]

$$\frac{P;E \vdash_{\mathsf{token}} t}{P;E \vdash \mathsf{Object}\langle t\rangle}$$

[TYPE C]

$$\frac{P \vdash \mathsf{class}\ cn\langle f_{1..n}\rangle \cdots \\ P \vdash_{\mathsf{token}} t_{1..n}}{P;E \vdash cn\langle t_{1..n}\rangle}$$

$\boxed{P;E \vdash cond}$ $\boxed{P;E \vdash e{:}\tau}$

[COND EQ]

$$\frac{P;E \vdash e_1 \\ P;E \vdash e_2}{P;E \vdash e_1{==}e_2}$$

[COND NEQ]

$$\frac{P;E \vdash e_1 \\ P;E \vdash e_2}{P;E \vdash e_1{!=}e_2}$$

[EXP VAR READ]

$$\frac{E = E_1, \tau\ y, E_2 \\ \tau = c\langle t_{1..n}\rangle}{P;E \vdash y{:}\tau}$$

[EXP FIELD READ]

$$\frac{\begin{array}{c} E = E_1, \tau_y\ y, E_2 \quad \tau_y = c_y\langle t^y_{1..m}\rangle \\ \tau_f = c_f\langle t^f_{1..n}\rangle \quad P \vdash (\tau_f\ fd) \in \tau_y \\ P;E \vdash_{\mathsf{token}} t^y_j \quad P;E \vdash_{\mathsf{token}} t^f_1 \end{array}}{P;E \vdash y.fd{:}\tau_f[t^f_1/t^y_{f(1)}]\cdots[t^f_m/t^y_{f(m)}]}$$

$\boxed{P;E \vdash s}$

[STMT NEW]

$$\frac{E = E_1, \tau\ x, E_2 \quad \tau = c\langle t_{1..n}\rangle \\ P;E \vdash c\langle f_{1..n}\rangle}{P;E \vdash x = \mathsf{new}\ c\langle t_{1..n}\rangle}$$

[STMT READ/COPY]

$$\frac{E = E_1, \tau\ x, E_2 \\ P;E \vdash e{:}\tau}{P;E \vdash x = e}$$

[STMT LABEL]

$$\frac{P;E \vdash wf}{P;E \vdash \ell{:}}$$

[STMT GOTO]

$$\frac{P;E \vdash wf}{P;E \vdash \mathsf{goto}\ \ell}$$

[STMT IF]

$$\frac{P;E \vdash \ell_1{:}\quad P;E \vdash \ell_2{:} \\ P;E \vdash cond}{P;E \vdash \mathsf{if}cond\ \mathsf{then}\ \ell_1\mathsf{else}\ \ell_2}$$

[STMT WRITE]

$$\frac{\begin{array}{c} E = E_1, \tau_x\ x, E_2 \quad E = E'_1, \tau_y\ y, E'_2 \\ \tau_x = c_x\langle t^x_{1..n}\rangle \quad \tau_y = c_y\langle t^y_{1..m}\rangle \\ P;E \vdash_{\mathsf{token}} t^x_1 \quad P;E \vdash_{\mathsf{token}} t^y_1 \\ P;E \vdash (\tau_y\ fd) \in \tau_x \end{array}}{P;E \vdash x.fd = y}$$

[STMT INVOKE]

$$\frac{\begin{array}{c} P;E \vdash mn\langle f_{1..r}\rangle(\tau_j\ y_j)_{j\in 1..n}\{\cdots\} \\ P;E \vdash_{\mathsf{token}} a_i \quad \tau_j = cn_j\langle f_{j_1..j_{m_j}}\rangle \quad \tau'_j = \tau_j[a_i/f_i] \quad a_{j_1} = f_{j_1}[a_i/f_i] \quad P;E \vdash_{\mathsf{token}} a_{j_1} \\ P;E \vdash e'_j{:}\tau'_j \quad P;E \vdash a_0{:}\tau_0 \quad \tau_0 = cn\langle f_{1..m_0}\rangle \quad meth_{mn} \in cn \end{array}}{P;E \vdash a_0.mn\langle a_{1..r}\rangle(e'_{1..n})}$$

Fig. 12. Type Rules

- **ParsS:** The parser subsystem, which contains code to read the input file, group characters into words, and recognize formatting commands.
- **PMapS:** The property management subsystem, which manages the data structures that control the translation between each Tagger formatting command and the corresponding Quark output.
- **ActS:** The action subsystem, which uses the property management subsystem to translate Tagger commands into Quark commands, then passes the output to the generation subsystem.
- **GenS:** The generation subsystem, which produces the output Quark document. This subsystem manages the translation of the Quark commands into a flat stream of output symbols. It is responsible for generating the surface syntax of the Quark document and producing the output file.
- **EngS:** The engine subsystem, which processes the Tagger commands and serially dispatches each command to the Act subsystem.
- **MainS:** The main subsystem, which initializes the system and implements the connection between the Pars subsystem, which reads the input file, and the Act subsystem, which processes the text and Tagger commands in the file.

Of the original 14 classes, six are subsystem entry point classes in the annotated version. Two more are abstract superclasses of subsystem entry point classes. Another two are used to transfer data between the Pars, Eng, Act, and Gen subsystems; their methods simply store and retrieve the transferred data. Another class reads in the configuration data that governs the translation from Tagger to Quark formatting commands; this class is encapsulated within the PMap subsystem. Another two store updatable processing state relating to the output document, for example the current position in an itemized list of paragraphs. These classes are encapsulated inside the Eng subsystem. The remaining class manages assertions.

In Figure 13, we present the call/return interaction model for Tagger. We can observe that the **GenS** subsystem is invoked by the **ActS**, **EngS** and **MainS** subsystems; our analysis guarantees that **GenS** is only called by these three subsystems. Note also that there is no edge between **PMapS** and **GenS**: the generator does not invoke the property management subsystem. In addition to the invocation relationships, this diagram presents the tokens that represent the objects that carry data between subsystems.

5.2   Tokens of Tagger

To present the other models, we need to discuss the token structure of Tagger. We have augmented Tagger with 16 tokens, some of which represent system classes, such as **EStrm**, the standard error output stream. The tokens are:

- **Gen, Eng, Pars:** These tokens represent objects that are required by the generator, engine, and parser, respectively.
- **NumStr, Ctr:** These tokens represent objects containing state for list counters used in the Tagger source.

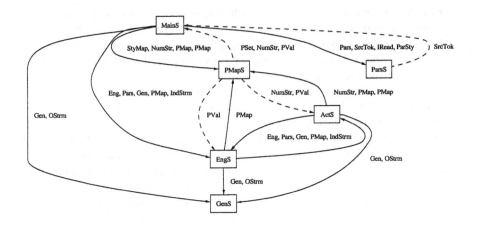

Fig. 13. Call/return model for Tagger

- **SrcTok:** This token represents objects containing the input characters read by the parser, and passed to the engine.
- **PMap, PList, PName, PVal:** These tokens are owned by the property management subsystem **PMapS**, and represent objects containing text properties and maps thereof.
- **StyMap, ParSty:** These tokens represent objects containing particular property maps, used for storing character and paragraph style information.
- **IRead:** This token represents the input stream object, from which Tagger reads its input data.
- **EStrm, OStrm:** These tokens represent the system output and error output stream objects.

In Figure 14 we show the object model for Tagger. This model illustrates the reachability relations in the heap, and records what state is held by which tokens. Note that a **Gen** object refers only to an **OStrm** object, which holds the output stream.

5.3   Combining Subsystems and Tokens

Our analysis makes both subsystem and token information available. We can combine this information to give the subsystem access and heap interaction models.

The subsystem access model is illustrated in Figure 15. We can observe, for instance, that the **EngS**, **ActS** and **ParsS** subsystems all use **SrcTok** tokens. This strongly suggests that they might use heap objects with **SrcTok** tokens to indirectly communicate between themselves: we expect that the parser subsystem must somehow share information with the action subsystem, and there are no direct interactions in the call/return model. In Figure 16 we present the heap interaction model for Tagger.

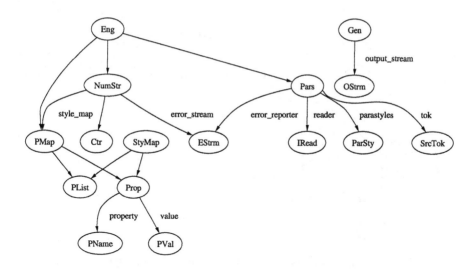

Fig. 14. Object model for Tagger

6 Related Work

We discuss related work in the areas of software model extraction, pointer analysis, and ownership types. We also briefly compare the models we extract with the models present in the Unified Modelling Language.

6.1 Modeling Extraction

Software models play a key role in most software development processes [28, 12]. Modeling is usually carried out during the design phase as a way of exploring and specifying the design. The design is then usually implemented by hand, opening up the possibility of inconsistencies between the design and the implementation. The software engineering community has long recognized the need for tools to help ensure that the software conforms to its design [17]. Automatic model extraction is a particularly appealing alternative, because it holds out the promise of delivering models that are guaranteed to correctly reflect the structure of the implementation.

There are tools currently on the market which can both automatically extract UML models from code and generate skeletal code from UML models, e.g. TogetherJ by TogetherSoft and Rational Rose. These tools use heuristics to extract (possibly unsound) UML design information from the source code. There is also a Java Specification Request underway[4] which would extend Java to permit developers to embed arbitrary metadata into their code, including for instance UML design information. While this embedding may facilitate the process of manually updating the design information to match the implementation, there is still no guaranteed connection.

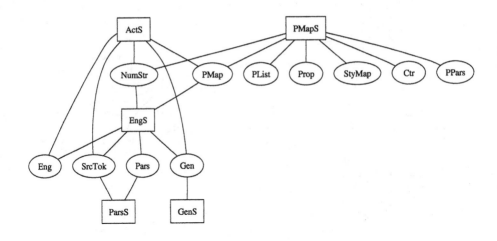

Fig. 15. Subsystem Access Model for Tagger

Control-Flow Interactions Most previous model extraction systems have focused on control-flow interactions. The software reflexion system [21], for example, automatically extracts an abstraction of the call graph and enables the developer to compare this abstraction with a high-level module dependency diagram.
Like our system, ArchJava [1] enables the extraction of software architecture
information embedded directly into program code. Its approach augments Java
with the software architecture concepts of components, connections, and ports;
ArchJava then enforces the constraint that all inter-component control transfers
must take place through ports (ensuring communication integrity). This enables
the automatic extraction of communication diagrams similar to our call/return
interaction models. Note in particular that ArchJava summarizes only control-
flow interactions; it does not handle heap-mediated interaction between compo-

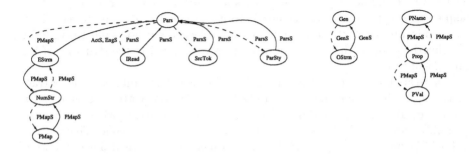

Fig. 16. Heap Interaction Model for Tagger

nents; our system, on the other hand, was designed to capture the structure of heap-mediated interaction between subsystems.

Our use of polymorphic token types and the associated analysis enables us to capture a wider range of design issues; specifically structural issues associated with referencing relationships between objects in the heap and information flow issues associated with method invocations. Most importantly, we also capture indirect information flow between subsystems that takes place via objects in the heap. To the best of our knowledge, all previous systems do not attempt to perform the analysis that would enable them to capture these kinds of dependences. This raises the possibility that the extracted models fail to accurately capture all important interactions.

Object Model Extraction Standard approaches for extracting object models from code treat each class as a unit. In type-safe languages, it is even possible to extract a (relatively crude) object model directly from the type declarations of the fields in the objects. Problems with this approach include conflation of different instances of general-purpose classes and overly detailed object models because of a failure to abstract internal data structures. Womble [18] attacks the latter failure by treating collection classes separately as relations between objects. Womble is also unsound in that the extracted model may fail to accurately characterize the referencing relationships. In contrast, our extracted object models are sound and avoid both conflation of instances of general-purpose classes and excessive detail associated with failing to abstract internal data structures.

6.2   Comparison with UML

We next compare our extracted models to UML models. A primary difference underlying the two approaches is that UML was designed solely as a design abstraction with (at least in principle) no formally precise connection with the code that implements the design. One of the primary goals of our approach, on the other hand, is to establish such a connection and to ensure that our extracted models are sound (i.e., correctly reflect all potential implementation behaviors). We view this connection as necessary to ensure that the models remain consistent with the implementation and therefore a useful source of information about the design. We have found that realizing such a connection caused our models to differ, in some cases substantially, from standard UML models.

Class Diagrams and Object Models UML class diagrams are designed, in part, to characterize relationships between objects in the heap. The standard interpretation of a UML object model is that each box represents a class and each arrow represents a relationship between instances of the involved classes. Our object models also capture this kind of structural information. But each box corresponds to a token, not a class, and the arrows represent relationships derived from object referencing relationships in the heap.

We found that the lack of a connection between the design and code can actually help the designer to deliver a clear, effective design — the designer has great flexibility to adjust the design to present the most important and relevant aspects of the envisioned implementation. In particular, UML allows designers to elide instances of auxiliary classes such as the list nodes in a collection. It also allows designers to draw two distinct boxes that correspond to the same class in the implementation — a clear case of the designer using multiple design elements that correspond to a single code element. We designed tokens, in part, to enable the designer to adjust the granularity of the extracted design in similar ways.

UML also allows the developer to present arbitrary relationships that may be implemented in a variety of ways. All of the relationships in our models, on the other hand, are derived from referencing relationships in the implemented data structures. While we support derived relationships that are implemented by multiple fields working together and enable the developer to hide irrelevant referencing relationships, our models do not capture relationships that do not have a concrete realization as references in the heap. As this discussion illustrates, we believe that any guaranteed connection will inevitably reduce the flexibility of expressing the design because of the constraints imposed by the enforcing the connection.

Interaction Diagrams and Call/Return Models UML interaction diagrams (sequence and collaboration diagrams) typically summarize the control-flow interactions which occur in one specific or several related executions of a program (a use case). Our call/return models also summarize these kinds of interactions, but because they are sound, they capture all potential interactions that may happen in *any* execution, not just the execution that corresponds to a given use case.

We note that this distinction reflects the different contexts in which UML and our system were developed. UML diagrams are primarily intended to be produced by designers. It is much easier and more productive for the designer to produce partial diagrams that capture important scenarios rather than tediously listing all possible interactions. An automated tool, however, has no problem enumerating all possible interactions. It is, of course, possible to eliminate any clutter by hiding interactions that may be considered irrelevant.

State Diagrams UML state diagrams capture the conceptual state transitions that objects take during their lifetimes in the computation. In our system, the state of an object can be represented by the token on the object and changed when there is a change in the object state. Currently, we support token changes only for objects which have at most one heap reference; in this case, the holder of the reference can change the token on the object. Because of problems associated with ensuring the soundness of such token changes in the presence of aliasing, we do not currently support token changes for objects that may have multiple references. Once we extend our system using roles [19] to allow controlled aliasing of objects, we will be able to generate transition diagrams for arbitrary objects as their tokens (and therefore their conceptual states) change throughout the computation. This discussion highlights another complication which arises because of our goal of establishing a sound connection between the design and the implementation.

Indirect Interaction Models We view our indirect interaction models as providing a substatial benefit missing in UML: they summarize the indirect interactions that may take place via objects allocated in the heap. We decided to support indirect interaction models both because of the importance of these kinds of interactions in many programs, and for completeness: we wished to allow developers to reason about the independence of different subsystems. Specifically, our goal was to ensure that if none of our models indicated a potential interaction between two subsystems, one subsystem could not affect the other subsystem.[6] We believe that UML would benefit from the introduction of a model that captured indirect heap interactions.

6.3   Pointer Analysis

Pointer analysis has been an active area of research for well over 15 years. Approaches range from efficient flow- and context-insensitive approaches [3, 27, 26, 23, 15, 11, 16] to potentially more precise but less efficient flow- and context-sensitive approaches [24, 29, 14, 8, 20, 25]. These approaches vary in whether they create a result for each program point (flow-sensitive analyses) or one result for the entire program (flow-insensitive analyses). They also vary in whether they produce a result for each calling context (context-sensitive analyses) or one result that is valid for all calling contexts (context-insensitive analyses). There are also flow-insensitive but context-sensitive analyses that produce a single parameterized result for each procedure that can be specialized for each different calling context [22].

From our perspective, a primary difference between existing pointer analysis algorithms and our approach is the flexibility our approach offers in selecting object representatives. Specifically, our polymorphic type system enables the developer to separate objects allocated at the same object creation site in the generated model. We believe this separation is crucial to delivering models that accurately reflect the conceptual purposes of the different objects in the computation. Of course, obtaining this additional precision requires the developer to provide the polymorphic type declarations.

Another difference is that because the type declarations in our programs characterize the points-to relations in the reachable region of the heap, there is no need to analyze the individual store and load instructions to synthesize a points-to graph. Instead, the analysis can simply propagate tokens to substitute token

---

[6] With the possible exception of timing channels.

variables out of the polymorphic types. The analysis needs to process the load and store instructions only to generate the heap interaction graph.

Our approach is quite flexible in the degree of context-sensitivity that it provides. It is possible to tune the analysis to produce a separate result for each combination of token variable and subsystem values, a result that separates subsystems but combines information within a single subsystem, or a single result for each method. Our implementation currently produces a separate result for each distinct instantiation of token variable and subsystem values.

6.4   Ownership Types

Ownership type systems are designed to enforce object encapsulation properties [10, 7, 6, 9, 2]. In this capacity, they can be used to ensure that objects from one instance of an abstraction are not used to inappropriately communicate with other instances of the same abstraction [5, 2]. For example, one might use ownership types in a multithreaded web server to ensure that the sockets associated with one server thread do not escape to be used by another server thread.

Our system focuses on extracting communication patterns. Encapsulation violations in our system therefore show up as unexpected communication. We would attack the problem of verifying encapsulation properties by enabling the developer to state desired properties, then checking the appropriate extracted model to verify that the program did not violate these properties.

7   Conclusion

The software engineering community has long recognized the need for tools to help ensure that the software conforms to its design. Our implemented system, with its polymorphic type system, analysis, and automatic model extractors, takes an important step towards this goal of verified design. Our models capture important information about the program; because they are automatically generated, they are guaranteed to accurately reflect the program's structure and behavior. The sound heap aliasing information provided by our combined type system and analysis enables the extraction of both structural object referencing models and behavioral models that characterize not only direct interactions that take place at method and procedure calls, but also indirect interactions mediated by objects in the heap.

We believe our approach holds out the promise of integrating the design effectively into the entire lifecycle of the software. Today, in contrast, design models tend to become increasingly less reliable (and therefore less relevant) as development proceeds into the implementation and maintenance phases. The potential result would be a more powerful and pervasive notion of design, leading to more reliable systems and more economical development.

Acknowledgements

The authors would like to thank Derek Rayside for much useful feedback on the paper.

References

[1] J. Aldrich, C. Chambers, and D. Notkin. Archjava: Connecting software architecture to implementation. In *24th International Conference on Software Engineering*, Orlando, FL, May 2002.

[2] J. Aldrich, V. Kostadinov, and C. Chambers. Alias annotations for program understanding. In *Proceedings of the 17th Annual Conference on Object-Oriented Programming Systems, Languages and Applications*, Seattle, WA, Nov. 2002.

[3] L. O. Andersen. *Program Analysis and Specialization for the C Programming Language*. PhD thesis, DIKU, University of Copenhagen, May 1994.

[4] J. Bloch et al. JSR175: A metadata facility for the Java™ programming language, Apr 2002.

[5] B. Bokowski and J. Vitek. Confined types. In *Proceedings of the 14th Annual Conference on Object-Oriented Programming Systems, Languages and Applications*, Denver, CO, Nov. 1999.

[6] C. Boyapati, R. Lee, and M. Rinard. Ownership types for safe programming: Preventing data races and deadlocks. In *Proceedings of the 17th Annual Conference on Object-Oriented Programming Systems, Languages and Applications*, Seattle, WA, Nov. 2002.

[7] C. Boyapati and M. Rinard. A parameterized type system for race-free Java programs. In *Proceedings of the 16th Annual Conference on Object-Oriented Programming Systems, Languages and Applications*, Tampa Bay, Florida, Oct. 2001.

[8] J. Choi, M. Burke, and P. Carini. Efficient flow-sensitive interprocedural computation of pointer-induced aliases and side effects. In *Conference Record of the Twentieth Annual Symposium on Principles of Programming Languages*, Charleston, SC, Jan. 1993. ACM.

[9] D. Clarke and S. Drossopoulou. Ownership, encapsulation and disjointness of type and effect. In *Proceedings of the 17th Annual Conference on Object-Oriented Programming Systems, Languages and Applications*, Seattle, WA, Nov. 2002.

[10] D. Clarke, J. Potter, and J. Noble. Ownership types for flexible alias protection. In *Proceedings of the 13th Annual Conference on Object-Oriented Programming Systems, Languages and Applications*, Vancouver, Canada, Oct. 1998.

[11] M. Das. Unification-based pointer analysis with directional assignments. In *Proceedings of the SIGPLAN '00 Conference on Program Language Design and Implementation*, Vancouver, Canada, June 2000.

[12] D. D'Souza and A. Wills. *Objects, Components, and Frameworks with UML: the catalysis approach*. Addison-Wesley, Reading, Mass., 1998.

[13] J. Ellson, E. Ganser, E. Koutsofios, and S. North. Graphviz. Available from http://www.research.att.com/sw/tools/graphviz.

[14] M. Emami, R. Ghiya, and L. Hendren. Context-sensitive interprocedural points-to analysis in the presence of function pointers. In *Proceedings of the SIGPLAN '94 Conference on Program Language Design and Implementation*, pages 242–256, Orlando, FL, June 1994. ACM, New York.

[15] M. Fahndrich, J. Foster, Z. Su, and A. Aiken. Partial online cycle elimination in inclusion constraint graphs. In *Proceedings of the SIGPLAN '98 Conference on Program Language Design and Implementation*, Montreal, Canada, June 1998.

[16] N. Heintze and O. Tardieu. Ultra-fast aliasing using CLA: A million lines of code in a second. In *Proceedings of the SIGPLAN '01 Conference on Program Language Design and Implementation*, Snowbird, UT, June 2001.

[17] D. Jackson and M. Rinard. The future of software analysis. In A. Finkelstein, editor, *The Future of Software Engineering*. ACM, New York, June 2000.

[18] D. Jackson and A. Waingold. Lightweight extraction of object models from byte-code. In *21st International Conference on Software Engineering*, Los Angeles, CA, May 1999.

[19] V. Kuncak, P. Lam, and M. Rinard. Role analysis. In *Proceedings of the 29th Annual ACM Symposium on the Principles of Programming Languages*, Portland, OR, Jan. 2002.

[20] W. Landi and B. Ryder. A safe approximation algorithm for interprocedural pointer aliasing. In *Proceedings of the SIGPLAN '92 Conference on Program Language Design and Implementation*, San Francisco, CA, June 1992.

[21] G. Murphy, D. Notkin, and K. Sullivan. Software reflexion models: Bridging the gap between source and high-level models. In *Proceedings of the ACM SIGSOFT 95 Symposium on the Foundations of Software Engineering*, Washington, DC, Oct. 1995.

[22] R. O'Callahan. *Generalized Aliasing as a Basis for Program Analysis Tools*. PhD thesis, School of Computer Science, Carnegie Mellon Univ., Pittsburgh, PA, Nov. 2000.

[23] R. O'Callahan and D. Jackson. Lackwit: A program understanding tool based on type inference. In *1997 International Conference on Software Engineering*, Boston, MA, May 1997.

[24] E. Ruf. Context-insensitive alias analysis reconsidered. In *Proceedings of the SIGPLAN '95 Conference on Program Language Design and Implementation*, La Jolla, CA, June 1995.

[25] A. Salcianu and M. Rinard. Pointer and escape analysis for multithreaded programs. In *Proceedings of the 8th ACM SIGPLAN Symposium on Principles and Practice of Parallel Programming*, Snowbird, UT, June 2001.

[26] M. Shapiro and S. Horwitz. Fast and accurate flow-insensitive points-to analysis. In *Proceedings of the 24th Annual ACM Symposium on the Principles of Programming Languages*, Paris, France, Jan. 1997.

[27] B. Steensgaard. Points-to analysis in almost linear time. In *Proceedings of the 23rd Annual ACM Symposium on the Principles of Programming Languages*, St. Petersburg Beach, FL, Jan. 1996.

[28] J. Warmer and A. Kieppe. *The Object Constraint Language: Precise Modeling with UML*. Addison-Wesley, Reading, Mass., Redwood City, CA, 1998.

[29] R. Wilson and M. Lam. Efficient context-sensitive pointer analysis for C programs. In *Proceedings of the SIGPLAN '95 Conference on Program Language Design and Implementation*, La Jolla, CA, June 1995. ACM, New York.

Higher-Order Hierarchies

Erik Ernst

Dept. of Computer Science, University of Aarhus, Denmark

Abstract. This paper introduces the notion of higher-order inheritance hierarchies. They are useful because they provide well-known benefits of object-orientation at the level of entire hierarchies—benefits which are not available with current approaches. Three facets must be adressed: First, it must be possible to create hierarchies incrementally based on existing hierarchies, such that commonalities are expressed via reuse, not duplication. Second, the hierarchies must themselves be organized into hierarchies, such that their relationships are made explicit and can be exploited in a type safe manner. Finally, it must be possible to write generic code that works on every hierarchy derived from the hierarchy for which it was written. This paper presents a language design that supports such a notion of higher-order hierarchies. It has been implemented in context of a full-fledged, statically typed language.

1 Introduction

Consider people working in a company. All of them would be employees. They might also be managers, accountants, project managers, secretaries, etc. We could model such concepts with classes and use the resulting class hierarchy in a number of business applications. However, a payroll system would emphasize different properties of each concept than a workflow system. There might also be differences in the appropriate class hierarchies in different systems.

With current technology we end up writing a number of separate, but similar, inheritance hierarchies, and there would be insufficient support for expressing commonalities: We would redundantly express that a `Secretary` is-a `Clerk` is-an `Employee` in each of those hierarchies; we would redundantly implement some generic functionality on the classes like printing, or basic business rules; we would redundantly apply certain design patterns [9] to express, e.g., that `ProjectManager` is a *role* that can be played by an `Employee`; and we would redundantly write multiple copies of common algorithms working on members of these hierarchies, because the individual classes in the hierarchies do not have useful type relations with the "same" classes in other hierarchies.

In other words, we regress to the bad old copy-then-modify approach in order to express a number of similar phenomena, thus eliminating core object-orientation benefits: There is no incremental specification among hierarchies (corresponding to inheritance in traditional OO), and we cannot write statically type safe generic code which is reusable across different hierarchies (corresponding to polymorphism and late binding in traditional OO). In a dynamically

L. Cardelli (Ed.): ECOOP 2003, LNCS 2743, pp. 303–328, 2003.
© Springer-Verlag Berlin Heidelberg 2003

typed language like Smalltalk [10] we could actually write generic code working in context of multiple hierarchies. However, we would still have to manually maintain the consistency in the protocols of corresponding classes across the different hierarchies—i.e., type safety—and object creation would have to happen by sending 'new' messages to dynamically selected classes (as opposed to standard object creation which uses compile-time constant class names) in order to create instances from the correct hierarchy.

This paper describes a solution to these problems, based on support for hierarchies of hierarchies. It has been implemented in context of the language gbeta [5], and it is integrated with the rest of the language.

The main contributions of this work are the concept of higher-order hierarchies, which is a language integrated mechanism that goes beyond earlier inheritance hierarchy manipulation mechanisms; the underlying idea of using constraints to define the meaning of virtual classes, thus greatly enriching the expressiveness and flexibility of higher-order hierarchies; a step towards a formalization of the semantics of virtual classes built on constraints; the concrete language design supporting higher-order hierarchies; and the implementation of this design in context of a full-fledged programming language.[1]

Let us briefly consider the notion of *higher-order* entities. In a functional language like Haskell [13], functions abstract over expressions. Higher-order functions take other functions as arguments or return functions as results, and they express the high-level structure of computations in an elegant, reusable manner. The basic idea is to apply the function concept to itself, thus introducing *functions of functions*. In this paper the topic is how to deal with the relations among hierarchies, when organized into *hierarchies of hierarchies*. Therefore, we chose the term 'higher-order hierarchies' to describe our approach.

To what *level* are higher-order constructs actually useful? Functions of functions are very useful; functions of functions of functions are used more sparingly, and even higher levels become even harder to understand and manage. We believe that support for higher-order constructs should be general—such that there is no fixed limitation on the number of levels—but we also believe that the first few levels will be much more important in practice than the higher levels. In this paper we will focus on level two, i.e., hierarchies of hierarchies of classes, but the language design and implementation does actually support the general case.

The transition to higher-order versions of the well-known features of ordinary hierarchies can be characterized as follows:

Incrementality: An ordinary hierarchy is built incrementally, by creating a new class C' based on an existing class C (or based on multiple classes, in case of multiple inheritance). The higher-order version of this is to incrementally create a new class hierarchy H' based on an existing hierarchy H (or possibly several). This may include the incremental creation of a new class $H'.C_i$ based on $H.C_i$—such that C_i is extended, but occupies the same position in H' as in H; it may also include addition of classes in new leaf positions

---

[1] This language is gbeta, and the implementation is freely available. The source code is open source and it can be fetched from http://www.daimi.au.dk/~eernst/gbeta/.

in H', thus *extending* the hierarchical structure; and it may include certain *modifications* to the hierarchical structure.

Hierarchical Structure: An ordinary hierarchy is a set of classes with a structure among them, namely the subclassing relation. In this paper we assume that the subtyping relation includes the subclassing relation, such that subclass implies subtype (gbeta, e.g., has this property). This means that the incremental specification automatically provides us with a subtyping hierarchy. Since types do not express everything, we need to assume an appropriate conceptual modeling and programming discipline, and on that assumption it is safe to use instances of a subtype where instances of a supertype are expected. This is known as the Liskov Substitution Principle [17] (LSP). In the higher-order setting, the incremental specification of hierarchies along with the second order subtyping hierarchy among hierarchies ensures that a subhierarchy can—assuming LSP—be used in contexts where a superhierarchy is expected.

Polymorphism and Late Binding: Instances of a class C or of any subclass C' can be treated identically, because of subtype polymorphism. This means that a given algorithm can work on instances of an unbounded number of subclasses of a statically known class. Late binding—i.e., choosing method implementations based on the dynamic class of the receiver object, not the statically known class—enables a generic algorithm to treat different objects differently, accommodating their actual properties. Similarly, a hierarchy with a subtype T' of a given type T may be used where a hierarchy of type T is expected, by means of a polymorphic reference to the hierarchy. Note that we are not substituting a single class for another single class; we are substituting a set of classes along with their *relations* to each other (subclassing, associations, etc.) for a set of similar classes having similar relations to each other. Late binding in the second-order setting includes late binding of method implementations as in the first-order setting, but it also includes late binding of classes, such that newly created objects will be instances of classes from the actual hierarchy being used, not the statically known one. The third-order setting includes late binding of hierarchies, etc.

The rest of this paper is organized as follows. Section 2 presents a simple example based on a higher-order hierarchy. A number of subsections present the development of this example, gradually exposing the mechanism. Section 3 presents a step towards a formal model of the underlying virtual class mechanism, and proves two important properties related to type soundness. Finally, Sec. 4 covers related work, and Sec. 5 concludes.

2   The Main Example

We first present the design and the properties of higher-order hierarchies via examples. We start out with a simple example and extend it in a number of steps, thus thematizing important properties of the mechanism. The examples are related to language processing (compilers, refactoring tools, etc.).

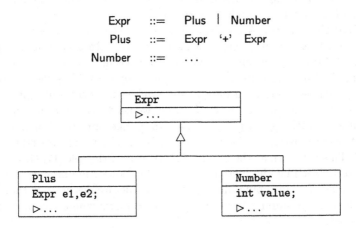

Fig. 1. Grammar and abstract syntax hierarchy for 'Expression'

The examples are in **gbeta**, but they are not presented using standard **gbeta** syntax (which is similar to the syntax of BETA [21], i.e., quite unusual compared to main-stream languages). Instead, we use a syntax which is similar to the syntax of the Java™ programming language [14], but of course extended with constructs available in **gbeta** and necessary for the expression of higher-order hierarchies. These constructs will be described when they are used.

Section 2.1 presents the simplest hierarchy. In Sec. 2.2 this hierarchy is extended, and in Sec. 2.3 two hierarchies are composed. Finally, Sec. 2.4 describes ways in which the structure of a hierarchy can be modified.

2.1 A Basic Abstract Syntax Tree

Consider a very simple programming language 'Expression' with the grammar given in Fig. 1, along with a class hierarchy modeling its abstract syntax.

In order to keep the examples minimal, the classes only contain very few features. The only remarkable property of the class hierarchy is that each class in the hierarchy is *extensible*. We indicate that a class is extensible by adding '▷ ...' below the list of features. An extensible class has the ability to be extended in a subhierarchy in a similar manner as by subclassing; the crucial difference is that a subclass has a different name, but an extensible class keeps the same name under extensions. The hierarchy is expressed in source code as follows:

```
class Expression {
  virtual class Expr {}
  virtual class Plus extends Expr { Expr e1,e2; }
  virtual class Number extends Expr { int value; }
}
```
Pgm. 1

The hierarchy consists of virtual classes [20, 33, 6, 12]. Being a virtual class is the same thing as being extensible, as described above. A virtual class is an attribute of an object, so in order to express a hierarchy of virtual classes we declare an enclosing class, here `Expression`, and each instance of the enclosing class will then provide the virtual classes by ordinary feature access—i.e., by "dotting into" the object. We use the term *hierarchy repository* for such an object which is used to hold a class hierarchy.

Assuming that E denotes an instance of `Expression` or a subclass thereof then `E.Expr`, `E.Plus`, and `E.Number` denote a set of classes belonging together and satisfying the declared subclassing—and hence subtyping—relations: `E.Plus` is a subclass and subtype of `E.Expr`, etc. If E2 is another instance of `Expression` or a subclass then `E2.Expr`, `E2.Plus`, and `E2.Number` would be another set of classes belonging together in the same manner.

However, we cannot assume any subclassing or subtyping relations between `E2.Plus` and `E.Expr`, or any other pair of virtual classes belonging to different enclosing objects. As a result, a reference to an instance of `Expression` or any other hierarchy repository object must be immutable (in Java: `final`), such that expressions like `E.Plus` and `E.Expr` will indeed refer to virtual classes belonging to the same enclosing object. Consequently, the static analysis of gbeta keeps track of immutability during type checking.

Polymorphic access to a hierarchy of virtual classes is achieved as a consequence of polymorphic access to the enclosing object. Knowing that E is an instance of `Expression` or a subclass, we also know that the hierarchy contained in E will be a subhierarchy of the hierarchy statically known from the declaration of the class `Expression`.

At this point we need to introduce the semantics of virtual classes in gbeta. Details can be found in [6], here we just present the special case which is used in the examples of this paper. A virtual class in gbeta is an immutable member v of an enclosing class C with a value which is a class W, similar to an inner class in Java. W is not statically known, it is computed based on the actual enclosing object in a process similar to late binding of method implementations. A gbeta virtual class is not *overridden* in subclasses of C, but subclasses of C may *enhance* it, with an effect that is similar to multiple inheritance. It might be appropriate to describe the mechanism as 'vertical multiple inheritance'. Here is an example:

```
class C { virtual class V extends ColorPoint; }
class D extends C { furtherbound class V extends UndoPoint; }
```
Pgm. 2

In an instance of D, the virtual class V is a class that extends both `ColorPoint` and `UndoPoint`. You may think of this as a process of constraint solving: The declaration in class C requires that V extends `ColorPoint`, the declaration in class D requires that V extends `UndoPoint`, and the result is that all requirements are satisfied.

A subhierarchy is created from a given hierarchy by zero or more steps of furtherbinding applied to each virtual class, so properties preserved by virtual furtherbinding will carry over from the statically known hierarchy to the actual, dynamic hierarchy provided by E. In particular, if a virtual class such as Expr in context of the statically known class of the enclosing object has a feature foo, then the actual class E.Expr will also have such a feature. Moreover, if foo is a method accepting an argument of type Plus then the foo method provided by E.Expr will accept an argument of type E.Plus. In short, we can safely use an actual, dynamic hierarchy in the same way as we would have used the statically known hierarchy, as long as we keep hierarchies from different enclosing objects isolated from each other.

So far, the properties of gbeta virtual classes described here are the same as the properties we have described in [6, 7]. In particular, the internal consistency among a set of classes in an object (virtual classes and/or ordinary ones) is a property of *family polymorphism*, which has been presented in [7]. The difference between this paper and our earlier work is that we are now exploring the possibilities provided by virtual classes inheriting from each other. This means that we can build hierarchies of virtual classes, and it introduces the notion of subhierarchies, as described in the next section.

2.2   Introducing Pretty-Printing

We extend the hierarchy in Pgm. 1 with support for storing a comment in each node as follows:

```
class CommentExpr extends Expression {
  furtherbound class Expr { String comment; }
}
```
Pgm. 3

The effect of this is as shown in Fig 2. It is important to note that we have *not* created a subclass of Expr, we have created a new hierarchy built from the hierarchy in Fig. 1 by extending the member of the hierarchy which is called Expr. As a consequence (since we are extending the root of the hierarchy), all node classes in the new hierarchy will have a comment instance variable. Note that we obtain a fresh copy of all classes in the hierarchy, preserving their subclass relations, but we only need to mention the classes which are being extended. Note that extensions can be made to any (extensible, i.e., virtual) class in the hierarchy.

In the next step, we extend the hierarchy with the ability to *pretty-print* expressions. A new method print is added, with different implementations in each class of the hierarchy. We only need to write the method implementations as in ordinary hierarchies: If the method implementation in Expr had been appropriate for the class Number as well then we would just not mention class Number in class PrintExpr and the (invisible) fresh copy of Number would then inherit print from Expr. However, in this case we do need an implementation in all three classes. Here is the source code:

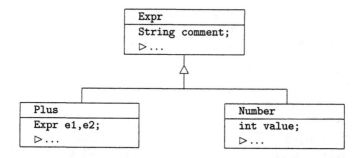

Fig. 2. Extending the hierarchy to hold a comment at each node

```
class PrintExpr extends CommentExpr {
  furtherbound class Expr {
    void print() {
      if (comment.length>0) System.out.print("// "+comment);
    }
  }
  furtherbound class Plus {
    void print() {
      super(); e1.print(); System.out.print("+"); e2.print();
    }
  }
  furtherbound class Number {
    void print() { super(); System.out.print(value); }
  }
}
```
Pgm. 4

In gbeta we would use an INNER statement in Expr.print, and we would not
have super() in print methods of subclasses of Expr, but since we have chosen
to express program fragments in a style that is similar to Java for main-stream
readability, we also felt that a Java style method implementation would be the
most consistent choice. It makes no difference with respect to the hierarchies
discussed. The hierarchy resulting from the extension in Pgm. 4 is shown in
Fig. 3.

The important observation in connection with this extension is that it is
possible to extend many classes of a hierarchy simultaneously. One typical application of this—which is also the one we see here—is to introduce a new method
into a virtual class C somewhere in the hierarchy, and at the same time insert
a number of implementations of this method in some subclasses of C. The result is that the class C and its subclasses in the new hierarchy support the new
method.

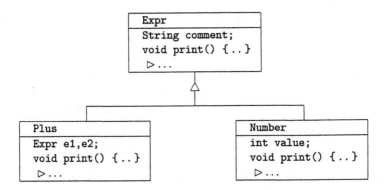

Fig. 3. Extending the hierarchy to support pretty-printing of expressions

2.3   Combining Hierarchies

Consider the following extension of the original hierarchy in `Expression`, supporting *evaluation* of expressions:

```
class EvalExpr extends Expression {
   furtherbound class Expr { int eval() {} }
   furtherbound class Plus {
      int eval() { return e1.eval()+e2.eval(); }
   }
   furtherbound class Number { int eval() { return value; } }
}
```
Pgm.
5

This is very similar in structure to the extension in Pgm. 4. Like this, we could create many different independent extensions of a hierarchy repository class like `Expression`.

Assume that we have a number of subhierarchies of a given hierarchy, e.g., the extensions `PrintExpr` and `EvalExpr` of `Expression`. It may then be useful to *combine* some of the extensions into a new subhierarchy supporting the features of all the contributing hierarchies. The propagating combination mechanism in gbeta supports this in a general sense. For a detailed description of this mechanism, please see [6].

In this paper we will only use propagating combination in a restricted manner where it may be considered as a kind of multiple inheritance that combines nested, virtual classes. The syntactic form of the combination operator in gbeta is the ampersand ('&'), but in this context we will use the symbol '⊕' to denote the combination operation, in order to preserve a syntactic style which is compatible with that of Java where '&' already has a different meaning. We may now combine the existing hierarchies as follows:

```
class CombinedExpr extends PrintExpr ⊕ EvalExpr {}
```
Pgm.
6

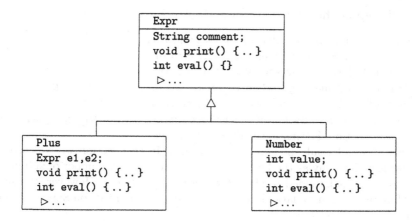

Fig. 4. Combining two independent extensions of the hierarchy

The resulting hierarchy is a subhierarchy of the one in `PrintExpr` and of the one in `EvalExpr`, and it provides features as shown in Fig. 4.

The effect of combining the enclosing classes `PrintExpr` and `EvalExpr` is that each of the nested virtual classes `Expr`, `Plus`, and `Number` is created by combination of the corresponding virtual classes in `PrintExpr` and `EvalExpr`. As a result, the hierarchy in `CombinedExpr` supports all of the methods from each of the hierarchies combined, with method implementations located in the "same" classes of the combined hierarchy as in the superhierarchy they came from. Hierarchy polymorphism now allows generic code expecting to work on an `EvalExpr` syntax tree, or on a `PrintExpr` syntax tree, to actually work on a `CombinedExpr` tree at run-time.

Type checking based on family polymorphism then ensures that different class repositories are kept apart, so we don't end up with a `Plus` from `CombinedExpr` having two `Number` nodes from `PrintExpr` under it. This must indeed also be prevented, since `eval` on the `Plus` node would try to invoke `eval` on the `Number` nodes, but since they are from `PrintExpr` they do not have an `eval` method.

Note that the example outlines a way to structure a complex system like a compiler modularly: Write a basic hierarchy expressing the abstract syntax trees along with methods and state used by all phases of the compiler; then write a subhierarchy for each phase, e.g., for type checking and for code generation; finally compose a complete compiler by composing hierarchies. Note that this allows us to mix and match features, and by hierarchy polymorphism we can write generic code which will work with many different variants of the compiler— e.g., an extended front end used for syntax coloring in an Integrated Development Environment as well as the complete compiler in that same IDE.

2.4 Changing the Structure of a Hierarchy

We have seen that higher-order hierarchies allow us
to create a fresh copy of a given hierarchy containing extended classes. However, we can also enrich
the structure of a hierarchy when we create a subhierarchy of it. To save space we use a more compact graphical representation of inheritance hierarchies in this section. For instance, all the hierarchies

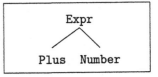

Fig. 5. Base

from Sec. 2.1–2.3 would be shown as in Fig. 5. In this section we will use the
Expression hierarchy as the basis from which we create a number of subhierarchies, so Fig. 5 is intended to show the hierarchy in Fig. 1. However, the same
kind of hierarchy manipulations could be made on ExprPrint, on ExprEval, and
so on.

One possibility for creation of a subhierarchy is to add leaf classes, as shown
in Fig. 6. We can add leaves to classes
which are leaves in the base hierarchy,
or to internal classes. This could, for instance, be used to extend an application
domain oriented hierarchy of classes with
a number of implementation classes. Different extensions of the base hierarchy of
this kind could then provide different im-

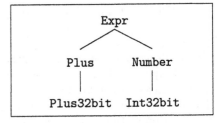

Fig. 6. Add leaf

plementations of the application domain hierarchy, allowing for dependencies between the implementation classes, and with family polymorphism used to ensure
that objects belonging to different hierarchies—hence with different implementation strategies—would not be used together. The source code:

```
class AddLeaf extends Expression {
  virtual class Plus32bit extends Plus { ... }
  virtual class Int32bit extends Number { ... }
}
```
Pgm.
7

We can also add a new root, and an intermediate class in the hierarchy, as shown
in Fig. 7. For example, we might want to
extend the Expression language into a language with both expressions and statements.
We could then add a new root, Ast, to represent more general abstract syntax trees, and
a child of Ast, Stm, to represent statements.
Similarly, we might want to insert a class,
BinExp, to represent binary expressions and
thereby opening opportunities for inheriting
common code from BinExp to Plus and new

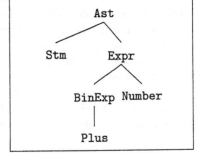

Fig. 7. Add non-leaf

siblings we might add, such as Minus or Divide. In source code:

```
class AddNonLeaf extends Expression {
  virtual class Ast { ... }
  virtual class Stm extends Ast { ... }
  furtherbound class Expr extends Ast {}
  virtual class BinExp extends Expr { ... }
  furtherbound class Plus extends BinExp {}
}
```
Pgm. 8

In general, we just need to specify the edges in the graph that we want, e.g., we want BinExp to be a subclass of Expr and Plus to be a subclass of BinExp. This is possible because it does not contradict the inherited relations: Plus must be a subclass of Expr, and this requirement is still satisfied because it is a subclass of BinExp which is again a subclass of Expr, and the subclass relation is transitive. Had we instead asked for Expr being a subclass of Plus, then the program would have been rejected with an error message about circular dependencies. As we shall see in Sec. 3, it is actually possible to allow for circular dependencies, but this would require fixed-point iteration on the class computations, and we feel that it would be more programmer friendly to avoid having to explain the notion of fixed-points. It is possible that the opposite choice is better, even though it is likely to be harder to generate efficient code for, so this issue has not yet been settled entirely.

3   A Small Step towards a Formal Model

It is highly non-trivial to formalize the full semantics of gbeta, but in this section and its subsections we will try to establish a couple of formal arguments concerned with specific aspects of the semantics. We need to describe the informal semantics of gbeta, through a stepping stone which is a small object calculus, and then we can reason about crucial special cases of the semantics of that calculus.

The core of the semantics of gbeta is the propagating combination mechanism, described in [6]. This mechanism could also be characterized as the semantics of virtual classes in gbeta. We present a small calculus, $\mathbf{Obj_{gb}}$, exhibiting a projection of the semantics of gbeta, in the sense that it mimics the propagating combination in gbeta except that the *ordering* of mixins in each class is ignored. Classes and mixins in gbeta will be introduced below, and $\mathbf{Obj_{gb}}$ will be introduced in Sec. 3.1.

The purpose of introducing $\mathbf{Obj_{gb}}$ is to prove two crucial properties of virtual classes called *monotonicity* and *stability*. Stability means that declared subclassing relations between virtual classes will hold in enclosing objects which are instances of subclasses; monotonicity means that virtual classes grow along with the class of the enclosing object. This explanation is slightly misleading because of family polymorphism, but we will make it more precise later.

The rest of this section introduces the basic concepts of gbeta, in order to support the argument that $\mathbf{Obj_{gb}}$ is a faithful simplification of the semantics of gbeta virtual classes.

```
fun combine (p: mixin list) ([]: mixin list) = p
  | combine [] q = q
  | combine (xp as x::p) (yq as y::q) =
    if x=y then x::(combine p q)
    else if not (member x q) then x::(combine p yq)
    else if not (member y p) then y::(combine xp q)
    else raise Inconsistent;
fun member x [] = false
  | member x (y::ys) = (x=y) orelse member x ys;
```

Fig. 8. The function `combine` which computes gbeta class combination, delivering p & q from arguments p and q

As mentioned in Sec. 2.3, gbeta supports class combination (a generalization of multiple inheritance) by means of the '&' operator.[2] The semantics of this operator can be characterized in several ways [6, 8]. Here we give an operational characterization by means of an algorithm in Standard ML [26], as shown in Fig. 8.

As the algorithm suggests, gbeta *classes* are total orders of mixins (which may also be considered as lists, consisting of distinct elements). A gbeta *mixin* is a pair consisting of (1) a class body, i.e., the {...}-enclosed piece of syntax that specifies the difference between a class and its superclasses, and (2) the identity of the enclosing part object. A *part object* is an instance of a mixin. A gbeta *object* is a list of part objects, $[o_1, \ldots o_n]$; it is created as an instance of a class $[m_1, \ldots m_n]$, with each part object o_i created as an instance of the corresponding mixin m_i in the class.

Note that enclosing part objects always correspond to enclosing syntax: If a class body B is syntactically enclosed by a class body B', and if m is a mixin containing B as its class body and o' as its enclosing part object, then B' is guaranteed to be the class body of the mixin of o'. This means that we can think nested objects when reading nested constructs in source code. In the example below, if we have an instance myY of Y created in context of an instance myX of X then myY will contain exactly one part object; it will be an instance of the mixin corresponding to the class body marked '2' and located in the single part object that myX contains, which is again an instance of a mixin containing the class body marked '1'. Here is the example:

```
class X {1 class Y {2 ... } Y myY = new Y(); }     Pgm.
X myX = new X();                                    9
```

Mixins are values, so two mixins are equal iff they refer to the same class body and have the same enclosing part object (a mixin is not an object, and does not have its own object identity). The fact that a mixin includes the enclosing

---

[2] Shown as ⊕ in Pgm. 4.

part object (not just the type of it) is the basis for family polymorphism, and it requires that the static analysis of gbeta keep track of the identity of certain objects.

The design of $\mathbf{Obj}_{gb}$ is such that classes can only be looked up in the current object, or in a (directly or indirectly) enclosing object. This ensures that we can reason about initialization of the attributes of one object at a time. Note that this is sufficient to express the examples in this paper, as well as a host of other things. The extension to real family polymorphism need only affect the type declarations for instance variables, but $\mathbf{Obj}_{gb}$ does not include instance variables (it allows only declaration of classes, and creation of instances). The addition of instance variable declarations supporting family polymorphism would not invalidate the proofs of $\mathbf{Obj}_{gb}$ properties, since the value of a class attribute would never depend on any instance variables. However, we would need to use richer run-time paths (introduced in Sec. 3.1 below) in order to express the semantics of creation of instances nested in objects (as in new myX.Y() where the class Y is nested in the object myX), and in order to be able to type check instance variable assignment and usage when the type of the instance variable is nested in an object (as in myX.Y myY = ...;).

3.1 The Calculus

The syntax of the object calculus $\mathbf{Obj}_{gb}$ is shown in Fig. 9. An $\mathbf{Obj}_{gb}$ program is a class body, a Body, which may contain class declarations, Decl, nested to any depth, followed by statements, Stmt. Every declaration is a declaration of a virtual class. Occurrences of identifiers which define a name are called name declarations, NameDcl, and non-defining occurrences are called name applications, NameApl. The right hand side of a declaration is an expression, Expr, which may be the name of a class, a NameApl, a class body, or the combination of two expressions using the combination operator, ' ∪ '.

The informal semantics of an $\mathbf{Obj}_{gb}$ program is as follows: Create an object which contains one part object which is an instance of the mixin whose class body is the outermost Body of the program, and whose enclosing part object is irrelevant (it will not be used). Initialize the attributes of this primary object by evaluating right hand sides of declarations. Then execute each statement of the body of the object. To execute a statement S, lookup the class having the

Program	::=	Body
Body	::=	'[' Decl* 'do' Stmt* ']'
Decl	::=	NameDcl ':' Expr
Stmt	::=	NameApl
Expr	::=	NameApl | Body | Expr ' ∪ ' Expr

Fig. 9. Grammar of the object calculus $\mathbf{Obj}_{gb}$

NameDcl S, stopping with an error if it does not exist, then create an instance of that class, and execute its statements. We leave the order of the statements unspecified (it is a set in Fig. 10 below) since it makes no difference.

Note that the semantics of the combination operator '$\cup$' is standard set union. Hence, if A is a class (a set of mixins), and B is also, then A $\cup$ B is the union of the two sets. In gbeta, the set of mixins in a combination p & q is exactly the union of the set of mixins in p and the set of mixins in q; so the $\mathbf{Obj_{gb}}$ class combination mimics gbeta class combination, except that the order of mixins is ignored.

Before we proceed with a description of the lookup process, we need to introduce the semantic entities of $\mathbf{Obj_{gb}}$, as shown in Fig. 10. An object is a finite set of part objects; a part object is a finite map from names to classes—the state of the part object—together with the mixin from which it was created; and a mixin is the enclosing part object, a body id, BodyID, a finite map from names to expressions (the declarations), and a set of names (the statements). Each name application, NameApl, is enriched with a so-called Path by static analysis, as described below. A BodyID is the unique identity of an occurrence of a Body construct in the program. Even if two different pieces of Body syntax are identical as text strings, they must both have a unique body id. Note that late binding of classes (and of methods, in full gbeta) is achieved by the *same* attribute having different values in instances of different classes, not by letting one attribute definition be the 'active one' and the other definitions 'overridden'. This kind of late binding is a necessary precondition for being able to ignore the order of mixins in a class: In a given object $\{o_1, \ldots o_n\}$, no matter in which mixin instance o_i we look up foo, it will have the same value.

The lookup process is directed by static analysis. The calculus is parameterized by *some* static analysis process which takes a program and annotates every name application, NameApl, with a specification of exactly which name declaration in which part object is the meaning of this name application at runtime. This specification is known as a 'run-time path' in gbeta, and it consists of a number of steps. A similar concept is used in $\mathbf{Obj_{gb}}$, but each step is a bit simpler than in gbeta run-time paths.

$$
\begin{aligned}
\text{Object} &= \text{SetOf(PartObject)} \\
\text{PartObject} &= \text{State} \times \text{Mixin} \\
\text{State} &= \text{NameDcl} \hookrightarrow \text{Class} \\
\text{Class} &= \text{SetOf(Mixin)} \\
\text{Mixin} &= \text{PartObject} \times \text{BodyID} \times (\text{NameDcl} \hookrightarrow \text{Expr}) \times \text{SetOf(NameApl)} \\
\text{NameApl} &= \text{NameDcl} \times \text{Path} \\
\text{Path} &= \text{ListOf(BodyID)}
\end{aligned}
$$

Fig. 10. Semantic entities for $\mathbf{Obj_{gb}}$

For $\mathbf{Obj_{gb}}$ each NameApl n is annotated with a path, which is a non-empty sequence of BodyIDs, and with the NameDcl (the simple, pathless name) that n resolves to. The meaning of a path $[\iota_1, \ldots, \iota_k]$ is that we select the part object o_1 of the current object having a mixin m_1 with BodyID ι_1, then proceed to the enclosing part object o_2' of the mixin of that part object, then repeat for $\iota_2 \ldots \iota_{k-1}$, and finally proceed to the part object o_k in the object containing o_k' (the enclosing part object of o_{k-1}), and selecting the part object o_k having mixin m_k with BodyID ι_k in that object.

In short, we follow a step by going to the specified part object and out to the enclosing part object; and we follow a path by following its steps. In the last step we don't go out, but we lookup the attribute with the given NameDcl in the selected part object.

The static analysis is *correct* if the $\mathbf{Obj_{gb}}$ program is either rejected as erroneous, or it can be executed and will never cause failure of a lookup operation. Note that it is trivial to ensure statically that a given Body construct does actually contain a declaration with the requested NameDcl, because that is a purely syntactic issue. However, it is non-trivial to select paths such that every part object traversed will actually exist in every execution of the program.

It is important to realize that the semantics of lookup in $\mathbf{Obj_{gb}}$ (and gbeta) ensures that the question of whether there will be a 'message-not-understood' error is reduced to the question of whether each run-time path describes a sequence of part objects that do actually exist. This again means that type safety is established by ensuring that each object accessed does indeed contain every part object that we want to visit in it. In the case of $\mathbf{Obj_{gb}}$ it is sufficient to ensure that all the enclosing objects contain at least the predicted part objects, because no other objects can be reached during lookup.

We will not attempt to describe the full static analysis of $\mathbf{Obj_{gb}}$, but we will argue that the static analysis has a couple of correctness *preserving* properties, namely the monotonicity and the stability property mentioned in the introduction of Sec. 3. To approach that goal we will consider a simple special case.

3.2 Self-Contained Objects

Consider the case where an object O consists of part objects $\{o_1, \ldots o_n\}$ with mixins $\{m_1, \ldots m_n\}$ such that every name application in the bodies of the mixins has a run-time path with lenght exactly one. This is the case where the object is *self-contained* in the sense that its attributes can be initialized without reference to any other object. Instances of **Expression** and its subclasses in Sec. 2 all have this property. Let us describe the initialization process in greater detail.

To do this it is sufficient to model the object as a partial function, φ, from a finite set of names to the set of sets of body ids, i.e., NameDcl $\hookrightarrow$ SetOf(BodyID).[3] The domain of φ is the set of all NameDcls occurring in the Body constructs of the mixins $\{m_1, \ldots m_n\}$. This means that the value of each attribute is not

---

[3] We use the notation $A \hookrightarrow B$ to denote a partial function from A to B defined in a finite subset of A

a class as specified in Fig. 10, but it is simply a set of body ids. Each body id stands for a Mixin, but: We do not need the enclosing part object since no paths contain more than one step; we do not need the declarations of the nested mixins since we will only initialize each attribute with its class value—we need the declarations of nested mixins as soon as we create instances, but we do not do that here; and we do not need the statements of nested mixins, because we do not execute them.

With this heavily simplified model it becomes much less cumbersome to describe the semantics of attribute initialization. The semantics is that we solve the constraint system implied by the following interpretation: Each declaration is a constraint on the NameDcl that its value must be a class which contains *at least* the mixins denoted by the right hand side of the declaration. In the cases where the same name is declared in multiple mixins, that name has multiple constraints associated with it. As with the definition of the $\mathbf{Obj_{gb}}$ combination operator '∪' which mimics the gbeta combination operator '&', this produces the same result as the semantics of gbeta virtual classes, except that the ordering of mixins in each virtual class is ignored.

The correct initialization process is a constraint solving process in which all constraints are satisfied, with the smallest possible sets of mixins for each name. This is well-defined, as we shall see below. The constraint set is produced as follows:

- For each declaration $d : n$ where n is a name, add the constraint $d \supseteq n$
- For each declaration $d : b$ where b is a body, add the constraint $d \supseteq \{b'\}$ where b' is the body id of b
- For each declaration $d : e_1 \cup e_2$ where e_1 and e_2 are expressions, add constraints as if we had had the declaration $d : e_1$ and the declaration $d : e_2$

For a given constraint set S, define the function F_S with functionality and definition as follows:

$$F_S : (\mathsf{NameDcl} \hookrightarrow \mathsf{SetOf(BodyID)}) \to (\mathsf{NameDcl} \hookrightarrow \mathsf{SetOf(BodyID)})$$
$$F_S(\varphi) = \varphi' \quad \text{where} \quad \varphi'(n) = \varphi(n) \cup \left(\bigcup_{c \in S(n)} \varphi(c.r) \right)$$

where $S(n)$ is the set of constraints in S whose left-hand side is the name n, and $c.r$ is the right hand side of the constraint c. In other words, F_S takes an assignment of names to sets of mixins, and produces another assignment of names to sets of mixins where, for each name n, the values of the right hand sides of constraints on n have been added to the value of n.

Finite sets with the subset relation form a complete partial order, so the functions of type NameDcl $\hookrightarrow$ BodyID form a complete partial order by pointwise ordering (one assignment φ is smaller than another assignment φ' if they are defined for the same names, and $\varphi(n) \subseteq \varphi'(n)$ for all names n in the common domain). F_S is a continuous function because it is monotonic and the range is finite, so the standard Fixed-Point Theorem (e.g. [35, p.71]) allows us conclude that there is a least fixed-point for F_S, and that we can find it be repeatedly applying F_S to $\varphi_\perp$, which is the assignment that maps every name in the domain to the empty set.

This is a faithful projection of the semantics of gbeta virtual classes in the sense that if all the gbeta class combinations succeed then the resulting value of virtual class attributes will be associated with the same sets of body ids as the ones produced by the constraint solving process in $\mathbf{Obj_{gb}}$. Class combinations in gbeta fail iff there are circularities in the requested inheritance structure. As long as hierarchy repository classes are statically known at the point where instances of them are created, this problem can be detected statically. Detecting it in the general case is an issue that has not yet been fully resolved, but [8] is one step in the right direction.

However, we may need to transform a gbeta program before $\mathbf{Obj_{gb}}$ can faithfully mimic it, because $\mathbf{Obj_{gb}}$ supports *only* virtual classes. If the gbeta program contains two class attributes with the same name used in the same object which are not contributions to the same virtual attribute, then we must systematically rename one of them so they have different names. We could for instance have two simple class attributes with the same name and in the same class, and the semantics would then be shadowing, not virtual combination. However, such a renaming process is easy, given a gbeta program with annotations from static analysis.

Now we can proceed to prove the first property of $\mathbf{Obj_{gb}}$, in the special case of a self-contained object:

Proposition 1 (Monotonicity). *Assume that O is a self-contained object containing part objects $\{o_1, \ldots o_n\}$ with mixins $\{m_1, \ldots m_n\}$, where o_i is an instance of m_i. Assume that O has an attribute with name n and value V. Then an object O' containing a superset of part objects $\{o_1, \ldots o_n, o'_1, \ldots o'_m\}$ for an $m \geq 0$ will have an attribute named n, and its value will be a superset of V.*

Proof. The proof is an easy induction in the number of iterations in the fixed-point computation: Note that the constraint set S of the object O is a subset of the constraint set S' of O'. In the beginning the value of each attribute is the empty set. For each step, i.e., for each natural number i, $F_S^i(\varphi_\perp)$ is smaller than $F_{S'}^i(\varphi_\perp)$, where $\varphi_\perp$ is an assignment that maps all defined names to the empty set. Hence, the least fixed-point of F_S is also smaller than that of $F_{S'}$. □

The significance of this result is that it is correct for a static analysis of $\mathbf{Obj_{gb}}$ to use an approximation from *below* for the set of mixins in the value of each attribute, and then proceed to reason about nested classes and objects which are instances thereof. In other words, it is sound to assume that the value of a virtual class is a subclass of the statically known value. The other result can now also be stated and proved:

Proposition 2 (Stability). *Assume that O is a self-contained object. Assume that O has an attribute with name declaration n' whose right hand side contains the name application n. The value of n' will then be a superset of the value of n.*

Proof. This is an easy consequence of the values of attributes being a fixed-point for F_S: Let φ_∞ be the solution, i.e., the fixed-point of F_S. Then $F_S(\varphi_\infty) = \varphi_\infty$, and according to the definition of F_S, $\varphi_\infty(n')$ is equal to the union of a number of sets where $\varphi_\infty(n)$ is one of the sets, and consequently $\varphi_\infty(n') \supseteq \varphi_\infty(n)$.   □

The significance of this result is that it is guaranteed to be true that one attribute v is a subclass of another attribute w if we know just one declaration of v with w somewhere on the right hand side. Tracing this back to gbeta, this is the reason why the declarations in Fig. 7 will actually ensure that the requested subclassing relations—such as Plus **is-a** BinExp—are satisfied, also in arbitrary subhierarchies.

3.3   Beyond Self-Contained Objects

We need to divide the computation of attribute values in an $\mathbf{Obj_{gb}}$ program into separate phases, and $\mathbf{Obj_{gb}}$ has been designed exactly to make that easy. First, every name application in an expression that must be evaluated during object initialization is resolved to a part object in the current object or an enclosing part object (not a sibling object, nor an object which is nested deeper than the name application itself). Consequently, each part object is always created in a context where all lookup-reachable part objects have already been created, and all their attributes computed.

This means that we just need to extend the fixed-point computation from the previous section with constraints where the values of attributes of enclosing objects are added to each attribute of the new object which uses such enclosing attributes. The new constraints will have existing names on the left hand side (namely some of the attributes which are being initialized), and constant values on the right hand side. Fixed-point iteration proceeds as before, and the result satisfies the following additional stability property: If an attribute with name n' has a right hand side which contains the name n of some attribute of a different object, then the value of n' will be a superset, i.e., subclass, of the value of n. This means that declared subclass relations are also stable across object boundaries towards enclosing objects in $\mathbf{Obj_{gb}}$.

There is still a large amount of work to do before gbeta has been fully formalized, and properties like type soundness indisputably proven. We are working towards that goal, taking the small steps we can. However, in the mean time, the implementation of the language is available, and readers who think that there might be, e.g., type safety issues are invited to try it out!

4   Related Work

William R. Cook mentions inheritance of entire hierarchies in his thesis [4], but he describes it in such a way that the discussion related to multiple inheritance below applies, so we will not cover it separately. Creation of variants of hierarchies by means of a virtual class used as the root of a hierarchy is covered briefly in [20], and we discuss this below under 'Virtual Classes'. Other than that we are not aware of treatments of hierarchies of hierarchies as an integrated language mechanism.

However, there are a number of other language features which may be used to solve similar problems, several of which are related to first-order manipulation of hierarchies. We discuss each of them in the following.

Multiple Inheritance. It is possible to create a derived hierarchy from a given hierarchy using multiple inheritance, as supported by C++ [31], Eiffel [23] and a number of other languages. In Fig. 11 we show an example of this, based on the hierarchy used in Sec. 2. We create a subclass Expr2 of the given class Expr, and similarly for Plus and Number. This establishes the **is-a** relations shown as dotted lines in Fig. 11, but it does not estab-

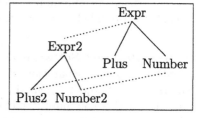

Fig. 11. Multiple inheritance

lish the internal structure of the derived hierarchy, e.g., Plus2 **is-an** Expr2, so we have to manually reconstruct the entire subclass structure in the derived hierarchy. We must also specify every class of the derived hierarchy even if we only want to write new declarations in a few of them. Moreover, the internal type structure among the classes is not preserved in new hierarchy: If Expr has a method foo accepting an argument of type Plus then Expr2 can inherit foo due to the dotted-line subclass relations, but the argument type will not be Plus2, it will be Plus, so we cannot use the possibly extended interface of Plus2 without by-passing static type checking. In other words, it doesn't work.

The 'Visitor' Pattern. An important application of higher-order hierarchies is to create variants of a given hierarchy with extensions, such as additional methods. The 'Visitor' pattern [9, p. 331–344] is a well-known device which effectively enables post-hoc addition of new methods to a given hierarchy. However, this pattern

- does not support addition of new state (instance variables) to classes in the visited hierarchy
- does not support inheritance—in the terminology of [9], we can write an implementation of visitExpr, but this implementation is not going to be used in place of visitPlus if visitPlus is not defined, in other words 'Plus does not inherit from Expr with respect to visitor-methods'
- requires every extension to apply to the same hierarchy—if we want to add a method to Plus and its subclasses using a visitor framework based on Expr, then we must effectively add the method to Expr and all its *other* subclasses, possibly producing an error message such as 'Do not call this method on this class!' In short, the granularity is too rigid.
- requires changes to every visitor class if a new class is added to the visited hierarchy

In contrast, higher-order hierarchies do support addition of state, inheritance of added methods (and state), and modifications of, including extensions to, the hierarchy. To add a new class to the hierarchy along with implementations of various methods, we need to write a subhierarchy mentioning only that single class and those method implementations. Moreover, higher-order hierarchies enable coexistence of many different related hierarchies. This means that it is no problem for two different extensions of a hierarchy to coexist, even if they use contradicting design assumptions in the internal relations between member classes. This is one of a number of benefits associated with the better separation of concerns provided by higher-order hierarchies.

Aspect Oriented Software Development. It is a very prominent goal in AOSD to improve separation of concerns, already expressed for Composition Filters [1], for Subject-Oriented Programming [11], and for AOP [16]. Many approaches in this community, including AspectJ [15], support quantification of source code elements, by means of such devices as expressions containing wild cards, matching declared names and method argument lists. It is also a prominent feature of AOSD approaches that it is possible to modify the meaning of existing source code entities without actually editing them. These two features enable insertion of both state and methods into an existing inheritance hierarchy, in a manner which is in some ways more flexible than that of gbeta (e.g., there is no wild card based matching in gbeta). An important difference is that AOSD approaches generally enable *modifications* to existing hierarchies, whereas higher-order hierarchies create *separate copies* of existing hierarchies.[4] The modification approach ensures that client code can use the extended hierarchy without being changed (it is a non-intrusive change), and the separate-copy approach ensures that multiple different variants of a hierarchy can coexist in the same program. Conversely, a modification approach makes such coexistence impossible, and the separate-copy approach requires either polymorphism or client code changes for client code to be able to use an extended hierarchy.

'New' considered harmful. At this point we must insert a general remark about the 'new' operator as known from main-stream object-oriented languages. Ordinary polymorphism allows client code to operate on objects without being intimately dependent on the nature of those objects—it is enough to know that they are instances of some subclass of a statically known class. This is a cornerstone of the information hiding capabilities of object-oriented languages. However, every 'new' statement in a language like Java contains a denotation of a specific class and the new object will be an instance of *exactly* that class. In other words, the

---

[4] This does not mean that, e.g., AspectJ must be implemented by means of source code modification. It means that, e.g., if we introduce a method foo into a class Bar then the Bar with the extension and the Bar without the extension cannot coexist in the same program—when we add foo, Bar is modified. This is also the reason why client code can use the modified version of Bar without being changed.

information is *not* hidden in connection with creation of new objects. This constitutes a major breach in the information hiding capabilities of object-oriented languages, and a significant portion of the client code inflexibility that aspect oriented approaches seek to repair by means of "invisible" changes to existing classes is a consequence of this problem.

Hierarchy repository objects are one step towards a solution to this problem, ensuring not only polymorphic (information hiding) access to hierarchies, but also consistency among the classes in the hierarchy.

Combination of Inheritance Hierarchies. The paper [28] with exactly this title presents an approach to combine hierarchies. The paper gives a very interesting discussion about the software engineering considerations around correctness of hierarchy combination, and the combination examples given are similar in structure to the simple examples we have given. Moreover, the approach is then formalized in a manner that is highly independent of the concrete language in which the class hierarchies are written. However, the approach is first-order, in the sense that there is no representation of hierarchies as such at the language level. This means that it only works for a flat name space containing all the classes involved (no nesting), there is no support of coexistence of multiple variants of a given class hierarchy in the same program, and hence the issue of hierarchy polymorphism and generic code using it does not even arise. It is claimed that it could be implemented to work without access to the source code of the classes being combined, but we cannot see how the proposed implementation could correctly handle re-binding of names, as when the following two versions of a class C are combined:

```
int x;
class C { void m() { x+=1; } } // first version
class C { float x; } // second version
class C { float x; void m() { x+=1; } } // result
```

Pgm. 10

The problem is that the generated code for the method 'm' must be changed in a non-trivial manner when the meaning of the expression 'x' changes type and allocation status. From this we conclude that the approach is essentially built on source-code manipulation, and it is up to an ordinary compiler of the language to generate code for method bodies such that it corresponds to the merged program. In summary, even though that paper superficially seems to present much the same results as the ones presented in this paper (11 years ago, even), we would claim that our higher-order hierarchies are integrated into the language in a much more deep sense. Nevertheless, the paper is certainly interesting and well-written!

Constraints in Type Systems. The type system for Cecil [3] is based on constraints, and type checking is based on constraint solving [18]. However, Cecil type constraints are used only to declare expected types of various declarations and expressions, and to check whether a given program satisfies all the declared constraints.

In contrast, constraints in gbeta are used operationally, to *construct* entities like classes, such that the constraints are satisfied. The consequence is that we can create a variant of a few classes in a hierarchy and let the constraint solver propagate the modifications to the rest of the hierarchy. With the approach where the constraints are only *checked* and not *satisfied* by the language semantics, we would need to mention each of the affected classes and explicitly update them.

To see the significance of this, consider the following analogous situation: Imagine a version of Java with interfaces but without subclassing. In such a language we would have to copy and paste state and implementation from each class to each of its would-be subclasses (according to the declared interfaces), and we would have to maintain consistency among all these duplicated declarations. So, at least, the pair of subtyping vs. subclassing clearly illustrates that it makes a difference for programmers whether declared relations are being merely checked or they are being automatically satisfied.

Layers. There are several proposals built on the idea of layered designs wherein hierarchies may to some extent be manipulated. Mixin Layers [30] uses mixins containing nested classes to enable flexible combination of slices of several classes; the main vehicle in the paper is C++ template programming, but the ideas apply to other languages as well. Adaptive Plug-and-Play Components [24] (AP&PCs) support the expression of collaboration diagrams in terms of abstract class graphs which may be applied to concrete class graphs in such a way that class and method names are mapped to other names, and associations are mapped to object graph navigation paths. Jiazzi [22] is a component system for Java that supports the 'open class pattern' which enables type-safe composition of different classes with the same name in multiple components. These approaches provide sophisticated support for composition, but there is no notion of hierarchies as first-class language entities, of subhierarchies, nor of hierarchy polymorphism.

With delegation layers [29] there is a notion of virtual classes which is closely related to the one in gbeta, and the paper actually shows and explains a virtual class (UEdge) which inherits from another virtual class. Due to the many similarities between this approach and gbeta, especially the fact that Delegation Layers are based on family polymorphism, we believe that higher-order hierarchies can be expressed here. It is a very interesting experiment to combine family polymorphism with delegation, but we must remark that the lowering/lifting mechanism which is so crucial in this approach seems to be somewhat impractical because of the demands it puts on programmers.

The On-Demand Remodularization of [25] also uses family polymorphism, and it presents a very convincing case for a mechanism that connects generic functionality with application code based on a collaboration interface specifying a provided and an expected interface, along with implementations of the provided interface (by generic code) and of the expected interface (by connection to application code). However, these concepts can be expressed directly in gbeta (except for the so-called wrapper recycling which must be implemented manually), so these features are essentially already in gbeta.

Virtual Classes. The notion of virtual classes (more precisely: virtual patterns) was introduced in the language BETA [20] many years ago, and this concept was the basis from which the virtual classes in gbeta were developed. In recent years a number of papers have been published [2, 34, 19, 12] deepening the concept, especially by means of formal analysis. A language like SCALA [27] also supports the moral equivalent of virtual attributes by means of so-called type refinements. However, all these approaches to virtual classes are based on the requirement that a virtual furterbinding must specify a subclass of the inherited specifications for that virtual—which means that there is no constraint solving involved, only constraint checking—and a virtual class is *not* allowed to inherit from another virtual class. This makes it impossible to create a hierarchy of virtual classes, and hence this makes it impossible to create higher-order hierarchies.

However, it is mentioned in [20] that usage of a virtual class as the root of a class hierarchy nested inside an enclosing class would be useful because it enables the creation of variants of that hierarchy by furtherbinding the virtual class. This idea seems to be very similar to the one presented in this paper, and it would actually be able to express the first hierarchy extension (where a new feature was added to the root of the hierarchy). Nevertheless, the underlying language design was very different from gbeta, and as a consequence it could not express similar things as our higher-order hierarchies. First, BETA never allowed inheritance from virtual to virtual, and hence only the root of a hierarchy could be extensible (e.g., we could not add implementations of a new method in classes inside the hierarchy). Second, when inheriting from a virtual it was not allowed to furtherbind a nested virtual (e.g., even if the language were extended to allow a virtual to inherit from a virtual, we could still not implement that new method). Finally, BETA never supported composition of classes (multiple inheritance), and the proposals for adding multiple inheritance to BETA [32] did not have the needed properties. Hence, the composition of hierarchies would not be within reach without a deep generalization of BETA—which is by the way exactly what gbeta is.

5   Conclusion

We have presented the notion of higher-order inheritance hierarchies, supporting incremental creation of subhierarchies, organization of hierarchies into a higher-order hierarchy of hierarchies, and enabling reusable generic code, based on polymorphic access to hierarchies via 'hierarchy repository objects'. This enables simultaneous extensions of a hierarchy of classes in a manner which is more flexible than usage of the 'visitor' pattern, among other things because it is possible to add a class to the hierarchy without changing existing classes or methods. Aspect oriented approaches support a greater flexibility in the modification of a given hierarchy, but the result is that the same hierarchy is modified. In contrast, with higher-order hierarchies a new hierarchy is created incrementally, capable of coexisting with other subhierarchies in the same program. For large systems, we believe that coexistence of independently created variants of a given entity is important. Moreover, higher-order hierarchies allow for extensive reorganizations of the inheritance relations in a given hierarchy, in the creation of subhierarchies. This enables the expression of commonalities—such as inherited methods signatures, method implementations, or state—into different subhierarchies, where traditional approaches would not be able to express any useful type relations among hierarchies with different structure. At the technical level, we think that it is an interesting, novel feature of higher-order hierarchies that they are based on constraint solving, such that inheritance relations may be specified in a more declarative and abstract manner.

References

[1] Mehmet Ak sit. *On the Design of the Object-Oriented Language Sina.* PhD thesis, University of Twente, Enschede, the Netherlands, 1989.

[2] K. Bruce, M. Odersky, and P. Wadler. A statically safe alternative to virtual types. *Lecture Notes in Computer Science*, 1445:523–549, 1998.

[3] Craig Chambers. *The Cecil Language, Specification and Rationale.* Dept. of Comp.Sci. and Eng., Univ. of Washington, Seattle, Washington, 1997.

[4] W. R. Cook. *A Denotational Semantics of Inheritance.* PhD thesis, Brown University, 1989.

[5] Erik Ernst. *gbeta – A Language with Virtual Attributes, Block Structure, and Propagating, Dynamic Inheritance.* PhD thesis, DEVISE, Department of Computer Science, University of Aarhus, Aarhus, Denmark, June 1999.

[6] Erik Ernst. Propagating class and method combination. In Rachid Guerraoui, editor, *Proceedings ECOOP'99*, LNCS 1628, pages 67–91, Lisboa, Portugal, June 1999. Springer-Verlag.

[7] Erik Ernst. Family polymorphism. In Jørgen Lindskov Knudsen, editor, *Proceedings ECOOP'01*, LNCS 2072, pages 303–326, Heidelberg, Germany, 2001. Springer-Verlag.

[8] Erik Ernst. Safe dynamic multiple inheritance. *Nordic Journal of Computing*, 9(2002):191–208, fall 2002.

[9] Erich Gamma, Richard Helm, Ralph Johnson, and John Vlissides. *Design Patterns – Elements of Reusable Object-Oriented Software.* Addison-Wesley, Reading, MA, USA, 1995.

[10] Adele Goldberg and David Robson. *Smalltalk–80: The Language.* Addison-Wesley, Reading, MA, USA, 1989.

[11] William Harrison and Harold Ossher. Subject-oriented programming (A critique of pure objects). In *Proceedings OOPSLA'93, ACM SIGPLAN Notices*, volume 28, 10, pages 411–428, October 1993.

[12] Atsushi Igarashi and Benjamin C. Pierce. Foundations for virtual types. In *Proceedings ECOOP'99. Also in informal proceedings of the Sixth International Workshop on Foundations of Object-Oriented Languages (FOOL6)*, 1999.

[13] Simon Peyton Jones. *Haskell 98 Language and Libraries: The Revised Report.* Cambridge University Press, 2003. To appear.

[14] Bill Joy, Guy Steele, James Gosling, and Gilad Bracha. *Java(TM) Language Specification (2nd Edition)*. Addison-Wesley Publishing Company, 2000.

[15] Gregor Kiczales, Erik Hilsdale, Jim Hugunin, Mik Kersten, Jeffrey Palm, and William G. Griswold. An overview of AspectJ. In *Proceedings ECOOP'01*, LNCS 2072, pages 327–353, Heidelberg, Germany, 2001. Springer-Verlag.

[16] Gregor Kiczales, John Lamping, Anurag Mendhekar, Chris Maeda, Cristina Lopes, Jean-Marc Loingtier, and John Irwin. Aspect-oriented programming. In Mehmet Aksit and Satoshi Matsuoka, editors, *Proceedings ECOOP'97*, LNCS 1241, pages 220–242, Jyväskylä, Finland, 9–13 June 1997. Springer.

[17] Barbara Liskov. Data abstraction and hierarchy. *ACM SIGPLAN Notices*, 23(5):17–34, May 1988. Revised version of the keynote address given at OOPSLA '87.

[18] Vassily Litvinov. Constraint-based polymorphism in Cecil: Towards a practical and static type system. In Craig Chambers, editor, *Proceedings OOPSLA'98*, *ACM SIGPLAN Notices*, volume 33, 10, Vancouver, October 1998. ACM Press.

[19] Ole Lehrmann Madsen. Semantic analysis of virtual classes and nested classes. In Linda M. Northrop, editor, *Proceedings OOPSLA'99*, *ACM SIGPLAN Notices*, volume 34, 10, Denver, October 1999. ACM Press.

[20] Ole Lehrmann Madsen and Birger Møller-Pedersen. Virtual classes: A powerful mechanism in object-oriented programming. In *Proceedings OOPSLA'89*, *ACM SIGPLAN Notices*, volume 24, 10, pages 397–406, October 1989.

[21] Ole Lehrmann Madsen, Birger Møller-Pedersen, and Kristen Nygaard. *Object-Oriented Programming in the BETA Programming Language*. Addison-Wesley, Reading, MA, USA, 1993.

[22] Sean McDirmid, Matthew Flatt, and Wilson Hsieh. Jiazzi: New-age components for old-fashioned Java. In *Proceedings of OOPSLA'01*, volume 36(11) of *SIGPLAN Notices*, pages 211–222, New York, NY, November 2001. ACM.

[23] Bertrand Meyer. *Object-oriented Software Construction*. Prentice Hall, New York, N.Y., second edition, 1997.

[24] Mira Mezini and Karl Lieberherr. Adaptive plug-and-play components for evolutionary software development. *ACM SIGPLAN Notices*, 33(10):97–116, October 1998.

[25] Mira Mezini and Klaus Ostermann. Integrating independent components with on-demand remodularization. In Cindy Norris and Jr. James B. Fenwick, editors, *Proceedings of OOPSLA'02*, volume 37, 11 of *ACM SIGPLAN Notices*, pages 52–67, New York, November 4–8 2002. ACM Press.

[26] R. Milner, M. Tofte, R. W. Harper, and D. MacQueen. *The Definition of Standard ML*. MIT Press, 1997.

[27] Martin Odersky. Report on the programming language Scala. Technical report, Ecole Polytechnique Federale de Lausanne, 2002.

[28] Harold Ossher and William Harrison. Combination of inheritance hierarchies. In *Proceedings OOPSLA'92*, pages 25–40, October 1992.

[29] Klaus Ostermann. Dynamically composable collaborations with delegation layers. In *Proceedings ECOOP'02*, LNCS 2374, pages 89–110, Malaga, Spain, 2002. Springer-Verlag.

[30] Yannis Smaragdakis and Don Batory. Implementing layered design with mixin layers. In Eric Jul, editor, *Proceedings ECOOP'98*, volume 1445 of *LNCS*, pages 550–570, Brussels, Belgium, July 1998.

[31] Bjarne Stroustrup. *The C++ Programming Language*. Addison-Wesley, 3rd edition, 1997.

[32] Kristine Stougård Thomsen. *Multiple Inheritance, a Structuring Mechanism for Data, Processes and Procedures.* Datalogisk afdeling, AArhus Universitet, Århus, Denmark, 1986. DAIMI PB-209.

[33] Kresten Krab Thorup. Genericity in Java with virtual types. In *Proceedings ECOOP'97*, LNCS 1241, pages 444–471, Jyväskylä, June 1997. Springer-Verlag.

[34] Mads Torgersen. Virtual types *are* statically safe. In *5th Workshop on Foundations of Object-Oriented Languages (FOOL)*, at http://pauillac.inria.fr/~remy/fool/program.html, January 1998.

[35] Glynn Winskel. *The Formal Semantics of Programming Languages – an Introduction.* Foundations of Computing Series. MIT Press, London, England, 1993.

Two-Dimensional Bi-directional Object Layout

Yoav Zibin* and Joseph (Yossi) Gil

Technion—Israel Institute of Technology
{zyoav,yogi}@cs.technion.ac.il

Abstract. C++ object layout schemes rely on (sometimes numerous) compiler generated fields. We describe a new language-independent object layout scheme, which is space optimal, i.e., objects are contiguous, and contain *no compiler generated fields* other than a single type identifier. As in C++ and other multiple inheritance languages such as Cecil and Dylan, the new scheme sometimes requires extra levels of indirection to access some of the fields. Using a data set of 28 hierarchies, totaling almost 50,000 types, we show that the new scheme improves field access efficiency over standard implementations, and competes favorably with (the non-space optimal) highly optimized C++ specific implementations. The benchmark includes a new analytical model for computing the frequency of indirections in a sequence of field access operations. Our layout scheme relies on whole-program analysis, which requires about 10 microseconds per type on a contemporary architecture (Pentium III, 900Mhz, 256MB machine), even in very large hierarchies.

1 Introduction

A common argument raised by proponents of the single inheritance programming model is that multiple inheritance incurs space and time overheads and inefficiencies on the runtime system [1, 7]. A large body of research was targeted at reducing the multiple inheritance overhead in operations such as dynamic message dispatch and subtyping tests (see e.g., [17, 18, 19] for recent surveys). Another great concern in the design of runtime systems for multiple inheritance hierarchies is efficient object layout. To this end, both general purpose [9] and C++ language specific [5, 4] object layout schemes were previously proposed in the literature.

The various C++ layout schemes are not space-optimal since they introduce (sometimes many) compiler generated fields into the layout. They are also not time-optimal since access to certain fields (in particular, those defined in virtual bases) requires several memory dereferences. This paper revisits the object layout problem in the general, language-independent setting. Our new object layout scheme is space optimal, i.e., objects are contiguous, and contain *no compiler generated fields*. Hence, in terms of space, it is superior to C++ layout schemes. It is also superior in terms of field access efficiency to the space-optimal *field dispatching* technique[1] employed by many object oriented languages.

---

* Contact author.

[1] In the field dispatching technique we encapsulate fields in accessor methods.

L. Cardelli (Ed.): ECOOP 2003, LNCS 2743, pp. 329–350, 2003.

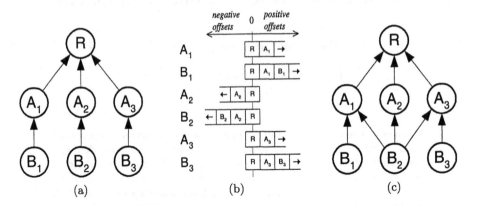

Fig. 1. A small single inheritance hierarchy (a), a possible object layout for this hierarchy (b), and a multiple inheritance hierarchy in which there is no contiguous layout for all objects (c)

We say that the layout is *two dimensional, bi-directional* since all objects can be thought of as being laid out first in a two-dimensional matrix, whose rows (also called *layers*) may span both positive and negative indices. The layout algorithm ensures that the populated portion of each such layer is consecutive, regardless of the object type. The particular object layout in one-dimensional memory is a cascade of these portions.

A data set of 28 hierarchies, totaling almost 50,000 types, was used in comparing the field access efficiency of the new scheme with that of different C++ specific layouts. Our analytical cost model shows that in this data set, the new scheme is superior to the standard C++ layout and to the simple inlining algorithm [4]. Even though the new layout is not C++ specific, it competes favorably in this respect with aggressive inlining [4], arguably the best C++ layout scheme.

To better understand the intricacies of object layout, consider Figure 1a, which depicts a small single inheritance hierarchy.

A possible object layout of the types defined in this hierarchy is shown in Figure 1b. The fields of A_1 are laid out just after R. The layout of B_1 adds its own fields in increasing offsets. All types inheriting from A_1 and B_1 will have positive directionality. Types A_2 and B_2 are laid out in negative offsets. This should also be the directionality of any of their descendants. Types A_3 and B_3 and all of their descendants have positive directionality.

Figure 1b demonstrates a degenerate case of the two-dimensional bidirectional layout scheme, in which there is only one layer. This layer is populated either in negative or positive offsets. In the general case, there are multiples layers, which may use for the same object type both positive and negative offsets, or even be empty.

Consider now the multiple inheritance hierarchy of Figure 1, obtained by adding multiple inheritance edges from B_2 to A_1 and A_3. Here and henceforth, inheritance is assumed to be *shared* (`virtual` in the C++ jargon). Thus, in the figure, type B_2 has a *single* R sub-object. We believe that repeated inheritance, i.e., where type B_2 has two R sub-objects, is a rarity, or as one wrote: "repeated inheritance is an abomination".[2]

With the addition of multiple inheritance, a layout for B_2 becomes difficult, since at the same positive offsets immediately following R we expect to find both the fields of A_1 and the fields of A_3. This difficulty is no coincidence, and is in fact a result of the strong conformance requirement (or fixed offsets [9]) which we implicitly made:

> **The Strong Conformance Requirement:** Every type must be laid out in the same offset in all of its descendants.

If the layout of A_1, A_2 and A_3 is required to be contiguous, then the fields of each of these types must be laid out adjacent to R. Since the layout of R in memory has only two sides, then it must be that at least two of A_1, A_2 and A_3 are laid out at the same side of R. This is not a problem as long as these two types are never laid out together, as is the case in single inheritance. The difficulty is raised in multiple inheritance, specifically, when there is a common descendant of these two types.

Thus, we see that it is sometimes impossible to maintain the strong conformance requirement and contiguous object layout. Our new scheme resolves the conflict by sacrificing the strong conformance requirement. In particular, each object is laid out in one or more layers, where each layer uses a bidirectional layout. The above difficulty is removed by placing (say) type A_3 in a different layer.

We note that separate compilation discovers too late that two base types compete for the same memory location, i.e., after the layout of these base types was determined. For this reason, our layout scheme, just as all other optimizing layouts, relies on whole program analysis.

Outline Pertinent definitions are given in Section 2, which also lists some of the standard simplifications of the object layout problem. Section 3 describes the criteria used in evaluating object layout schemes, using these to place our result in the context of previous work. The actual layout, which comes in three versions is described in Section 4. Section 5 presents the algorithm for computing the actual layout. Section 6 describes the data-set used in the benchmark, while Section 7 gives the experimental results. Finally, conclusions and directions for future research are given in Section 8.

Epilog We have recently learnt that similar results were independently obtained by Pugh and Weddell and described in a 1993 technical report [10]. Their work suggests a similar layout algorithm, using fields instead of types, and includes several theoretical bounds on complexity. Our work takes a more empirical slant.

---

[2] Words of an anonymous reviewer to [5].

2   Definitions

Leading to a more exact specification of the problem, this section makes precise notions such as a hierarchy, incomparable types, and introduced and accessible fields in a type.

A *hierarchy* is specified by a set of types $\mathcal{T}$, $n = |\mathcal{T}|$, and a partial order, $\preceq$, called the *subtype relation* which must be reflexive, transitive and anti-symmetric. Let $a, b \in \mathcal{T}$ be arbitrary. Then, if $a \preceq b$ holds we say that a is a *subtype* of b and that b is a *supertype* of a. If neither $a \preceq b$ nor $a \succeq b$ holds, we say that the types are *incomparable*. Also, if there does not exist c such that $a \preceq c \preceq b$ and $c \neq a$, $c \neq b$, then we say that a is a *child* of b and that b is a *parent* of a.

A hierarchy is *single inheritance* if each $a \in \mathcal{T}$ has at most one parent, and *multiple inheritance* otherwise.

The set of ancestors of a type $a \in \mathcal{T}$ is $\mathrm{ancestors}(a) \equiv \{b \in \mathcal{T} \mid a \preceq b\}$. We denote the number of ancestors of a by θ_a. Note that $a \in \mathrm{ancestors}(a)$.

Types in a hierarchy may *introduce* fields, which can be thought of as unique names or selectors. We assume that there is no *field overriding*, i.e., that the same field name can only be used once in each type. Although C++ (and other languages) allow a derived class to reuse the name of a `private` field defined in a base class, our assumption is trivially satisfied by simple renaming.

Stated differently, our demand is that no run time dispatching process is required to select the particular "implementation" of a field name. This is precisely the case in statically typed languages, where the field name and the static object type uniquely determine the introducing class.

The problem of object layout in dynamically typed languages is not very interesting and excluded from the domain of discourse. In languages such as SMALLTALK, fields access is restricted to the methods of the defining object. With this restriction, the strong conformance requirement does not need to be satisfied[3]: The object layout problem then becomes trivial, even with the face of multiple inheritance. If however a dynamically typed language supports non-private fields, then there must be a runtime check that the accessed field is defined in the object. Such checks are related to subtyping tests and even to a more general dispatching problem which received extensive coverage in the literature [17, 18, 19].

For simplicity, we assume that all fields are of the same size. For a type $t \in \mathcal{T}$, let $|t|$ denote the number of fields introduced in t. The *accessible* fields of a type include all fields introduced in it and in any of its proper supertypes.

Given a type hierarchy, the *object layout problem* is to design a *layout scheme* for the objects of each of the types in the hierarchy, and a method for accessing at runtime the accessible fields of each type. Specifically, given a field f and an object address o of type t, the runtime system should be able to compute the

---

[3] In fact, even the weak conformance requirement (defined later in Section 3) is not satisfied.)

address of o.f. The selector f is a compile time constant, while o is supplied only at runtime.

3 The Object Layout Problem

A layout scheme is evaluated by the following criteria.

1. *Dynamic memory overhead.* This is extra memory allocated for objects, i.e., memory beyond what is required for representing the object's own fields. Ideally, this overhead is zero. However, holes in a noncontiguous object layout contribute to this overhead. Another overhead of this kind are compiler generated fields, e.g., virtual function table pointers (VPTRs) in C++.

   Note that the semantics of most object oriented languages dictates that the layout of each object must include at least *one type identifier*. This identifier is used at runtime to identify the object type, for purposes such as dynamic message dispatch and subtyping tests. This identifier can be conveniently thought of as a field defined in a common root type (e.g., type R in Figure 1), and therefore is not counted as part of the dynamic memory overhead. However, if a scheme allocates multiple type identifiers, as is the case with the C++ standard layout, then all but the first identifier contribute to this overhead.

2. *Field access efficiency.* This is the time required to realize the field access operation o.f. Ideally, fields can be accessed in a single machine instruction, which relies on a fixed offset (from the object base) addressing mode. Layout schemes often rely on several levels of indirection for computing a field location in memory.

   It is common that all fields introduced in a certain type are laid out consecutively. Since f is supplied at compile time, the type t' in which f was introduced can be precomputed. The main duty of the runtime system is to find the location in memory in which the fields of t' are laid out in t, the type of o.

3. *Static memory overhead.* These are the tables and other data-structures used by the layout which are shared between all objects of a certain type. This overhead is usually less significant than the dynamic memory overhead, and therefore it seems worthwhile to maximize sharing. On the other hand, retrieving the shared information comes at the cost of extra indirections, and may reduce field access efficiency.

4. *Time for computing the layout.* This is the time required for computing the layout, which could be exponential in some schemes.

Object layout in a single inheritance hierarchy can simultaneously optimize all the above metrics. As can be seen in Figure 1b, both static and dynamic memory overheads are zero. Field access efficiency is optimal with no dereferencing. Also, the computation of the layout is as straightforward as it can be.

A trivial layout scheme for multiple inheritance which maintains the strong conformance requirement is that the layout of each type reserves memory for *all* fields defined in the hierarchy. Static memory overhead, time for computing the layout, and field access efficiency are optimized. However, dynamic memory overhead is huge since each object uses memory of size $\sum_{t\in\mathcal{T}}|t|$, regardless of its actual type, which usually has far fewer accessible fields.

Pugh and Weddell [9] investigated more efficient layout schemes which still fulfill the strong conformance requirement. The dynamic memory overhead of their main bidirectional object layout scheme is in one case study only 6%, compared to 47% in a unidirectional object layout. The authors also showed that the problem of determining whether an optimal bidirectional layout exists is NP-complete.

At the other extreme stands what may be called *field dispatching* layout scheme, which is employed by many dynamically typed programming languages including Cecil [2] and Dylan [12]. In this scheme, the layout of type t is obtained by iterating (in some arbitrary order) over the set ancestors(t), laying out their fields in order. Since the strong conformance property is broken, we encapsulate fields in accessor methods. If a field position changes in a subtype, we override its accessor. The dynamic memory overhead in this scheme is zero.

Dispatching on accessor methods can be implemented by an $n \times n$ *field dispatch matrix* which gives the base offset of a type in the layout of any of its descendants. This static memory overhead can be reduced if the matrix is compressed by e.g., techniques used for method dispatching (see e.g., [18] for a recent survey). A different implementation is found in the SmallEiffel compiler [16], in which a static branch code over the dynamic type of the object finds the required base offset.

The main drawback of field dispatching is in reduced field access efficiency. In the matrix implementation, field access requires at least three indirections in the simplest version, and potentially more with a compressed representation of the matrix.

An interesting tradeoff between the two extremes is offered by the memory model of C++ [6]. C++ distinguishes between `virtual` and *non-virtual* bases.[4] For non-virtual bases, C++ uses a relaxed conformance requirement. Let $t_1, t_2, t_3 \in \mathcal{T}$ be such that t_1 is a non-`virtual` base of t_2, and t_3 is an arbitrary subtype of t_2.

The Weak Conformance Requirement: The offset of t_1 with respect to t_2 is fixed in all occurrences of t_2 within $t_3 \preceq t_2$.

In other words, although the offset of t_1 is not the same in all of its descendants, it is fixed with respect to any specific descendant t_2, regardless of where that descendant is found. Consequently, to find the location of t_1 within t_3 it is sufficient to find the address of t_2 within t_3.

The weak conformance requirement can be maintained together with object contiguity in many multiple-inheritance hierarchies, specifically those with no

---

[4] We are not so interested in the textbook [14] difference between the two. Instead, we say that a type is a virtual base if two or more of its children have a common descendant.

virtual-bases. However, since a type is not always located at the same offset, it is necessary to apply a process called this -adjustment [13] in order to access a field introduced in a supertype. For example, a method of t_2 cannot be invoked on an object of type t_3, without first correcting the pointer to the object, coercing it to type t_2.

The this -adjustment model incurs many penalties other than the time required for the addition. For example, the runtime system must apply null checks before a pointer can be corrected. Also, a conversion from an array of subtypes to an array of supertypes cannot be done constant time. Moreover, an object may contain multiple type-identifiers, (VPTRs in the C++ jargon) contributing to dynamic memory overhead. Also, the pointers to the same object may have different values which is a serious hurdle for garbage collectors (and for efficient identity testing).

In hierarchies with virtual bases, even the weak conformance requirement cannot be satisfied together with object contiguity. In these cases, C++ uses *virtual base pointers* (VBPTRs) to tie memory segments of the same object. Gil and Sweeney [5] give a detailed description of VBPTRs. We only mention that VBPTR can be stored directly in the objects, as in the "standard" C++ implementation, contributing to dynamic memory overhead, or moved to the static memory, at the cost of increasing field access time. Also, in order to be able to access fields at constant time, an implementation must store (a potentially quadratic number of) *inessential* VBPTRs. We note that referencing fields through VBPTRs also requires this -adjustment, and that a virtual base does have a VPTR.

Gil and Sweeney [5] proposed several optimizations of the standard C++ layout, which were then empirically evaluated by Eckel and Gil [4], whose main yardstick was dynamic and static memory overhead. The main optimization which contributes to field access efficiency is *simple-inline* which tries to reduce the number of virtual bases by conforming transformations of the hierarchy. *Aggressive-inline* does the same, using a maximal-independent set heuristic as procedure for finding a close to optimal set of transformations. The *bidirectional object layout* optimization reduces dynamic memory overhead but does not contribute to field access efficiency.

For the purpose of illustration, Figure 2 depicts a type hierarchy and its aggressive-inline C++ layout. The same hierarchy will be used below in Section 5 for demonstrating the new two-dimensional bi-directional layout. A C++ programmer is allowed to denote some of the inheritance edges as virtual. In the figure, inheritance edges ⟨B, A⟩ and ⟨C, A⟩ are virtual so that F has a single A sub-object. The virtual edges that were *inlined* in the aggressive-inline layout are marked in bold, while the other non-inlined virtual edges are dashed. The cells with a dot in Figure 2b represent VPTRs (VBPTRs were not drawn since they can be stored either in a class or in all of its instances).

The new scheme incurs *no dynamic memory overhead*. In this respect it is at least as good as any other layout scheme, and strictly better than all C++ implementations (which may include more than one VPTR). The most

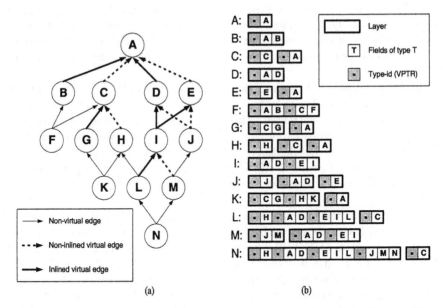

Fig. 2. A type hierarchy (a) with its aggressive-inline C++ layout (b)

interesting criterion for comparison with C++ and field dispatching is therefore field access efficiency. We shall see that the new scheme competes favorably even with the highly optimized and language specific aggressive-inline layout scheme.

Our results indicate that the time for computing the new layout is small—about 10 μSec per type (see Section 7). We also find that the static memory overhead is small compared both to field dispatching and various C++ techniques.

The new layout is *uniform*, in the sense that (unlike C++) the runtime system does not need any information on the static type of an object pointer in order to access any of its fields. Consider an object o and a field f. Then, the sequence of machine instructions for the field access operation o.f depends only on the selector f, and is the same regardless of the type of o. This is in contrast to languages such as C++ in which, depending on the static type of o, access to field f is either direct, or through indirection.

4   Two-Dimensional Bi-directional Object Layout

In the two-dimensional bi-directional object layout strategy each field defined in the type hierarchy has a two-dimensional address $\langle \ell, \Delta \rangle$. Coordinate ℓ, $1 \le \ell \le L$, is the field's *layer*, where L is the number of layers used by the type hierarchy. (The assignment of types into layers is the subject of Section 5.) Coordinate Δ is an integral offset of the field in its layer. We say that the layout is bidirectional since this offset may be either positive or negative.

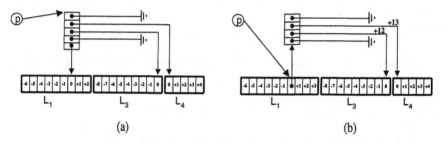

Fig. 3. The canonical (a) and the compact (b) two-dimensional bi-directional layout of an object from a 5-layer hierarchy. Layers L_2 and L_5 are empty in the depicted object

All fields introduced in the same type t are laid out consecutively: Their layer is the same as ℓ_t, the type's layer, while their offset is fixed with respect to Δ_t, the offset of the type. This section describes the actual object layout, which has three versions: the simple and not so efficient *canonical* layout, which is included for purpose of illustration, the general purpose *compact* layout, which we expect to be used in most cases, and the highly-optimized *inlined* layout which is applicable in some special cases.

In the *canonical* layout each object is represented as a pointer to a *Layers Dispatch Table* (LDT) of size L. Entry i, $i = 1, \ldots, L$, of the LDT points to the ith layer of the object.

The canonical layout is demonstrated in Figure 3(a) for the case $L = 5$. The object depicted in the figure represented by a pointer p to its LDT, which stores pointers to layers L_1, L_3, and L_4. The type of the object is such that it has no fields from the second and the fifth layers. Hence the corresponding entries of the LDT are null.

In general, layers are two directional, and may store fields with both negative and positive offsets. Such is layer L_1 in the figure, with offsets in the range $-6, \ldots, +2$. However, the type of the object depicted has no fields with positive offsets in layer L_3. Similarly, layer L_4 has no fields with negative offsets.

We can see in the figure that each of the layers is contiguous. More precisely, if an object has a field at a certain layer in offset $\Delta > 0$, then it also has fields in all offsets $0, \ldots, \Delta - 1$. By placing the layers and the LDT next to each other we obtain a contiguous object layout. The pointers from the LDT to the layers can then be stored as relative offsets.

A compiler algorithm for producing the runtime access code in the canonical layout is presented in 5canonical. Take note that the type t, the layer ℓ_t, and the offsets Δ_t and Δ_f are computed at compile time. A *single* memory dereference is required to compute the field *address*.

It is important to notice that the occupied entries in each layer depend only on the object *type*. Therefore, an offset-based LDT is identical in all objects of the same type and can be shared. The *compact* version of object layout is obtained

---

Algorithm 1 An algorithm for generating field access code in the canonical layout

---

Given f, a name of a field of type int, and a pointer p to an object which uses the *canonical layout*, generate the code sequence (using pseudo-C++ notation) for accessing field f in p.

1: Let t be the type in which f was defined
2: Let ℓ_t be the unique layer of t // ℓ_t *is a positive integer*
3: Let integer Δ_t be the offset of t
4: Let Δ_f be the offset of f within its type // Δ_f *is a non-negative integer*
5: **Output**
```
int *layer_ptr = ((int **)p)[ℓt − 1];
int &r = layer_ptr[Δt + Δf];
```

---

by employing this sharing and by letting the object pointers reference the first layer directly, which tends to be the largest in our algorithm for assigning fields to layers.

Figure 3b gives an example of the compact layout of the same object of Figure 3a. In the figure we see the same three non-empty layers: L_1, L_3 and L_4. However, the object pointer p now points to offset 0 in layer L_1. At this offset we find the *object type identifier*, which is a pointer to the shared LDT. Notice that the size of layer L_1 was increased by one to accommodate the object type identifier. Also, there are now only four entries in the LDT, which correspond to layers $L_2, \ldots, L_5$.

Algorithm 2 An algorithm for generating field access code in the compact layout

---

Given f, a name of a field of type int, and a pointer p to an object which uses the *compact layout*, generate the code sequence (using pseudo-C++ notation) for accessing field f in p.

1: Let t be the type in which f was defined
2: Let ℓ_t be the unique layer of t // ℓ_t *is a positive integer*
3: Let integer Δ_t be the offset of t
4: Let Δ_f be the offset of f within its type // Δ_f *is a non-negative integer*
5: **If** $\ell_t = 1$ **then**
6:     **Output**
```
int &r = ((int *)p)[Δt + Δf];
```
7: **else**
8:     **Output**
```
int *p1 = *((int **)p);
int layer_offset = p1[ℓt − 2];
int &r = p[layer_offset + Δt + Δf];
```

Algorithm 2 is run by the compiler to generate the code sequence for accessing a field in the compact layout. If the compiler determines that the field is in the first layer, then the field can be accessed directly—*no* memory dereferences are required for computing its address. If the field however falls in any other layer, then memory must be dererenced once to find the LDT, and then again to find the layer offset. Also, in this case, the addressing mode for the final field access is slightly more complicated since it must add compile- and runtime- offsets.

The LDT in the example of Figure 3 includes only four entries, all of which are byte-size integers (assuming of course that the object size is less than 256 bytes). The entire LDT can be represented as a single 32 bit words. The *inlined* layout is obtained from the compact layout by inlining the LDT into the object's first layer. At the cost of increasing object space, inlining saves a level of indirection in fetching LDT entries. Note that even if the LDT is stored inside the object, each object must include at least one type identifier for purposes such as subtyping tests and dispatching. Therefore, even in this simple example, the inlined layout uses more space than the compact layout.

5   Computing Type Addresses

This section is dedicated to the algorithm for assigning field addresses. The main constraint to maintain is that all layers are contiguous in all types. It is always possible to find such an assignment, since each field can be allocated its own layer (as done in field dispatching).

Our objective is an assignment which minimizes L, the number of layers. One reason for doing so, is that the memory required for LDTs is $L \times n$. LDTs are source for static memory overhead in the compact layout, and dynamic memory overhead in the inlined layout.

However, our most important motivation is reducing the *likelihood of LDT fetches*, or in other words, inefficiency of field access. If the number of layers is one, then all fields can be retrieved without any dereferences. We note that if the number of layers is small, then an optimizing compiler might be able to pre-fetch and reuse layer addresses to accelerate field access.

Note first that each layer has a positive and a negative *semi-layer*, and that these semi-layers are independent for the purpose of allocation. To understand the constraints of allocation better, consider Figure 4a which gives the object layout for our running example.

We see in the figure that the hierarchy uses a total of two layers and three semi-layers. The first layer has at offset 0 the object type identifier and a positive and negative semi-layers. The second layer uses only the positive semi-layer. The arrows in the figure indicate the place where the semi-layer may continue.

Figure 4b shows the allocation of types to semi-layers which generates this layout: Seven types A, C, F, H, K, L, and N are in semi-layer 1 (positive side of the first layer). Semi-layer 2 (negative side of the first layer) includes five types: B, E, G, J, and M. Only D and I are in semi-layer 3 (positive side of the second

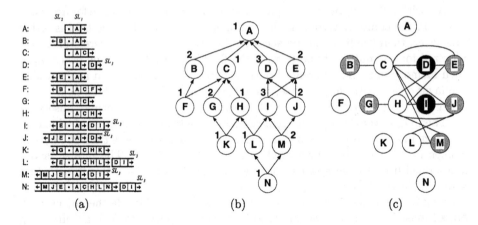

Fig. 4. The two-dimensional bi-directional object layout of the running example (a), the allocation of types in it to semi-layers (b), and the conflict graph with its coloring (c)

layer). The layout of type N for example, makes use of all three semi-layers, while the layout of D uses just semi-layers 1 and 3.

Notice the following points: (**i**) Semi-layers 1 and 2 comprising the first layer are in a fixed offset. Semi-layer 3 occurs at different offsets in different types. (**ii**) Each type is always placed in the same location in its layer. For example, E is located in the first location in semi-layer 2 in the layouts of all of its descendants: E, I, J, L, M, and N. (**iii**) The same location in the same semi-layer can be used for different types. For example, the first location of semi-layer 1 stores also the fields of B in the layout of F, and the fields of G in the layout of K. (**iv**) Types are allocated to semi-layers in descending subtyping order. For example, we see that types A, C, H, L and N are placed in this order in semi-layer 1 in the layout of N and that $A \succeq C \succeq H \succeq L \succeq N$.

The general question is whether two arbitrary types $a, b \in \mathcal{T}$ can be allocated to the same semi-layer, and what should their relative ordering in that semi-layer should be. Suppose first, without loss of generality, that $a \preceq b$. Then, whenever a appears, so does b. Therefore, with the absence of other constraints, we can allocate a and b into the same semi-layer, and a must be placed after b in this semi-layer. If however a and b are incomparable, then they could be allocated to the same semi-layer, and even to the same location in the level, as long as they do not occur together in the layout of any third type c. In other words, the allocation is allowed as long as a and b have no common descendants.

Figure 4c shows the *conflict graph* of our running example, where two types are connected by an edge if they are incomparable, yet have a common descendant. We see in the figure that no edges are incident on A. This is because A is the root, and as such is comparable with all types in the hierarchy. Also, no edges are incident on the leaves F, K and N. The edge between C and E , for example, is due to their common descendant L.

A node coloring of the conflict graph provides a legal allocation. We of course seek a minimal coloring of this graph. Figure 4c gives a coloring of the conflict graph of the running example. A total of three colors are used: White nodes are allocated to semi-layer 1, grey to semi-layer 2, and black to semi-layer 3.

Algorithm 3 shows the general procedure for address allocation. Using a graph coloring heuristic, the algorithm computes the number of layers for the layout. Also, for each type t in the input hierarchy the algorithm returns ℓ_t, its layer and Δ_t, the base offset in the layer at which its fields are allocated. If $\Delta_t \geq 0$, then fields are allocated in ascending addresses. Otherwise, t is in the negative semi-layer, and field are placed in the addresses below Δ_t.

Algorithm 3 Produce the compact two-dimensional bi-directional layout of a hierarchy

---

Given a hierarchy T and $\preceq$, return the number of layers L, and compute ℓ_t and Δ_t for each type $t \in T$

1: Let $E \leftarrow \emptyset$ // E is the set of edges in the undirected conflict graph
2: **For all** $t \in T$ **do** // Consider all possible common descendants
3:    **For all** $p_1, p_2 \in$ ancestors(t) **do** // p_1 and p_2 have a common descendant t
4:       **If** $p_1 \npreceq p_2$ and $p_1 \nsucceq p_2$ **then** // p_1 and p_2 are incomparable
5:          **If** $\{p_1, p_2\} \notin E$ **then** // A new conflict edge found
6:             $E \leftarrow E \cup \{\{p_1, p_2\}\}$

7: Let $G \leftarrow \langle T, E \rangle$ // G is the graph of conflicts between types
8: Let $\phi : T \mapsto [1, \ldots, s]$ be a coloring of the nodes of G

9: **For all** $t \in T$ **do** // Compute the offset and the semi-layer of t
10:    $\Delta_t \leftarrow 0$ // Compute the total size of proper ancestors in the same semi-layer as t
11:    **For all** $p \in$ ancestors(t), $p \neq t$ **do**
12:       **If** $\phi(p) = \phi(t)$ **then** // Ancestor p is in the same semi-layer as t
13:          $\Delta_t \leftarrow \Delta_t + |p|$
14:    $\ell_t \leftarrow \lceil \phi(t)/2 \rceil$ // Layer l hosts colors $2l - 1$ and $2l$
15:    **If** $\phi(t)$ mod $2 = 0$ **then** // Even colored objects are laid out in negative semi-layers
16:       $\Delta_t \leftarrow -\Delta_t - 1$ // Offsets of negative semi-layers start at -1
17:    **else if** $\phi(t) = 1$ **then**
18:       $\Delta_t \leftarrow \Delta_t + 1$ // Offset 0 in layer 1 is reserved for the type-identifier

19: **Return** $\lceil s/2 \rceil$

Lines 3–3 compute the edges in the conflict graph. In the main loop, we consider the ancestors of each candidate. There is a conflict between any two of its ancestors if they are incomparable. The runtime of the inner loop should (empirically) be close to linear, since the average number of ancestors in our hierarchies is small.

Next (lines 3–3) we compute the conflict graph and a coloring of it. We use a simple, greedy heuristic for finding this coloring. A favorable property of this heuristic is that the color groups tend to come out in descending order, i.e., $|\phi^{-1}(i)| \geq |\phi^{-1}(i+1)|$ for $i = 1, \ldots, s - 1$. Since fields in the first layer can be accessed in a single indirection, the first layer should be as large as possible.

The next command block computes the layer of each type t, and its (positive or negative) offset within this layer. Lines 3–3 compute the total size of types which precede t in its semi-layer. After computing the layer number (line 3) we turn to making the necessary corrections to the offset. In general, positive semi-layers use offsets $0, +1, +2, \ldots$, while negative semi-layers use offsets $-1, -2, \ldots$ (lines 3–3). However, layer 1 is special since it contains the type identifier at offset 0 (lines 3–3).

6   Data Set

For the purpose of evaluating the multi-layer object layout scheme, we used an ensemble of 28 type hierarchies, drawn from eight different programming languages, and spanning almost 50,000 types. The first 27 hierarchies[5] were used in our previous benchmarks. A detailed description of their origin, respective programming language, and many of their statistical and topological properties can be found elsewhere [17, 18]. (Even though multiple-inheritance of fields is not possible in JAVA, the JAVA hierarchies are still useful in characterizing how programmers tend to use multiple inheritance.) To these we added Flavors, a 67-type hierarchy representing the *multi-inheritance core* of the Flavors language [8] benchmark used by Pugh and Weddell [9, Fig. 5].

Together, the hierarchies span a range of sizes, from 67 types (in IDL and Flavors) up to 8,793 types in MI: IBM SF, the median being 930 types. The hierarchies are relatively shallow, with heights between 9 and 17. Most types have just one parent, and the overall average number of parents is 1.2. In these and other respects, the hierarchies are not very different from balanced binary trees [4]

The number of ancestors is typically small, averaging less than 10 in most hierarchies. Exceptions are the Geode and the Self hierarchies, which make an extensive use of multiple inheritance. In Geode, there are 14 ancestors in average to each type, and there exists a type with as many as 50 ancestors. Self has 31 ancestors in average per type. The topology of Self is quite unique in that almost all types in it inherit from a type with 23 ancestors. Table 1 below gives (among other information), the number of types in each hierarchy, and the maximal and average number of ancestors.

---

[5] IDL, MI: IBM XML, JDK 1.1, Laure, Ed, LOV, Cecil2, Cecil-, Unidraw, Harlequin, MI: Orbacus Test, MI: HotJava, Dylan, Cecil, Geode, MI: Orbacus, Vor3, MI: Corba, JDK 1.18, Self, Vortex3, Eiffel4, MI: Orbix, JDK 1.22, JDK 1.30, MI: JDK 1.3.1, and MI: IBM SF.

Table 1. Statistics on the input hierarchies, including the number of colors and layers found by 5TD compared with the maximal anti-chain lower bound

Hierarchy $\langle \mathcal{T}, \preceq \rangle$	$n = \lvert\mathcal{T}\rvert$	ω [6]	s [7]	$\lceil\omega/2\rceil$	$\lceil s/2\rceil$	$\max(\theta_t)$ [8]	$\text{avg}(L_t)$ [9]	$\text{avg}(\theta_t)$ [10]
Flavors	67	3	4	2	2	13	1.6	4.9
IDL	67	2	2	1	1	9	1.0	4.8
MI: IBM XML	145	5	5	3	3	14	1.5	4.4
JDK 1.1	226	2	2	1	1	8	1.0	4.2
Laure	295	3	3	2	2	16	1.1	8.1
Ed	434	12	13	6	7	23	3.2	8.0
LOV	436	13	14	7	7	24	3.5	8.5
Cecil2	472	8	8	4	4	29	2.0	7.4
Cecil-	473	8	8	4	4	29	2.0	7.4
Unidraw	614	3	3	2	2	10	1.0	4.0
Harlequin	666	14	14	7	7	31	1.9	6.7
MI: Orbacus Test	689	3	4	2	2	12	1.3	3.9
MI: HotJava	736	14	15	7	8	23	2.0	5.1
Dylan	925	3	3	2	2	13	1.1	5.5
Cecil	932	6	6	3	3	23	1.7	6.5
Geode	1,318	21	22	11	11	50	5.1	14.0
MI: Orbacus	1,379	11	11	6	6	19	1.6	4.5
Vor3	1,660	6	6	3	3	27	1.6	7.5
MI: Corba	1,699	6	7	3	4	18	1.3	3.9
JDK 1.18	1,704	12	12	6	6	16	1.2	4.3
Self	1,802	24	24	12	12	41	10.7	30.9
Vortex3	1,954	8	8	4	4	30	1.7	7.2
Eiffel4	1,999	15	15	8	8	39	2.2	8.8
MI: Orbix	2,716	6	6	3	3	13	1.1	2.8
JDK 1.22	4,339	14	14	7	7	17	1.5	4.4
JDK 1.30	5,438	15	15	8	8	19	1.5	4.4
MI: JDK 1.3.1	7,401	21	21	11	11	24	1.5	4.4
MI: IBM SF	8,793	13	13	7	7	30	2.3	9.2

7   Experimental Results

This section presents the results of running 5TD on our data set. Since this algorithm depends on a graph-coloring heuristic (Line 3), we would like first to be assured by the output quality. We remind the reader that if a graph has a clique of size k, then it cannot be colored by fewer than k colors. Although it is not easy to find cliques in general graphs, some cliques can be efficiently found in conflict graphs. Consider a type t and its set of ancestors ancestors(t). Let $P_t \subseteq$ ancestors(t) be a set of types which are pair-wise incomparable. Then any $t_1, t_2 \in P_t$ are in conflict, and the set P_t is a clique in the conflict graph. Finding a maximal set of incomparable nodes in a hierarchy is a standard procedure of finding a maximal anti-chain in a partial order [15].

Table 1 compares the number of colors and layers with the predictions of the lower bound thus found.

Let $\omega_t = \max\{\lvert P_t\rvert \mid P_t \subseteq$ ancestors(t) is a set of pair-wise incomparable types$\}$, i.e., ω_t is the size of the maximal anti-chain among the ancestors of t. Then, $\omega = \max_{t \in \mathcal{T}}\{\omega_t\}$ is a lower bound on the number of colors (or semi-layers), and $\lceil\omega/2\rceil$ is a lower bound on the number of layers L. We see in the table that $s > \omega$ only in seven hierarchies: Flavors, Ed, LOV, MI: Orbacus Test, MI: HotJava, Geode and MI: Corba. In these seven cases, $s = \omega + 1$, so the number of colors was off by at most one from the lower bound. Further, as the next two columns indicate, the situation that the number of layers is greater than the prediction of the lower bound, occurs in only three hierarchies: Ed, MI: HotJava and MI: Corba.

It is also interesting to compare the number of colors and the number of layers with the maximal number of ancestors, denoted $\alpha = \max(\theta_t)$. As expected, the number of colors is never greater than the maximal number of ancestors, and is typically much smaller than it. The number of entries in the LDT is even smaller, since every two colors are mapped to a single layer.

The maximal number of layers in the field dispatching technique is exactly α, since each layer is a singleton. The field dispatch matrix can be compressed using method dispatching techniques, such as selector coloring [3, 11]. A lower bound on the space requirement of selector coloring is $n \times \alpha$. We therefore have that the static memory of our layout scheme $n \times L$ is superior to that of the field dispatch matrix compressed using selector coloring.

The next two columns of Table 1 give another comparison of hash-table implementation of the LDT with a hash table implementation of the field dispatch matrix. We see that the number of layers which each object uses is typically small. No more than 3.5 in all but the Self and Geode hierarchies. In all hierarchies, we see that the average number of ancestors is much greater than the average number layers. This shows that the **(i)** Algorithm 3 is successful in compressing multiple types into layers, and consequently that **(ii)** the LDT places weaker demands than the field dispatch matrix on static memory.

The theoretical complexity of Algorithm 3 is $O(n^3)$, since lines 3–3 may iterate in certain hierarchies over a fixed fraction of all possible type triplets. The runtime of the simple greedy graph-coloring heuristic is $O(n^2)$. In practice however, the algorithm runs much faster. By applying some rather straightforward algorithmic optimizations, e.g., considering in line 3 only types which have more than one parent, the run times were reduced even further.

On a Pentium III, 900Mhz machine, equipped with 256MB internal memory and running a Windows 2000 operating system, Algorithm 3 required less than 10 mSec in 19 hierarchies. Seven hierarchies required between 10 mSec and 50 mSec. The worst hierarchy was MI: IBM SF which took 400 mSec. The total runtime for all hierarchies was 650 mSec, which gives on average 13μSec of CPU time per type. The runtime of C++ aggressive-inline procedure on the same hardware is much slower. For example, aggressive inline of MI: IBM SF took 3,586 mSec, i.e., about 9 times slower. Simple inline of MI: IBM SF took 2,294 mSec, which is still much slower.

The most important criterion for evaluating a layout scheme is field access efficiency.

Since the hierarchies were drawn from different languages and were not associated with any application programs, we were unable to directly measure the actual cost of field access in the various layout schemes. We can however derive other metrics to compare the costs of the new layout technique with that of prior art.

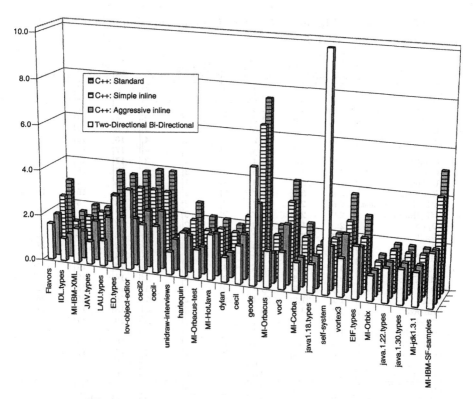

Fig. 5. Average no. of layers in different hierarchies

For example, the number of layers used by a given type, gives an indication on the number of different dereferences required to access *all* the object fields. The corresponding metric in C++ is the number of virtual bases, which can be accessed only by dereferencing a VBPTR.

Figure 5 compares the average number of layers of the new scheme with that of the standard C++ implementation, the simple inlined implementation and the aggressive inlined implementation. In making the comparison we bear in mind that the new scheme is both language-independent and space-optimal—properties which the C++ schemes do not enjoy.

We see in the figure that with the exception of Self hierarchy (which as we mentioned above has a very unique topology), the new layout scheme is always superior to the standard- and simple-inlined implementation of C++. Moreover, the new scheme is superior or comparable with the aggressive-inline layout scheme, with the exception of four hierarchies: Ed, LOV, Geode and Self. Comparing the *maximal*- rather than the *average*- number of layers yields similar results.

Table 2 shows the extra dynamic memory consumed by the various C++ layout schemes, specifically for VPTRs.

Table 2. No. of VPTRs using standard C++ layout, simple inline (S-Inline), and aggressive inline (A-Inline)

Hierarchy	Average			Median			Maximum		
	C++	S-Inline	A-Inline	C++	S-Inline	A-Inline	C++	S-Inline	A-Inline
Flavors	3.4	3.2	2.4	3	3	2	9	8	5
IDL	1.9	1.6	1.2	2	2	1	3	2	2
MI: IBM XML	2.8	2.8	2.0	2	2	1	9	9	6
JDK 1.1	2.1	2.0	1.8	2	2	2	4	4	3
Laure	3.9	3.2	2.3	4	3	2	8	7	5
Ed	5.2	5.0	4.2	4	4	4	16	16	12
LOV	5.6	5.5	4.6	5	5	4	17	17	13
Cecil2	4.6	4.4	3.4	3	3	3	17	15	9
Cecil-	4.6	4.3	3.5	3	3	3	17	15	9
Unidraw	1.4	1.4	1.4	1	1	1	4	3	3
Harlequin	3.6	3.2	2.7	2	2	2	21	19	16
MI: Orbacus Test	2.5	2.1	1.7	2	2	1	8	6	5
MI: HotJava	2.9	2.9	2.7	2	2	2	17	17	15
Dylan	2.0	1.9	1.3	2	2	1	7	6	5
Cecil	3.7	3.5	2.7	3	3	2	16	13	8
Geode	9.9	9.5	8.3	9	9	7	32	31	27
MI: Orbacus	2.8	2.6	2.2	2	2	1	13	12	11
Vor3	4.6	4.2	3.5	4	3	3	17	14	11
MI: Corba	2.6	2.3	1.7	2	2	1	14	12	10
JDK 1.18	1.9	1.9	1.7	2	2	1	14	13	12
Self	21.2	21.2	21.1	22	22	22	26	25	25
Vortex3	4.4	3.8	3.4	3	3	3	18	15	11
Eiffel4	3.7	3.4	3.1	2	2	2	20	17	16
MI: Orbix	1.5	1.4	1.3	1	1	1	7	7	6
JDK 1.22	2.4	2.3	2.1	2	2	2	16	15	14
JDK 1.30	2.4	2.3	2.1	2	2	2	17	17	16
MI: JDK 1.3.1	2.3	2.3	2.0	2	2	1	23	22	21
MI: IBM SF	5.8	5.8	3.6	6	6	3	16	16	13
Total	4.2	4.0	3.3	-	-	22	32	31	27
Median	3.2	3.0	2.4	2	2	2	16	14.5	11
Minimum	1.4	1.4	1.2	1	1	1	3	2	2
Maximum	21.2	21.2	21.1	22	22	22	32	31	27

Curiously, the four hierarchies in which the new scheme does not perform as well, Ed, LOV, Geode and Self, are exactly the hierarchies in which the C++ schemes, including the highly optimized aggressive inline waste the most amount of dynamic memory.

We also offer a more sophisticated theoretical model for comparing the performance of various schemes of object layout which involve indirection to access various fields. Suppose that a certain field was retrieved from a certain layer. Then, a good optimizing compiler should be able to reuse the address of this layer in retrieving other fields from this layer. Even in the standard C++ layout, the compiler may be able to reuse the address of a virtual base to fetch additional fields from this base.

For a fixed type t, and for a sequence of k field accesses, we would like to compute $A_t(k)$, the expected number of extra dereferences required to access these fields. Since much empirical data is missing from our ensemble of hierarchies, we were inclined to make two major simplifying assumptions:

1. *Uniform class size.* The number of fields introduced in each type is the same. Although evidently inaccurate, this assumption should not be crucial to the

results. We do expect that most classes introduce a small number of fields, with a relatively small variety.

2. *Uniform access probability.* The probability of accessing any certain field is fixed, and is independent of the fields accessed previously, nor of the type in which the field is defined. This assumption is clearly in contradiction to the *principle of locality of reference.*

   However, as we shall see, locality of reference improves the performance of layout schemes. It is not clear whether this improvement contribute more to any specific scheme.

The θ_t ancestors of t are laid out in L_t different layers or virtual bases, such that layer i (virtual base i) has $\theta_t(i)$ ancestors. The first layer can always be accessed directly. Access to a field in layer i in step k requires a dereference operation, if that layer was not accessed in steps $1, \ldots, k-1$.

Let $X_t(i)$, $i = 2, \ldots, L_t$ be the random binary variable which is 1 if a field of level i was not referenced in any of the steps $1, \ldots, k$. Then,

$$\mathbf{Prob}[X_t(i) = 1] = \mathbf{Exp}(X_t(i)) = \left(1 - \frac{\theta_t(i)}{\theta_t}\right)^k.$$

Additivity of expectation allows us to sum the above over i, obtaining that the expected number of levels (other than the first) which were not referenced is

$$\sum_{i=2}^{L_t} \left(1 - \frac{\theta_t(i)}{\theta_t}\right)^k.$$

Using the linearity of expectation, we find that the expected number of referenced levels, i.e., the number of dereferences is simply

$$A_t(k) = (L - 1) - \sum_{i=2}^{L_t} \left(1 - \frac{\theta_t(i)}{\theta_t}\right)^k. \tag{1}$$

Averaging over an entire type hierarchy, we define

$$A(k) = \frac{1}{n} \sum_{t \in \mathcal{T}} A_t(k) \tag{2}$$

Figure 6 gives a plot of $A(k)$ vs. k in four sample hierarchies in the layout schemes field dispatching, standard C++ layout, simple inline (S-Inline), aggressive inline (A-Inline), and two-dimensional bi-directional (TDBD). Values of $A(k)$ were computed using (1) and (2) in the respective hierarchy and object layout scheme. For field dispatching, we set $\theta_t(i) = 1$.

It is interesting to see that in all hierarchies and in all layout schemes, the expected number of dereferences is much smaller than the number of actual fields accessed. It is also not surprising that $A(k)$ increases quickly at first and slowly later. As expected, the new scheme is much better than field dispatching. The graphs give hope of saving about 75% of the dereferences incurred in

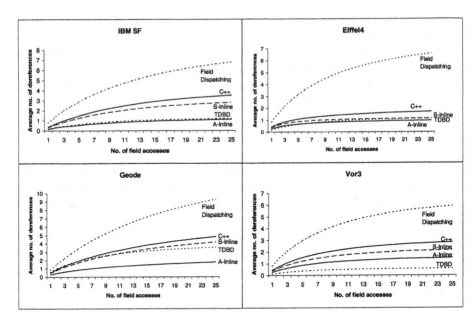

Fig. 6. Average no. of dereferences vs. no. of field accesses in four hierarchies

field dispatching. (Note however that the model does not take into account any optimizations which runtime systems may apply to field dispatching.)

The other, C++ specific techniques are also more efficient than field dispatching. We now turn to comparing these with our scheme. In the Vortex3 hierarchy the new scheme dramatically improves the expected number of dereferences compared to any of the C++ layout schemes. The new scheme is also the best in smaller k values in the Eiffel4 hierarchy, and is comparable to aggressive inline with greater values of k. Another typical behavior is demonstrated by MI: IBM SF, in which the new scheme is almost the same as aggressive-inline. In the Geode hierarchy which is one of the two hierarchies in which the two-dimensional bi-directional scheme cannot find a good partitioning into a small number of layers, we find that aggressive inline gives the best results in terms of field access efficiency. Still, even in this hierarchy the new scheme is better than the standard C++ implementation and the simple-inline outline heuristic.

8   Conclusions and Open Problems

The two-dimensional bi-directional object layout scheme enjoys the following properties: (i) the dynamic memory overhead per object is a single type-identifier, (ii) the static memory per type is small: at most 11 cells in our data set, but usually only around 5 cells, (iii) small time for computing the layout: an average of 13 μSec per type in our data set, and (iv) good field access efficiency as predicted by to our analytical model: the new scheme always improves upon the field dispatching scheme and on the standard C++ layout model. Even compared to the highly optimized C++ layout, after performing aggressive inline, the new scheme still compares favorably.

We note that the new scheme does not rely on this -adjustment, and in the few hierarchies the aggressive-inline C++ won, it was with the cost of large dynamic memory overheads, e.g., as much as 21 VPTRs on average in the Self hierarchy.

The one-dimensional bi-directional layout of Pugh and Weddell's [9] realizes field access in a single indirection, but it may leave holes in some objects. In comparison, our two-dimensional bi-directional layout has no dynamic memory overheads, but a field access might require extra dereferences. In the Flavors hierarchy Pugh and Weddell reported 6% dynamic memory overhead (assuming a single instance per type). Our scheme uses only two layers for this hierarchy, and the probability that a field access would require extra dereferences is only 0.19.

Directions for future work include empirical study of frequencies of field accesses, and further reducing the static memory overheads. In dynamically typed languages where fields can be overloaded, the layout algorithm must color fields instead of types. Empirical data should be gathered to evaluate the efficiency of the layout algorithm in such languages.

References

[1] T. Cargill, B. Cox, W. Cook, M. Loomis, and A. Snyder. Is multiple inheritance essential to OOP? Panel discussion at the Eighth Annual Conference on Object-Oriented Programming Systems, Languages, and Applications (OOP-SLA'95) (Washington, DC), Oct. 1993.

[2] C. Chambers. The Cecil language, specification and rationale. Technical Report TR-93-03-05, University of Washington, Seattle, 1993.

[3] R. Dixon, T. McKee, M. Vaughan, and P. Schweizer. A fast method dispatcher for compiled languages with multiple inheritance. In *Proceedings of the 4th Annual Conference on Object-Oriented Programming Systems, Languages, and Applications*, pages 211–214, New Orleans, Louisiana, Oct. 1-6 1989. OOPSLA'89, ACM SIGPLAN Notices 24(10) Oct. 1989.

[4] N. Eckel and J. Y. Gil. Empirical study of object-layout strategies and optimization techniques. In *Proceedings of the 14th European Conference on Object-Oriented Programming*, number 1850 in Lecture Notes in Computer Science, pages 394–421, Sophia Antipolis and Cannes, France, June 12–16 2000. ECOOP 2000, Springer Verlag.

[5] J. Y. Gil and P. Sweeney. Space- and time-efficient memory layout for multiple inheritance. In *Proceedings of the 14th Annual Conference on Object-Oriented Programming Systems, Languages, and Applications*, pages 256–275, Denver, Colorado, Nov.1-5 1999. OOPSLA'99, ACM SIGPLAN Notices 34(10) Nov. 1999.

[6] S. B. Lippman. *Inside The C++ Object Model.* Addison-Wesley, 2nd edition, 1996.

[7] B. Magnussun, B. Meyer, and et al. Who needs need multiple inheritance. Panel discussion at the European conference on Technology of Object Oriented Programming (TOOLS Europe'94), Mar. 1994.

[8] D. A. Moon. Object-oriented programming with flavors. In *Proceedings of the 1ˢᵗ Annual Conference on Object-Oriented Programming Systems, Languages, and Applications*, pages 1–8, Portland, Oregon, USA, Sept. 29 - Oct. 2 1986. OOP-SLA'86, ACM SIGPLAN Notices 21(11) Nov. 1986.

[9] W. Pugh and G. Weddell. Two-directional record layout for multiple inheritance. In *Proceedings of the ACM SIGPLAN'90 Conference on Programming Language Design and Implementation (PLDI)*, pages 85–91, White Plains, New York, June 1990. ACM SIGPLAN, ACM Press. SIGPLAN Notices 25(6).

[10] W. Pugh and G. Weddell. On object layout for multiple inheritance. Technical Report CS-93-22, University of Waterloo—Department of Computer Science, May 1993.

[11] A. Royer. Optimizing Method Search with Lookup Caches and Incremental Coloring. In *Proceedings of the 7ᵗʰ Annual Conference on Object-Oriented Programming Systems, Languages, and Applications*, pages 110–126, Vancouver, British Columbia, Canada, Oct.18-22 1992. OOPSLA'92, ACM SIGPLAN Notices 27(10) Oct. 1992.

[12] A. Shalit. *The Dylan Reference Manual: The Definitive Guide to the New Object-Oriented Dynamic Language*. Addison-Wesley, Reading, Mass., 1997.

[13] B. Stroustrup. *The Design and Evolution of C++*. Addison-Wesley, Reading, Massachusetts, Mar. 1994.

[14] B. Stroustrup. *The C++ Programming Language*. Addison-Wesley, Reading, Massachusetts, 3ʳᵈ edition, 1997.

[15] W. T. Trotter. *Combinatorics and Partially Ordered Sets: Dimension Theory*. The Johns Hopkins University Press, 1992.

[16] O. Zendra, C. Colnet, and S. Collin. Efficient dynamic dispatch without virtual function tables: The SmallEiffel compiler. In *Proceedings of the 12ᵗʰ Annual Conference on Object-Oriented Programming Systems, Languages, and Applications*, pages 125–141, Atlanta, Georgia, Oct. 5-9 1997. OOPSLA'97, ACM SIGPLAN Notices 32(10) Oct. 1997.

[17] Y. Zibin and J. Y. Gil. Efficient subtyping tests with PQ-encoding. In *Proceedings of the 16ᵗʰ Annual Conference on Object-Oriented Programming Systems, Languages, and Applications*, pages 96–107, Tampa Bay, Florida, Oct. 14–18 2001. OOPSLA'01, ACM SIGPLAN Notices 36(10) Oct. 2001.

[18] Y. Zibin and J. Y. Gil. Fast algorithm for creating space efficient dispatching tables with application to multi-dispatching. In *Proceedings of the 17ᵗʰ Annual Conference on Object-Oriented Programming Systems, Languages, and Applications*, pages 142–160, Seattle, Washington, Nov. 4-8 2002. OOPSLA'02, ACM SIGPLAN Notices 37(10) Nov. 2002.

[19] Y. Zibin and J. Y. Gil. Incremental algorithms for dispatching in dynamically typed languages. In *Proceedings of the 30ᵗʰ ACM SIGPLAN-SIGACT symposium on Principles of programming languages (POPL'03)*, pages 126–138. ACM Press, 2003.

LeakBot: An Automated and Lightweight Tool for Diagnosing Memory Leaks in Large Java Applications

Nick Mitchell and Gary Sevitsky

IBM T.J. Watson Research Center
19 Skyline Drive
Hawthorne, NY 10532 USA
{nickm,sevitsky}@us.ibm.com

Abstract. Despite Java's automatic reclamation of memory, memory leaks remain an important problem. For example, we frequently encounter memory leaks that cause production servers to crash. These servers represent an increasingly common class of Java applications: they are *large scale* and they make *heavy use of frameworks*. For these applications, existing tools require too much expertise, and, even for experts, require many hours interpreting low-level details. In addition, they are often too expensive to use in practice. We present an automated, adaptive, and scalable tool for diagnosing memory leaks, called LeakBot.

LeakBot incorporates three new techniques. First, it automatically ranks data structures by their likelihood of containing leaks. This process dramatically prunes the set of candidate structures, using object reference graph properties and knowledge of how leaks occur. Second, it uses Co-evolving Regions to identify suspicious regions within a data structure and characterize their *expected* evolution. Third, it uses the first two methods to derive a lightweight way to track those regions' *actual* evolution as the program runs. These techniques are mutually beneficial: we need only monitor what is highly ranked, and, because the tracking is so cheap, a region's rank can be continually updated with information from production machines. Finally, this whole process can be done without user assistance.

We demonstrate LeakBot's effectiveness on a number of large-scale applications that we have analyzed as part of the ongoing consulting practice our group maintains. We have found that the ranking analysis scales (e.g. written in Java, it analyzes 10^6 objects in 30 seconds with a 300M heap), is selective (e.g. it prunes that set to three candidate leak roots), and is accurate (it discounts non-leaking roots). The CER generation completes in tens of seconds. The lightweight tracking refines the rankings, while lowering throughput by less than 5%.

1 Introduction

Despite automatic garbage collection, memory leaks remain an important problem for many Java applications. A memory leak occurs when a Java program

L. Cardelli (Ed.): ECOOP 2003, LNCS 2743, pp. 351–377, 2003.

inadvertently maintains references to objects that are no longer needed, preventing the garbage collector from reclaiming space. Memory leaks are easy to spot, but are often difficult to diagnose. We can determine that a memory leak is likely to exist by using a black-box analysis, monitoring the heap after each round of garbage collection. We observe a downward-sawtooth pattern of free space (every collection frees less and less) until the application grinds to a halt for lack of space.

A number of diagnosis tools exist that help the user look inside the black box to determine the root cause of a leak. They rely on a combination of heap snapshot differencing [26, 19, 30], and allocation and/or usage tracking at a fine level of detail [27, 29, 11, 4, 21, 24]. We have used tools in both of these categories as part of an active consulting practice our group maintains helping solve memory leaks in large stand-alone Java applications and in IBM customer *e-Business* systems (web-based transaction processing systems built on an application server framework, such as J2EE[1] [28]). We have found that these techniques are not adequate for these large-scale applications.

In our experience, to diagnose a memory leak, the user must look for a set of candidate data structures that are likely to have problems. Finding the right data structures to focus on is difficult; as we will see in Section 2, when exploring the reference graphs of large applications, issues of noise, complexity, and scale make this a daunting task. For example, e-Business servers intentionally retain a large number of objects in caches. Existing approaches require that the user manually distinguish these cached objects from truly leaking ones. In general, these approaches swamp the user with too much low-level detail about individual objects that were created, and leave the user with the difficult task of interpreting complex reference graphs or allocation paths in order to understand the larger context. This interpretation process requires a lot of expertise; even for experts, it usually takes many hours of analysis work to find the root cause of a leak. Moreover, these techniques will in some cases perturb the running application too much to be of practical value, especially in production environments.

1.1   A Summary of the Contributions of LeakBot

We propose a way around these difficulties: raise the level of analysis from individual objects to regions within data structures. This approach has two beneficial consequences. First, it enables automated discovery and simple presentations of what is really causing the leak. Second, it enables lightweight and automated tracking of how whole data structures evolve. To realize these benefits, we have developed three new techniques: a way to rank data structures automatically by their likelihood of containing leaks, a way to identify suspicious regions within a data structure and characterize their *expected* evolution, and a lightweight way to track those regions' *actual* evolution as the program runs. We present an implementation of these techniques in an automated and lightweight memory leak

---

[1] J2EE may more accurately be described as a large collection of libraries and frameworks, covering many different areas of functionality such as database access, session management, directory access, asynchronous messaging, etc.

detection tool called LeakBot. We demonstrate that these techniques work well on several large-scale Java applications. Furthermore, we explain how they are especially powerful when used in combination.

Our first step in finding leaks is to identify the few data structures in which leaks are likely to be occurring. We introduce the concept of a *leak root*, which is the head of a data structure containing regions exhibiting unbounded growth. Section 3 discusses why finding candidate leak roots is not straightforward: data structures are complex, and their properties do not have a simple linear effect on the importance of that data structure. We present a method for ranking candidate leak roots which combines, in a non-linear fashion, a collection of structural and temporal properties of the object reference graph. This method uses no knowledge of any particular framework. Section 3.6 demonstrates the effectiveness of the model on three representative IBM customer applications. For example, on a customer form-processing server application, it finds two candidate leak roots from a heap containing one million live objects. In addition, it does so quickly: the ranking process completes in under thirty seconds.

Under one leak root there may be multiple *regions* evolving in different ways. In Section 4 we introduce the notion of Co-evolving Regions, as a way to identify these distinct regions and concisely model the essence of their evolution. To this purpose, we introduce the *owner-proxy* and *change-proxy*, waypoints along each member's path from the leak root. We show how these waypoints are useful for a number of purposes. First and foremost, they classify members into Co-evolving Regions, and allow us to rank regions according to whether they leak. They are also useful for summarizing the structural highlights and severity of each region's growth for the user.

The two previous steps work by analyzing two snapshots[2] of the reference graph taken early in the run. A user could stop there, and operate in an *off-line* mode. But, in order to refine the results of those previous steps, it is sometimes necessary to acquire more information as the application runs. However, in practice, taking additional full reference graph snapshots either often, or late into an application's run, is far too expensive on large-scale applications.

In Section 5 we show how to acquire additional information *selectively*, using the results of the previous steps. In this *on-line* mode, we can be selective in two ways. First, we need only monitor the few most highly ranked regions. Second, we need only track a small subset of an entire region in order to determine how the entire region evolves. We show how to use the owner-proxy and change-proxy to derive a short path that LeakBot can periodically traverse to detect how a region evolves. The number of hops in this traversal is very small in relation to the size of large, leaking data structures.

LeakBot uses the on-line findings to refine the analyses and user presentation. For example, it characterizes each Co-evolving Region according to its actual evolution, and tells the user which containers are growing (i.e. are likely sources

---

[2] A reference graph snapshot is a list of currently live objects, including, for each object, its identifier, data type, and outgoing references. By live we mean objects that are not collectible by the garbage collector.

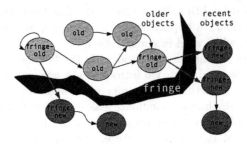

Fig. 1. The *fringe* is the boundary between older and recently created objects

of leaks), which are alternating in size (e.g. a cache with a flux of constituent objects, or a database connection pool), and which have reached a plateau (e.g. a data structure fully initialized at application startup time). It uses the characterization trend to update the rankings, and also presents this information to the user to assist in understanding the dynamic behavior of each region. Finally, the updated rankings allow LeakBot to adaptively adjust the frequency with which it explores each region.

We have implemented LeakBot in two components. The ranking and CER generation occur in an *analyzer* that runs independently of the target application. The *tracing agent* attaches to the application using JVMPI [15]. In on-line mode, the agent takes the initial snapshots and periodically samples the CERs.

2   Diagnosing Leaks in Large Java Applications

The applications that motivated the work in this paper have properties, common to many Java applications today, that make memory leak diagnosis especially difficult. These applications make heavy use of reusable frameworks and libraries,[3] often from many sources. These *framework-intensive* applications contain large amounts of code where the inner workings are not well understood by the developers, let alone those doing the problem determination. Server-side e-Business applications make use of particularly large frameworks, and introduce additional analysis difficulties due to their high degree of concurrency, scale, and long-running nature.

Before LeakBot, we used existing tools to help diagnose leaks as part of our consulting practice. HPROF [29] works by categorizing each object according to its allocation call path and type, as shown in Table 1. Many tools work by dividing the heap into old and new objects, under the assumption that older objects are expected to be more permanent. The user manually tries to discover why newer, supposedly temporary objects are being retained, by exploring what we call the *fringe*, the boundary between old and new objects, as shown in Figure 1. Below, we describe the many difficulties we encountered when using these tools.

---

[3] For convenience we will use the term framework to mean a framework or library.

Table 1. The output of HPROF on a toy example. It divides the heap objects based on allocation site (`stack trace`) and type

	percent		live		alloc'ed		stack	class
rank	self	accum	bytes	objs	bytes	objs	trace	name
1	97.31%	97.31%	10280000	10000	10280000	10000	1995	byte array
2	0.39%	97.69%	40964	1	81880	10	1996	object array
3	0.38%	98.07%	40000	10000	40000	10000	1994	MemoryConsumer
4	0.16%	98.23%	16388	1	16388	1	1295	character array
5	0.16%	98.38%	16388	1	16388	1	1304	character array

Perturbation: In tracking the call stack of every allocation, HPROF can reduce the throughput of a web-based application by five to ten times. Heap differencing tools that acquire full heap snapshots late into a leak can cause a system with a large heap size to pause for tens of seconds. For servers these slowdowns or pauses can cause timeouts, significantly changing the behavior of the application. On production servers, this level of service degradation is completely out of the question.

Noise: Given a persisting object, it is difficult to determine whether it has a legitimate reason for persisting. For example, caches and resource pools intentionally retain objects for long periods of time, even though the objects may no longer be needed. This is especially relevant to e-Business applications, where numerous resource management mechanisms (such as database connection pools and web page fragment caches) are used behind the scenes to ensure good transaction performance. Some other common examples of noise are: session information that is retained for a fixed time period in web-based systems, in case the user returns later; containers that have lazy removal policies; objects that appear to persist only because they are part of a transaction that was in progress when the application's state was captured. Noise can be especially problematic when diagnosing slow leaks in long-running systems; noise effects can dwarf the evidence needed to diagnose a slow leak until very late in the run.

Existing techniques provide little assistance in this area. An aggregate view, such as that shown in Table 2, dividing the heap into old, new, and fringe objects, gives us little insight for determining which objects exist due to the flux in and out of caches, which are from a transaction in progress, and which are leaks. Existing approaches leave the user with the hard work of digging through reference graphs or call stacks manually. Users must rely on their own, often limited knowledge of how the application and frameworks manage their data, in order to segregate objects by their likely usage.

Data Structure Complexity: Knowing the type of leaking object that predominates, often a low-level type such as String, does not help explain why the leak occurs. This is because these Strings are likely to be used in many contexts,

Table 2. Number of non-collectible instances in a leaking customer Websphere application. We have divided the heap as shown in Figure 1

class name	old	new
java.lang.ref.Finalizer	20246	17084
java.lang.String	223266	9453
xerces...TextImpl	9035	7676
character array	202782	5290
xerces...AttrImpl	6258	5135
object array	17165	3255
java.util.Hashtable$Entry	56745	3244
xerces...NamedNodeMapImpl	3667	2713
xerces...ElementImpl	3204	2123
integer array	4410	2064
java.util.Vector	6394	1993
xerces...DeferredTextImpl	960	1209
java.util.ArrayList	215	1151
com.bank...log.Record	1	1045

class name	fringe-new
java.util.HashMap$Entry	322
java.lang.String	243
java.util.Hashtable$Entry	95
com.ibm...CredentialsImpl	20
com.bank...MessageModel	20
byte array	15
character array	14
xalan...KeyTable	12
java.util.Hashtable	11

and even may be used for multiple purposes within the same high-level data structure, such as a DOM document. In addition, presented with the context of low-level leaking objects, it is easy to get lost quickly in extracting a reason for leakage. A single DOM object contains many thousands of objects, with a rich network of references among them. Without knowledge of the implementation of frameworks, it is difficult to know which paths in the reference graph to follow, or, when analyzing allocation call paths, which call site is important.

3   Finding Candidate Leak Roots

Consider a buggy e-Business application where each transaction places items into a global ActiveOrders structure, but forgets to remove some of them when the transaction is complete. In this simple example, shown in Figure 2, Book's are removed properly, but CD's are inadvertently left connected.

We may distinguish between a data structure that contains a leak, in this example ActiveOrder's, and the actual leaking substructures, in this case the CD objects and everything they point to. In general, a single data structure may contain more than one different type of leak, in addition to regions that are stable or are in flux but not growing. In this section we describe a technique for discovering the overall data structures that are likely to contain leaks. Our eventual goal is the discovery and characterization of the leaking regions themselves, which we describe in Section 4 and 5.

Definition 1. *A leak root is the object at the head of a data structure which is leaking in one or more ways.*

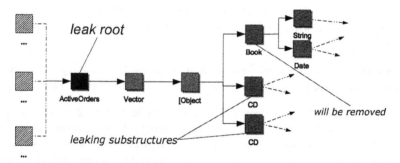

Fig. 2. If every transaction leaks a CD object, then `ActiveOrders` is probably the best *leak root*: the most indicative, highest-level object responsible

Our approach to finding leaks is to first identify candidate leak roots. We do this by ranking each object based on a mixture of structural and temporal properties of the object reference graph, using a small number of snapshots gathered while the application is running. Each candidate leak root may then be used as a proxy for a data structure containing leaks, and ultimately as one of the attributes describing each leaking region.

3.1 An Overview of Leak Root Ranking

A number of requirements influence the design of our ranking scheme. First, it must be a good discriminator of leak roots. The discovery process should not propose many more candidates than actual leaks in the program. In addition, it is not enough for the ranking to be merely an ordering; it must be a meaningful ranking as well. If one object is much more likely than another to be a leak root, this should be reflected in those objects relative ranks.

Second, the ranking must be resilient to the time at which the snapshots were taken. We would like the ranking to do a good job with input taken early in a programs run. This allows for quicker turnaround in test environments. and it is a practical concern for production settings, where taking snapshots late in a run with a severe memory leak can be prohibitively expensive.

Finally, it is important that the ranking scale to large object reference graphs, both in its memory and time consumption. We achieve this by filtering many objects down to a small set of candidates in a succession of three steps, each utilizing different criteria. Each ranking step applies an increasingly expensive algorithm to a successively smaller set of candidate leak roots. Each algorithm assigns a number between zero (definitely not a candidate) and one (a highly probable leak root), and each subsequent step only applies to objects ranked above a chosen threshold. The final rank of an object indicates its goodness as a leak root. We term this final rank the `leakroot` rank, or $\mathcal{L}$.

In our example above, the algorithm would identify the `ActiveOrders` object as a likely leak root. A number of considerations lead us to rank this object higher than other objects in the graph (for example, higher than the Vector). The ranking algorithms which led to this choice are the realization of the following four observations.

Observation 1 (Binary Metrics) *Structural and temporal reference graph attributes can definitively rule out many objects, but definitively rule in none.*

We can easily eliminate some of the objects in Figure 2 from any further consideration. For example, in Java, array objects do not automatically grow. Therefore, we can rule out the object array, [Object. Section 3.3 provides a collection of binary (yes or no) metrics which eliminate a large number of objects from further consideration. We will show how eight binary metrics typically reduces the set of candidates from a million to a few hundred objects.

Of the remaining candidates, however, we cannot with absolute assurance assign them a rank of one. Based on a few heap snapshots, we cannot know that the application will not eventually remove the Order objects from the Vector (just as e-Business applications eventually clear out cached user sessions). At best, we can say the an object is a good candidate and, with additional evidence, that it is increasingly likely to be so. Also, for the reasons of noise described in Section 2, there are typically many such *possibly* leaking structures in the reference graph. We should prioritize those not immediately ruled out.

Observation 2 (Mixture Metrics) *For those objects not ruled out yet, some reference graph attributes are positive indicators, in favor of candidacy, and some are negative indicators. But no one attribute either stands out or always applies.*

Data structures and leaks have many forms, thus the importance of each attribute varies. Consider the importance of the size of a candidate, treated as a data structure.[4] Increasing size is a positive indicator, in favor of candidacy. But it is not always indicative in every leak situation, since not all big data structures leak. For example, we analyzed a customer's business-to-business gateway application. Typical of many applications, the top five data structures by size were all caches and resource pools. They ranged from 200kB to 1.5MB in size. The known leak root, on the other hand, was (at one point) only 64kB large. In another typical example, an e-Business form processing application with two leaks, one leak showed up as the largest data structure, while the other leak showed up only as the 85th-largest; the second case turned out to be a slow leak.

Observation 3 (Gating Functions) *Some positive indicators are much more positive than others; ibid for negative.*

If the binary metrics prune the candidates down to a hundred, the mixture model must do better than just ordering those hundred by likelihood. Instead, we starkly differentiate those that are very likely from those that are less so. We accomplish this differentiation by applying nonlinear gating functions to the values of the reference graph attributes.

---

[4] Note that this alone would be an advance over existing tools.

For example, one criterion that helps rank an object is the number of objects it owns which are referenced by on-stack variables. Owning such objects is a negative indicator, because it implies that this data structure is changing in size only because the heap sample happened to capture some operations in progress. We'd like this indicator to follow a very sharp curve: owning just a few on-stack roots should highly discount the candidate; owning none shouldn't discount the candidate at all. This is an example of applying a "low-pass" gating function to a reference graph attribute. Section 3.4 shows how other attributes are gated with high-pass or band-pass gates.

Observation 4 (Fixpoint Metrics) *The rank of an object depends on the rank of other objects.*

We have found two main cases when metrics based only on reference graph attributes are insufficient. First, when one data structure leaks, all of its enclosing leak as well. However, if the *only* reason we think the enclosing data structures leak is due to that one data structure, then we have falsely identified multiple leak roots for a single leak. However, there are common cases where, looking only at the members and reachability of a candidate leak root, we will be left in this situation (for example, when a candidate has multiple parents).

The second reason stems from the need to combat the noise effects described in Section 2. Consider a leak of the form that objects of type B leak under an object A, and where each B is itself a complex data structure which is populated during (but not after) a transaction. Therefore, if a graph snapshots is acquired concurrently with transactions, then it will appear as if objects of type B are leaking: e.g. in one snapshot they are empty (newly created), and in the second they are fully populated. In this common scenario, object A will appear to leak (because of the true leak of B's into A); but a large number of B's will also be identified, falsely, as candidate leak roots by the attribute-based metrics.

3.2   Reference Graph Attributes

The first two ranking steps use metrics based on a collection of reference graph attributes. While most of these attributes have a well-understood meanings [17], we define them here, to avoid confusion.

Single-Entry Equivalence Given an arbitrary graph G, we compute a reduced graph G' where a node in G' represents all nodes in G in the same single-entry (but not necessarily single-exit) region. The edges are collapsed in the obvious way. In the applications we have studied, the collapsed graph has about one eighth as many nodes of the original graph. For example, many character arrays are each pointed to by a single `String` object; we can collapse each pair of objects into a single node in G'.

GC Roots Those objects referenced by sources other than fields of Java objects. Examples of these GC roots include references from local variables currently on the Java or native stack, JNI references from native code, references from currently-held monitors.

Reachability The *reachers* of an object o is the union of all paths from some set of objects to o. To make this computation efficient, the ranker computes reachability on the single-entry collapsed graph. In addition, rather than computing all-points reachability, the ranker only computes a small reachability vector. Each element of the vector counts the number of GC roots of a particular type that reach that single-entry subgraph.

Unique Ownership One object o *dominates* o' if any path from a GC root which includes o' also includes o. In the other direction, the objects *uniquely owned by* an o is the set of all objects dominated only by it; we denote this by M_o. Again, so that this analysis scales, the ranker computes dominance on the single-entry reduced graph (see Appendix A).

Age The age of an object is the snapshot in which that object was first witnessed by LeakBot. The fringe of an object reference graph is the set of objects in the latest generation immediately pointed to by objects in earlier generations. We say an object is *on the fringe* if it is a new object pointed to by an older one. In this discussion, we say an object is *new* if it comes from the latest generation, and otherwise it is *older*.

Size We distinguish between the allocation size and the data structure size of an object. The latter is the total size of its uniquely owned objects.

3.3   Binary Metrics (Ranking Step 1)

The step-1 rank of a candidate object is the *product* of the eight metrics of that object. Each metric is computationally easy-to-compute and each takes on a value of zero or one. Thus, if any metric assigns a value of zero, then that the object is not a candidate. Otherwise, the binary metrics are "agnostic" to that candidate, and it is passed on to the next ranking step. The following binary metrics evaluate to zero for objects with certain structural (S_1 through S_4) and temporal (T_1 through T_4) reference graph attributes. We show how, together, these metrics quickly eliminate most objects from further consideration.

Binary Metrics Based on Structural Graph Attributes

S_1 **Leaf Nodes:** these objects cannot possibly be the root of a leaking data structure. Note that a leaf node may eventually point to another object, and commence leaking. But we rely on the fact that it has not yet.

S_2 **Arrays:** objects which are arrays; in Java, arrays are allocated with a fixed size, therefore, a leak involving growth of an array must have that array as part of a larger data structure (which reallocates the array when it reaches its maximum size).

S_3 **Internal Nodes:** objects which aren't the head of a single-entry region. From every single-entry region, we choose one (the head) as a representative of that region, and disregard the rest. For example, the Vector in Figure 2 is filtered out using this property. In many cases, this will keep us from identifying more than one leak root for the same leak.

Table 3. For five applications, this table shows the *cumulative* effectiveness (from left to right) of the four binary metrics based on structural graph attributes

| | # objects | fraction remaining | | | |
		S_1	S_2	S_3	S_4
phone company	267,956	67%	59%	9%	6%
IDE	350,136	61%	55%	9%	7%
brokerage	838,912	65%	62%	7%	3%
brokerage2	1,015,112	71%	70%	2%	1%
finance	1,320,953	60%	56%	11%	8%

S_4 **Non-owners:** objects which uniquely own nothing. An object may be a non-leaf node, but only share ownership of objects with many others. These objects tend to be located close to GC roots, such as class loaders. We ignore them, and instead favor the objects they point to (directly or indirectly) which *do* own objects. The parents of the `ActiveOrders` object in Figure 2 have this property.

Binary Metrics Based on Temporal Graph Attributes

T_1 **No Age Intersection:** the object owns only older, or only new objects. If we have witnessed no objects added to a data structure in any of the reference graph snapshots, then this object is a very likely the owner of a pool, or some other unchanging structure. Likewise, if we see no older objects as of the latest graph sample, then we very likely have caught a transient data structure, perhaps due to an in-progress transaction. In either case, we can safely ignore this object.

T_2 **New Arrays Only:** the object owns only new object arrays, but no new objects inside those arrays. For example, an empty hashtable used only during program initialization may still own a large, but empty array.

T_3 **No Fringe:** the object owns no objects on the fringe. Some objects may own both new and older objects, but they own none on the fringe. This is likely to be an artifact of shared ownership. To avoid these artifacts, we favor the objects which own both older, new, *and* fringe objects.

T_4 **No Datatype Intersection:** the set of data types of older owned objects intersected with the same for new objects is empty. For example, a generic object cache may contain ten strings in one reference graph sample and fifteen integers in a later sample. This data structure passes most of the other binary filters, but nonetheless isn't very likely to be leaking.

Table 3 and Table 4 give five examples of the effectiveness of the binary metrics, for the structural and temporal metrics respectively. These five examples come from engagements we've been involved with; four are large IBM customers, and one (IDE) is an internal IBM application. In each case, the input to the binary metrics was a pair of full reference graph snapshots. We had warmed up

Table 4. The cumulative filtering effectiveness (from left to right) of the four binary metrics based on temporal graph attributes (T_1, T_2, T_3, T_4). S_i shows the number of objects left after applying all four structural metrics; see Table 3

	# objects	S_i	number remaining			
			T_1	T_2	T_3	T_4
phone company	267,956	16,346	73	73	72	29
IDE	350,136	25,653	99	99	29	10
brokerage	838,912	26,291	97	82	81	67
brokerage2	1,015,112	12,020	102	102	64	17
finance	1,320,953	106,900	579	519	518	242

the applications various amounts (e.g. with `financial` we warmed up the system with only five minutes of typical load, whereas for `brokerage2` we warmed up the system with 30 minutes of typical load). We took the first snapshot, performed additional load (roughly the same as the warmup load), and took the second snapshot.

On the `finance` application, the second snapshot had around 1.3 million live objects, and the combination of the eight binary metrics filtered out all but 242 objects. This number is somewhat higher than for the other applications because we had warmed up the application for a much shorter period of time than for the others. Nonetheless, the binary metrics are effective. As we discussed earlier, resilience to input early in a program's run is an important design criteria. Our experience has shown that, given input from early in a program's run, the binary metrics typically filter down to several hundred candidates.

3.4   A Mixture of Gated Metrics (Ranking Step 2)

Of the (typically) several hundred remaining candidates, not all are equally likely. Thus, we rank them by the unweighted sum of a collection of gated metrics.

As pointed out in Observations 2 and 3, no one metric is an overwhelming indicator of candidacy, but selected reference graph attributes can be very strong negative indicators. To reflect this observation, we *gate* each attribute. The particulars of each gating function depend on the attribute, but each has the following characteristics. For extreme values of the attribute, gates are either strongly against or agnostic to that object's candidacy (but never strongly in favor). If an attribute has a strongly negative extreme, the gate assigns a negative rank. By agnostic, we mean that, all other things being equal, we should assign the object a rank of one. In-between, the gates use a superposition of cubic exponential gating functions to implement either high-pass, low-pass, or band-pass filters on the attribute's value. Space does not permit a full exposition of each attribute's gate, but we describe them for several of the following attributes.

G_1 **On-Stack Ownership:** We discount data structures that are growing only because we caught operations in progress based on the number of objects owned that are referenced by on-stack GC roots.

G_2 **On-Stack Reachability:** We discount those objects reachable from on-stack roots, because the entire data structure may be transient.

G_3 **Ownership Counts:** S_4 has already filtered out objects which own nothing. Here, we favor objects which own both a greater number and size of objects. We consider number and size separately: owning one large array isn't as indicative of problems as owning many smaller objects. But comparing two objects which own the same number, we somewhat favor the one of larger data structure size.

G_4 **New Ownership:** T_1 has already filtered out objects which own no new objects. Here, we favor objects which own a greater number of newer objects.

G_5 **Array Ownership:** The larger the number of object arrays compared to objects, the less likely the candidate. Also, if a data structure contains no object arrays, we have found it to be less likely (though not entirely unlikely) to be a root of leaks. Therefore, for this criterion, the number of object arrays in a data structure, we must apply a band-pass gating function to array ownership: not too large a fraction of object arrays, and not too small.

G_6 **Fringe Ownership:** If an object owns many objects on the fringe, that is a sign that the leak is progressing quickly. All other things being equal, we favor these candidates over others.

G_7 **Fringe Datatype Uniformity:** Single leaks tend to have a fairly uniform datatype on the fringe. [5] If there is only a plurality of datatypes on the fringe, this is an indication either that this data structure may have multiple leaks, or that it is a general-purpose data structure with a constantly-changing constituency (like a cache). In the former case, we'd like to favor the smaller data structures which contain the individual leaks (if not heavily discounted by other metrics). We want to ignore the latter case entirely.

G_8 **Datatype Intersection:** As explained earlier, we strongly discount objects without high overlap in owned datatypes from one sample to the next.

G_9 **Dominance Frontier:** Data structures that are highly embedded in larger ones tend not to leak. Rather, leaking data structures extend ownership all the way down to graph leaf nodes. Therefore, we discount an object which owns many objects with a non-empty dominance frontier.

3.5   Iterative Fixpoint Ranking (Ranking Step 3)

Finally, LeakBot updates the step-2 rank to account for the interactions identified in Observation 4. We account for interactions using an iterative algorithm which inflates or discounts the rank of one object based on its rank relative to the rank of related candidates. The algorithm starts with all objects whose rank, so far, lies above a specified threshold (see Appendix B). It then iterates until no candidate's rank changes appreciably. We have found that, in nearly every case, no more than three iterations are required.

Initially, the step-3 rank of every object equals its step-2 rank. At each iteration, choose a candidate o, and compute the three metrics from o.

---

[5] This is the *change proxy* introduced in Section 4.

F_1 **Immediate Domination Residue:** the sum of the step-3 ranks of each object o immediately dominates.

F_2 **By-Type Immediate Domination Residue:** as F_1, but sum the maximum by datatype.

F_3 **Immediate Dominator Residue:** the maximum of the step-3 ranks for every object in immediate dominators from, but not including o.

Let r_o be the current step-3 rank of o. Update r_o as follows. If $F_1 \approx 0$, then no sub-structures are better candidates than the current object; continue to the next iteration with no changes. If $F_1 = r_o$, then o is a candidate mainly because exactly one of its sub-structures is a good candidate; discount r_o by 50%. Otherwise (if $F_1 > r_o$) multiple of o's sub-structures contribute to o's candidacy; if $F_2 = F_1$ then there are two independent problems in sub-structures, and so discount r_o by 50%; otherwise, we are witnessing the falsely-identified leaks described in Observation 4, and so discount each of the falsely identified candidates by 50%. We perform similar updates based on F_3. If $F_3 = 0$, then no larger structure is a good candidate, so continue with no changes. If $F_3 \gg r_o$, then there is an enclosing data structure which is a much better candidate than o; discount r_o by 50%.

3.6   Examples of the Ranker in Use

We have applied LeakBot in off-line mode to a variety of applications, both large GUI applications and e-Business applications. We have used it for a number of purposes: to diagnose known leaks, to check whether an application has leaks before shipping it, and to verify that fixes for known leaks do in fact work. Here, we share three of these experiences. In each of these examples, the input to LeakBot was a trace containing two snapshots of the heap, with a number of suspected leaking operations separating the two snapshots.

Discovering and Diagnosing a Leak In this example, we analyzed a large GUI integrated development environment, heavily dependent on frameworks, for leaks. We tested opening and closing an editor window, thinking that this should be a "round trip" scenario: all resources for the editor window should go away when it is closed. We performed a total of three operations: we warmed up the IDE with two operations, took a heap snapshot, then performed one more operation, and finally took a second heap snapshot. Table 5(a) shows that, from 350 thousand live objects, the ranker chooses only three with non-zero leakroot, and only one with leakroot above 0.5. We were surprised to find these highly-ranked suspects. It turns out that LeakBot had identified a previously unreported leak. With a 90MB heap, the structural computation takes 5 seconds, and the metric computation takes another 5 seconds (on a 1.2GHz Pentium3-M).

For comparison, we enabled HPROF, and exercised the application similarly. We started the application with the option -Xrunhprof:heap=sites, and used the IBM 1.3.1 JVM. After we had issued eighteen leaking operations, we examined the HPROF output. Recall that HPROF aggregates allocations by call site

Table 5. Examples of the leak root ranking, showing the objects with highest rank ($\mathcal{L}$), with those at the head of actual leaks annotated (*)

(a) IDE

class name	$\mathcal{L}$
(*)WorkbenchPage	0.719
WidgetTable	0.446
ResourceBundle	0.31

(b) IDE- bug fixed

class name	$\mathcal{L}$
WidgetTable	0.430
DeltaDataTree (#1)	0.322
DeltaDataTree (#2)	0.320

(c)   auction- no leak

class name	$\mathcal{L}$
DDRMain	0.396
ibm.LogUtil	0.265

(d) brokerage

class name	$\mathcal{L}$
APCache	0.830
TemplateCache	0.805
AntiVirus	0.757
Record	0.596
(*)XSLTransform	0.582

(e) brokerage2

class name	$\mathcal{L}$
(*)EventNotifier	0.848
ibm.CachedTargets	0.579
(*)FormProperties	0.572

(f) brokerage2-bug fixed

class name	$\mathcal{L}$
ibm.CachedTargets	0.271
ibm.ORB	0.234

and type. It ranks these aggregations by the number of non-collectible bytes due to that call site and type. Table 6 shows the top five, all of which are primitive arrays. The first leaking application-typed aggregate, of type StyleRange, has rank 45. However, given the rate at which this application was leaking StyleRange objects, we would have to perform around 200 leaking operations before its aggregate floated to the top. In contrast, as we have shown, LeakBot is robust to the quality of the input: leakroot does well with many fewer extant leaks: after only three leaking operations, it has identified the leak as the top suspect.

Checking for a Leak before Shipping In this case, we applied the ranker to a high-volume e-Business application. We now know this application is leak free. At the time, however, we needed to verify this before the application went into production. We applied the ranker to a previously acquired trace, collected while the application was running a workload mix of various web transactions. Of seven hundred thousand objects, the ranker assigns 11 a non-zero leakroot; it assigns only two objects a leakroot above 0.25, and none above 0.4. Table 5(c) shows the leakroot metric for those two objects. With a 300MB heap, the structural analysis (computing the reduced object reference graph, and the dominator and reachability relations) took 10 seconds, the metric computation took 15 seconds.

Verifying that a Fix to a Known Leak Works Our third demonstration is from a leaking e-business form-processing application. The developers had already implemented fixes to two leaks, but wanted two types of assurance: first, that the patches indeed fixed the problem, and second, that there were no remaining leaks. The customer could not afford to discover, after deploying the fixes and running in production for several days, that there were still leaks. We

Table 6. A subset of the output of HPROF on the IDE application from Table 5(a). The head of the structures which are leaking is ranked 640th

	percent		live		alloc'ed		stack	class
rank	self	accum	bytes	objs	bytes	objs	trace	name
1	5.27%	5.27%	639600	39	2279600	139	1522	character array
2	4.57%	9.84%	554488	7339	559752	7540	2262	character array
3	4.35%	14.20%	528192	6762	589504	7294	1530	character array
				...				
640	0.01%	85.45%	1152	18	1152	18	19766	EditorManager$Editor

first applied LeakBot's ranker to the server running a known-buggy version of the code. Table 5(e) shows the result: from one million live objects, the ranker finds ten with non-zero `leakroot`, five with `leakroot` above 0.3, and only three above 0.5. With a 300MB heap, the structural and metric computations took 15 seconds each (on a 1.2GHz Pentium3-M). The same analysis applied to the fixed code appears in Table 5(f). This time, the ranker assigns 9 objects a non-zero `leakroot`, and it assigns no objects a `leakroot` greater than 0.3.

4   Co-evolving Regions: Patterns within Leaking Structures

Section 3 identifies leaks by finding candidate leak roots, objects which head data structures that possibly contain leaks. However, there are several reasons why this information is too coarse. For example, one leak root may identify more than one leak. In addition, leakage isn't the only way a data structure can change. There is a variety of ways in which evolution happens. For example, one data structure can have distinct regions that evolve as leaks (grow without bound), as caches or pools (bounded size, changing constituency), that may never change (e.g. a preloaded data structure), that may shrink (e.g., if used for initialization), or that may switch between these various types of evolution. This section refines from the level of a data structure to the level of *regions* within that structure.[6] We desire to identify regions that are as big as possible, but that still evolve in a single, coherent way. We term such regions *Co-evolving Regions* (CERs).

Coherency of evolution is determined by several factors. First, the region should only exhibit one type of evolution: either monotonic growth, monotonic shrinkage, bounded-changing constituency, and bounded-fixed constituency. Second, as a region evolves, different of its elements are, or once were, on the fringe. Those fringe elements must share a similar to each other. Third, all members of a region must share a similar relationship to the region's leak root.

This section presents a mechanism for finding *likely*[7] Co-evolving Regions. To find CERs, we develop an equivalence relation for objects owned by a leak

---

[6] In [7], they discuss the "geometry of containment".

[7] Likely, not certainly. Section 5 shows how to adapt regions as the program runs.

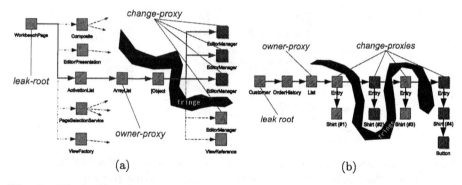

Fig. 3. The leak-path does not solely indicate co-evolution. The elided path of leak root, owner-proxy, and change-proxy is a better indicator

root. To every object owned by a candidate leak root we assign a Region Key, a tuple of features reflecting the important components of equivalence. We define similarity of Region Keys, and classify a leak root's members based on Region Key similarity. Finally, we describe how to prioritize the Co-evolving Regions using a simple ranking algorithm.

4.1   Region Keys

Two members are part of the same CER based in part on their paths from their leak roots. As there may be many such paths, we identify one.

Definition 2. *The* leak-path, P_m, *of m owned by leak root o is the reverse of the path of immediate dominators from the m to o.*

The entire leak path is too rigid a specification to be useful for classifying objects into regions. For example, Figure 3 shows the structure of two leaks, an array leak (from the application covered in Section 3.6) and a linked list leak. In the array example, both the `EditorManager` objects and all their constituents should be part of the same CER, and yet their paths are, in large part, different. In the linked list example, even the leak-paths of only the highest-level leaking objects (the `Entry`'s) can be very different. And yet, in both examples, members of one region have *somewhat* similar leak-paths.

Eliding Leak-Paths via the Owner-Proxy and Change-Proxy. While the leak-path in its entirety does not indicate co-evolution, there is an elided version which does. We identify important "waypoints" in every leak-path, that indicate similarity of evolution [12]. Every object between the waypoints is effectively a wildcard for determining in which region a member belongs. The only parts of the path which do matter are the leak root, two concepts we now introduce: the owner-proxy, and the change-proxy.

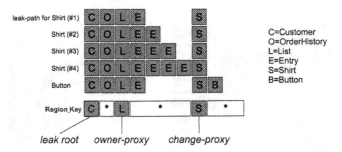

Fig. 4. Some leak-paths from Figure 3(b). The Region Keys for the `Shirts` and `Buttons` are the same, so they are part of one Co-evolving Region

The owner-proxy is a stable object on the old side of, and in close proximity to, the fringe. The change-proxy is that indicator of updates to the region; for this, we choose the largest stable object on the new side of the fringe. For example, Figure 4 shows the leak-paths for several of the objects in Figure 3(b). It illustrates how the waypoints define wildcarded subpaths of the each leak-path. The change-proxy for the `Shirt` and `Button` objects is the same, because, every leak to that region is indicated by the addition in a similar way.

Definition 3. *The* distance-from-fringe *of an object o on a leak-path P_m is the number of hops from o to an object on the other side of the fringe. It is positive for objects on the old side of the fringe, and negative for those on the new side. We'll denote this by $d_{o,m}$. Also let $c_{o,m}$ be the number of fringe crossings along P_m from m to o. Finally let t_o be the expected lifetime of object o.*

For example, along the highlighted leak-paths in Figure 3(a), [`Object` has a distance of 1, and the `EditorManager` objects have distance -1. When computing the Region Key for m, we have found that a simple model of expected lifetime works very well in practice. Assume that arrays and objects with the same data type as the chosen change-proxy have an expected lifetime of 0, that new objects have 1, and that old objects have 10.

Definition 4. *The* change-proxy *of a new member m, C_m is that object o in P_m that maximizes $-t_o/d_{o,m}/(1+c_{o,m})$. The* owner-proxy, *O_m, maximizes $t_o/d_{o,m}$.*

Consider finding the owner-proxy and change-proxy for the `Shirt` object in the linked list example shown in Figure 3(b). We use the lifetime model defined above. It's leak-path contains all seven objects in the figure. In determining the change-proxy, the ratios specified in the above definition for each element in P_m are $(-0.833, 1.25, -2.5, +0.333, -5, +1, +0.5)$, indicating the best choice of change-proxy is the right-most `Entry` object. For the owner-proxy, the ratios specified in the above definition for each element in P_m are $(+3.33, +5, 0, 0, 0, 0, -0.125)$ indicating the best choice of owner-proxy is the `List` object. A similar process for the leak in Figure 3(a) will determine that the

`ArrayList` from is the owner-proxy of every `EditorManager` object: the `[Object` array is closer to the fringe, but has a much shorter expected lifetime, and the objects further upstream have equal lifetimes but larger distances.

Definition 5. *The Region Key of an object m belonging to leak root L is the tuple (L, O_m, C_m). The Region Key for m and m' are equal (i.e. objects m and m' belong to the same co-evolving region) if $L = L'$, $O_m = O_{m'}$, and the datatype of C_m is the datatype of $C_{m'}$.[8]*

Using Region Keys to Find Co-evolving Regions. For every leak root candidate L whose rank lies above a desired threshold, we compute Co-evolving Regions as follows. To L we associate a set of regions. To each region, we associate two numbers to measure a region: the total number of bytes which belong to that region, and the number of distinct data structures within that region. The latter is a useful metric, because it estimates the number of leaking operations which led to that region's current constituency.

Definition 6. *The* dump-size *of a region is the number of Region Keys that map to that region (using Definition 5's). The* proxy-size *of a region is the number of distinct change-proxy objects over all Region Keys which map to that region.*

Then, for each $m \in M_L$ whose P_m has spans the fringe (i.e. $c_{L,m} > 0$), do the following. Compute m's Region Key as described above, and insert it into L's region set. If an equivalent Region Key already exists, increment that region's dump-size. If an equivalent Region Key with the same change-proxy exists, increment that region's proxy-size.

For example, using this process, in the IDE application from Section 3.6, the highest-ranked candidate leak root (the `WorkbenchPage` object) has two regions. The proxy-size of the known leaking region is precisely the number of leaking operations that had been performed: three (recall from that section that we had performed three suspected leaking operations).

4.2   Ranking Regions

Finally, not all regions are equally likely to leak, so we rank them. When comparing one region to another, we consider three criteria. First, if one region's leak root has been ranked higher than another, this influences the relative ranking of the regions similarly. Second, if one region has a higher proxy-size than another, we favor the larger one. We do not use dump-size, because we'd prefer to rank based on an estimate of the number of leaking operations which have been performed, rather than the byte-size of the leak. Finally, if one region's proxy-size is growing faster than another's, we favor the faster one. This third criterion allows for updating the region ranks as we gather more information from the running application. A region's rank is the the unweighted average of

---

[8] More generally, either C_m is assignable to the datatype of $C_{m'}$ or vice versa.

these three elements. Unlike the leak root ranking described in Section 3 where a root's rank was bounded at one, we allow a region's rank to grow without bound. This allows for differentiating regions based on their leak rate, whereas bounding at one would asymptote all leaking regions to the same rank.

5   Cheap, Adaptive, Online Exploration of Regions

We have described the analyses of Sections 3 and 4 assuming an off-line usage scenario: acquire snapshots, find candidate leak roots, and then find co-evolving regions within highly-ranked candidates. We could very well stop here. An immediate benefit of having found regions that are likely to co-evolve is that LeakBot can present a high-level *schematic* of the suspected problematic regions of the reference graph. However, we'd like to know more than just the structure of problematic regions. We'd also like to know how those regions actually evolve.

In off-line mode, our estimates of actual evolution are limited by the information in initial snapshots. Recall that we desire to acquire initial snapshots as early into the run as possible. On the other hand, if LeakBot remains connected to the program under analysis, it can present a more refined view of how regions actually evolve.

A principal constraint of LeakBot is that it must minimally perturb the program's behavior. Region Keys, in addition to helping us find Co-evolving Regions, can also help us derive lightweight probes to discover how these regions actually evolve. To this gather information, the LeakBot agent periodically traverses selected subgraphs of the object reference graph of the running application. It reports important structural changes back to the analyses of the previous sections. With the updated analysis (closing the feedback loop), we update the traversals as described below.

For example, to efficiently detect leaks of data structures into an array, we needn't keep track of every element in those leaking data structures. Instead, it is sufficient to periodically examine the references from the array, to a depth of one. There is no need to look any deeper into each leaking data structure, since we can just count the array contents by datatype. However, there is another case we must consider. In Java, an array is of bounded size. Thus, if the Co-evolving Region has monotonic growth, we would expect occasional reallocations of the array; when adding to an `ArrayList`, the underlying array is a transient object. Therefore, we must start the traversal from `ArrayList`, not the array. Observe that the same traversal also detects elements having been removed from the array. In addition, it can be used to inform us of when a *relinking* has occurred — that is, when one path element has been replaced by a new one. Observe that this traversal (in this case) follows precisely the path between owner-proxy and change-proxy.

This example shows that, to know how a Co-evolving Region evolves, we must derive a set of traversals that detect certain *updates*: additions, removals, and relinking. In some cases, one traversal can detect more than one of these

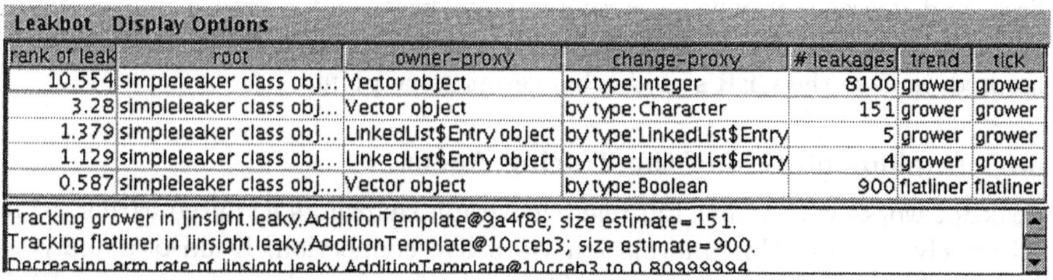

Fig. 5. Screenshot of the LeakBot tool. Each row corresponds to one suspect region. For each region, we show its region rank ("rank of leak"), the proxy-size ("# leakages"), and a summary of the trend and tick of that region's evolution

updates. If, when doing the actual traversal, we witness an evolution, we say that update has been detected.

For every region, we keep a histogram of detected updates. We use this to estimate a region's evolution trend. For example, if only addition updates have been detected for a region, we say that region is a monotonic grower. If a roughly equal mixture of addition and removal updates have been detected, we classify the region as an *oscillator*. If only removal updates, it is a *shrinker*. If no updates, then it is a *flatliner*. Figure 5 shows the actual tool in action. The table has one row per Co-evolving Region, and indicates for each its current proxy-size and evolution trend.

Note that, in some cases, such as Figure 3(b), that traversal would be much longer than necessary: as the list in that example grows, so does the traversal. The solution to this problem of finding *efficient* traversals involves defining a family of short traversals which explore the fringe as it evolves. Space does not permit discussion of this topic, and therefore we leave it to future work. Nonetheless, the owner-proxy and change-proxy can still be used to define these traversals without a full dump of the object reference graph.

5.1 Tracing Adaptively

LeakBot first publishes the traversals to the tracing agent. The tracing agent spawns a thread that cycles through the unique traversals and periodically (once per second) performs at most one every time it wakes up. The agent assigns, to each unique traversal, a *sample bias* which lies between 0 and 1, and is initially 1. The bias is the probability that, when a traversal's turn comes up, the agent will actually perform the traversal. For every traversal, the agent determines whether any of that traversal's associated updates have been detected. It reports any detected updates (i.e. as an element having been added, removed, or relinked) back to the analyzer. For example, when an addition update is detected, the analyzer updates the proxy-size of that region.

LeakBot adaptively adjusts the sample bias of the traversals. Since we are interested in tracking leaks, we increase the bias whenever an addition template fires, and decrease it whenever no template fires, and decrease it even more so when a removal template fires. LeakBot ensures that no CER is completely ignored, in case the CER's mode changes at some point.

5.2   Implementation of the Tracing Agent

LeakBot works with either full reference graph snapshots acquired earlier, or it selectively acquires this information via a live connection. LeakBot's analyzer can parse previously acquired trace files in the Sun heapdump format, the IBM heapdump format, or the Jinsight [18] format. The agent relies on the JVMPI [15] profiling interface to gather information from the JVM.

JVMPI identifies objects by their memory address. Therefore, to maintain unique object identifiers in between initial snapshots, the agent needs to listen to object move and free events. This slow down garbage collection by as much as a factor of two. Luckily, LeakBot allows this interval to be very short. Once we have identified CERs, we no longer listen to move and free events. Instead, we use weak references to maintain persistent identifiers just for the elements of traversal paths — a very small number of weak references in relation to the entire reference graph. Therefore, once tracing begins, we do not measurably perturb the garbage collection. In addition, because the sampling process itself is so infrequent and selective, the cost of the sampling is also very small. In fact, the only measurable slowdown is the cost of having a JVMPI agent *attached*, not of listening to events. For example, when attached, some JVMs use a slower object allocator. This overhead can run as high as several percent, which still meets our design constraint.

6   Additional Related Work

This section categorizes and discusses the related research we have encountered.

Type Assistance: Some recent work use static semantics to enforce and detect ownership using ownership types[6, 5]. Perhaps, knowing aspects of data structure flux at compile-time, such as the allocation site of constituents, and the sites at which members are added or removed, or substructures relinked, we could insert instrumentation at just those sites.

Heap Analysis: Some have studied the interaction between the application's and the runtime's use of objects [22, 23]. They break an object's lifetime into several phases, such as the time after allocation and before first use, and the time between last use and collection ("drag"). Glasgow Haskell [10] as of version 5.03 has built-in support for this type of analysis, which it calls "biographical profiling." Other works study how liveness information [1, 13] or reachability [14] can benefit conservative garbage collection. As with static analysis, it is conceivable that LeakBot could leverage these findings in its ranking. However, they gather the information via a pre-pass profiling run, which doesn't fit with our goal of analysis on production machines.

Debugging Memory Problems by Tracing: Others have explored instrumenting allocation sites [3, 11, 29] and instrumenting field access and modification [24, 25] in order to assist in tracking down memory-related errors. Some of these [24, 25] using the notions introduced by [22], strive to automatically fix the problems, by instrumenting field updates to remove "dragging" references to array elements. In addition to high overhead, these techniques do not address the issues of ease of tool use in framework-intensive environments. While static assistance could possibly guide the instrumentation points to reduce runtime cost, it would have to be very precise in order to be useful.

Glasgow Haskell supports a form of heap analysis called "retainer profiling" to help fix memory consumption problems due persisting, but unevaluated closures. At least as of version 5.04, this profiling is based only on reachability, has a fixed maximum-size retainer set, and exploring multi-hop ownership requires multiple passes. In addition, retainer profiling is done on a per-class basis, with classes specified on the application command-line. For long-running, framework-intensive servers we think this approach is too restrictive.

Debugging via Tracing: Some approaches instrument the application [16] or debugger [2]) to alert the tool user to specific conditions specified by the tool user. Based on the specified conditions, these tools insert or activate instrumentation to gather the relevant information. This is akin to the interaction between the analyzer and tracing agent in LeakBot, except that in LeakBot the requests for information gathering have been automated, and are specific to the evolution of whole data structures.

Discovering Static Properties with Tracing: Several works collect and analyze traces to establish properties of programs which are difficult to establish with static analysis [8, 9]. As with other work we have discussed, collecting the required traces can be expensive. Perhaps detecting invariant properties of data structures could assist LeakBot in ranking the objects or refining the CERs.

7   Conclusion

We had two design goals for LeakBot. First, it should be usable by non-experts, and by experts without many hours to burn. Second, it should be feasible to apply on production machines. In our consulting practice with IBM customers, we happily found that these two goals are not at odds. In fact, we found a synergy between them. Being selective about what the tool presents to the user (because those are the aspects which best explain the problem) facilitates being selective about what it traces.

In this paper we have presented a tool called LeakBot, which we have demonstrated to achieve these goals. We have used LeakBot successfully in our consulting practice to assist in problem determination on large IBM customer applications. It has quickly identified that leaks do or do not exist, verified that bug fixes actually fix problems, and assisted in diagnosing and expediting the resolution of known leaks. We were able to analyze applications with millions of live objects, and trace the ongoing evolution of suspicious data structures with negligible impact on the transaction throughput of those server applications. LeakBot implements four contributions presented in this paper:

Raising the Level of Analysis. Our technique presents results, and performs analysis at the level of data structures, not individual objects. This enables discovery and presentation of high-level properties, both structural and temporal, of those data structures.

A Way to Automatically Find Problematic Data Structures. We define the concept of leak roots, objects that are likely to be at the head of these structures: they contain one or more leaks. We identify a set of important structural and temporal properties of data structures, and introduce a nonlinear combination of them that prioritizes objects based on the likelihood that they are leak roots. Without any knowledge of specific frameworks, it quickly finds a small set of candidate leak roots out of millions of live objects.

Concise Models of Data Structure Evolution. We introduce Co-evolving Regions, sub-structures whose members exhibit coherent evolution behavior. We identify salient features — the leak root, the owner-proxy, and the change proxy — that concisely describe this similarity. These features not only group members into regions, but they also aid in explaining the regions to a user, and in observing the actual evolution in a cheap way.

A Lightweight Tracing Agent. We show how to use Co-evolving Regions to automatically derive tracing schemes to detect when elements are added to, removed from, or repositioned within a region. To track these changes, we derive traversals from the owner-proxy and change-proxy.

An Adaptive Loop that Combines Ranking and Evolution Tracing to Mutual Benefit. Ranking informs the tracing: it identifies a small set of data structures that we need to track. Tracing informs the ranking: it identifies new temporal properties of those data structures. These new findings refine the rankings, which in turn allows the tracing agent to focus on only the relevant regions.

We continue to validate these techniques in our consulting practice. For example, as new frameworks come along, we may need to refine the model LeakBot uses for object ranking; new data structure or temporal properties, or new ways of combining them may be appropriate. We also continue to refine the CERs, and their use in the adaptive agent. Other areas of future work include using the high-level properties that LeakBot uncovers to develop better presentations, and exploring additional applications of CERs beyond memory leak diagnosis.

Acknowledgements

We appreciate the assistance of Matthew Arnold, Jong-Deok Choi, and Harini Srinivasan at IBM T.J. Watson Research Center in the refinement of the presentation of this paper.

References

[1] O. Agesen, D. Detlefs, and J. E. B. Moss. Garbage collection and local variable type-precision and liveness in Java virtual machines. In *Programming Language Design and Implementation*, 1998.

[2] J. K. A. W. Appel. Traversal-based visualization of data structures. In *Symposium on Information Visualization*, pages 11–18, 1998.

[3] D. R. Barach, D. H. Taenzer, and R. E. Wells. A technique for finding storage allocation errors in c-langage programs. *ACM SIGPLAN Notices*, 17(5), May 1982.

[4] Borland software corporation optimizeit™.

[5] C. Boyapati, R. Lee, and M. Rinard. Ownership types for safe programming: preventing data races and deadlocks. In *Object-oriented programming, systems, languages, and applications*, 2002.

[6] D. Clarke, J. Noble, and J. Potter. Simple ownership types for object containment. In *European Conference on Object-Oriented Programming*, 2001.

[7] J. S. Dong and R. Duke. The geometry of object containment. *Object-oriented Systems*, 2:41–63, 1995.

[8] M. Ernst, W. G. Griswold, Y. Kataoka, and D. Notkin. Dynamically discovering pointer-based program invariants. In *International Conference on Software Engineering*, 1999.

[9] S. Hangal and M. S. Lam. Tracking down software bugs using automatic anomaly detection. In *International Conference on Software Engineering*, May 2002.

[10] The Glasgow Haskell compiler user's guide. http://haskell.cs.yale,edu/ghc.

[11] R. Hastings and B. Joynce. Purify — fast detection of memory leaks and access errors. In *USENIX Proceedings*, pages 125–136, 1992.

[12] B. Hayes. Using key object opportunism to collect old objects. In *Object-oriented programming, systems, languages, and applications*, 1991.

[13] M. Hirzel, A. Diwan, and A. Hosking. On the usefulness of liveness for garbage collection and leak detection. In *European Conference on Object-Oriented Programming*, 2001.

[14] M. Hirzel, J. Hinkel, A. Diwan, and M. Hind. Understanding the connectivity of heap objects. In *International Symposium on Memory Management*, 2002.

[15] http://java.sun.com/products/jdk/1.2/docs/guide/jvmpi/jvmpi.html.

[16] R. Lencevicius. On-the-fly query-based debugging with examples. In *Automated and Algorithmic Debugging*, 2000.

[17] S. S. Muchnik. *Advanced Compiler Design and Implemtnation*. Morgan Kaufmann, 1997.

[18] W. D. Pauw, E. Jensen, N. Mitchell, G. Sevitsky, J. Vlissides, and J. Yang. Visualizing the execution of Java programs. In *Software Visualization, State-of-the-art Survey*, volume 2269. Springer-Verlag, 2002.

[19] W. D. Pauw and G. Sevitsky. Visualizing reference patterns for solving memory leaks in Java. *Concurrency: Practice and Experience*, 12:1431–1454, 2000. previously appeared in ECOOP 1999.

[20] G. Ramalingam. On loops, dominators, and dominance frontiers. *ACM Transactions on Programming Languages and Systems*, 24(5):455–490, 2002.
[21] Rational software corporation quantify^{TM}.
[22] N. Rojemo and C. Runciman. Lag, drag, void and use — heap profiling and space-efficient compilation revisited. In *International Conference on Functional Programming*, pages 34–41, 1996.
[23] C. Runciman and N. Rojemo. New dimensions in heap profiling. *Journal of Functional Programming*, 6(4):587–620, July 1996.
[24] R. Shaham, E. K. Kolodner, and M. Sagiv. Automatic removal of array memory leaks in java. In *Computational Complexity*, pages 50–66, 2000.
[25] R. Shaham, E. K. Kolodner, and M. Sagiv. Estimating the impact of heap liveness information on space consumption in Java. In *International Symposium on Memory Management*, June 2002.
[26] Sitraka Inc. JProbe^{TM} Profiler with Memory Debugger ServerSide Suite.
[27] Heap Analysis Tool. http://java.sun.com/people/billf/heap.
[28] Java 2 Platform, Enterprise Edition. http://java.sun.com/j2ee.
[29] Sun Microsystems HPROF JVM profiler.
[30] S. Wilson and J. Kesselmann. *Java^{TM} Platform Performance Strategies and Tactics*. Addison Wesley, June 2000.

A   Handling Multiple Ownership

We detail two solutions to multiple ownership. One generalizes the definition of ownership, and the other prunes the reference graph so that multiple ownership does not occur.

First, we can generalize unique ownership to k-ownership, which is the number of objects owned by this object and k other objects. Thus, 0-ownership is equivalent to the unique ownership described above. We can derive this new relation by weakening dominance to allow for k-dominance. In this case, the dominator tree becomes a diamond-free graph (i.e. a tree with neither cross nor back edges).

In practice, however, computing k-dominance may be too expensive. Alternatively, we can use a technique similar to [20]: reduce the graph to a depth-first spanning tree. Since there are many such trees for one graph, we provide heuristics which guide which non-tree edges are more favorable to prune than others. For example, we populate the start set (of graph roots) in priority order: we give highest preference to first class objects, then objects referenced by on-stack GC roots, then every other graph root. Another example heuristic: for objects on the fringe, we make sure that if we clip any incoming edges, we clip edges which do not cross the fringe in preference to those which do. Note, however, that by pruning these edges, the ranking algorithm loses shared ownership information. Therefore, this pruning trades off speed of analysis with completeness of information.

B   Choosing a Threshold for Leak Root Ranks

In our implementation, we have designed the gating functions so that most objects with a step-2 rank below 0.4 are fairly certain not to be leak roots. In off-line mode, we tend to set the threshold at least to 0.4 under the assumption that the snapshots we have are all the information we will get. In online mode, we can leverage the online evolution tracker described in Section 5: set the threshold lower, and use evolution tracking to quickly confirm or deny the candidacy of all non-zero ranked leak roots.

Java Subtype Tests in Real-Time

Krzysztof Palacz and Jan Vitek

S^3 Lab, Department of Computer Sciences, Purdue University

Abstract. Dynamic subtype tests are frequent operations in Java programs. Naive implementations can be costly in space and running time. The techniques that have been proposed to reduce these costs are either restricted in their ability to cope with dynamic class loading or may suffer from pathological performance degradation penalizing certain programming styles. We present R&B, a subtype test algorithm designed for time and space constrained environments such as Real-Time Java which require predictable running times, low space overheads and dynamic class loading. Our algorithm is constant-time, requires an average of 10.8 bytes per class of memory and has been shown to yield an average 2.5% speedup on a production virtual machine. The Real-Time Specification for Java requires dynamic scoped memory access checks on every reference assignment. We extend R&B to perform memory access checks in constant-time.

1 Introduction

Dynamic subtype tests are a staple of modern object-oriented programming languages. In Java subtype tests are executed in a variety of contexts, such as checked casts, array updates, exception handling and `instanceof` queries. The language runtime system is responsible for maintaining data structures to encode the subtype relation and efficiently answering queries. Subtype tests can be performed in linear time by traversing the type hierarchy. Unfortunately such implementations lead to unpredictable performance. This problem remains in many state-of-the-art implementations which have a constant-time fast path and a slow path which falls back on a form of hierarchy traversal.

The lack of predictability is particularly bothersome in real-time settings because giving the time bound of a simple instruction such as an array store requires making non-trivial assumptions about the concrete types of objects and knowledge of the implementation technique used by the VM. In this paper, our goal is to engineer a subtype test algorithm for memory-constrained real-time systems which satisfies the following requirements:

- Queries must run in constant time.
- Space overhead must not significantly increase system footprint.
- Preemption latency must be small and bounded.

In general-purpose virtual machines, such as Hotspot or Jikes, unpredictable performance is also a nuisance because it impacts programming style. For instance,

L. Cardelli (Ed.): ECOOP 2003, LNCS 2743, pp. 378–404, 2003.

in many application subtype tests may be slower for interface than classes (usually if the number of implemented interfaces is larger than some VM-specific constant). This situation reinforces folklore about the cost of using interfaces and suggests that they should be avoided for performance critical activities.

The issue of implementation of subtype tests for object oriented languages has been addressed by many authors from both theoretical and applied communities [6, 15, 1, 7, 5, 11, 14, 18, 19, 2, 20, 17]. A number of non-incremental techniques for compact and constant time subtype tests have been proposed [7, 14, 17, 20]. Production virtual machines that implement fast incremental algorithms [2, 6] can, in special cases, exhibit suboptimal performance.

In this paper we investigate simple techniques based on well-known algorithms and strive to find a compromise between these three requirements. We reduce the amount of work needed upon class loading so that in most cases there is no recomputation; we guarantee fast and constant time subtype tests[1] and require very little space per class.

We also report on a proof-of-concept implementation of our algorithm, called R&B, in which we integrated R&B in a production virtual machine, the Sun Microsystems Research VM (or EVM). And we show that for that particular implementation we reduced space consumption and improved running times by an average of 2.5%. We had to change only about 100 lines in the original code of the VM and optimizing just-in-time compiler.

In this paper, we also discuss two extensions to R&B, one extension is a *combined encoding* which unifies the treatment of classes and interfaces, and the other extension is an algorithm for checking memory accesses. Memory access checks are mandated by the Real-Time Specification for Java (RSTJ) [4] on each reference assignment. We observe that these checks are a special case of subtype tests and that it is thus relatively straightforward to apply R&B to this problem. The technique described here has a slow path of two loads and two compares which is faster than previous work [3, 12, 8]. Moreover, we only need one word of storage per memory area.

2   Subtype Tests in Java

We start by presenting the subtype test algorithm used in EVM. Subtype tests are mandated by the Java language specification for most checked cast expressions, type comparisons, array stores, and exception handler determination. In all of these cases, one of the following two primitive functions is evaluated:

```
instanceof( o, T)    returns true if o.class <: T
checkcast( o, T)     throws exception if not o.class <: T
```

We write A <: B to mean that type A is a subtype of B. The first function checks that an object is an instance of a given type and the second, that it is assignable

---

[1] Recomputation can create short pauses, but these are infrequent enough that we argue that they will not impact overall throughput. Furthermore R&B is thread safe allowing the runtime to be preempted at any time by a real-time thread.

to that type. These functions treat null values differently. On a null, an instance test returns false, while a cast succeeds. Java also defines a subtyping relation for arrays based on equality of their dimensions and subtyping of element types.

In the remainder of this paper we abstract those differences and focus on the core functionality of subtype testing as implemented by the subtypeof procedure of Fig. 1. EVM's type test algorithm treats class and interface queries differently. For classes, the hierarchy is traversed until the requested class is located or the root is reached. For interfaces, a per-type array of implemented interfaces is scanned. The basic scheme is optimized in two straightforward ways. The subtype test logic is guarded by an equality test so as to catch cases when both argument types are the same. To exploit type locality of tests a per-type cache is added. This cache always holds the last type that tested positively as a subtype of the given type. EVM's optimizing compiler inlines the code of subtypeof (but not implements or extends). The equality test in is inlined because it is cheap. The branch on the kind of the type pr (either a class or an interface) may

```
type_info {
   type_info    parent;
   type_info[]  interfaces;
   type_info    cache; }


subtypeof( type_info cl, type_info pr ) {
   if ( cl == pr || cl.cache == pr ) return true;
   if ( isInterface( pr ) )          return implements( cl, pr);
   else                              return extends( cl, pr); }


implements( type_info cl, type_info pr ) {
   for( int i = 0; i < pr.intefaces.length; i++)
      if ( cl == pr.interfaces[i] )
         { cl.cache = pr; return true; }
   return false; }


extends( type_info cl, type_info pr ) {
   for ( type_info pcl = cl.parent; pcl != null; pcl = pcl.parent)
      if ( pcl == pr )
         { cl.cache = pr; return true; }
   return false; }
```

Fig. 1. EVM Subtype test: hierarchy traversal, one-entry cache and equality test

be resolved if pr is loaded. The algorithm is simple and performs well, though in pathological cases the performance of tests may vary greatly.

3   Runtime Behavior of Subtype Tests

A suite of twelve Java programs was used to characterize the runtime behavior of subtype tests in practice. The data was obtained by running these programs on an instrumented version of EVM. This benchmark suite is part of larger collection available from www.ovmj.org.

Runtime program size. While the average size of programs in the benchmark suite (inclusive of the JDK libraries) is close to ten thousand classes and interfaces, in practice a much smaller number is used – and, thus, loaded. This difference is significant because designing an algorithm based solely on static characteristics would be overly pessimistic. As can be seen, Table 1 includes counts of classes and interfaces that are loaded by the VM during the test runs, respectively in columns #class and #itf. The relatively small numbers of loaded types suggests that in a typical situation the size of data structures may not be a bottleneck. Table 1 also illustrates the average number of implemented interfaces (avgit) and the depth of the inheritance hierarchy defined as the number of classes between a type and the hierarchy root (ichain). While averages are low, it should be noted that in one benchmark there were as many as twelve implemented interfaces. The inheritance chain length suggest that the average iteration count of hierarchy traversal is less than two. We believe that the architecture of the benchmark programs accounts for some of the variations among programs. For instance CO has few interfaces because its implementors chose to minimize their number to avoid the (supposed) higher cost of interface dispatch. By contrast, EH has a clean design with a rich type hierarchy, a large number of interfaces and deep inheritance chains. Finally, it should be noted that this data is not a predictor of subtype test performance as we will see later.

Hierarchy shape. The shape of a class hierarchy can be further characterized by the number of *runtime leaf* classes it contains. A runtime leaf class is one for which no subclass was dynamically loaded during the benchmark run. Fig. 2 shows that, on average, over 80% of loaded classes are leaves. Runtime leaf classes may, of course, have subclasses that simply were not loaded in a given run.

Test frequencies. The benchmark programs performed an average of 320K tests per second as measured by instrumenting the optimizing JIT compiler and the interpreter and running on a SunBlade 100. Fig 3 breaks down subtype tests between instanceof and checkcast. As can be expected, casts occur more frequently in programs that manipulate generic data structures, such as the Generic Java compiler (GJ). At the other extreme, the bytecode analysis framework used in CO uses its own template macro expansion mechanism to generate container types thus avoiding casts. We have observed that the number of casts will be

Table 1. Benchmark suite. The number of classes dynamically loaded during the benchmark run is #class, the number of interfaces is #itf. avgit is the average number of implemented interfaces, and i-chain is the average inheritance chain height

	Name	Description	#class	#itf	avgit	ichain
EH	enhydra	Html2Java	313	113	2.6	2.7
CA	cap	Javac stress test	264	21	0.9	1.6
GJ	gj	Java compiler	328	27	0.7	1.6
KA	kawa	Scheme interpreter	511	19	0.6	2.2
BL	bloat	Bytecode optimizer	362	28	0.5	1.8
JE	jess	Expert shell	410	33	1.0	1.5
JA	javasrc	Html generator	232	22	0.6	1.7
XM	XML	XML tool	327	78	0.7	1.6
TO	toba	Java-to-c compiler	220	16	0.4	1.6
RH	rhino	Javascript interp.	305	21	0.6	1.7
SO	soot	Optimization fmk	641	102	1.2	2.2
CO	confined	Confinement check	467	29	0.3	1.6

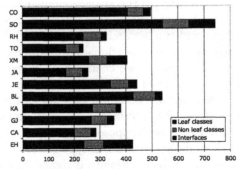

Fig. 2. Breakdown of dynamically loaded classes and interfaces. Leaf classes do not have subclasses

much higher if the optimizing compiler is turned off. This is accounted for by common programming idioms that are easily optimized by the JIT, *e.g.* the use of instanceof to guard a cast. Overall, the variability in test frequencies is most likely due to programming style; for instance, in CO the inner loop is a visitor pattern over a complex instruction hierarchy and each iteration requires several tests. The data also shows that almost 90% of the tests are extends tests.

Test sites. The EVM JIT compiler emits an average of four hundred subtype test sequences per program. Fig. 4 shows that all but three of the benchmarks have less than 500 test sites. This is surprisingly low and suggests that code size increase due to inlining is likely to be negligible. No correlation between the number of sites and dynamic occurrences of tests could be established. Because the number of sites is so small, compiler implementors may even choose to keep track of test sites during program execution. As more information becomes available, the original code can be patched to remove the extra interface check.

Success rate. A test is considered successful if it returns true (instanceof) or does not throw an exception (checkcast). Fig. 5 shows that 90% of tests are successful. Clearly any implementation should optimize for success, but considering the frequency of tests the costs of the slow path can not be ignored.

Cache effectiveness. EVM uses a two element cache composed of an array cache and an object cache. The array cache is used to record the last successful cast performed on an array store, the object cache is used for all other tests. The average hit rate is 84.5%, but as can be seen in Fig. 6 these results can be highly variable. Hit rates can be as low as 50.3% (EH) or as high as 99.9% (JE). While these numbers confirm the usefulness of caches they also demonstrate that it is not a panacea.

Miss costs. The cost of a cache miss depends on the number of comparisons required by the implements() and extends() functions. Average iteration counts, with caches turned off, appear in Table 2. The first counts the levels of inheritance traversed, the second the number of interfaces tested. The numbers are surprisingly high for some benchmarks, *e.g.*, EH in which an average of 7.6 interfaces are tested per cache miss. The implication is that pathological cases with important performance perturbations are quite likely to occur.

Selftests. A selftest is a test of the form subtypeof(A, A). On average 59% of the subtype tests evaluated in the benchmark suite are selftests. Fig. 7 also shows that the large majority of these selftests are performed on leaf classes.

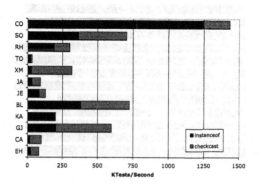

Fig. 3. Subtype tests per second

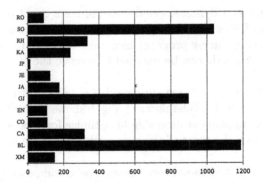

Fig. 4. Subtype tests sequences emitted by the JIT

Table 2. Iterations of the hierarchy traversal algorithm

	EH	CP	GJ	BL	JE	XM	TB	RH	CO	JA
extends	1.03	1.67	1.40	3.21	1.05	1.99	0.95	1.00	1.39	2.54
implements	7.64	0.66	0.00	0.64	1.98	1.00	1.98	1.75	0.64	1.00

Conclusions. Several conclusions should be drawn from this data. First, the run-time type hierarchy is more important then the compile time hierarchy. While many benchmark programs consist of many classes, the portion actually used is small. It would appear that at runtime it is common to encounter a shallow hierarchy with few interfaces. Selftests and caches are important for good performance, however they are not sufficient. Finally, there are surprisingly few test sites suggesting that code bloat is unlikely to be an issue.

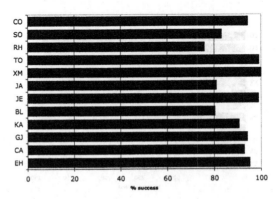

Fig. 5. Ratio of successful subtype tests. An `instanceof` test is successful if it returns `true` and `checkcast` if it does not throw an exception

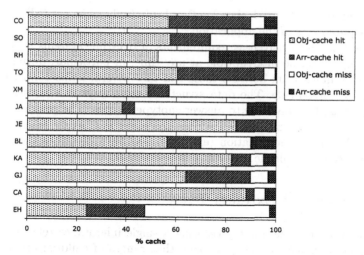

Fig. 6. Effectiveness of a two element cache. The first two bars denote, respectively, hits in the object cache and the array cache. The last two bars indicate misses in the object and array cache. Values are normalized wrt. successful subtype tests

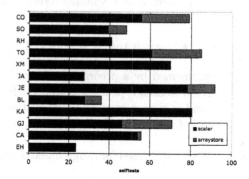

Fig. 7. Frequency of selftests. The first bar denotes the ratio of tests subtype(A,A) where A is a leaf. The second bar is the ratio of selftests for non-leaf classes

4   The R&B Algorithm

The algorithm presented in this paper, called R&B for *ranges and buckets*, has the following characteristics. Subtype tests are run in constant time. Caches can be added to the basic algorithm to yield different configurations, their tradeoffs are studied in Section 7. Space requirements are small. Each class and interface has a single word reserved for extends tests and, on average, 2.8 bytes for implements tests. The algorithm is incremental in nature. Type information may be recomputed eagerly (at each class load) or lazily (only when needed), depending on the requirements of the application.

To meet the responsiveness requirements of real-time systems it is essential that the algorithm be interruptible at any time, in particular, during updates to the type information because these can take several milliseconds. In R&B, updates are thread safe. The data structures are always in a consistent state and can be used at any time to answer subtype queries. The presentation of is structured as follows. Section 5 describes the range numbering scheme used for checking the inheritance relation (extends). Section 6 describes the bucketing technique used for multiple subtyping (implements).

5   Range-Based Extends Tests

A well-known technique for representing a single inheritance relation is based on assigning a range to each type such that ranges of children are subranges of their parents' ranges and ranges of siblings are disjoint. The technique was first described by Schubert et al. [15] and independently rediscovered by the implementors of Modula-3.

Subtype tests are, essentially, range inclusion checks which can be computed in constant time and constant space. Assuming that each class is described by two variables called *low* and *high*, a test whether type A is a subtype of B becomes:

$$B <: A \quad \Leftrightarrow \quad A.low < B.low \wedge B.high < A.high \tag{1}$$

The range assignment is performed by a preorder walk on the inheritance tree. A consecutive number is given to each type's low bound the first time the type is encountered. The high bound is chosen so as to be larger than the maximum of the type's low bound and all of it's children's high bounds. A sample assignment is shown in Fig. 8.

Several questions need to be addressed for range-based queries to be practical.

1. How many bits are required to represent ranges?
2. How can the impact of class loading be minimized?
3. How can thread safety be ensured?

The first question is important for long running systems because these may load many more classes than the applications in the benchmark suite. It would be advantageous to pack the ranges in a single word. With a naive encoding this would restrict VM to 32,768 classes. Note also, that the encoding of Section 9 requires packed ranges. Class loading is frequent and implies recomputing the range assignment each time a new class is added. The cost of computing the assignment should be minimized. Finally, in a real-time setting, a real-time thread may be released while the range assignment is in the middle of being recomputed. The algorithm should be designed so as to ensure that it can be preempted without invalidating the type information.

5.1   Refining the Encoding

We now consider how to refine the encoding to address the three questions mentioned above. For a subtype query such as o instanceof T, we call type T the *provider* and the type of the object o the *client*. Thus we refer to the left hand-side of a test *client* <: *provider*, as the client position, and the right-hand side the provider position.

Observe that both high bounds are not needed. Thus equation (1) can be written:

$$\text{B} <: \text{A} \quad \Leftrightarrow \quad \text{A.low} < \text{B.low} \land \text{B.low} < \text{A.high} \tag{2}$$

The low bound is the only information required from the client. Furthermore, A.low < B.low can be safely weakened to A.low ≤ B.low without invalidating the result. The invariants that must be maintained in cases where B is a subclass of A are, thus, A.low ≤ B.low < A.high.

The key insight to limit the growth of ranges and reduce the cost of recomputing the assignment is that the high bounds can be computed on demand. As long as the low bound has been initialized, the type can be used in the client position of subtype queries. The refined extends test function will thus perform a subrange check and, only if the test fails, will the validity of the provider be verified. If it is not valid, *i.e.* the high bound is zero, the high bound is computed — we say the type is *promoted* — and the test is attempted one more time. Fig. 9 gives pseudocode for extends tests. The type_info data structure contains two 16 bit values, **high** and **low**. An equality check is added because it

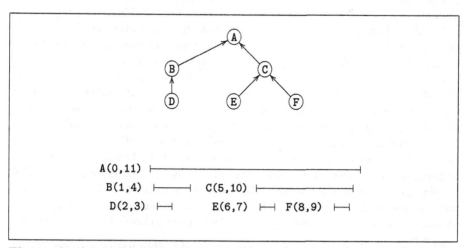

Fig. 8. A valid range assignment for an inheritance hierarchy. The class A is the root, all of its subclasses have subranges. Siblings such as B and C have disjoint ranges

```
type_info {
    ushort high;
    ushort low;
    type_info parent; }


extends( type_info cl, type_info pr) {
    if ( cl == pr ||
        pr.low <= cl.low && cl.low < pr.high)    return true;
    if ( invalid( pr) )
        { promote( pr); return extends( cl, pr);}
    return false; }


invalid( type_info t) { return t.high == 0; }
```

Fig. 9. Extend test

will obviate the need to promote leaf types[2]. Tests of the form extends(A, A) will be shortcircuited by the equality check.

5.2 Range Assignment

Every time a new class[3] is added to the system, the class is inserted in the hierarchy using the insert() procedure shown in Fig. 10. Thus every type starts out with an invalid range, but in a state that allows it to be used in the client position. The algorithm only recomputes the range assignment on calls to the promote() routine. In our benchmarks, promote() is called on average eleven times per program (one promotion for every 40 loaded classes, or one promotion per 13 million tests). The cost of promotion is linear in the number of types as will be shown next. Promotions can also be triggered eagerly upon class loading, in which case the extends procedure of Fig. 9 need not check for validity.

Consider the hierarchy of Fig. 11.a which is the result of several calls to insert(). All classes have the same invalid range $[1, 0]$. The first subtype test, extends(F, C) forces a relabeling. Fig. 11.b shows that C is promoted which triggers the promotion of its parent A. The query extends(F, C) can now evaluate to true as $2 \leq 2 \wedge 2 < 3$. The second test, extends(H, C), will succeed without promotion. Note that children of C still have an invalid range since it has

---

[2] The only case when leaf types have to be promoted is when testing extends(A, B) and B is a leaf. Of course, tests of this kind always fail, so there is, in fact, no need to promote a leaf.

[3] Interfaces are subclasses of Object but they do not need to be promoted because they can never be in the provider position.

```
insert( type_info t) {
    t.high = 0;
    t.low = ( t.parent == null ) ? 1 : t.parent.low; }
```

Fig. 10. Adding a class to the hierarchy

not been necessary to distinguish them so far. Fig. 11.c, shows the result of evaluating extends(F, E). Since E is invalid it has to be promoted. extends(F, E) fails as $3 \leq 4 \land 4 < 4$ is false. Next, we evaluate extends(H, H) which is trivially true. Finally extends(G, D) is evaluated in Fig. 11.d. After this step no more promotions will be required.

The pseudocode of our implementation is given in figures 12 and 13. The basic data structure representing types, type_info, was inherited from the EVM. It includes a reference to the parent of the class or interface, siblings and first child. Whenever promote() is invoked, the algorithm starts by flattening the hierarchy in an array of entry records (flatten()). Leaf classes are stored once, non-leaves are stored twice, once before all of their subclasses and once after. Ranges are allocated by increasing a counter for all non-leaf entries. This algorithm is doing slightly more than is strictly necessary because we recompute the assignment for the entire tree each time.

5.3   Thread Safety and Real-Time

We now argue that the algorithm of Fig. 13 is thread safe. The promote() procedure maintains the following invariants. If A is the type information before a promotion and A' is the same after a promotion we have:

$$\texttt{A.low} \leq \texttt{A'.low} \ \land \ \left(\texttt{A.high} = 0 \ \lor \ \texttt{A.high} \leq \texttt{A'.high} \right) \tag{3}$$

Furthermore, for any pair of type A and B we have:

$$\texttt{A.low} \leq \texttt{B.low} \ \Rightarrow \ \texttt{A'.low} \leq \texttt{B'.low} \tag{4}$$

These invariants follow from the fact that ranges are assigned in the order classes occur in the siblings list. The order of siblings is not modified during insertion because types are always added at the end of the sibling list of their parent and no other operation modifies this order.

To ensure that the data structures are consistent at every step of the update we schedule write to the type_info according to a preorder right-to-left tree traversal. High bounds are always written before low bounds and before any bounds of children. Consider the updates between Fig. 11.a and Fig. 11.b. Types A, C, F, E, H have to be updated. The following order ensures that they are valid at every step:

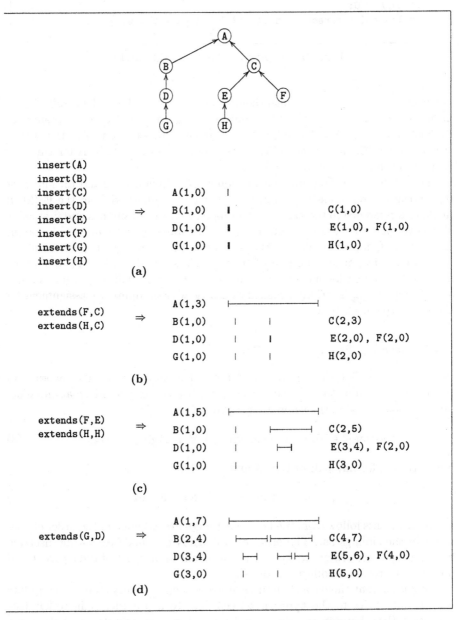

Fig. 11. Allocating bounds for a small hierarchy

```
int MINRANGE = 1, MAXRANGE = 0xffff;
char FIRST='f', LAST='l', IGNORE='i';

type_info root;
entry[] array;
int array_pos;

entry {
    char type;
    type_info class;
    ushort position; }

type_info {
    ushort high;
    ushort low;
    boolean isInterface;
    type_info super, nextSibling, firstChild; }
```

Fig. 12. Data structures, constants and global variables

1. $A.high = 3$,
2. $C.high = 3$,
3. $F.low = 2$,
4. $H.low = 2$,
5. $E.low = 2$,
6. $A.low = 1$.

The state immediately after (4) may cause one to wonder about validity of the approach since we have $E(1,0)$ and $H(2,0)$. However the state is still valid, since both types are still recognized as subtypes of $A(1,3)$. And any attempt to evaluate extends(H, E) will block until the promote() procedure returns.

In a real-time Java VM, a real-time thread should never have to block. This can be achieved by configuring R&B to perform eager range assignment. Every time a new class is loaded the entire hierarchy will be recomputed. This imposes an added cost to class loading, but this cost is acceptable because real-time threads are not expected to trigger class loading (unless a way is found to bound the costs of class loading).

6   Bucket-Based Implements Tests

Our algorithm for subtype tests in a multiple inheritance type hierarchy (required for implements tests) is a variant of the packed encoding algorithm [17], extended to handle dynamic hierarchy extensions. Implements tests have the form:

$$o <: I$$

```
synchronized promote() {
   array = new entry[SizeOfHiearchy*2];
   array_pos = 0;
   if (root.isValid()) root.setRange( MINRANGE, MAXRANGE);
   root.flatten();
   allocateRange();
   updateClasses();
   array = null; }

flatten() {
   if (firstChild == null) add( IGNORE);
   else
       { add(FIRST); firstChild.flatten(); add( LAST); }
   if (nextSibling != null) nextSibling.flatten(); }

add( char c) {
   entry e = new entry();
   e.type = c;
   e.class = this;
   e.position = 0;
   array[ array_pos++ ] = e; }

allocateRange() {
   int position = 0;
   for (int pos = 0; pos < arr_pos; pos++) {
       if (array[pos].type != IGNORE) {
           char prev = array[pos - 1].type;
           char this = array[pos].type;
           if (!(prev == LAST && this == LAST)
                 && !(prev == FIRST && this == LAST))   position++;
       }
       array[pos].position = position;
   } }

updateClasses() {
   for (int pos = array_pos - 1; pos >= 0; pos--) {
       entry e = array[pos];
       if (e.type == LAST || e.type == IGNORE)
           if (e.class.low != e.position)
               e.class.low = e.position;
       else if ( e.class.high != e.position)
           e.class.high = e.position;
   } }
```

Fig. 13. Computing the range assignment

```
type_info {
    byte[] display; }

interface_info {
    byte iid;
    byte bucket; }
implements( type_info cl, interface_info pr) {
    return cl.display[ pr.bucket ] == pr.iid; }
```

Fig. 14. Implements test

where the client o is an instance of some class C and the provider I is an interface type. In this approach, every interface is represented by two numbers that we call a bucket (bucket) and an interface identifier (iid). The algorithm will maintain the following invariants for any two distinct interfaces I and J,

$$I <: C \land J <: C \; \Rightarrow \; \text{I.bucket} \neq \text{J.bucket} \tag{5}$$

$$I <: J \; \Rightarrow \; \text{I.bucket} \neq \text{J.bucket} \tag{6}$$

$$\text{I.bucket} \neq \text{J.bucket} \lor \text{I.iid} \neq \text{J.iid}. \tag{7}$$

Our goal is to find heuristics that minimize the number of buckets. For each class the runtime system maintains a *display*, i.e., an array of iids indexed by bucket. If a class does not implement any interfaces from a given bucket the display element for that bucket contains an iid of 0. The subtype test is performed by comparing the provider interface's iid against the value stored in the class' display at bucket and hence require one array access and a compare, as illustrated in Fig. 14.

This test returns the correct answer provided that any two interfaces with a common subtype are never assigned to the same bucket. Our algorithm satisfies this requirement while striving to keep the number of buckets low since the total space taken up by the displays is proportional to the number of interfaces in the system times the number of buckets. The number of interfaces in a given bucket is typically small (obviously bounded by the total number of interfaces in the system, *cf.* Table 1), hence one byte can be used to encode the interface iid. In case of overflow a new bucket will be allocated.

Dynamic class loading can violate the invariant that interfaces with common subtypes belong to distinct buckets because a newly loaded class may implement two interfaces which did not have, up to this point, a common subtype. In this case it is necessary to recompute the assignment of interfaces to buckets. This may be done by the algorithm given in [17], however, we present a simpler approach that gives satisfactory results in practice.

When a class C is loaded, we first determine if the invariant has been violated. To achieve this, we check if any of the existing buckets contains more than one interface implemented by C. If this is not the case, then the invariant is not violated and no recomputation is needed. Otherwise the following procedure is performed for each bucket b that contains k interfaces implemented by C: $k - 1$ new buckets are created, one superinterface of C is left in b and the remaining $k - 1$ interfaces are assigned to one of the new buckets. New buckets receive the next available bucket number. Subsequently the remaining interfaces from b are assigned to the new buckets so that both b and the new buckets contain approximately the same number of interfaces.

When an interface is moved from bucket b_1 to bucket b_2 its iid remains unchanged and the iid is added to b_1's *exclusion list*. If an interface is later assigned to b_1, it will never receive an iid that appears on b_1's exclusion list. Once all buckets are processed we iterate over all the loaded classes and reallocate their displays. Existing entries in the displays remain unchanged and new entries are added to account for the new buckets. This means that in a given class's display an iid identifying the same interface may appear more than once, first at the index corresponding to its original bucket and, then, at the indices corresponding to the buckets it has been subsequently moved to.

When an interface is loaded, we have to choose which bucket to assign it to. When no buckets have been created yet or all buckets are full (i.e., all numbers within the iid range are used or appear on the bucket's exclusion list) we have to add a new bucket. Otherwise we choose the bucket with the fewest interfaces among m most recently created buckets and add the interface to it. Here m is a small integer constant, five in our implementation. This heuristic is based on the observation that the most often implemented interfaces such as Cloneable and Serializable are loaded early during VM initialization and, hence, have low bucket numbers. A class implementing an interface defined in the application code is likely to also implement one of the system interfaces, hence putting these two interfaces in the same bucket would likely require the bucket to be divided. On the other hand, two interfaces loaded from application code are less likely to be implemented by the same class, and can, therefore, be put in the same bucket. The iid of the interface is chosen to be the next number from the iid range that is not assigned yet to any interface in the bucket and does not appear on the bucket's exclusion list.

We now argue that the implements tests algorithm is also thread-safe. This follows from the following facts:

- provider's iid never changes,
- provider's bucket number is changed before displays are reallocated,
- existing entries in displays never change.

The test given in Fig. 14 can use either old values of client.display and provider.bucket or their new values, denoted client.display' and provider.bucket'. We have the following cases.

- client.display and provider.bucket: client and provider must have been loaded prior to the test and the answer is correct;
- client.display' and provider.bucket': correct by construction;

- `client.display'` and `provider.bucket`: the client display contains the same entry both for the old and the new bucket number, thus the test returns the correct answer;
- `client.display` and `provider.bucket'`: this case will never occur if all displays are updated before the `provider.bucket` fields are written and memory barrier is issued between these two steps.

Therefore, in all cases the test returns the same answer. In many virtual machines threads are only stopped at GC safe points. In such systems thread safety is atomic if we assume that safe points are not inserted in the middle of subtype test sequence.

7   Experimental Results

We implemented our algorithm in the Sun Labs Virtual Machine for Research (EVM). EVM uses a one-element general-purpose cache and a one-element array store cache. The subtype test algorithm used by EVM is the one described in Section 2. The just-in-time compiler emits inline code to check the cache and a call to the out-of-line test routine. We made several modifications to the baseline EVM build. To evaluate the benefits of caching we removed the inlined cache checks emitted by the SPARC JIT for `instanceof` and `checkcast` tests as well as array stores (the SunNoCache configuration). We experimented with two configurations of our algorithm. In the UsJIT configuration we preserved the original cache checks emitted by the JIT but replaced the rest of the test code with an inline type equality test followed by out-of-line calls to our `extends()` and `implements()` routines. In the UsINL configuration we removed the original caches and changed the JIT to emit the fast path of our extends test. We used lazy range assignment in both configurations. We performed our experiments on a Sun Blade 100 workstation with a 500 MHz SPARC-IIe processor and 384 MB RAM.

The speedup results are summarized in Fig. 15. These were obtained because the average over five runs and are displayed as percentage speedups over the baseline EVM configuration (higher is faster). The results show that UsJIT is better on average than the baseline, with speedups up to 4.3% and on average of 2.5%. Inlining of the subtype test does not appear to pay off and performs slightly worse than the baseline. This clearly indicates that caches are important for performance.

The number of range promotions and bucket recomputations for each program are shown in Fig. 16. They show clearly that recomputation is infrequent. The individual costs of recomputation are given in Fig. 17. The recomputation times are small and mostly linear in the number of classes in the system.

We have also computed the space required to store the metadata as well the code size emitted by the JIT. Fig. 18 gives the breakdown of costs. While we can not guarantee constant space for the type information data, we note that the average size required is 10.8 bytes per class of which eight bytes are fixed overhead. The increase in code size is modest. Our representation is smaller than EVM's which requires three words per class and does not share type displays.

8   Combined Encoding

We now outline an alternative approach to our algorithm which we call *combined encoding*. It unifies the treatment of extends and implements checks. While not as space efficient, its implementation is somewhat simpler. Each loaded class and interface is placed in a bucket and receives an iid within the bucket. First, MAX_INLINE buckets are reserved for classes only. MAX_INLINE is a small constant, such as eight. If class C has an inheritance chain of length $d <$ MAX_INLINE then C will be put in bucket d. If $d >=$ MAX_INLINE the class is treated as if it were an interface. Interfaces are assigned a bucket according to the algorithm described in Section 6. Classes in the first MAX_INLINE buckets never change their bucket assignment. Hence, for these classes, the packed encoding technique reduces to Cohen's algorithm.

Fig. 19 illustrates our combined encoding. The key idea is that inl_parents field is a display *inlined* in the type_info structure. It may be padded with zero entries if necessary. Note that we use short integers as bucket in the first MAX_INLINE buckets because these buckets are likely to grow large. When the provider is known at compile time to be a non-leaf class from one of the inlined buckets, its bucket number and iids are guaranteed not to change and the

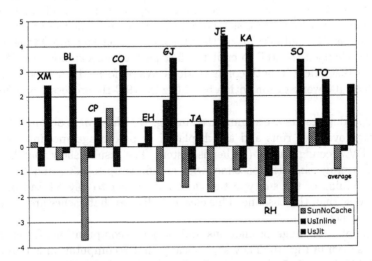

Fig. 15. Performance of the proposed subtype test techniques as percentage speedup over the baseline. The baseline is the unmodified EVM system. SunNo-Cache is the EVM with cache turned off. UsInline is a variant of our algorithm with inlining of the subtype test sequence and no caches. UsJit is the variant with caches. The last category shows average speed ups. UsJit exhibits a 2.5% average improvement (as compared to the base line)

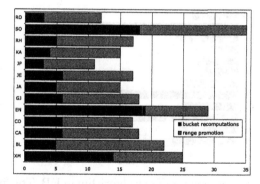

Fig. 16. Number of recomputations of implements and extends metadata. Class loading creates invalid ranges which may result in recomputations, for buckets recomputation is triggered if a new class introduces a conflict in bucket assignments

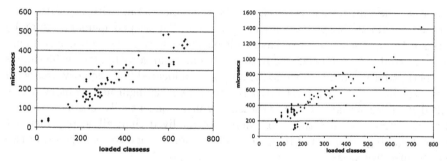

Fig. 17. Range and bucket recompute times as a function of the number of classes and interface loaded in the system at recompute time

subtype test can be executed in three instructions (load client's display element, compare and branch).

The code can be implemented as either a runtime routine or inlined. Dynamic subtype testing using truncated and padded Cohen displays has been explored in [2, 6]. However, these algorithms did not guarantee constant-time tests.

9   Real-Time Java Scoped Memory Access Checks

The Real-Time Specification for Java (RTSJ) [4], introduces the concept of scoped memory to Java. Scoped memory is similar in principle to the familiar notion of stack-based allocation that is present in languages like C, and C++ and to the region construct of ML [16]. The semantics of scoped areas are defined in [4]. The salient features are described below. After a scoped memory area is entered by a thread all subsequent allocations come from that scoped memory area. When a thread exits a scope, and there are no more active threads within

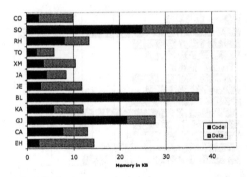

Fig. 18. Memory of requirements of our algorithm in KB. The first bar denotes the space required for the inlined test sequences, the second bar denotes subtype metadata. The average memory cost per class is 10.8 bytes for data structures

the area, the entire memory area can be reclaimed along with all objects allocated within it. Scoped areas can be nested. The scoped memory hierarchy forms a *tree* as each scope can have multiple subscopes. Because a scoped memory area could be reclaimed at any time, a memory area with a longer lifetime is not permitted to hold a reference to an object allocated in a memory area with a shorter lifetime. The RTSJ further defines two distinguished memory areas, called HeapMemory and ImmortalMemory which, conceptually, act as a root to the scope tree and are, thus, considered longer lived than all scoped memory areas. Fig. 20 gives all valid reference patterns for a scope tree composed of two scoped memory areas.

RTSJ implementations such as jRate and jTime enforce the RTSJ reference semantics by means of scope checks. These scope checks are performed each time

```
type_info {
    short inl_parents[MAX_INLINE];
    byte[] other_parents;
    short iid;
    short bucket; }


subtypeof( type_info cl, type_info pr) {
    buckets = ( pr.bucket < MAX_INLINE ) ?
                    cl.inl_parents : cl.other_parents;
    return buckets[ pr.bucket ] === pr.iid; }
```

Fig. 19. Combined encoding test sequence

a reference is stored in memory. Much like subtype tests, predictability in space and time is essential.

A range-based encoding can be used straightforwardly to implement dynamic scope checks. Consider the following assignment:

$$x.f = y;$$

The assignment is only allowed if the region in which y is allocated is longer lived than the region of x, we write this x.region <: y.region. Assuming every object has an added **region** field holding a reference to some scoped memory area, the code of the write barrier is given in Fig. 21.

We now outline a variant of the algorithm of Section 5 adapted for implementing access checks that ensure constant time and space performance and with a test sequence short enough to inline.

Range computation. Ranges are computed eagerly when a scoped memory area is entered. When an area that contains no threads is first entered from a scoped area S, that area becomes the parent of the newly entered region. The same area can be entered from different parent scopes at different times, however, there can never be two parents at the same time. While eager computation may seem costly, we recall that the cost is linear in the number of memory areas and in practice we have not encountered application scenarios that would require more than a handful of them. Thus, computing the assignment is unlikely to be prohibitive or a major part of the bookkeeping associated with region management. To reduce the need for recomputing ranges, each memory area caches the range it was last assigned, a new range will be computed only if it is entered from a different parent. The following changes to the algorithm are needed:

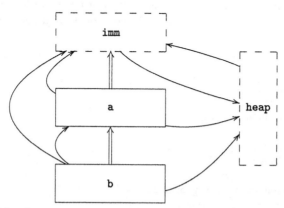

Fig. 20. Valid reference patterns. Double arrows indicate parent relations between scopes, *e.g.* a is a parent of scope b. Single arrows represent allowed reference patterns, *e.g*, a reference to a can be stored in a field of an object allocated in b

```
rx = x.region;
ry = y.region;
if ( extends( rx, ry) )
    x = y;
else
    fail();
```

Fig. 21. Scoped memory access check

1. Heap and immortal memory are always assigned the maximum range to allow them to reference each other and scoped memory areas to reference both of them.
2. Sparse ranges are used to limit the need for recomputing ranges.
3. Bounds of inactive scoped memory areas are cleared when recomputing the range assignment.
4. When an inactive memory area is entered, an extends check is performed against the cached range, if the extends check is successful, ranges need not be reassigned.

The last point will drastically reduce the need to recompute the range assignment because the most common RTSJ coding idiom is to use a scoped area to repeatedly perform the same computation in a periodic task. The representation of ranges is discussed next.

Scope checks. Eager range computation obviates the need to check for promotions as any newly allocated object will reside in a region with a valid range. The scope check sequence is thus made much simpler. We shorten the sequence further by packing both bounds in the same word and performing the range check in a single compare. Fig. 22 shows the code of the compact test. The check

```
region_info {
    unsigned prange;
    unsigned crange; }

MSK = 0x80008000;
RES = 0x00008000;

extends( region_info r, region_info s) {
    return ( r == s ) ? true :
            ( provider.prange - client.crange) & MSK == RES; }
```

Fig. 22. Compact scope access check

assumes that an equality test is always performed first. Furthermore, memory areas have two range fields one called `prange` constructed as `(low<<16)|high|MSK` and the other called `crange` constructed as `(low<<16)|high`. Furthermore, the `insert()` procedure of Section 5 is modified so that children are always allocated a low range value of `parent.low + 1`. This ensures that if `client <: provider` then the client's low bound is larger than it's provider.

Previous works on implementing access checks have relied on hierarchy traversal [3, 12] and Cohen's encoding [8]. Hierarchy traversal is clearly unacceptable because its performance is a function of the depth of a scoped memory area in the scope tree. Corsaro and Cytron's [8] approach has a slow path that requires three loads and three compares (this is assumes the addition of an equality test). The check outlined here is faster and more compact.

10 Related Work

Constant time (CT) techniques. The simplest constant time algorithm treats the subtype relation as a large sparse N^2 binary matrix where N is the number of types as discussed in [17]. For large programs matrices can grow to the megabyte range. Furthermore there is no clear strategy for incremental update. Despite these disadvantages, the simplicity of the binary matrix approach has motivated its use in practice [13, 9]. Attempts to reduce the space requirements of binary matrices while retaining the constant time access can be viewed as techniques for compressing the matrix.

CT for single subtyping. One particularly effective idea due to Cohen [7] is a variation of Dijkstra's "displays" [10]. Each type is identified by a unique type identifier, `tid`, which is simply a number. The runtime type information data structure also records the complete path of each type to the root as a sequence of type identifiers. The key trick is to build, for each type x, an array of $card(ancestors(x))$ type identifiers so that for each ancestor y, the `tid` of y is stored at an offset equal to $level(y)$ in the array. With this encoding, type inclusion tests reduce to a bound-checked array access and a comparison operation. The bound check is necessary if array sizes are not uniform. This approach is being used for extends checks in the Jikes RVM as described in [2] and in Wirth's Oberon.

CT for multiple subtyping. The hierarchical encoding proposed by Krall, Horspool and Vitek [14] is another constant time technique which represents each type with a set of integers chosen so that

$$x <: y \quad \Leftrightarrow \quad \gamma(y) \subseteq \gamma(x)$$

where $\gamma(x)$ maps type x to its set representation. Thus, the set of a subtype has to be a superset of the set representing its parent. This slightly counterintuitive relation allows a natural representation as bit vectors. In the bit vector representation the test function becomes $\gamma(x) \wedge \gamma(y) = \gamma(y)$, thus a type is a subtype of another if the bit pattern of the parent occurs in the child. The problem of finding optimal bit vector encodings for partial ordered sets is NP-hard [11] and there are some classes of partial ordered sets where an optimal encoding is as large as the number of types with only one supertype. The graph coloring algorithm of [14] is both fast and generates compact sets for most hierarchies (less than 32 bits). Unfortunately, there is no obvious way to support incremental recomputation. Another technique for compacting subtype hierarchies is the *packed encoding* of Vitek, Horspool and Krall [17]. In the binary matrix encoding, there is a one-to-one mapping from types to matrix indices. Each type has a column and a row of the matrix. In the packed encoding, columns for unrelated types are merged. This reuse of columns is similar in spirit to the reuse of genes in hierarchical encoding and to the levels of Cohen's algorithm. Subtype tests with packed encoding run as fast as with Cohen's algorithm, space usage is somewhat higher because there are some empty entries in the arrays holding type ids. This technique is the basis of our treatment of interfaces. Zibin and Gil have published several recent papers improving these techniques [20].

Incremental techniques. Currently the most efficient subtype test algorithms used in production virtual machines are the ones by Click and Rose [6] and the Jikes RVM team [2]. Both are variants of Cohen displays with a slow path that may require scanning a linear list of types. The techniques are slightly more space consuming than our approach since they inline some of the metadata in the class data structure. Zibin and Gil have presented several incremental algorithms that provide alternatives to the bucketing technique used here [21]. Since the space overhead of the data for implements test is very low in our benchmarks, we have not evaluated their techniques.

11   Conclusion

In this paper, we have presented R&B, a subtype test algorithm that can perform subtype tests in constant time and which has fairly modest space requirements. R&B supports incremental modifications to the type hierarchy and is thread safe. This algorithm has all the properties required for addition to a real-time virtual machine. We have evaluated R&B on a production VM and shown that it is possible to get predictable performance and at the same time improve both time and space (though this was not our goal). On average our benchmarks ran 2.5% faster and required less memory than the baseline virtual machine. Last but not least, this was achieved without adding unnecessary complexity to the virtual machine (about 100 lines of original code were modified).

Acknowledgments

This work is supported by grants from DARPA, and NSF (CCR–9734265). The authors thank Dave Detlefs for his help with EVM and EVM team for producing an excellent system. Some of the programs from our benchmark come from the

Ashes suite, we thank the McGill Sable research group for making these available. Finally, we thank David Holmes, Urs Hölzle, Alex Garthwaite, Doug Lea, Bill Pugh, Michael Hind and Scott Baxter for their comments.

References

[1] Hassan Aït-Kaci, Robert Boyer, Patrick Lincoln, and Roger Nasr. Efficient implementation of lattice operations. *ACM Transactions on Programming Languages and Systems*, 11(1):115–146, 1989.

[2] B. Alpern, A.Cocchi, and D. Grove. Dynamic type checking in Jalapeno. In *Java Virutal Machine Research and Technology Symposium*, April 2001.

[3] William S. Beebee, Jr. and Martin Rinard. An implementation of scoped memory for real-time Java. *Emsoft - LNCS*, 2211, 2001.

[4] Greg Bollella, James Gosling, Benjamin Brosgol, Peter Dibble, Steve Furr, and Mark Turnbull. *The Real-Time Specification for Java*. Java Series. Addison-Wesley, June 2000.

[5] Yves Caseau. Efficient handling of multiple inheritance hierarchies. In *Proc. Conference on Object Oriented Programming Systems, Languages & Applications, OOPSLA'93*, Published as SIGPLAN Notices 28(10), pages 271–287. ACM Press, September 1993.

[6] Cliff Click and John Rose. Fast subtype checking in the HotSpot VM. In *Java Grande 02*, November 2002.

[7] Norman H. Cohen. Type-extension type tests can be performed in constant time. *ACM Transactions on Programming Languages and Systems*, 13(4):626–629, 1991.

[8] Angelo Corsaro and Ron K. Cytron. Efficient memory-reference checks for real-time java. In *Proceedings of Languages, Compilers, and Tools for Embedded Systems (LCTES'03)*, 2003.

[9] J. Dean, G. DeFouw, D. Grove, V. Litvinov, and C. Chambers. Vortex: An optimizing compiler for object-oriented languages. In *Proc. Conference on Object Oriented Programming Systems, Languages & Applications, OOPSLA'96*. ACM Press, October 1996.

[10] E. W. Dijkstra. Recursive programming. *Numer. Programming*, (2):312–318, 1960.

[11] Michel Habib and Lhouari Nourine. Tree structure for distributive lattices and its applications. *Theoretical Computer Science*, 165:391–405, 1996.

[12] Teresa Higuera-Toledano and Valerie Issarny. Analyzing the performance of memory management in rtsj. In *Proceedings of the Fifth International Symposium on Object-Oriented Real-Time Distributed Computing (ISORC'02)*, 2002.

[13] Andreas Krall and Reinhard Grafl. CACAO – a 64 bit JavaVM just-in-time compiler. In Geoffrey C. Fox and Wei Li, editors, *PPoPP'97 Workshop on Java for Science and Engineering Computation*, Las Vegas, June 1997. ACM.

[14] Andreas Krall, Jan Vitek, and R. Nigel Horspool. Near optimal hierarchical encoding of types. In *Proc. European Conference on Object-Oriented Programming, ECOOP'97*, Lecture Notes in Computer Science. Springer-Verlag, June 1997.

[15] M. A. Schubert, L.K. Papalaskaris, and J. Taugher. Determining type, part, colour, and time relationships. *Computer*, 16 (special issue on Knowledge Representation):53–60, October 1983.

[16] Mad Tofte and Jean-Pierre Talpin. Region based memory management. *Information & Computation*, 132(2):109–176, February 1997.

[17] Jan Vitek, Andreas Krall, and R. Nigel Horspool. Efficient type inclusion tests. In *Conference on Object-Oriented Programming Systems, Languages and Applications, OOPSLA'97*, October 1997.

[18] Niklaus Wirth. Type extensions. *ACM Transactions on Programming Languages and Systems*, 10(2):204–214, 1988.

[19] Niklaus Wirth. Reply to "type-extension type tests can be performed in constant time". *ACM Transactions on Programming Languages and Systems*, 13(4):630, 1991.

[20] Yoav Zibin and Joseph Gil. Efficient subtyping tests with PQ-Encoding. In *Conference on Object-Oriented Programming Systems, Languages and Applications, OOPSLA'01*, October 2001.

[21] Yoav Zibin and Joseph Yossi Gil. Fast algorithm for creating space efficient dispatching tables with application to multi-dispatching. In *Proceedings of the 17th ACM conference on Object-oriented programming, systems, languages, and applications (OOPSLA-02)*, volume 37, 11 of *ACM SIGPLAN Notices*, pages 142–160. ACM Press, November 4–8 2002.

Growing XQuery

Mary Fernández[1] and Jérôme Siméon[2]

[1] AT&T Labs – Research
180 Park Ave., Florham Park, NJ 07932, USA
mff@research.att.com
http://research.att.com/info/mff
[2] Bell Laboratories
600 Mountain Avenue, Murray Hill, NJ 07974, USA
simeon@research.bell-labs.com
http://www-db.research.bell-labs.com/user/simeon/

Abstract. XQuery is a typed, functional language for querying XML data sources. XQuery has features of both traditional query languages and modern functional languages. In this paper, we introduce XQuery from both a "programming language" and a "query language" perspective and consider how these features impact the implementation and the evolution of XQuery. We conclude with a discussion of features currently missing from XQuery, but that we expect users will soon demand.

1 Introduction

XML [43] is a flexible format that can represent many classes of data: structured documents with large fragments of marked-up text; homogeneous records such as those in relational databases; and heterogeneous records with varied structure and content such as those in object-oriented and hierarchical databases. XML makes it possible for applications to handle all these classes of data simultaneously and to exchange such data in a simple, extensible, and standard format. One measure of XML's impact is the proliferation of industry-specific XML vocabularies [15]. Numerous industry groups, including automotive, health care, and telecommunications, publish document type definitions (DTDs) and XML Schemata [44], which specify the format of the XML data to be exchanged between their applications. Ultimately, the goal is for XML to be the "lingua franca" of data exchange, making it possible for data to be exchanged regardless of where it is stored or how it is processed.

For the past (almost) four years, we have been actively involved in defining XQuery 1.0 [49], a query language for XML designed to meet the diverse needs of applications that query and exchange XML. XQuery 1.0 and its sister language XPath 2.0 are designed jointly by members of the World-wide Web Consortium's XSLT and XML Query working groups. Group members are from software vendors, large user communities, and industrial research labs. Broadly speaking, they represent two major software industries and user communities, each of which significantly influence XQuery's design and definition. The "document-processing" community contributes their experience in designing languages and

L. Cardelli (Ed.): ECOOP 2003, LNCS 2743, pp. 405–430, 2003.
© Springer-Verlag Berlin Heidelberg 2003

tools (e.g., editors, formatters, browsers, and text-search engines) for processing structured documents. In particular, several members helped define the Standard Generalized Markup Language (SGML), from which XML is descended. The "database" community contributes their experience in designing query languages, storage systems, and query engines for data-intensive applications. In particular, several members helped define SQL [16], the standard query language for relational database systems. Each community has also unique and sometimes conflicting requirements for XQuery. Document-processing applications typically require a rich set of text-processing operators and the abilities to search for text that spans XML markup, to query and preserve the relative order of XML document fragments, and to rank approximate search results. Database applications typically require a rich set of operators on atomic types (e.g., numbers, dates, strings), the ability to compare, extract, and transform values in large XML databases, and the ability to construct new XML values that conform to a given schema. Chamberlin gives an excellent overview on these and other influences on the design of XQuery [10].

XQuery, the result of the collaboration of these two communities, is a typed, functional language that supports user-defined functions and modules for structuring large queries. It contains XPath 2.0 [48] as a sublanguage. XPath 2.0 supports navigation, selection, and extraction of fragments of XML documents, and is also an embedded sublanguage of XSLT 2.0 [52]. XQuery also includes expressions to construct new XML values, and to integrate or join values from multiple documents.

Interestingly, XQuery has as much in common with modern programming languages as it does with traditional query languages. User-defined functions and modules, for example, are not features typical of query languages. XQuery's design is also due to the influence of group members with expertise in the design and implementation of other high-level languages. This smaller "programming language" community advocated that XQuery have a static type semantics and that a formal semantics of XQuery be part of the W3C standard. As a result, XQuery has a complete formal semantics [50], which contains the only complete definition of XQuery's static typing rules.

Even though not yet completely specified, XQuery has generated an astounding level of interest from software vendors, potential users, and computer-science researchers. The XML Query working group Web page[1] lists twenty-three publicly announced implementations, many of which are embedded in products that integrate data from legacy databases. The interest of the database-research community in XML, and XQuery in particular, is also overwhelming. Every major database research conference has at least one track on XML and related technologies, and demonstration sessions are rife with XQuery applications. Numerous workshops accommodate the overflow of research papers.

One reason for this flood of activity is that *semi-structured data*, of which XML is one example, is substantially different than relational data, which has been the focus of database research for the past twenty years. These differ-

---

[1] http://www.w3.org/XML/Query

ences challenge most of what database researchers know about storing data and processing queries. Vianu provides a thorough survey of the theoretical issues related to semi-structured data, including schema and constraint languages; type checking of queries; and complexity of query evaluation and checking query containment [41].

If the response to XML by the database community is a flood, the response by the programming-language community is more like a babbling brook. Influential contributions focus on language expressiveness and type checking. XDuce [25] is a statically typed functional language for XML whose key feature is regular expression pattern matching over XML trees. The XQuery type system incorporates some of the structural features of XDuce's type system, as well as the named typing features of XML Schema. Siméon and Wadler formalize the semantics of named typing and establish the relationship between document validation and type matching in XQuery [36]. Cardelli and Ghelli have proposed a tree-based logic [8] as a foundation for expressing the semantics of query languages and schemata for semistructured data. Such a logic can be used to establish the complexity of problems such as query containment and type checking and thus influence development of practical algorithms, much as the the first-order logic serves a foundation for relational query languages. Hosoya and Pierce survey a variety of languages that process XML, focusing on the expressiveness of their type systems and the complexity of type checking [25]. Other contributions address efficient implementation of document validation [11] and XML parsing [26].

Query languages do not exist in isolation of their evaluation environment, which is often a high-level programming language, but the barrier between the query language and its host language is usually high and wide. An impedance mismatch typically exists between the query language's data model and its representation in the programming language's data types, making it difficult (or impossible) to guarantee the type safety of operations in the host language. There are several approaches to addressing this problem. One strategy is identifying a type-safe "embedding" of a data model (and possibly query language) in the host language (e.g., SQL tables in Haskell [31], OQL in Java [3], XML in Java [14], and XML in Haskell [42]). Another strategy is to ignore the barrier entirely by incorporating more programming language features into the query language [32], or to identify a programming language that can serve as a query language [40]. Implementing "hybrid" languages requires understanding implementation techniques for both programming and query languages.

1.1 Growing a Language

"If we add just a few things – generic types, operator overloading, and user-defined types of light weight ... — that are designed to let users make and add things of their own use, I think we can go a long way, and much faster. We need to put tools for language growth in the hands of the users."
— Guy Steele, "Growing a Language", 1999 [39]

In other work, we have focused on XQuery's static type system [18], on XQuery's formal semantics [19], and on the relationship between XQuery's core language and monads [20]. In this paper, we consider how XQuery may grow from an already powerful *query* language for XML into a *programming language* for XML-aware applications. History shows that successful query languages *do* grow, but often inelegantly. SQL-99 [29] is so large that no implementation supports the complete standard. As Guy Steele envisioned for Java, our vision is that XQuery grow elegantly with the addition of several flexible language features instead of numerous ad-hoc ones. An important open question is what these features should be.

We begin in Section 2 with the basics of XML and XQuery and present an example query that integrates data from two XML sources. We focus on the "query language" characteristics of XQuery in Section 3 and on the "programming language" characteristics of XQuery in Section 4. A critical barrier to XQuery's growth is identifying efficient evaluation strategies for queries on large XML data sources. XQuery's programming-language features make evaluation even more challenging. To familiarize the reader with these issues, we outline the stages of compilation and optimization in an "archetypal" XQuery implementation in Section 5. In Section 6, we look forward to XQuery 2.0 and consider some new features including update statements, exception handling, higher-order functions, and parametric polymorphism – features that require the knowledge and creativity of the programming language community. Our hope is that this tour will encourage readers to take a closer look at XQuery.

2 XML and XQuery Basics

XML often serves as an exchange format for data that is stored in other representations (e.g., relational databases, Excel spreadsheets, files with ad-hoc formats, etc.) or that is generated by application programs (e.g., stock-quote service or on-line weather service). An application may publish the data it wants to exchange as an XML document, or it may provide a query interface that produces XML. In our examples, we assume the data is published in an XML document. The example document in Figure 1 contains a book catalog represented in XML. The document has one top-level catalog element, which contains book elements.

An XML *element* has a name and may contain zero or more *attributes* and a sequence of zero or more properly nested *children* elements, possibly interleaved with character data. An attribute has a name and contains a *simple value*, i.e., character data only. In Figure 1, the book element contains two attributes: an isbn number and a year. All of an element's attributes must have distinct names, but their order is insignificant – so changing the attributes to year followed by isbn does not change the element's value. By contrast, an element's children may share the same names, and their relative order is significant. The book element contains a title element followed by an author, a publisher, a retail_price, and a list_price. The review element is an example of *mixed* content in which character data is interleaved with elements: The title element is embedded in the text of the

```
<?xml version="1.0" encoding="ISO-8859-1" ?>
<catalog>
  <book isbn="156352578X" year="2000">
    <title>No Such Thing as a~Bad Day</title>
    <author>Hamilton Jordan</author>
    <publisher>Longstreet Press, Inc.</publisher>
    <retail_price currency="USD">15.40</retail_price>
    <list_price currency="USD">22.10</list_price>
    <review reviewer="Library Journal">
      This book is the moving account of one man's successful battles
      against three cancers...<title>No Such Thing as a~Bad Day</title>
      is warmly recommended.
    </review>
  </book>
  <!-- More books here -->
</catalog>
```

Fig. 1. A book catalog represented in XML

review. This document is *well-formed*, because its elements are properly nested and the attributes of each element have unique names.[2]

XQuery expressions operate on *values* in the XML data model [46], not directly on the character data in XML documents. A value is a sequence of individual *atomic values* or *nodes*. Sequences are central to XQuery, so much so that one atomic value or node and a sequence containing that item are indistinguishable. An atomic value is an instance of one of the the twenty-three XML Schema primitive types (e.g., xs:string, xs:decimal, xs:date, et al) [45]. A node is either a document, element, attribute or text [3]. A document node has a value; an attribute or element node has a name, a value, and a *type annotation*; and a text node has a string value. A node's type annotation specifies that the node is valid with respect to a type defined in a schema.

Although XQuery only requires that input documents be well formed, data-exchange applications often require that some structure be imposed on documents. There are a number of standard schema languages for XML, including: DTDs, part of the original W3C recommendation defining XML [43]; XML Schema, a W3C recommendation which supersedes DTDs [44, 45]; and Relax NG, an Oasis standard [13]. XML Schema features both named and structural types [36], with structure based on tree grammars, whereas all other XML schema languages only express structural constraints. XQuery's type system is based on XML Schema, so it supports both named and structural types. In this paper, we describe only essential features of XML Schema, including named simple types and complex types, global attributes and elements, and atomic simple

---

[2] The XML specification defines several other constraints for well-formedness.

[3] For simplicity, we omit comment and processing-instruction nodes.

types. We omit anonymous types, local elements and attributes, and derivation of new types by restriction and by extension.

XML Schema's syntax is XML, making it difficult to read, and the same type can be modeled using different constructs, making it a poor notation for types. Instead, we use XQuery's internal type notation, which is concise and orthogonal. Figure 2 defines a schema for book catalogs in XQuery type notation. A schema is a collection of mutually referential declarations of *simple, complex, element* and *attribute* types.

A simple-type declaration associates a name with an atomic type, a list of atomic types, or a union of atomic types. Atomic types include XML Schema's twenty-three primitive types. The simple-type declaration on line 13 in Figure 2 specifies that the simple-type name ISBN is associated with the atomic type xs:string.

A complex-type declaration associates a name with a model of *node types*. A node type is a document type, a named element or attribute type, or the text type. The complex type declaration on line 2 associates the name Catalog with the model containing one or more book elements, and the declaration on lines 4–12 associate the name Book with the model containing one isbn and one year attribute, one title element followed by one-or-more author elements or one-or-more editor elements, followed by one publisher element, one retail_price element, an optional list_price element, and zero-or-more review elements. In general, atomic and node types can be combined with the infix operators for sequence (,), union (|), and interleave (&), and the post-fix operators zero-or-one (?), one-or-more (+), or zero-or-more (*).

An attribute declaration associates a name with a simple type (lines 14,18, 24, and 29 contain examples), and an element declaration associates an element name with a simple or complex type (lines 1, 3, 16, 17, 19–22, and 28 contain examples).

XQuery expressions operate on data-model values, not directly on documents. Given an (external) document and a type (from a schema), *validation* produces an (internal) data-model value in which every element and attribute node is annotated with a simple or complex type, or it fails. Validation guarantees that a node's content matches the node's type annotation.

2.1   An Example Query

A common application of XQuery is to integrate information from multiple XML data sources. Our example query in Figure 3 integrates information from the Barnes and Ignoble book catalog with information about book sales from the Publisher's Weekly trade magazine. For each author in the catalog, the query produces the total number of and the total sales receipts for books published by the author since 2000. The query illustrates most of XQuery's key features: path expressions for navigating, selecting, and extracting XML values; constructors for creating new XML values; let expressions for binding variables to intermediate results; for expressions for iterating over sequences and for constructing new sequences; and functions for modularizing queries.

```
1. define element catalog of type Catalog
2. define type Catalog { element book + }

3. define element book of type Book
4. define type Book {
5.   ( attribute isbn & attribute year ) ,
6.   element title ,
7.   ( element author + | element editor + ),
8.   element publisher ,
9.   element retail_price ,
10.  element list_price ? ,
11.  element review *
12. }

13. define type ISBN restricts xs:string
14. define attribute isbn of type ISBN

15. define type Name restricts xs:string
16. define element author of type Name
17. define element editor of type Name

18. define attribute year of type xs:integer
19. define element title  of type xs:string
20. define element publisher of type xs:string

21. define element retail_price of type Price
22. define element list_price of type Price

23. define type Currency restricts xs:string
24. define attribute currency of type Currency
25. define type Price {
26.   attribute currency , xs:decimal
27. }

28. define element review of type Review
29. define attribute reviewer of type xs:string
30. define type Review {
31.   attribute reviewer , ( text | element )*
32. }

33. define type Vendor {
34.   attribute type of type xs:string ,
35.   element name of type xs:string ,
36.   element total-sales *
37. }
38. define element vendor of type Vendor

39. define type Sales {
40.   element author ,
41.   element count of type xs:integer ,
42.   element total of type xs:decimal
43. }
44. define element total-sales of type Sales
```

Fig. 2. Schema in XQuery type notation for book catalog in Figure 1

Figure 3 contains an XQuery *main module*. A main module consists of im-ported schemas, user-defined functions, and one main expression, whose value is the result of evaluating the module. The schema imported on line 1 corresponds to the book catalog schema in Figure 2 and is imported as the default schema, which means unprefixed names of nodes and types refer to definitions in the given schema. The schema imported on line 2 corresponds to a schema for book

```
1.  import schema default element namespace = "http://book-vendors.com/catalog.xsd"
2.  import schema namespace sls = "http://book-trade.com/sales.xsd"

3.  define function sales-by-author ($cat as element catalog,
4.                    $sales as element sls:sales) as element total-sales *
5.  {
6.   for $name in fn:distinct-values($cat/book/author)
7.   let $books := $cat/book[@year >= 2000 and author = $name],
8.      $receipts := $sales/sls:book[@isbn = $books/@isbn]/sls:receipts
9    order-by $name
10.  return
11.     <total-sales>
12.        <author> { $name } </author>
13.        <count> { fn:count($books) } </count>
14.        <total> { fn:sum($receipts) } </total>
15.     </total-sales>
16. }

17. let $bi := fn:doc("http://www.bni.com/catalog.xml"),
18.     $pw := fn:doc("http://www.publishersweekly.com/sales.xml")
19. return
20.    <vendor type="retail" name="Barns and Ignoble">
21.      { sales-by-author($bi/catalog, $pw/sls:sales) }
22.    </vendor>
```

Fig. 3. An XQuery main module

sales and is associated with the prefix sls, which means all elements and types prefixed with sls refer to this schema. We will discuss schemas and typing more in the Section 4.

The function sales-by-author (lines 3–16) is the work-horse of this module. It takes a catalog element and a sls:sales element, and for each author in the catalog, returns a total-sales element containing the author's name, the total number of and the total sales of books that the author published since January, 2000.

This function has several examples of *path expressions*, so we describe those first. The path expression $cat/book/author on line 6 extracts all the author children of book children of the catalog element bound to the variable $cat. Path expressions may conditionally select nodes. The path expression on line 7:

$cat/book[@year >= 2000 and author = $name]

extracts all book children of the catalog element that have a year attribute with value greater-or-equal to 2000 and that have at least one author child whose content equals the value bound to the variable $name. In database parlance, this path expression *self-joins* the authors and books in the catalog source and *selects* those books published since 2000. Similarly, the path expression on line 8:

$sales/sls:book[@isbn = $books/@isbn]/sls:receipts

joins the books selected by the path expression on line 7 with the sls:books from the sales source. The nodes are joined on their isbn attribute values. The path expression then extracts or *projects* the sls:receipts elements.

The let expression on lines 7–8 is a classic functional let: It binds the variable on the left-hand-side of := to the value on the right-hand side, then evaluates its body (lines 9–15) given the new variable binding.

Returning to line 6, the function fn:distinct-values[4] takes a sequence of atomic values, possibly containing duplicates, and returns a sequence with no duplicates. When applied to the sequence of author nodes, it returns their string contents with duplicates eliminated. Given this sequence of author names, the for expression on line 4 binds the variable $name to each string in the sequence of author names, evaluates the let expression on lines 5–12 once for each binding of $name, and concatenates the resulting values into one sequence. The for expression corresponds to a monad over sequences of atomic values and nodes [20].

The order-by expression on line 7 guarantees that the sequence produced by the return expression is in sorted order by the authors' names. The return expression on lines 8–13 is evaluated once for each binding of $name. The element constructor on lines 9–13 constructs one total-sales element, and in turn its subexpressions construct one author, one count, and one total element, which contain the author's name, the total number of books published in 2000, and the sum of all book receipts, respectively.

The main expression on lines 17–22 applies the function sales-by-author to the book catalog published by Barns and Ignoble and to the book sales data published by Publisher's Weekly magazine – of course, the function could be applied to any pair of elements that are valid instances of the catalog and sls:sales elements. The function fn:doc accesses the XML document at the given URL, validates it, and maps it into a document-node value. Documents typically contain references to the schemas against which they should be validated. The book catalog is validated against the schema book-catalog.xsd, and the sales document is validated against the schema book-sales.xsd. This correspondence is not explicit in the query, but instead is established by the environment in which the query is evaluated. For example, the fn:doc function might be implemented by a database in which pre-validated documents are stored.

A document node represents an entire XML document and therefore does not correspond to any data in the document itself. The path expression $bi/catalog selects all catalog elements that are children of the document node. The path expression $pw/sls:sales is similar. Lastly, the element constructor on lines 20–22 constructs a new vendor element, which contains the result of applying the function sales-by-author to the values of the path expressions $bi/catalog and $pw/sls:sales.

This quick introduction should give the reader a sense of XQuery's expressiveness and capabilities. For the reader interested in more details, we recommend Robie's XQuery tutorial [34].

3   XQuery as a Query Language

XQuery has many characteristics of traditional query languages, such as SQL, Datalog [2], and OQL [9]. First, Its data model is restricted to those values that XML can represent, that is XQuery's data model includes sequences of nodes

---

[4] The fn is the namespace prefix that denotes XQuery's built-in functions [47].

and atomic values, but excludes, for example, sets, bags, and nested sequences, because they are not intrinsic to XML.

Second, almost all XQuery operators and expressions either construct or access values in the data model, and common idioms for constructing and accessing values are built-in to the language to improve ease of use. For example, XQuery's equality and inequality operators have a fairly complex implicit semantics. This equality expression evaluates to true if the book bound to $book contains at least one author child whose content equals the string "Hamilton Jordan":

```
$book/author = "Hamilton Jordan"
```

Thus, the (in)equality operators are existentially quantified over sequences of items: The operators are applied to pairs of items drawn from their operands. If any one item evaluates to a node, the node's (atomic-valued) content is extracted and then compared to the other operand. This implicit semantics improves ease-of-use for the query writer, especially when writing queries over XML documents with irregular structure. The query writer writes the same expression whether a book has zero, one, or multiple author children. Other expressions in XQuery's user-level syntax also have rich implicit semantics. Although convenient for a user, this rich semantics can complicate typing and evaluation, so the semantics of user-level expressions is made explicit by *normalization* into a smaller core language. Typing, optimization, and evaluation operate on this smaller core language. We discuss normalization and other compilation steps in Section 5.

Third, XQuery is strongly typed, meaning that the types of values and expressions must be compatible with the context in which the value or expression is used. For example, this expression raises a type error because an isbn attribute contains a string, which cannot be compared to an integer:

```
$book[@isbn = 156352578]
```

All implementations of XQuery must support dynamic typing, which checks during query evaluation that the type of a value is compatible with the context in which it is used and raises a type error if an incompatibility is detected. Static typing is an optional feature of XQuery implementations and more common in programming languages than in query languages. We discuss static typing in the next section.

Lastly, XQuery is declarative, thus its semantics permits a variety of evaluation strategies. Recall that the function sales-by-author *self-joins* the authors and books in the catalog source, *selects* those books published since 2000, *joins* those books with the sales receipts, *projects* the books' receipts, *groups* the resulting books and receipts by author, *aggregates* the total number of books and total receipts, and *orders* the results by the author's name. From a query-language perspective, this function is very expressive and consequently may be difficult to evaluate efficiently. Although it is easy to produce a naive evaluation strategy for this query – simply interpret the query on an in-memory representation of the documents – for all but the smallest input documents, the naive strategy will be prohibitively slow. Because XQuery is declarative, its semantics does not enforce an order of evaluation, and this flexibility permits implementations to use a variety of evaluation strategies. For example, the following expression, in which i1 ... ik are integer values:

```
for $i in (i1, i2,..., ik) return 100 div $i
```

is equivalent to the following sequence expression, which evaluates the body of the for expression once for each value in the integer sequence:

```
(100 idiv i1), (100 idiv i2), ... (100 idiv ik)
```

Because each integer-division expression is independent of all others, they can be evaluated in any order, or even in parallel. We discuss evaluation strategies in Section 5.

Flexible evaluation order permits some expressions to be non-deterministic. For example, the following expression may raise a divide-by-zero error or evaluate to true, depending on which disjunct is evaluated first:

```
(1 idiv 0 < 2) or (3 < 4)
```

The if-then-else conditional expression, however, enforces an evaluation order, thus the or expression above is not equivalent to the following if-then-else, because the else branch is only evaluated if the conditional expression evaluates to false:

```
if (1 idiv 0 < 2) then fn:true()
else if (3 < 4) then fn:true()
else fn:false()
```

XQuery's formal semantics [50] specifies formally where an evaluation order must be enforced and where it is flexible, and it also guarantees that an expression either raises an error or evaluates to a unique value.

4   XQuery as a Programming Language

Despite its similarity to other query languages, XQuery has two significant characteristics more common in programming languages: it is statically typed and it is Turing complete. We consider the impact of these features next.

Static typing, in general, refers to both *type checking* and *type inference*. For each expression in a query, type checking determines if the type of the expression is compatible with the context in which it is used, and type inference computes the type of the expression based on the types of its subexpressions. Neither type checking nor type inference are difficult for languages like SQL and Datalog. The types include only atomic types and tuples of atomic types, and simple inspection of the query determines the type of each expression. As a compositional, object-based language, static typing of OQL is more difficult than static typing of SQL, but less so than static typing of XQuery. OQL types include records, objects and collection (sets, lists, and bags), but does not include regular expressions over types, construction of objects with new types, or user-defined functions or modules. These features make static typing of XQuery like static typing of high-level programming languages.

We expect the reader is familiar with static typing's numerous benefits. Most modern compiled languages (Java, C++, C#, ML, Haskell, etc.) provide static typing to help build large, reliable applications. Static typing can help by detecting common type errors in a program during static analysis instead of the developer discovering those errors when the program is run. Static typing in XQuery serves the same purpose and can detect numerous common errors. For example, it detects the type error in this expression from Section 3 in which a string is compared to an integer:

```
$book[@isbn = 156352578]
```

It can also detect the misspelling of isbn as ibsn in the path expression $book/@ibsn. Assuming that $book has type element book, the static type inferred for $book/@ibsn is the empty sequence, because a book element contains no ibsn attributes. A static type error is raised whenever the type of an expression (other than the literal empty sequence ()) is empty. XQuery's static typing rules also detect when a newly constructed element will never validate against the expected type for that element. In the query Figure 3, the vendor element constructed contains a name *attribute*, but the vendor element type in the schema in Figure 2 expects a name *element* – static type checking detects this error. In addition, static type analysis can help yield more efficient evaluation strategies. We discuss those benefits in the next section.

Given these benefits, it may come as a surprise that static typing is an optional feature of XQuery. One reason is that there is a tension between writing queries that operate on well-formed documents and that are also statically well-typed. In Section 2, we stated that XQuery only requires input documents to be well formed, but also stated that all data-model values be labeled with a type. To represent well-formed documents in the data model, all nodes are labeled with types indicating that no additional type information is known – well-formed elements are labeled with xdt:untypedAny and well-formed attributes are labeled with xdt:untypedAtomic. Assuming that $book has static type element book of type xdt:anyType, the following expression is ill-typed:

```
$book/list_price - $book/retail_price
```

The reason is that the static typing rules for arithmetic operators require that each operand be zero-or-one atomic value. A well-formed book element may have an arbitrary number of list_price and retail_price children, and therefore contain an arbitrary number of atomic values. Because static typing examines a query's expressions, not the values that those expressions produce, static typing a *conservative* analysis. Even though during evaluation every well-formed book element may contain exactly one list_price and one retail_price, static analysis must assume otherwise. To write statically well-typed queries over well-formed data, the query writer must explicitly assert the expected structure of the document. The following expression asserts *statically* that *dynamically* the book element will contain one list_price and one retail_price:

```
fn:one($book/list_price) - fn:one($book/retail_price)
```

This permits static typing to proceed assuming the correct types. If during evaluation, the book does not have the expected structure, a dynamic error is raised. XQuery is designed to be easy to use on both well-formed and validated documents. Because these assertions make writing queries over well-formed documents burdensome, static typing is optional.

XQuery is Turing complete, because it does not restrict recursion in user-defined functions. XML documents support recursive structure and therefore some form of recursion is necessary. For example, here is a schema that describes a parts manifest, in which a part element may contain other part elements.

```
define element part {
    attribute name of type xs:string ,
    attribute quantity of type xs:integer ,
    element parts *
}
```

And here is a parts manifest conforming to the above schema:

```
<element part name="widget" quantity="1">
    <element part name="nut" quantity="100"/>
    <element part name="bolt" quantity="100"/>
</element>
```

Any query that must preserve the recursive structure of the document can only be expressed by a recursive function.

From a database-theory perspective, Turing completeness is heresy. Many optimizations for relational queries require solving the *query containment* problem: Given two queries Q_1 and Q_2 and a schema S, for all databases D such that D is an instance of S, is $Q_1(D)$ contained in $Q_2(D)$, i.e., $\forall D$ s.t. $D : S, Q_1(D) \subset Q_2(D)$? Numerous results from database theory characterize the complexity of query containment based on the expressiveness of the query language. Answering the question has practical implications. Query optimizers use containment to determine whether the result of a new query is contained in a pre-computed *view* – thus potentially reducing the cost of evaluating the new query. Evaluation strategies also use containment to rewrite queries so that they may better utilize physical indices.

Answering the containment question for a Turing-complete program is equivalent to solving the halting problem(!), so to establish containment results for XQuery, we must consider subsets of the language. Most results are restricted to containment of path expressions, which express a very limited form of recursion (i.e., navigation via the descendant and ancestor axes) and do not construct new values. The UnQL [7] query language supports mutually recursive functions over trees, but requires that recursion alway proceed down the tree, thus guaranteeing termination. Considering such a subset of XQuery may help make some queries more amenable to analysis.

5   Implementing XQuery

Most implementations of XQuery are not generic, stand-alone processors, but are designed with particular applications or goals in mind. Examples include processors that operate on streams of XML data [4, 23] and ones that query data stored in relational databases and publish it in XML[17]. These implementations are designed for speed and/or scalability, but not necessarily completeness. Our own implementation, called Galax[24] and the IPSI XQuery processor [21] aim for completeness and are the only implementations to date that support static typing. All processors, regardless of how they work, must preserve the XQuery semantics as described in the language and formal semantics documents [49, 50], otherwise they do not implement XQuery! But how they achieve this result is an open and highly competitive area. In this section, we describe an "archetypal" XQuery architecture, which loosely corresponds to the Galax architecture.

5.1   Archetypal Architecture

Figure 4 depicts the query-processing stages of archetypal architecture. The first four query-processing stages (top of diagram) are common in compilers for high-level languages. The later stages (bottom of diagram) are common in interpreters for query languages. *Parsing* takes an expression in XQuery's user-level syntax and yields an abstract syntax tree (AST). We do not discuss this stage further. *Normalization* takes the AST of the user-level expression and maps it into an AST of XQuery's smaller *core* language, which is a proper subset of the user-level language. This stage makes the implicit semantics of user-level expressions explicit in the core language. The optional *static typing* stage takes the core AST and yields the same AST in which every expression node is annotated with its static type. *Logical optimization* takes the core AST (with or without static type annotations) and applies logical rewriting rules, such as common-subexpression elimination, constant folding, hoisting of loop-invariant expressions, etc., and if static types are known, type-specific simplifications.

The first four stages typically are independent of the physical representation of documents, whereas the last three depend on the representation. A fast-path to a complete implementation is building a simple interpreter for the typed XQuery core. We initially took this path in Galax, but are now extending Galax to include the later stages. *Compilation* takes a (typed) core AST and compiles it into an algebraic query plan that depends on the physical operators available for accessing the document. Whereas the core AST is a "top-down" representation of the original expression, the algebraic query plan is a "bottom up" representation. *Physical optimization* takes a query plan and improves it by utilizing any available indices. Lastly, the *evaluation* stage interprets the optimized query

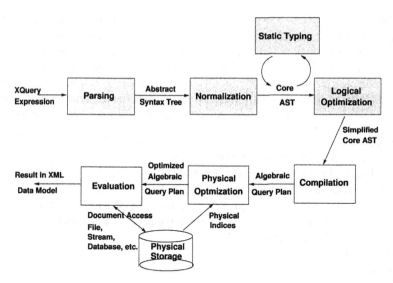

Fig. 4. Archetypal Architecture

plan and yields an XML value in the data model, which is returned to the environment in which the query was evaluated. We illustrate the normalization, logical optimization, and physical optimization stages on a simplified version of the query in Figure 3.

Our example architecture figure excludes the document-processing stages, which are highly implementation dependent. An implementation typically will provide a few methods for accessing documents, for example, in the file system, on the network [1, 23], in native XML databases with specialized indices [12, 6, 30], or in relational databases [5, 35], but most do not provide all possible methods. Our example architecture assumes that documents are stored in a relational database.

5.2   Normalization

To illustrate normalization, we consider a variant of the query in Figure 3 that computes the number of books published by each author since 2000:

```
for $name in distinct-values($cat/book/author),
let $books := $cat/book[@year >= 2000 and author = $name]
return
  <total-sales>
    <author> { $author } </author>
    <count> { count($books) } </count>
  </total-sales>
```

Recall from Section 3 that many user-level expressions have a complex implicit semantics. This semantics improves ease-of-use when writing queries over

XML documents whose structure may not be known, but complicates static typing and compilation into algebraic query plans. Normalization rewrites each user-level expression into an expression in the core syntax that has the same semantics but in which each subexpression has a very simple semantics. By necessity, normalization precedes static typing, so the rewritings are independent of typing information. For example, the path expression $cat/book[@year >= 2000] in the query above is is normalized into the following core expression:

```
for $_c in $cat return
  for $_b in $_c/child::book return
  if (some $v1 in fn:data($_b/attribute::year) satisfies
        some $v2 in fn:data(2000) satisfies
          let $u1 := fs:promote-operand($v1,$v2) return
          let $u2 := fs:promote-operand($v2,$v1) return
              op:ge($u1, $u2))
  then $_b
  else ()
```

The implicit iteration in each step of the path expression is made explicit in the nested for expressions. The axis (or direction) in which path navigation proceeds is also made explicit – in this case, it is the child axis. The implicit existential quantification of the predicate expression is made explicit in the nested some expressions, and the automatic extraction of atomic values from a sequence of atomic values or nodes is handled by the fn:data function. Before applying the overloaded greater-than-or-equal operator, the pair of atomic values are promoted to comparable types, if possible. For example, promoting a float and decimal yields two floats, and promoting a decimal and date would raise a type error, because they are incomparable. If the book element bound to $_b satisfies the conditional expression, the conditional evaluates to the book element, otherwise it evaluates to the empty sequence (). The for expressions yield a single sequence of all the book elements.

From the very small example above, we can see that normalization yields large core expressions in which each sub-expression has a simple semantics. For simplicity, we have omitted other explicit operations, e.g., that guarantee the result of every path expression is in document order. After normalization and static typing, logical optimizations can further simplify the core expression.

5.3   Logical Optimization

Many standard optimizations for functional languages, such as elimination of common subexpressions, constant propagation and folding, function inlining, and elimination of unused variables, are applicable to XQuery. For example, he normalization of $cat/book[@year >= 2000] in the last section can be simplified to:

```
for $_c in $cat return
  for $_b in $_c/child::book return
  if (some $v1 in fn:data($_b/attribute::year) satisfies
        let $u1 := fs:promote-operand($v1,2000) return
        let $u2 := fs:promote-operand(2000,$v1) return
          op:ge($u1, $u2))
  then $_b
  else ()
```

The application of fn:data to the constant integer 2000 simplifies to the constant itself, the existential quantification over the constant is eliminated, and the constant is propagated to its uses. Without additional type information, the above expression cannot be further simplified, because we do not know, for example, the type of values contained in an year attribute.

Static type information can be used to further simplify expressions. Assuming that $cat has type element catalog of type Catalog, the static types of the other expressions are as follows:

$$\$cat : \text{element catalog of type Catalog}$$
$$\$cat/child::book : \text{element book} +$$
$$\$\_b : \text{element book of type Book}$$
$$\$\_b/attribute::year : \text{attribute year of type xs:integer}$$
$$fn:data(\$\_b/attribute::year) : \text{xs:integer}$$
$$\$v1 : \text{xs:integer}$$
$$\$u1 : \text{xs:integer}$$
$$\$u2 : \text{xs:integer}$$

Given this information, the above expression is simplified to:

```
for $_b in $cat/child::book return
if (op:integer-ge(fn:data($_b/attribute::year), 2000))
then $_b
else ()
```

The first for expression is eliminated (because its input sequence is a single element). Similarly, the existential quantification over the year attribute's single xs:integer value is eliminated. Because both arguments to fs:promote-operand are integers, the promotions are eliminated, and the overloaded op:ge operator is replaced by the monomorphic op:integer-ge. Even these basic simplifications can substantially reduce the size and complexity of query plans. Although not illustrated by this example, another important logical optimization is determining when the order of values produced by an expression is insignificant. Knowing that order is insignificant can yield more efficient evaluation plans – we return to this issue in the next section.

Returning to the example query that computes the number of books published by each author since 2000, the simplified core expression assuming static typing is:

```
for $name in
  distinct-values(for $_b in $cat/child::book return
                  fn:data($_b/child::author))
return
let $books :=
  for $_b in $cat/child::book return
  if (op:integer-ge(fn:data($_b/attribute::year), 2000)
      and
      some $_a in $_b/child::author
      satisfies fn:data($_a) = $name)
  then $_b
  else ()
return
  <total-sales>
    <author> { $name } </author>
    <count>  { fn:count($books) } </count>
  </total-sales>
```

Although this expression is substantially simpler than the core expression that is dynamically typed, a naive evaluation strategy is quadratic in the number of distinct author names and books (i.e., each book in the catalog is accessed once for each author in the catalog). Clearly, this is impractical for any document in which the set of books and authors exceed main memory.

5.4   Physical Optimization

Efficient evaluation strategies are possible if the physical representation of the XML documents is taken into account. Typically, an evaluation plan is composed of algebraic operators specialized to the access methods provided by the storage system. A common technique is to store XML documents in relational tables and use operators that process streams of tuples. This strategy can take advantage of high-performance relational query engines. Native XML databases with custom indices over trees and algebras for utilizing these structures also exist [27, 30], but are yet to be shown effective on very large-scale data.

For our small example, we assume the book catalog document is stored in a relational database containing the two tables:

```
BookTable(bid, title, year)
AuthorTable(bid, name, idx)
```

The BookTable table contains one tuple for each book; each tuple contains the book's year, its title, and a key field (bid) that uniquely identifies the book in the catalog document. The AuthorTable table contains one tuple for each author in each book. The bid field is the unique identifier of the book, name is the name of the author, and idx is the ordinal index of the given author in the book's sequence of authors. We chose this representation, because it is simple. There are numerous techniques for "shredding" XML document into relational tables [35], and with each technique, there are corresponding trade-offs in query performance [5].

Given the relational representation above, the compilation stage rewrites the core expression into a tree (or graph) of operations that consume and produce streams of tuples. We assume the following standard operations:

- **Scan** produces each tuple in a table.
- **Select** takes a stream of tuples and a predicate and produces a stream of tuples that satisfy the predicate.
- **Project** takes a stream of tuples and a set of field names and produces a stream of tuples that contain the specified fields.
- **Join** takes two tuple streams and a join predicate, and produces tuples from the Cartesian product of the two input streams that satisfy the join predicate.
- **Map** takes an input tuple stream and a variable, binds the variable to each tuple in the stream, and evaluates an expression given the variable binding, which yields a result tuple. The operator yields the result tuple extended with the variable bound to the input tuple.
- **Group-by** takes a stream of tuples and a grouping expression and produces one tuple for each distinct value in the grouping expression. Each such tuple contains the group-by value and the partition of (nested) tuples for which the grouping expression has the given value.

A naive compilation strategy takes the core expression and mechanically produces a query-evaluation plan composed of the above operators. The query plan for our example query is:

```
Map(
  AUTHOR-BOOKS ;
    Map(
      AUTHOR ;
      distinct(
        Project(A1.name,
          Join(Scan(A1 in AuthorTable),
               Scan(B1 in BookTable),
               A1.bid = B1.bid)
        )
      ),
      Select(Join(Scan(A2 in AuthorTable),
                  Scan(B2 in BookTable),
                  A2.bid = B2.bid),
             B2.year >= 2003 AND A2.author = AUTHOR)
      As BOOKS
    ),
    <total-sales>
      <author> { AUTHOR-BOOKS.AUTHOR } <author>
      <count> { count(AUTHOR-BOOKS.BOOK) } </count>
    </total-sales>
)
```

The variables A1, A2, B1, and B2 denote *tuples* in the AuthorTable and Book-Table tables, respectively. Path navigation is compiled in to scans over tables and joins over the author and book tuple streams. The predicate in the path expression is compiled into a select operation. The outer for expression over distinct author names is compiled into a map operation and the the inner let expression into the outer map operation. Obviously, this query plan is not better than naive evaluation of the core expression, but given this representation, we can now apply database optimization techniques. For example, query unnesting techniques can be applied, and the nested query can be converted into a group-by operation. One possible query plan is as follows:

```
Map(
  AUTHOR-BOOKS ;
  GroupBy(
    Select(Join(Scan(A1 in AuthorTable),
                Select(Scan(B1 in BookTable), B1.year >= 2000)
                A1.bid = B1.bid)) As BOOKS,
    A1.name As AUTHOR
  ),
  <total-sales>
    <author> { AUTHOR-BOOKS.AUTHOR } </author>
    <count>  { count(AUTHOR-BOOKS.BOOKS) } </count>
  </total-sales>
)
```

This plan applies the selection predicate early and performs only one join over the author and book tables.

This example illustrates that there are many strategies for evaluating even the simplest XQuery expressions and that choices made in each stage can influence the result of later stages. Although we have described a processing model in which early stages are independent of later stages, the physical operators available may influence decisions made in earlier stages, for example, when or if to apply function inlining or unrolling of tail-recursive function calls. Understanding the interaction between earlier "programming language" stages and later "query processing" stages is an important and open problem when implementing XQuery.

6   Growing XQuery

We cannot predict what XQuery 2.0 will be, but we observe that XQuery 1.0 is growing already. Requirements for fulltext operators already exist [51], and we expect more special-purpose operators will follow. XL [22], a programming language for web services, is based on XQuery. Xduce, a cousin of XQuery, is becoming Xtatic, a programming language for XML [25]. Our own experiences with Galax constantly reveal opportunities in which a richer XQuery semantics would permit our users to build more XML applications faster and more reliably.

We expect that some (many?) of our working-group colleagues will object to our suggestions that XQuery evolve into a programming language for XML. But we believe it is prudent to consider version 2.0 features now, before many incompatible feature sets emerge.

We focus on features already in demand and those that we believe will help XQuery grow in a disciplined way: updates, exception handling, higher-order functions, and parametric polymorphism. Even if XQuery were to have all these features, it still has to co-exist within a variety of environments. We conclude with a discussion of XQuery's interface to other host languages.

Update statements are conspicuously absent from XQuery 1.0, and are the most frequently requested feature. Database programmers rightly expect the ability to query *and* update XML. Updates were excluded from XQuery 1.0, because they require substantial study to get right, and thus would delay delivery of XQuery 1.0. Lehti has proposed an update language for XQuery [28] in which an insert, delete, or replace statement specifies how to update a node or location, and a path expression denotes the node or location to update. This statement updates our example book catalog by inserting a new book element:

```
insert
  <book isbn="0399127380" year="1982">
    <title>Crisis: The Last Year of the Carter Presidency</title>
    <author>Hamilton Jordan</author>
    <publisher>Putname Pub Group</publisher>
    <retail_price currency="USD">1.94</retail_price>
  </book>
before $cat/catalog/book[@isbn="156352578X"]
```

Update statements are an imperative feature, but more restricted than pointers in imperative languages or reference values in functional languages, making it possible to retain some benefits of declarativeness, such as flexible evaluation order. To permit reordering of update and query statements, it must be possible to determine "non-interference" between statements. A formal semantics of updates would help establish criteria for non-interference, and thus should be specified before officially adding updates to XQuery.

Another feature missing from XQuery is exception handling. XQuery's built-in functions may raise errors, and user-defined errors can be raised by calling the function fn:error, which takes any atomic value or node as an argument. For example, this expression raises an error containing a myerror element:

```
fn:error(<myerror>An error in my query</myerror>)
```

There is no expression, however, for catching and handling errors – errors are propagated to the environment in which the expression is evaluated. As more libraries of XQuery functions are created and used, the ability to detect and recover from errors becomes an important usability issue. The working group debated a proposal for an exception-handling expression. A try expression takes an expression and zero or more catch branches labeled with types, and conditionally evaluates a branch if the expression raises an error value that matches the branch's type. For example, the expression below either evaluates to the value of *Expr* or if *Expr* raises an error, and the error value matches element myerror, the try evaluates to the string "My error", otherwise any other error is re-raised.

```
try (Expr)
catch $err as element myerror return  "My error"
default $err return fn:error($err) {-- Re-raise the error --}
```

One reason the try-catch expression was excluded from XQuery 1.0 is its potential interaction with updates. It was not immediately clear what the semantics of updates should be in the presence of exceptions and exception handling. For example, should exception handling enforce a transactional semantics (i.e., the ability to rollback or commit) on update statements? Because we cannot yet answer these questions, we decided to study updates and exception handling together in XQuery 2.0.

Although XQuery is a functional language, it does not support higher-order functions or parametric polymorphism – two of the most powerful programming constructs in languages like O'Caml, Standard ML, and Haskell. In higher-order languages, functions are first-class values and, for example, can be bound to variables and passed as arguments to other functions. Higher-order functions promote code reuse, much as method overriding promotes code reuse in object-oriented languages. Parametric polymorphism permits a function to have one definition but to operate on values of different types. Higher-order functions and parametric polymorphism are most powerful when combined. For example, this O'Caml signature for the function quicksort takes a list of values of any type 'a, a comparison function that takes two 'a values and returns an integer, and returns a list of 'a values in sorted order.

```
quicksort : 'a list -> ('a * 'a -> int) -> 'a list
```

XQuery 1.0 has ad-hoc polymorphism. All the infix operators and many built-in functions are overloaded, e.g., the arithmetic operators can be applied to any numeric type. Users can simulate polymorphism by constructing a new type that is the union of a fixed set of types and then define a function that expects the union type. But this requires that the input types be known in advance of writing the function, which defeats much of the usefulness of polymorphism. Like exception handling, higher-order functions and parametric polymorphism become more important as users write more libraries. For example, we can imagine an XQuery library that constructs and processes SOAP messages [38], which consist of generic headers and application-specific payloads. An XQuery library for SOAP could take as arguments functions that construct and process the application-specific payloads. Not surprisingly, as higher-order functions and parametric polymorphism increase expressiveness, they also increase the complexity of static typing and evaluation. But because XQuery is a functional language, they are natural features to consider.

In Section 1, we noted that query languages, no matter how expressive or complete, are usually evaluated within a host programming language. In general, the host language provides the application's interface to the query language, and vice versa. For example, a host language might convert a user's request posted in a form into a query expression and convey the query results to the user through a GUI. In our experience with Galax, the application programming interface (API) is often the first experience a user has with XQuery. The API must be lightweight enough for new users to understand, but complete enough so that experienced users can exercise all the features of the underlying implementation. We have designed a traditional functional API to Galax, but an important open question is what the boundary should be between XQuery and its host languages. Despite attempts to tightly couple SQL's and OQL's data models with host type systems and to embed SQL in a host language, in practice, the barrier between query and host language remains solid.

Designing XQuery 1.0 has been both an invigorating and exhausting experience. The requirements of vendors, expectations of users, and scrutiny of academics has added equal amounts of challenge and frustration. We believe the resulting language will be a success, and that with success, users will demand that XQuery grow to meet their XML programming needs. We hope to influence that growth by adding a small number of powerful language features. In that way, we hope to put the tools for XQuery's growth in the hands of its users.

Acknowlegments We are privileged to work with the talented and dedicated members of the W3C XML Query Working Group. In particular, we thank Philip Wadler, friend and colleague, for many years of fruitful collaboration on XQuery.

References

[1] S. Abiteboul, O. Benjelloun, I. Manolescu et al. "Active XML: Peer-to-Peer Data and Web Services Integration", Proceedings of Conference on Very Large Databases (VLDB) 2002, pp 1087–1090.

[2] S. Abiteboul, R. Hull, and V. Vianu. *Foundations of Databases*, Addison-Wesley, 1995.

[3] S. Alagic. "Type-Checking OQL Queries In the ODMG Type Systems", Transactions on Database Systems, 24(3), 1999, pp 319–360.

[4] I. Avila-Campillo et al. "XMLTK: An XML Toolkit for Scalable XML Stream Processing", Informal proceedings of PLAN-X: Programming Language Technologies for XML, Oct. 2002.

[5] P. Bohannon, J. Freire, P. Roy, and J. Siméon. "From XML Schema to Relations: A Cost-Based Approach to XML Storage", International Conference on Data Engineering, 2002, pp 209-218.

[6] R. Kaushik, P. Bohannon, J. Naughton, and H. Korth. "Covering indexes for branching path queries" Proceedings of ACM SIGMOD Conference 2002, pp 133–144.

[7] P. Buneman, S. Davidson, G. Hillebrand, and D. Suciu. "A Query Language and Optimization Techniques for Unstructured Data", Proceedings of ACM SIGMOD Conference, 1996, pp 505–516.

[8] L. Cardelli and G. Ghelli. "A Query Language based on the Ambient Logic", Mathematical Structures in Computer Science, 2003.

[9] R. G. Cattell et al. *The Object Database Standard: ODMG 2.0.* Morgan Kaufmann, 1997.

[10] D. Chamberlin, "Influences on the Design of XQuery", in *XQuery from the Experts: A Guide to the W3C XML Query Language*, edited by H. Katz, Addison-Wesley, 2003.

[11] T. Chuang, "Generic Validation of Structural Content with Parametric Modules", Proceedings of ACM SIGPLAN International Conference on Functional Programming, 2001, pp 98–109.

[12] C. Chung, J. Min, and K. Shim, "APEX: an adaptive path index for XML data", Proceedings of ACM SIGMOD Conference 2002, pp 121–132.

[13] J. Clarke and M. Makoto. RELAX NG specification, Oasis, 2001, http://www.oasis-open.org/committees/relax-ng/spec-20011203.html.

[14] R. Connor et al. "Extracting Typed Values from XML Data, OOPSLA Workshop on Objects, XML, and Databases, 2001.

[15] R. Cover. The XML Cover Pages: XML Industry Sectors, http://www.xml.org/xml/industry_industrysectors.jsp.

[16] H. Darwen (Contributor) and C. J. Date. *Guide to the SQL Standard : A User's Guide to the Standard Database Language SQL*, Addison-Wesley, 1997.

[17] M. Fernandez, Y. Kadiyska, D. Suciu et al. "SilkRoute: A framework for publishing relational data in XML", Transactions on Database Systems 27(4), 2002, pp 438-493.

[18] M. Fernández, J. Siméon and P. Wadler. "Static Typing in XQuery", in *XQuery from the Experts: A Guide to the W3C XML Query Language*, edited by H. Katz, Addison-Wesley, 2003.

[19] M. Fernández, J. Siméon and P. Wadler. "Introduction to the Formal Semantics", in *XQuery from the Experts: A Guide to the W3C XML Query Language*, edited by H. Katz, Addison-Wesley, 2003.

[20] M. Fernández, J. Siméon and P. Wadler. "A Semi-monad for Semi-structured Data", International Conference on Database Theory, 2001, pp. 263–300.

[21] P. Fankhauser, T. Groh and S. Overhage. "XQuery by the Book: The IPSI XQuery Demonstrator", International Conference on Extending Database Technology (EDBT), 2002, pp 742–744.

[22] D. Florescu, A. Grünhagen and D. Kossmann. "XL: a platform for Web Services", Conference on Innovative Data Systems Research (CIDR) 2003, Online Proceedings.

[23] D. Florescu, C. Hillary, D. Kossmann, et al. "A Complete and High-performance XQuery Engine for Streaming Data", Proceedings of Conference on Very Large Databases (VLDB) 2003, to appear.

[24] M. Fernández, J. Siméon et al. Implementing XQuery 1.0: The Galax Experience Demonstration track, Proceedings of Conference on Very Large Databases (VLDB) to appear, 2003, http://db.bell-labs.com/galax/.

[25] H. Hosoya and B. Pierce. "XDuce: A Statically Typed XML Processing Language", ACM Transactions on Internet Technology, to appear, 2003.

[26] Q. Jackson. "Efficient Formalism-Only Parsing of XML/HTML Using the S-Calculus", ACM SIGPLAN Notices, 38(2), Feb. 2003.

[27] H. V. Jagadish et al. "TAX: A Tree Algebra for XML", Workshop on Databases and Programming Languages, LNCS 2397, 2002, pp. 149–164.

[28] P. Lehti. "Design and Implementation of a Data Manipulation Processor for an XML Query Language", Technische Universität Darmstadt Technical Report No. KOM-D-149, http://www.ipsi.fhg.de/ lehti/diplomarbeit.pdf, August, 2001.

[29] SQL, Parts 1 – 13, International Organization for Standards (ISO), Technical reports ISO/IEC 9075-1:1999 through ISO/IEC 9075-13:1999.

[30] H. V. Jagadish, S. Al-Khalifa, A. Chapman, et al. "TIMBER: A Native XML Database", The VLDB Journal, 11(4), 2002, pp 274–291.

[31] D. Leijen and E. Meijer. "Domain Specific Embedded Compilers", USENIX 2nd Conference on Domain-Specific Languages, 1999, pp 109-122.

[32] P. Manghi et al. "Hybrid Applications over XML: Integrating the Procedural and Declarative Approaches", ACM CIKM International Workshop on Web Information and Data Management (WIDM'02), 2002.

[33] F. Neven. "Automata Theory for XML Researchers", ACM SIGMOD Record, 31(3), Sept. 2003.

[34] J. Robie. "An Introduction to XQuery", in XQuery from the Experts: A Guide to the W3C XML Query Language edited by Howard Katz, Addison-Wesley, 2003.

[35] J. Shanmugasundaram, K. Tufte, G. He, et al. "Relational Databases for Querying XML Documents: Limitations and Opportunities", Proceedings of Conference on Very Large Databases (VLDB) 1999, pp 302–314.

[36] J. Siméon and P. Wadler. "The Essence of XML", ACM Symposium on Principles of Programming Languages, 2003, pp 1–13.

[37] F. Simeoni et al. "Language Bindings to XML", IEEE Internet Computing, 7(1), Jan./Feb. 2003.

[38] SOAP 1.2 Part 1: Messaging Framework, W3C Proposed Recommendation, May 2003. http://www.w3.org/TR/2003/PR-soap12-part1-20030507/.

[39] G. Steele. "Growing a Language", Journal of Higher-Order and Symbolic Computation, 12(3), Oct 1999, pp 221-236.

[40] V. Tannen, P. Buneman and S. Naqvi. "Structural Recursion as a Query Language", Workshop on Databases and Programming Languages, 1991, Morgan Kaufmann, pp 9-19.

[41] V. Vianu. "A Web Odyssey: from Codd to XML", Proceedings of ACM Symposium on Principles of Database Systems, pp 1–16, 2001.

[42] M. Wallace and C. Runciman. "Haskell and XML: generic combinators or type-based translation?", Proceedings of ACM SIGPLAN International Conference on Functional Programming, 1999, pp 148–159.

[43] Extensible markup language (XML) 1.0. W3C Recommendation, February 1998. http://www.w3.org/TR/REC-xml/.

[44] XML Schema Part 1: Structures. W3C Recommendation, May 2001.

[45] XML Schema Part 2: Datatypes. W3C Recommendation, May 2001.

[46] XQuery 1.0 and XPath 2.0 data model. W3C Working Draft, May 2003. http://www.w3.org/TR/query-datamodel/.

[47] Xquery 1.0 and xpath 2.0 functions and operators version 1.0. W3C Working Draft, May 2003. http://www.w3.org/TR/xpath-operators/.

[48] XPath 2.0. W3C Working Draft, May 2003. http://www.w3.org/TR/xquery/.

[49] XQuery 1.0: An XML Query Language. W3C Working Draft, May 2003. http://www.w3.org/TR/xquery/.

[50] XQuery 1.0 and XPath 2.0 Formal Semantics. W3C Working Draft, May 2003. http://www.w3.org/TR/query-semantics/.

430 Mary Fernández and Jérôme Siméon

[51] XQuery and XPath Full-text Requirements W3C Working Draft, May 2003.
http://www.w3.org/TR/xmlquery-full-text-requirements/.
[52] XSL Transformations (XSLT) Version 2.0. W3C Working Draft, May 2003.
http://www.w3.org/TR/xslt20/.

Discovering Algebraic Specifications from Java Classes[*]

Johannes Henkel and Amer Diwan

University of Colorado at Boulder
Boulder CO 80309, USA
{henkel,diwan}@cs.colorado.edu
http://www.cs.colorado.edu/~{henkel,diwan}/

Abstract. We present and evaluate an automatic tool for extracting algebraic specifications from Java classes. Our tool maps a Java class to an algebraic signature and then uses the signature to generate a large number of terms. The tool evaluates these terms and based on the results of the evaluation, it proposes equations. Finally, the tool generalizes equations to axioms and eliminates many redundant axioms. Since our tool uses dynamic information, it is not guaranteed to be sound or complete. However, we manually inspected the axioms generated in our experiments and found them all to be correct.

1 Introduction

Program specifications are useful for both program development and understanding. Gries [20] describes a programming methodology that develops axiomatic program specifications along with the code itself. At least anecdotal evidence suggests that programs that are developed using Gries' methodology are relatively bug free and easier to maintain. However, developing formal program specifications is difficult and requires significant mathematical maturity on the part of programmers. For this reason, programmers rarely develop full formal specifications with their code.

Recent work proposes tools that automatically discover likely specifications based on program runs [15, 1, 23, 44]. These tools allow programmers to benefit from formal specifications with much less effort. Our research is inspired by these tools. To our knowledge, however, our methodology is the first to tackle high-level functional specifications of significant software components. The main shortcoming of prior tools such as Daikon [15] is that they refer to the inner state of software components when specifying pre- and postconditions.

Our tool discovers algebraic specifications [22] from Java classes. Algebraic specifications can describe *what* Java classes implement without revealing implementation details. Our approach is as follows. We start by extracting the

---

[*] This work is suported by NSF grants CCR-0085792 and CCR-0086255, and an IBM Faculty Partnership Award. Any opinions, findings and conclusions or recommendations expressed in this material are the authors' and do not necessarily reflect those of the sponsors.

L. Cardelli (Ed.): ECOOP 2003, LNCS 2743, pp. 431–456, 2003.

signatures of classes automatically using the Java reflection API. We use the signatures to automatically generate a large number of terms, using heuristics to guide term generation. Each term corresponds to a legal (i.e., does not throw an exception) sequence of method invocations on an instance of the class. We then evaluate the terms and compare their outcomes. These comparisons yield equations between terms. Finally, we generalize these equations to axioms and use term rewriting to eliminate redundant axioms. Note that we can systematically generate more terms if we have low confidence in our axioms.

We evaluate our approach on a variety of classes. Our experiments reveal that our approach is effective in discovering specifications of Java classes even when it does not have access to any implementation details of the classes. Since we employ mostly dynamic techniques, the specifications that we discover are unsound. However, our experiments reveal that the axioms that we discover are actually correct and useful in understanding the behavior of the classes.

The remainder of the paper is organized as follows. Section 2 motivates the need for algebraic specifications. Section 3 describes our approach and an implementation of our approach. Section 4 presents case studies that demonstrate the usefulness and effectiveness of our current prototype. Section 5 discusses extensions to our prototype. Section 6 reviews related work. Finally Section 7 concludes.

2   Motivation

Fig. 1 contains the Java source for an integer stack implementation. Even though the concept of an integer stack is simple, the details of the implementation are tricky. In particular, the implementations of push and pop may need to resize the internal array which involves copying the contents of one array to another.

There are two levels in understanding this code: *What concept* does it implement and *in which way* does it implement the concept. To understand *what concept* the IntStack class implements, one needs to know:

- the pop method returns the int value that was used as the argument to the most recent call to push.
- after applying pop, the state of the stack is equivalent to the state before the most recent push.
- pop will throw an exception if applied to an empty stack.

To understand *in which way* the IntStack class implements the concept, one needs to know:

- The inner state of the integer stack is modeled as an array int [] state containing the stack elements and an integer int size maintaining a pointer to the first free index in the state array.
- push checks whether state is large enough to accommodate one more value and if not, allocates a new state array that is twice as big as the old one and copies the old elements over. After potentially scaling the state array,

```
public class IntStack {
    private int [] store;    private int size;
    private static final int INITIAL_CAPACITY=10;
    public IntStack(){
        this.store = new int[INITIAL_CAPACITY];
        this.size=0;
    }
    public void push(int value){
        if(this.size ==this.store.length){
            int [] store = new int[this.store.length*2];
            System.arraycopy(this.store,0,store,0,this.size);
            this.store = store;
        }
        this.store[this.size]=value;
        this.size++;
    }
    public int pop(){
        int result = this.store[this.size-1];
        this.size--;
        if(this.store.length > INITIAL_CAPACITY && this.size*2
                 < this.store.length){
            int [] store = new int[this.store.length/2];
            System.arraycopy(this.store,0,store,0,this.size);
            this.store = store;
        }
        return result;
    }
}
```

Fig. 1. An integer stack implementation in Java

push adds the new value at the position of size in the state array and increments size by 1.

– ...

By discovering algebraic specifications [21] which do not reveal the implementation, yet characterize the interfaces, we are addressing the first level of understanding: *What concept?* Other tools, e.g. Daikon [15], are more useful for the second level, since their specifications characterize implementation details such as the resizing of the state array. Fig. 2 shows an algebraic specification of the Java integer stack discovered by our tool. The first part of the algebraic specification (called the *signature*) gives the type of the operations on the integer stack. The second part of the specification gives the axioms that describe the behavior of the integer stack. The first axiom states that applying the *pop* operation to a stack returns the value that has been pushed previously. The second axiom states that the *pop* operation yields the abstract state in which the stack was before *push* was applied. The third axiom specifies that applying *pop* to the empty integer stack results in an exception. We will further explain these axioms and the syntax that we use in Section 3.1. Note that these axioms refer only to the *observable* behavior of the stack and not to the internal implementation details.

TYPE *IntStack*
FUNCTIONS
$\quad$ *IntStack* : $\rightarrow$ *IntStack* $\times$ *void*
$\quad$ *push* : *IntStack* $\times$ *int* $\rightarrow$ *IntStack* $\times$ *void*
$\quad$ *pop* : *IntStack* $\rightarrow$ *IntStack* $\times$ *int*
AXIOMS
$\forall s$: *IntStack*, i : *int*
$\quad$ $pop(push(s,i).state).retval = i$
$\quad$ $pop(push(s,i).state).state = s$
$\quad$ $pop(IntStack().state).retval \rightsquigarrow \text{ArrayIndexOutOfBoundsException}$

Fig. 2. An algebraic specification for `IntStack` (Fig. 1) as discovered by our tool

The algebraic specifications discovered by our tool have many uses:

- **Reverse Engineering and Program Understanding.** As the example illustrates, algebraic specifications discovered by our tool can be useful for program understanding.
- **Program Documentation.** A programmer can use our tool to document code that he/she has written. In this case, the programmer may want to start with specifications generated by our tool and edit them if necessary.
- **Prototyping.** Let's suppose the developer wants to implement an efficient integer stack. In this case, the developer can start with a slow and simple (and more likely to be correct) integer stack, use our tools to generate the specifications, and use the specifications to guide and test the efficient final implementation (e.g. [14, 12]).
- **Automatic Test Generation.** The specifications discovered by our tool can be used to automatically generate test cases (e.g. [14, 12]). For example, using the specification in Fig. 2, one can generate the following test case

$$pop(pop(push(push(IntStack()\bullet state\bullet 7)\bullet state\bullet 9)\bullet state)\bullet retval = 7$$

Since this test case has been derived from the first two axioms in Fig. 2, if this test fails, one will know that at least one of these axioms does not hold. By generating more test cases for these particular axioms, the tool will be able to characterize the circumstances under which a particular axiom fails to hold and therefore determine the difference between specification and implementation.
- **Debugging.** If our tool generates axioms that do not make sense, it may indicate a bug in the implementation. For example, the following axiom most likely indicates a bug in the implementation since it says that applying pop four times to any stack causes an exception:

$$\forall \bullet : Stack \; (\; pop(pop(pop(pop(\bullet)\bullet state)\bullet state)\bullet state)\bullet state \rightsquigarrow \text{Exception} \;)$$

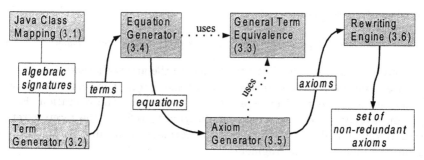

Fig. 3. Architectural overview of our tool for discovering algebraic specifications

3 Approach

Fig. 3 gives an overview of our approach. We start by generating terms in an algebra derived from a Java class (Sections 3.1 and 3.2). Terms represent sequences of invocations of methods on an instance of a class. We use these terms to generate equations. For example, we may find that two terms evaluate to the same value. We use *observational equivalence* [14] to determine if values produced by two terms are equal (Section 3.3): We consider them the same if they behave the same with respect to their public methods. Thus, observational equivalence abstracts away from low-level implementation details and only considers the interface. We discover equations (Section 3.4) and then generalize the equations by replacing subterms with universally-quantified typed variables (Section 3.5). This generalization results in axioms. However, these axioms may or may not be true. To determine (with some probability) that the axioms are true, we check them by generating test cases. Finally, we rewrite our axioms to eliminate many redundant axioms (Section 3.6).

3.1 Mapping Java Classes to Algebras

While algebraic specifications have been used to describe object-oriented systems, previous work assumed that a method invocation either has no side effects or that it does not return a value [29]. Our mapping from Java classes to algebras can represent methods with both side effects and return values.

Consider the Java *IntStack* class in Fig. 1. Note that the *pop* method not only returns a value (i.e., it is an *observer*) but also modifies the internal state of the receiver of the *pop* message. To represent such side effects and return value at the same time, each operation in the algebra returns two entities: a reference to the receiver and the normal return value.

More precisely, given a Java method named m defined in class cls with n arguments $arg_1 \cdot arg_2 \cdot \cdots arg_n$ of types $type(arg_1) \cdot type(arg_2) \cdot \cdots type(arg_n)$ and return type *returntype*, we construct the signature of an algebraic operation m within an algebra *cls* as follows:

$$m : cls \times type(arg_1) \times \cdots \times type(arg_n) \rightarrow cls \times returntype \qquad (1)$$

The receiver argument (typed *cls*) to the left of the arrow characterizes its original state. The receiver type to the right of the arrow represents the possibly modified state of the receiver as a result of evaluating the operation. For an operation invocation, we use *.state* qualification to refer to the receiver return value and *.retval* qualification to refer to the normal return value. As an example, consider the following Java fragment.

```
IntStack s = new IntStack(); s.push(4); int result=s.pop();
```

pop(push(IntStack()•state•4)•state)•retval denotes the integer value stored in result, while *pop(push(IntStack()•state•4)•state)•state* denotes the state of s at the end of the computation. Similarly, the first axiom in Fig. 2 refers to the return value of a *pop*, while the second axiom refers to the state of the stack after a *pop*.

Since constructors do not take an implicit first argument, we leave out the object state from the algebraic signature. Also, for constructors, *returntype* is always *void*. The signature for constructor c of class cls looks as follows:

$$c : void \times type(arg_1) \times \cdots \times type(arg_n) \rightarrow cls \times void \qquad (2)$$

The algebra mapping described here (and implemented in our tool) does not have a means of capturing side effects to arguments other than the receiver of methods. We could generalize our mapping given in Equation 1 to take side effects to arguments into consideration by returning not just the possibly modified receiver but also all the (potentially modified) arguments:

$$\begin{aligned} m : cls \times type(arg_1) \times \cdots \times type(arg_n) \\ \rightarrow cls \times returntype \times type(arg_1) \times \cdots \times type(arg_n) \end{aligned} \qquad (3)$$

Our implementation cannot handle side effects on static variables and some interactions between objects, i.e. where an object $\bullet_1$ modifies the state of an owned object $\bullet_2$, but the state of $\bullet_2$ cannot be observed through $\bullet_1$. We handle terms that throw exceptions, but we do not capture the (possibly) modified state of an object if an exception has been thrown. The $\rightsquigarrow$ operator distinguishes exception throwing terms from regular terms (e.g., the third axiom in Fig. 2).

In contrast to previous algebraic tools, where users of the tools needed to define elaborate mappings from Java/C++ classes to algebras [29], our implementation for extracting algebraic signatures from Java classes is fully automated and retrieves all the information that is necessary from the Java reflection API.

3.2   Generating Ground Terms

This section considers how to generate terms in an algebra obtained from a Java class. The output of the term generator is an endless stream of terms. The quality

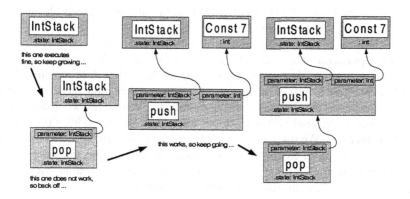

Fig. 4. Growing terms incrementally

of the generated terms is important since the terms are our test cases and thus
a critical ingredient for successful dynamic invariant detection [15]. The term
generator may either systematically generate all terms up to a given size [10]
or randomly generate terms based on some distribution function (e.g., having
a bias towards shorter terms).

Our terms satisfy two properties. First, terms do not throw exceptions when
evaluated. Second, all terms return the state of an object, but never a return
value. For example, we will generate $pop(push(IntStack()$•$state$•$5)$•$state)$•$state$
but not $pop(push(IntStack()$•$state$•$5)$•$state)$•$retval$ because it computes a return
value, not a state. During equation generation we also generate terms that return
values and throw exceptions (Section 3.4).

Our prototype implementation represents terms as trees with nodes representing operation application, constructor application, array construction, constants, and free variables. The children of each term are its arguments. Each node
is represented by a Java object containing a reference to the appropriate Java
reflection API object that is needed for evaluation. For example, an operation-
application node may contain a pointer to the `java.lang.reflect.Method` instance representing the pop method of class IntStack.

Growing Terms We grow terms incrementally, beginning with a constructor.
Fig. 4 shows how we generate a term for the *IntStack* algebra. We begin by
selecting the constructor *IntStack*. We execute the term using Java reflection.
Since it executes without throwing any exception, we continue to extend it by
selecting an operation that can be applied to the existing term. When we grow
the term with a *pop* and evaluate the result, it throws an exception. We back-
track and now choose *push*. *push* requires an argument, so we generate a term
that returns a value of that particular type, in this case the integer constant
7. This time, the term executes without throwing an exception. Thus we can

keep growing the term. We then extend the term with *pop*, which also executes without throwing an exception.

Since the goal of the term generator is to explore the state space of instances of a class, operations that do not modify the state of the receiver need not be part of any terms. We can determine that an operation does not modify the state of the receiver by either using a compile-time mod-ref analysis or a run-time heuristic. The run-time heuristic works as follows. Whenever we grow a term, we keep the new term only if the last operation of the term modifies the internal state of the receiver. We use a hash sum of the serialized inner state to determine if an operation changes the inner state. Although this process does not remove all the operation applications that do not modify the observable state of the object,[1] it significantly improves the quality of terms.

Generating Arguments for Terms We can use terms themselves as object arguments for any operations in a term. However, in the interest of efficiency and quality of ultimate results, we identify two special cases that we handle differently: arguments of a primitive type (such as integer) and arguments that are instances of immutable classes (i.e., classes, such as Object, that do not have any modifying operations).

For arguments of a primitive type, we maintain a precomputed set of constant nodes that have values of the primitive type (e.g., values between 0 and 10). Whenever we need an argument of a primitive type, we select one value from the set. If our set is too small, we will not explore enough of the state space and may end up missing some axioms. If the set is too large, the tool will become too inefficient for practical use or, if a random selection of test cases is used, our terms will populate the state space too sparsely. Our approach for primitive types works well for types such as integers and booleans.[2]

Our approach for generating arguments of immutable classes is similar to that for primitive types: we precompute a set of values of that type. An *immutable class* is a class that has no methods for modifying the state of an instance after creation (e.g., Object and String classes in Java). For example, instead of using *push(ObjStack()•state• Object()•state)•state* we prefer to generate *push(ObjStack()•state•obj@4)•state* where obj@4 is an object in the precomputed set. While *Object()•state* in the first term will generate a new instance of Object each time it is evaluated, the second term contains the particular instance obj@4 of Object as a constant. As we elaborate in Section 3.4, our technique of using constants for immutable classes allows us to exploit reference equality for instances of immutable classes which avoids the high cost incurred by the traditional EQN method [14]. However, if we use reference equality, we need to make sure that we still have some chance of computing the same instance when comparing two terms. For example,

$$pop(push(ObjStack()•state•obj@9)•state)•retval \quad \text{and}$$
$$pop(push(push(ObjStack()•state•obj@4)•obj@9)•state)•retval$$

---

[1] Just the serialized inner state being different does not guarantee that the objects before and after the applications are different in any externally observable way.

[2] We have no experience with floating point values.

would both compute the same instance, namely obj@9. Thus, analogously to primitive types, it is important to pick a set that is neither too big nor too small.

For non-immutable classes, we can not safely replace subterms with a particular instance as a precomputed constant, since then the potentially modified state of the instance would be used in the next evaluation of the term. For example, if we execute the term $push(\text{IntStack@4}\bullet 9)\bullet state$ multiple times, we will compute a different inner state each time.

Algorithm 1 describes how we determine if a class is immutable. Intuitively, we generate a number of instances of the class, apply all operations to each instance, and look at the hash code of the serialized instance before and after operator application.[3] If the hashes are the same for a sufficiently large number of instances, then we can be confident that the class is immutable. An alternative to this approach is to use a compile-time mod-ref analysis. If the mod sets of all methods of a class (except constructors) are empty then the class is immutable.

Algorithm 1 Class immutability

CLASS-IMMUTABLE(C) **begin**
Require: C is a class
  repeat
    $i \leftarrow$ instance of C
    for all operations op in class C **do**
      $hashBefore \leftarrow$ SERIALIZE-AND-HASH(i)
      $hashAfter \leftarrow$ SERIALIZE-AND-HASH(op(i))
      if $hashAfter \neq hashBefore$ **then**
        return false
      end if
    end for
  until confident of outcome
  return true
end

3.3 Term Equivalence

To compare whether or not two ground terms are the same, we use a variation of Doong and Frankl's EQN method [14]. EQN tries to determine whether two terms evaluate to observationally equivalent values. Doong and Frankl define that two values are *observationally equivalent* if they behave the same when we apply arbitrary operations to both of them. Two values can be observationally

---

[3] If the operator requires arguments, one may need to generate many test cases for these arguments as well to become confident.

equivalent even though they have different internal representations. For example, consider the IntStack implementation in Java from Fig. 1, where *pop* is implemented as

```
public int pop(){
    return this.store[--this.size];
}
```

In this case, applying 11 *push* operations and 2 *pop* operations results in a different inner state compared to 9 *push* operations,[4] even though both values are observationally equivalent if the first 9 pushed values were the same.

The EQN method for observational equivalence is effective but inefficient since it needs to apply many operations to both terms in order to gain confidence that they are indeed the same. Thus, we identify two special cases that we can handle quickly: primitive types and immutable classes. Algorithm 2 describes how we dispatch between the three possibilities. In Algorithm 2, the parameters

---

Algorithm 2 General term equivalence dispatch

GTE-DISPATCH(t_1, t_2) **begin**
Require: t_1, t_2 are terms of the same type T.
  if T is a primitive type **then**
    return PRIMITIVE-EQUALS(t_1,t_2)
  else
    if REFEQ-APPLIES(t_1, t_2) **then**
      return EVAL(t_1)$=_{ref}$EVAL(t_2)
    else
      return EQN(t_1,t_2)
    end if
  end if
end

---

for GTE-DISPATCH are terms, not the values computed by the terms. This is necessary since each of PRIMITIVE-EQUALS, REFEQ-APPLIES and EQN needs more than a single sample of what the terms evaluate to. EVAL($\bullet$) denotes the result of the evaluation of $\bullet$ and $=_{ref}$ checks reference equality.

GTE-DISPATCH is conservative in that it is accurate whenever it exposes non-equivalence. It may be inaccurate when it finds equivalence.

We now describe the algorithms for the three cases in more detail.

Equivalence for Primitive Types Consider the question whether *pop* (*push*(*IntStack*()$\bullet$*state*$\bullet$4))$\bullet$*retval* and 4 are equivalent terms. We can confirm equivalence by checking that both terms evaluate to 4.

Now consider the term *hashCode*(*IntStack*()$\bullet$*state*)$\bullet$*retval*. Since the *hashCode* function will compute a different value for each *IntStack* instance, the term will

---

[4] Recall that the *IntStack* uses an array representation with an initial size of 10 elements.

Algorithm 3 Equivalence for primitive types

PRIMITIVE-EQUALS(t_1, t_2) **begin**
Require: t_1, t_2 are terms computing values of the same primitive type.
  $result_{1a} \leftarrow$ EVAL(t_1), $result_{1b} \leftarrow$ EVAL(t_1)
  $result_{2a} \leftarrow$ EVAL(t_2), $result_{2b} \leftarrow$ EVAL(t_2)
  $consistent_1 \leftarrow result_{1a} =_{val} result_{1b}$
  $consistent_2 \leftarrow result_{2a} =_{val} result_{2b}$
  if not $consistent_1$ **and not** $consistent_2$ **then**
    return true
  end if
  if not $consistent_1$ **or not** $consistent_2$ **then**
    return false
  end if
  return $result_{1a} =_{val} result_{2a}$
end

---

evaluate to a different value each time. To identify such cases, Algorithm 3 evaluates each term twice. If both terms evaluate to the same value both times then they are equal. If only one of the terms evaluates to the same value both times, then the two terms cannot be equal. Finally, if both terms evaluate to different values each time they are evaluated, then we assume that they are equal.

Algorithm 4 Checking for reference equality

REFEQ-APPLIES(t_1, t_2) **begin**
Require: t_1, t_2 are terms of the same reference type.
  return EVAL(t_1) $=_{ref}$ EVAL(t_1)
        and EVAL(t_2) $=_{ref}$ EVAL(t_2)
end

Comparing the References Computed by Terms Since our algorithm currently handles only side effects to instance variables of receivers and we use instances of immutable classes from a fixed set (Section 3.2), there may be many situations where we can use reference equality rather than resorting to the more expensive observational equivalence algorithm (Section 4). Thus, we use a heuristic similar to that for primitive types (Algorithm 4): we evaluate each term twice and see if each term evaluates to the same value in both evaluations. If they do, then we can simply compare the references that they return. If they do not, then we use the observational equivalence procedure. For example, for the terms $pop(push(ObjStack()\bullet state\bullet obj@123)\bullet retval$ and obj@123, REFEQ-APPLIES returns true, while it returns false for

$$pop(push(ObjStack()\bullet state\bullet obj@123)\bullet state$$

and $ObjStack()\bullet state$.

Algorithm 5 Observational equivalence

EQN(t_1, t_2)
Require: t_1, t_2 are terms, evaluating to instances of some class C
  if   SERIALIZE-AND-HASH(EVAL(t_1))$=_{val}$SERIALIZE-AND-HASH(EVAL(t_2))
  then
     return true
  end if
  repeat
     Generate a term stub stb, with an argument of type C
     for all observers ob applicable to evaluation results of stb **do**
        $stubapp_1 \leftarrow stb(t_1)$, $stubapp_2 \leftarrow stb(t_2)$
        $obsapp_1 \leftarrow ob(stubapp_1,\ldots).retval$, $obsapp_2 \leftarrow ob(stubapp_2,\ldots).retval$
        if not GTE-DISPATCH($obsapp_1,obsapp_2$) **then**
           return false
        end if
     end for
  until confident of outcome
  return true

Observational Equivalence Algorithm 5 shows pseudocode for our version of EQN.[5] EQN approximates observational equivalence of two terms of class C as follows. First, it checks if both terms evaluate to objects with identical inner state by using SERIALIZE-AND-HASH which serializes an object and computes a hash value of that serialization. If the objects have the same inner state, we can safely assume that they are observationally equivalent.

If SERIALIZE-AND-HASH fails to prove equivalence we test for observational equivalence. We start by generating term stubs that take an argument of type C and apply the stubs to $\bullet_1$ and $\bullet_2$. We then pick an observer[6] and apply it to both terms. We compare the outputs of the observers using GTE-DISPATCH (Algorithm 2). If GTE-DISPATCH returns false, then we know that $\bullet_1$ and $\bullet_2$ are not observationally equivalent, otherwise we become more confident in their equivalence.

For example, consider applying this procedure to terms from the *IntStack* algebra. An example of a stub is $\bullet \bullet \bullet push(push(\bullet \bullet 2)\bullet state\bullet 3)\bullet state$ and an example of an observer is *pop*. If $\bullet_1$ is $push(IntStack()\bullet 3)\bullet state$, the application of the stub and the observer yields

$$pop(push(push(push(IntStack()\bullet state\bullet 3)\bullet state\bullet 2)\bullet state\bullet 3)\bullet state)\bullet retval$$

---

[5] This algorithm could run into an infinite recursion. This can be cured by adding a recursion limit which we left out for clarity.

[6] An observer is an operation op such that the type of $op(\ldots).retval$ is not void.

3.4   Finding Equations

The form of the equations determines the form of the algebraic specifications that our system will discover. Our current implementation handles only equalities. This is a limitation of our current implementation and not of our approach.

We can easily add new types of equations and can enable or disable equation types. So far we have added three kinds of equations to our implementation:

- **State Equations: Equality of Distinct Terms.** For example,

$$pop(push(IntStack()\bullet state \bullet 4) \bullet state) \bullet state = IntStack() \bullet state$$

  is a state equation. These equations are useful in characterizing how operations affect the observable state of an object. We generate these equations whenever we find that two distinct terms are equivalent. An approach that is able to find some but not all state equations is as follows. We take all terms produced by the term generator, evaluate them, and hash the evaluation results in a table. Whenever we detect a conflict in the hash table we have a possible equation. Note that since hashing does not use full observational equivalence, this method will only find some of the state equations. We call the optimized equation generator state/hash, while the more general generator (using observational equivalence) is called state/eqn.

- **Observer Equations: Equality of a Term to a Constant.** These equations take the following form (*obs* is an observer and c is a constant of primitive type):

$$obs(term_1 \bullet arg_2 \bullet \hspace{-0.5em}\cdots\hspace{-0.5em} arg_n) \bullet retval = c$$

  Observer equations characterize the interactions between operations that modify and operations that observe. For example,

$$pop(push(IntStack() \bullet state \bullet 4) \bullet state) \bullet retval = 4$$

  is an observer equation.

  To generate observer equations we start with a term and apply an operation that returns a constant of a primitive type. We form an equation by equating the term to the constant.

- **Difference Equations: Constant Difference between Terms.** These equations take the following form (*obs* is an observer, *op* is an operation computing a value of a primitive type, and *diff* is a constant of a primitive type):

$$op(obs(term_1 \bullet state) \bullet retval \bullet diff) \bullet retval = obs(term_2) \bullet retval$$

  For example, given the operation *size* with the signature

$$size : IntStack \rightarrow IntStack \times int$$

which returns the size of the integer stack, we could formulate the following equation.

$$IntAdd(size(IntStack()•state)•1)•retval$$
$$= size(push(IntStack()•state•3)•state)•retval$$

In this example, *op* is *IntAdd* (i.e., integer addition) and *diff* is 1.

To generate such axioms, we generate two terms, apply an observer to both terms, and take their difference. In practice, we found that difference equations with a small value for *diff* are the most interesting ones. Therefore, we only generate such an equation if *diff* is lower than a fixed threshold. This technique filters out most spurious difference equations.

3.5 Generating Axioms

Our axioms are 3-tuples ($•_1••_2••$), where $•_1$ and $•_2$ are terms and $•$ is a set of universally-quantified, typed variables that appear as free variables in $•_1$ and $•_2$. An equation is simply an axiom with $• = \{\}$.

The generation of axioms is an abstraction process that introduces free variables into equations. For example, given the equation

$$IntAdd(size(IntStack()•state)•retval•1)•retval$$
$$= size(push(IntStack()•state•3)•state)•retval \tag{4}$$

our axiom generator can abstract *IntStack()•state* into the quantified variable $•$ of type IntStack and 3 into $•$ of type int to discover the axiom

$$\forall• : IntStack \ \forall• : int$$
$$IntAdd(size(•)•retval•1)•retval = size(push(•••)•state)•retval \tag{5}$$

Algorithm 6 describes the axiom generator, with minor optimizations left out for clarity. To generate an axiom for a particular algebra, we first use any of the equation generators as described in Section 3.4 to come up with an equation. We then compute the set of all subterms of *term₁* and *term₂*. For example, given the terms *push(IntStack()•state•4)•state* and *IntStack()•state*, the set of subterms would be {*push(IntStack()•state•4)•state• IntStack()•state• 4*}. We then initialize $•$ as the set of universally-quantified variables, so that for each subterm there is exactly one corresponding universally-quantified variable in $•$. The loop then checks for each subterm, whether we can abstract all occurrences to a free variable. First, we replace all occurrences of the subterm with a free variable. Then, we generate test cases, where each test case replaces all the free variables in the terms with generated terms. We compare whether *term₁* and *term₂* are equivalent under all test cases. If not, we undo the replacement of the particular subterm. At the end, we eliminate all free variables that do not occur in the terms and return the axiom.

Algorithm 6 Axiom generation

---

generateAxiom(*Algebra*) **begin**
  $(term_1, term_2) \leftarrow$ generate an equation in *Algebra*
  Subterms $\leftarrow$ the set of unique subterms occurring in $term_1$ and $term_2$
  $V \leftarrow$ a set of typed, universally-quantified variables $x_1, ..., x_n$
      with one x_i for each $subterm_i \in Subterms$
  for $x_i \in V$ **do**
    Replace each occurrence of $subterm_i$ with the variable x_i in $term_1$ and $term_2$
    Generate a large set of test cases *testset* where each test case is a set of
        generated terms $\{test_1, ..., test_n\}$, such that $test_j$ can replace $x_j \in V$
    for $testcase \in testset$ **do**
      Set all $x_j \in V$ to the corresponding $test_j \in testcase$
      if EQN-DISPATCH($term_1, term_2$)= false **then**
        Undo the replacement of $subterm_i$ in $term_1$ and $term_2$
        Stop executing test cases
      end if
    end for
  end for
  Eliminate all x_i from V which occur neither in $term_1$ nor in $term_2$
  return the axiom $(term_1, term_2, V)$
end

3.6 Axiom Redundancy Elimination by Axiom Rewriting

The axiom generator (Section 3.5) generates many redundant axioms. For example, for the *IntStack* algebra, our generator may generate both

$$\forall \bullet_6 : IntStack \bullet \forall \bullet_6 \bullet \bullet_6 : int$$
$$pop(pop(push(push(\bullet_6 \bullet \bullet_6) \bullet state \bullet \bullet_6) \bullet state) \bullet state) \bullet state = \bullet_6 \tag{6}$$

and

$$\forall \bullet_7 : IntStack \ \forall \bullet_7 : \bullet \bullet \bullet \bullet pop(push(\bullet_7 \bullet \bullet_7) \bullet state) \bullet state = \bullet_7 \tag{7}$$

We eliminate redundant axioms using term rewriting [35]. We use axioms that satisfy these two requirements as *rewriting rules*: (i) the left and right-hand sides must be of different length; and (ii) the free variables occurring in the shorter side must be a subset of the free variables occurring in the longer side. When using a rewrite rule on an axiom, we try to unify the longer side of the rewrite rule with terms in the axiom. If there is a match, we replace the term with the shorter side of the rewrite rule.

Whenever we are about to add a new axiom we note if any of the existing rewrite rules can simplify the axiom. If the simplified axiom is a rewrite rule we try to rewrite all existing axioms with this rule. If the rewriting makes an axiom redundant or trivial we throw it away. If a rewritten axiom yields a rewrite rule then we use that rule to simplify all existing axioms. This process terminates since each rewriting application reduces the length of the terms of the axioms that it rewrites, which means that in general, the addition of an axiom can only lead to a finite number of rewriting and elimination steps.

We now sketch how to rewrite the example Axioms (6) and (7) as shown above. Suppose that Axiom (6) already exists and we are about to add Axiom (7). First, we try to rewrite Axiom (7) using Axiom (6) as a rewriting rule. Unfortunately since the left (longer) term of Axiom (7) does not unify with any subterm in Axiom (6) rewriting fails. We find that Axiom (7) does not already exist and it is not a trivial axiom so we add it to the set of known axioms. Since Axiom (7) is a rewriting rule, we try to rewrite all existing axioms, namely Axiom (6). We find that the left side of Axiom (7) unifies with the following subterm of Axiom (6)

$$pop(push(push(\bullet_6 \bullet\bullet_6)\bullet state \bullet\bullet_6)\bullet state)\bullet state$$

with the unifier

$$\{\bullet_7 \rightarrow push(\bullet_6 \bullet\bullet_6)\bullet state\bullet \ \bullet_7 \rightarrow \bullet_6\} \bullet$$

Therefore, we instantiate the right side of Axiom (7) with the unifier we found and obtain

$$push(\bullet_6 \bullet\bullet_6)\bullet state$$

which we use as a replacement for the subterm that we found in Axiom (6). Therefore, Axiom (6) rewrites to

$$\forall\bullet_6 : \ IntStack\bullet\forall\bullet_6 : int \ (\ pop(push(\bullet_6 \bullet\bullet_6)\bullet state)\bullet state = \bullet_6\ ) \tag{8}$$

which is equivalent to Axiom (7). Since the rewritten Axiom (6) is identical to Axiom (7), we eliminate Axiom (6). In summary, we end up with Axiom (7) as the only axiom in the final set of axioms.

4   Evaluation of Our Prototype

We conducted our evaluations on a Pentium 4 1.4 GHz workstation with 512 MB of RDRAM running SuSE Linux 8.1 and Sun JDK 1.4.1. We configured our system as follows: As a default, we used a term size of 5 for the equation generators[7] and a test case size of four.[8] For HashMap, we chose a term size of 4 for all equation generators except for the observer equation generator, where a size of 6 was beneficial. We configured the system for HashSet in the same way as HashMap, except that we found that a test case size of 3 was sufficient. We also configured three distinct instances of Object and similar small pools for primitive types.

Table 1 describes the our benchmark programs. Column "# op" gives the number of operations in the class and "# observ" gives the number of operations that are observers (i.e., operations with a non-void return type).

Section 4.1 gives performance characteristics for our system. Section 4.2 presents data that suggests that our tool is successful in exercising most of the class under consideration and is thus likely to be mostly sound. Finally Section 4.3 discusses some axioms that our tool discovers.

---

[7] Term size is defined as the number of nodes in the tree representing the term. For example, the size of $push(IntStack().state, 4).state$ is 3.

[8] This means that test cases can have up to $5+4 = 9$ nodes in their term representation.

Table 1. Java classes used in our evaluation

Java Class	Description	Source	# op	# observ.
IntegerStack	minimal integer stack	Henkel	11	5
IntegerStack2	efficient integer stack (Fig. 1)	Henkel	11	5
ObjectStack	same as above but for objects	Henkel	11	5
FullObjectStack	another Object stack	Henkel	15	8
IntegerQueue	a FIFO queue for integers	Henkel	15	8
ObjectMapping	a mapping between objects	Henkel	15	9
ObjectQueue	a FIFO queue for objects	Henkel	15	8
LinkedList	linked list	Sun JDK 1.4.1	39	30
HashSet	hash set	Sun JDK 1.4.1	23	17
HashMap	hash map	Sun JDK 1.4.1	22	15

Table 2. Timings for our benchmark programs

benchmark	# before rewriting	# final axioms	time
IntegerStack	116	18	8.48 sec
IntegerStack2	142	18	6.69 sec
ObjectStack	116	9	8.22 sec
FullObjectStack	145	27	12.97 sec
IntegerQueue	404	28	1.59 min
ObjectMapping	194	24	8.97 sec
ObjectQueue	404	24	1.59 min
LinkedList	1045	116	2.37 min
HashSet	6830	74	1.75 h
HashMap	8989	71	15.28 h

4.1 Performance of the Tool

Table 2 gives the overall performance of our system. For each benchmark, we display the number of axioms before rewriting, after rewriting and the time it took to generate the axioms. The table shows that our redundancy reduction by rewriting is very effective. It also shows that our system is fast for all of the classes except for HashSet and HashMap. HashMap is more demanding since many of its operations take two arguments, which enlarges the state space. Running our system with smaller test term sizes for these classes takes less time, but introduces erroneous axioms which can 'infect' many other correct axioms during the rewriting.

We see from Table 2 that LinkedList has the most axioms (116). While 116 axioms is quite a lot, it is worth noting that the Java standard implementation of linked list has a large number of operations (39) and thus, 116 axioms is not excessive.

Fig. 5 explores the performance of our system in detail. Fig. 5a gives the time to generate all terms of sizes 10 (first column) and 11 (second column) respectively. We see that the number of terms does increase significantly with

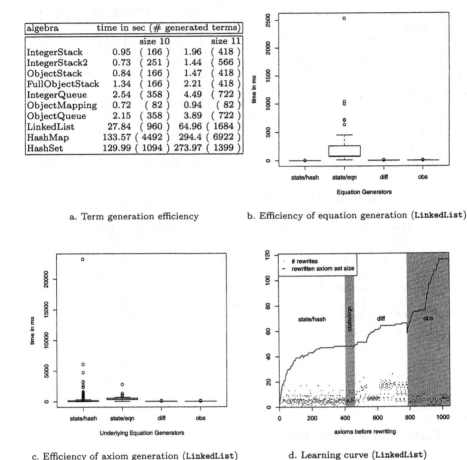

algebra	time in sec (# generated terms)			
	size 10		size 11	
IntegerStack	0.95	(166)	1.96	(418)
IntegerStack2	0.73	(251)	1.44	(566)
ObjectStack	0.84	(166)	1.47	(418)
FullObjectStack	1.34	(166)	2.21	(418)
IntegerQueue	2.54	(358)	4.49	(722)
ObjectMapping	0.72	(82)	0.94	(82)
ObjectQueue	2.15	(358)	3.89	(722)
LinkedList	27.84	(960)	64.96	(1684)
HashMap	133.57	(4492)	294.4	(6922)
HashSet	129.99	(1094)	273.97	(1399)

a. Term generation efficiency

b. Efficiency of equation generation (LinkedList)

c. Efficiency of axiom generation (LinkedList)

d. Learning curve (LinkedList)

Fig. 5. Efficiency and effectiveness of our tool

term length, even though we prune away many useless terms. We also see that classes with a large number of terms (e.g., HashSet) are the ones that take the most time in our system.

Fig. 5b and c are box plots that give the distribution of the time to generate the different kinds of equations and axioms for LinkedList. As an example, consider the state/eqn plot in Fig. 5b. The box denotes the interquartile range, which contains the 50% of the values that fall within the second and third quartile. The line inside the box is the median, which overlaps with the bottom of the box due to a strong bias towards low values. Values above the whisker are outliers. From Fig. 5b and c we see that the state axioms and equations are the most expensive to generate with state/eqn being the slowest. For the most part, observer and difference equations and axioms are fast to generate and all equations and axioms of those type take approximately the same time. These results suggest that it may be worthwhile to try other orderings or kinds of equations in order to speed up the equation and axiom generation.

Fig. 5d gives insight into the behavior of our tool when discovering axioms for LinkedList. The x axis denotes time in terms of axioms generated by the axiom generator. The "learning curve" is the number of axioms that have been discovered and rewritten. Note that this curve does not ascend monotonically, as the discovery of one axiom can lead to the elimination of numerous other axioms. The dots denote the number of rewriting events per discovered axiom. We run our system as follows: first, we discover state axioms using the hash table optimization (state/hash), then we generate the general state axioms (state/eqn), then we generate the difference axioms and finally the observer axioms. The shaded areas in Fig. 5d denote these different zones.

4.2   Coverage Measurements

Since our system is based on a dynamic approach it is neither sound nor complete. One way in which our system can fail to be sound is if the generated terms do not adequately exercise the full range of behavior of the class under consideration. In this section we use basic block coverage to determine the effectiveness of our term generator in exploring the class code.

Overall, we find that our terms yield a high coverage: 100% for ObjectStack, FullObjectStack, IntegerQueue, IntegerStack2, ObjectMapping, and ObjectQueue; 62.5% for IntegerStack; 72.8% for LinkedList; 84.6% for HashSet; and 73.3% for HashMap. When our coverage is less than 100% it is often because our terms do not adequately explore the argument space for operations (e.g., for *LinkedList* we did not generate a term that called removeAll with a collection that contains a subset of the receiver's elements). Other reasons include: dead code (e.g., some code in LinkedList.subList); corner cases (e.g., corner cases for initialCapacity in HashTable).

We are currently using these results and observations to improve our tool.

Table 3. Representative selection of example axioms

1	$intPlus(0,1).retval = 1$
2	$\forall x_0 : HashMap\ (\ size(x_0).state = x_0\ )$
3	$\forall x_0 : HashMap\ (\ putAll(x_0,x_0).state = x_0\ )$
4	$\forall x_0 : HashMap, \forall x_1, \forall x_2 : Object\ (\ get(put(x_0,x_1,x_2).state, x_1).retval = x_2\ )$
5	$\forall x_0 : Object\ (\ get(put(HashMap().state, Object@0, x_0).state, Object@1).retval = \text{null}\ )$
6	$\forall x_0 : LinkedList, \forall x_1 : Integer\ (addAll(x_0,x_1,LinkedList().state).state = x_0\ )$

4.3   Manual Inspection of Axioms

To make sure that the axioms discovered by our tool were correct, we manually verified the generated axioms for all classes and found no mistakes in the axioms. The axioms though many for some classes (e.g., *LinkedList*), were relatively easy to read (at most an hour of our time per class).

Table 3 gives a few sample axioms from our tool. Axiom 1 in Table 3 is a trivial one and arises because our tool does not have background axioms for integer arithmetic.

Axiom 2 says that invoking *size* on a *HashMap* does not modify its internal state. Our system generates such axioms for each pure observer (i.e., an operation that has a non-void return value and does not change the state of the object), for example, it finds 16 such axioms for *LinkedList*.

Axiom 3 says that if we add all mappings of a *HashMap* into an equivalent *HashMap*, the receiver's state does not change. Axiom 4 gives a partial characterization of the *get* and *put* operations.

Axiom 5 is one of the axioms that could be more abstract if our tool would support conditional axioms: Instead of using the constants Object@0 and Object@1, the axiom could then be rewritten into

$$\forall \bullet_0 \bullet\bullet_1 \bullet\bullet_2 : Object$$
$$\bullet_1 \neq \bullet_2 \Rightarrow get(put(HashMap()\bullet state\bullet\bullet_1 \bullet\bullet_0)\bullet state\bullet\bullet_2)\bullet retval = \text{null}$$

Axiom 6 points out an incompletely specified behavior in the documentation for *LinkedList*. *addAll* adds all elements in the third argument to $\bullet_1$ at position $\bullet_0$. Axiom 6 says that no matter what position we specify, adding an empty list to $\bullet_1$ does not modify $\bullet_1$. In other words, *addAll* does not verify that $\bullet_0$ is within the bounds of the list.

Finally, it is worth noting that while we can manually verify that the axioms generated by our tool are correct, it is much harder to verify that our tool generates all the axioms needed to fully specify the interface of a class.

5   Limitations and Future Work

The limitations of our implementation fall into three categories: unsoundness, incompleteness, and inefficiency. Our future work will strive for improvements in each of these areas. Note that given a time limit, better efficiency will allow us to execute more tests and discover more axioms and thus improve soundness and completeness.

- **Limited Side Effects.** We currently allow only side effects to the receiver of a method. This means that our specifications may be unsound since non-equivalent states are considered equivalent, and they may be incomplete because some side-effects are not described. Section 3.1 sketches how to deal with side effects to non-receiver arguments. We are also planning to model some interactions between objects that we are currently unable to capture.

- **Arguments to Methods Are Naively Generated.** Currently, our methodology for choosing arguments for methods is insensitive to the body of a method. We plan to use domain analysis [31] to select arguments more carefully in order to achieve better coverage faster. Also, we plan to extended domain analysis beyond simple types. This will improve the efficiency of our tool.
- **No Support for Conditional Axioms.** Support for conditional axioms would enhance completeness. We can support conditional axioms by changing the abstraction mechanism in the axiom generator (Section 3.5). More specifically, if a particular test case does not satisfy an axiom, we can add it to an exception set and then derive a constraint for the conditional axiom from the exception set. capture the same information.
- **Measuring Unsoundness and Incompleteness.** We plan to use the axioms to emulate the data types that they describe. This can be achieved by re-generating implementations from our discovered specifications (e.g., [33, 38]). Using the generated implementation in parallel with the original implementation for realistic benchmark programs will allow us to study the soundness and completeness of our tool in practice.

6   Related Work

We now describe related work in algebraic specifications, dynamic invariant detection, automatic programming, static analysis, and testing.

6.1   Algebraic Specifications

We drew many ideas and inspirations from previous work in algebraic specifications for abstract data types [22]. Horebeek and Lewi [28] give a good introduction to algebraic specifications. Sannella *et al.* give an overview of and motivation for the theory behind algebraic specifications [41]. A book by Astesiano *et al.* contains reports of recent developments in the algebraic specification community [5].

Antoy describes how to systematically design algebraic specifications [3]. In particular, he describes techniques that can help to identify whether a specification is complete. His observations could be used in our setting; however, they are limited to a particular class of algebras.

Prior work demonstrates that algebraic specifications are useful for a variety of tasks. Rugaber *et al.* study the adequacy of algebraic specifications for a reengineering task [38]. They specified an existing system using algebraic specifications and were able to regenerate the system from the specifications using a code generator. Janicki *et al.* find that for defining abstract data types, algebraic specifications are preferable over the trace assertion method [6, 30]

6.2 Dynamic Invariant Detection

Recently, there has been much work on dynamic invariant detection [15, 44, 1, 23]. Dynamic invariant detection systems discover specifications by learning general properties of a program's execution from a set of program runs.

Daikon [15] discovers Hoare-style axiomatic specifications [27, 20]. Daikon is useful for understanding *how* something is implemented, but also exposes the full complexity of a given implementation. Daikon has been improved in many ways [16, 17, 13] and has been used for various applications including program evolution [15], refactoring [32], test suite quality evaluation [24], bug detection [23], and as a generator of specifications that are then checked statically [36].

Whaley *et al.* [44] describe how to discover specifications that are finite state machines describing in which order method calls can be made to a given object. Similarly, Ammons *et al.* extract nondeterministic finite state automatons (NFAs) that model temporal and data dependencies in APIs from C code [1]. These specifications are not nearly as expressive as algebraic specifications, since they cannot capture what values are returned by the methods.

Our preliminary studies show that the current implementation of our tool does not scale as well as some of the systems mentioned above. However, we are unaware of any dynamic tool that discovers high-level specifications of the interfaces of classes. Also, unlike prior work, our system interleaves automatic test generation and specification discovery. All previous systems require a test suite.

6.3 Automatic Programming

Automatic programming systems [7, 9, 8, 2, 25, 43] discover programs from examples or synthesize programs from specifications by deduction. The programs are analogous to our specifications in that our specifications are high-level descriptions of examples. Algorithmic program debugging [42] is similar to automatic programming and uses an inductive inference procedure to test side-effect and loop-free programs based on input output examples and then helps users to interactively correct the bugs in the program. Unlike the above techniques whose goals are to generate programs or find bugs, the goal of our system is to generate formal specifications (which could, of course, be used to generate programs or find bugs).

6.4 Static Analysis

Program analyses generate output that describes the behavior of the program. For example, shape analyses [39] describe the shape of data structures and may be useful for debugging. Type inference systems, such as Lackwit [37] generate types that describe the flow of values in a program. Our system is a dynamic black-box technique that does not need to look at the code to be effective. However, various static techniques can be used to guide our system (for example, we have already experimented with mod-ref analyses).

6.5 Testing

Woodward describes a methodology for *mutation testing* algebraic specifications [45]. Mutation testing introduces one change ("mutations") to a specification to check the coverage of a test set. Woodward's system includes a simple test generation method that uses the signatures of specifications.

Algebraic specifications have been used successfully to test implementations of abstract data types [18, 40, 29, 4]. One of the more recent systems, Daistish [29] allows for the algebraic testing of OO programs in the presence of side effects. In Daistish, the user defines a mapping between an algebraic specification and an implementation of the specification. The system then checks whether the axioms hold, given user-defined test vectors. Similarly, the system by Antoy *et al.* [4] requires the users to give explicit mappings between specification and implementation. Our system automatically generates both the mapping and the test suite.

Our work builds upon Doong and Frankl's definition of observational equivalence and we were inspired by their algorithm for generating test cases from algebraic specifications [14]. Their system semi-automatically checks implementations against generated test cases. Later work improved on Doong and Frankl's test case generation mechanism [12] by combining white-box and black-box techniques. Our tool can potentially benefit from employing static analysis of the code when generating test cases (white box testing).

In addition to the above, prior work on test-case generation [26, 11, 34] is also relevant to our work, particularly where it deals with term generation. Also, methods for evaluating test suites or test selection [46, 19] are relevant. We do not use these techniques yet but expect that they will be useful in improving the speed of our tool and the quality of the axioms.

Korat is a system for automated testing of Java programs [10]. Korat translates a given method's pre- and post-conditions into Java predicates, generates an exhaustive set of test cases within a finite domain using the pre-condition predicate and checks the correctness of the method by applying the post-condition predicate. Our approach for generating terms borrows ideas from Korat.

7 Conclusion

We describe a dynamic approach for automatically discovering algebraic specifications from Java classes. These specifications are in the form of axioms in terms of public methods of classes. Thus, they describe the observable behavior of classes and are not burdened by implementation details. Since our approach is dynamic our system is neither sound nor complete. However, compared to other dynamic systems, our system generates its own test cases (terms) and can thus keep generating more terms until it attains adequate confidence in the discovered axioms. For example, our system may determine that the basic block coverage for the test cases is inadequate and may decide to generate further test cases.

Our experiments with a number of Java classes reveals that our system generates axioms that are both correct and useful for understanding and using these classes. Our experiments also reveal some situations when our approach fails to discover certain axioms. More specifically, we find situations where conditional axioms would be useful.

Finally, our approach is not specific to Java but can be applied to other object-oriented languages that have sufficient reflection capabilities.

Acknowledgements

We thank Michael Burke, Dan Connors, Daniel von Dincklage, Matthias Hauswirth, Martin Hirzel, James Martin, Christoph Reichenbach, William Waite, Alexander Wolf, and the anonymous POPL and ECOOP reviewers for their insightful comments and suggestions on the paper and on earlier versions.

References

[1] Glenn Ammons, Rastislav Bodik, and James R. Larus. Mining specifications. In *Proceedings of the 29th ACM SIGPLAN-SIGACT Symposium on Principles of Programming Languages*, pages 4–16, 2002.

[2] Dana Angluin. Inference of reversible languages. *Journal of the ACM (JACM)*, 29(3):741–765, 1982.

[3] S. Antoy. Systematic design of algebraic specifications. In *Proceedings of the Fifth International Workshop on Software Specification and Design*, Pittsburgh, Pennsylvania, 1989.

[4] S. Antoy and D. Hamlet. Automatically checking an implementation against its formal specification. *IEEE Transactions on Software Engineering*, 26(1), January 2000.

[5] E. Astesiano, H.-J. Kreowski, and B. Krieg-Brückner, editors. *Algebraic Foundations of Systems Specification*. Springer, 1999.

[6] W. Bartussek and D. L. Parnas. Using assertions about traces to write abstract specifications for software modules. In *Information Systems Methodology: Proceedings, 2nd Conference of the European Cooperation in Informatics, Venice, October 1978; Lecture Notes in Computer Science*, volume 65. Springer Verlag, 1978.

[7] A. W. Biermann. On the inference of turing machines from sample computations. *Artificial Intelligence*, 3:181–198, 1972.

[8] Alan W. Biermann. The inference of regular Lisp programs from examples. *IEEE Transactions on Systems, Man, and Cybernetics*, 8:585–600, August 1978.

[9] Alan W. Biermann and Ramachandran Krishnaswamy. Constructing programs from example computations. *IEEE Transactions on Software Engineering*, 2(3):141–153, September 1976.

[10] C. Boyapati, S. Khurshid, and D. Marinov. Korat: Automated testing based on java predicates. In *International Symposium on Software Testing and Analysis*, Rome, Italy, July 2002.

[11] U. Buy, A. Orso, and M. Pezze. Automated testing of classes. In *Proceedings of the International Symposium on Software Testing and Analysis*, Portland, Oregon, 2000.

[12] H. Y. Chen, T. H. Tse, F. T. Chan, and T. Y. Chen. In black and white: An integrated approach to class-level testing of object oriented programs. *ACM Transactions on Software Engineering*, 7(3), July 1998.

[13] Nii Dodoo, Alan Donovan, Lee Lin, and Michael D. Ernst. Selecting predicates for implications in program analysis.
http://pag.lcs.mit.edu/~mernst/pubs/invariants-implications.pdf,
March 2002.

[14] R. Doong and P. G. Frankl. The ASTOOT approach to testing object-oriented programs. *ACM Transactions on Software Engineering*, 3(2), April 1994.

[15] Michael D. Ernst, Jake Cockrell, William G. Griswold, and David Notkin. Dynamically discovering likely program invariants to support program evolution. *ACM Transactions on Software Engineering*, 27(2):1–25, February 2001.

[16] Michael D. Ernst, Adam Czeisler, William G. Griswold, and David Notkin. Quickly detecting relevant program invariants. In *Proceedings of the 22nd International Conference on Software Engineering*, pages 449–458, June 2000.

[17] Michael D. Ernst, William G. Griswold, Yoshio Kataoka, and David Notkin. Dynamically discovering program invariants involving collections. TR UW-CSE-99-11-02, University of Washington, 2000. revised version of March 17, 2000.

[18] J. Gannon, P. McMullin, and R. Hamlet. Databstraction implementation, specification and testing. *ACM Transactions on Programming Languages and Systems*, 3(3):211–223, 1981.

[19] Todd L. Graves, Mary Jean Harrold, Jung-Min Kim, Adam Porter, and Gregg Rothermel. An empirical study of regression test selection techniques. *ACM Transactions on Software Engineering and Methodology (TOSEM)*, 10(2):184–208, 2001.

[20] David Gries. *The science of programming*. Texts and monographs in computer science. Springer-Verlag, 1981.

[21] J. V. Guttag, J. J. Hornig, S. J. Garland, K. D. Jones, A. Modet, and J. M. Wing. *Larch: Languages and Tools for Formal Specification*. Springer Verlag, 1993. (out of print).

[22] J. V. Guttag and J. J. Horning. The algebraic specification of abstract data types. *Acta Informatica*, 10:27–52, 1978.

[23] Sudheendra Hangal and Monica S. Lam. Tracking down software bugs using automatic anomaly detection. In *Proceedings of the International Conference on Software Engineering*, pages 291–301, May 2002.

[24] Michael Harder, Benjamin Morse, and Michael D. Ernst. Specification coverage as a measure of test suite quality. Septermber 25, 2001.

[25] Steven Hardy. Synthesis of Lisp functions from examples. In *Proceedings of the Fourth International Joint Conference on Artificial Intelligence*, pages 240–245, 1975.

[26] Richard Helm, Ian M. Holland, and Dipayan Gangopadhyay. Contracts: specifying behavioral compositions in object-oriented systems. In *Proceedings of the European conference on object-oriented programming on Object-oriented programming systems, languages, and applications*, pages 169–180. ACM Press, 1990.

[27] C. A. R. Hoare. An axiomatic basis for computer programming. *Communications of the ACM*, 12(10):576–580, 1969.

[28] Ivo Van Horebeek and Johan Lewi. *Algebraic specifications in software engineering: an introduction*. Springer-Verlag, 1989.

[29] M. Hughes and D. Stotts. Daistish: Systematic algebraic testing for OO programs in the presence of side-effects. In *Proceedings of the International Symposium on Software Testing and Verification*, San Diego, California, 1996.

[30] R. Janicki and E. Sekerinski. Foundations of the trace assertion method of module interface specification. *ACM Transactions on Software Engineering*, 27(7), July 2001.

[31] B. Jeng and E. J. Weyuker. A simplified domain-testing strategy. *ACM Transactions on Software Engineering*, 3(3):254–270, July 1994.

[32] Yoshio Kataoka, Michael D. Ernst, William G. Griswold, and David Notkin. Automated support for program refactoring using invariants. In *International Conference on Software Maintenance*, Florence, Italy, 2001.

[33] Huimin Lin. Procedural implementation of algebraic specification. *ACM Transactions on Programming Languages and Systems*, 1993.

[34] Vincenco Martena, Alessandro Orso, and Mauro Pezze. Interclass testing of object oriented software. In *Proc. of the IEEE International Conference on Engineering of Complex Computer Systems*, 2002.

[35] John C. Mitchell. *Foundations of Programming Languages*. MIT Press, 1996.

[36] Jeremy W. Nimmer and Michael D. Ernst. Automatic generation of program specifications. In *Proceedings of the 2002 International Symposium on Software Testing and Analysis (ISSTA)*, Rome, July 2002.

[37] Robert O'Callahan and Daniel Jackson. Lackwit: A program understanding tool based on type inference. In *International Conference on Software Engineering*, pages 338–348, 1997.

[38] Spencer Rugaber, Terry Shikano, and R. E. Kurt Stirewalt. Adequate reverse engineering. In *Proceedings of the 16th Annual International Conference on Automated Software Engineering*, pages 232–241, 2001.

[39] Mooly Sagiv, Thomas Reps, and Reinhard Wilhelm. Parametric shape analysis via 3-valued logic. *ACM Transactions on Programming Languages and Systems*, 24(3):217–298, May 2002.

[40] S. Sankar. Run-time consistency checking of algebraic specifications. In *Proceedings of the Symposium on Testing, Analysis, and Verification*, Victoria, British Columbia, Canada, September 1991.

[41] Donald Sannella and Andrzej Tarlecki. Essential concepts of algebraic specification and program development. *Formal Aspects of Computing*, 9:229–269, 1997.

[42] Ehud Y. Shapiro. *Algorithmic Program Debugging*. ACM Distinguished Dissertation 1982. MIT Press, 1982.

[43] Phillip D. Summers. A methodology for lisp program construction from examples. *Journal of the ACM (JACM)*, 24(1):161–175, 1977.

[44] J. Whaley, M. C. Martin, and M. S. Lam. Automatic extraction of object-oriented component interfaces. In *Proceedings of the International Symposium of Software Testing and Analysis*, 2002.

[45] M. R. Woodward. Errors in algebraic specifications and an experimental mutation testing tool. *IEEE Software Engineering Journal*, 8(4):237–245, July 1993.

[46] Hong Zhu, Patrick A. V. Hall, and John H. R. May. Software unit test coverage and adequacy. *ACM Computing Surveys (CSUR)*, 29(4):366–427, 1997.

A Refinement Algebra
for Object-Oriented Programming

Paulo Borba, Augusto Sampaio, and Márcio Cornélio

Informatics Center, Federal University of Pernambuco
Recife, PE, Brazil
Fax: +55 81 32718438
{phmb,acas,mlc2}@cin.ufpe.br

Abstract. In this article we introduce a comprehensive set of algebraic laws for ROOL, a language similar to sequential Java but with a copy semantics. We present a few laws of commands, but focus on the object-oriented features of the language. We show that this set of laws is complete in the sense that it is sufficient to reduce an arbitrary ROOL program to a normal form expressed in a restricted subset of the ROOL operators. We also propose a law for data refinement that generalises the technique from traditional modules to class hierarchies. Together, these laws are expressive enough to derive more elaborate rules that can be useful, for example, to formalize object-oriented design practices; this is illustrated through the systematic derivation of a refactoring from the proposed laws.

1 Introduction

The laws of imperative programming are well-established and have been useful both for assisting software development and for providing precise algebraic programming language semantic definitions [1, 2]. In fact, besides being used as guidelines to informal programming practices, programming laws establish a sound basis for formal and rigorous software development methods. Moreover, algebraic laws have proven to be an important tool for the design of correct compilers and code optimisers [3].

Other programming paradigms have also benefited from algebraic semantics which give a sound basis for program derivation and transformation. The laws of Occam [4], for example, exhibit nice and useful properties of concurrency and communication. Algebraic properties of functional programming are elegantly and deeply addressed in [5]. An algebraic approach to reasoning about logic programming is presented in [6]. Even unifying theories [7] have been proposed to classify and study different paradigms, considering a variety of semantic presentations in an integrated way: denotational, operational and algebraic.

In spite of all these efforts, the laws of object-oriented programming are not yet well-established. Some laws have been informally discussed in the object-oriented literature [8, 9]. Some others have been formalised to the degree that

L. Cardelli (Ed.): ECOOP 2003, LNCS 2743, pp. 457–482, 2003.

they can be encoded in refactoring tools [10, 11], but they have not been formally proved to be sound or complete in any sense. Opdyke [10] proposes a set of preconditions for application of refactorings, whereas Roberts [11] goes a step further introducing postconditions for them. The definition of correctness used by Roberts is based on test suites. There are no formal proofs that refactoring a program preserves its behavior or that it continues meeting its specification. In fact, there seems to be no comprehensive, provably sound, set of laws to help developers understand and use the properties of medium grain programming units, and of mechanisms such as classes, inheritance, and subtyping. Furthermore, some of the laws of imperative programming are not directly applicable to corresponding small grain object-oriented units and constructs. For instance, due to dynamic binding, the laws of procedure calls are not valid for method calls.

Small grain object-oriented constructs have been considered [12, 13], but medium grain constructs have been largely neglected. A great deal of work, as those presented in [14, 15, 16, 17], has already been carried out on transformations for design models in the Unified Modelling Language (UML) [18], but those naturally do not consider programming and behavioral specification constructs. Although those UML transformations are proved sound with respect to a formal semantics, no completeness result has been reported to our knowledge.

In this article we describe a comprehensive set of laws for ROOL (Refinement Object-Oriented Language) [19, 20], which is based on the sequential subset of Java [21] but has a copy semantics. While we illustrate a few laws that deal with the imperative features of the language, we concentrate on laws for its object-oriented features. Besides clarifying aspects of the semantics of ROOL, the laws serve as a basis (interface) for deriving more elaborate rules for practical applications of program transformation. Indeed, we show how the proposed laws can be used to derive refactorings [8] which capture informal object-oriented design and maintenance practices. In addition to algorithmic refinement, we introduce a law for data refinement that allows change of data representation in class hierarchies, contrasting with traditional laws that deal with a single program module [2].

An important contribution of this work is to show that the proposed set of laws for the object-oriented features of ROOL is complete in the sense that it is sufficient to transform an arbitrary program into a normal form expressed in terms of a small subset of the language constructs, following the usual approach adopted for imperative and concurrent languages [1, 4], among others. Using the laws, we describe and justify a strategy for reducing programs to normal form. This does not suggest a compilation process for ROOL; its sole purpose is to prove a completeness result and therefore suggest that our set of laws is expressive enough to derive the more elaborate and useful transformation rules mentioned above. Programs in the normal form defined here have the same type hierarchy as the original program, but with no method declarations, and attribute declarations appearing only in **object**, ROOL's universal class.

This article is organised as follows. We first give an overview of ROOL (Section 2). After that we characterise the normal form and introduce a set of laws for the object-oriented features of ROOL, explaining and justifying how they can be used to define a strategy for reducing an arbitrary program to normal form (Section 3). Some additional laws of commands and expressions, and a law for refining class hierarchies, are presented in Section 4. Then we show how the proposed laws can serve as a basis for proving refactorings (Section 5). Finally, we summarise our results and discuss topics for further research (Section 6).

2   An Overview of ROOL

ROOL is an object-oriented language based on the sequential subset of Java [22] with a copy semantics rather than a reference semantics. The copy semantics significantly simplifies reasoning and still allows us to consider parts of Java programs that do not have reference aliasing. ROOL has been specially designed to allow reasoning about object-oriented programs and specifications, hence it mixes both kinds of constructs in the style of Morgan's refinement calculus [2].

A program in ROOL is written as $cds \bullet c$, for a *main* command c and a set of class declarations cds. Classes are declared as in the following example, where we define a class called *Client*.

> **class** *Client* **extends** *Object*
>   **pri** *name* : *string*; **pri** *addr* : *Address*; ...
>   **meth** *getStreet* $\widehat{=}$ **res** *r* : *string* $\bullet$ $\tilde{\ }$*addr.getStreet*(*r*) **end**;
>   **meth** *setStreet* $\widehat{=}$ **val** *s* : *string* $\bullet$ $\tilde{\ }$*addr.setStreet*(*s*) **end**;
>   **new** $\widehat{=}$ *addr* := **new** *Address* **end**;
> **end**

Subclassing and single inheritance are supported through the **extends** clause. The built-in **object** class is a superclass of any other class in ROOL, so the **extends** clause above could have been omitted. Besides the **pri** qualifier for private attributes, there are visibility qualifiers for protected (**prot**) and public (**pub**) attributes, with similar semantics to Java. For simplicity, ROOL supports no attribute redefinition and has only public methods, which can have value and result parameters. The list of parameters of a method is separated from its body by the symbol '$\bullet$'. Constructors are declared by the **new** clause and do not have parameters. In contrast to Java, ROOL adopts a simple semantics for constructors: they are syntactic sugar for methods that are called after creating objects of the corresponding class.

In addition to method calls, as illustrated in the *Client* class, the body of methods and constructors may have imperative constructs similar to those of the language of Morgan's refinement calculus. This is specified by the definition of the commands of ROOL:

$$
\begin{aligned}
c \in Com ::= {}& le := e \mid c; \; c & \text{assignment, sequence} \\
\mid {}& x : [\psi_1, \psi_2] & \text{specification statement} \\
\mid {}& pc(e) & \text{parameterized command application} \\
\mid {}& \textbf{if } []i : 1 .. n \bullet \psi_i \rightarrow c_i \textbf{ fi} \; \text{alternation} \\
\mid {}& \textbf{rec } X \bullet c \textbf{ end} \mid X & \text{recursion, recursive call} \\
\mid {}& \textbf{var } x : T \bullet c \textbf{ end} & \text{local variable block} \\
\mid {}& \textbf{avar } x : T \bullet c \textbf{ end} & \text{angelic variable block}
\end{aligned}
$$

where le are the expressions allowed to appear as target of assignments and as result arguments. These expressions are defined later. A specification statement $x : [\psi_1, \psi_2]$ is useful to concisely describe a program that can change only the variables listed in the frame x, and when executed in a state that satisfies its precondition ψ_1 terminates in a state satisfying its postcondition ψ_2. The frame x lists the variables whose values may change. Like the languages adopted in other refinement calculi, ROOL is a specification language where programs appear as an executable subset of specifications.

Methods are seen as parameterized commands, which can be applied to a list of arguments to yield a command (the entry '$pc(e)$' in the description of commands). Therefore method calls are represented as the application of parameterized commands:

$$
\begin{aligned}
pc \in PCom ::= {}& pds \bullet c & \text{parameterization} \\
\mid {}& le.m \mid ((N)le).m & \text{method calls} \\
\mid {}& \textbf{self}.m \mid \textbf{super}.m \\
pds \in Pds \; ::= {}& \varnothing \mid pd \mid pd; \; pds & \text{parameter declarations} \\
pd \in Pd \quad ::= {}& \textbf{val } x : T \mid \textbf{res } x : T
\end{aligned}
$$

A parameterized command $pds \bullet c$ has parameters pds that are used in the command c. The parameterized command $le.m$ is a call to method m with target object le. Parameters can be passed by value (**val**) or by result (**res**).

The conditional (alternation) command is written in the same style as in Dijkstra's language. ROOL also provides recursion and variable blocks. Angelic variables are similar to local variables, but they have their initial values angelically chosen so that c succeeds. Data types T are either primitive (**bool**, **int**, and others) or class names. For simplicity, we consider that methods cannot be mutually recursive, but classes can.

For building expressions, ROOL supports typical object-oriented constructs:

$$
\begin{aligned}
e \in Exp ::= {}& \textbf{self} \mid \textbf{super} & \text{special 'references'} \\
\mid {}& \textbf{null} \mid \textbf{new } N & \text{null 'reference', object creation} \\
\mid {}& x \mid f(e) & \text{variable, built-in application} \\
\mid {}& e \textbf{ is } N \mid (N)e & \text{type test, type cast} \\
\mid {}& e.x \mid (e; \; x : e) & \text{attribute selection and update}
\end{aligned}
$$

where **self**, **super** and **is** have similar semantics to `this`, `super` and `instanceof` (which does not require exact type matching) in Java, respectively. The update '$(e_1; \; x : e_2)$' denotes a copy of the object denoted by e_1 but with the attribute x mapped to a copy of the value of e_2, in a similar way to update of arrays in the refinement calculus [2]. So, despite its name, the update expression, similarly to all ROOL expressions, has no side-effects; in fact, it creates a new object instead of updating an existing one. Variables can, however, be updated through the execution of commands, as in $o := (o;\ x : e)$, which is semantically equivalent to $o.x := e$, and updates o. Expressions such as **null**.x and (**null**; $x : e$) cannot be successfully evaluated; they yield the special value **error** and lead the commands in which they appear to *abort*, as explained in the sequel.

The expressions that are allowed to appear as the target of assignments and as result arguments, define the *Le* (*left expressions*) subset of *Exp*:

$$le \in Le ::= le1 \mid \textbf{self}.le1 \mid ((N)le).le1 \qquad\qquad le1 \in Le1 ::= x \mid le1.x$$

From a theoretical point of view, ROOL can be viewed as a complete lattice whose ordering is a refinement relation on specifications. The bottom (**abort**) of this lattice is the worst possible specification:

$$\textbf{abort} = x : [\textbf{false}, \textbf{true}]$$

It is never guaranteed to terminate (precondition **false**), and even when it does, its outcome is completely arbitrary (postcondition **true**). It allows any refinement; for instance, programs setting x to arbitrary values. On the other extreme we have the top (**miracle**) of the lattice; it is the best possible specification

$$\textbf{miracle} = x : [\textbf{true}, \textbf{false}]$$

which can execute in any state (precondition **true**) and establishes as outcome the impossible postcondition **false**.

Although these extreme specifications are not usually deliberately written (**miracle** is not even feasible as an executable program), they are useful for reasoning. For instance, it is normally useful in program derivation or transformation to assume that a condition b holds at a given point in the program text. This can be characterized as an *assumption* of b, designated as $\{b\}$, defined as follows:

$$\{b\} = : [b, \textbf{true}]$$

Note that, if b is **false**, an assumption reduces to **abort**. Otherwise it behaves like a program that always terminates and does nothing, denoted by **skip**:

$$\textbf{skip} = : [\textbf{true}, \textbf{true}]$$

Further considerations about specification statements, ROOL, and its formal semantics based on weakest preconditions are given elsewhere [2, 19, 20]. In the next section, we define algebraic laws for the object-oriented features of ROOL, and show that these laws are complete in the sense that they can be used to define a normal form for ROOL. We give more details about the language constructs only when necessary.

3   A Normal Form for Class Hierarchies

In order to show that the proposed set of laws is comprehensive, we define a reduction strategy (based on the laws) whose target is a normal form described in terms of a restricted subset of the ROOL operators.

Definition 1 *(Subtype Normal Form) A* ROOL *program cds • c is in Subtype Normal Form if it obeys the following conditions:*

- *Each class declaration in cds, except* **object**, *has an empty body; the inheritance and subtype clause* **extends** *might be included, but no declaration of methods, constructors or attributes is allowed in subclasses.*
- *The* **object** *class may include only attribute declarations, each with either a primitive type or* **object** *itself.*
- *All local declarations in the main command c are declared with either a primitive type or* **object**.
- *No type cast is allowed in c.*

Although this normal form still preserves some object-oriented features (the subtype hierarchy, object creation and type test) it is substantially close to an imperative program. In particular, the **object** class, the only one with explicitly declared elements, takes the form of a recursive record, as only attributes are permitted. As no methods are allowed, the main command c also looks very much like an imperative program, although object creation and type test can still be used.

Further reduction could lead to the complete elimination of all object-oriented features, in which case the natural normal form would be the imperative subset of ROOL extended with recursive records. A reduction to such a form would require some sort of encoding in the style of a mapping from an object to a relational model, as an extra variable (attribute or field) would be necessary to keep the type information. We target the Subtype Normal Form, which is sufficiently close to an imperative program, and the additional laws for a reduction to a pure imperative program can be easily identified, as further discussed in Section 4.

The reduction strategy involves the following major steps:

- Move all the code (attribute and method declarations) in *cds* to the **object** class;
- Change all the declarations of object identifiers to type **object**;
- Eliminate casts;
- Eliminate method calls and declarations.

In the remainder of this section we present the reduction strategy in detail, as a sequence of simple and incremental steps.

3.1   General Assumptions

Before we start the detailed presentation of the reduction strategy, we introduce some simple and syntactic conditions that will ensure the applicability of the laws and the convergence of the overall strategy. The following conditions are assumed:

1. In the set of class declarations *cds*, two distinct classes are not allowed to declare attributes with the same name.
2. Similarly, two distinct classes in *cds* are not allowed to declare methods with the same name, except in the case where a method of a superclass is being redefined.
3. All references to an attribute or method *op* are of the form *e.op*, for any expression *e*, including **self**.

The first two conditions are necessary to ensure that the laws to move attributes and methods up in the inheritance hierarchy are always applicable, not generating name conflicts. The third condition allows a uniform treatment of attribute and method occurrences. The roles of these conditions are further motivated in the detailed normal form reduction steps which follow. It is important to note that they do not impose any significant constraint on our approach; they can be easily achieved by simple automatic purely syntactic transformations. Moreover, our laws are also valid for programs that do not satisfy these conditions. The conditions are only necessary for simplifying the normal form reduction process, which will not need intermediate steps for simply renaming methods and attributes.

3.2 Make Attributes Public

Aiming to move all the code up to **object**, the first step in our reduction strategy (process) would be to move attributes up. But before that we should make sure that they are either public or protected, otherwise method declarations in the subclasses might become invalid. For simplicity, we make all attributes public so that we have to deal only with this case in the remaining steps of the reduction process.

In order to make attributes public, we apply two laws. The following one indicates that a protected attribute can be turned into a public one, and vice-versa, provided that the attribute is only directly used by its class and the associated subclasses. This proviso is necessary to guarantee that the law relates valid ROOL programs. We use the notation '**prot** $a : T$; *ads*' to denote the set of attribute declarations containing '**prot** $a : T$' and all the declarations in *ads*, whereas *ops* stands for the declarations of operations (object constructor and methods). Equivalence of sets of class declarations cds_1 and cds_2 is denoted by $cds_1 =_{cds,c} cds_2$, where *cds* is the context of 'auxiliary' declarations for cds_1 and cds_2, and *c* is the main program. This is just an abbreviation for the corresponding behavioural program equivalence: $cds_1 \, cds \bullet c = cds_2 \, cds \bullet c$ [20].

Law 1 ⟨change visibility: from protected to public⟩

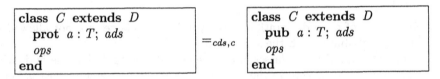

provided

(←) $B.a$, for all $B \leq C$, appears only in *ops* and in the subclasses of C in *cds*.

The typed name $B.a$ refers to uses of the attribute name a via expressions of type B. So when we write that $B.a$ does not appear in *ops* we mean that *ops* does not contain any expression in the form $e.a$ for any expression e of type B, strictly (that is, the type of e cannot be a subclass of B). The subclass relation is denoted by $\leq$, or $\leq_{cds}$ when the set of auxiliary class declarations *cds* is not clear from the context.

Since we want to turn protected attributes into public ones, we should apply Law 1 from left to right. In this direction, the condition for applying the law is trivially valid since a protected attribute can only appear inside its class and the associated subclasses. In fact, the above condition is relevant only when applying the law in the other direction, for turning a public attribute into a protected one. That is why we write '(←)' before the condition. We also write '(→)', when a proviso is necessary only for applying a law from left to right, and '(↔)', when it is necessary in both directions.

For turning the private attributes into public ones, we apply the following law from left to right. The proviso is trivially valid for similar reasons to the ones discussed for the previous law.

Law 2 ⟨change visibility: from private to public⟩

class C extends D
  pri $a : T$; *ads*
  ops
end
	$=_{cds,c}$	class C extends D
		  pub $a : T$; *ads*
		  ops
		end

provided

(←) $B.a$, for all $B \leq C$, does not appear in *cds*, *c*.

Another obvious law related to the previous ones allows us to change attribute visibility from private to protected. This is omitted here since it is not necessary in our reduction strategy; it can also be trivially derived from the previous two laws.

By exhaustively applying Laws 1 and 2 to all classes in *cds*, in any order, we turn all protected and private attributes into public ones.

3.3 Move Attributes Up

After making all attributes public, we can move them up to the **object** class. This is justified by the following law. It establishes that we can move a public attribute from a subclass to a superclass as long as this does not generate a name conflict, such as when a superclass and one of its subclasses declare an attribute with the same name[1]. This law also indicates that we can move the attribute in the other direction provided that it is used only as if it were declared in the subclass, otherwise we would obtain an invalid program.

Law 3 ⟨move attribute to superclass⟩

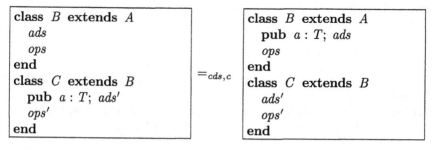

provided

> (→) The attribute name a is not declared by the subclasses of B in cds;
> (←) $D.a$, for all $D \leq B$ and $D \not\leq C$, does not appear in cds, c, ops or ops'.

Notice that, according to the special notation $D.a$ previously introduced, the second condition above precludes an expression such as **self**.a from appearing in ops, but does not preclude **self**.$c.a$, for an attribute '$c : C$' declared in B. The last expression is valid in ops no matter a is declared in B or in C.

Starting from the bottom of the class hierarchy defined by cds and moving upwards in the hierarchy towards **object**, the exhaustive application of this law, from left to right, will move all attributes to **object**. The name conflicts that could be generated during this process are avoided because, as mentioned in Section 3.1, we assume that no two classes declare attributes with the same name; this can be easily achieved by renaming attributes. Therefore the condition for applying the law from left to right becomes trivially valid.

3.4 Trivial Cast Introduction

To enable and simplify the next steps, we generate a uniform program text in which occurrences of an identifier are cast wherever possible. Casts will not be introduced only for primitive type identifiers and for occurrences of identifiers as targets of assignments or result arguments, since this is not allowed in ROOL. This step is necessary, for instance, to guarantee that method bodies are valid

---

[1] ROOL does not allow attribute redefinition or hiding as in Java.

when moved to a superclass. For example, a method body such as $x :=$ **self** would not be valid in a superclass, assuming that the type of x is a subclass C, but the corresponding body with a cast, $x := (C)$**self**, would be valid.

The following law formalizes the fact that any expression can be trivially cast with its own type. The notation $cds, N \rhd e : T$ asserts that the expression e that can appear in the body of a method in class N has type T. Similarly, the notation $cds, N \rhd c = d$ indicates that the equation $c = d$ holds inside class named N, in a context defined by the set of class declarations cds. Instead of a class name, we use **main** in the notations above for asserting that the typing or equality holds inside the main program.

Law 4 ⟨introduce trivial cast in expressions⟩
If $cds, A \rhd e : C$, then

$$cds, A \rhd e = (C)e$$

This is formalised as a law of expressions, not commands. It can be considered as an abbreviation for several laws of assignments, conditionals, and method calls that deal with each possible pattern of expressions. For example, it abbreviates the following laws all with a similar antecedent to Law 4.

$$cds, A \rhd (le := e.x) = le := ((C)e).x$$
$$cds, A \rhd le.m(e) = le.m((C)e)$$

This is equally valid for left-expressions, which are a form of expression.

The previous two laws are sufficient to introduce trivial casts in an arbitrary ROOL program. As a result, all non-assignable object expressions are cast, either because they were originally cast, or because casts were introduced by the current step of our reduction strategy. An additional observation, however, is that the transformations described by the above laws (as well as subsequent laws which relate commands) must be carried out not only inside classes, but also in the main program.

3.5 Eliminate Super

Before moving methods up to **object**, we should also make sure that their bodies do not contain references to **super**, otherwise the program semantics could not be preserved. Indeed, when moving a method up, instead of referring to a method m of an immediate superclass C we might end up referring to the method m of a superclass of C. Furthermore, the resulting program could even be invalid, since **super** cannot appear in **object**.

Our approach for eliminating **super** relies on the following law, which indicates that we can replace a method call using **super** by a copy of the method's body declared in the superclass, provided the body does not contain **super** nor private attributes, which would not be visible in the subclass.

Law 5 ⟨eliminate **super**⟩
Consider that CDS is a set of two class declarations such as the following:

```
class B extends A
  ads
  meth m ≘ pc end; ops
end
class C extends B
  ads'
  ops'
end
```

If **super** and the private attributes in *ads* do not appear in *pc*, we have that

$$cds\ CDS, C \rhd \textbf{super}.m = pc$$

where '*cds CDS*' denotes the union of the class declarations in *cds* and *CDS*.

However, notice that a method called via **super** is not always declared in the immediate superclass of the class where the call appears. In this situation Law 5 cannot be applied. So, in order to avoid that situation, we apply the following law before eliminating **super**. It basically says that we can introduce or remove a trivial method redefinition.

Law 6 ⟨introduce method redefinition⟩

<table>
<tr>
<td>

```
class B extends A
  ads
  meth m ≘ pc end; ops
end
class C extends B
  ads'
  ops'
end
```

</td>
<td>=</td>
<td>

```
class B extends A
  ads
  meth m ≘ pc end; ops
end
class C extends B
  ads'
  meth m ≘ super.m end;
  ops'
end
```

</td>
</tr>
</table>

provided

(→) *m* is not declared in *ops'*.

Strictly, we cannot define a method as **meth** $m \hateq \textbf{super}.m$. A method declaration is an explicit parametrised command, so that, above, *pc* has the form (*pds* • *c*); the redefinition of *m* should be **meth** $m \hateq (pds \bullet \textbf{super}.m(\alpha pds))$, where *αpds* gives the list of parameter names declared in *pds*. For simplicity, however, we adopt the shorter notation **meth** $m \hateq \textbf{super}.m$.

In fact, for eliminating **super**, we first introduce several method redefinitions using **super** itself. This is exhaustively done by applying Law 6, from left to right, whenever the proviso is valid, for all methods of all superclasses in *cds*, starting from **object** and moving downwards in the class hierarchy.

After introducing the trivial method redefinitions, every class will redefine (trivially or not) all the methods in its superclass. So we can exhaustively apply Law 5, from left to right, for eliminating all method calls using **super**. This elimination process starts at the immediate subclasses of **object** and move downwards. As the methods of **object** cannot refer to **super**, and all attributes are already public at this point, the conditions of Law 5 are valid for the immediate subclasses of **object**. After eliminating **super** from those classes, the conditions will be valid for their immediate subclasses and so on.

3.6   Move Methods Up

After introducing trivial casts and eliminating **super**, we can safely move methods up to **object**. This is justified by two laws. We apply the first one when the method declaration that we want to move up is a redefinition of a method declared in the immediate superclass. This law states that we can merge the two method declarations into a single one in the superclass. The resulting method body uses type tests to choose the appropriate behaviour. As mentioned in Section 3.1, **self** is not omitted in calls and selections of methods and attributes of the same class where they appear.

Law 7 ⟨move redefined method to superclass⟩

$$
\begin{array}{l}
\textbf{class } B \textbf{ extends } A \\
\quad ads \\
\quad \textbf{meth } m \mathrel{\widehat{=}} pds \bullet b \textbf{ end}; \\
\quad ops \\
\textbf{end} \\
\textbf{class } C \textbf{ extends } B \\
\quad ads' \\
\quad \textbf{meth } m \mathrel{\widehat{=}} pds \bullet b' \textbf{ end}; \\
\quad ops' \\
\textbf{end}
\end{array}
\quad =_{cds,c} \quad
\begin{array}{l}
\textbf{class } B \textbf{ extends } A \\
\quad ads \\
\quad \textbf{meth } m \mathrel{\widehat{=}} pds \bullet \\
\qquad \textbf{if } \neg(\textbf{self is } C) \;\rightarrow\; b \\
\qquad [\!] \; \textbf{self is } C \;\rightarrow\; b' \\
\qquad \textbf{fi} \\
\quad \textbf{end}; \; ops \\
\textbf{end} \\
\textbf{class } C \textbf{ extends } B \\
\quad ads' \\
\quad ops' \\
\textbf{end}
\end{array}
$$

provided

    (↔) **super** and private attributes do not appear in b';
        super.m does not appear in ops';
    (→) b' does not contain uncast occurrences of **self** nor expressions in
        the form $((C)\textbf{self}).a$ for any private or protected attribute a in ads';
    (←) m is not declared in ops'.

Most of these provisos are necessary to guarantee that the application of the law to a valid ROOL program yields a valid program as well. The exceptions are those concerning **super**; the semantics of expressions and commands that use this construct might be affected by moving code from a subclass to a superclass, or vice-versa, as discussed in Section 3.5.

    The other law that justifies moving methods up should be applied when the method that we want to move is not a redefinition. In this case we can only move a method up if this does not introduce a name conflict[2]. The law indicates

---

[2] ROOL supports method overriding but not method overloading in general. Hence we cannot have different methods in the same class, or in a class and a subclass, with the same name but different parameters.

that we can move a method down too, if this method is used only as if it were defined in the subclass.

Law 8 ⟨move original method to superclass⟩

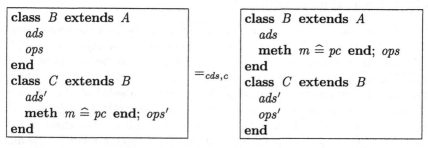

provided

(↔) **super** and private attributes do not appear in pc;
   m is not declared in any superclass of B in cds;

(→) m is not declared in ops, and can only be declared in a class D, for
   all $D \leq B$ and $D \not\leq C$, if it has the same parameters as pc;
   pc does not contain uncast occurrences of **self** nor expressions in
   the form $((C)\textbf{self}).a$ for any private or protected attribute a in
   ads';

(←) m is not declared in ops';
   $D.m$, for all $D \leq B$, does not appear in cds, c, ops or ops'.

The conditions for applying this law are similar to the ones of Laws 7 and 3. Only the first two are necessary to preserve semantics. The others guarantee that we relate only syntactically valid programs. We preclude superclasses of B from defining m because this could affect the semantics of commands such as '$b.m(...)$', for a b storing an object of B, when moving the declaration of m.

Using Laws 7, 8, and 4 we can move all method declarations to **object**. We start from the bottom of the class hierarchy defined by cds and move upwards to **object**. In a given class C, it does not matter if we move first the methods that do not call other methods declared in C; even the calls for methods of C not declared in its superclass will be valid in the superclass since at this point the occurrences of **self** are all cast. In order to maintain that, we need to apply Law 4 immediately after applying Law 7, since the last one introduces two uncast references to **self**.

Following this process, the conditions for applying Law 7 from left to right are valid because, at this phase of the reduction to normal form, all attributes are already public and declared in **object** (so ads' is empty), and all method bodies do not use the **super** construct nor have uncast references to **self** (which is a non-assignable expression). This also explains why some of the conditions for applying Law 8 from left to right are valid too. In order to understand why the other conditions are valid, recall from Section 3.1 that method names cannot be reused and notice that, after eliminating **super** (see Section 3.5), every class redefines the methods in its superclass. So if a method m is declared in C but not in B, we can then assume that it is not declared in any superclass of B.

3.7   Change Type to Object

After moving all the code up, we eliminate type casts from the entire program. This is the purpose of this and the following step. One immediate condition to eliminate type casts in general is that all the identifiers (attributes, local variables and parameters names) that have a class type[3] must have the same type. In order to illustrate that, consider a class A, a subclass B of A, and the following declarations: '$a : A$' and '$b : B$'. Then, in ROOL (as well as in Java) the assignment of a to b must be cast, as in '$b := (B)a$'. Therefore, unless we replace the types of those identifiers with a single type, we will not be able to get rid of arbitrary type casts. The natural candidate type to play this role is the **object** class.

Surprisingly, perhaps, changing the type of an identifier to a superclass of its declared type can be justified provided all the occurrences of such an identifier in non-assignable expressions—that is, when not used as target of assignments and result arguments—are cast with its original type. The reason is that in this case one cannot distinguish between an identifier being declared with its original type or with a supertype of this type. The apparent paradox comes from the fact that eliminating casts requires changing the types of identifiers, and that may require the introduction of type casts. Nevertheless, as seen in Section 3.4, the introduction of such casts is trivial, because the casts are always to the declared types of the identifiers.

Here we need some laws to formalize the fact that the types of identifiers for attributes, variables, and value parameters can be replaced with a supertype if all occurrences of these identifiers in non-assignable expressions are cast. In such cases, the change of type will cause no interference, as already explained. As an example, we present a law for attributes. The laws for variables and parameters are similar. For a result parameter, we require, in addition, the types of the corresponding arguments to be greater than or equal to the new parameter type.

Law 9 ⟨change attribute type⟩

$$
\boxed{\begin{array}{l} \textbf{class } C \textbf{ extends } D \\ \quad \textbf{pub } a : T;\ ads \\ \quad ops \\ \textbf{end} \end{array}} \quad =_{cds,c} \quad \boxed{\begin{array}{l} \textbf{class } C \textbf{ extends } D \\ \quad \textbf{pub } a : T';\ ads \\ \quad ops \\ \textbf{end} \end{array}}
$$

provided

---

[3] Recall that primitive type expressions cannot be cast.

($\leftrightarrow$) $T \leq T'$ and every occurrence of a in non-assignable expressions of
  ops, *cds* and *c* is cast with T or any subtype of T declared in *cds*;
($\leftarrow$) every expression assigned to a, in *ops*, *cds* and *c*, is of type T or any
  subtype of T; every use of a as result argument is for a corresponding
  formal parameter of type T or any subtype of T.

The exhaustive application of this law (together with those for variables and
parameters), from left to right, instantiating the type T' with **object**, allows
the replacement of the types of all identifiers with the **object** class. Recall that
at this point all identifiers having a class type are trivially cast, so the conditions
of the law are valid.

3.8 Cast Elimination

As the types of the identifiers were changed to **object**, the trivial casts introduced by the step described in Section 3.4 are not trivial anymore. Furthermore,
the program might include arbitrary casts previously introduced by the programmer. Therefore, we need new laws for eliminating nontrivial casts.

It is also worth observing that a type cast plays two major roles. At compilation time, casting is necessary when using an expression in contexts where
an object value of a given type is expected, and this type is a strict subtype
of the expression type. For example, if '$x : B$', $C \leq B$ and a is an attribute
which is in C but not in B, then the selection of this attribute using x must
be cast, as in $((C)x).a$. If a were declared in B, then the cast would not be
necessary concerning compilation purposes, but once it is there it cannot simply
be eliminated, because a cast also has a run time effect.

At run time, if the object value of a cast expression does not have the required
type, then the expression evaluation results in **error** and the command in which
this expression appears behaves like **abort**. Therefore, in the example discussed
above (and assuming the attribute a is in class B) although the cast could be
directly eliminated regarding its static effect, it still has a dynamic effect when
the object value of x happens to be of type B but not of type C.

In order to be able to eliminate a cast while still preserving its dynamic
behaviour, we use assumptions. Recall, from Section 2, that the assumption
$\{b\}$ behaves like **skip** if b is true, and as **abort** otherwise. The following laws
deal with the elimination of type casts in expressions. However, unlike Law 4
which deals with casts regardless of their contexts, here we need to consider the
particular context in which the cast is used, in order to determine whether it
can be eliminated. The static requirements of type casts are captured by the
antecedent of each law, while the dynamic behaviour of the cast is replaced
by an assumption. For example, the following law removes casts in assignment
statements, while the next law eliminates casts in method calls.

Law 10 ⟨eliminate cast of expressions⟩
If $cds, A \ \triangleright \ le : B$, $e : B'$, $C \leq B'$ and $B' \leq B$, then

$$cds, A \ \triangleright \ le := (C)e \ = \ \{e \text{ is } C\}; \ le := e$$

Law 11 ⟨eliminate cast of method call⟩
If $cds, A \rhd e : B$, $C \leq B$ and m is declared in B or in any of its superclasses in cds, then

$$cds, A \rhd ((C)e).m(e') = \{e \text{ is } C\};\ e.m(e')$$

These are just two possible cases. Observe that a type cast might occur arbitrarily nested in an expression. Therefore, in order to deal with cast elimination in general, it is convenient to reduce expressions to a simple form, so that we can then consider only a fixed number of patterns. This form is basically as defined in the BNF for expressions (see Section 2), with the replacement of arbitrary expressions (denoted by e) with variables. The reduction of an arbitrary expression to this form is a reduction strategy in itself. Nevertheless, it is a very standard one, and is not presented here; this kind of reduction strategy can be found elsewhere [3].

The laws to deal with the elimination of casts in the remaining expression patterns are very similar to the previous two laws, so are omitted here. Observe that, at this stage of our reduction strategy, all casts can be eliminated. The static role of each cast is trivially fulfilled as a consequence of the fact that the type of each identifier is **object**, and that all methods and attributes of the entire program have been moved to the **object** class. Therefore, the provisos of each law are always satisfied. Complementarily, the dynamic effect of each cast is preserved by the assumption on the right-hand side of each law. As a result, the exhaustive application of these laws eliminates all casts in the program.

3.9   Method Elimination

The purpose of this step is to eliminate all method calls and then all method declarations, keeping in the **object** class only attribute declarations. For method call elimination, observe that we need only a simple law which can be regarded as a version of the the *copy rule*. The reason is that we have already dealt with dynamic binding in Section 3.6, when moving methods all the way up to **object**. Therefore, in general the body of each method is a large conditional whose guards resolve the possible dynamic binding aspects. In fact, there are no method redefinitions at this point, since all methods are already in **object**.

Law 12 ⟨method call elimination⟩
Consider that the following class declaration

    class C **extends** D
      ads
      meth $m \hat{=} pc$ **end**; *ops*
    end

is included in cds. Then

$$cds, A \rhd e.m(e') = \{e \neq \textbf{null} \wedge e \neq \textbf{error}\};\ pc[e/\textbf{self}](e')$$

provided

($\leftrightarrow$) $cds, A \rhd e : C$; m is not redefined in cds and does not contain references to **super**; and all attributes which appear in the body of m (i.e., pc) are public.

Note that a method call $e.m(e')$ aborts when e is **null** or **error**. Thus, we need the assumption $\{e \neq$ **null** $\land\ e \neq$ **error**$\}$ on the right-hand side of the above law which also aborts when e is **null** or **error**; otherwise, the assumption behaves like **skip** and the method body behaves the same as its invocation.

After all calls of a method are replaced with its body, the method definition itself can be eliminated. Similarly to the notation introduced in Section 3.2, in the following law $B.m$ stands for calls of the method m via expressions of type B, strictly.

Law 13 $\langle$method elimination$\rangle$

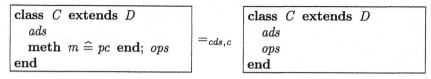

provided

($\rightarrow$) $B.m$ does not appear in cds, c nor in ops, for all B such that $B \leq C$.
($\leftarrow$) m is not declared in ops nor in any superclass or subclass of C in cds.

In this step, we should apply Law 12 exhaustively for eliminating all method calls. Before doing so, however, we need to eliminate all recursive calls. This should be done by defining the recursive methods using the recursive command **rec** $X\ \bullet\ c$ **end**, in such a way that recursive calls become references to X. The law that can be used to perform this change is standard and omitted.

After eliminating all method calls, Law 13 is then applied to remove method definitions. There is no particular order to be followed; methods can be eliminated in any order. Even in the case where a method m invokes a method n, it is possible to eliminate m first, as in every place where m is invoked we can replace this invocation by the body which includes an invocation to n; but this is no problem since n is still in scope. Remember that at this point there are no private attributes, method redefinitions or references to **super**.

3.10   Summary of the Strategy

The main result of this work is captured by the following theorem which summarizes the overall reduction strategy.

Theorem 1 *(Reduction strategy) An arbitrary* ROOL *program satisfying the conditions stated in Section 3.1 can be reduced to Subtype Normal Form.*

Proof: *From the application of the steps described in sections 3.2–3.9, in that order.*

The proof of the above theorem is straightforward because the details of the strategy concerning its convergence in terms of the applicability of the laws is discussed in each individual step.

4   Additional Laws and Data Refinement

Although our normal form reduction strategy has hopefully uncovered an interesting and expressive set of laws, it might be surprising that some additional laws were not necessary in our reduction process. Note that this is a consequence of the fact that our subtype normal form preserves classes, attributes, type tests, and object creation. As explained in Section 3, we decided to aim at this normal form because its reduction process is entirely algebraic, whereas reduction to a pure imperative form requires some sort of encoding of the object model data into, for instance, a relational one. Nevertheless, some additional laws necessary for reduction to a pure imperative form can be easily identified.

The next two laws deal with classes and attributes. Law 14 removes a class declaration provided it is not used.

Law 14 ⟨class elimination⟩

$$cds\ cd_1 \bullet c = cds \bullet c$$

provided

($\rightarrow$) The class declared cd_1 does not appear in cds and c;
($\leftarrow$) The name of the class declared in cd_1 is distinct from those of all classes declared in cds; the superclass appearing in cd_1 is either **object** or declared in cds; and the attribute and method names declared by cd_1 are not declared by its superclasses in cds, except in the case of method redefinitions.

If a private attribute is not read or written inside the class in which it is declared, we can remove it by using Law 15.

Law 15 ⟨attribute elimination⟩

class B extends A
pri $a : T$; ads
ops
end

$=_{cds,c}$

class B extends A
ads
ops
end

provided

($\rightarrow$) $B.a$ does not appear in ops;
($\leftarrow$) a does not appear in ads, and it is not declared by a superclass or subclass of B in cds.

Another construct preserved by our normal form is the type test (**is**). Two simple laws of type test are presented below. These are actually laws of expressions, which usually refer to the context in which the expression occurs. Law 16 asserts that the type test **self is** N is true when appearing inside the class named N.

Law 16 ⟨**is** test true⟩

$cds, N \rhd$ **self is** $N =$ **true**

Complementary to Law 16, Law 17 asserts that the test **self is** M is false inside a class N, provided N is not a subclass of M, and vice-versa.

Law 17 ⟨**is** test false⟩
If $N \not\leq M$ and $M \not\leq N$, then

$cds, N \rhd$ **self is** $M =$ **false**

Apart from the laws of the object-oriented features of ROOL, laws of imperative commands are also necessary in practical applications of program transformation. These laws are simple adaptations of those found in the literature [1, 4] and are not the focus of this work. However, as an example of an imperative law of ROOL, we present Law 18 that allows us to simplify an alternation whose guarded commands are the same in all branches of the alternation, assuming that the disjunction of all guards of the alternation is true.

Law 18 ⟨**if** identical guarded commands⟩
If $\lor\, i : 1 .. n \bullet \psi_i =$ **true**, then

if $[\!]\, i : 1 .. n \bullet \psi_i \;\to\; c$ **fi** $\;=\; c$

As another example of law for an imperative command, Law 19 states that the order of the guarded commands of an alternation is immaterial.

Law 19 ⟨**if** symmetry⟩
If π is any permutation of $1 .. n$, then

if $[\!]\, i : 1 .. n \bullet \psi_i \;\to\; c_i$ **fi** $\;=\;$ **if** $[\!]\, i : 1 .. n \bullet \psi_{\pi(i)} \;\to\; c_{\pi(i)}$ **fi**

For the transformation of programs, in general, we also need to apply class refinement. The traditional techniques of data refinement deal with modules that encapsulate the variables whose representations are being changed. In our approach, this is extended to consider hierarchies of classes whose attributes are not necessarily private: they can be protected or public. Law 20 allows us to introduce new attributes in a class, relating them with already existing attributes by means of a coupling invariant CI. The application of this law changes the bodies of the methods declared in the class and in its subclasses. The changes follow the traditional laws for data refinement [2].

Law 20 ⟨superclass attribute-coupling invariant⟩

class A ˜extends C		class A ˜extends C
$\quad adsa;$		$\quad adsc;$
$\quad ops$	$\preceq_{cds,c}$	$\quad CI(ops)$
end		**end**
cds'		$CI(cds')$

> **where**
>> CI distributes over language constructs modifying commands according to traditional data refinement laws;
>
> **provided**
>> $B.a$, for all $B \leq A$ and public attribute a in $adsa$, does not appear in cds or c;
>>
>> CI refers only to public and protected attributes in $adsa$;
>>
>> cds' only contains subclasses of A, and cds contains no subclasses of A.

By convention, the attributes denoted by $adsa$ are abstract, whereas those denoted by $adsc$ are concrete. The coupling invariant CI relates abstract and concrete states. The notation $CI(cds')$ indicates that CI acts on the class declarations of cds'. The application of CI to a class declaration changes the methods of such a class according to the laws of data refinement [2]: every guard may assume the coupling invariant; every command is extended by modifications to the new variables so that the coupling invariant is maintained. These transformations are also done in the class A; this is indicated by the notation $CI(ops)$. In order to apply this law, the public attributes in $adsa$ must not be accessed in the command c nor in any method of the classes in cds. Also, the coupling invariant CI must refer only to public and protected attributes in $adsa$, since these must be visible in the subclasses of A.

This law for data refining class hierarchies together with laws of commands and laws of the object-oriented features of ROOL form a solid basis for proving more elaborate transformations of object-oriented programs, as illustrated in the next section.

5   Formal Refactoring

In this section we present how the laws used for the reduction of ROOL programs to the normal form serve as a basis for justifying program transformations. We are particularly interested in the application of these laws to prove refactorings. Here we present the proof of the refactoring ⟨Pull Up/Push Down Field⟩. In fact, we represent these refactorings by a single law. Applying this law from left to right corresponds to the first refactoring; the reverse direction corresponds to the other one. Here we prove the derivation of this refactoring from left to right, which allows us to move attributes from subclasses to their common superclass. The attributes might have different names, but their types have to be the same. Here we consider public attributes as this is the most general case; private and protected attributes can be turned into public ones using Laws 2 and 1, respectively.

Refactoring 1 ⟨Pull Up/Push Down Field⟩

class $A\tilde{}\,$**extends** D
    $adsa$
    $opsa$
end
class B **extends** A
    pub$\tilde{}\,x : T$; $adsb$
    $opsb$
end
class C **extends** A
    pub$\tilde{}\,y : T$; $adsc$
    $opsc$
end
cds'
	$=_{cds,c}$	**class** $A\tilde{}\,$**extends** D
		    pub$\tilde{}\,z : T$; $adsa$
		    $opsa$
		end
		class B **extends** A
		    $adsb$
		    $opsb[z/x]$
		end
		class C **extends** A
		    $adsc$
		    $opsc[z/y]$
		end
		$cds'[z, z/x, y]$

provided

($\leftrightarrow$) cds' contains only the subclasses of B and C in which there are occurrences of x and y;

($\rightarrow$) The attribute name z is not declared in $adsa$, $adsb$, $adsc$, nor in any subclass or superclass of A in cds and cds'; and the attribute names x and y are not declared by $adsb$, $adsc$, nor by any subclass of A in cds;

  $N.x$, for any $N \leq B$, does not appear in cds or c, and $N.y$, for any $N \leq C$, does not appear in cds or c;

($\leftarrow$) $N.z$, for any $N \leq A$, $N \not\leq B$, and $N \not\leq C$, does not appear in cds or c;

  x (y) is not declared in $adsa$, $adsb$ ($adsc$), nor in any subclass or superclass of B (C) in cds and cds'.

The first step of the proof is to apply Law 3 twice. Each application of this law moves the attributes x and y of classes B and C, respectively, to their common superclass A. Notice that, the attributes are public as required by Law 3. For simplicity, we omit cds' in the derivation because modifications to the operations of classes in cds' are similar to those done to $opsb$ and $opsc$. We use $cds'[z, z/x, y]$ to denote that occurrences of x and y in operations of classes in cds' are replaced with z.

class A **extends** D
    pub $x : T, y : T$; $adsa$
    $opsa$
end
	class B **extends** A
	    $adsb$
	    $opsb$
	end
		class C **extends** A
		    $adsc$
		    $opsc$
		end

The next step is to prepare A and its subclasses for data refinement. This preparation consists of the exhaustive application of a law that we omit here since it is well known. This law [2] transforms assignments of the form $t :=$ **self**.x into its corresponding specification statement $t : [\textbf{true}, t = \textbf{self}.x]$. This transformation occurs in all subclasses of A in which there are occurrences of the abstract variables x and y in assignments. After these changes the operations of classes A, B, and C are denoted by $opsa'$, $opsb'$, and $opsc'$, respectively.

We then apply Law 20, introducing the attribute z (the concrete representation of both x and y) into A. The coupling invariant CI, relating z with x and y, is given by the predicate $((\textbf{self is } B) \Rightarrow z = x) \wedge ((\textbf{self is } C) \Rightarrow z = y)$.

class A extends D	class B extends A	class C extends A
pub $z : T$;	$adsb$	$adsc$
pub $x : T, y : T$; $adsa$	$CI(opsb')$	$CI(opsc')$
$CI(opsa')$	**end**	**end**
end		

The application of CI changes guards and commands of classes A, B, and C according to the laws of data refinement presented by Morgan [2]. Guards are augmented so that they assume the coupling invariant. The new guard may be just a conjunction of the old guard with the coupling invariant. We augment specifications so that the concrete variable appears in the frame of the specification and the coupling invariant is conjoined with the pre and post conditions. In this way, the specification statement $t : [\textbf{true}, t = \textbf{self}.x]$ becomes $t, z : [CI, t = \textbf{self}.x \wedge CI]$. An assignment to an abstract variable of the form $\textbf{self}.x := exp$ is augmented to $\textbf{self}.x, \textbf{self}.z := exp, exp$. These changes are also applied to classes in cds' that, for simplicity, we omit here. Since the attributes x and y are new in class A, there are no occurrences of them in $opsa'$. Consequently, we can reduce $CI(opsa')$ just to $opsa$ by using refinement laws [2].

The next step is the elimination of occurrences of abstract variables in the subclasses of A. We proceed with diminishing assignments of the form $\textbf{self}.x, \textbf{self}.z := exp, exp$ to $\textbf{self}.z := exp$, as we are replacing the variables that constitute the abstract state with the variables that compose the concrete state. For specification statements of the form $t, z : [CI, t = \textbf{self}.x \wedge CI]$ we apply Laws 16 and 17 that simplify the conjunction of the coupling invariant. Inside B, Law 16 states that the test **self is** B is true because we are refining the class B. On the other hand, Law 17 states that the test **self is** N, for a class N that is not a superclass or a subclass of B is false inside B. This simplifies the coupling invariant to the predicate $(\textbf{true} \Rightarrow z = x) \wedge (\textbf{false} \Rightarrow z = y)$ which is trivially $z = x$. The specification statement, at this moment, is $t, z : [z = x, t = \textbf{self}.x \wedge z = x]$ which is refined by the assignment $t := \textbf{self}.z$, which is actually $t := \textbf{self}.x[z/x]$, a renaming of the original code in $opsb$. Guards must be algorithmically refined.

We proceed in the same way with the commands of C that are augmented with concrete variables and that assume the coupling invariant. As the coupling invariant relates abstract and concrete variables via an equality between attribute names, the classes B and C that we obtain after the elimination of abstract variables are the same as the original except that all occurrences of x and y in the commands are replaced with z.

Since the abstract attributes are no longer read or written in B or C and their subclasses, where they were originally declared, we can remove them from A. First we apply Law 2, from right to left, in order to change the visibility of these attributes to private, since they are are not read or written outside the class in which they are declared. Then we apply Law 15 that allows us to remove a private attribute that is not read or written inside the class it is declared. We proceed in the same way for C.

class A extends D	class B extends A	class C extends A
pub $z : T$; $adsa$	$adsb$	$adsc$
$opsa$	$opsb[z/x]$	$opsc[z/y]$
end	**end**	**end**

This finishes the proof of the refactoring ⟨Pull Up Field⟩. The reverse direction corresponds to the refactoring ⟨Push Down Field⟩, whose proof is similar to the one presented here. As both sides are refinement of each other, we conclude that they are equal.

6   Conclusions

Defining a rich set of algebraic laws for object-oriented programming seems a desirable and original contribution. Although the laws presented here are for a particular language (ROOL), they will hopefully be of more general utility. In particular, although ROOL is based on copy semantics, whereas most practical object-oriented programming languages are based on reference semantics, the laws for the object-oriented features of ROOL, presented here, do not rely on this design decision. In contrast, some command laws (like those for combining assignments) do rely on copy semantics.

Strategies for normal form reduction such as the one introduced here are usually adopted as a measure of *completeness* of a set of proposed laws, not as the final aim for a practical programmer. In fact, our strategy aims to make a program less object-oriented and does not suggest good development practices or compilation strategies. However, when applied in the opposite direction, the laws used to define the strategy serve as a tool for carrying out practical applications of program transformation. Our completeness result, together with the proposed law for data refinement of class hierarchies, suggests that the proposed set of laws is expressive enough to derive transformation rules that capture informal design practices, such as refactorings, as illustrated in the previous section and in Cornélio's thesis [23].

One aspect which became evident when defining the laws presented here is that, associated with most of them, there are very subtle side conditions which require much attention. Uncovering the complete side conditions has certainly been one of the difficult tasks of our research. This can be contrasted with more practically-oriented work in the literature which focus on the transformations without paying must attention to correctness or completeness issues, as already discussed in Section 1.

Perhaps another interesting issue of this research is the particular approach taken for the reduction strategy, by moving all the code (attributes and methods) all the way up to the **object** class. An alternative would be to move the code down, to the classes in the leaves of the inheritance hierarchy. This has, nevertheless, been shown unsuitable for a systematisation based on algebraic laws. The reason is that moving a single attribute or method from a superclass to a subclass might have great contextual impact, whereas moving declarations up is more controllable, as it causes less effects on other code. The particular approach adopted has allowed us to separate concerns to a great extent, helping to tackle the overall task. For example, the elimination of method invocation (Law 12) has been dissociated from dynamic binding (Law 7), as well as from the behaviour of **super** (Laws 5 and 6).

A common criticism to the algebraic style is that merely postulating algebraic laws can give rise to complex and unexpected interactions between programming constructions; this can be avoided by linking the algebraic semantics with a mathematical model in which the laws can be verified. The command laws of ROOL have already been proved correct with respect to a weakest precondition semantics for the language [20]. The complete link between the algebraic semantics presented here and the weakest precondition semantics of ROOL is the subject of a complementary work [23].

Another complementary work [24], recently completed, to our research is the mechanisation of the reduction strategy, as well as the mechanical proofs of some refactorings, using the Maude [25] term rewriting system.

Acknowledgements

We thank our collaborators Ana Cavalcanti and David Naumann for many discussions that contributed to the research reported in this article. We also thank the anonymous referees for the detailed comments that helped to improve this article. Part of the work reported here was carried out when the first two authors were visiting the Stevens Institute of Technology. The authors are partly supported by CNPq, grants 521994/96–9 (Paulo Borba), 521039/95–9 (Augusto Sampaio), and 680032/99-1 (Dare CO-OP and CO-OP projects, jointly funded by PROTEM-CC and the National Science Foundation).

References

[1] Hoare *et al*, C. A. R.: Laws of programming. Communications of the ACM **30** (1987) 672–686

[2] Morgan, C.: Programming from Specifications. second edn. Prentice Hall (1994)

[3] Sampaio, A.: An Algebraic Approach to Compiler Design. Volume 4 of Algebraic Methodology and Software Technology. World Scientific (1997)

[4] Roscoe, A., Hoare, C. A. R.: The laws of occam programming. Theoretical Computer Science **60** (1988) 177–229
[5] Bird, R., de Moor, O.: Algebra of Programming. Prentice Hall (1997)
[6] Seres, S., Spivey, M., Hoare, T.: Algebra of logic programming. In: ICPL'99, New Mexico, USA (1999)
[7] Hoare, C., Jifeng, H.: Unifying Theories of Programming. Prentice Hall (1998)
[8] Fowler, M.: Refactoring—Improving the design of existing code. Addison Wesley (1999)
[9] Lea, D.: Concurrent Programming in Java. Addison-Wesley (1997)
[10] Opdyke, W.: Refactoring Object-Oriented Frameworks. PhD thesis, University of Illinois at Urbana-Champaign (1992)
[11] Roberts, D.: Practical Analysis for Refactoring. PhD thesis, University of Illinois at Urbana Champaign (1999)
[12] Mikhajlova, A., Sekerinsk, E.: Class refinement and interface refinement in object-oriented programs. In: Proceedings of FME'97. Volume 1313 of Lecture Notes in Computer Science., Springer-Verlag (1997) 82–101
[13] Leino, K. R. M.: Recursive Object Types in a Logic of Object-oriented Programming. In Hankin, C., ed.: 7th European Symposium on Programming. Volume 1381 of Lecture Notes in Computer Science., Springer-Verlag (1998)
[14] Evans, A.: Reasoning with UML class diagrams. In: Workshop on Industrial Strength Formal Methods, WIFT'98, Florida, USA, IEEE Press (1998)
[15] Evans, A., France, R., Lano, K., Rumpe, B.: The UML as a formal modeling notation. In Bézivin, J., Muller, P. A., eds.: The Unified Modeling Language, UML'98 - Beyond the Notation. First International Workshop, Mulhouse, France, June 1998, Selected Papers. Volume 1618 of LNCS., Springer (1999) 336–348
[16] Lano, K., Bicarregui, J.: Semantics and transformations for UML models. In Bézivin, J., Muller, P. A., eds.: The Unified Modeling Language, UML'98 - Beyond the Notation. First International Workshop, Mulhouse, France, June 1998, Selected Papers. Volume 1618 of LNCS., Springer (1999) 107–119
[17] Gogolla, M., Richters, M.: Transformation rules for UML class diagrams. In Bézivin, J., Muller, P. A., eds.: The Unified Modeling Language, UML'98 - Beyond the Notation. First International Workshop, Mulhouse, France, June 1998, Selected Papers. Volume 1618 of LNCS., Springer (1999) 92–106
[18] Booch, G., Jacobson, I., Rumbaugh, J.: The Unified Modelling Language User Guide. Addison-Wesley (1999)
[19] Cavalcanti, A., Naumann, D.: A weakest precondition semantics for an object-oriented language of refinement. In: FM'99 - Formal Methods. Volume 1709 of Lecture Notes in Computer Science. Springer-Verlag (1999) 1439–1459
[20] Cavalcanti, A., Naumann, D.: A weakest precondition semantics for refinement of object-oriented programs. IEEE Transactions on Software Enginnering **26** (2000) 713–728
[21] Arnold, K., Gosling, J.: The Java Programming Language. Addison Wesley (1996)
[22] Gosling, J., Joy, B., Steele, G.: The Java Language Specification. Addison-Wesley (1996)
[23] Cornélio, M. L.: Applying Object-oriented Refactoring and Patterns as Formal Refinements. PhD thesis, Informatics Center, Federal University of Pernambuco, Brazil (To appear in 2003)
[24] Lira, B. O.: Automação de Regras para Programação Orientada a Objetos. Master's thesis, Centro de Informática, Universidade Federal de Pernambuco, Brazil (2002)

[25] Meseguer, J.: A logical theory of concurrent objects and its realization in the
Maude language. In Agha, G., Wegner, P., Yonezawa, A., eds.: Object-Oriented
Programming. MIT Press (1993) 314–390

Object-Oriented Reading Techniques for Inspection of UML Models – An Industrial Experiment

Reidar Conradi[1], Parastoo Mohagheghi[2], Tayyaba Arif [1], Lars Christian Hegde[1],
Geir Arne Bunde[3], and Anders Pedersen[3]

[1] Department of Computer and Information Science
NTNU, NO-7491 Trondheim, Norway
conradi@idi.ntnu.no
[2] Ericsson Norway - Grimstad
Postuttak, NO-4898 Grimstad, Norway
parastoo.mohagheghi@eto.ericsson.se
[3] Agder University College
NO-4876 Grimstad, Norway

Abstract. Object-oriented design and modeling with UML has become a central part of software development in industry. Software inspections are used to cost-efficiently increase the quality of the developed software by early defect detection and correction. Several models presenting the total system need to be inspected for consistency with each other and with external documents such as requirement specifications. Special Object Oriented Reading Techniques (OORTs) have been developed to help inspectors in the individual reading step of inspection of UML models. The paper describes an experiment performed at Ericsson in Norway to evaluate the cost-efficiency of tailored OORTs in a large-scale software project. The results showed that the OORTs fit well into an incremental development process, and managed to detect defects not found by the existing reading techniques. The study demonstrated the need for further development and empirical assessment of these techniques, and for better integration with industrial work practice.

1 Introduction

The Unified Modeling Language (UML) provides visualization and modeling support, and has its roots in object-oriented concepts and notations [4]. Using UML implies a need for methods targeted at inspecting object-oriented models, e.g. to check consistency within a single model, between different models of a system, and between models and external requirement documents. Detected defects may be inconsistencies, omissions or ambiguities; i.e. any fault or lack that degrades the quality of the model.

L. Cardelli (Ed.): ECOOP 2003, LNCS 2743, pp. 483–500, 2003.

Typically software inspections include an individual reading step, where several inspectors read the artifacts alone and record the detected defects. An inspection meeting for discussing, classification and recording defects follows this step. Individual reading of artifacts (the target of this paper) strongly relies on the reader's experience and concentration. To improve the output of the individual reading step, checklists and special reading guidelines are provided. Special Object-Oriented Reading Techniques (OORTs) have been developed at the University of Maryland, USA, consisting of seven individual reading techniques (sec. 2.2). In each technique, either two UML diagrams are compared, or a diagram is read against a Requirements Description.

Modeling in UML is a central part of software development at Ericsson in Grimstad. With increased use of UML, *review* and *inspection* of UML models are done in all development phases. While reviews are performed to evaluate project status and secure design quality by discussing broader design issues, formal inspections are part of the exit criteria for development phases. In the inspection process in Ericsson, individual inspectors read UML diagrams using different views, with checklists and guidelines provided for each type of view or focus.

Ericsson primarily wants to increase the *cost-efficiency* (number of detected defects per person-hour) of the individual reading step of UML diagrams, since inspection meetings are expensive and require participation of already overloaded staff. Ericsson further wants to see if there is any correlation between developer experience and number of defects caught during individual reading. Lastly, Ericsson wants to improve the relevant reading techniques (old or new) for UML diagrams, and to find out whether the new reading techniques fit into their incremental development process.

Before introducing the OORTs in industry, systematic empirical assessments are needed to evaluate the cost-efficiency and practical utility of the techniques. Following a set of student experiments for assessment and improvement of the techniques at The University of Maryland and NTNU [17][6], we conducted a small controlled experiment at Ericsson. The experiment was performed as part of two diploma (MSc) theses written in spring 2002 at the Agder University College (AUC) and The Norwegian University of Science and Technology (NTNU) [5][1]. The original set of OORTs from The University of Maryland were revised twice by NTNU for understandability, evaluated and re-evaluated on two sample systems, and then tailored to the industrial context.

The Ericsson unit in Norway develops software for large, real-time systems. The Requirements Descriptions and the UML models are big and complex. Besides, the UML models are developed and inspected *incrementally*; i.e. a single diagram may be inspected several times following successive modifications. The size of the inspected artifacts and the incremental nature of the software development process distinguish this industrial experiment from previous student experiments. The cost-efficiency of inspections and the types of detected defects were used as measures of the well-suitedness of the techniques. Other steps of the inspection process, such as the inspection meeting, remained unchanged.

Results of the experiment and qualitative feedback showed that the OORTs fit well into the overall inspection process. Although the OORTs were new for the inspectors, they contributed to finding more defects than the existing reading techniques, while their cost-efficiency was almost the same. However, the new techniques ought to be simplified, and questions or special guidelines should be added.

The remainder of the paper is structured as follows: Section 2 describes some state of the art and the new OORTs. Section 3 outlines the overall empirical approach to assess the OORTs. Section 4 summarizes the existing practice of reviews and inspections at Ericsson and some baseline data. Section 5 describes the experimental steps and results, analyzes the main results, and discusses possible ways to improve the new OORTs and their usage. The paper is concluded in section 6.

2   The Object-Oriented Reading Techniques (OORTs)

2.1   A Quick State of the Art

Inspection is a technique for early defect detection in software artifacts [8]. It has proved to be effective (finding relatively many defects), efficient (relatively low cost per defect), and practical (easy to carry out). Inspection cannot replace later testing, but many severe defects can be found more cost-efficiently by inspection. A common reading technique is to let inspectors apply complimentary perspectives or views [2][3]. There are over 150 published studies, and some main findings are:

It is reported a net productivity increase of 30% to 50%, and a net timescale reduction of 10% to 30% [9, p.24].

Code inspection reduces costs by 39%, and design inspection reduces rework by 44% [11].

Ericsson in Oslo, Norway has previously calculated a net saving of 20% of the total development effort by inspection of design documents in SDL [7].

As software development becomes increasingly model-based e.g. by using UML, techniques for inspection of models for completeness, correctness and consistency should be developed. Multiple models are developed for complex software systems. These models represent the same system from different views and different levels of abstraction.

However, there exist no documented, industrial-proven reading techniques for UML-based models [16]. The closest is a reported case study from Oracle in Brazil [13]. Its aim was to test the practical feasibility of the OORTs, but there was no company baseline on inspections to compare with. The study showed that the OORTs did work in an industrial setting. Five inspectors found 79 distinct defects (many serious ones), with 2.7 defects/person-hour (totally 29 person-hours, but excluding a final inspection meeting). Few qualitative observations were collected on how the OORTs behaved.

2.2   The OORTs

As mentioned, one effort in adapting reading techniques for the individual reading step of inspections to object-oriented design was made by the OORT-team at University of Maryland, USA [17]. The principal team members were:

- Victor R. Basili and Jeffrey Carver (The University of Maryland)
- Forrest Shull (The Fraunhofer Center – Maryland)
- Guilherme H. Travassos (COPPE/Federal University of Rio de Janeiro)

Special object-oriented reading techniques have been developed since 1998 to inspect ("compare") UML diagrams with each other and with Requirements Descriptions in order to find defects. *Horizontal reading techniques* are for comparing artifacts from the same development phase such as class diagrams and state diagrams developed in the design phase. Consistency among artifacts is the most important focus here. *Vertical reading techniques* are for comparing artifacts developed in different development phases such as requirements and design. Completeness (traceability of requirements into design) is the focus. UML diagrams may capture either *static* or *dynamic* aspects of the modeled system. The original set of OORTs has seven techniques, as in Figure 1:

OORT-1: Sequence Diagrams vs. Class Diagrams (horizontal, static)
OORT-2: State Diagrams vs. Class Descriptions[1] (horizontal, dynamic)
OORT-3: Sequence Diagrams vs. State Diagrams (horizontal, dynamic)
OORT-4: Class Diagrams vs. Class Descriptions (horizontal, static)
OORT-5: Class Descriptions vs. Requirements Descriptions (vertical, static)
OORT-6: Sequence Diagrams vs. Use Case Diagrams (vertical, static/dynamic)
OORT-7: State Diagrams vs. (Reqmt. Descr.s / Use Cases) (vertical, dynamic)

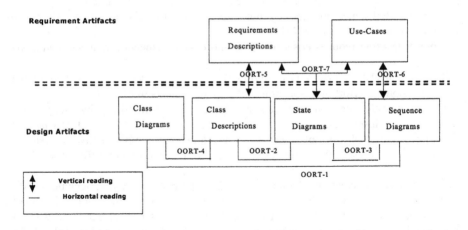

Fig. 1. The seven OORTs and their related artifacts, taken from [18]

The techniques cover most diagrams when modeling a system with UML. In addition, Requirements Descriptions are used to verify that the system complies with the prerequisites. Each technique compares at least two artifacts to identify defects in them (but requirements and use cases are assumed to be defect-free here). The techniques consist of several steps with associated questions. Each technique focus the reader on different design aspects related to consistency and completeness, but not on e.g. maintainability and testability. In student experiments, each reader either did

---

[1] Class Descriptions include textual descriptions of goals and responsibilities of a class, list of functions with descriptions of each function, attributes, cardinalities, inheritance, and relations.

four "dynamic" OORTs or four "static" ones, and with OORT-6 in common. That is, we had two complementary *views*, a dynamic and a static one.

Defects detected by the techniques are classified either as Omission (missing item), Extraneous information (should not be in the design), Incorrect fact (misrepresentation of a concept), Ambiguity (unclear concept), Inconsistency (disagreement between representations of a concept), or Miscellaneous (any other defects). In [18], severity of defects may be either Serious (It is not possible to continue reading. It needs redesign), Invalidates (the defects invalidates this part of the document) or Not serious (needs to be checked).

To get more familiar with the techniques, a short description of OORT-1 is given in the following: The goal of this technique is to verify that the Class Diagram for the system describes classes and their relationships consistently with the behaviors specified in the Sequence Diagrams. The first step is to identify all objects, services and conditions in the Sequence Diagram and underline them in different colors. The second step is to read the related Class Diagram and see whether all objects are covered, messages and services found, and constraints fulfilled. To help the reader, a set of questions is developed for each step.

3   The Overall Empirical Method

Developing a method solid enough to be used in the industry takes time and effort through various experiments and verification of results. A set of empirical studies at University of Maryland and NTNU has used the empirical method presented in [14] for improving a development process from the conceptual phase to industry. The method is divided into four studies where each study step has some questions that need to be answered before the next level can be reached:

1. Feasibility study -- Did the process provide usable and cost-effective results?
2. Observational study -- Did the steps of the process make sense?
3. Case study: Use in real life cycle -- Did process fit into the lifecycle?
4. Case study: Use in industry -- Did process fit into industrial setting?

Previous studies at The University of Maryland have emphasized steps 1-3, using students. There is also an undocumented student study from University of Southern California, where the OORTs were tailored to the Spiral Model, i.e. step 3. Previous student experiments at NTNU [6] have applied steps 1 and 2.

The mentioned case study at Oracle in Brazil was the *first* industrial study, emphasizing step 4 and feasibility. It applied more or less the original version of the OORTs, i.e. with no tailoring to the industrial context. Regrettably, we were not aware of this study before our experiment.

The study at Ericsson was the *second* industrial study, with emphasis on step 4 and with a direct comparison of Ericsson's existing inspection techniques. It used a revised and tailored version of the OORTs. We will call it an *experiment* and not a case study, as it was very close to a controlled experiment.

4   The Company Context

The goal of the software development unit at Ericsson in Grimstad, Norway is to build robust, highly available and distributed systems for large, real-time applications, such as GPRS and UMTS networks. SDL and the proprietary PLEX languages have recently been replaced by UML and e.g. Java or C++. UML models are developed to help understanding the structure and behavior of the system, for communicating decisions among stakeholders, and finally to generate code to some extent [10].

The Ericsson inspectors are team members working on the same software system. They have extensive experience with and good motivation for inspections. The artifacts in the student experiments represented complete, although small systems. In contrast, Ericsson's UML models are developed incrementally and updated in each delivery with new or changed requirements. I.e., diagrams are inspected in increments when any complete revision is done. The artifacts at Ericsson are also of industrial calibre:

- The Requirements Descriptions are in many cases large and complex, including external telecommunication standards, internal requirement specifications, and/or change requests.
- The inspected UML diagrams are often huge, containing many classes, relationships or messages - indeed covering entire walls!

4.1   State of the Practice of Reviews and Inspections

Ericsson has a long history in inspecting their software artifacts; both design documents and source code. The inspection method at Ericsson is based on techniques originally developed by Fagan [8], later refined by Gilb [9], adapted for Ericsson with Gilb's cooperation, and finally tailored by the local development department. Below, we describe the existing Ericsson review and inspection process for UML diagrams.

A review is a team activity to evaluate software artifacts or project status. Reviews can have different degrees of formality; i.e. from *informal meetings* (to present the artifacts) and *walkthroughs* (to discuss design issues and whether the design meets the requirements) to *frequent reviews* (more formal intermediate checks for completeness and correctness). Reviews act as internal milestones in a development phase, while formal *inspections* are performed at the end of an activity and act as exit criteria.

Each inspection has an associated team. The team consists of a moderator, several inspectors, at least one author, and possibly a secretary. For optimal performance, Ericsson guidelines state that a team should consist of 5 to 7 persons. The moderator is in charge of planning and initiating the inspection process. He chooses the artifacts to be inspected (with incremental development also their versions), and assigns inspectors to different views (see below). Before the inspection meeting, inspectors individually read the artifacts and mark the defects, usually directly in the inspected artifact. Requirements Descriptions, UML diagrams and source code are usually printed out for easy mark-up. If a diagram is too large to be printed out, the inspector takes separate notes on the defects and related questions.

Ericsson uses *views* during inspections, where a view means to look at the inspected artifact with a special focus in mind. Examples are *requirement* (whether a design artifact is consistent with requirements), *modeling guideline* (consistency with such guidelines), or *testability* (is the modeled information testable?). For each view, the inspectors apply checklists or design rules to help discovering defects.

An example of a modelling guideline is: The interface class will be shown as an icon (the so-called "lollipop") and the connection to the corresponding subsystem, block or unit proxy class shall be "realize" and not "generalize". An example of a design rule is: A call back interface (inherited from an abstract interface) shall be defined on the block or subsystem level (visibility of the interface). Such guidelines and rules enforce that the design model will contain correct interfaces to generate IDL files.

Only two different classifications for severity of defects are used, Major and Minor. A Major defect (most common) will cause implementation error, and its correction cost will increase in later development phases. Examples include incorrect specifications or wrong function input. A Minor defect does not lead to implementation error, and is assumed to have the same correction cost throughout the whole process. Examples are misspelling, comments, or too much detail.

In spite of a well-defined inspection process and motivated developers, Ericsson acknowledges that the individual reading step needs improvement. For instance, UML orientation is poor, and inspectors spend too little time in preparatory reading - i.e. poor process conformance, see below.

4.2   Inspection Baseline at Ericsson

A post-mortem study of data from inspections and testing was done at the Ericsson development unit outside Oslo, Norway in 1998 [7]. The historical data used in this study is from the period from 1993 to 1998, and also covered data for code reviews and different test activities (unit test, function test, and system test). The results confirm that individual design reading and code reviews are the most cost-efficient (economical) techniques to detect defects, while system tests are the least cost-efficient.

While the cost-efficiency of inspections is reported in many studies, there is no solid historical data on inspection of UML diagrams, neither in the literature nor at Ericsson. As part of a diploma thesis at AUC, data from 38 design and code inspections between May 2001 and March 2002 were analyzed; but note that:

Design (UML) and code inspections were *not* distinguished in the recorded data.

In the first 32 inspections logs, only the *total* number of defects was reported, covering both individual reading and inspection meetings. Only the last 6 inspections had distinct data here.

Table 1. Ericsson baseline results, combined for design and code inspections

	%Effort Individual Reading	%Effort Meeting	Overall Efficiency (def./ph)	Individual Reading Efficiency (def./ph)	Meeting Efficiency (def./ph)
All 38 inspections	32	68	0.53	-	-
6 last inspections	24	76	1.4	4.7	0.4

The data showed that most of the effort is spent in inspection meetings, while individual reading is more cost-efficient. For the 6 last inspections:

- 24% of the effort is spent in individual reading, finding 80% of the defects. Inspection meetings took 76% of the effort but detected 20% of defects. Thus, individual reading is 12 times more cost-efficient than inspection meetings.
- Two of these inspections had an extra high number of defects found in individual reading. Even when this data is excluded, the cost-efficiency is 1.9 defects/person-hour for individual reading and 0.6 defects/person-hour for meetings, or a factor 3.

There has been much debate on the effect of inspection meetings. Votta reports that only 8% of the defects were found in such meetings [19]. The data set in this study is too small to draw conclusions, but is otherwise in line with the cited finding.

5   Ericsson Experiment and Results

The experiment was executed in the context of a large, real software project and with professional staff. Conducting an experiment in industry involves risks such as:

- The experiment might be assumed as time-consuming for the project, causing delay and hence being rejected. Good planning and preparation was necessary to minimize the effort spent by Ericsson staff. However, the industrial reality at Ericsson is very hectic, and pre-planning of all details was not feasible.
- The time schedule for the experiment had to be coordinated with the internal inspection plan. In fact, the experiment was delayed for almost one month.
- Selecting the object of study: The inspected diagrams should not be too complex or too trivial for running the experiment. The inspected artifacts should also contain most of the diagrams covered by the techniques.

PROFIT - PROcess improvement For IT industry – is a cooperative, Norwegian software process improvement project in 2000-2002 where NTNU participates. This project is interfaced with international networks on empirical software engineering such as ESERNET and ISERN. For the experiment at Ericsson, PROFIT was the funding backbone.

The OORTs had to be modified and verified before they could be used at Ericsson. Therefore the NTNU-team revised the techniques in two steps:

1. Comments were added and questions rephrased and simplified to improve understandability by making them more concise. The results in [1] contain concrete defect reports, as well as qualitative comments and observations.
2. The set of improved techniques were further modified to fit the company context. These changes are described in section 5.2.

Students experienced that the OORTs were cost-efficient in detecting design defects for two sample systems, as the OORTs are very structured and offer a step-by-step process. On the other hand, the techniques were quite time-consuming to perform. Frustration and de-motivation can easily be the result of extensive methods.

In addition, they experienced some redundancy between the techniques. Particularly OORT-5 and OORT-6 were not motivating to use. A lot of issues in OORT-5 and OORT-6 were also covered by OORT-1 and OORT-4. OORTs-6/7 were not very productive either.

The experiment was otherwise according to Wohlin's book [20], except that we do not negate the null hypotheses. The rest of this section describes planning and operation, results, and final analysis and comments.

5.1   Planning

Objectives: The inspection experiment had four industrial objectives, named **O1-O4**:

- **O1 – analyze cost-efficiency and number of detected defects,** with **null hypothesis** *H0a: The new reading techniques are as cost-efficient and help to find at least as many defects as the old R&I techniques.*   ("Effectiveness", or fraction of defects found in inspections compared to all reported defects, was not investigated.).

- **O2 – analyze the effect of developer experience,** with **null hypothesis   H0b:** Developer experience will positively impact the number of detected defects in individual reading.

- **O3 – help to improve old and new reading techniques for UML,** since Ericsson's inspection guidelines had not been properly updated after the shift in design language from SDL to UML. No formal hypothesis was stated here, and results and arguments are mostly qualitative.

- **O4 – investigate if the new reading techniques fit the incremental development process at Ericsson.** Again, qualitative arguments were applied.

Relevant Inspection Data: To test the two null hypotheses *H0a* and *H0b*, the *independent* variable was the individual reading technique with two treatments: either the existing review and inspection techniques (R&I) or the OORTs modified for the experiment. The *dependent* variables were the effort spent, and the number and type of detected defects in the individual reading step and in the inspection meetings (see below on defect logs). Data in a questionnaire (from the OORT-team at Maryland) over developer experience was used as a *context* variable. To help to evaluate objectives *O3* and *O4*, all these variables were supplemented with qualitative data from defect logs (e.g. comments on how the OORTs behaved), as well as data from observation and interviews.

Subjects and Grouping: Subjects were the staff of the development team working with the selected use case. They were comprised of 10 developers divided in two groups, the *R&I-group* applying the previous techniques and the *OORT-group* applying the new ones. A common moderator assigned the developers to each group. A slight bias was given to implementation experience in this assignment, since Ericsson wanted all the needed views covered in the R&I-group (see however Figure 2 in 5.2). The R&I-group then consisted of three very experienced designers and programmers, one newcomer, and one with average experience. The OORT-group consisted of one team leader with good general knowledge, two senior system architects, and two with average implementation knowledge. Inspection meetings were held as usual, chaired by the same moderator. Since both groups had 5 individuals, the experimental design was balanced. Both groups had access to the same artifacts.

Changes to the OORTs: As mentioned, the OORTs were modified to fit Ericsson's models and documents, but only so that the techniques were comparable to the original ones and had the same goals. The main changes were:

- **Use Case Specifications:** Each use case has a large textual document attached to it, called a Use Case Specification (UCS), including Use Case Diagrams and the main and alternative flows. This UCS was used instead of the graphical Use Case Diagram in OORT-6 and OORT-7.
- **Class Descriptions:** There is no explicit Class Description document, but such descriptions are written directly in the Class Diagrams. In OORT-2, OORT-4 and OORT-5, these textual class descriptions in the Class Diagrams are used.
- **OORT-4:** Class Diagram (CD) vs. Class Description (CDe). The main focus of this technique is the consistency between CD and CDe. As Class Descriptions are written in the same Class Diagram, this technique seems unnecessary. However, the questions make the reader focus on internal consistency in the CD. Therefore all aspects concerning Class Descriptions were removed and the technique was renamed to "*Class Diagram for internal consistency*".
- **OORT-5:** Class Description (CDe) vs. Requirements Descriptions (RD). Here, the RD is used to identify classes, their behaviors and necessary attributes. That is, the RD nouns are candidates for classes, the RD verbs for behaviors, and so on. The technique was not applicable in Ericsson, due to the large amount of text that should be read. But Ericsson has an iterative development process, where they inspect a small part of the system at one time. The UCS could substitute the RD for a particular part of the system, but the focus of the specification and the level of abstraction demanded major changes in the technique, which would make the technique unrecognizable. Therefore a decision was made to *remove OORT-5*. Thus, we had *six OORTs* to try out.

Defect Logging: To log defects in a consistent and orderly manner, one template was made for the R&I-group and a similar one for the OORT-group – both implemented by spreadsheets. For all defects, the inspectors registered an explanatory name, the associated artifact, the defect type (Omission, Extraneous etc.), and some detailed comments. The OORT-group also registered the technique that helped them to find the defect. Ericsson's categorization of Major and Minor was not applied (we regretted this during later analysis). These changes in defect reporting were the only process modification for the R&I-group. The amount of effort spent by each inspector, in individual reading and inspection meetings, was also recorded for both groups. We also asked for qualitative comments on how the techniques behaved.

5.2   Operation, Quantitative Results, and Short Comments

It was decided to run the experiment in April or May 2002, during an already planned inspection of UML diagrams for a certain use case, representing the next release of a software system. The inspected artifacts were:

- Use Case Specification (UCS) of 43 pages, including large, referenced standards.
- Class Diagram (CD), with 5 classes and 20 interfaces.
- Two Sequence Diagrams (SqD), each with ca. 20 classes and 50 messages.
- One State Diagram (StD), with 6 states including start and stop, cf. below.

Problem note 1: When the actual use case and its design artifacts were being prepared for the experiment, a small but urgent problem occurred: For this concrete use case (system) there was *no State Diagram (StD)!* Such diagrams are normally made, but not emphasized since no code is generated from these. Luckily, the UCS contained an Activity Diagram that was a hybrid of a StD and a data flow chart. Thus, to be able to use the OORTs in their proposed form, a StD was hastily extracted from this Activity Diagram. However, the StD was now made in the analysis and not in the design phase, so the reading in OORT-7 changed focus. The alternative would have been to drop the three OORTs involving State Diagrams, leaving us with only three OORTs. The R&I-group had access to, but did not inspect this StD.

The experiment was executed over two days. In the beginning of the first day, the NTNU students gave a presentation of the experimental context and setup. For the OORT-group, a short introduction to the techniques was given as well. Since we had few inspectors, they were told to use *all the available six OORTs (excluding OORT-5)*, not just four "dynamic" ones or four "static" ones as in previous experiments (again, we regretted this later).

Each participant filled out a questionnaire about his/her background (e.g. number of projects and experience with UML). The R&I-group was not given any information on the OORTs. The 10 participants in this experiment were the team assigned to the use case, so they had thorough knowledge of the domain and the UML models at hand.

When all participants had finished their individual reading, they met in their assigned teams for normal inspection meetings. During these meetings, each defect was discussed and categorized, and the moderator logged possible new defects found in the meetings as well. At the end of the meetings, a short discussion was held on the usability of the techniques and to generally comment on the experiment.

Problem note 2: One inspector in the OORT-group did only deliver his questionnaire, not his defect log. Thus the OORT-data represents 4, not 5 persons. The number of defects from the OORT group is therefore lower than expected (but still high), while the OORT effort and cost-efficiency data reflect the reduced person-hours.

Table 2 shows the number of distinctive defects found in individual reading and inspection meetings, both as absolute numbers and relative frequencies. It also shows the effort in person-hours for individual reading and meetings. Defects reported in more than one defect log are called *overlaps* (in column four), and 8 "overlap defects" were reported for the OORT-group.

The cost-efficiency (defects/person-hours) of the individual reading step, the inspection meetings and the average for both groups is shown in Table 3 below.

Table 2. Summary of collected data on defects from the Ericsson experiment

	Indiv. read. defects	Meet. defects	Over-laps	% Indiv. read. defects	% Meet. defects	Person-hours Indiv. read.	Person-hours Meet.
R&I-group	17	8	0	68	32	10	8.25
OORT-group	38	1	8	97	3	21.5	9

Table 3. Cost-efficiency of inspections as no. of detected defects per person-hour

	Cost-eff. Indiv.read. (defects/ph)	Cost-eff. Meeting (defects/ph)	Cost-eff. Average. (defects/ph)
R&I-group	1.70	0.97	1.37
OORT-group	1.76	0.11	1.28

Table 4. Defect Distribution on defect types

Defect Type	R&I-group Indiv.read.	R&I-group Meeting	OORT-group Indiv.read.	OORT-group Meeting
Omission	3	2	12	1
Extraneous	-	3	6	-
Incorrect fact	10	3	1	-
Ambiguity	-	-	5	-
Inconsistency	2	-	12	-
Miscellaneous	2	-	2	-
Total	17	8	38	1

The cost-efficiency (defects/person-hours) of the individual reading step, the inspection meetings and the average for both groups is shown in Table 3 below.

Short comment: Incorrect facts reported by the R&I-group were mostly detected in the two Sequence Diagrams showing the interactions to realize the use case behavior. These defects were *misuse of a class or interface*, such as wrong order of operation calls or calling the wrong operation in an interface (Incorrect fact was originally defined as misrepresentation of a concept). The group argued that the interface is misrepresented in the Sequence Diagram, and thus the defects are of type Incorrect fact.

For the OORT-group the defects were also classified based on the question leading to find them. OORT-1 and OORT-2 helped finding most defects. OORT-7 did not lead to detection of any defects whatsoever.

Problem note 3: The inspectors mentioned that some defects were detected by more than one technique and only registered the first technique that lead to them. However, the techniques were time-consuming, and one of the developers did not do OORT-6 and OORT-7, while others used little time on these latter two.

As mentioned, the participants filled in a questionnaire where they evaluated their *experience* on different areas of software development on an ordinal scale from 0 to 5, where 5 was best. A total score was coarsely calculated for each participant by simply adding these numbers. The maximum score for 20 questions was 100. Figure 2 shows the number of defects reported by each participant and their personal score for 9 participants (data from the "misbehaving" fifth participant in the OORT-group was not included). The median and mean of these scores were very similar within and between the two groups, so the groups seem well balanced when it comes to experience. For the R&I-group, the number of reported defects increases with their personal score, while there is no clear trend for the OORT- group!

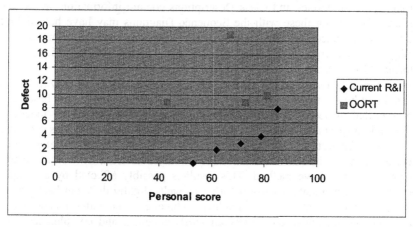

Fig. 2. Relationship between numbers of defects reported in individual reading and personal scores ("experience") for 9 participants

5.3   Further Comments, Interpretation and Analysis

Here, we first comment deeper on some of the results, also using qualitative feedbacks. Then we assess the objectives and hypotheses, and lastly analyze the validity threats. A general reminder is that the data material is very meager, so any conclusion or observation must be drawn with great care.

Comments on Old vs. New Reading Techniques: All in all, the R&I-group only found 68% of their defects in individual reading. This is considerably less then the 98% of the defects found by the OORT-group in this step. The meeting was less prosperous for the latter group, which is the expected result. The R&I-group inversely detected 32% of their defects in the inspection meeting, which is high but not cost-efficient. However, the OORT-group spent twice the effort on individual reading, and therefore the cost-efficiency is almost the same. Furthermore, the OORTs were new for the inspectors, and this may hurt cost-efficiency.

The OORT-group found much more Omissions and Inconsistencies than the R&I-group. The OORTs are based on comparing UML diagrams with each other and with requirements, and this may result in finding many more Omissions and Inconsistencies. In contrast, the R&I techniques do not guide inspectors to find "defects", which do not degrade the behavior of the system. An example is possible

Inconsistencies between a Class Diagram and a Sequence Diagram (in OORT-1), since no code is generated from a Sequence Diagram during design. However, Inconsistencies in other artifacts related to the State Diagram (as in OORT-2 and OORT-3) are important also for implementation.

The R&I-group detected 10 defects of type Incorrect fact, all being important for implementation, while the OORT-group detected only *one* such defect. The registered defects included both misrepresentation of concepts and misuse of them, such as interface misuse being commented for Figure 4. Finding Incorrect facts may be based on previous knowledge of the system, and inspectors in the R&I-group had better insight in implementation details. Another reason is, that for the inspected system, internal design guidelines and Class Descriptions contain information on the use of interfaces. Comparing these with the Sequence Diagrams may have helped finding violations to interface specifications, such as wrong order of operation calls. This technique is not currently in the set of OORTs, while the R&I techniques ask for conformance to such design guidelines.

One interesting result of the experiment was the total *lack of overlap* between defects found by the two groups. The N-fold inspection method [12] is based on the hypothesis that inspection by a single team is hardly effective and N independent teams should inspect an artifact. The value of N depends on many factors such as cost of additional inspections and the potential expense of letting a defect slip by undetected. Our results showed that each team only detected a fraction of defects as anticipated by the above method. This result is possibly affected by a compound effect of the two elements discussed earlier as well: slightly different background of inspectors and different focus of reading techniques. The latter meant, that the OORTs focused on consistency between UML diagrams and completeness versus requirements, while the R&I techniques focused on conformance to the internal guidelines. The experiment therefore suggests concrete improvements in the existing R&I techniques.

Lastly, defect severity (e.g. Major, Minor, and possibly Comment or as defined by the OORTs) should be included for both techniques. Defect types might also be made more precise – e.g. to distinguish Interface error, Sequencing error etc.

Comments on the New Reading Techniques: Some OORTs helped to detect more defects than others. The inspectors mentioned that some defects were found by more than one technique, and were therefore registered only once for the first OORT. Such redundancies should be removed.

Some UML diagrams of the inspected system contain "more" information than others. Modeling is also done differently than assumed in the original set of OORTs - cf. the "Ericsson" changes to OORT-4 and removal of OORT-5.

As mentioned, for the inspected system we had to improvise a State Diagram from an Activity Diagram already standing in the Use Case Specification. But again, making an explicit and separate State Diagram proved that the new OORTs really work: 16(!) defects were totally identified using OORT-2 and OORT-3, comparing the State Diagram with, respectively, Class Descriptions and Sequence Diagrams.

The participants in the OORT-group said it was too *time-consuming* for each to cover all the OORTs, and some (often the last) techniques will suffer from lack of attention. A possible solution is to assign only a subset of the techniques to each participant, similarly to Ericsson's *views* and to what was done in earlier student experiments. A more *advanced UML editor* might also catch many trivial inconsistencies, e.g. undefined or misspelled names, thus relieving human inspectors from lengthy and boring checks.

Finally, we should *tailor* the reading techniques to the context, i.e. project. For instance, the OORTs were successful in detecting Omissions and Inconsistencies by comparing UML diagrams with each other and with the requirements. But they did not detect e.g. misuse of interfaces and inconsistencies between the models and the internal guidelines. A natural solution is to include questions related to *internal guidelines and design rules,* and then e.g. compare Sequence Diagrams with class and interface descriptions as part of a revised OORT-1.

Evaluation of O1/H0a – Cost-Efficiency and Number of Defects: Our small sample prevents use of standard statistical tests, but we can anyhow assess *H0a* (and *H0b* below). The cost-efficiency of the old and new techniques seems rather similar, and in line with that of the baseline. The OORTs seem to help finding more defects in the individual reading step than the R&I techniques, respectively 38 and 17 defects. Even without defects (indirectly) related to the new State Diagram, 22 defects were reported using the OORTs. Thus the null hypothesis *H0a should be accepted.*

Evaluation of O2/H0b – Effect of Developer Experience on Number of Defects: From Figure 2 we see that the number of reported defects from the individual reading step increases with the personal score for the R&I-group. This may indicate that the R&I techniques rely on the experience of the participants. But there is no clear relationship for the OORT-group. Thus the null hypothesis *H0b should be accepted for the R&I-group,* but we cannot say anything for the OORT-group. The effect for the OORT-group is surprising, but consistent with data from The University of Maryland and NTNU [6], and will be documented in Jeffrey Carver's forthcoming PhD thesis.

Evaluation of O3 – Improvement of Reading Techniques for UML: The new OORTs helped Ericsson to detect many *defects not found* by their *existing* R&I techniques. However, both the old and new reading techniques varied a lot in their effectiveness to detect defects among different diagrams and diagram types. This information should be used to improve both sets of reading techniques. Actually, there were many comments on how to improve the OORTs, suggesting that they should be shortened and simplified, have mutual redundancies removed, or include references to internal design guidelines and rules. Thus, although the original set of OORTs had been revised by NTNU in several steps and then tailored for Ericsson, the experiment suggests further simplification, refinement, and tailoring.

Evaluation of O4 – Will Fit in the Incremental Development Process: Although the OORTs were originally created to inspect entire systems, they work well for an *incremental* development process too. The techniques helped to systematically find inconsistencies between new or updated UML diagrams and between these diagrams and possibly changed requirements. That is, they helped inspectors to see the revised design model as a whole.

Validity Evaluation: Threats to experimental validity are classified and elaborated in [15] [20]. Threats to validity in this experiment were identified to be:

- *Internal validity*: There could be some compensatory rivalry; i.e. the R&I-group could put some extra effort in the inspection because of the experiment. Inversely, the OORT-group may do similar in a "Hawthorne" effect. Due to time/scheduling constraints, some participants in the OORT-group did not cover all the techniques properly, e.g. OORT-6 and OORT-7.
- *External validity*: It is difficult to generalize the results of the experiment to other projects or even to other companies, as the experiment was done on a single use case. Another threat was that the OORTs were adapted for Ericsson, but we tried to keep the techniques as close to the original set as possible.
- *Construct validity*: The OORT-group had knowledge of the R&I techniques and the result for them could be a mix of using both techniques.
- *Conclusion validity*: The experiment is done on a single use case and it is difficult to conclude a statistical relationship between treatment and outcome. To be able to utilize all the techniques, a simple State Diagram was extracted the day before the experiment. The R&I-group did not look at this particular diagram, while the OORT-group reported 16 defects related to this diagram and to indirectly related artifacts. The inspectors were assigned "semi-randomly" to the two groups, which roughly possessed similar experience. The adding of ordinal scores to represent overall inspector experience is dubious, but this total score was only used qualitatively (i.e. is there a trend? - not how large it is).

6   Conclusions

The studied Ericsson unit incrementally develops software for large-scale real-time system. The inspected artifacts, i.e. Requirements Descriptions and UML models, are substantially larger and more complex than those used in previous academic experiments. For Ericsson it is interesting to see if these techniques could be tailored to their inspection needs in the individual reading step.

Below we sum up the objectives of the experiment and how they have been reached:

- **O1 and H0a – cost-efficiency and detected defects:** The cost-efficiency of the old R&I techniques and the new OORTs seems very similar. The new ones helped to find more than twice as many defects as the old ones, but with no overlaps with the defects found by the old techniques.
- **O2 and H0b – effect of developer experience on detected defects:** There is probably a positive trend for the old R&I techniques, but we do not know for the new ones. The result may term "expected", but the reasons are not quite understood.
- **O3 - improvement of old and new reading techniques:** Although the new OORTs have shown promising results, the experiment suggests further modifications of both general and specific issues. We have for both the old and the new reading techniques identified parts that could be included in the other.
- **O4 – fit into an incremental process:** To our surprise this went very well for the OORTs, although little attention and minimal effort was spent on this.

To conclude: In spite of very sparse data, the experiment showed a need for several concrete *improvements*, and provided many unforeseen and valuable *insights*. We also should expect a learning effect, both for the reading techniques and for Ericsson's inspection process and developers, as a result of more OORT trials. We further think that the evaluation process and many of the experimental results can be *reused* in future studies of inspections of object-oriented design artifacts in UML.

Some final challenges: First, how to utilize inspection data actively in a company to improve their inspection process? Second, how to convince the object-oriented community at large, with its strong emphasis on prototyping and short cycle time, to adopt more classic quality techniques such as inspections?

Acknowledgements

We thank Ericsson in Grimstad for the opportunity and help to perform the experiment with ten of their designers and several managers, who all were highly motivated. We also thank the original OORT-team in USA for inspiration and comments. The study was partially funded by two public Norwegian research projects, namely PROFIT (sec. 5) and INCO (INcremental and COmponent-based development, done jointly by University of Oslo and NTNU). Thanks also goes to local colleagues at NTNU.

References

[1]   Arif, T., Hegde, L.C.: Inspection of Object-Oriented Construction. Diploma (MSc) thesis at NTNU, June 2002. See http://www.idi.ntnu.no/grupper/su/su-diploma-2002/Arif-OORT_Thesis-external.pdf.

[2]   Basili, V.R., Caldiera, G., Lanubile, F., and Shull, F.: Studies on reading techniques. Proc.   Twenty-First Annual Software Engineering Workshop, NASA-SEL-96-002, p. 59-65, Greenbelt, MD, Dec. 1996.

[3]   Basili, V.R., Green S., Laitenberger, O., Lanubile, F., Shull, F., Sørumgård, S., Zelkowitz, M. V.: The Empirical Investigation of Perspective-Based Reading, Empirical Software Engineering Journal, 1(2):133-164, 1996.

[4]   Booch, G., Rumbaugh, J., Jacobson, I.: The Unified Modeling Language User Guide. Addison-Wesley, 1999.

[5]   Bunde, G.A., Pedersen, A.: Defect Reduction by Improving Inspection of UML Diagrams in the GPRS Project. Diploma (MSc) thesis at Agder University College, June 2002. See http://siving.hia.no/ikt02/ikt6400/g08/.

[6]   Conradi, R.: Preliminary NTNU Report of the OO Reading Techniques (OORT) exercise in course 7038 on Programming Quality and Process Improvement, spring 2000, v1.12. Oct. 2001, 80 p.

[7]   Conradi, R., Marjara, A., Hantho, Ø., Frotveit, T., Skåtevik, B.: A study of inspections and testing at Ericsson, Norway. Proc. PROFES'99, 22-24 June 1999, p. 263-284, published by VTT.

[8]   Fagan, M. E.: Design and Code Inspection to Reduce Errors in Program Development. IBM Systems Journal, 15 (3):182-211, 1976.

[9]   Gilb, T., Graham, D.: Software Inspection. Addison-Wesley, 1993.

[10]   Jacobson, I., Christerson, M., Jonsson, P., Övergaard, G.: Object-Oriented Software Engineering: A Use Case Driven Approach, Addison-Wesley, revised printing, 1995.

[11]   Laitenberger, O., Atkinson, C.: Generalized Perspective-Based Inspection to handle Object-Oriented Development Artifacts. Proc. ICSE'99, Aug. 1999, IEEE CS-Press, p. 494-503.

[12]   Martin, J., Tsai, W.T.: N-fold Inspection: A Requirements Analysis Technique. Communications of the ACM, 33(2): 225-232, 1990.

[13]   Melo, W., Shull, F., Travassos, G.H.: Software Review Guidelines, Technical Report ES-556/01, Aug. 2001, 22 p. Systems Engineering and Computer Science Department, COPPE/UFRJ, http://www.cos.ufrj.br (shortly reporting OORT case study at Oracle in Brazil).

[14]   Shull, F., Carver, J., Travassos, G.H.: An Empirical Method for Introducing Software Process. Proc. European Software Engineering Conference 2001 (ESEC'2001), Vienna, 10-14 Sept. 2001, ACM/IEEE CS Press, ACM Order no. 594010, ISBN 1-58113-390-1, p. 288-296.

[15]   Sommerville, I.: Software Engineering. Addison-Wesley, sixth ed., 2001.

[16]   Travassos, G.H., Shull F., Carver J., Basili V.R.: Reading Techniques for OO Design Inspections, Proc. Twenty-Forth Annual Software Engineering Workshop, NASA-SEL, Greenbelt, MD, Dec. 1999, http://sel.gsfc.nasa.gov/website/sew/1999/program.html.

[17]   Travassos, G.H., Shull, F., Fredericks, M., Basili, V.R.: Detecting Defects in Object-Oriented Designs: Using Reading Techniques to Increase Software Quality. Proc. OOPSLA'99, p. 47-56, Denver, 1-5 Nov. 1999 (in ACM SIGPLAN Notices,34(10), Oct. 1999).

[18]   Travassos, G.H., Shull, F., Carver, J., Basili, V.R.: Reading Techniques for OO Design Inspections. University of Maryland Technical Report CS-TR-4353. April 2002 (OORT version 3), http://www.cs.umd.edu/Library/TRs/CS-TR-4353/CS-TR-4353.pdf.

[19]   Votta, L.G.: Does Every Inspection Need a Meeting? Proc. ACM SIGSOFT'93 Symposium on Foundation of Software Engineering (FSE'93), p 107-114, ACM Press, 1993.

[20]   Wohlin, C., Runeson, P., Höst, M., Ohlsson, M.C., Regnell, B., Wesslén, A.: Experimentation in Software Engineering, an Introduction. Kluwer Academic Publishers, 2000.

Author Index

Lecture Notes in Computer Science

For information about Vols. 1–2646
please contact your bookseller or Springer-Verlag

Vol. 2687: J. Mira, J.R. Álvarez (Eds.), Artificial Neural Nets Problem Solving Methods. Proceedings, Part II. 2003. XXVII, 820 pages. 2003.

Vol. 2688: J. Kittler, M.S. Nixon (Eds.), Audio- and Video-Based Biometric Person Authentication. Proceedings, 2003. XVII, 978 pages. 2003.

Vol. 2689: K.D. Ashley, D.G. Bridge (Eds.), Case-Based Reasoning Research and Development. Proceedings, 2003. XV, 734 pages. 2003. (Subseries LNAI).

Vol. 2691: V. Mařík, J. Müller, M. Pěchouček (Eds.), Multi-Agent Systems and Applications III. Proceedings, 2003. XIV, 660 pages. 2003. (Subseries LNAI).

Vol. 2692: P. Nixon, S. Terzis (Eds.), Trust Management. Proceedings, 2003. X, 349 pages. 2003.

Vol. 2693: A. Cechich, M. Piattini, A. Vallecillo (Eds.), Component-Based Software Quality. X, 403 pages. 2003.

Vol. 2694: R. Cousot (Ed.), Static Analysis. Proceedings, 2003. XIV, 505 pages. 2003.

Vol. 2695: L.D. Griffin, M. Lillholm (Eds.), Scale Space Methods in Computer Vision. Proceedings, 2003. XII, 816 pages. 2003.

Vol. 2697: T. Warnow, B. Zhu (Eds.), Computing and Combinatorics. Proceedings, 2003. XIII, 560 pages. 2003.

Vol. 2698: W. Burakowski, B. Koch, A. Bęben (Eds.), Architectures for Quality of Service in the Internet. Proceedings, 2003. XI, 305 pages. 2003.

Vol. 2701: M. Hofmann (Ed.), Typed Lambda Calculi and Applications. Proceedings, 2003. VIII, 317 pages. 2003.

Vol. 2702: P. Brusilovsky, A. Corbett, F. de Rosis (Eds.), User Modeling 2003. Proceedings, 2003. XIV, 436 pages. 2003. (Subseries LNAI).

Vol. 2704: S.-T. Huang, T. Herman (Eds.), Self-Stabilizing Systems. Proceedings, 2003. X, 215 pages. 2003.

Vol. 2706: R. Nieuwenhuis (Ed.), Rewriting Techniques and Applications. Proceedings, 2003. XI, 515 pages. 2003.

Vol. 2707: K. Jeffay, I. Stoica, K. Wehrle (Eds.), Quality of Service – IWQoS 2003. Proceedings, 2003. XI, 517 pages. 2003.

Vol. 2709: T. Windeatt, F. Roli (Eds.), Multiple Classifier Systems. Proceedings, 2003. X, 406 pages. 2003.

Vol. 2710: Z. Ésik, Z, Fülöp (Eds.), Developments in Language Theory. Proceedings, 2003. XI, 437 pages. 2003.

Vol. 2711: T.D. Nielsen, N.L. Zhang (Eds.), Symbolic and Quantitative Approaches to Reasoning with Uncertainty. Proceedings, 2003. XII, 608 pages. 2003. (Subseries LNAI).

Vol. 2712: A. James, B. Lings, M. Younas (Eds.), New Horizons in Information Management. Proceedings, 2003. XII, 281 pages. 2003.

Vol. 2713: C.-W. Chung, C.-K. Kim, W. Kim, T.-W. Ling, K.-H. Song (Eds.), Web and Communication Technologies and Internet-Related Social Issues – HSI 2003. Proceedings, 2003. XXII, 773 pages. 2003.

Vol. 2714: O. Kaynak, E. Alpaydin, E. Oja, L. Xu (Eds.), Artificial Neural Networks and Neural Information Processing – ICANN/ICONIP 2003. Proceedings, 2003. XXII, 1188 pages. 2003.

Vol. 2715: T. Bilgiç, B. De Baets, O. Kaynak (Eds.), Fuzzy Sets and Systems – IFSA 2003. Proceedings, 2003. XV, 735 pages. 2003. (Subseries LNAI).

Vol. 2716: M.J. Voss (Ed.), OpenMP Shared Memory Parallel Programming. Proceedings, 2003. VIII, 271 pages. 2003.

Vol. 2718: P. W. H. Chung, C. Hinde, M. Ali (Eds.), Developments in Applied Artificial Intelligence. Proceedings, 2003. XIV, 817 pages. 2003. (Subseries LNAI).

Vol. 2719: J.C.M. Baeten, J.K. Lenstra, J. Parrow, G.J. Woeginger (Eds.), Automata, Languages and Programming. Proceedings, 2003. XVIII, 1199 pages. 2003.

Vol. 2720: M. Marques Freire, P. Lorenz, M.M.-O. Lee (Eds.), High-Speed Networks and Multimedia Communications. Proceedings, 2003. XIII, 582 pages. 2003.

Vol. 2721: N.J. Mamede, J. Baptista, I. Trancoso, M. das Graças Volpe Nunes (Eds.), Computational Processing of the Portuguese Language. Proceedings, 2003. XIV, 268 pages. 2003. (Subseries LNAI).

Vol. 2722: J.M. Cueva Lovelle, B.M. González Rodríguez, L. Joyanes Aguilar, J.E. Labra Gayo, M. del Puerto Paule Ruiz (Eds.), Web Engineering. Proceedings, 2003. XIX, 554 pages. 2003.

Vol. 2723: E. Cantú-Paz, J.A. Foster, K. Deb, L.D. Davis, R. Roy, U.-M. O'Reilly, H.-G. Beyer, R. Standish, G. Kendall, S. Wilson, M. Harman, J. Wegener, D. Dasgupta, M.A. Potter, A.C. Schultz, K.A. Dowsland, N. Jonoska, J. Miller (Eds.), Genetic and Evolutionary Computation – GECCO 2003. Proceedings, Part I. 2003. XLVII, 1252 pages. 2003.

Vol. 2724: E. Cantú-Paz, J.A. Foster, K. Deb, L.D. Davis, R. Roy, U.-M. O'Reilly, H.-G. Beyer, R. Standish, G. Kendall, S. Wilson, M. Harman, J. Wegener, D. Dasgupta, M.A. Potter, A.C. Schultz, K.A. Dowsland, N. Jonoska, J. Miller (Eds.), Genetic and Evolutionary Computation – GECCO 2003. Proceedings, Part II. 2003. XLVII, 1274 pages. 2003.

Vol. 2725: W.A. Hunt, Jr., F. Somenzi (Eds.), Computer Aided Verification. Proceedings, 2003. XII, 462 pages. 2003.

Vol. 2726: E. Hancock, M. Vento (Eds.), Graph Based Representations in Pattern Recognition. Proceedings, 2003. VIII, 271 pages. 2003.

Vol. 2727: R. Safavi-Naini, J. Seberry (Eds.), Information Security and Privacy. Proceedings, 2003. XII, 534 pages. 2003.

Vol. 2731: C.S. Calude, M.J. Dinneen, V. Vajnovszki (Eds.), Discrete Mathematics and Theoretical Computer Science. Proceedings, 2003. VIII, 301 pages. 2003.

Vol. 2733: A. Butz, A. Krüger, P. Olivier (Eds.), Smart Graphics. Proceedings, 2003. XI, 261 pages. 2003.

Vol. 2734: P. Perner, A. Rosenfeld (Eds.), Machine Learning and Data Mining in Pattern Recognition. Proceedings, 2003. XII, 440 pages. 2003. (Subseries LNAI).

Vol. 2743: L. Cardelli (Ed.), ECOOP 2003 – Object-Oriented Programming. Proceedings, 2003. X, 501 pages. 2003.

Vol. 2745: M. Guo, L.T. Yang (Eds.), Parallel and Distributed Processing and Applications. Proceedings, 2003. XII, 450 pages. 2003.

Vol. 2749: J. Bigun, T. Gustavsson (Eds.), Image Analysis. Proceedings, 2003. XXII, 1174 pages. 2003.

Vol. 2750: T. Hadzilacos, Y. Manolopoulos, J.F. Roddick, Y. Theodoridis (Eds.), Advances in Spatial and Temporal Databases. Proceedings, 2003. XIII, 525 pages. 2003.